The Emergence of

Women's Voices in ISKCON

A Collection of Letters, Articles, Papers,

and Conference Reports from 1988 to 2020

Compiled and edited by Pranada devi dasi

For Vaishnavis around the world,
may you find shelter
at the lotus feet of Srimati Radharani and Her servants.

"If Krishna does give me some more time, I would like to do something for the women, to SUPPORT the women, to give a strong VOICE to the WOMEN."

— Yamuna Devi

TO GIRIRAJ MAHARAJ
JUST WEEKS BEFORE PASSING AWAY

A few weeks before Yamuna Devi passed away, Giriraja Maharaja asked her if there was anything she wanted to do if Krishna gave her more time. At first she said she was ready to go. Then she said, "If Krishna does give me some more time, I would like to do something for the women, to support the women, to give a strong voice to the women."

The Bond of Love: Srila Prabhupada and his Daughters
is a book of the memories of over 300 of Srila Prabhupada's female disciples.
Release date: Vyasa-puja 2020. It is available from Book Wrights Press here:
https://www.bookwrightspress.com/wp1/product-category/books/

For more information about advocacy and activities for women in ISKCON visit the
Vaishnavi Ministry at www.vaishnaviministry.org, or contact the international Minister
or your local Ministry representative.

International Vaishnavi Minister
Radha devi dasi
radha16108@gmail.com

Brazil
Gitamrta devi dasi
gitamrtadd@gmail.com
+55 83 98643 9410

Australia
Krishnarupa devi dasi
krishnarupa.acbsp@gmail.com
+61 416 179 733

North America
Govindapriya devi dasi
www.vaishnaviministryna.com
+1 4083980483

Mexico
Alaksya devi dasi
alaksya.soultools@gmail.com
+52 5581595181

UK
Madhavi devi dasi
madhavi@krishnatemple.com

South Africa
Krsangi Radhe devi dasi
prabashnee@mweb.co.za

Russia/CIS
Sati devi dasi & Ekanga devi dasi
ruvaishnaviministry@gmail.com
https://satibts.wixsite.com/rusvaishnavi/ostavit-soobshenie
Domestic abuse reports: Zaschitadevi@yandex.ru

The print version of *The Emergence of Women's Voices in ISKCON* is available through Book
Wrights Press here https://www.bookwrightspress.com/wp1/product-category/books/

On the Cover
Photo taken by Megha Rupa dasi at the Festival of Joy in Dallas, Texas, 2019.
Devotees left to right: Vrnda Priya dasi, Kalindi dasi, Radha Kunda dasi.

Cover Design: Mayapriya devi dasi, www.bookwrightspress.com

Contents

Foreword
by Anuttama dasa

One of my *vartma-pradarshaka-gurus* was a young woman. She was only an acquaintance, someone I chatted with for an hour or so on a sunny afternoon in Ann Arbor, Michigan in 1975. I was a recent college dropout and working as a bartender. I rose late, but started each day with reading the Bible and *Be Here Now*, accompanied by prayer and chanting. On Sundays I attended the local Methodist Church, or a Buddhist retreat, and occasionally the Hare Krishna temple. I never met her again, that wise young woman, but she planted a seed within my heart when she told me boldly, "If you are serious about spiritual life, you should go to Boulder, Colorado."

Somehow that instruction stayed with me. Later, after more than a month of hitchhiking and spiritual seeking across the western United States, I found my way to Boulder. I lived a few days with a Buddhist community. Then I moved into the Hare Krishna temple in Denver.

There too, women played a vital role. I lived as a *brahmachari* for the next ten years. I kept a respectful distance from the "mothers." But I knew that the ladies, or "mothers," in the community were as dedicated as any man or "prabhu." They served on the altar, cooked for the Deities and the devotees, went on *harinama,* managed departments, and sold as many – actually more – books as the men did. Many of the women in the community, I noted, expressed more kindness to me than did the men.

In 1983, I was asked to return to Boulder to open a "preaching center" near the University of Colorado along with my friend Jitari dasa and two senior Vaishnavi disciples of Srila Prabhupada, Palika dasi and Rangavati dasi. The women cooked, distributed books, went on *harinama,* preached, cleaned, gave classes, raised funds, counseled local youth, and were full partners in all our services. Without these two women, Boulder ISKCON of the mid-1980's would not have existed.

When I became president of the Denver temple in 1986, my awareness of the capacity and devotion of Srila Prabhupada's women disciples and grand-disciples, his "secret weapons" in spreading Krishna consciousness, only increased. During my seven years as president women were leaders in every capacity. Women served as department heads, on the temple board, gave classes in the temple, raised funds, they (still) led in book distribution, and generally set a high standard of devotion in the community. I learned to depend upon the women in Denver as much as, and some cases far more, than the men.

The fairer sex became an even more vital aspect of my life in 1986. As a married man, I soon realized how valuable is the partnership of a Krishna conscious wife. Thirty four years later, Rukmini devi dasi, who has two articles in this publication, continues to be my closest confidant, and my life's companion in assisting Srila Prabhupada in his mission.

In 1993, I was asked to move to Washington, D.C. where I became the National Director, then International Director, of ISKCON Communications, and later a member of the ISKCON Governing Body Commission (GBC). As Communications Director, my understanding of the essential role that women play in ISKCON again increased manyfold. I learned that most women have inherent abilities in communicating and building relationships that most men struggle to emulate. As GBC, I worked "shoulder to shoulder" with Vaishnavi leaders like Sudharma dasi, Malati dasi, and Radha dasi, also all featured in this volume, who proved to me that women are often as, or more, intelligent and better managers than we of the "stronger" sex.

I was especially blessed to serve with Jahnavi Haggard, a dear spiritual daughter who served as the first Executive Director of Children of Krishna. She was a major factor in ISKCON's efforts to reach out the youth who had been victims of mistreatment and abuse. She cared deeply for all generations of ISKCON's family. Jahnavi remains an inspiration to me even today, and she is sorely missed since her departure from this world some years ago.

Today, my GBC zone includes five women temple presidents. Five women presidents! I am honored to support and serve with them. If there was a competition, I would rate these women among the top presidents across the ISKCON world. They are smart, strong, visionary, compassionate, systematic, determined, and highly devoted.

During my almost five decades of service in ISKCON, I've thus had the honor of serving with dozens of exceptional women. I am glad to see that the writings of many of these Vaishnavis are featured in this volume. Practically every service I have performed has profited from the cooperation, support, friendship, and leadership of women in ISKCON.

From promoting child protection; to creating policies against domestic abuse; to dialoguing with anti-cult organizations; to reaching out to academics, media and governments; to promoting religious freedom; to producing movies; to serving in a multitude of various committee assignments; to promoting appropriate policies and laws in the GBC. In each and every one of these service areas I, and ISKCON, have benefitted immeasurably from Vaishnavi leadership.

I believe most men in ISKCON have similar stories, and have similarly benefitted from the contributions of ISKCON's Vaishnavis. However, for complex reasons, many of which are discussed in this volume, women have often been minimized, misunderstood, under-appreciated, and relegated to secondary roles.

None of this is acceptable in ISKCON. Our Movement is founded on Lord Krishna's declaration of the equality of all souls. Lord Chaitanya advented to break open the storehouse of love of God and welcomed all people "young men, old men, women and children" to take part. Srila Prabhupada went against the supposed norms of contemporary India as well as "Vedic culture" when he consciously and purposefully empowered and engaged his female disciples in chanting the Gayatri mantra, performing

Deity service, leading public kirtans in India and across the globe, giving classes on the *shastra,* accompanying him on preaching tours, and more.

The volume you are about to read documents some of those many, many engagements and contributions. It represents the voices of Vaishnavis across the world who have been – and will continue to be – pillars in the ISKCON Society. As mothers, grandmothers, daughters, wives, teachers, preachers, GBC members, gurus, book distributors, board members, temple presidents, *sankirtana* devotees, and more, we are all indebted to their contributions and their commitment. I pray that this important book will increase awareness of the countless contributions of these noble women throughout our Society, and that it will help smooth the path for women devotees in the future.

For those women who have suffered indignities or worse in the past, I offer my deepest apologies. I do so on behalf of all your (god)brothers, sons, fathers, and fellow devotees for anything we may have done knowingly or unknowingly that were impediments to your progress and the awakening of your natural love for the Lord.

For women devotees of the present and into the future, I remind you of the true story of a young Vaishnavi who was sitting with Srila Prabhupada when he said to room full of his students, "I want all of my disciples to open temples." This 16-year old girl, a recent initiate, inquired, "Even the girls Swamiji?"

Prabhupada responded, "Yes, why not? Even the girls."

I, too say, "Yes, why not, even the girls." And, perhaps – based on my experience – I will add: "Especially the girls."

July 16, 2020
Kamika Ekadasi

In the sixteenth century, Sri Chaitanya Mahaprabhu initiated the greatest spiritual and social revolution in modern history when He established that anyone could be purified to the highest level of consciousness through Krishna's holy names. The four *varnas* of traditional Vedic society, described by Krishna in the *Bhagavad-gita,* create a hierarchical social structure. The idea that anyone, even those outside Vedic society, could reach the highest level is a fundamental challenge to social hierarchy.

When Srila Prabhupada brought this revolution to the western world in 1966, he entered a society ripe for change. Young adults in the U.S. in the 1960s were disillusioned by material culture and frustrated by the emptiness of material achievements. Many were distraught at the brutal oppression of African Americans in the southern part of the United States. Others objected to the millions of lives sacrificed in the America's pointless proxy war with China in Vietnam. These young people, convinced of the futility of material life, heard a message of hope in Srila Prabhupada's words.

By worshipping Krishna through the holy names, he instructed them, human society could be united and find lasting peace. All living beings are equally sons and daughters of the same Father, he said. The highest bliss, Srila Prabhupada promised, is found in remembering our true identity as servants of Lord Krishna.

Srila Prabhupada quietly overturned countless ages of Vedic tradition when he accepted female disciples into ISKCON ashrams and gave them the Gayatri mantra. To his students, unaware of the usual role of women in Vedic society, his egalitarian mood was entirely consistent with his teachings. Knowing that we are not this body and that the soul may change from male to female bodies in different lifetimes, they were unsurprised when Srila Prabhupada gave his female disciples equal access to transcendental knowledge and spiritual practices.

In India, however, many of Srila Prabhupada's godbrothers were shocked at the notion of a *sannyasi* accepting unmarried women as disciples and accepting personal service from them. Moreover, prior to Srila Prabhupada, no guru in the Gaudiya Vaishnava line had ever given women the Gayatri mantra. Prior to Srila Prabhupada, *pujaris* in our lineage were men, with only a few, rare exceptions. Srila Prabhupada, initiating women as *brahmanas,* engaging them as his personal cooks, and training them as his first *pujaris,* turned tradition on its head. He understood how best to spread the teachings of Sri Chaitanya Mahaprabhu throughout the world and was confident in engaging Vaishnavis in new ways. He demonstrated that the mercy of Sri Chaitanya Mahaprabhu is for everyone and that engaging the beleaguered citizens of Kali-yuga supersedes the need to maintain tradition.

And yet, Srila Prabhupada never forgot that the *daivi-varnashrama* system, given to humankind by Lord Krishna Himself, is the best social arrangement for encouraging people to become God conscious. Nor did he forget that men and women have certain duties and needs related to their gender. Women, he taught, require protection. The young Vaishnavis who surrendered to him, knew the dangers of rape, domestic violence, sexual harassment, and other ills inflicted on women in modern society. They did not need convincing to accept his protection. Nor did they quarrel with his view that motherhood is a vital duty that only women can fulfill. Srila Prabhupada never struggled in balancing the unique needs and duties of his Vaishnavis against the desire to engage them "equally with their brothers" in Krishna consciousness.

As ISKCON developed, however, Srila Prabhupada's disciples became aware that social roles for women in India differed significantly from those in America. The place of Vaishnavis, formerly seen as sisters and equal members of a spiritual family, became defined in terms of marriage and motherhood. As ISKCON's leadership began to include more and more celibate monks, Vaishnavis found themselves overlooked and their voices ignored.

This is the point at which I joined ISKCON. When I was a young devotee, Vaishnavis stood at the back of the temple and we were last in line for everything, from receiving the fire of the ghee lamp, to receiving *prasadam* at meals. At one temple I visited, Vaishnavis were forbidden from speaking in the *prasadam* hall for fear that our voices would unduly agitate the *brahmacharis* at the other end of the room.

I cannot say that I accepted these practices without question, but my profession and educational background gave me access to senior devotees and service that engaged my propensities. For the most part, I was content to accept the restricted place of Vaishnavis in ISKCON as a necessary evil on the path to Krishna.

My viewpoint changed after the birth of my daughter. In one brief moment, she helped me see that limitations on Vaishnavis were no minor inconvenience but a potent message about who belongs in Krishna consciousness. During the *guru-puja* kirtan one morning when she was still a toddler, she began pulling me toward the front of the temple, anxious to stand before Krishna and offer her prayers. Seeing the crowd of *brahmacharis* in front of the altar, I resisted. She refused to take no for an answer and in an attempt to quickly and quietly explain my reluctance I told her that the *brahmacharis* would be mad if I stood by them. My daughter was not satisfied by this explanation. She marched up to the nearest *brahmachari* and punched him as hard as she could.

At that point I realized, while I might be willing to tolerate limitations on my access to Krishna, those limitations affected all of the young girls growing up in our movement, all of the women who came to the temple for the first time and were repelled by what looked like discrimination, and all of the Vaishnavis who had been denied service, opportunity and spiritual experiences based on their bodily designation. Standing in the back of the temple room, accepting unnecessary restrictions on my activities in Krishna consciousness, might not hurt me significantly, but I could not support a system that did not make room for my daughter or the millions of other girls like her.

For over 20 years now, I have been examining this tension between the egalitarian message of Sri Chaitanya Mahaprabhu and the recognition that men and women can legitimately differ in their needs and social roles. I have heard from Srila Prabhupada's Vaishnavis about the love with which he engaged them in services that were later denied to them. I have spoken with religious scholars about the changes in women's roles in ISKCON after the departure of Srila Prabhupada. I have deeply considered the perspective of those who emphasize the need to institute *varnashrama-dharma* in ISKCON and the social and spiritual benefits of traditional societies.

Ultimately, I have learned that we must honor both sides of the wonderful gift Srila Prabhupada has given us. Sri Chaitanya Mahaprabhu has broken open the storehouse of love of God and everyone deserves the opportunity to serve Srila Prabhupada and Sri Chaitanya according to their propensities. This is, as Srila Prabhupada explained, our right as eternal servants of Lord Krishna.

At the same time, we cannot forget that the service of motherhood is essential to the development of a spiritual society. Unless we value this service and value the Vaishnavis who perform it, we will struggle to build spiritual communities. Nor can we forget that Vaishnavis have unique needs, including the need for protection. But protecting Vaishnavis does not equal limiting their service. Srila Prabhupada always protected his spiritual daughters. That protection never prevented him from giving Vaishnavis opportunities to speak in public, lead kirtan, give classes on the scriptures, perform worship of the Deities in the growing number of temples he founded, and in numerous other services.

In attempting to implement the principles of *daiva-varnashrama-dharma* in the modern world, we are breaking new ground. What a modern *daiva-varnashrama* society will look like is still unknown. But the principle that everyone has the right to use their talents and propensities in Krishna's service transcends social considerations. While we may adjust to time, place, and circumstance in the way service opportunities are offered, it is essential that all devotees be encouraged to serve the Lord according to our individual natures.

We can embrace different social roles for Vaishnavas and Vaishnavis, understanding that those roles are complementary and both are essential. But within these roles, which can vary around the world, we must permit devotees to use their personal natures and talents in service. Ultimately, we must create communities where our love for one another ensures that differences between men and women never become a barrier to anyone's spiritual development. In the revolutionary mood of Sri Chaitanya Mahaprabhu, following the example of Lord Nityananda and Haridasa Thakura, we must fall at the feet of everyone we meet and beg them to engage themselves in service to Lord Krishna and His devotees.

Introduction
by Pranada dasi

The Emergence of Women's Voices in ISKCON conveys the understanding that women were once silent and then began speaking up. This contradicts a current prevailing impression that women in ISKCON should acquiesce to the rules and roles of *stri-dharma* – the *dharma* of women according to *varnashrama* – and should finally and quietly take their place.

The actual history is vastly different. From around 1972 until 1988, women were nearly completely silent about the roles handed down to them and how they were treated. During this time, managers in ISKCON corralled women to the back of temple rooms, stopped them from giving classes and leading kirtans, chanting *japa* in temple rooms, and serving in managerial capacities, gave them fewer living facilities or provided no *ashrama* facilities, took away *pujari* services, such as offering an *arati* during a well-attended ceremony like *mangala-arati* in certain temples, and implemented other social and service restrictions.

For more than a decade, we women graciously, humbly, and with dedication followed the dictates and mandates our brothers had enforced, even though their rules were often in direct contraposition to Srila Prabhupada's guidance and example.

In changing what Prabhupada had laid out for us in relation to what women could do and how they should be treated, ISKCON managers conducted a *stri-dharma* "social experiment." I am fairly certain the experiment wasn't intentionally orchestrated to do harm. Rather, in tracing the history, it appears that some men in leadership roles (several s*annyasis* in particular), after visiting India and inculcating a vague idea about "proper" social standards for women, made changes in ISKCON to bring women into line with what they thought were "Vedic" or "dharmic" ideals.

Women embraced this social experiment with an open heart and continued to serve with integrity. They were (and are) integral parts to the spreading and maintenance of the Krishna consciousness movement: generally they collected the greater portion of funds in most temples, and kept the *sankirtana,* kitchens, *pujari* rooms, altars, festivals, and childcare humming along. Though this was so, women were required not to be seen nor heard and to be submissive to every man, not just their husbands. Women kept their heads down and covered and their mouths shut.

My sisters and I thought complying with our brothers and their needs was the Krishna conscious approach. After all, humility is the price to pay for love of God. As Srila Prabhupada's daughters and in great appreciation for what he gave us, we would give our lives to try to please him. Who cared what services we could or couldn't do, or whether our brothers claimed accolades for the services we performed? We could even tolerate when they spoke ill of us, which they did often.

We had pity on them, too. We were sorry that their senses were so disturbed that they had to put us down to control their sex urge. For some reason, our brothers had to personify their challenges in us and thus belittle, mock, demoralize, and attempt to erase us. Still, we knew that advancement on the path was an internal process and our brothers couldn't take *that* away from us.

For a large percentage of women, the social norms enacted in ISKCON produced social anxiety, a deep lack of confidence, feelings of tremendous shame, insecurity, learned hopelessness, self-hate, anxiety, depression, and physical and psychological abuse.

As a group, as a generalization, our brothers largely failed us. We weren't protected; our children weren't protected. The current demand that women submit to a continued, or renewed, *stri-dharma* experiment carelessly ignores that the experiment was already conducted and that it failed miserably, and not because the women weren't compliant or quiet. We also ignore that women still acutely feel the pangs of prejudice and oppression, as evidenced by questions posed to me at a recent international Vaishnavi online conference.

The discussion about women's roles centers squarely on (mis)conceptions of *varnashrama*. The various papers within this anthology respond to the notion that *varnashrama* is required for bhakti. I can briefly state that this idea counters Srila Rupa Gosvami's definition of pure bhakti, which emphatically states that pure bhakti is free of any tinge of *karma* or *jnana*, a sentiment Krishna Himself declares in *Gita* (18.66): surrender fully to Me giving up all of your preconceptions about *dharma*. Just engage in bhakti to Me in full surrender.

As we'll hear, Srila Prabhupada engaged women in all the services that some would like to deny women in the name of *stri-dharma*. To see this for yourself you can view the narrated slideshow produced by Visakha and Malati Prabhus here https://www.youtube.com/watch?v=Rxhqk9mTGe4. It is striking to see what Srila Prabhupada approved for women to do in his presence.

It is also incumbent on us to recognize that proponents of *stri-dharma* have cherry-picked what to implement and what to leave aside, yet claim "their" *varnashrama* is pure and necessary. *Varnashrama* orders us to properly propitiate demigods on a regular basis. We cannot leave the house except under stringent guidelines. One must eat, sleep, urinate – perform all bodily functions – exactly following elaborate rules. The list of dos and donts is lengthy and has little to do with *bhakti*. On more than one occasion, Srila Prabhupada said it was impossible to institute *varnashrama*,[1] but he had no problem demonstrating how we could live the moral and virtuous bhakti life of *bhagavata-dharma*.

As we cannot manufacture a religion by accepting and rejecting various tenets of it, we cannot claim to have a *varnashrama* system by subjectively choosing some things and leaving aside others. We cannot, for instance, focus largely on women's roles and ignore what *grihastha* men and *sannyasis* are mandated within the system. It is a whole system that doesn't work if you miss even one minute detail. King Nriga was an exemplary follower of every minute detail of *varnashrama,* but a slight misstep – even unknowingly – created havoc for him. Partially implementing *varnashrama* already created havoc as we'll hear in this book from women who have first-hand experience.

Adherents of *stri-dharma* extol the glory of India's culture as a reason to accept their modified version of *varnashrama.* But in order to claim that India models a glorious social culture, we have to ignore the fact that *varnashrama* is no longer practiced on its home soil; the remnants of the culture have been polluted due to several hundred years of Muslim rule, to name one influencing factor.

India as a beacon to a model social culture is no more. In 2019, the Thomson Reuters Foundation stated India is "the most dangerous country for women" in the world, pointing to dowry deaths, honor killings, rape, sex trafficking, forced child marriage, acid throwing, and the fact that 70% of women are victims of domestic violence. A crime against women is committed every three minutes according to India's National Crime Records Bureau – and most domestic violence acts go unreported. India's distinctions also include the highest rate of female infanticide in the world.

To identify our Society's morals based on the sensibilities of a sacred culture, the only example we can turn to is Srila Prabhupada. He was unequivocal. Repeatedly. Over and over, when he was approached for clarification about women's roles, responsibilities, and *seva* opportunities he gave the same answer: the girls are as good as the boys; there is no difference on the spiritual platform; bhakti has nothing to do with birth. He wanted the girls preaching and doing all the actitivities boys were doing including *arcana,* opening temples, and acting as guru; he gave them *diksha.*

In the recent online Vaishnavi conference someone asked me why we female disciples of Srila Prabhupada were silent. I acknowledge it took us a while to find our voices, but we did not remain silent. Unfortunately, by the time we found the courage to speak, social behaviors were entrenched and a warped view of women was deeply embedded into the individual and group psyche, which continues to this day to varying degrees.

In addition, initially changes were slow and what little was changed was often made reluctantly or begrudgingly. Subsequently, a change would be made in a temple and then sometimes retracted. When we first began speaking, the vast majority of our godbrother-leaders simply ignored us. The prevailing mood was that only a few women were discontent and surely they would be quiet or go away (many women had already left the Movement) making it unnecessary for them to respond.

It took several years of active, focused dialogue to garner the public support of a handful of godbrothers – Anuttama dasa, Bhaktitirtha Swami, Bir Krishna Swami, and Mukunda Maharaja – a step that required significant courage on their parts. At the time, most of our other godbrothers remained silent or resisted, unable to respond to their sisters with the same kind of compassion and favor Srila Prabhupada had freely and profusely given all the "boys and girls." And while these men are no longer the vast majority, many in power still find it difficult to welcome women's full participation. Often leaders do not instruct their disciples and followers how to treat women with courtesy or Vaishnava regard, therefore subtle and gross disrespectful, dismissive, and demeaning behaviors persist in many temples. This is especially problematic in our main centers in Mayapur and Vrindavan because devotees from around the world go there to learn how to behave in Krishna consciousness. And there, unfortunately, sexist behaviors are prominent.

While Srila Prabhupada's daughters spent years raising awareness and educating, holding conferences, seeking resolutions, and writing many papers, we only began the journey toward social-spiritual health for women and children in our Movement.

Men and women in ISKCON should not allow the mistreatment of women to continue or to be repeated in any center, in any temple, in any home. To change paradigms and entrenched social behaviors – especially ones that seem to be supported by *shastra* and guru – requires a solid understanding of complex issues. And in this dialogue we have the drawback that we start from a presumption that women are less intelligent. Therefore, if we want to be taken seriously, if we are grappling with a current circumstance or event in our local temple, if we want change, if we want to advocate for our sisters, we will have to know our topic. Luckily, this is not difficult with the publication of this anthology.

The essays in this anthology will bring light to devotees around the world. They are as applicable today as they were yesterday and can be used as a road map for moving into the future. Your senior sisters and brothers, who have poured out their wise hearts to you here, thought deeply about this topic. They knew Srila Prabhupada and lived under his roof. This is not only an important book of history, but a useful resource – a veritable encyclopedia of responses to misconceptions about women and their role in Krishna consciousness. Refer regularly to this comprehensive reference; you will stand on solid ground in good company.

One of the most important contributions this book can make is giving you the information and the wisdom of our experience to stand strong against everything that is opposed to bhakti. To be sure, prohibiting services based on the body is a violence directly contrary to Bhakti Devi Herself.

In closing, I bring attention to one anomaly. Some have claimed that women spoke up because they wanted position and power. We should note, however, that no woman ever made a power grab. And those women who have been asked to take on higher-profile service positions (in addition to their loving responsibilities as wives and mothers) – because of their Krishna-given talents and devotion – have proven their worth. Devotees, serving as leaders now and in the past include Ananda Vrindavan dasi, Dina Sarana dasi, Jaya Sri dasi, Kosarupa dasi, Krishnarupa dasi, Kusha dasi, Lila Shuka dasi, Malati dasi, Mathura Mandala dasi, Mukhya dasi, Prasanta dasi, Radha dasi, Rukmini dasi, Sandamani dasi, Sudharma dasi, Tadit dasi, Vaibhavi dasi, Visakha dasi, Vraja Lila dasi, Yamuna dasi – surely I'm forgetting some here, there are too many to name, and I don't even know them all! It would be unfortunate for our Movement should we lose these devotees and their services because of a consideration about their external body.

It is my heartfelt hope that you will be inspired and motivated to continue the work that Prabhupada's daughters began. Too often I still hear the tears of women around the world as they contend with discrimination, mistreatment, cruelty, disrespect, and, yes, even abuse.

I pray that we (women and men) will stop the pollution of Gaudiya Vaishnavism with the *smarta*-like mentality of trying to import concepts of sexism, racism, sectarianism, and other forms of prejudice and bigotry. Srila Prabhupada pointed out the history of how so many Hindus converted to Islam because they were disheartened and demoralized by the behavior and strictures of arrogant *smartas* who tried to control their "exalted" positions within *varnashrama* by excluding others. Envy has no place in spiritual life.

The matter is in our hands. Do we want to show the world the nobility of Gaudiya Vaishnavism and its beautiful ideals of universal appeal regardless of race, sex, or caste? It is our greatest honor to represent these sacred teachings to the world. Will we represent them not only by our own spiritual practices but also how we treat our women and children? I hope so and I hope this anthology offers us assistance in our forward march.

May this book give you vision, determination, and courage to advocate for your mothers, sisters, daughters, granddaughters, and generations of women to come so that everyone has full access to the practice of bhakti according to all their talents and desires to serve.

May you find your voice; may it be strong. And may you find your voice sooner than we found ours.

A Note about the Structure of this Book

When I opened Yamuna Devi's Word file with the piece she read at the Women's Ministry GBC presentation in 2000, I was immediately stuck by her intentional choice of font. *Of course!* I thought. Yamuna was a master calligrapher, which meant she had a refined sense of taste for typography. And here in her document – which most likely no one else but her would see – she had chosen an elegant, old-style serif typeface.

I was moved by remembering her consistent attention to detail in everything she did. I also considered the symbolism of using the same font she used in this anthology. It would be a way to honor her and remember her last wish to give a strong voice to women.

Thus I have used Sabon, a typeface whose origins stem from the fifteenth century, for the text of this book. I have paired Sabon, a serif font, with Karla, a sans serif typeface, for the titles and headings. I believe Yamuna would have appreciated the combination. In this way, we find her touch throughout the print and PDF version of the book. The other digital versions change the font based on the device used.

I have arranged the material in this anthology in chronological order as clearly shown in the Table of Contents by indicating the year the pieces were released. However, some content was better placed in the Appendixes. For instance, there was no sense in placing each *Priti-laksanam* newsletter in the book itself. Other pieces were books unto themselves and couldn't be inserted into the main text.

Since this is a digital book, I'm able to give you links to audio recordings, videos, and other PDFs, thus increasing your access to complimentary or supportive material.

For those who purchase the print book, please refer to the digital version for your downloads.

June 2020

[1] Lecture on *Gita* 3.18-30 given on December 30, 1968; lecture on *Bhagavatam* 3.25.14 given on November 14, 1974; lecture on *Bhagavatam* 6.1.24 given on July 8, 1975.

The Untold Story of How I Found My Voice
by Pranada dasi

As a pioneer voice for women in ISKCON, I have been repeatedly asked why I spoke up. To all but a handful of people, I have made only general replies; I've never publicly answered this question. But now, as I'm compiling this anthology, it's clear the book needs an introduction to the first entry – my letter to Saudamani dasi – which was the initiating event that led to the emergence of women's voices in ISKCON. With the following account, we find the reason for all the essays in this book.

To help me gain courage to write, I considered these points:

(a) history is being forgotten,

(b) what did happen to women, and by extension our children, should never happen again, ever, and,

(c) while some of the more abusive behaviors against the first-generation women in ISKCON have been ameliorated, demeaning, dismissive, and prejudiced behavior toward women continues in many temples.

For these reasons, I decided to give an uncensored, personal account of what urged me to speak up for women in ISKCON.

1984

Mangala-arati is only a couple of hours away, but I still can't sleep. From my sleeping bag on the floor my eyes remain fixed on the ceiling as vivid scenes, one after another, explode in full color and emotion in the dark night. They repeat over and over. I toss and turn and cry.

Until tonight I hadn't realized just how much the past years have affected me. Each time a godbrother had taken credit for a service I had offered, I took the opportunity to be humble. I didn't care, I was eager for service. I took on more and more responsible services and became proficient in managing. I blissfully soared in absolute joy giving every ounce of energy, all my abilities, every minute – my very self – to Srila Prabhupada and Krishna. Sacrifice had brought me so much happiness and I just wanted to give more!

But the strangest things started to happen. A godbrother told me he didn't like that I was so enthusiastic to take on services so he took away my service of managing the tape ministry for a guru. When he couldn't find a replacement, I was asked to take it back up. I was also typing the letters for a GBC-guru. Another devotee said he wanted to get a replacement though I typed well, timely, and reliably. There was never a backlog, never a delay. This devotee, too, said he just didn't like that I was doing so much and therefore he was going to look for a replacement. The weeks passed and he couldn't find a replacement, so he resorted to periodically threatening to take away the service.

At the time, I was working on the final two volumes of the *Srila Prabhupada-lilamrta* as the typesetter, proofreader, and production manager of Gita-Nagari Press, as we were short staffed and we were on a tight deadline. All of a sudden one day, in pursuance of the many "promises" that services would be taken from me, I was told that a man was taking over my responsibilities as the production manager. The appointed devotee had no experience in book production. But I acquiesced and spent many days training him in all facets of the service. Surprisingly to me, he wasn't keen on the work and simply didn't do it. He wouldn't show up to the office day after day, week after week. He knew I was capable of handling the work and that I would do it. He, however, kept the position as the production manager, which made it difficult for me to get the work done. He would receive communications from team members and the printers and not pass them on to me. Aspects of production fell between the cracks and the schedule almost came to a full halt until I was put back in that service. These are but two examples of a plethora of scenarios.

As these memories swirl around, I chastise myself: *You're not being humble.* This thought tortures me. How can I make advancement unless I'm humble? My mind darts around looking for ways to pacify myself. But it races over dozens of memories without letting up. *Why is my mind doing this? Is what is coming up the root of the current depression that I've been unable to shake?*

Before I can think about it, another memory rushes onto the ceiling. I'm walking outside on a temple property, and a man spits on the ground in my direction. I've seen other men spit at my sisters, sometimes right on them. I assume this response is to the oft-quoted statement that one should spit at the thought of sex life, but they're spitting *at* human beings.

Now the stairway of the Santo Domingo temple comes into view. It's 1977 and I'm six months pregnant. As I start down the stairs, I slip and begin tumbling down. The *brahmachari* walking up the stairs simply presses his back against the wall to make sure he doesn't touch me. Another *brahmachari* refuses to share with me some milk from the one cup a day that is offered to the Deities.

The stairway triggers memories of hallways. I see myself facing the wall and pressing myself up against it so that a *brahmachari* can pass freely without the slightest possibility of accidentally touching me and to spare him from seeing the front of me. I'd seen several other women do this and it became the unspoken "proper etiquette."

The scene switches to women lined up at the *prasadam* table for lunch. Most men come late. As they saunter in, they simply step in front of the last man, but in front of the first woman. If we had been the first person in line, we're now toward the end of a long line. No mind that our children are hungry and crying and that, again today, there may not be enough *prasadam* for the women. We already know that if there was any special preparation it would only be served to the men, who sometimes relish it with statements they make out loud, while asking for seconds.

This triggers another *prasadam* memory. I've injured my back and barely able to walk. My services are in a house that is a mile away from the temple. I'm unable to walk to the temple for lunch, nor can I ride in their car with the *brahmacharis*, who go every day. After going hungry for a few days, I gain the courage to ask them if they could bring me a plate of *prasadam*. The only one who doesn't flat-out ignore me, laughs and says, "Definitely not." So for months I go without a mid-day meal. By the time I make it to the temple there are only leftovers which are insufficient, but I learn to make do.

My mind moves to a *harinama* on Hollywood Boulevard in Los Angeles. As usual, and considered normal, the women and children are at the back of the procession. Intoxicated men harass us, sometimes grabbing our arms or trying to hug or kiss us, and we have concern about our children in their strollers.

Stop looking for all the problems, Pranada, I chastise myself. But my mind is not letting up. I wonder if I'm losing my mind. I've never experienced torment like this and I'm not clear why all of this is demanding my attention. *Why are you focusing on what you feel are wrongs against you? They're minor, after all. This isn't the attitude of a devotee.*

I'm not going mad; I'm not making up the memories. I begin to acknowledge these are suppressed memories. But they're rising in a disorienting flurry. Until now, I had made light of, or intentionally forgot, each incident. *What is actually bothering me?* I wonder. *What is my subconscious trying to say?* There's not enough time to carefully ponder, the memories are coming too fast and I can't stop them.

Now a voice is asking for me to consider other points. *Yes, it's true,* I acknowledge. The daily *Bhagavatam* classes in all the temples that I've lived in are sessions for belittling women, even though half of the audience is women. These lengthy diatribes go on even if the verse isn't about women. A day couldn't go by without some verbal assault about women.

I wonder why the speaker cannot balance the statements from *shastra* that are so affronting. So many statements are sweeping generalizations that hardly apply to every woman. Oftentimes even not the majority! The texts were written *for men* so it's understandable why they take pot shots at women – to fortify a man's practice. But times have changed, and by Srila Prabhupada's doing, women are practicing now, too. So the principle the text is teaching applies to us, but in reverse: we have to be careful of attraction and attachment to men, who are also foolish, cycling in *samsara*. But no one talks like this. There are an equal number of verses about men's shortcomings, but the speakers seem to have amnesia about these. Not every word here is absolute, but no one explains the distinction between relative and absolute statements. And definitely no one makes mention that the devotee women are not ordinary women. Such hateful behavior!

My mind scans over the years. Everything associated with women has been demeaned: the women themselves, men who are married to them, and their children. Of course I have known this, but haven't focused on it; I was too absorbed in service, nothing else mattered.

Then I have this startling thought: *Do you see what you've done? In response to how women are viewed, you've tried to become a man!* I pass my hand over the stubbles of hair on my head and pull on my *shikha. For years, you've been wearing white dhotis with the thinnest border wrapped like a sari.*

For the first time I catch a raw glimpse of myself: I look like a man; I've tried to become a man. It occurs to me that this was a reasonable, yet subconscious, strategy. After all, as a single mom, I was the lowest of the low in the social hierarchy and I knew that to have a place in what ISKCON had become, I had to do more and better than anyone else. And I did. I was doing the amount of service that two or three people were doing and I was doing it well, happily, and enthusiastically. *Well,* I thought, *whatever psychology may be amiss, there's nothing else more important than service. But why do my brothers keep taking it away? Why can't I do what I'm good at doing? They won't accept me even though I've practically changed into a man!*

Tulasi Dasa's quote, "You can beat a dog, a drum, or a woman until you get a nice sound," that passed around ISKCON, surfaces to my mind and along with it, memories of women confiding in me their anguish. Women had told me how their husbands had used this quote to support beating them.

The night ends like this. I rise for *mangala-arati* and go about my day. But as I lay down to go to sleep the next night – and the next and the next and the next – the ceiling becomes a cinema screen again and again and again. I cannot stop the rush of memories. No amount of philosophical reasoning or praying calms my mind nor stops the memories that seem to need to spill out of me. I'm being forced to come to terms *with all of them.*

The ceiling now shows the scene of my godsisters trying to find a place to chant *japa.* It's below freezing outside. The temple room has two large heaters, but only men are allowed to chant in the temple room. In one temple where I lived, women were allocated the unheated shoe room (yes, filled with shoes, we would scoot some aside to find a spot to sit), in another an unheated room off the temple room. Many women would go to their rooms, an unsuitable place for attentive *japa,* where I would see them get distracted or take rest instead of chanting.

I see Jadurani on the *vyasasana* in Los Angeles giving *Bhagavatam* class. There are rumbles outside the class by some men who are upset that she's speaking. Their complaints have nothing to do with the quality of her class, they just don't want her to speak. In Hawaii, Kirtanananda Swami complains to Prabhupada about it and asks if they can stop Jadurani from giving class, but he doesn't agree. However Jadurani is never asked to give class again.

In 1977, the temple moved from the city in Puerto Rico up to the mountains in Gurabo. There were two buildings on the new property, one in good condition and another that had been uninhabited for years and was infested with large rats. Women were given this building and the men stayed in the newer building. At night we took turns keeping guard with a broom. As rats jumped off the rafters, we'd hit them to make them land on the floor and not on our beds. We had two babies and rats are known to eat around infants' mouths.

At least we had a place to stay. There were temples that didn't have facility for women at all, though every temple had living arrangements for men.

On the ceiling, I now see my dearest friend, T., a huge collector, sneak out in the middle of the night to leave Krishna consciousness in 1983. She is one of the casualties who couldn't tolerate the mistreatment. Though only one of the many women I have seen leave, her departure hits me hard because we were so close. Now in my mind's eye I see many women who visit a temple turn around and walk out aghast. These memories tear at my heart and I cry.

I wish I could sleep before *mangala-arati*. I then remember other *mangala-aratis*. We're in the back of the temple barely able to see the Deities. If my son misbehaves during *arati*, his punishment is that he has to go to the back of the temple and be with the women. The children know they are being demoted. *Oh, Krishna, the children are hearing the classes! How could I have missed the significance of this point?*

On the ceiling, a picture flashes of a godsister who brought me a wedding ring. As this image surfaces – for the first time since it happened in 1976 – my body shakes. *What is it? Why does this memory disturb me even more than the others?* A flood of associated memories overwhelm me.

When the Los Angeles airport was closed, I was told I'd be joining Y.'s newly formed woman's party to collect money. Another women, also assigned to the party, came up to me. Opening the palm of her hand, she extended me a ring saying, "Essentially you'll be marrying Y. This ring is for you." I declined the ring and the chance to marry a married man since I was already married! But I wasn't taken off the party. Our little group drove up to Berkeley so we could be trained by the women on Jiva's women's party and Y. could be trained by Jiva.

One evening, after lights were out, D., who lay in her sleeping bag next to mine, whispered, "Do everything you're asked without question – whatever it is. Otherwise there are consequences. You heard N. broke her arm? She didn't fall as they say, Jiva *beat* her! He beats who he wants and has sex with many of the women. There's this idea that he's married to a few of the women."

"Can't you do anything?"

"Who would I tell? What would Jiva do to me if I said something?"

"Before we came up here G. told me I was to think I was marrying Y. and I was supposed to wear a ring but I wouldn't take it." I whisper back.

As I remember these scenes I begin sobbing. *Why didn't I say something to someone, anyone, at the time about what was happening to these women?* I try to appease myself. *You were shocked and terrified and barely 18.* When I had returned back to LA, I was able to get off of Y.'s party. I wonder how much more the women went through!

Some months prior to the trip to Berkeley in 1976, two or three women had separately (and quietly) come up to me to tell me that all the women in Los Angeles were planning to hide during Tamal Krishna Maharaja's upcoming visit and suggested I might like to follow suit because he was trying to get all the women sent to Australia.

"Prabhupada wouldn't do that, would he?" I had asked. No one was sure.

Now the scene on the ceiling shifts. I'm at the West 55th Street temple. It's 1978, a few months after Srila Prabhupada passed away. My son is six months old, I just turned 20 a few days earlier. Having newly arrived in New York, I ask if I can go on book distribution, my favorite service. In the conversation, a couple of women tell me that the women's party in New York is wonderful. "T. dasa," they say, "even makes sure all the women have sanitary napkins for their menstruation." I know this is news because not all women have easy access to basic needs. "And also," they continue, "he is nothing like D., who is worse than Jiva by far."

This sends shivers up my spine. I had heard whispers about the New Vrindavan women's party but these New York devotees have heard more about the physical and psychological abuse the women are braving to do their service for Srila Prabhupada in New Vrindavan.

I don't say a word. What do you say to this kind of information?

The next memory surfaces. I gasp. *I remember. I remember!*

Srila Prabhupada had appeared to me in a dream after I arrived at West 55th Street. I had never dreamt of him before, and this dream had shook me up. Prabhupada was distressed and told me that the dissension between the men and women would ruin his movement. He was perplexed and disturbed and wanted it to stop. He looked at me pleading – as if *I* was to do something.

What could I possibly do? Some years later when the *Lilamrta* was published, I had heard how unhappy Srila Prabhupada was with the disagreements between traveling *sannyasis/brahmacharis* and *grhastha* temple presidents. But it was Prabhupada first in my dream who announced his concern and dissatisfaction to me.

His look haunts me now. I have pushed the dream away for years but here it is with the same petition. How can I respond? *What can I do?*

But I can't answer the questions. Something else dawns on the horizon of my awareness. *Everything. I have pushed* everything *out of my mind.* I know these memories will never go back into hiding. *But what am I going to do with all of this?* Feeling crushed by these memories, I cry more.

The next scene begins. In 1978, some years after I first met the women on Jiva's party, I returned to Berkeley to find all of them wearing white *saris*. I thought only a few were "married" to Jiva, but every woman on the party is now in white. It had become public knowledge that Jiva had psychologically, physically, and sexually abused many of them. In their wisdom, the managers gave Jiva *sannyasa*, essentially promoting him. I thought *sannyasa* was awarded to those who had control of sex desire. But then strange and scary things were happening within ISKCON's social structure, which manifested as a dissonance towards women. The young women wore white making the statement they would never marry. They were still the major financial support for the temple, working long hours collecting money. *What were the managers doing for the women who had been so abused? How were my sisters now?*

Pretty soon I imagine the conditions each woman likely had to endure and it overwhelms me; I *feel* what I imagine to be their pain in my body. *Really, maybe I am going insane.*

As the night ends I know I have to speak to someone, but who? Who will be safe to speak with? During the day I would look at different godsisters and try to assess if I could speak with them. After some days, I venture a conversation with one godsister, but I'm careful not to reveal everything on my mind.

"You're not making up the problems and inequities," she assures me.

This short conversation calms me and gradually the sleepless nights stop. But a problem remains. I begin noticing more and more injustices toward women as if I have newly developed antennae. For the longest time, I had brushed aside my experiences and ignored what I was seeing by classifying them as anomalies.

Now I wonder if *any* godsister has been immune. I think of a few who probably haven't experienced much of the situation, like those who are married or living outside the temple. I know that the wives of some temple presidents were spared. I know not all men have intentionally set out to hurt women, many seem oblivious, but they *have and continue to participate* in this system by their silence, and the situation is atrocious.

As I cautiously begin speaking with godsisters, I learn about the depth of their buried pain: I'm not alone – not even slightly.

A commitment develops within me and grows stronger. I will accept what happens to me and look for Krishna's hand in my life. I want to respond with humility and advance in Krishna consciousness. *But, I cannot be quiet about the abuses my godsisters endure. I will speak honestly.*

Yet I can't find my voice. I'm absolutely terrified. What will happen to me if I speak up? I could lose everything. My spiritual family means everything to me. Where would I be without shelter here? I have no material possessions, but I could lose my spiritual standing and my spiritual family. How can I go against the social rules instituted throughout the *entire* Movement?

While wrestling with this growing internal unrest, I was faced with another striking issue: marriages were arranged for women who didn't want to marry and/or who didn't want to marry the man chosen for them.

And now it was my turn. I sat on the ground shocked and disoriented in 1985. The devotee in front of me had announced my authority's decision to have me married. During our 30-minute conversation, I had said, "No, I'm not getting married," three or four times. I wondered how long it would take for him to understand my decision. To make sure I was off the hook and help him find a partner for this man, I gave the names of three other women who I knew wanted to marry him. Finally, the *brahmachari*-messenger said, "Actually, you don't have an option. The fire sacrifice is in three weeks."

And that was that. No, I wouldn't go against my highest authority. But this was devastating and only exponentially increased my conviction that something was askew with how women were being dealt with in ISKCON.

1986

As I continue private conversations with older godsisters, a picture of ISKCON before the sexism emerges. It's a story completely unknown to me and I have been a devotee for eleven years!

Though I had seen Jadurani give a couple of classes, she was stopped soon after I joined the Los Angeles temple. Now I was learning that it was common for women to give classes, just like men, as soon as they joined the temple: they were trained to speak just like their brothers! In fact, Prabhupada himself had asked women to give classes and they gave classes in front of him.

My sisters told me that Prabhupada had asked women to lead kirtans, which they led in the presence of *sannyasis* and thousands of people. Therefore, the prevailing attitude that renounced men could not hear a women devotee sing was another concoction.

Prabhupada had asked Yamuna and Govinda dasi to sit on the GBC, but Tamal Krishna Maharaja had protested so vehemently that the women declined. Women had been *pujaris* in India. Women stood side by side their brothers in temples, not in the back of the temple room. When men had complained about women chanting *japa* in the temples, in a letter to Ekayani on December 3, 1972 and a morning walk in Australia, Srila Prabhupada said that those who were agitated should go to the forest. Women used to offer flower petals to Prabhupada on his *vyasasana* during his *guru-puja*. Women, on Prabhupada's request, offered *dandavats*. So many things had changed and most devotees had no idea!

How did this happen? Some godsisters explained that as the number of *sannyasis* grew in ISKCON the misogyny also grew. *Sannyasis* who had visited India came back making changes. Other godsisters questioned what was actually Vedic and which behaviors were inculcated into Indian society due to Muslim influence. Bhaktivinoda Thakura writes that the Mohammedan rule of India from 1206 to 1757 was a calamity that greatly diminished the standard of *varnashrama* and polluted the culture in many ways. So I find some truth in their statements. Regardless if I could sort that issue out, Prabhupada knew Vedic culture more than the new *sannyasi*-converts: his discretion trumped theirs.

As each piece of history was revealed I grew more and more astonished and dismayed. ISKCON's social and even spiritual barriers for women didn't reflect what Srila Prabhupada had established for us. It was an act of dismantling what Srila Prabhupada had established. We needed a social transformation back to what Prabhupada had given us.

Some of the stories shocked me. One woman relayed how she was near the *vyasasana* doing a service just before Srila Prabhupada began his class. A *sannyasi* who didn't appreciate her presence among the men struck her on the back with his *danda*. Luckily for him, Prabhupada didn't see.

Another godsister told me that there was tension between her and a godbrother-*sannyasi* who was unappreciative of her involvement in the temple management – a service Srila Prabhupada had given her. Trying to diffuse the situation, she went to the godbrother and paid obeisance. He chose not to return the obeisance, and while she was on the ground in front of him, he kicked her in the stomach.

And, oh, the stories of the beatings in so many marriages! And the extreme emotional abuse women endured after marrying men who'd been indoctrinated as *brahmacharis* to hate women and who were ill-equipped to evolve their thinking. So many men had not come to ISKCON as chauvinists, but now they were misogynists.

I started to become angry. Very angry!

Help me, I asked one sister after another. *We have to expose what is going on.* I felt I needed the public support of at least one other person. But everyone declined: they were too frightened.

Finally, I approached Yamuna. She soberly looked at me and said, "You don't know what you're up against, Pranada."

"But I do, Yamuna. That's why I need help."

With that, tears welled up in her eyes. She placed her hand over her heart. "I can't, Pranada. It would break my heart."

I knew what she meant. In previous conversations she had described events that had already broken her heart and sent her into seclusion and she couldn't bear more.

But during this year, I finally found my voice. My voice was weak and timid, but I spoke.

I was in a meeting with three men discussing a service. They were dependant on my participation because I was the only one in the group who knew the details of project. K. dasi wasn't present in the meeting, but was a key team member. They had choice words about her – the same kinds of things I had heard said about me over the years.

"She's independent, and that's just unacceptable," one said, and the other two agreed with him pointing out her numerous "faults." They begin to talk about removing her from some of the services and "putting her in her place." This went on for a good half an hour.

I knew K.; I worked with her. By "independent," they meant she was intelligent, competent, dedicated, and could think for herself. She wasn't willy-nilly doing whatever she wanted, she was competent and they were threatened by that.

I said, "You ought to be cautious about disrespecting someone who is your key team member. Your bravado about finding someone else could get you and the service into trouble."

I couldn't find courage to say more in the meeting, but I wrote them a long letter detailing why their attitude and behavior was wrong. I questioned why they felt so threatened by a woman. I explained why I wouldn't tolerate their comments and behavior, and if they ever criticized K. again – or if they made any attempt to take away her services – then I would not be available to consult with them or answer any questions. Period. They definitely needed me at least for the moment, and therefore my statement carried weight.

I trembled as I sealed the envelope. But I was happy; I was advocating for my godsister. *If each of us did this,* I thought, *it could make a difference!* I said what needed to be said. Trying to reassure myself I thought, *If I'm courageous, maybe it will give strength to other women. Maybe the abusive situation that long ago got out of hand for women in ISKCON can change.*

For some reason, the meeting was a turning point for me, I think because I was watching first-hand the way those devotees intended to unravel K.'s life for no reason except that she was a woman and they wanted control. I had experienced it before and suspected how they spoke behind closed doors, but now I saw it in action. My taking a stand upended their plans to harm K., and they stopped their negative statements about her.

I would no longer watch devotees in male bodies treat *any* of my sisters like this anymore. And the behavior had to be stopped where it started: in the classes. After listening to countless *Bhagavatam* classes in which men disparaged women, I decided I didn't have to sit in them any longer. What a feeling of liberation! And if I stayed in class, I could raise my hand after the class and question what was said or make comments. So I began doing that. *All the time.* I took off the gag on my mouth and stepped out of the dark closet where I had been fearfully hiding.

I was convinced that reinstating services for women would go a long way in shifting demoralizing attitudes and behaviors – for men and women – and bring balance back to ISKCON making for stronger preaching. Besides self-purification, Prabhupada wanted us to preach.

As I was coming to terms with all these thoughts, I wondered how to bring attention to the plight of women and change the social structure. I was still looking for *one person* to publicly stand with me.

I approached Saudamani and explained my distress, what I had learned, and asked her if she would help me. She wanted to know what I wanted changed. She didn't say change wasn't possible, or that she couldn't help – she wanted to know what I wanted changed! No one had opened a door until this moment. I got excited.

"Everything, Saudamani, everything should be changed. Women should be giving *Bhagavatam* classes, leading kirtans, standing on the side of their godbrothers, they can initiate disciples," . . . I quickly rattled off a long list.

"What one thing, if changed, could have the biggest impact?"

I knew she had something in mind, "Tell me."

"*Bhagavatam* class," she said. "If devotees see that women are as devoted, mature, and as intelligent as men, it will be much harder to depersonalize women and mistreat them. Write me a letter with all your points and I'll write you a reply. Then we can send the letters into the GBC."

1988

As I began writing my letter to Saudamani, my son's teacher came to me. She was having trouble disciplining him. He wouldn't follow her instructions saying, "I don't have to listen to you because you're a woman. I'm more intelligent than you." At ten years old he felt emboldened to treat a teacher and an elder like this thanks to the prevailing speech and attitudes in ISKCON! How was I going to undo the indoctrination? This incident was strong confirmation that I must speak.

And in case I still had any hesitation, while I was composing my letter, a godsister called and told me that several boys had returned from the Vrindavan *gurukula*. They had been sexually abused and that it was *hush-hush*. I simply could not believe what she was telling me. How could this happen in our Movement? How could this happen?

She confided that one or two of the mothers had approached some authorities, but the women's claims were being denied or made light of by them. In fact, these mothers were told to keep quiet! These Vaishnavis were not only beside themselves because of what their sons had gone through, but they weren't being heard! Where was the hope of justice and rectifying the situation?

I was furious.

It wouldn't have been possible for these children to be abused and for the abuse to remain unaddressed if these mothers had not been systematically and thoroughly demoralized and intimidated for years.

With this news, I was no longer frightened by what would happen to me for speaking up. I had lived through too much, seen too much, heard too much, knew too much.

I wasn't going to be quiet.

My letter to Saudamani and her reply were sent to the GBC.

Additionally, I put forward an agenda item to the GBC body requesting that they pass a law allowing women to give *Bhagavatam* class. In what I took as a sophisticated, political move, the GBC responded that there was no need to put a ruling on the books allowing women to give class because there was no rule stating they couldn't give class. I was filled with dread: my godbrothers fully intended to ignore the immensity of the situation. It was no longer a matter of them not being aware. It was now verified. They now knew and weren't going to help.

Savvy herself, Saudamani said, "So let's start giving classes." My heart sank. I wasn't trained in speaking, but I forged ahead ignoring the panic – for my sisters. She and I began speaking on the *Bhagavatam*. As soon as one of us would sit on the *asana,* men would stand up and walk out. There was a lot of rumbling in the hallways. Conversations were trigged around the Movement.

Our letters emboldened some women. Manasa Ganga dasi, a new devotee, came to me asking why women weren't allowed to chant *japa* in the temple room. "No good reason," I had told her. She wrote a letter to the devotees in Philadelphia asking to change the standard. It worked. Women were allowed to chant in the temple room after having been prohibited for nearly a decade. Now, this second change in the Philadelphia temple fueled further conversations across the United States and elsewhere. "What were these women up to?" devotees started asking.

Someone anonymously wrote me saying they wanted me to die and indicated they would like to make sure it happened. M. from New York sent a note saying I was destroying Srila Prabhupada's movement. His sentiment was expressed by *many*. All kinds of slurs about me – a lot of them – began flying around. I was shaken, but not enough to be quiet. I kept thinking that when devotees really understood what was going on for women, their hearts would melt and we could be a closer family.

Back to Godhead magazine moved to San Diego. As servants of the magazine, my husband, son, and I went too.

KK was waiting for me. She wanted change in San Diego – and around the world – and she wanted it *now*. She suggested I do something to get all the women in ISKCON to go on strike and bring the Movement to a screeching halt. "In just three days everything would be completely stopped," she said passionately. Yes, of course it would. We knew that all too well. But I told her we would do more by raising the consciousness of devotees and educating them. I didn't want to harm the preaching.

Well, since that wasn't possible, she wanted to know how to change the *darshana* standard so that women could see the Deities during *aratis* by standing side by side with the men. I told her to follow ISKCON's system of addressing grievances. First she should approach her temple president. I suggested she write a letter and gave her various points to highlight. The temple president took his time to respond to her letter, only to tell her she had to go to her GBC representative. The GBC man told her she had to take the matter to the GBC chairman. The GBC chairman said she was to discuss the matter with her temple president. Her letter writing campaign took months (this was before email), but she didn't give up.

To me, it appeared that the GBCs and temple president were speaking, because at last, the temple president clearly felt pressured and finally conceded to her request. He drew an imaginary line on the side of temple room about ten feet behind the altar. He told us to stay on this side and that if we *once* stepped over the line he would repeal the privilege. Most women stayed in the back, unsure if they wanted to be seen as rebelling against the men. They heard the rumblings about me.

Battered women started knocking on my door. One came in distress that her husband was raping her nearly every night. Another came with a black eye and bruises. I began educating myself about resources available to these devotees, and gave them moral support and common-sense advice.

But where was real change in ISKCON? In Philadelphia, Saudamani gave classes and women chanted *japa* in the temple room. Now in San Diego women could stand on the side of the temple room to see the Deities. After a full year there was little overall improvement for women. What could I do now?

1989

I didn't know Sudharma well, but I went up to her on the sidewalk in San Diego and revealed my frustrations. Would she help me do something to change the situation for women in ISKCON? Unbeknownst to me, she was intimately familiar with abuse of women in ISKCON. She had been spared much, but she had been on Jiva's party.

"Oh, Sudharma, will you help me, please?"

"Yes. But I'm leaving for the east coast now. Mukunda Maharaja has asked me to head up ISKCON's PR department for the Robin George case. The original $32 million verdict just got reduced to $9 million, but that means we could still lose several temples. Give me a couple of months and let's reconnect."

That day we forged an alliance that would bear fruit. After a few months we had a plan. I would launch the *Priti-laksanam* newsletter and send it to devotees and managers around the world to fuel the dialogue and continue grassroots education. Sudharma, who was now regularly speaking to temple presidents and GBCs because of her important service on the Robin George case, would begin speaking with each person about the situation of women in ISKCON. When opportunities arose, she would take up the topic with each of them as relationships developed. It was a slow, painstaking but methodical process that we embarked on.

Devotees from around the world wrote me, either expressing support or their anger. Visiting *sannyasis* would ask me why I was speaking up. Some of them were genuinely moved by my answers and shifted their perspective. Suhotra Swami in Germany wrote, encouraging me to carry on. Sridar Swami and Satsvarupa dasa Goswami said they supported my work. But these were private statements.

My frustration peaked at certain points. Just when I thought some devotees were understanding what the issues were, I was shown they didn't understand at all. One *sannyasi* asked me to take up a managerial service in a prominent project. "But Maharaja," I said, "You're going against your strong views about women, who you believe are less intelligent. Remember? How could I possibly take up that service?" He replied – in all seriousness – that I was an exception; that I was intelligent. I got sick to my stomach.

Managers were asking me to be on various ISKCON boards. I became the token woman. Should I decline the offers or take up the services to show devotees that women were capable of offering these services?

Sudharma and I focused on our avenues of work patiently, gradually raising awareness, understanding, and sympathy around the world.

Priti-laksanam was widely distributed. For every one magazine I mailed out, it was read by three more devotees. It contributed to changing the mindset of many. Unquestioned behaviors were no longer automatic for some people. But the unspoken rules of behavior and restrictions in service remained firmly in place.

1994

Sudharma kept having to remind me to find patience. She was making progress with our godbrothers, she assured me. I knew why they were taking her seriously and therefore suspected she just might have a chance. The Robin George case, if lost, would mean ISKCON would lose several key temples in North America. Sudharma's contribution was significant. Our godbrothers couldn't deny how expert and capable she was and how much difference she was making in the long battle to save the temples. As she demonstrated her capacities she was given more credence. As her relationships with our brothers deepened, she was able to discuss in greater depth about the situation for women. Now, some of them really and finally understood, and several publicly supported change. Mukunda Maharaja, Bir Krishna Maharaja, and Bhaktitirtha Maharaja were willing to help Sudharma bring the discussion into the GBC meeting rooms and Bhaktitirtha Swami suggested that we establish a Ministry, not a council, for women. Thus in 1994, the North American Women's Ministry was formed with a voting seat and Sudharma became the Minister.

1995

Sudharma knocked on my door. When I opened it she didn't make a move to enter, but just stood there grinning, probably exhausted from lengthy North American GBC meetings.

"What, Sudharma, what?!"

"A woman was just voted onto a seat on the highest managerial body in North America."

I burst into laughter, jumped up and down, and grabbed her into a hug.

Sudharma had just been unanimously elected by the body as the executive officer for ISKCON North America. The seat entitled her to be a guest on the international GBC body in Mayapur. She was welcomed as an executive officer – the highest position on the North American managerial body. This spoke directly to her qualifications that had become so self-evident in her work on the Robin George case with the leaders in North America. The devotees had so much respect for her, they easily included her.

Ten years after I began fretting and five years after beginning work with Sudharma, we crossed a significant milestone and broke through the invisible ceiling for women. The previous year she was able to establish the North American Ministry with a voting seat. And now this year she was an executive director on the NA GBC body. Maybe we could permanently re-establish what Srila Prabhupada had given to us, forever dismantling debilitating ideas that the material body should dictate service and preaching opportunities.

Just as we were set to really make progress, I fell ill and could only help Sudharma on the sidelines, limping along to some meetings and conferences. She forged ahead, leading the way after gathering the support and help of special souls like Anuttama dasa, Bhaktitirtha Swami, Bir Krishna Swami, Kusha dasi, Mukunda Maharaja, Prasanta dasi, Radha dasi, Rukmini dasi, Visakha dasi, Vraja Lila dasi, and others. And, of course, we always had the quiet, loving support of Yamuna Devi.

Sudharma Prabhu went on to establish the International Women's Ministry in 1996, now known as the Vaishnavi Ministry.

It is of interest to note that Tamal Krishna Maharaja, who was the emblem of anti-woman thought and behavior and to whom many current-day predominant leaders hold in high esteem, welcomed Sudharma Prabhu onto both the NA and International GBC bodies. As we know, he initially protested the presence of women on the GBC when Srila Prabhupada formed it.

1996

In September at North America's first Vaishnava-Christian Dialogue, I sat at a table with Tamal Krishna Maharaja and Ravindra Svarupa dasa in East Freeport, MA, eating lunch *prasadam* between sessions. Unexpectedly, Tamal Krishna Goswami thanked me for my work of educating devotees about Vaishnavis. He point blank told me that he supported all my efforts to initiate change for women *in all spheres of ISKCON participation including as gurus* – a belief which he had already demonstrated in welcoming Sudharma to the GBC. He said that he had changed his views about women by interacting with highly intelligent women in academia (some more intelligent than him, he told me), by observing how much our outreach was being hindered by ISKCON's sexist attitudes that weren't supported shastrically, and by personal realizations about how much harm he did to his godsisters, many of whom were highly competent. He was genuinely repentant.

The next part of the story can only be told by Sudharma Prabhu, to whom I offer *koti dandavats* and deep gratitude for her devotion, selflessness, and loving desire to include as many godsisters as possible in our crusade to end the silence and re-empower women.

Short of Sudharma writing something, this anthology and the GBC resolutions passed during her tenure from 1994 to 2000 will have to suffice to tell the rest of the story. Luckily, some of her memories and reflections are in the Epilogue of this anthology.

1988

Pranada dasi's Letter to Saudamani dasi

At the time the letters were published, the ideas were novel and few devotees were even aware of many of the quotes I cited. There was no Vedabase, and Srila Prabhupada's letters were newly published, thus few devotees had read them.

These letters sent a bit of a shock wave through ISKCON. No one had publicly countered the internationally-accepted restrictions, exclusions, and oppression of women in ISKCON. The letters were given to all GBC members with a request to pass a resolution that women be allowed to give Srimad-Bhagavatam *classes in ISKCON temples. My letter was also published in the* Vaishnava Journal, *a now defunct publication that had a fairly broad reading base, and the letter was translated into different languages.*

Because women had remained silent as their services were gradually taken away from them, the institutional memory of how Srila Prabhupada had engaged his daughters had all but been erased. My letter was the first attempt to remind the devotees of the scope of services Srila Prabhupada requested of women and encouraged them to do.

January 17, 1988
Dear Saudamani Prabhu,

Please accept my humble obeisances. All glories to Srila Prabhupada.

In light of our conversation the other day, I want to share with you some further thoughts I have been having about the role of women in the Krishna consciousness movement, and how I perceived that their role as Prabhupada saw it has been misunderstood.

I am sincerely trying to understand Srila Prabhupada's desires in this connection, and I am getting much realization from the various quotes I will include here. I know you will find these statements by Srila Prabhupada extremely thought-provoking. They are revolutionary in terms of what the movement has come to expect from devotee women, who are most often viewed as less intelligent, inferior, and personifications of *maya*. Based on this view, women were once seen as valuable to the movement only if they could collect money. That has changed for various reasons, but being in a woman's body still bars devotees from doing many services they may be qualified to do. This stereotyped understanding of women as inferior even leads many devotees to think that it is entirely appropriate for women to be beaten by their husbands. This mentality derives from a misinterpretation of the Vedic scriptures. The mentality is prevalent, and it is obvious by the way men speak to and about women, and how they behave toward them. At different times, Srila Prabhupada tried to give a balanced, correct understanding of the position of women, but somehow devotees have not imbibed it.

During Srila Prabhupada's 1975 U.S. tour, when he was strongly challenging the women's liberation movement, Prabhupada explained that the scriptural quotes describing women as less intelligent are material; they do not apply on the spiritual platform. In other words, materially a woman is less intelligent, but spiritually there is no difference between men and women. In fact, Prabhupada laughingly commented to some women disciple during a room conversation in Philadelphia that when a woman becomes a devotee, her brain expands. Also, Visakha Prabhu related to me that on a morning walk when she was present, Prabhupada was speaking very strongly about women, and at the end of his comments he said, "But not devotee women; they are Vaishnavas." In other words, anyone, male or female, who once surrenders to Krishna becomes intelligent. Srila Prabhupada used to quote a verse from *Chaitanya-charitamrita* that says, "One who is a devotee of Krishna is most intelligent."

Concerning the point that women are the agents of *maya*, Srila Prabhupada explained that when the term woman is used in the *shastra* is doesn't necessarily mean the female sex:

"Two things: woman and money. If we become attracted . . . The woman means for woman the man is woman. Not that woman means a particular class. Woman means that which is enjoyable. In this material world the man is enjoyable and the woman is enjoyable. So for both of them, *visayinam . . . yosit. . .* This body is superfluous. The bodily structure, it can be changed. Perhaps you know, now in medical science they can change the woman's body into man's body, and the man's body into woman's . . . We are not these bodies, this dress. It is a man's dress. I can transform into a woman's dress with a sari, but that does not mean that I am a woman. So, every one of us, living entities, we are part and parcel of the Supreme Lord. The outward dress, man and woman, that is dress." (Lecture on *Srimad-Bhagavatam* 1.7.11, September 10, 1976)

In the following letter Prabhupada explains that while previously only men would take up spiritual life and preaching, that has been changed in recent Gaudiya Vaishnava history – and it pleases Srila Prabhupada and Lord Chaitanya:

"Personally I am so much engladdened that the pairs of young boys and girls whom I have placed in householder life are doing so nicely in the Western world. When Lord Chaitanya delivered Jagai and Madhai He was also a householder, but when Jagai and Madhai were actually reclaimed, His wife, Vishnupriya, was not there. But in this case and in many other cases also, I find that my disciples combined together, husband and wife, are doing this preaching work so nicely. So I am especially proud how my householder disciples are preaching Lord Chaitanya's Mission. This is a new thing in the history of the *sankirtana* movement. In India all the *acharyas* and their descendants later on acted only from the man's side. Their wives were at home because that is the system from old times that women are not required to go out. But in *Bhagavad-gita* we find that *women are also equally competent like the men in the matter of Krishna Consciousness Movement.* Please therefore carry on these missionary activities, and prove it by practical example that there is no bar for anyone in the matter of preaching work for Krishna Consciousness." (Letter to Himavati dasi, December 2, 1969) [italics added]

Removing all bars and opening the preaching doors for everyone is the special mercy of Lord Chaitanya, and this is the principle Srila Prabhupada applied to spread the Krishna consciousness movement all over the world. How can we expect to spread Krishna consciousness on the scale Srila Prabhupada did, engaging all classes of people, unless we realize this principle and practice it? Srila Prabhupada is quite explicit about this point in the *Chaitanya-charitamrita:*

"Since both the boys and girls are being trained to become preachers, those girls are not ordinary girls but are as good as their brothers who are preaching Krishna consciousness. Therefore, to engage both boys and girls in fully transcendental activities is a policy intended to spread the Krishna consciousness movement. These jealous fools who criticize the intermingling of boys and girls will simply have to be satisfied with their own foolishness because they cannot think of how to spread Krishna consciousness by adopting ways and means which are favorable for this purpose. Their stereotyped methods will never help spread Krishna consciousness. . . . we are thoroughly instructing both men and women how to preach, and actually they are preaching wonderfully. . . . Both men and women are preaching the gospel of Lord Chaitanya Mahaprabhu and Lord Krishna with redoubled strength." (Cc. *Adi-lila* 7.32 and 7.38, purports)

Because of the present mentality prevailing in the movement, women have been restricted in their preaching activities by being restricted from various services. I will not go into detail here because it would increase the length of this letter too much. But after reading this letter from Satsvarupa dasa Goswami that a godsister recently shared with me, I felt really encouraged that we may be able to change this unfortunate situation and develop a proper understanding.

"First, I would like to express my admission of the fact that some men have misused the Krishna conscious philosophy regarding the place of women. The Vedic philosophy and the Vedic cultural context certainly recommend protection of women through all stages of her life. But the idea of a demeaning, insulting attitude toward women, treating them as less intelligent, inferior, as persons who may be beaten, is certainly obnoxious and is not Krishna conscious. I think you have accurately described that a male chauvinistic attitude of conditioned souls has been implanted on top of the Krishna conscious philosophy by a wrong interpretation. Thus we have a hypocritical misuse of the philosophy. I think it is only fair that mature women devotees, as well as men devotees, rectify this wrong. Since we are trying to rectify so many wrong directions we have taken in ISKCON, in regard to our approach to the public, and in other matters, this also should be rectified. And it will require admitting mistakes wherever they occurred by whoever made them." (December 13, 1987)

This wrong mentality has woven itself deeply into the thinking of the majority of devotees. This is a big mistake, and it goes against Srila Prabhupada's spirit, as he expresses it here in a 1968 room conversation in Seattle:

"Now another thing, that girls should not be taken as inferior. You see? Sometimes . . . Of course, sometimes scripture we say that 'Woman is the cause of bondage.' So that should not be, I mean to say, aggravated. That should not be aggravated, that 'Woman is inferior,' or something like that. So the girls who come, we should treat them nicely. I heard that G., after his wife left him, he became a woman-hater. That is not good. After all, anyone who is coming to Krishna consciousness, man or woman, if very fortunate. The idea of addressing – 'prabhu' means 'you are my master.' 'Prabhu' means master. And Prabhupada means many masters who bow down at his lotus feet. So everyone shall treat others as 'my master.' This is the Vaishnava understanding. That is stated in Bhagavata . . . . So, in spiritual life there is nothing like this sexist. The more we forget sex life that means we are advancing in spiritual life. So this should be the attitude: Women, godsisters, they should be nicely treated . . . That should be our policy everywhere."

Missing this spirit, we are committing a great violence to the prosperity of the Krishna consciousness movement and the individual spiritual lives of the devotee women. To what extent? I think greatly, and from my experience in talking with devotee women all over the movement, I think we'll hear more and more how this is so. Of course, I have personally seen many women leave our movement and many unable to join because of this problem. To me this is most regrettable and painful.

I also have personal experience how this "off" mentality is affecting our children. A known cure for a little's boy's misbehavior in *arati* will be to threaten that he must "stand with the women" – a humiliating, horrible fate, even though his own mother is probably there! Recently, Patita Pavana told me he didn't have to follow his teacher's instructions because (verbatim) "She's a woman, and women are less intelligent. I'm smarter than her." Therefore, it's all right to be disrespectful – that's logical enough for a ten-year-old, or, it seems, for many thirty-five year olds. He imbibed this from *Bhagavatam* classes and the display of the male devotees' general attitude toward women. However, these lessons he has learned are faulty in that they have not taught him how to respect all devotees of the Lord. Without respect he can not have submissiveness, thus he's missing out on a spiritual principle intrinsic to our whole philosophy. How will he absorb Krishna consciousness, since his mother and his schoolteacher are women? In fact, the mother is a guru, who is giving Krishna consciousness and encouraging her children on the spiritual path all their lives. Many devotees have experience that our teenagers are able to confide more confidentially in their mothers than their fathers. If our children have imbibed this wrong mentality about women, thus having their respect undermined, how will they fare?

One godsister told me that her daughter (at 3 or 4) didn't want to go to nursery in a skirt because girls weren't allowed to lead *kirtans* and do so many things she wanted to do. Why should this child experience this squashing of her spiritual aspirations? Rather, whatever spark of Krishna consciousness is there should be fanned, not smothered.

Blinded by our misconceptions, we are committing great violence to our own children. We are thoroughly implanting in their heads material duality. I find it very sad.

We have already discussed at length how this attitude has contributed to difficulties in a number of marriages in the movement. Marriage requires that the parties respect one another as devotees. If there are to be good, God-centered marriages, then there must be solid Vaishnava relationships. If men see women as less intelligent, like animals (or children), and not as devotees of Krishna, how can they have Vaishnava relationships with them?

There is much more to be said about these particular ISKCON social ills, and our movement as a whole, as well as the individuals within it, will have to come to terms with them. We will have to see changes in the near future. But I wanted to specifically talk to you now about one particular, but very important, matter: devotee women not being allowed to give *Srimad-Bhagavatam* class. I feel this practice is symbolic of the mentality we have been discussing – and it is with several, strong quotes by Prabhupada that we can refute this policy as complete, unadulterated *maya*.

I am completely convinced about Prabhupada's desires in this regard. There is certainly good reason for women to desire to give class, and it is the movement's duty to train them for this preaching work. We need so many experienced preachers. We know that our realization of the philosophy deepens the more we speak it. This is an essential principle Prabhupada addresses in the First Canto, Chapter One, text 6:

"To hear and explain them [these literatures] is more important than reading them. One can assimilate the knowledge of the revealed scriptures only by hearing and explaining. Hearing is called *sravana*, and explaining is called *kirtana*. The two processes of *sravana* and *kirtana* are of primary importance to progressive spiritual life. Only one who has properly grasped the transcendental knowledge from the right source by submissive hearing can properly explain the subject."

Prabhupada wrote a few letters where he explicitly stated that women can and should give *Bhagavatam* classes. These are most solid evidences, and after reading them I cannot understand how we so drastically deviated from this point.

"Regarding lecturing by woman devotees: I have informed you that in the service of the Lord there is no distinction of caste or creed, color, or sex. In the *Bhagavad-gita*, the Lord especially mentions that even a woman who has taken seriously is also destined to reach Him. We require a person who is in the knowledge of Krishna, that is the only qualification of a person speaking. It doesn't matter what he is. Materially a woman may be less intelligent than a man, but spiritually there is no such distinction. Because spiritually everyone is pure soul. In the absolute plane there is no such gradation of higher and lower. If a woman can lecture nicely and to the point, we should hear her carefully. That is our philosophy. But if a man can speak better than a woman, the man should be given first preference. But even though a woman is less intelligent, a sincere soul should be given proper chance to speak, because we want so many preachers, both men and women." (Letter to Jai Govinda dasa, February 8, 1968)

"So far as girls or boys lecturing in the morning, that doesn't make any difference. Either girl or boy devotees may deliver lecture if they choose to do. We have no such distinction of bodily designations, male or female. Krishna Consciousness is on the spiritual platform." (Letter to Shyama dasi, October 21, 1968)

"So you please continue your devotional service, cooking, etc., and you can also keep giving *Bhagavatam* class if you like. Women in our movement can also preach very nicely. Actually male and female bodies, these are just outward designations. Lord Chaitanya said that whether one is *brahmana* or whatever he may be if he knows the science of Krishna then he is to be accepted as guru. So one who gives class, he must read and study regularly and study the purport and realize it. Don't add anything or concoct anything, then he can preach very nicely. The qualification for leading class is how much one understands about Krishna and surrendering to the process. Not whether one is male or female. Of course women, generally speaking are less intelligent, better she has heard nicely then she will speak nicely." (Letter to Malati dasi, December 25, 1974)

About this last quote I have an interesting story. I obtained a copy of the outline for the "Strong Speaking" course from the Vrindavan classes J. Swami led this year. To my surprise this letter was discussed at one of these classes. The topic was, Should women give class? My copy had notes written on it by one of the students, who gave his understanding of the outcome of the classes' discussion. The notes said that there would be two acceptable circumstances to having a woman speak: (1) If all men in the temple had gone out preaching and only women and children remained, or (2) students had come to a Sunday Feast to hear about "The Lady's role in Krishna consciousness."

With all honesty, I cannot imagine how they reached their conclusion, and I have to doubt this interpretation of Prabhupada's straightforward instruction. I wrote to J. Swami about this, but I have not received a reply.

Though we can't bring ourselves to ask a godsister to speak, Srila Prabhupada himself wouldn't hesitate to ask his women disciples to speak – because he practiced what he preached. We find in the *Lilamrta* that Prabhupada asked women devotees to speak on many different occasions. In this next letter Prabhupada expresses his appreciation of Jadurani Prabhu's speaking ability:

"When I get to Montreal, I shall take selected pictures from Jadurany and as well as some of the pictures by Gourasundar and Govinda published in BTG. Jadurany has now become a nice preacher. I have report from Satsvarupa that she gives lectures very nicely. If we open a pavilion I shall take Jadurany also at that time, so she will deliver nice lectures." (Letter to Mahapurusha, March 28, 1968)

I remember Jadurani Prabhu giving enlivening lectures full of shastric references as late as 1975 in Los Angeles under Srila Prabhupada's auspices. In fact, that same year in Hawaii Kirtanandana Swami and another *sannyasi* complained to Srila Prabhupada about it. Prabhupada's response was (as related at that time to Jadurani by Ramesvara): "A preacher is spiritual and designation of 'women' and '*sannyasa*' are material." Unfortunately, shortly afterwards the temple president stopped asking her to give class –

the men had become perturbed and agitated. But Prabhupada had something strong to say about that problem at an earlier time. In New York, 1972, women were prohibited from chanting in the temple during the *japa* period. Apparently, on the plea that the men were agitated, they tried (and ultimately have been successful) excluding women from the temple room. Prabhupada was quite furious about this restriction.

" . . . and I have noted the contents with great concern. I do not know why these things inventions are going on. That is our only business, to invent something new programme? We have already got our Vaishnava standard. That is sufficient for Madhavacharya, Ramanujacharya, it was sufficient for Lord Chaitanya, six Gosvamis, for Bhaktivinoda Thakur, for my Guru Maharaja Bhaktisiddhanta Sarasvati, for me, for all big, big saints and *acharyas* in our line – why it shall be inadequate for my disciples so they must manufacture something? That is not possible. Who has introduced these things, that women cannot have chanting *japa* in the temple, they cannot perform the *arati* and so many things? If they become agitated, then let the *brahmacharis* go to the forest, I have never introduced these things. The *brahmacharis* cannot remain in the presence of women in the temple, then they must go to the forest, not remaining in New York City, because in New York there are so many women, so how they can avoid seeing? Best thing is to go to the forest for not seeing any women, if they become so easily agitated, but then no one will either see them and how our preaching work will go on?" (Letter to Ekayani dasi, December 3, 1972)

Prabhupada remarkably points out here that our whole disciplic succession supports the standards he introduced in ISKCON regarding women. How have we become more advanced than all the *acharyas* about "keeping women in their place," at the cost of our preaching endeavor?

Prabhu, let me, in closing, include a few quotes about women becoming gurus. I want to put these forth as supporting evidence that devotee women can give a *Bhagavatam* class. It is sound common sense that if a woman can initiate she can preach the *Bhagavatam* philosophy – to anyone.

First, there is a precedent in our Gaudiya Vaishnava *sampradaya*. Jahnava devi, Lord Nityananda's wife, and Hemlata Thakurani, Shrivasa Thakura's daughter, both gave formal *diksha* to male devotees. This is documented in the *Bhakti-ratnakara* and the *Prema-vilasa,* as explained to me by Nandarani Prabhu, who recently returned from her BBT Research in Delhi.

How does that apply to ISKCON, though? Srila Prabhupada expressed his desires explicitly in this letter of December 3, 1968, to Hansadutta:

"I want all of my spiritual sons and daughters will inherit this title of Bhaktivedanta, so that the family transcendental diploma will continue through the generations. Those possessing the title of Bhaktivedanta will be allowed to initiate disciples. Maybe by 1975, all of my disciples will be allowed to initiate and increase the numbers of generations. That is my program."

I happened upon this letter describing women as capable of becoming spiritual masters of their husbands:

"The actual system is that the husband is the spiritual master to his wife, but if the wife can bring her husband into practicing the process, then it is all right that the husband accepts the wife as spiritual master. Chaitanya Mahaprabhu has said that anyone who knows the science of Krishna, that person would be accepted as spiritual master, regardless of any material so-called qualifications, such as rich or poor, man or woman, or Brahmin or *shudra*." (Letter Silavati dasi, June 14, 1969)

Srila Prabhupada reaffirms this in *Teachings of Lord* Chaitanya:

"Whatever position one may have, if he is fully conversant with the science of Krishna, Krishna consciousness, he can become a bona fide spiritual master, initiator or teacher of the science. In other words, one can become a bona fide spiritual master if he has sufficient knowledge of the science of Krishna, Krishna consciousness. The position does not depend on a particular position in society or on birth. This is the conclusion of Lord Chaitanya Mahaprabhu, and it is in accordance with the Vedic injunctions."

In fact, all the quotes in the Vedic literature about becoming guru by qualification and not by birth also apply to women. Srila Prabhupada – with reference to Lord Chaitanya's teachings and example – preached so strongly against the idea that one is disqualified from spiritual practices because of birth. If spiritual life depended on birth, even the men in our movement wouldn't be able to worship the Deity. Isn't it just as incorrect to say that someone is disqualified from becoming guru and speaking on the *Bhagavatam* because of having taken birth as a woman?

The English language does not afford us the use of a singular pronoun that refers to either men or women (any human being). So sometimes when the word he is used, it is misunderstood to refer only to men. When Lord Chaitanya states, "One who knows the science of Krishna is guru." He doesn't mean that only men can become qualified. At one point our movement thought that only *sannyasis* could become guru, and we came to realize that this was "blatantly ashastric."

As you know, I have been thinking these things over for a couple of years, and I feel it is time to correct these mistakes. As a first step to rectify this wrong in our movement, I think that there should be a GBC resolution stating that women can give *Srimad-Bhagavatam* classes, or better yet, that they should be included on *Srimad-Bhagavatam* class schedules. They should be asked to give classes. Of course, I'm well aware that there is no resolution stating that they can't. So, why a GBC resolution? Because I feel that this problem is very deep-rooted, and I also feel that by addressing the point of women giving classes, we will take our first practical step in dealing with the larger issues. Women being denied the right to give *Bhagavatam* class has become an unspoken, unwritten law of ISKCON. It is enforced uniformly. However, it is unwritten because it cannot be philosophically justified. Because this policy is completely contrary to Prabhupada's instructions, it must be corrected by a GBC resolution.

Women devotees should be seen as teachers and preachers, and they should be respected. They are Prabhu also, and they should be addressed as such. If women started giving *Bhagavatam* classes, this would greatly help foster this vision, enabling us to discard our current vision of women as lowly, etc., and help establish a healthier, more prosperous condition of our Society. At present this unaddressed problem is a hurdle for our movement to overcome. Our spiritual growth, individually and collectively, depends on our purity and knowledge of our spiritual truths. If we misunderstand Srila Prabhupada's orders, then our growth will be slowed or stunted.

Many women have come to the Krishna consciousness movement with sincere desires to advance in spiritual life. Have the women had to perform any less austerity than the men in becoming devotees? Is their sincerity in Krishna consciousness tested any less severely than the men's? Is it tested in a different way? Is their adherence to the process of Krishna consciousness something other than realization of the philosophy of Krishna consciousness? Are they any less eager to preach? Does Krishna make a distinction that men are more dear for preaching than women? Why should women be denied the basic function of a devotee to speak among the devotees?

After all, our main principle is that we are spirit souls, not men or women, and the soul is to be engaged in spiritual service. If we deny services on the basis of the body, how is that a spiritual principle? How will that help spread the Krishna consciousness movement all over the world to everyone? And how will this denial of services be spiritually healthy or encouraging to the women devotees?

I think devotees all over the movement should seriously reflect upon these questions. Please let me know what you think of these things.

Your servant,
Pranada dasi

P.S. I just received a response from J. Swami. He explained that there was no final conclusion reached in their Vrindavan class, but he expressed that some of the arguments raised by the students against women giving class were:

1.   Women giving class would be contrary to *varnashrama*.
My comment: What do you think about the idea that a woman's giving *Bhagavatam* class would be contrary to the *varnashrama* institution?

2.   The examples in our *sampradaya* (such as Jahnava devi) of women taking on such roles of spiritual leadership are rare.
My comment: It is also rare for *mlecchas* and *yavanas* to become Vaishnavas, but we don't start out with a defeatist mentality by not even trying to become transcendentally situated. That would be quite ridiculous and would leave us without any members in the Krishna consciousness movement. If J. Swami is implying that since it's rare surely no

Vaishnava in ISKCON will make it, then we may point out that Prabhupada gave *brahmana* initiation (to women also) because he accepted that we were on the transcendental platform – we were Vaishnavas (at least aspiring ones) by our attempting to surrender to Krishna and follow his instructions. He always encouraged us to keep endeavoring to come to the transcendental situation of becoming Vaishnavas, and he clearly explained that it is possible by Krishna's mercy – as much for women as for men.

3.   No one could recall any woman giving a temple class in front of Srila Prabhupada.
My comment: Srila Prabhupada asked his women disciples to speak their realization at engagements and Vyasa-puja ceremonies in front of him set a precedent. If J. Swami is trying to say that there is a difference between speaking at an engagement and a *Bhagavatam* class, then I would have to ask what the difference is. Prabhupada made clear that we should hear from one who can speak about Krishna, he didn't say if it was a woman, then we would only hear her speak at an engagement. An interesting aside: Prabhupada would personally ask women to lead *kirtans* in his presence. Revolutionary today! But why?

4.   Prabhupada's letter should be understood according to time and place; a letter to Malati encouraging after her husband left may not be intended for general application.
My comment: As for Prabhupada's letter being understood according to time and place – in the letters that I have quoted here Prabhupada is explaining our philosophy. He is demonstrating spiritual vision based on the *Bhagavatam* philosophy. He isn't only telling so-and-so to do such-and-such at a certain time for his or her personal progress. He is speaking and applying the philosophy of Krishna consciousness. Why else would he so pointedly tell Jai Govinda dasa to hear a woman devotee carefully if she was speaking *krsna-katha*?

5.   D. dasa played an undefeatable "trump card" by stating that Srila Prabhupada told Jadurani women shouldn't give the temple class if the men get disturbed.
My comment: I called Jadurani Prabhu about this "Prabhupada said." She said that Prabhupada never told her that.

February 14, 1988
Ekadasi

Dear Pranada Prabhu,

Please accept my humble obeisances. All glories to Srila Prabhupada.

I really like your letter of January 17, 1988 concerning the role of women in ISKCON, and in particular, about their giving *Srimad-Bhagavatam* classes. Your ideas are very clearly expressed, and your points are well documented. It is hard to imagine an honest devotee not being moved by your letter to seriously consider helping to change things and encourage the authorities to include qualified women on *Srimad-Bhagavatam* schedules.

May I have your permission to circulate the letter? (I would like to send some copies to India with my husband for the GBC members to read.) Also, if you can bear with my lack of writing talent, I would like to share some thoughts I have on the subject. You can give me some feedback, so I can further refine them.

We have made many mistakes in conducting Srila Prabhupada's ISKCON. The mood now is toward rectification. And the rectification is to understand purely what Srila Prabhupada wanted – and to implement purely what Srila Prabhupada wanted. So we are doing this in many areas. The discrepancies in the role given women in ISKCON is not a small thing we can set aside until "more important" problems are solved. It is especially not a small issue to disobey the instructions of Srila Prabhupada when that disobedience offends half the Vaishnava population of the movement. And really what is at the heart of it is the only issue: our enemy *maya* in her form of false ego and lust is preventing us from spreading love of Krishna with full strength.

It is not a matter of the men vs. the women and now the women vs. the men. It is a matter of *maya* vs. Krishna consciousness. We are stunted in our growth: men, women, and children.

The devotee comes to the movement willing to admit that he is not God – Krishna is God. But influenced by *maya*, he can try to establish himself as top devotee. It worries me: the "flowery words of the Vedas" can provide various quotations that if misunderstood can give our men the false impression of categorical superiority over all women devotees. What a handicap in trying to actually realize humility. Having eliminated all the women from the competition as top devotee, then one can feel strengthened to compete with the other men. This goes on, too – "Whose disciple are you? Are you a Prabhupada disciple? How long have you been a devotee? What is your *ashrama*? What is your *varna*?" Sort of, "How big a deal are you?"

I don't mean to suggest that all our ISKCON men suffer this illusion of categorical superiority over women; I don't mean to suggest that only our ISKCON men have difficulty with false ego. What concerns me is that we have unwritten laws and attitudes that are mixed in the training we give our devotees that act to negate our task of rooting out our false ego. An unwary man can be trained to think: he is superior to half the Vaishnavas – just for a start. And an unwary woman can be tricked into thinking herself unable to aspire for full, pure devotional service.

We must not be envious of one another. We must have faith that devotional service is completely spiritual and, as such, can expand unlimitedly. Another devotee's advancement will not impede my advancement. In fact, the more devotees are demonstrating and preaching pure devotional service without artificial limitations imposed by our conditioned perspective, then the more the spiritual energy will expand outward and outward and outward to the whole universe. There really can be an ecstatic Hare Krishna explosion!

This is the *sankirtana* movement. The *yuga-dharma* is *sankirtana*. We need to have every man, woman, and child enlivened to preach Krishna consciousness. Lord Chaitanya, as the perfect devotee, is teaching us to feel lower than the straw in the street. Srimati Radharani is teaching us to help the other devotees serve Krishna. When we remove the obstacles to devotional service imposed on our women devotees, how can we not all benefit? When Srila Prabhupada's movement finally "gets itself together," and we begin to "take off" it will be breath-taking. I seriously think this "woman issue" is as big a boil as our misunderstanding of the guru issue.

How vulnerable to illicit sex we become if we view women as vehicles for exploitation, the serf class of devotees! It reminds me of the Christians who use the Bible's reference to man having "dominion" over the beasts as justification for eating them. By the misuse of the meaning of the word protection, we have justified abuse, exploitations, prejudice, and hording of various devotional activities from other devotees – women are simply sense objects to be used by men. And all too often this can mean gross illicit sex indulgence. In fact, it is my observation that when we have had instances of heavy enforcement of women being kept in their so-called place, it has been accompanied by illicit sex.

I think of the first ten years of ISKCON as our spiritual childhood. The "boys and girls" were all jumbled together because we didn't yet understand that materially we need to make distinction and carefully orchestrate male/female interaction patterned on a mutually respectful mother/son relationship. (I am not arguing for some casual, loose intermingling of the men and women in our Society. What I am talking about is being sure that we are all given equal access to this spiritual process.)

I think of the second ten years of ISKCON as our spiritual adolescence. The "off" position given to women in this movement could be forgiven in the name of our immaturity. Adolescence is typically a confused time concerning the male/female duality. And it is a painful period.

But now we must grow up! From within our movement and from without we are being forced to recognize the rights and responsibilities of the woman devotee to preach and work to spread Krishna consciousness with any and all of her God-given talents, according to Srila Prabhupada's instructions.

My hope is that the men and women of this movement will pray, discuss, and clarify the role of women in this movement and come together to facilitate that role.

"In human society all over the world there are millions and billions of men and women, and almost all of them are less intelligent because they have very little knowledge of spirit soul. Almost all of them have a wrong conception of life, for they identify themselves with the gross and subtle material bodies, which they are not, in fact." (*Srimad-Bhagavatam* 2.3.1, purport)

What can be done practically? We say that spiritually male and female are equal. Even in the purport to the infamous "the hearts of a woman is like that of a fox" *Bhagavatam* verse where Srila Prabhupada quotes Chanakya Pandita's advise, "Never place your faith in a woman or a politician," Srila Prabhupada asserts equality on the spiritual platform:

"Chanakya Pandita has advised, *visvaso maiva katavvah strisu raja kulesu ca*: "Never place your faith in a woman or a politician.' Unless elevated to spiritual consciousness, everyone is conditioned and fallen, what to speak of women, who are less intelligent than men. Women have been compared to *shudras* and *vaishyas* (*striyo vaishyas tatha shudrah*). *On the spiritual platform, however, when one is elevated to the platform of Krishna consciousness, whether one is man, woman, shudra or whatever, everyone is equal.*" (*Bhag.* 9.14.36, purport) [underline added]

How can we demonstrate that we practice the spiritual equality we preach? It seems to me that we must show that in ISKCON the various devotional activities are available to everyone.

We teach someone he or she is not the body. He or she is spirit soul. And the soul is not inactive. So what does a spirit soul do? The spirit soul performs devotional service! We must be careful to facilitate devotional service. Lord Chaitanya has broken into the storehouse of love of Godhead. And He is distributing love of Godhead freely. It has fallen on us to distribute devotional service, and we must not pilfer the goods and horde them for ourselves like dishonest servants. We must practice devotional service and teach others. Women, as well as men, must be visible hearing, chanting, and worshiping the Deity.

Devotees must engage in the nine processes of devotional service. In *The Nectar of Devotion* – especially Chapters Twelve and Thirteen – Srila Prabhupada discusses various devotional activities of the devotee. In the beginning of Chapter Thirteen, Srila Prabhupada writes, "Rupa Gosvami has stated that five kinds of devotional activities –

namely residing in Mathura, worshiping the Deity of the Lord, reciting *Srimad-Bhagavatam*, serving a devotee and chanting the Hare Krishna mantra – are so potent that a small attachment for any one of these five items can arouse devotional ecstasy even in a neophyte." We should encourage all the devotees – men and women – to participate in these devotional activities.

As far as women giving *Srimad-Bhagavatam* classes, I agree this is a good first step toward dealing with the larger issue of the women's role in ISKCON. *Srimad-Bhagavatam* class – during the morning program – amongst the devotees is most special of all. Hearing nicely sparks the desire to preach, and preaching creates the necessity to hear nicely . . . the transcendental dialectic. I'm sure the possibility of having to prepare and deliver *Srimad-Bhagavatam* class will result in better reading and hearing among the ladies. And I'm sure there are ladies among us who can learn to give *Srimad-Bhagavatam* classes that will enlighten and enliven the devotees.

I'm afraid, however, that many qualified women may shy away from giving class, being intimidated by the stigma that women can't give class. Of course, women are supposed to be shy. On the other hand, Prabhupada encouraged women to be bold preachers. Does giving *Bhagavatam* class imply that a women isn't shy? Giving *Srimad-Bhagavatam* class is a valuable facility to improve one's speaking ability and realization.

So, I think women should be encouraged to give *Bhagavatam* class. I have seen very shy girls – even young, shy Indian girls from Guyana and Trinidad - learn to successfully approach men and women on the streets and in the airport to give them *Srimad-Bhagavatams* and collect donations in return. And after being on the receiving end of devotees' sharing their realizations of devotional service and *Srimad-Bhagavatam*, it is only natural that the devotee women will want to return the favor, and can overcome the small obstacle of their feeling awkward about speaking.

This letter is getting long – and writing is not my medium (that's for sure). I would much prefer an opportunity for some friendly discussion and debate amongst the devotees.

But I do want to briefly add some ideas in response to the arguments against women giving class as raised by J. Swami's students.

1. Women giving class would be contrary to *varnashrama*.

If we are going to successfully demonstrate *varnashrama* within our Society in order to give proper example for society in general, we must get straight the difference between our obligation to perform various spiritual activities like *japa*, *Srimad-Bhagavatam* class, worshiping the Deity, accepting and becoming initiated by a bona fide guru – and the various roles we can play based on our *guna* and *karma*. There is confusion about this. We must distinguish between what I will refer to as our Vaishnava activities and our *varnashrama* roles.

Exactly what roles women should play and whether or not they have their own *varnas* and *ashramas* is open to discussion. I ran across a paper on this subject written by Urmila Prabhu from Detroit. I know there was a lot of discussion about this in Gita-nagari when my husband and Muralivadala Prabhu conducted the "Varnashrama Town Meetings" there. So these things should be carefully worked out.

But how can someone seriously argue that in the name of demonstrating *varnashrama*, only those who are qualified by birth should give classes, worship the Deity, etc.? As you pointed out in your letter, if our spiritual life depended on birth, even most of the men in our movement wouldn't be able to worship the Deity or give classes.

A devotee may rise early, chant, worship the Deity, perhaps give *Srimad-Bhagavatam* class, and then later in the day do carpentry work or art work, which are traditionally *shudra* activities – this is not a mixed message. As spirit souls we are all equal, and we are encouraged to perform Vaishnava activities. In fact, these practices will give us strength to perform various roles in Krishna consciousness. We aren't trying to recreate the caste system. Srila Prabhupada didn't go to all this trouble to make us into Hindus. We are aspiring to become devotees of Krishna – situated transcendentally.

Even for a woman to properly demonstrate the role of chaste wife, she needs to chant sixteen good rounds, hear *Srimad-Bhagavatam,* and worship the Deity. Can you imagine how utterly tedious it would be to play wife and mother all day or all one's life without being Krishna conscious? And it hardly seems like a full-time career. Most *grihastha* men who have their household life well ordered are eager to minimize the household duties of their wives and engage them in direct Krishna conscious preaching activities.

I feel there is real confusion about what is Vedic, what is the women's role in *varnashrama*, what is Krishna consciousness.

We might begin an investigation of this issue with *Srimad-Bhagavatam,* Seventh Canto, Part Three, Chapter Eleven, verses 25-29. The chapter is titled "The Perfect Society: Four Social Classes." The verses I mention discuss women's role.

In Vrindavan 1976 Chandrika Prabhu gave me a list of eighteen qualities of a chaste woman. She told me that Srila Prabhupada gleaned this list from his purports of these particular verses soon after completing the Seventh Canto. He apparently told Rupa-vilasa Prabhu that the girls should be trained in these qualities: (1) service, (2) good disposition, (3) dedication, (4) dressing nicely, (5) cleanliness (personal), (6) house cleaning & decorating, (7) modesty, (8) sense control, (9) truthfulness, (10) speaking nicely, (11) affectionate behavior according to time and circumstance, (12) not being greedy, (13) satisfaction in all circumstances, (14) expertise in household affairs, (15) *being fully conversant with religious principles, (16) careful, (17) following the footprints of the goddess of fortune in serving her husband, and (18) not following a husband who is fallen.

*Srila Prabhupada said this was the most important quality of a chaste woman.

This list is very nice because it saves us from having to speculate and concoct what it means to be chaste.

One wonders – given the present ISKCON misconception of what it means to be a chaste woman – if we would find Rukmini or Draupadi chaste. We hear how Rukmini helped Krishna fight the princes and Jarasandha, and how she drove the chariot as Krishna stole her away from Sisupala.

Do you recall the description of Draupadi knocking Jayadratha off the chariot when he tried to kidnap her?

Have you ever read that wonderful description from *Mahabharata*, Chapters 232 & 233 (Draupadi Satyabhama Sambhava Parva)? Draupadi is telling Satyabhama all that she is dealing with in running Yudhisthira's treasury and affairs. Incredible. Talk about women in management.

The main point is that we have to understand with a cool head what Srila Prabhupada is saying about *varnashrama* and our spiritual practices. We don't want to concoct anything, like Kirtananandana Swami giving women *sannyasa*, which definitely violates the instructions of scripture and further instruction from Prabhupada.

I agree with your argument that the quotations from Srila Prabhupada's letters in support of women giving class are all making philosophical points. They are not just specific instructions. It is interesting that at the Prabhupada disciple's meeting in New York City a year ago, New Vrindaban used a similar argument to refute using Srila Prabhupada's letters to support the argument that our recent zonal *acharya* system was not Srila Prabhupada's desire. They wanted to limit the discussion to what was in the books or lectures. The counter argument that prevailed was that his letters can function as *sadhu* (as in *guru, shastra,* and *sadhu*).

Thank you for your patience in listening to me. I hope we can have some further discussions soon.

Your servant,
Saudamani-devi dasi

Japa in the Temple Room for All
by Manasa Ganga dasi

The following letter was presented to the devotees in Philadelphia and a majority vote allowed women to chant in the temple room after ten years being prohibited. News of this change in Philadelphia spread quickly in ISKCON, which fueled a growing "unrest" from many quarters about changes for women in ISKCON.

October 1988

TO: All Devotees of ISKCON Philadelphia
RE: Women and Men Chanting Japa in the Temple Room during Japa Period

Dear Prabhus,

Please accept my humble obeisances. All glories to Srila Prabhupada.

I would like to propose that an important policy set by Srila Prabhupada, but ignored during the last ten years, be reestablished. This policy states that women, not just men, are to chant in the temple room during *japa* period.

The writing of this proposal has been prompted by several factors. The most immediate reason is that winter is encroaching and women devotees have no warm, spiritually inviting area in which to chant. However, this proposal is not merely a plea to alleviate physical hardship for the women, although that is important; it is also an attempt to address some of the underlying philosophical misconceptions and deviations that have contributed to the existing discriminatory practices towards women within ISKCON, policies like that pertaining to the *japa* issue that are contrary to Prabhupada's teachings. Obviously, any attempt to fully analyze these issues in so short a paper is bound to be cursory; therefore, this paper (like Pranada and Saudamani Prabhus' letter of last winter) is offered as a prelude to invite open and principled discussion.

I sincerely hope that this paper will not be misconstrued as promoting a mundane war between the sexes or as an indulgence in the reactive and dualistic tendency of "oneupmanship;" my earnest intent here is to try to understand, express and act upon what is philosophically correct. Also, it can been seen that what is best for our spiritual lives individually will, in turn, reap the best results for us collectively – the individual and collective work in tandem. If as a group we can begin working with the same under-standing of what it means to be members of a Vaishnava community – of what it means in practice for everyone to be afforded equal spiritual opportunity – and if we can begin working together rather than at the expense of one another, then we will have a chance of overturning the heavy onslaught of ignorance as kali-yuga progresses. Without this shared understanding and mutual respect, our unity is necessarily divided, our strength diminished, and our potential for causalities much greater. As Prabhupada stressed over and over again, central to our preaching success is cooperation.

Vaishnavism: A Tradition of Spiritual Enfranchisement

The current policy that exists – of having men chant in the temple room and women outside – is one that has evolved through the years as the only acceptable practice, but is not a policy that Prabhupada approved of. In fact, he adamantly opposed it. Philosophically, there are reasons why Prabhupada opposed excluding women in this way. In essence, such sectarianism is in contradistinction to the spiritual tradition of Vaishnavism.

Throughout the history of the Krishna consciousness movement, we have been taught by guru, *shastra*, and *sadhu* that our tradition is one of enfranchisement (of allowing everyone the right to take part), not of hierarchical exceptionalism as has been historically characterized by impersonalist traditions.

In the forefront of the battle against the disenfranchisement policies practiced by the impersonalists was Lord Chaitanya. He propounded a communistic model of spiritual practice, laying the ground work for a future, worldwide movement which is to have at the core of its philosophy the practice of nondiscrimination. This vision of equality is expressed in the 7th chapter of the *Chaitanya-charitamrita*, in the section describing the merciful preaching activities of the Pancha-tattva.

"In distributing love of Godhead, Chaitanya Mahaprabhu and His associates did not consider who was a fit candidate and who was not, nor where such distribution should or should not take place. They made no conditions. Wherever they got the opportunity the members of the Pancha-tattva distributed love of Godhead." [Cc . *Adi* 2.7.23]

Because Lord Chaitanya's preaching mission was unconditionally motivated, he was criticized by the Mayavadis for slumming – for preaching to and converting the *mlecchas* and *yavanas*. Yet by making great devotees out of such lowly persons, Lord Chaitanya rendered moot the practice of spiritual biases based on external physical make-up. Spiritual parity is such an important aspect of Vaishnavism that three texts later Prabhupada underscores the same point again:

"Here again it may be emphasized that although jealous rascals protest that Europeans and Americans cannot be given the sacred thread or *sannyasa,* there is no need even to consider whether one is a gentleman or a rogue because this is a spiritual movement which is not concerned with the external body of skin and bones. Because it is being properly conducted under the guidance of the Panca-tattva, strictly following the regulative principles, it has nothing to do with external impediments." [Cc. *Adi* 2.7.26]

Srila Prabhupada's Instructions

Srila Prabhupada tried to impart to us this mood of enfranchisement,[1] by allowing everyone, regardless of one's bodily designation, the opportunity to perform any service which would fully engage a person's propensities and thereby best enable that person to advance in Krishna consciousness. This insistence on inclusiveness extended to allowing everyone the privilege to chant in the temple room – the most spiritually auspicious room – during *japa* period.

Now, however, many years later, many senior devotees have forgotten, and younger devotees are unfamiliar with, Prabhupada's unequivocal and uncompromising instructions in this matter. To reacquaint us with what Prabhupada wanted, the following quote from a letter Prabhupada wrote to Ekayani dasi in 1972 is given below. This letter was written in response to a decision by authorities at the New York temple to exclude women from the temple room during *japa* period:

"... I do not know why these things inventions are going on. That is our only business, to invent something new programme? We have already got our Vaishnava standard. That is sufficient for Madhvacharya, Ramanujacharya, it was sufficient for Lord Chaitanya, Six Gosvamis, for Bhaktivinoda Thakur, for my Guru Maharaja Bhaktisiddhanta Sarasvati, for me, for all big, big saints and acharyas in our line – why it shall be inadequate for my disciples so they must manufacture something? That is not possible. Who has introduced these things, that women cannot have chanting *japa* in the temple, they cannot perform the *arati* and so many things That is not possible. Who has introduced these things, that women cannot have chanting. If they become agitated, then let the *brahmacharis* go to the forest, I have never introduced these things. The *brahmacharis* cannot remain in the presence of women in the temple, then they must go to the forest, not remaining in New York City, because in New York there are so many women, so how they can avoid seeing? Best thing is to go to the forest for not seeing any women, if they become so easily agitated, but then no one will either see them and how our preaching work will go on?" (Letter to Ekayani dasi, December 3, 1972)

Taking the "Direct" Meaning of Prabhupada's Instructions

An often-used argument to avoid adhering to these instructions is that chanting in the presence of the opposite sex is distracting. The rationale often used to justify this position is that "we are not on a very elevated platform." This line of reasoning, however, has potentially dangerous ramifications; it can be used as a basis for modifying any one of Srila Prabhupada's instructions. It is akin to what Srila Bhaktisiddhanta Sarasvati Thakura describes in the *Chaitanya-charitamrita* as *aksana-vrtti*. *Aksana-vrtti* means "indirect meaning," and it is mentioned in reference to how the Mayavadis give distorted interpretations of the Vedic literature. Instead of accepting Krishna's instructions in a simple, straightforward way, they go to great lengths to create all sorts of convoluted, misleading mental puzzles in an attempt to justify their interpretations of the scriptures.

But Srila Prabhupada cautions us against the dangers of this mental jugglery:

"The Vedic literature is to be considered a source of real knowledge, but if one does not take it as it is, one will be misled. For example, *Bhagavad-gita* is an important Vedic literature which has been taught for many years, but because it was commented upon by unscrupulous rascals, people derived no benefit from it, and no one came to the conclusion of Krishna consciousness. Since the purpose of *Bhagavad-gita* is now being presented as it is, however, within four or five years thousands of people all over the world have become Krishna conscious. That is the difference between direct and indirect explanations of Vedic literature. Therefore Sri Chaitanya Mahaprabhu said, *mukhya-vrttye sei artha parama mahattva:* to instruct Vedic literature according to its direct meaning, without false commentary, is glorious. Unfortunately, Sri Sankaracharya, by the order of the Supreme Personality of Godhead, compromised between atheism and theism in order to cheat the atheists and bring them to theism, and to do so he gave up the direct method of Vedic knowledge and tried to present a meaning which is indirect." [Cc. 2.7.110]

Similarly, we must learn to hear and act on the instructions of guru, *shastra* and *sadhu* exactly as they are presented – as *mukhya-vrtti* – without qualification or manipulation. To concoct one's own meaning is referred to by Prabhupada as being "overly intelligent." Therefore, if Srila Prabhupada says both women and men should chant in the temple room, then women and men should chant in the temple room. And if someone is too agitated to do so, then the instruction for that is also there.

Changing One's Consciousness is A Practical Activity

One more point needs to be made about the belief that "we are not yet elevated enough to chant in the same room with the opposite sex." Inherent in this line of reasoning is a fundamental misconception of how change of consciousness actually occurs. Essentially, the methodology employed here is a nondialectical form of reification. It says (like the consciousness-raising groups that began in the 1960s) that consciousness precedes practice: "Let me first understand who I am and then later I'll change things." As opposed to: "Let me begin changing things so I can begin to find out who I am." In effect, reification is a form of psychological alienation because it takes a feature of one's thinking and imposes it upon reality, reifying it as the truth. But this is not how reality works! Prabhupada taught us that by practice we can learn to do anything. Just as learning to chant unoffensively results from a concerted effort to do just that, so does learning to concentrate one's mind to not be distracted by those around us come from practice. One learns to become respectful of all living entities by engaging in the activity of honoring them, not by waiting for the day when one's consciousness becomes more elevated.

This process of changing one's consciousness is described in the *Bhagavad-gita* [12.12] as *abhyasa-yogena*, which means "by the practice of devotional service." By following the rules and regulations under the guidance of a spiritual master, we revive what's already there all along – our dormant love for Krishna. In a class on this text, Ravindra Svarupa Prabhu explains this intrinsic nature of reality: "The process of *abhyasa-yogena* is the revival of what's already there. It's not putting something in, or importing something into our psyche. It's clearing away the garbage so it can be reawakened. It's not first that I revere Krishna and then bow down, but rather that I bow down and then learn to revere Him by bowing down. William James said, 'It's not that we feel afraid and then start to run, but that we start to run and then feel afraid.' It's practical or pragmatic.

"What we do is we go through the form of the thing, and then our feelings fill that form. . . By engaging in this practice, the senses actually become purified. It's the education of the senses in Krishna consciousness, and somehow it involves us as a whole person – mind, senses, intelligence. That's the way it works.

"Prabhupada used the example also, although it may sound strange, that in India where marriages are arranged, a young girl may not have seen or met her husband, but the practice is that she begins to serve him – cook the food and things like that, and by that practice actual feelings of love and attachment arise. If you go through these practices, then it evokes the feelings and realizations."

Similarly, if we hope to rise above the dualism of seeing one another as male or female, and to begin to relate to one another as Vaishnavas, then we must be on the clearing platform; we must practice relating to one another in that way. Prabhupada gave us The Morning Program (his precise, practical meaning of *abhyasa-yogena*), and he told us that if we follow this program rigidly we will not fall into *maya*. Let us take heed of the words "follow rigidly." Faithfully attending The Morning Program consists of *mangala arati, japa* period, greeting the Deities, *guru-puja* and *Srimad-Bhagavatam* class. According to Prabhupada's instructions, the *japa* segment of our program is faulty: it is a "new programme" tainted by "manufactured invention." If women are not chanting in the temple room during *japa* period, then we have not yet understood the meaning of *abhyasa-yogena*.

Other Relevant Considerations

Although Prabhupada's instructions alone are sufficient reason for restoring his former program, there are also practical, moral and preaching considerations that should be mentioned. They are:

(1) During most of the year, and especially during the winter months, there is no adequate space in which the women can chant . This lack of facility is to their spiritual detriment. It forces them to disperse to their rooms for warmth. By not being able to chant in the association of other devotees, women are deprived of that collective strength which Prabhupada so strongly recommended. Alone in their rooms, women have a tendency either to fall asleep or to chant with less attention. Thus, women become more susceptible prey to *maya*.

(2) The extent to which a society is civilized can be judged by how it treats its women and children. As a Society whose philosophy strongly states that women are to be protected, and that Vaishnava women in particular are to be related to with respect – as devotees of Krishna, not as objects of lust or disdain – it is vitally important that our daily activities and organizational policies reflect our philosophy. The title "mother" must become more than merely a token appellation. Otherwise, those whom we are trying to preach to will (and many, in fact, do) view us as hypocritical.

Therefore, protection must be understood and tangibly applied on a spiritual as well as a material level. Spiritually, it should be insisted that women, as the more "vulnerable" sex, utilize the devotional serenity (and security) of the temple room during *japa* period so as to optimally augment their spiritual growth. By viewing one another as godsister and godbrother, a positive attitude is cultivated, not a negative one that views women or men as sources of distraction or temptation. It is precisely this negativity towards women – this tendency to relate on a material platform – that Prabhupada forcefully counters in his letter.

Materially, women's well-being should also be considered. It is only courteous that they be given at least minimal physical conditions for performing *sadhana-bhakti*. Also, from the vantage of preaching, it reflects poorly on our organization when guests see men stay in the warm temple room, while women remove themselves to the cold foyer. It violates even basic Western rules of etiquette.

(3) The coming and going of devotees through the foyer area during *japa* period creates a disruptive and unserious atmosphere. Devotees – both men and women – tend to have conversations in this area, thereby hampering one's ability to concentrate and take one's own *japa* seriously.

(4) There are temples throughout the movement where for years men and women have chanted in the temple room together, separated only by dividers or balconies (but not sound barriers). I have been told that in Miami and Vancouver, women and men chant together without any physical dividers, confining themselves to opposite sides of the temple room. One devotee from Vancouver told me that "being distracted" was simply not an issue, and she was genuinely surprised to find out that her temple was an exception. Perhaps in the beginning of instituting this change, there might be a heightened sense of "otherness" since such a to-do has been made about it, but the fact is that men and women chant in the company of one another in many other circumstances – riding in the same car together, in the temple room at other times of the day, and at festivals – yet no one protests in these situations.

Conclusion

This proposed reenactment of Prabhupada's desires should not be seen as a "taking away from the men," but rather as the opportunity to qualitatively boost the spiritual strength of our community. By insisting that we strictly and respectfully relate to one another as godbrother and godsister, and rigorously rout out the diseased tendency to relate on a less platform, not only will women be given greater opportunity to develop their full spiritual potential, but the overall spiritual climate and attractiveness of the

Krishna consciousness movement – for both men and women in and outside the movement – will be enhanced. As always, our individual and collective spiritual success lies in pleasing our spiritual master. Therefore, let us ensure our future success by owning up to our past mistakes and rectifying a longstanding error.

Your servant,
Manasa Ganga dasi

In consultation with:
Pranada dasi
Sasvata Pavana dasi
Suci dasi

Notes
Srila Prabhupada discusses the unfortunate historical consequences of spiritual disenfranchisement of the shudras *by the* brahmanas *in India in "The Supreme Destination is for Everyone" (Rome 5/26/74).*

Srila Prabhupada: In the beginning, we do not ask anybody to become initiated or a *brahmana*. No. We simply ask the person to join the chanting. This is our process. We should strictly follow this process. In the beginning, we should not ask that you do this and do that. It is not possible. But everyone should be given chance. Because in the Kali-yuga, there is no reformatory system. Everybody is born *shudra*, and less than that, *chandala*. So, this has been neglected also. It's not that because all people have fallen, they are less than *shudra* and *chandala*, let me chant Hare Krishna. No. This is not. The duty of Vaishnava is to reclaim the fallen souls. Just like it is said in the *Bhagavad-gita* [9.32]:

> mam hi partha vyapasritya
> ye 'pi syuh papa-yonayah
> striyo vaisyas tatha sudras
> te 'pi yanti param gatim

Krishna says, "Anyone who can come to My shelter, never mind if he is the lowest of the lowest – lowborn. *Striyo vaishyas tatha*. He may even be women, and the mercantile community, and *shudra*. They are also considered as *papa-yoni*. *Papa-yoni* means whose brain is not very developed. That is *papa-yoni*. . . . The supreme destination, back to Godhead, back to home is for everyone. It is not that just God, God means for everyone. God does not say, "Only the *brahmana* class of men please come here. Others are (?)." No, no. He means everyone, even the lowest of lowest, the lowborn – *papa-yonayah* – women, *shudra*, or *vaishya*, or everyone. Krishna says that everyone has got the potential of coming to Me, of going back to home, back to Godhead. Then one to serve Krishna. Who then makes them qualified to go back home, back to Godhead. That is Vaishnava, those who are actually very sincere servants of Krishna. It is their duty. Krishna says that everyone is competent to come to Me if he is following the rules and regulations. *Vyapasritya*. What is the meaning of *vyapasritya*?

Answer: Particularly taking shelter.

Srila Prabhupada: Yes, particularly. One should be willing to go back to home, back to Godhead and take shelter particularly or His representative. Such person can be elevated. But unfortunately in India, although the *Bhagavad-gita* is there they neglect it. The so-called *brahmanas* and so-called *goswamis,* they neglected this process. Just like in India, the Mohamedans who claim to be partisan, Pakistan and Hindustan. There are a number of Mohamedans, they protested that India is going to be independent but we do not wish to participate with the Hindus. We must be separate. Why? Because they have got a bad experience that the Hindus did not treat them very well.

Even *shudra* in South India, it was the process, so bad process, if the *shudra* is walking on the street he has to cry, "I am a *shudra* passing on the street. Please close your door." The *brahmanas* would close their doors so they would not even see a *shudra* then everything will be spoiled – their food grains and everything. They were closed. Now, the reality in South India, the communists. Communists mean the so-called low-class people, the *shudras* and *chandalas* are now in a majority. They formed the government. On principle, as soon as some *brahmana* comes for government service he will be rejected.

So the *brahmanas* are now hiding themselves because they cannot get any job. This is foolish. This negligence is not Vedic culture because they neglected. These Mohamedans grown in India, they were not imported from Afghanistan or Turkey or any Mohamedan country. They were Indians. But they were not given any facility for spiritual culture. The *brahmanas* monopolized it. Although they would not do anything. They were all degraded by the state, they would keep these *shudras* and *chandalas* downtrodden. . . .

Therefore, when Aurangzeb passed a law, jijaya tax. "JiJaya" tax means all the non-Mohamedans would be taxed now. These low-class people were so neglected, they thought – it was natural – "Why should we pay this tax? We are no very much well-treated by the Hindus. So what is the use of remaining Hindu and pay the tax?" So wholesale this neglected class of man became Mohamedan.

This is this history. Otherwise, this Mohamedan did not come from the Mohamedan countries. In this way, a Mohamedan community was formed gradually and this British government took advantage of this ill-feeling between Hindu and Mohemadans. Anyway, this is the policy of the politicians. Because they are not given . . . our point is that Krishna says everyone should be given chance how to come back home, how to approach Krishna.

So who's duty it is? It is the duty of Krishna's servant. Just like Prahlada Maharaja. Prahlada Maharaja said, "My Lord, I do not wish to go back to home, back to Godhead, alone. I want to take all of them who are godless, or not devotees. I want to take them."

1990

On Chivalry in ISKCON and the Rights of Our Mother
by Jagannatha Krishna dasa

One of the most redeeming qualities of a gentleman is chivalry, typified by religiousness, morality, courtesy, honor, courage, justice, and readiness to help the weak. And who amongst us men in the West will allow themselves to be thought of as ungentlemanly? Dare I say none? However, every day, tacitly, most men of the ISKCON movement participate in an institution which perpetuates an ungentlemanly mentality: relegating the entire female population of the community to the back of the temple room.

Some will say, "Oh, you're disrupting Vedic culture," or "That's the Vedic standard." But in my travels throughout the whole of India, north, south, east and west, I have never seen a shred of evidence to support this notion. At Udupi there is equal access to the Deity for men and women; at Tirupati; at Jagannatha Puri (though I haven't personally seen); at Trivandrum, equal access; at Srirangam, the same; at Dvaraka I have seen women <u>allowed priority</u>, as well as children; at Guruvayur, the tradition of equality for men and women is again upheld. Yet at the Krishna-Balaram Mandir, the representative stronghold of the Brahma-Gaudiya-Vaishnava *sampradaya,* we do something entirely different. Some years ago I asked one *sannyasi* at Mayapur, Bhakti Vidya-purna Swami, "Where did this policy originate? It's not Vedic, is it?" His Holiness replied, "No, not really. It comes from the Muslims." And I suddenly remembered seeing this in my travels in South East Asia: women are trained almost like possessions, without rights, and shunned to the periphery of the mosque, out of sight, and – in essence – out of mind. The only cultural precedent I can find for this peculiar habit is not Vedic, not Indian, not even Western, but Islamic, and not particularly worthy of being followed. So who is actually disrupting Vedic culture?

Nor have I seen any definitive shastric statements supporting this pretense of corralling the fairer sex out of *darshana's* view, although I've sincerely sought it. Nothing from Srila Prabhupada's books, nothing from his lectures, nor from his letters. I've given up looking.

What I have found is a wealth of philosophical and personal statements from Srila Prabhupada and his books to the contrary. In a minute I'll share some of the more pertinent with you.

Others will complain that there isn't enough room and the geography of the temple is not well suited to having both the men and the woman in the front. Yet in various temples around the world devotees remark that ecstatic *kirtans* regularly occur where there is such a division, and resident devotees can't conceive of it being otherwise. (Such is the case at New Mayapur, where the women have more of the temple room than the men.) On *harinama-sankirtana* in the streets of London and other cities I've often experienced the most ecstatic kirtans walking two by two. During those times we're so enlivened and absorbed in the holy name, no one who is not otherwise obsessed is worried about whether the women are on one side and the men on the other. In some temples in Italy, women are protected by being pushed to the front, along with the men, where they can hear the kirtan as well, and the popular account is that this increases the pleasure of the passersby. Conversely, I can't count the times I've been asked, "Hey, don't you have any women in your movement? Oh, why are they in the back?" as a sometimes cowering and timid huddle of women get shoved in the wake of the often oblivious *brahmacharis* . . . Another unconscious self-inflicted blow to our otherwise sincere attempts to share the holy name with others.

Most people in the West outside of ISKCON will agree that denying the women and female children equal access to the Deities smacks of blatant chauvinism. Or do we think we're completely above the criticism of the secular world to ignore that? At this point can we afford to be? Wasn't it Srila Prabhupada's philosophy to adopt expedient normative social customs to avoid causing disturbances in the preaching? And in the context of modern social values, pushing women to the back, and hence a lower rung of society, is an archaic and destructive institution that I feel acts not to foster purity – as is intended – but serves merely to disrupt what could otherwise be a sanctified mood of love, camaraderie and friendship within the temple, without which there is no possibility of attracting new devotees.

"Separating men and women is disrupting a mood of purity?" some may ask. "We have to keep the *brahmacharis* and women separate." The *brahmacharis* are "the backbone" of ISKCON some have wrongly said, and therefore we have to separate them. Yes we all agree – separation between men and women must be there, but during the kirtan separation does not mean forcing the women to stare at the backs of gyrating youths, who can also be seen as sense objects, some of whom seem to exhibit a distinct awareness of the presence of women. Separation does not perforce entail obscuring the ladies' view of Their Lordships. If I were in a woman's shoes I would feel slighted.

And so, I know, do many women, within and outside of ISKCON. For instance, my sister, Kirsten, who just completed her doctorate in plant biology and botany at the University of Texas at Austin, remarked some years back after visiting the Boston temple, "I appreciate your philosophy and I agree with what you say, but your treatment of women makes it all seem a travesty. I don't mean to be rude, but I feel that women are equal to men, not in ability exactly, but in opportunity, and it seems as though you're denying the obvious by keeping up your policy of pushing the women to the back."

Kirsten is married, a vegetarian, doesn't drink or smoke, and believes in reincarnation, *karma*, and a personal Deity. She is a prime candidate for entering devotional service. But she won't come to the temple. Why? Here is another close-to-home example, from an acquaintance of mine in San Diego, Rebecca Hickox, a graduate from Harvard Law School, practicing attorney and full-time mother. She described to Krishna Kumari dasi, mentioned in a recent issue of *Priti-laksanam*, that many of her professional female colleagues have expressed interest in Krishna consciousness, but "all of them are hesitant to come to the temple or to get involved because of the discrimination against women they see."

In her letter to KK dasi of January 11, 1990 she writes, "The matter most often raised by outsiders is the question of why women stand at the back of the temple room during *arati*. A number of visitors I have brought to the temple at various times (students, attorneys, my mother, my brother) and others who have talked about the movement with me have mentioned this phenomenon as something that troubles them about Krishna consciousness. The fact that women stand in the rear of the temple room is seen as an indication that women are discriminated against in the movement . . . Finally, fostering an artificial separation between men and women has not prevented devotees from falling down. Plenty of illicit affairs have taken place, even between devotees who regularly took their assigned places at the front or the back of the temple room." Krishna Kumari also mentions in this context another devotee, Allen Rider, an intelligent young man with whom I've spent several Sunday feasts talking in the past. Allen is a journalist for San Diego's popular Beach and Bay Press, and laments that his girlfriend no longer comes to the temple because of this discrimination. This is a brief sample, though in my eyes, devastating.

For those of us who are interested in increasing the preaching, doesn't this seem like a justified starting place?

Srila Prabhupada said, "For God there is no discrimination. Women, men have equal rights to become godly and go back home back to Godhead . . . " [1] "It doesn't matter whether one is a woman or a mercantile class of man or a *shudra*. It doesn't matter . . . But Krishna is opening the path for everyone . . . [2] The general spiritual progress of state and community depends on the chastity and faithfulness of its womanhood . . . Therefore both children and women require protection . . . Being engaged in various religious practices women will not be misled into adultery . . . "[3] From these quotes it seems that the prime responsibility of the men and leaders of any society, including ISKCON is to protect the women by offering them the utmost absorption in spiritual activities. Hence it's my resolute conviction that the responsibility of the management in ISKCON is to provide for every individual – irrespective of sex or class – and protect them by enabling them to make as much spiritual advancement as possible, which necessarily includes having equal access to the mercy of the Lord. In the Fourth Canto, Srila Prabhupada writes, "It is said that when women are protected they remain an always auspicious source of energy to man."[4]

What values are we instilling in our children? The boys grow up feeling that it's alright to herd their female peers to the rear. The *gurukula* boys will carry this latent condescending attitude with them to the outside world in later years unless we redress it. (This goes against my grain as an aspiring gentleman, and everything that my parents and teachers taught me as a child.) Then the girls are unconsciously indoctrinated in a gradually demeaning self-esteem that acclimates them to viewing such abuse and disrespect as normative and acceptable. Modern Western psychologists and analysts term this as "formative codependency," an often unconscious behavioral pattern that spawns a self-inflicted, though artificial image of oneself, as deserving abuse or warranting harsh and emotionally dysfunctional treatment. Most of us have experienced how one becomes habituated to such behavior and the relationships where we stage it.

For the children who aren't on the spontaneous platform, to be denied normal access to the Deities is a kind of violence. Most children don't come back to the temple to see Krishna in the daytime and so the morning kirtan is all they have to go on for the rest of the day, without *japa*. Must we force them to remain in the temple, obliged to stare at the back of twirling *brahmacharis* instead of their worshipful Lords? It's a disgrace I wouldn't subject my children to. Is it any wonder why so many women leave the temple room then? Must we deprive our children the taste of service to Radha's and Krishna's lotus feet they so badly need and deserve? Have we the right to deny the *gurukula* girls the proximity to the Deity, the memory of Whom will sustain their fertile brains throughout their fragile, vulnerable and formative years? How else will they grow strong as the pure souls we need them to be? If we disregard their needs, they won't help this grappling movement progress.

An alternative scenario resulting from this policy which is prevalent in the temple atmosphere, is men and women mutually ignoring each other. This is also pathological. As preachers, distributing books, meeting guests, chanting on *harinama-sankirtana,* teaching school, managing families, etc., we can't simply ignore half of the community because they're in bodies of the opposite gender. We have to support each other, encourage each other, help each other, without over familiarity.

We hear that in a healthy society men need respect from their female counterparts, but they'll probably never get it from a population they insist upon systematically disrespecting.

Lord Kapiladeva tersely warns in the 29th Chapter of the Third Canto, *Bhagavatam*, that those who fail to see the Supersoul in every living being, act out of envy for the bodies of others. They create false divisions and a mentally concocted, artificially separatist mentality that breeds false friends and false enemies which in turn, leads to an utterly disturbed mind. The Lord says, "Such a person can never please Me, despite opulent temple worship." If we're above the bodily concept, then please let's try to start showing it in practice. Give ourselves a chance. Then later in the Fourth Canto, Chapter 3, text 21, Lord Shiva describes to Sati that "One who is conducted by false ego and thus always distressed, both mentally and sensually, cannot tolerate the opulence of self-realized souls. Being unable to rise to the standard of self-realization, he envies such persons as much as demons envy the Supreme Personality of Godhead." One group of words used here is *hrda-atura-indriyah,* which literally translates to "enemies in the heart, springing from sensuality." Although this is referring to Daksha, a devotee, and may seem like a remote correlation, when we try to take away something from a devotee, big or small, young or old, male or female, take it as a sign of envy – subtle or gross. And according to Lord Shiva, to envy a devotee is ultimately to envy Krishna; *param padam dvesti yathasura harim.*

In the words of our local *pandita,* Rohininandana Prabhu, "There is a problem of male chauvinism in our Society, which I believe is a great stumbling block to our preaching. Before we can begin to rectify this problem, we must regret we have been party to it; and before we can feel regret, we must realize that this problem actually exists."

As the title of my talk suggests, in keeping with Srila Prabhupada's teachings and the paradigm of sane society he offered us, isn't it time we reevaluate our conceptions of what it means to be a mother?

On a morning walk in Nairobi, 10/30/75, a devotee explained to Srila Prabhupada the attitude held by some men about chanting in the temple room when women are present:

Devotee: "What I mean to say is that he says that he does not want to chant with women in the temple room. I have seen this before. He says, 'I do not want to chant in a room with women. I'd rather be away from the women.'"

Srila Prabhupada: "That means he has got distinction between men and women. He is not a *pandita. Pandita* means *darshinah.* He is a fool. That's all. He is a fool. So what is the value of his word? He is a fool. He should always consider, 'There is a woman, that's all right. She is my mother.' That's all. *Matrvat para daresu.* Suppose you sit down with your mother and chant. What is the wrong? But if he is not so strong, then he should go to the forest. Why should he live in the Nairobi city? On the street there are so many women. He'll walk on the street closing the eyes? [Laughter] This is all rascaldom. They are all rascals. They are not devotees. Simply rascals."

Administering the shift in the UK from men and women on each side of the temple to women in the back after *guru-puja,* subtly changes my consciousness from one of seeing my godsisters and aunts as my mother, deserving protection, fairness and equal access to the Lord, to one of derision, condescension, and bodily consciousness. Switch. They're now women, with women's bodies, no longer my mother. For I'm sure I'm not alone in saying I would never send my mother to the back of the temple room. If I want to practice what I preach, *pandita sama darshina,* where better place is there to start than in the morning, in the association of our family members and fellow soldiers in the temple room? When the *brahmacharis* go out to preach on the streets, don't they sometimes have to approach women and treat them carefully, listening to them, in a gentlemanly demeanor? And how many times have I seen the very same preachers come home to the temple to let doors slam in the women's faces, force them to sit on the dirty floor of the *harinama* van while the men sit in comfortable seats, and relegate them to the unsafe position of the back of the *harinama* party? How many times have I seen *brahmacharis* preach the tokenism of equality on the street, and then refuse to serve women when the opportunity arises in the temple, speak disparagingly about them or to them while ushering them to the back of the temple room? To me this is not what Srila Prabhupada wanted. It's nothing short of disgraceful.

One devotee recently said to me, "Could you do me a favor and tell that devotee that I have a name and I'm a person. He just waved to me like I was meat or an object or something and said . . . Oh when you're finished, give the keys to that *mataji*.' I hate to be called *mataji*," she said. "It makes me feel like dirt."

How, after 12 years in the movement can this unfortunate lady associate two apparently diametric terms; meat and *mataji*? One may wave a macho hand, as we often do, and say, "Oh, she's just disturbed. Get her married and she'll get over it." One may also say that this is purely reactionary and distended, an attitude engrained after years of bad conditioning. But how did she get there? And why the hatred for the word *mataji*? A full-time preacher, without any record of trouble or fall-down, comes to equate meat with *mataji*. However sour the grapes may be, this represents to me a symptom of what I seem to often be hearing from many devotees, not only women; that we men don't have the faintest idea of what it means to honor our mothers. We give a dog a bad name and hang it; "lusty woman," "disturbed *mataji*" or "unmarried woman means unbalanced woman." This is one example of what happens when women don't feel protected. We inadvertently drive them crazy and we label them as such.

Viewing women in such a distorted and destructive way helps breed ill-will and instability in our families too. Is there any correlation between the haphazard and sometimes misogynous "training" our *brahmacharis* are fed and the appalling failure of our marriage institution? I'm convinced there is, directly. We would like to set the pattern for other religions to follow, but sadly, we're more to blame than the "*karmis*" upon whom we generously shower our self-righteous banter. Conceiving of women as our mother intones such respect, veneration and concern, that a *brahmachari* properly indoctrinated in this mood will naturally and without effort make his fellow devotee women feel appreciated, respected and comfortable, a condition necessary where even the average woman will exercise her normal virtues of humility, tenderness and service.

Srila Prabhupada said, "Protection of women maintains the chastity of society . . . "[5] How can we afford to disrespect our mother? It's social and spiritual suicide. " . . . even by insulting them one loses one's duration of life." [6] We're spiritually dependent upon the women in a variety of ways, therefore Vaishnava etiquette does not exclude them.

I needn't say that most of us in the West have never had any training or idea what it means to properly honor our mothers, so it's no wonder that we drag our carelessness – and often scorn – for our original mothers into our devotee relationships.

We men are always priding ourselves on how much more intelligent we are and how many more times lusty the women are, how much more difficult it is to practice spiritual life in a woman's body, etc., etc. So therefore – in following the codes of even mundane chivalry – shouldn't the women be given even more priority for *darshana*? Shouldn't they be allowed first digs, considering their disadvantage? That is what I've seen in India, and not the other way around. The men will often stand to the back – admiringly or mopingly, whichever the case may be – while the women sit and chant together before the Deity, leading and responding with intense devotional song. I've seen this in several temples in Jaipur, namely Radha-Govinda Mandir and Radha-Gopinatha temple, as well as at the Dauji temple near Mathura, the main Varsana temple, and the Srinathaji temple in Nathdwar. I reiterate, nowhere outside of our ISKCON temples have I ever seen women pushed to the back. Not even in the Christian churches, with divisions between pews, which lend themselves quite well to segregation, do you see the women being shuffled anywhere (except perhaps first in line when receiving the sacrament, if you're Catholic). Are they on the bodily platform, or are we?

Here is some specific, direct historical evidence in favor of this equality, quoted again from *Priti-laksanam*:

"K. dasi, who joined the movement in Denver in 1973, had some interesting experiences to relate . . . When she joined there was a very Krishna conscious mood at the Denver temple with men and women devotees working very cooperatively and dedicatedly to spread Srila Prabhupada's mission. Men and women stood side by side during *kirtana* with an aisle separating them, women were on the schedule to offer *mangala arati,* etc. She said that no one, to her knowledge, thought anything was wrong with these standards, and she said that the women were chaste, not loud or frivolous. Kurusrestha Prabhu was temple president. Satsvarupa Maharaja at that time thought that the temple was the best example of a Krishna conscious temple in America and invited Srila Prabhupada to come, which he did.

"What happened after this is typical of what happened time after time in temples all across America between 1974 and 1975. This experience for many, many women in this movement was as big a mistake as placing big *vyasasanas* for certain of Srila Prabhupada's disciples in temples around the world. Srila Prabhupada arrived with an entourage of GBC men, *sannyasis*, and other leaders. She said that upon entering the temple, the leaders surrounding Srila Prabhupada immediately told the temple president that the women were supposed to stand in the back. She said that the mood in which the *sannyasis* did this was one of frustration, anger, and resentment, in a mood like keeping African Americans in the back of a bus. The temple president's wife approached Srila Prabhupada and humbly complained that we are not Vedic women, we are not used to this. Srila Prabhupada said, "No. No. This is not necessary. The ladies do not have to stand in back." Srila Prabhupada instructed this to the leaders surrounding him and the ladies came back to the front of the altar to one side of the men.

"As soon as Srila Prabhupada left, the *sannyasis* who remained, immediately ordered the temple president to put all the women in the back of the temple room. K. dasi said that Kurusrestha Prabhu did not want to do this, but did it anyway in the mood of respecting the order of 'higher authorities' You can inquire from dozens of devotees living in temples across America at that time. It was in this abrupt manner that leaders 'introduced' the standard that women belong in the back of the temples. I cannot find any quotes or information anywhere that Srila Prabhupada wanted our women in the back . . ."

K. dasi eventually became so discouraged that she left Denver temple and moved to the L.A. temple, where she served for the next seven years. In a famous letter to Ekayani dasi, December 3, 1972, Srila Prabhupada again emphatically squelches deviant attempts to banish women from complete access to the temple facilities: "I do not know why these things inventions are going on. That is our only business, to invent something new programme? We have already got our Vaishnava standard. That is sufficient for Madhyacharya, Ramanujacharya, it was sufficient for Lord Chaitanya, six Goswamins, for Bhaktivinoda Thakura, for my Guru Maharaja Bhaktisiddhanta Saraswati, for me, for all big big saints and acharyas in our line – why it shall be inadequate for my disciples so they must manufacture something? That is not possible. Who has introduced these things, that women cannot have chanting *japa* in the temple, they cannot perform the arotik and so many things? If they become agitated, then let the brahmacharies go to the forest, I have never introduced these things. The brahmacharies cannot remain in the presence of women in the temple, then they may go to the forest, not remaining in New York City, because in New York there are so many women, so how they can avoid seeing? Best thing is to go to the forest for not seeing any women, if they become so easily agitated, but then no one will either see them and how our preaching work will go on?"

If Srila Prabhupada was so stern and uncompromising about women chanting *japa* in the temple with men, I can assure you without a shadow of a doubt, that he would uphold the same standard of rights on the issue of women having *darshana* during *kirtana*.

Who has the prerogative to legislate and perpetuate a deviation from Srila Prabhupada's instructions so severe that devotees and guests – male and female alike – would avoid coming to the temple, leave kirtan early in disgust, and wind up emotionally soured and embittered for years? Srila Prabhupada said, "Our leaders should be careful not to kill the spirit of enthusiastic service which is individual and spontaneous and voluntary."[7]

Please, Prabhus, in all earnestness, think carefully about this issue and put yourself in the shoes of the women who feel this way.

Lastly, and leaving aside all of the politics, philosophy, and historical precedents, Srila Prabhupada said, "If we simply preach, then all difficulties will be resolved in due course of time."[8] If we feel bothered by the presence of women next to us during our morning worship, remember they have to look at you too. We all have specific needs, but if we can become even marginally conscious of each other's needs and we learn to act upon respecting them, then there is no room for sectarianism, partisanship, separatism or envy.

Please forgive me for my pedantic and long-winded presentation. I'm sorry to speak so strongly, self-righteously. I know I'm preaching to myself as much as to anyone else in this. I'm hoping you'll see through my faulty and bellicose words and objectively deliberate on the things I've laid before you.

Thank you for your patience. Hare Krishna.

Footnotes
[1] Johannesburg, Oct. 22, 1975; *Bhagavatam* lecture 5.5.2
[2] New York, Nov., 1968; *Bhagavatam* lecture 4.21.33
[3] *Bhagavad-gita* (purport)
[4] *Bhagavatam* 4.21.4
[5] *Bhagavatam* (purport) 1.8.5
[6] Ibid
[7] Letter to Karandhara, Dec. 22, 1972
[8] Letter to Tamala Krishna Goswami, January 21, 1976

Damsels in Distress ask,

"Where are our Knights in Shining Armor?"

by Sita devi dasi

We are all well aware of the fact that men and women are different; we each have different contributions to make to society. What these specific differences are can be the source of endless debate and discussion, something that perhaps is helpful at some point. But I feel that overriding whatever those differences may be, the men and women in ISKCON have something far more important in common: conjointly we make up the International Society for Krishna Consciousness. And this is no small thing.

To have the men and women in our Society emotionally or psychically at war with one another is merely tiring both of us out, perhaps even mortally wounding some of us. We need to put down this sword that divides us in two and instead tend to our battle scars.

The problem is neither a "women's issue" nor a "men's problem." It is one that we all share. And one that is ultimately going to hurt the greater ISKCON society more than it will hurt anyone of us individually. Damaging not only our internal relationships with one another, but the image that we present to the public.

As a contemporary poet, Anne Waldman, has written:

"The problem with you
Is the problem with me
The problem thinking we're so different
The problem is how to perceive . . . "

I feel that at the root of this gender war, there is actually a problem we all share in relating and communicating on all fronts. It's rare to find a devotee who leaves ISKCON because they've lost their belief in Srila Prabhupada or Krishna. Most apostates cite that their relationships with other devotees went amiss, discouraging them.

An academic researcher in America recently conducted a survey of many new religious movements. He concluded that while ISKCON had the most philosophically sound basis, it sorely lacked personal warmth and closeness in its interpersonal dealings.

This shows in many ways, manifesting as cliquishness. Undoubtedly most of us have experienced it from one side of the fence or the other at some time: *sankirtana* devotees are superior to *pujaris, sannyasis* more advanced than householders, Prabhupada disciples distinct from newer recruits. The list goes on and on of how we divide devotees into hierarchies of good and bad, us and them, right and wrong. This serves to breed suspicion, contempt and fear. Hardly the basis of love and trust that Srila Prabhupada wanted us to operate from.

I don't intend this to be a challenge to anyone. My motive here is to help our Society learn from its past mistakes. In fact it is extremely painful to reveal personal experiences, putting myself in a vulnerable position.

Of course in our own groups women can easily gripe about present circumstances; we sometimes even laugh at the ridiculousness of past ones. But if we dare to bring them to the attention of our authorities we risk being labelled as women's libbers. A few of us have tried this and have found it makes our lives even more unbearable. Since we intend to continue living within this ISKCON society for the rest of our lives, most of us therefore keep quiet to keep the peace.

But I sense that the mood in ISKCON is changing; there are men who are beginning to take us into consideration when making decisions.

By now you may be wondering what I'm even talking about. What problem? Haven't the women had enough to eat over the years? Or places to sleep? Or opportunities to chant Hare Krishna? Or is it that we've been subjected to physical abuse of some kind?

While most of us can't complain about anything like starvation or torture, most of us have, each in very different ways and under different circumstances, received debilitating blows from the men in our Society. These blows haven't been dealt by any physical weapons. Rather this weapon has been something far more subtle: an attitude that has caused us, over repeated exposure to it, to feel as if we are not wanted within this Society.

Some of you may balk at this. "Of course we want women to become Krishna conscious!" you may say indignantly. And indeed, were I to ask any man in this Movement whether they wanted me to remain in ISKCON or leave, I am certain every one of them would encourage me to stay.

But yet, an altogether different message comes across in the behavior patterns of many of these same men. I went to India to see Srila Prabhupada during a festival in the 1970s, a festival many of you perhaps also attended. Not having many opportunities to be with him, I was looking forward to being able to worship him daily.

Yet I was told that I must cut *subjis* during my *japa* and through *guru-puja* while the men chanted their rounds and took darshan. I daily finished that task in time to come into class after the Sanskrit had been chanted. In doing so I got a very clear message about how important it is for me to practice *sadhana*.

During those same pilgrimages, I watched all the *sannyasis* and men board the first buses to go on *parikrama*, leaving one bus to carry four times the amount of women and children it would hold. And once we'd arrive at the pilgrimage site, the men would already be sitting and listening to someone speak about the holy place while we ladies were still trailing behind. Once we'd breathlessly catch up with them, it would be just in time for them to get up and push on to the next spot. From this I got a message that I'm not really able to appreciate the transcendental nature of the *dhamas*.

During that festival I heard an announcement after the morning program that all devotees desiring to take Srila Prabhupada's Bhaktishastri exam should report to a particular room. But when another godsister and I were turned away from the door because "everyone understood the exam was only for the men," I got the message that philosophical study is not for me either.

When during a feast I saw that the men who'd transferred the *prasadam* had forgotten to bring the women five of the preps, while the men all had second and third helpings; and when a hurricane blew the tarpaulin off the roof on which the ladies were staying, blowing our trunks and baggage onto the ground below, and instead of offering us their own rooms to stay in, the men told us ladies to huddle in the *prasadam* hall that night; and while at the same time severe blockages in the ladies toilets had all of us wading through flooded stool waters in order to bathe, I got an impression that my material welfare is also not very important.

These are just a few of the messages we have been given, not necessarily deliberately or even consciously, by the men. Yet, I am certain that no one man has diabolically stayed up nights dreaming up schemes to torment the ladies.

Because most of you do not look to see what the ladies are doing during *japa*, you probably didn't even know that we weren't given a *japa* period during the Mayapur festivals. And of course you just did what you were told to do, board your own bus, so how could you know that many of us were left behind? And you most likely were absorbed in studying in preparation for the Bhaktishastri exam, unaware of the drama we were experiencing on being turned away from the door. And since the men were served *prasadam* in another tent, you had no idea the ladies weren't being fed. So, we are not personally blaming any of you.

As a matter of fact, when something of this nature occurs, there are usually one or two men around who we do complain too. And these men are generally extremely sympathetic. Unfortunately they are inevitably not in any sort of position to effect a change or rectify the mistake. Although it does have to be said that there have been times when men who have been in charge of us have dismissed us, neglecting to hear our pleas for help. All these things have exerted a powerful psychological effect upon the women in our Society. One, I would say that has convinced us that we are not really wanted around you, but that you are simply tolerating our presence.

Has that been healthy for us? Is it healthy for any of you? As a result of picking up these subtle messages from our brothers, have we developed into the kind of devotees we should be? Into the soft Vaishnavis Srila Prabhupada would want us to be? We are wounded women and we'd like to ask your help so that our wounds may not become infected any more than they already are. It is evident to me that until our pain has been recognized, until our brothers take compassion on us and ask "what ails thee?" we will not be healed. By sharing our dreams of a future that incorporates values of the heart together we can hopefully perfectly fit in the template of devotional service Srila Prabhupada has given us.

Equal Rights?

What is it that we want from you? Mostly we just want to be treated like persons. But you may say, are women not already being treated this way? Have we not been given equal treatment to the men? We distributed books side-by-side with them, we cooked feasts just as they did, we worshipped the Deities and attended lectures as they did, and even some places are allowing us to again give classes or lead kirtans.

But this is not what we are talking about here. We are speaking about the unique qualities that woman possesses which we feel are not being valued. Generally we protect something which we consider valuable. Does the fact that we don't feel protected have something to do with the feeling that we're not valued?

Our Society in many subtle ways seems to denigrate feminine qualities. And as a result, a woman is not likely to value herself as woman. She sees herself as somewhat lacking, inferior. She looks around and sees men achieving – men who may not even be as intelligent, creative, or as ambitious as perhaps she feels herself to be. This confuses her, but it confirms what she has observed: that women have no intrinsic value of their own – their value comes in relationship to men and to children. She buys into that myth and internalizes a feeling of self-loathing.

Her only option for recovering any sense of self-esteem is to identify with masculine values. But this also has a backlash, affecting her concept of herself as a woman, leading her to devalue other women.

For the last twenty years we have stood on the side lines and seen men being rewarded with position and prestige for their intelligence, drive, renunciation and dependability. And to the degree that any women have acted like these men, they may be similarly, but not equally rewarded.

But women will never be men. And it is my contention that most of the women who are trying to be the same as men are doing so at the expense of injuring their feminine nature.

I feel that it is imperative that devotee women reclaim their femininity as worthwhile. We must recognize our contribution to culture and society as intrinsically valuable. Women, because of our feminine nature, are usually more empathetic in relationships; we have a strong aesthetic orientation, and an altruistic desire to provide care. These are valuable assets for any society.

Women devotees need to understand that each one of us, male or female, has a unique role to play. This is crucial if women are to cease emulating men, or to cease belittling other women for the way they are choosing to adapt.

Can't We Take a Joke?

It has sometimes seemed to me that women have to deny their femininity in order to be real devotees. But is this necessarily so? Perhaps you might think that I'm extreme in drawing this conclusion. But here's where I got it from:

It's the mid-1970s and a group of *sannyasis* and *brahmacharis* are sitting around an office, laughing. A regular enough scene. Especially since they're laughing about a woman who was wearing ankle bells.

"What does she think she is?" one of the men says "A *gopi* or something?" Everyone chuckles.

"Doesn't she know she's just a bag of pus and blood and stool?" Another adds.

Everyone laughs harder, envisioning the absurdity of this foolish woman who is so deeply enmeshed in her body.

Another *sannyasi* glances out the window. He points to a devotee woman pushing an infant in a pram, another toddler in her arms. He chants the *Chaitanya-charitamrita* verse where Raghunatha dasa Goswami walked away from his family life just as if it were fresh stool. He repeats, "Fresh stool," for emphasis, drawing roars of guffaws.

Someone else says, "Look at her little piglets. More stool to wallow in." More laughter.

I was among that group of men. It was a common occurrence in the offices in which I happened to be the only woman working for several years. Did I tell them how offensive I found their behavior? Did I storm out of the room to register my disgust? Did I say anything in defense of my godsisters?

No. I laughed alongside them. They were my senior role mentors and spiritual authorities. Advanced devotees. And of course, I wanted to become an advanced devotee as well. To please Srila Prabhupada. Be renounced. Not attached.

And it soon became obvious to me that I couldn't be any of things if I acted like a woman. Or, as they were often wont to quote, "As long as I believed I was a woman."

So I joked with them. Mocked women who actually cared what colour *sari* they wore. Ridiculed the waste of Krishna's *laksmi* spent in purchasing earrings and bangles such women uselessly decorated their bodies with.

I thought it tedious to bother combing my hair, for what purpose did hair serve other than to drag a husband into mundane consciousness? And after all, it was only "stool." I certainly wanted to do whatever was necessary to get both me and my husband back to Godhead. So, along with other, more subtle things, I cut my hair off.

I was once in a car with my husband, with two *sannyasis* in the front seat. They were speaking about why another couple was not moving to our temple to serve as *pujaris*. The reason being that, in the words of one *sannyasi*, "the woman's *pujari*-ing days were over."

With a curl of his lip he said, "She's pregnant." Then he turned to me, seated a discreet distance of course away from my husband, and said, "You're not pregnant are you?"

"Of course not," I quickly answered, feeling my husband's piercing glances on me that I better not let it be known that we had ever, ever, ever, even considered trying for a child. So for emphasis I added, "No way I want one of those."

And for all this I was rewarded. I received a letter from my husband just before he took *sannyasa* saying, "Just think what a disturbance you could have been – like most women. What would have been the question of assistance? It could have been so different, so entangling, so dangerous."

Like a seal who has successfully jumped through a hoop, I was applauded. Clapped and patted on the back for my astute Krishna consciousness. So I learned that to gain that recognition, I had to continue giving up my innate feminine inclinations. Inclinations that needn't have even taken me away from Krishna.

Instead of a husband and children, I gained the association of sannyasis. I became known for being able to do substantial service whereas many of my other godsisters were wasting their lives caring for "stooly babies." I felt elevated as a woman who could even sometimes ask philosophical questions. That is when I wasn't succumbing to my womanly weakness of hankering and lamenting over having lost my husband.

But it wasn't all pats on the back. For not everyone was thrilled that I was becoming a surrogate man. Some men resented a woman speaking out occasionally with the same clarity of perception they had. And some men resented me fighting my own battles.

But I had no husband, and felt that all was fair in love and war. After all, I was only continuing to do as I'd been led to believe I should. So I went on, greedy in my pursuit of Krishna consciousness, stepping on toes, elbowing my way to Prabhupada and Krishna.

I even made myself ill doing this. Being split from my feminine side, I learned to override my body's needs, pushing it beyond exhaustion, ignoring my own intuition. In the middle of the day once, I left my office to lie down in the *ashrama* for an hour or so since I had my menses and was feeling quite unwell. Of course I felt guilty doing something so obviously womanly and selfish, but I physically couldn't stand on my feet just then.

But I'd not been in the *ashrama* for more than ten minutes when I received a message from my *sannyasi* authority that I was needed in the office. I told the woman bringing me the message that I was unable to move just then and I would be there in an hour or so. The message came back, more persistently this time, that I was not this body and I must be there right now. So dutifully, and not wishing to appear manipulative or wimpy, I overrode that pain to keep up with the men. I made my own body an object of derision.

Birds, Seals, Dolphins, or Whales?

But then one day I had a shock. I looked in my metaphorical mirror and realized that I was one of those women I so glibly scorned. But, at the same time I didn't have a clue any more what that meant. How did one graciously accept the body Krishna awarded me at birth, without feeling disgusted for it, without feeling shamed because its very existence obviously shouted to all and sundry my lust, without feeling hopeless of being able to go back to Godhead with it?

This is what I'm trying to deal with in my life right now. I'm trying to recapture my lost femininity, and trying to figure out how to fit it within the framework of devotional service as I've come to know that. The hair I cut off is growing back. Unfortunately there's other bits of me that aren't so easy to reclaim.

I don't like the fact that I've defeminized myself in order to fit into a world that seemed the exclusive domain of those in male bodies. I don't like it because it doesn't feel good and it isn't helping me become Krishna conscious. Contrary to getting me off the bodily platform, it's done exactly the opposite. And it's making it difficult for me to have healthy relationships with other devotees of either sex.

Now if I hear men speaking, even remotely like the conversations I've quoted above, you've undoubtedly seen me turn purple. I'll sometimes speak out inappropriately, or register my protest in other ways. But I'm not sure that many of my godbrothers or sisters understand just why I'm so upset about it.

I would like to think that my situation was extreme, a one-off freak of our Society. But I'm afraid it wasn't. There are other women who like me went to this extreme. And many, many more who jumped through different hoops of varying sizes.

It might be that no one explicitly told any of us to do any of these things, to adopt this mode of thought. And in some instances that may be right. But whether verbally we were instructed or not, we all got a message that having a woman's body is not an appropriate vehicle for taking up spiritual life. And since in our hearts we felt we were eternal parts and parcels of Krishna, who missed His transcendental association, and who longed to return to Him, we did whatever we thought we had to do to attain that. Foolishly, this was my response.

And then there are countless other women who took the shame heaped on them by their spiritual mentors, not even bothering to try to advance, just hoping and praying for a better birth next life.

A few years ago, one of my godsisters, Radha-priya Prabhu, was asked to address an audience about Krishna consciousness. She told me that she felt, "like a bird who has been kept in a cage for much of her life. Although the cage is reducing the bird's freedom to fly and experience the full pleasure of life, if the owner of the bird suddenly decides to open the cage door, the bird will be too afraid and unaccustomed to freedom to fly out."

"I felt very much like that bird, retreating further and further back into the corner of my cage at the sight of someone's demanding hand entering my door. However, I also felt that if the door were left ajar and I was given the time to become convinced that the people requesting me to come out were actually going to care for me and endeavor to understand me, that I could find the necessary confidence, in time."

But over the last four years, she's lived in a protected environment with her husband and children, and, in her own words, she has changed: "I have seen myself growing in confidence. In that safe environment I have developed creativity in my service and have discovered that I have ideas for preaching which previously I had not realized. This safe environment is created by living with someone who respects me as an individual with thoughts and feelings that matter."

Radha-priya is one of the lucky ones whose femininity is being respected by her husband. But very few of us know what it actually feels like to be comfortable being a woman as well as a devotee.

I've been told that if a woman has ignored her emotions while serving the needs of her family or community, there may come a point where she slowly begins to reclaim how she feels as a woman. At that time the mysteries of the feminine realm appear in her dreams; in synchronistic events; in her poetry, art and dance.

I think it therefore significant that a few days ago I had a dream that a woman was serving *prasadam* to the men. She sprinkled wheat germ over each of their bowls to give them extra energy. I could understand that women are able to give men energy by their feminine association in the same way that we as women are benefited and strengthened by male association. But when I opened my jar of wheat germ, I had a problem. The jar had been unused for so long that the grains were clinging to the sides of it with the webs tiny bugs had spun. I was unable to use it. Unable to add its energy and nourishment to my life, or to anyone else's.

This is how I feel about my femininity. I've shoved it so far back on the shelf so long ago that now when I want it, it's practically unusable. Was I being Vedic or *adharmic*? What would a "Vedic woman" have done had she been faced with these same circumstances in her life? I sincerely doubt it would have been anything like what I did.

What I would like to see is a new hoop for us to aspire to jump through. One that encourages us to become Krishna conscious as we develop those soft qualities of Vaishnava women. We need the strength we possess in our femininity to be rewarded, not our hardness. We need guidance and nurturing as we make our practice jumps, and allowances for our initial failures. I'd like to be given constructive feedback occasionally from the men to let me know how I'm doing.

Better yet, however attractive they are, do we still want the hoops at all? And what about dropping the hoops that are also being held up for men to jump through? Wouldn't it be preferable to just let all the seals swim freely in the ocean of devotional service that Srila Prabhupada introduced us all to? Let them swim alongside the dolphins and whales; let them bask in the shore alongside the penguins and sea-gulls. After all, Srila Prabhupada did build a house the whole world would live in. He wasn't interested in any of us becoming circus performers. He wanted us to become pure devotees.

Fairy Godmothers or Nasty Stepmothers?

At present many, many women are ambiguous about their identities within this Movement. You may feel inclined to say that our role is clear, you let us know what it is when you call us "*matajis.*"

But some of us have come to disdain that very word. At times we even hear it spoken to us as if it were a swear word, part of a phrase from the sixties: "Up against the wall mother." But why is this? We've learnt from Srila Prabhupada that all women other than a wife should be seen as "mother, *mata*." But the way our "sons" have treated us over the years has not made us feel cherished. Instead it's made many of us devalue ourselves. Would we honestly relegate our mothers to positions in the temple room where they were unable to see the Deities? Have them chant their *japa* in the corridors or up and down staircases?

This is supposed to be the *sankirtana* movement, with *harinama* a major celebration of the holy name. How many of you have ever gone out on a *harinama* party – staying at the back? Apart from the dangers of being accosted by drunks and hecklers, you can't hear the kirtana, and end up feeling just like a useless appendage dragging at the back. Doesn't make you feel too protected or respected.

One of my godsisters, Govardhana Prabhu, is also a mother. She told me of a time she visited Bhaktivedanta Manor for a feast day. All the devotees were being served from a central serving table which you had to queue in line. The queue itself was quite long, with the *brahmacharis* and *grihastha* men at the front, the women with their children at the back. She said, "We were standing there with our children who were pulling on our *saris* crying, 'we're hungry.' We were just standing there watching all the men going first to get served."

"On this particular occasion, I was still standing in the queue while some of the *brahmacharis* had finished taking *prasadam*. They came up and got back in the line again, ahead of the ladies. They were taking seconds."

"Although I knew with my intelligence that this was Krishna's temple and I wanted to be a devotee, and all that, with my heart I wanted to run a million miles. I just felt so sad that no one cared."

To my mind the saddest part about this is that it was most likely seen as a completely normal occurrence. It's something that we've grown up with in Krishna consciousness, quite normal. But I don't see it as fitting in with what we're supposedly being told. What's the use of calling us Mataji if you don't treat us like Mataji?

Govardhana Prabhu also recounted: "At Rathayatra last year only one tent had been booked for the Bhaktivedanta Players and anyone else who was on stage to use for changing into costumes. And guess who it was who had to get changed behind the stage in full view of anyone who happened to pass by? It wasn't the Bhaktivedanta players. It was me. Was that how to show respect for a woman?"

On a morning walk in Mauritius Prabhupada highlighted a difficulty we have with this concept:

Devotee: Srila Prabhupada, should we call all the women "mother"?
Prabhupada: Yes. And treat it like mother. Not only call, but treat it like mother.
Harikesa: Actually we have not even any idea how to treat mother.
Prabhupada: Learn it.

Perhaps an examination of just how we feel about our own mothers may give us some insight into why this is so. Mothers embody limitless nurturance. They provide sustenance for us while we are in their womb as well as offering us protection. At the same time many of us have also had the experience of how our mothers could almost be suffocating in their over-protectiveness.

According to present day psychologists, if a child sees his mother as the source of nurturance and support, he will experience her as a positive force. If she is perceived as neglectful or smothering, the child will experience her as destructive.

It's also been demonstrated that most adults respond to their own mothers in terms of the terrible destructive side. We fail to see her life in the context of the historical period in which she lived, her family background, and the opportunities available to women at that time. Many of our mothers were manipulated, contained and suppressed with the assistance of advertising, girdles and Valium. Yet, we often find it difficult to accept that our mothers did the best they could for us with the handicaps they had.

Many of us find it even difficult to forgive our mothers for the imagined and real hurts they inflicted upon us. And we carry this resentment and fear over to the whole issue of female power in general. We take our mother's nurturance for granted. This is evident in how we use, abuse and dominate even the Mother Earth every time we get the chance. The holes in her ozone and the forests we destroy demonstrate our enormous arrogance and disregard for her. In contemporary society because we subconsciously fear the power of mother, we do everything we can to denigrate and destroy it.

Is It Vedic?

And just because we're attempting to become Vaishnavas does not wipe out this conflict. As women we're often admonished to behave "Vedically," often used in the context of not acting assertively, etc. But let's compare how Indian society treats women.

Govardhana Prabhu has something to say on this point: "I've noticed that Indian people who you might say have some vestiges of Vedic culture left in them, treat their women differently. Very often when Indian ladies come to have darshan they are very beautifully dressed and made up. They are not at all denying their femininity. And they're confident. They walk right up to the Deities, make their offerings and offer their obeisances. They're not ashamed of themselves. Whereas if I walk into the temple I'm immediately thinking, 'where is it safe for me to be where I'll not disturb any man?' I'm always conscious of my body."

Govardhana's own story is interesting. She had put off visiting India for fifteen years because she felt that India, being the seat of Vedic culture, would accentuate this denigration of women even more than she'd experienced in the West. To her surprise, she was served *prasadam* by Bengali *brahmacharis* and passed the ghee lamp by them – things that had never happened to her in a Western ISKCON temple. "I was astounded." She said, "I felt my heart just melt. They were treating me like Mataji. All of a sudden it was okay to be a Mataji. That made me feel tremendous. For I don't want to be a man. I feel that whatever body I've landed with this time I'd rather do what I have to do with it. I don't want to imitate men."

She also described a time she participated in a function in a Hindu temple in Nottingham. Their *prasadam* room wasn't big enough to seat everyone at once. So the Indian men all stood at the side and chatted while the women and children took *prasadam*. They were taking pride in protecting their families, not having to prove that they were stronger or more important than the women.

Govardhana said about that incident, "We hear about women being simple, well, that little thing was enough to make those women so happy. And I have to say that just seeing that did more for me than listening to a hundred *Bhagavatam* lectures. It was living Krishna consciousness."

We're Just Conditioned Souls After All

So if this attitude is not Vedic in origin, there where does it come from? Could it possibly stem from influences we've assimilated from within our families of birth?

Virginia Woolf once wrote, "Everyone is partly their ancestors; just as everyone is partly man and partly woman." This is very much the case. As much as most of us would like to distance ourselves from our family of birth, adopting Lord Chaitanya's movement as our new family, we cannot deny that we continue to be influenced by attitudes and habits learned early in our lives.

Unfortunately, not all those habits are life-affirming. As women are taking more of a role in the world, the hearth of the family is becoming left unattended. Perhaps our own mothers were not there for us as much as we would have liked them to be. Perhaps we only had one parent in our family. Perhaps we may have even been abused by one of them. Perhaps Mum or Dad had behavioral problems that affected the tranquility within the family. All these things contribute to a deterioration of a nurturing connection with our parents.

In our own lives no doubt we can feel the pangs of this. But what of our own children? Will they not have a better go at it, having been born into families of loving Vaishnavas? Spiritually most certainly. But not necessarily emotionally. For if a devotee mother has been blocked from her own self-development and growth she may ignore or devalue her own daughter's competence. Or she may do the opposite and encourage her daughter to be a "special" or "gifted" child whose successes the mother will vicariously enjoy. Neither of these responses is especially healthy for either mother or daughter.

If husband and wife have not been able to reconcile their own sexuality in terms of Krishna consciousness, how are they possibly going to be able to communicate healthy attitudes and values to their children?

It's been proven that when an adolescent notices that his or her parents are uncomfortable with the outer signs of their emerging sexuality, they may reject their own changing body. They may use food to numb feelings of inadequacy, or alcohol, sex or drugs to alleviate the confusion and pain of being unacceptable. As they lose the ability to recognize the body's limitations, pain, and illness amass as the split between body, mind and spirit grows.

On the other hand, psychologists who study motivation have found that many successful women had fathers who nurtured their talent and made them feel attractive and loved at an early age. Woman are more likely to be self-determining when their fathers treat them as if they are interesting people, worthy and deserving of respect and encouragement. Women treated in this way don't feel their femininity is endangered by the development of talent.

No Such Thing as Love in this Material World

Is our own problem in reconciling spiritual principles within the context of a relationship having an adverse effect on our children in the ways catalogued above? What our Society's continued devaluation of women will lead to remains to be seen. But has it not already contributed in some way to the large number of unsuccessful marriages we've experienced?

Children need lots and lots of love. Srila Prabhupada mentions love in *gurukula* letters and conversations. "Discipline with love" he says, and "induce through happy, loving spirit." "The teacher must be expert in representing Krishna's loving compassionate nature," and "Everything should be done on the basis of love."

But love isn't a word very many devotees are comfortable using. We don't have the wide range of choice from *prema* to *kama* that exist in Sanskrit. For us one word is supposed to cover the feelings we have for God as well as for ice cream. As devotees, rather than use the same word we use for feelings we're attempting to cultivate for Krishna, we've adopted a pejorative term for the feelings one might have for their spouse and children: attachment.

And we use the word with the same tone of voice we often use the word "*mataji,*" spitting it off our tongues. Attached is not something we wish to be, attachment is not something we actively cultivate. This dilemma severely handicaps us when we attempt to be emotionally present for our children. For if "love" is something reserved only for the Supreme Lord, then what do we give our children?

Many parents solve this by interacting with our children and spouses as the perfect devotees we think we should be, and consequently, expect them to be perfect in return. But what does this impersonal relating do for the child? He's expected at times to be someone other than who he feels himself to be. As he grows up, he may rebel against this devotee business altogether or he may turn around and put his undigested, unexpressed shame on his own children.

Shame on You!

It's not only that children need to feel loved, they need to see love modelled between their parents as well. But this is difficult when we overlay renunciation on what are supposed to be affectionate relationships.

How many of us know couples where the husband is so wound up by inappropriate renunciation that he cannot even touch his wife's hand because he would immediately want her in bed? A good many of us I suspect, if it doesn't describe our own situations.

Such a husband ends up resenting his wife's womanly qualities, and she in turn feels shamed by her own natural femininity. And even though it is mentioned in the *Vedas* that it is in a woman's nature to dress nicely for her husband, how many of our husbands compliment or encourage their wives in that way?

One of my godsisters, Jaya Radhe Prabhu, is also concerned about the absence of love in our marriages. She told me, "It is easy for a man to 'renounce' family life and its nitty gritty responsibilities when love is absent. But is this renunciation – or merely a reaction to frustrated senses? I am sure that if there were more subtleties, more refinements, in the way a devotee man related with his wife, just little giving ways, and gentle behavior, he would not need to eventually explode into gross sense gratification. Or explode right out of the marriage. The all or nothing syndrome, *bhoga-tyaga*."

At What Price Submission?

If what Jaya Radhe and Govardhana Prabhus say is true, that women need to be able to feel feminine and appreciated within their relationships, then why don't more women stand up and just demand it from their husbands? Perhaps the title of a lecture that the Analytical Psychology Club of LA offered on the masculine principle might help us here. It was titled, "Knight in Shining Armor Seeks Damsel in Distress: Object Matrimony." It highlights how a man's sense of self is very often enhanced by rescuing a woman. But at what expense does the man gain this sense of strength? Is it that in order for a husband to be strong his wife must be weak?

Many of us have internalized this logic, deducing that if we somehow diminish ourself then our partner can be successful. And if he is successful then we can ride the crest of his spiritual attributes and thus to back to Godhead.

But then, in order for our relationships to survive in any way we must adopt a passive dependent stance. We do not speak out on needs we might have; most of us don't even let ourselves get as far as acknowledging that we even have any needs that are unmet. In doing this our unconscious motivation is to bolster and protect our husband's fragile ego.

And women who do dare to exercise their capacity for independent thinking and action, defining the terms of their own lives, are frequently accused of diminishing men, even of hurting children, or in some way being destructive to others. And this, of course, ladles heaps of guilt upon them.

So generally women put on masks to the men in their lives. They learn how to be compliant. They speak in polite tones of voice as they agree to practically anything a man proposes. But all the while such a woman may be seething underneath. She may be hiding daggers of rage about time sacrificed, confusion about betrayals left unaddressed, sadness for having abandoned herself for so long, and helplessness about taking the next step.

Superwomen?

It seems to me that we have to become some sort of pure devotee Superwomen in order to fit into the conception that the men in our movement have outlined for us. And personally, this is much too heavy a burden for one to live with anymore.

Marge Piercy, a poet, has written a poem entitled "For Strong Women." Part of it says,

"A strong woman is a woman at work, cleaning out the cesspool
of the ages, and while she shovels, she talks about how much she doesn't

mind crying, it opens the ducts of the eyes, and throwing up develops the stomach muscles, and she goes on shovelling with tears in her nose."

That describes the sort of strong women that many of us have become in order not to make any waves in this Society. But we're not happy; we're more like martyrs. Is this indeed the only thing that marriage is supposed to be bringing to us? I don't believe that any of us have a very clear definition of what marriage in Krishna consciousness actually means. My own opinion is that marriage is an opportunity for everyone, both men and women, to mature and grow both emotionally and spiritually. But in order for there to be growth in a union, much more must be brought to it than mere conquest of the woman by the man.

Marriage: Renunciation or Revelation?

Marriage requires patience, giving without thought to keeping accounts. When one partner says, "I gave this and so I am owed that," the marriage has not yet begun. Real sharing rests in a balanced recognition of sameness and difference; a discovery of balances and equalities.

Marriage is a relationship, a contract, a promise to help each other. It's not selfishness, that when the man feels satisfied (or just plain frustrated), he says, "Now I can renounce," not taking into account the other half of the marriage and her needs. Or the children's needs. Our philosophy is all about loving exchanges, and yet in our daily lives we seem to take those natural exchanges out of our primary relationships.

Any intimate relationship must be founded on the ability to be completely honest with our partner. But false renunciation of any sort is a form of dishonesty. How can love – whether for Krishna, Srila Prabhupada, one's wife and children, or the other devotees – flourish in an atmosphere of pretense? And where is there a chance of arriving at the Absolute Truth through a dishonest process?

Srila Prabhupada has described that if a snake sheds his skin naturally there will be no pain, but it you use a knife to skin him it will kill him. The standard of renunciation is not something which can be judged by one person – it has to be arrived at cooperatively by all members. We're all at different levels so what's too much for one person may not be enough for another.

Within the Catholic Church there was a polemic along similar lines in the early 1960s. Everyone will be familiar that Catholics firmly believe that the primary purpose of sex within a marriage was for procreation. A concept we also embrace. They had also institutionalized the ideal of celibacy, tending to emphasize the disruptive nature of sexuality both for the individual and for society at large.

As a result, their marriages were often dominated by rules and regulations. The Jesuits will be remembered as teaching that marriage was the salvation of the weak and that it was better to marry than burn in hell.

But dissatisfaction with this attitude towards marriage kept building up among the Catholic lay community, many of whom were experimenting with different attitudes. And when Pope John XXII came along, he listened to the laity as no other Pope had done before.

As a result, after Vatican II the Catholic Church changed its official stand. They now teach school children and counsel couples about to be married that each person should be recognized as being at different stages of development, and that marriage and the family are bedrocks of society, not something just for those who fail at celibacy. They've come to realize that feelings of shame or guilt are destructive. And that in order to love God and our neighbors (as the Bible admonishes), we must first love ourselves, have a strong sense of self-esteem and value what we are doing.

On the difficult issue of sexual "fall-downs" within a marriage, the Catholics have concluded that as a gift from God, the purpose of sexuality is the fostering of love. Following on from that they have come to recognize that the couple's mutual support is just as important as the function of procreation.

They have come to define that each individual should be encouraged, to exercise their own personal conscience in the matter of how they express their sexuality within the confines of their marriage, and that this should be mutually agreeable to both partners. According to a catholic ecclesiastical tract, "A human being's dignity requires them to act out of conscious and free choice as moved and drawn in a personal way from within, not by blind impulses or mere external restraint."

I think that we could learn much from the Catholic Church's history in respect to making our relationships more whole and holy. Things that will allow us to grow spiritually within our relationships with our spouses.

Our own scriptures tell us that intimate association with devotees is elevating. But just how many of our husbands actually see their wife's association as elevating? Does this mean that they perhaps are seeing them not so much as a devotee, but rather an object for their senses?

Should we not also be actively propagating marriage as the respectable, responsible, spirtualty dynamic, and yes loving, institution that it really should be? The *ashrama* that it is purported to be, not the second-rate solution for those too weak to be celibate.

Surrender versus Selfishness

A typical trait women possess is that we don't like to disappoint others. Consequently, we often give our assent to situations with little thought about how they will affect our own lives. This may even include agreeing to marry someone their authority has asked them to, agreeing not to marry but to continue with book distribution instead, agreeing not to have children, agreeing to have children, or any number of other similar major decisions.

Yet, if a woman braves her own feelings of selfishness and dares to ask to have a need met, she is often not only perceived by others as being demanding, needy and ungrateful, but shames herself into seeing herself in that way as well. This, coupled with our cultural background of seeing women – and in a particular, a woman's body – as a seductress, the cause of man's "original sin," has led us to many problems.

My godsister, Madhavi Prabhu, has some thoughts on this problem. If a woman feels loved – and physical affection is part and parcel of what makes her feel loved – she will usually be happy and content. She will remain "chaste" to her husband, and the children will be brought up in a healthy environment which is conducive for developing Krishna consciousness. Thus she and her children will feel protected. I don't mean to oversimplify, but this is an important aspect of our problems.

Madhavi Prabhu writes: "On the other hand, if a woman receives no affection, but her husband sees her for sex – when he 'falls down,' she lives in a hellish environment. Far from feeling protected and happy, she feels used and abused. And an ordinary woman can only take so much. Women by nature are very soft and vulnerable. And many of the women who join this Movement are exceptionally submissive and devoted to serving their husbands. So if he simply gives her the protective love she needs, everyone ends up happier. Society would not be a hellish condition, but rather a fertile ground for developing Krishna consciousness."

"A further extreme can result in out-and-out violent abuse of the woman, who is seen by the husband as the external cause of his "fall down." Because he wants to enjoy her, but can't touch her – he must hate her. And of course, if it wasn't for her presence, he could live a simple spiritual life, not have any sex desire, and even gain some prestige in society for his great capacity for renunciation."

"This situation of hating the object of desire can become so extreme (and indeed does) that only a pure devotee woman or a masochist could continue to tolerate it indefinitely. But many of us have tried for years – for the sake of 'chastity'."

"We, as women, need to have real relationships with the members of this Society. It is not that we should walk around feeling like objects, and that we must protect the men from becoming attracted to us, when we are supposed to be the ones who are protected."

On this topic, Govardhana Prabhu adds, "If this antagonism towards women is coming from agitation due to our past backgrounds, can we not be honest? Can we not call it that? Can we stop calling it Vedic?"

Lessons Learned

Despite the obviously noxious elements in my relationships with men, I must admit that I did gain confidence in my own intelligence and abilities through the support of my godbrothers. I gained a degree of freedom from traditional female roles by imagining a core of self that transcended femaleness. I truly believed that ultimately we are all spirit souls, eternal parts and parcels of Krishna.

Because we share a common spiritual goal, defined by our love for devotional service and our interest in the philosophy of Krishna consciousness, we are alike. But I foolishly extrapolated this to mean that I could become like my godbrothers.

I felt flattered to be occasionally told that I thought like a man. At the same time I experienced contempt for women who were satisfied living out traditional women's roles. I felt special, favored. But I realized that this has led to a betrayal of myself as a female.

I had a superior attitude toward other women, I wanted to think like a man; but of course I hated myself as a woman. I closed off large areas of myself in my quest to identify with men.

I realize now that in rejecting the feminine I've inhibited my growth as a woman and denied many inherent skills. I've also made lots of Vaishnava *aparadha* towards many of my sincere godsisters. That is what is motivating me to speak out now.

I would hope that none of the younger women who are joining us, who perhaps have been lured by the propaganda in the material world that women can and should equal men, will attempt to emulate the path I trod. Neither do I hope that the only other alternative is to sheepishly trail behind the so-called "submissive" women who are silently smoldering within.

In putting forward some of these feelings and concepts, and in pushing for reforms in various places within our Society, my godsisters and I have become labelled as "heavy" or some other denigrating term. We've heard devotees from other countries say that they know all about us and our lack of submission, our lack of chastity.

But the truth of the matter is that we are more than happy to take the role of women. More than happy to submit to the protection offered to us by our godbrothers. We welcome it, we beg for it. Please give it to us. So far we have not experienced it in any substantial way in our lives.

We do not claim to speak on behalf of all women within our Society. But neither are we isolated cases. Each one of us knows enough women with similar stories and experiences to justify the fact that we are not unique. Each of our stories vary slightly, the circumstances and our reactions to it differ as much as we each differ as individuals. But there is a common thread running in each of us: That we want to be devotees whatever the price, but up to now that price has been that we must flounder without protection from our godbrothers and continue to deny our intrinsic femininity.

But Not All Ladies Agree with You

Surprisingly much of the criticism levelled at me, or at women who are vocal like me, comes from other women. There are several causes for this as far as I can determine.

One is that we have successfully, over the last fifteen years at least, taught the newer ladies joining our Movement that being Krishna conscious is commensurate with renouncing your self-worth; that intrinsically men and their needs are more important in this spiritual Society; that women are more simple than men, and can participate in the movement but not to the same degree as men; that certain activities are the exclusive domain of those in male bodies and that this concept is coming from India and therefore Vedic; that marriage is a step-down from the advancement one was making in *brahmachari/brahmacharini* life; that there is not much benefit to be gained from being married other than to legally extinguish material desires; that in order to warrant being given protection by the men in our Society, a woman is required first to act in a chaste manner; that it is the woman's responsibility to ensure that no man in this movement feels any tinge of sexual feelings towards her.

And many of these ladies unfortunately have bought that lock, stock and barrel. So when we now tell them that this is not what we understand Krishna consciousness to be, they rightfully protest that we are "changing things."

Perhaps we are. But we feel that the present status quo is not what Srila Prabhupada intended it to be, that somewhere along the line, either due to our own dysfunctional backgrounds, or our misinterpretation of his instructions, or the inappropriateness of superimposing Vedic culture without adjustments on graduates of Western civilization, we have gone askew.

Being feminine is being both compassionate and instructive. Through it we can understand how to take care of ourselves. But all of us must avoid getting caught up in petty fights and the desire to dominate.

Another reason for the alarm of our godsisters can perhaps be understood in psychological terms. Many women who have had angry or emotional mothers are themselves afraid of their own anger and feelings. If they give these sentiments free reign they may be seen as being destructive or castrating. This repression of anger often prevents such women from seeing inequities in a male-defined system.

And when a woman is abused by a male in authority, she numbs herself to forget the humiliating pain associated with the trauma. She may even block remembrance of it from her conscious memory. But the pain does not disappear with its immediate cause. Nor does it go away if we somehow manage to "forget it." It merely becomes amour for the woman's wounded body, anaesthetizing her to her own instincts and intuition.

For centuries women have been told not to be "hysterical." If they feel strongly about something they were not lauded for their commitment and passion, but told that they were being unreasonable. If they expressed, a grievance with anger, they were told they were out of control. Most of us have learned to adjust our reactions to fit within this stereotype. But feelings that are not acknowledged don't go away; they go underground and bind us to the past.

Perhaps it is precisely because my godsisters and I have allowed ourselves to feel angry that we have been able to paint the pictures we've just given you. We know that anger is not an end in itself. It allows us to release some emotions that while buried eat away at us. But it does nothing for bringing about constructive change. For that reason we are approaching you, our godbrothers, our co-gardeners in Lord Chaitanya's garden.

When we feel heard, it's easier for us to accept our pain as it is, as part of life's natural process. When we feel heard, it doesn't eradicate the pain and humiliation, but in expressing our feelings to a receptive audience we can begin to heal our wounds. We then don't have to blame anyone; we can simply be with the suffering and thus heal naturally. Being permitted to just be with the pain, to go through a grieving process helps us to move through it.

We understand that it's important for us not to merely focus blame on others for this sorrow, but to deeply examine its cause and take responsibility for self-healing. Out of our own sadness we are beginning to develop compassion for those who have hurt us. Just the fact that you are taking the time to read this is a healing experience for us. Another factor one must take into consideration when hearing women who protest that that the issues this article focuses on does not reflect their opinions, is to look at who those women are. I would venture a guess that most of these women have been in a relationship for the bulk of their life in Krishna consciousness. They are very fortunate.

Women like me have had different experiences and have had to learn how to juggle various elements in order to stay on keel emotionally. We have had traumas with which we are trying to reconcile ourselves, such as raising orphaned children on our own, or understanding how Krishna allowed the abuse we suffered to go on. Our arguments should not be dismissed just because we are not in the majority. Our Society should be very happy if that is indeed the fact – that women such as us are the minority. But even if only one woman has had this experience, it is still relevant and should be taken into account.

It's All History

You may be tempted to dismiss everything I've presented here on the grounds that many of our predicaments happened over a decade ago, and now things are much different. Perhaps you might be assuaged to think that any of the men we might have made reference to are no longer practicing devotees. But we are unable to honestly assure you that the "offenders" and their "offenses" have been long rooted out of ISKCON.

It is undeniably true that things are changing. Were they not, we would not feel safe enough to come forward with these testimonies. But change is a slow and gradual process, one in which progress is measured in baby steps, not quantum leaps. We beg you not to turn a deaf ear on us. I have purposefully chosen not to dwell on a litany of current infringements of our womanhood. Rather, I wanted you to see something of the color of our background experiences so that in their light you might begin to understand who we are now, and perhaps derive a glimmer of a vision of how we can cooperatively move forward into the future.

The ability to preserve life is a feminine quality. This makes women ideal instigators for bringing a community together to work for our common good. Women are networkers, desiring to feel affiliated, part of a larger family. Over the ages, women have been the ones demanding protection for the young and less fortunate. So we are actually acting within our feminine role by trying to bring this to your attention.

On our own we can do something to help heal these wounds; but better yet is if our godbrothers support us. If with compassion and strength they help us to heal, we may learn how to reclaim our deep feminine spiritual wisdom. This will be a source of great wealth not only for the women, but for the men. For it is not only ourselves who are battle weary; the men must also be suffering as well.

A Fairy Tale?

I'd like to conclude with an English tale from the 14th Century. It's called "Gawain and Lady Ragnell." I feel that it can be instructive to our light.

One day King Arthur told his nephew, Gawain, that while out hunting alone he'd been accosted by a fearsome knight. This knight spared Arthur on the promise that he return in one year at the same spot. He was to return unarmed with the answer to the question, "What is it that women most desire, above all else?" If he had the correct answer, his life would be spared.

During the next twelve months Arthur and his nephew collected answers from one corner of the kingdom to the other. But Arthur was worried that none of them had the ring of truth.

A few days before he was to meet the knight, Arthur rode out alone into an oak grove. A huge, grotesque woman stopped him. She was almost as wide as she was high, her skin was mottled green and spikes of weed-like hair covered her head. Her face seemed more animal than human. She was Lady Ragnell. She told Arthur that she knew the correct answer, which she would give him if Gawain would become her husband.

Arthur was shocked and insisted that he could not give her his nephew. But she said that she had not asked him to give her the knight. Her condition was only if Gawain himself agreed to marry her would she help Arthur.

When Gawain came to hear of this, he was delighted to be able to spare his uncle's life. But King Arthur was despondent that his nephew was having to marry this supremely ugly woman on his account. Yet Gawain insisted that it was his decision.

So when King Arthur finally met the fearsome knight he first tried all his other answers, so that Gawain might be spared from marrying Lady Ragnell. But just as the knight lifted his sword to cleave Arthur in two, he said, "I have one more answer. What a woman desires above all else is the power of sovereignty, the right to exercise her own will." And thus he was spared, for that was indeed the correct answer.

Gawain's wedding to Lady Ragnell was held in a shocked and uneasy silence by the lords and ladies of the court. When in their own chambers, Lady Ragnell asked Gawain to kiss her, he did so without reservation. And there, true to all fairy tales, stood before him a slender young woman with starry eyes and a serene, smiling face. She told him that she had been cursed by her brother, the fearsome knight Arthur had met in the forest. She was only to be released from being a monstrous creature if the greatest knight in Britain willingly chose her for his bride.

Gawain asked her why her brother hated her so much, and she told him, "He thought me bold and unwomanly because I defied him. I refused his commands both for my property and my person."

Then she added that the spell was only partially broken. She said, "You have a choice my dear Gawain, which way I will be. Would you have me in this, my own shape, at night and my former ugly shape by day? Or would you have me grotesque at night in our chamber, and my own shape in the castle by day? Think carefully before you choose."

Gawain thought for a moment, finally telling her that it was a choice he could not make because it was her choice only to make. He told her that whatever she chose he would willingly support.

Ragnell was radiant, for his answer broke the evil spell completely. Ragnell explained: "My brother said that if my husband freely gave me the power of choice, the power to exercise my own free will, the wicked enchantment would be broken forever."

So Lady Ragnell and Gawain were united in a sacred marriage of two equals who had made a free and conscious choice to come together. She had been bewitched by her wicked brother for asserting her will and protecting her sexuality. Compassionate Gawain gave her the freedom to transform her disfigurement. She had the ability to save the king, and Gawain had the wisdom to recognize the sovereignty of the feminine. Together they found healing love.

If we want it to, this can be the story of our Society. Up to now you may have only been seeing us as grotesque and frightening. But if you shower us with compassion, we will freely change for you. You will be able to perceive our beauty and our gifts. And we will be grateful to have been saved from the wicked spell that this material world has kept us under for so long.

I am grateful to my godsisters for their solace and support in this work, as well as to their comments and advice. In particular; I'd like to thank Amekala-devi, Bhogini-devi, Govardhana-devi, Jagatam-devi, Jaya Radhe-devi, Madhavi-devi, Radha-priya-devi, Sri Kama-devi and the many godbrothers who have been honest enough and brave enough to lovingly validate and encourage me.

1991

Back to Godhead Articles

As debate in ISKCON intensified about the role of women in ISKCON, Back to Godhead *magazine ran five articles in the January 1991 issue on the topic. They are in the order they appeared in the magazine:*

Doing Things the "Prabhupada Way" by Pranada devi dasi;
A House for the Entire World by Sita devi dasi;
Srila Prabhupada and His Women Disciples by Visakha devi dasi;
Where Are Your Women Teachers? by Manasa Ganga devi dasi;
Krishna Knows What We Need by Jadurani devi dasi

We reprint them here in their entirety.

Doing Things the "Prabhupada Way"
by Pranada devi dasi

In discussing the role of women in our movement, we must understand Srila Prabhupada's teachings and the Vedic social ideal, and balance those with the precedents Srila Prabhupada himself set. It's a "hot topic," one on which even devotees may have spiritual differences of opinion.

In Vedic culture, women must be protected, they should be chaste and submissive, and they are naturally shy. Beyond this, Srila Prabhupada highlighted a woman's standing as a devotee of Krishna and a preacher in Lord Chaitanya's movement.

Srila Prabhupada was expert in applying Vedic culture and spirituality to the present day, as he showed by fine tuning the roles of his disciples, both men and women. For example, he wanted his *sannyasis* teaching in the world, not going to the forest for severe austerities. And he wanted his women disciples spreading Krishna consciousness too, not merely practicing it for themselves.

In many ways, Srila Prabhupada adjusted the traditional Vedic culture because we're in Kali-yuga and we are a Vaishnava preaching society. Our Movement is dynamic, not static; so as a young institution we face the challenge of striking the right balances.

How much should we stress that a woman be ideal in the Vedic sense? Should we stress it more than her role as a devotee or preacher? When do Vedic norms of behavior help protect women, and when do those norms slide into stereotyped definitions of shyness and submissiveness that turn women away or cut women off? Do we look at a woman's enthusiasm and competence in devotional service as a sign of good fortune or as a sign of independence and looseness?

Srila Prabhupada encouraged devotee women in all types of service. And because his vision for women was not stereotyped by traditional Vedic roles, women helped spread his movement all over the world.

But in the early '70s ISKCON adopted various changes meant, I suppose, to set a higher standard of Vedic custom. For example, in ISKCON's early years the women stood opposite (and separate from) the men during temple functions. Now they stand in the back, where it's difficult to see the Deities on the altar. Newcomers find this strange, and even cultured Indian ladies don't follow this policy, because it is foreign to them.

Other changes limited when women may lecture, offer *aratis*, offer flowers to Srila Prabhupada, and chant in the temple. Perhaps we should now look again at these changes, to see whether they fit what Srila Prabhupada desired.

We may also have to look again at some of our attitudes.

Srila Prabhupada spoke strongly about materialistic men and women, but he spoke differently about devotees both men and women. But now when men in ISKCON preach about women, they often seem to speak categorically, lumping together materialists and devotees.

What is the proper understanding about devotee women? Are they unintelligent? Or, as aspiring devotees, are they more intelligent than men who fail to devote themselves to Krishna? Speakers need to take care with the messages they send out. When the message to devotee women is that they're less intelligent creatures, or agents of illusion, doesn't that sap their inspiration to become Krishna conscious? And are those messages philosophically correct? If we want Krishna consciousness to spread, here's a place for some good Krishna conscious sensitivity.

Another point: Philosophically we have to accept that women can become *gurus*. Yet our movement does not have any women initiating. It's certainly not because of a lack of senior women devotees. Is it due to prejudice, or is it something the Vedic tradition tells us about women's psychophysical nature? How do we understand Srila Prabhupada's statement, in several letters, that his women disciples should also initiate?

Again, right now only men serve on ISKCON's Governing Body Commission. Is there a need to add senior devotee women to provide a balance, especially to see to the needs of women and children?

Overall, the women's issue in ISKCON concerns attitudes and behavior of how we relate to one another as devotees. We have to see one another as devotees, and then everything falls into place.

Srila Prabhupada stressed that to give women protection is essential for a progressive spiritual society. One way to judge a civilization is by how it treats its women. Does ISKCON provide women devotees the material and spiritual protection they need? We ought to make sure that it does.

This discussion within ISKCON is not an outcome of a battle of the sexes or a power struggle in the material world. It is a sincere attempt to look honestly into our hearts and correct wrongs if there are any, so that we can preserve and spread Srila Prabhupada's movement in its purest, most potent form.

In ISKCON we want to do things "the Prabhupada way." So why should we let our way of life in ISKCON depart from Srila Prabhupada's standards and attitudes about women? We shouldn't and certainly we won't.

We will solve the puzzle that confronts us in the "women's issue" by looking closely at Srila Prabhupada's caring, Krishna conscious dealings with his women disciples and following his mood. ISKCON consists of Srila Prabhupada's sincere followers. Srila Prabhupada is certainly guiding us, so it's just a matter of time before we address this topic and come to the right understanding.

Srila Prabhupada likened spiritual life to a razor's edge. That razor has to be handled carefully. Each of us must continually reevaluate our internal progress, and so it is too for the movement: As a group we must always reexamine how carefully we are following Srila Prabhupada's instructions. That will insure ISKCON's purity and longevity.

The present discussion about women's roles in ISKCON is an opportunity for such a reexamination. Our movement faces questions today and will continue to face them for the next ten thousand years as we grow, mature, and flourish. And just as by carefully polishing a diamond one brings out its natural, beautiful shine, the devotees in ISKCON, by advancing in Krishna consciousness, will show more and more examples of wonderful spiritual relationships in every sphere.

The topic of women's roles in ISKCON has only recently surfaced. As more devotees become aware of the discussion, surely we will deepen our understanding.

As Jadurani Prabhu points out later, our foremost meditation has to be on taking spiritual life seriously ourselves and teaching Krishna consciousness to others. For us as individuals, nothing is more important than this. And for us as a society of devotees, nothing is more important than working cooperatively to ensure the integrity of our movement. For Krishna consciousness, the world depends on us and we certainly won't let it down.

A House for the Entire World
by Sita devi dasi

Srila Prabhupada accepted women disciples lovingly into the familial embrace of his Hare Krishna movement, engaging us and encouraging us in all different types of service. He made us feel wanted and useful; we were devotees assisting in his endeavor to present Krishna to the world.

But something happened along the way to change ISKCON's perception of our role. It happened, I think, around 1975 or 1976, when our leaders were trying to relieve

Srila Prabhupada of the burdens of management and free him to concentrate on his *Srimad-Bhagavatam* translation.

ISKCON began adopting new rules, those rules Pranada Prabhu talks about. Some rules were timeless guidelines for *ashrama* life. Others, I'd say, were immature ways for twenty-year-old Westerners to handle their new attempts at celibacy.

Perhaps because it's hard for neophytes to distinguish their new spiritual realizations from their old material attitudes, some men found it easy to justify what we women joked about as the "mean swami syndrome."

And we women were emotionally and spiritually immature ourselves. We did not fully understand our roles, so we often accepted models of behavior that were not what Srila Prabhupada intended.

It's difficult for embryonic spiritual aspirants to perceive themselves as anything other than advanced. So we ISKCON devotees institutionalized patterns of behavior that to some extent made our family relationships dysfunctional.

What we need now, I suggest, are opportunities for Srila Prabhupada's disciples – men and women – to meet and formally discuss these issues so that our lines of dialogue and communication can open.

Now, wiser, I hope, both from age and from spiritual maturity, we can retrace our steps, recognize mistakes we've made along the way, and set things right.

Then, by our example we will be able to show the younger devotees Srila Prabhupada's original idea of a house in which the entire world can live.

As Srila Prabhupada fanned our infinitesimal sparks of devotional enthusiasm, we too must learn to appreciate one another's service to Srila Prabhupada, regardless of how inadequate that service might be.

As our Society develops, we should make sure it protects women from serious social neglect, makes it hard for men to abandon their wives and children, and provides support for women and children who need it. We should provide counseling to help devotees keep their marriages together, and we should see to it that devotees take their vows of marriage and *sannyasa* most seriously, in general ensuring that we never leave women unprotected.

I think I speak for many women who feel inclined to accept our role of being protected by men, who we in turn are inclined to serve. I don't want to usurp the managerial roles men have in our movement. I'm just searching for a clearer definition of my role within ISKCON.

Srila Prabhupada and His Women Disciples
by Visakha devi dasi

By a quirk of fate, when my family and I were living on an ISKCON farm some five years ago, I was assigned to once-a-week nursery duty. On my first day, I went to the nursery at the appointed time with my three-year-old daughter and received eight other lively three-year-olds as they were dropped off by their parents. I clapped my hands and said, "All right, children! Let's sit in a circle. We're going to have a *kirtana*!"

When they were seated, I asked, "Who would like to lead?" Immediately nine eager hands shot up, straining to get my attention, accompanied by a chorus of "Me!" "Me!" "Me!" Then the little boy sitting next to my daughter leaned over to her, his hand still raised, and said, "You can't lead because you're a girl."

I was so stunned by that comment that I can't remember what happened afterwards. At what other nursery, at least in the Western world, would a child have the notion that a girl couldn't lead others in singing simply because she was a girl? I think none.

Yet here, in a community of those attempting to practice Vaishnavism, a philosophy that acknowledges the spiritual equality of all living beings in all forms of life – we were shackled with "can do's" and "cannot do's" based on the particular body the soul was housed in.

On one hand our Vaishnava scriptures give explicit rules governing womanly conduct. Yet on the other hand the ultimate purpose of these rules is to enable all men and women to grow and blossom fully in Krishna consciousness.

For me, any seeming dichotomy this might raise is resolved when I think about the example of Srila Prabhupada, the embodiment of Vaishnava scripture. Since Srila Prabhupada's departure from this world thirteen years ago, little has been written about his unique exchanges with his female followers. This was a relationship free from any tinge of mundane romance or anti-woman sentiment. Srila Prabhupada, being free from sensual desires, did not feel his vow of celibacy threatened by his young female followers. And, being free from false ego, he had no need to assert male superiority or dominance.

In the atmosphere created by Srila Prabhupada's purity, a relationship grew. On Prabhupada's side it was full of caring and a continuous attempt to fan the spark of devotional service he saw within us. On our side it was fostered by a deep feeling of Prabhupada's concern for our spiritual advancement and well-being. We were full of excitement – how to serve him, how to please him, how to surrender more fully to him and so taste a tiny bit of the Krishna consciousness he was relishing at every moment.

I dearly wish that the little boy in the nursery and all the people behind the "you can't because" mentality in his mind could have seen Prabhupada as he asked my friend and godsister Yamuna Prabhu to lead *kirtana* time and time again – at gatherings of his disciples, at the homes of life members, and at programs with literally tens of thousands in attendance. Prabhupada pressed Yamuna into leading even when she had a sore throat and wanted to avoid it. He even asked me to lead once, and I can't sing worth a farthing. (Afterwards he said, "Visakha Prabhu, you have sung very nicely.") But what we could or couldn't do wasn't really a consideration. As women with Prabhupada, we held within us the most treasured knowledge: that Prabhupada wanted us to succeed. He wanted us to go back home, back to the spiritual kingdom, and he wanted us to be perpetually enlivened, determined, and patient in our quest of this goal. By his guidance, by his smile, by his selfless love for us, he all but carried us along. What stigma can shackle persons so propelled?

Pages could be filled with stories of Prabhupada's gentlemanly dealings and sweet exchanges with us women. I can only bow my head at the feet of my Lords, Sri Sri Radha Krishna, and thank Them for allowing me to have a little of Srila Prabhupada's association in this life. For without that, I couldn't understand what it means to be an aspiring woman devotee in an international society of aspiring devotees.

Where Are Your Women Teachers?
by Manasa Ganga devi dasi

The first preaching engagement I went to after being initiated was an experience I will always remember. In the fall of 1988, I and several other devotees, armed with *karatalas, mantra* cards, *prasadam,* and books, found our way to Temple University's branch campus in center city Philadelphia. Mostly adults filled the evening class on new religious movements. Except for one unfriendly student (a voice for impersonalism), the class responded well to the talk given by Ravindra Svarupa Prabhu. The students asked thoughtful, penetrating questions. Even after 2 hours, hands were still in the air.

I was thoroughly enjoying the lively, fast-moving dialogue, especially the philosophical deftness with which Ravindra Svarupa Prabhu defeated the one baiting antagonist. But then I was jolted from my track when a woman in the class abruptly turned to me and said, "I want to address this question to the only woman member of your organization present. I have the impression that the ISKCON church is male chauvinist. I have only seen men in the role of teacher. What is the role of women in your church? Do you have a function in teaching?"

I gulped, regretting I had not chosen a less conspicuous seat. The "women's issue" in ISKCON had caused many heated discussions among devotees, and for me it was still a touchy issue. I would have preferred to avoid the topic altogether, but now I was thrust on center stage with forty people awaiting an answer.

My heart accelerated as I quickly inventoried my scanty knowledge of Krishna consciousness, looking for an answer that would satisfy both the inquirer and me. After all, the student's assessment was to the point: women had not been encouraged to take up visible leadership in our movement. How was I going to explain why this was so?

My mind sped back over the years I had spent looking for the ideal philosophy that could wipe out the suffering and exploitation that millions of women face every day. I had evolved from a feminist perspective (seeing "men and patriarchal institutions" as the enemy), through Marxism-Leninism (seeing "the capitalists and their state" as the enemy), to finally finding Krishna consciousness (seeing "*maya* and my own impurities" as the enemy). My goal was to find a truly harmonious society in which all people, including women, could live with mutual care and respect and flourish to their fullest potential. I had recently concluded that such a society could only be one in which we give up self-centeredness and make Krishna the center of our lives.

As I gathered myself to speak, I was struck by the irony of the moment. Even though I felt, after years of searching, that I had found my home in ISKCON, I still felt the prejudices toward women that had initiated my search for truth years earlier. But now, instead of me seeing men as the enemy, they saw me as the enemy, as "Maya Devi," or illusion personified.

To be viewed as an embodiment of sin in the eyes of some male devotees would not have been so bad if it stopped there. But because I was seen as a temptress first and a devotee second, I was subtly or overtly denied or discouraged from a host of spiritual activities that I understood to be given to me by Srila Prabhupada. A frustrating dichotomy presented itself. On one hand, I was welcomed to clean, cook, and make flower garlands, services I enjoyed. But on the other hand I was told that because I am a woman I would disturb the minds of men (that is, sexually agitate them) if in their presence I chanted *japa* in the temple room, led *kirtana,* stood up near the Deities during *arati,* offered *puja* to Srila Prabhupada, gave *Srimad-Bhagavatam* class, was involved in higher levels of management, and so on. This dichotomy made me feel excluded, and a little schizoid, because I wanted to excel in *all* activities, not just those stereotypically designated as female.

ISKCON is supposed to be a house in which the whole world can live, so there must be room for all of me, not just the part that fits the female stereotype. Srila Prabhupada taught that Lord Chaitanya rejected the bodily-based caste system and affirmed spiritual enfranchisement for everyone. Enfranchisement is the heart and soul of Lord Chaitanya's *sankirtana* movement; it is why Srila Prabhupada came to the West. Srila Prabhupada confirms that anyone can be a Vaishnava:

"Sometimes persons criticize the Krishna consciousness movement because it engages equally both boys and girls in distributing love of Godhead . . . . But these rascals should consider that one cannot suddenly change a community's social customs. . . . These jealous fools who criticize the intermingling of boys and girls will simply have to be satisfied with their own foolishness because they cannot think of how to spread Krishna consciousness by adopting ways and means which are favorable for this purpose. Their stereotyped methods will never help spread Krishna consciousness." (*Chaitanya-charitamrita, Adi-lila,* 7.32)

If Srila Prabhupada accepts women and men equally, then how do I get enfranchised and get all of me into Lord Chaitanya's *sankirtana* movement?

Unfortunately, two years ago I didn't know how to answer that question. I acknowledged that in principle there is no service from which a woman is barred but in practice we are actually discouraged in some ways. But I felt that my answer was incomplete.

As the bell rang to end the class, I departed with the other devotees fortified with a new resolve: for the sake of preaching, I would learn to answer her question. As I continue to struggle, two years later, to follow the process Srila Prabhupada gave us, that answer is becoming clearer to me:

"Yes," I would now tell her, "there are men in ISKCON who are chauvinist in their behavior, and that's a problem that needs to be addressed, but that doesn't mean that the ISKCON church is male chauvinist. Srila Prabhupada, as a pure devotee, was above the dualities of male and female. So in that sense his teachings are radical. He brought us the gift of the *Vedas,* which teach that the purpose of human life is to realize that we are not these bodies but spirit souls meant for serving Krishna. The *Vedas* teach us how to achieve this goal and become free from sex life, which is the cause of death.

"To rise above the duality of male and female, we have to understand that the mind of the conditioned soul is perverse, because it is infused with the modes of material nature. The mind looks for so many ways to be the enjoyer, both grossly and subtly. It can even trick us into wanting to become spiritually advanced so it can enjoy having fame, respect, mystic potency, lots of followers, and so on. The conditioned mind leeches onto anything that will make it feel superior to others.

"In ISKCON, some men find mental satisfaction in thinking themselves superior to women. Well, where does this sense of superiority come from? Is Krishna speaking to us from within through the Supersoul, or is our mind subtly influenced by lust, greed, and anger because the false ego in us wants to feel important?

"To honestly determine the origin of our thoughts and feelings, we have to go to *guru* and *shastra* and carefully study what they say. A description of how our minds are conditioned is given in chapter fourteen of *Bhagavad-gita,* called The Three Modes of Material Nature. There Krishna speaks in detail about the categories He devised for running material nature: passion, goodness, and ignorance. They fit, respectively, with the basic cycle of nature: creation, maintenance, and destruction.

"When a soul takes on a material body, he is forced to act according to one or more of these three modes. And these modes act in all sorts of complicated ways.

"The modes of nature affect everything, including human psychology. In the mode of passion, the mind jumps here and there, unable to sit still. This agitated mind, restless, active, and wanting to create, finds ultimate expression in the sex act.

"In the mode of goodness, where things are maintained, one is calm, peaceful, and reflective. Knowledge and the ability to see things as they are is possible only in this mode. It is the steppingstone to spiritual awareness.

"In the mode of ignorance, one doesn't care about anything. The mind is neither active nor reflective. It is inert. This is the state reached through intoxicants.

"By studying this chapter in *Bhagavad-gita* we can learn to recognize these modes in ourselves and understand how they affect us. If a man acts to assert his superiority over women, he clearly is under the influence of the modes.

"In the mode of goodness, a person, through detachment, cultivates knowledge, which brings a sense of charitable superiority over those less knowledgeable. But in passion a person aggressively jockeys for some kind of position or control over others. And in ignorance one may be angry and violent.

"From this one could deduce that a male devotee who doesn't want to hear a qualified woman give class, lead *kirtana,* and so on, protesting that his mind becomes agitated, is affected by the mode of passion.

"But chauvinism – the desire to feel superior to others (racially, sexually, or however) – is antithetical to spiritual life. Not only does a transcendental person see all living entities as equal parts and parcels of Krishna, but because of humility he sees all other devotees as better servants of Krishna than himself.

"With this understanding of what makes some male devotees discriminate against women, I am better able to look at myself, for I face a similar struggle: to learn to control my mind and rise above the duality of seeing men as the ones excluding me from devotional service. I must look at the source of my anger and dissatisfaction, because ultimately no one who wants to get out of this material world is unfairly denied access to the means of getting out. As soon as we sincerely desire to get out of this material world, Krishna makes every possible arrangement, and *no one* and *nothing* can stand in Krishna's way, not even the male false ego. The facility for devotional service may not always come in the form we expect, but it will be there. That Krishna guarantees.

"Naturally, tests will come, and those tests are tailor-made with uncanny precision to goad the false ego. For me, learning to avoid becoming entangled in others' false egos has been the greatest challenge I have had to face. But I believe that with Lord Chaitanya's mercy it is possible to meet that challenge.

"The storehouse of knowledge that Lord Chaitanya has so mercifully unlocked for us is there ever ready for plundering. By distributing the holy name to the millions of lost souls, Krishna helps us transcend the dualities of male and female caused by the modes of material nature. And if we take His mission to heart, university students will soon no longer be asking, 'Where are your women teachers?' "

Krishna Knows What We Need
by Jadurani devi dasi

Obviously, having the body of a man or a woman is not a qualification or disqualification for spiritual activities. Srila Prabhupada wanted his women disciples to be as qualified as the men in teaching Krishna consciousness, and women should be offered full facilities for practicing Krishna consciousness and teaching it to others. This shouldn't even be a question of controversy.

But if there is some problem, or apparent problem, about the role of devotee women, women don't have to be worried. We can use all situations to our advantage in becoming pure devotees.

To give an example: When we go out to distribute books, some people take a book and some don't. We don't run after the ones who don't. We don't become discouraged by the no's. Instead, we concentrate on the yes's and pray to Krishna to help us be more Krishna conscious and present things better so that the no's, if He desires, will in time turn into yes's.

In the same way, if some devotee men don't want to hear us, we can go to other groups and speak to them about Krishna and train them through Srila Prabhupada's books.

We can *offer* our services anywhere, but who accepts our offer is up to Krishna.

The men in the temple are already hearing classes, chanting Hare Krishna, and making advancement. But other people may not be. So we can distribute books all over the world. We can preach on street corners, on television, in school auditoriums. We can invite people to the temple and speak about Krishna to them. If we have a house or apartment we can talk about Krishna to our family and neighbors. We can hold festivals and distribute books and *prasadam*.

If spreading Krishna consciousness is the real point, we can do it anywhere.

Krishna will recognize us. And when Krishna wants us to give a class in the temple or do other such things, He will arrange it.

We don't need to depend on any facility or position. Nor will such things guarantee our happiness or advancement in Krishna consciousness. Many devotees in the past had all sorts of facilities, but because of their own desires they left the movement, and now they have no spiritual power to speak about Krishna at all, or even to chant Hare Krishna. On the other hand, Haridasa Thakura was kept out of the Jagannatha temple, but that didn't stop him from becoming the greatest preacher of the holy name. Even *maya* herself was defeated by him and became his disciple.

Sometimes we use apparent "issues" as an excuse to be angry or resentful or as an excuse not to spread Krishna consciousness. When we come up against our own limits or shortcomings, we surrender to the "they" philosophy:

They don't encourage me enough.

They don't engage me in big enough programs.

They don't accept my suggestions.

In our modern materialistic society, we're trained from childhood to blame others for our troubles. Men blame women, women blame men, managers blame workers, workers blame managers.

But *we* are the architects of our own fortune.

About four years ago, I complained to a friend that certain devotees were causing me misery. So she answered that I myself was the cause.

"All right," I said, "I can understand that I may have been instrumental. But can't I say that those other devotees were the cause of my suffering?"

But she insisted that I was the cause.

This was hard to believe. But I wanted to believe her, because my own way of thinking wasn't making me happy or Krishna conscious. And then I remembered a verse in *Bhagavad-gita* (13.21) that confirmed her statements. *Purusah sukha-duhkhanam bhoktrtve hetur ucyate:* every living being causes his own happiness and distress.

The benefit of understanding that we are the cause of our own problems is that we can then take responsibility for the solutions.

We cause our own problems by our "overlording mentality," the mentality of trying to *control* everything. We forget that Krishna is supreme. So as a father sometimes puts a bad child in a reform school to get him to become good, Krishna spins us around like a merry-go-round just to bring us to our senses.

"Well," you may say, "That's just philosophy, but then there's real life. The philosophy is general, but we're dealing with specific issues."

But that would be to lose sight of the real issue.

If we go through any difficulty because of "women's issues," it is Krishna who is putting us into difficulty, and by knowing this we can serve Him without resentment.

Sometimes it looks as if Krishna, for no apparent reason, is withholding – withholding facility, position, profit, respect, knowledge, health, the results of our work, or whatever. But Krishna does it because He knows what we need to become purified.

Srila Prabhupada once said that if a devotee has an enemy – or thinks he has an enemy – the devotee thinks, "I am trying to become Krishna conscious. Why should this person be my enemy? Oh, I know: I have some impurity, and Krishna is trying to rectify me."

At every moment, the choice is ours: We can think dull, mundane thoughts or brilliant thoughts of Krishna's pastimes and ideas for spreading Krishna consciousness. We can pray in helplessness to develop all the devotional qualities and be used as transparent instruments for Krishna's will. No one can check us.

When we chant sixteen rounds of the Hare Krishna *mantra* on our beads, that comes to 28,000 names. So each day we have at least 28,000 opportunities to become pure devotees.

It's up to us individually how we identify ourselves. In 1966, while reading Srila Prabhupada's books, I once misunderstood he was saying that women couldn't make as much advancement as men. I was disturbed, so I told Srila Prabhupada. And his response was "If you think you are a girl, how can you make any advancement?"

According to the law of *karma*, the past makes the present, and the present makes the future. At present we are suffering because of our desires to lord it over material nature.

Who knows? A man who mistreated women in his last life may come back in this life as a mistreated woman. And – who knows? – maybe when I needlessly complain, I may be mistreating someone else.

If we act in Krishna consciousness at present, our future will be Krishna conscious.

1992

Building An All-Attractive ISKCON
by Pranada dasi

This paper was presented at the third annual ISKCON Communications Conference, Radhadesh, Belgium in 1992. It was the first time a woman spoke at the conference. It was later published in the first volume of the ISKCON Communications Journal.

Over the past ten years, I've experienced a growing pain in seeing devotees (adults and children) leave the Krishna consciousness movement. Each time someone I know leaves, I feel a deep loss and my heart breaks. Prabhupada once said not to be surprised that devotees leave but to be surprised that they stay, so it shouldn't come as a surprise to us that we have lost thousands of devotees over the years – perhaps more than the number we currently have in our temples. But Prabhupada didn't think lightly of the loss of even one devotee. In a letter to Upendra he wrote, "Those who have left the Society, I am always thinking of them." Prabhupada's heart went out to those who left, and he wanted them back. He pointed out that devotees are rare souls and that each one of us was trained with great difficulty. Many times he told us not to reject members so quickly, but to reform them, which requires great skill and tact.

Each person has free will and therefore we, as a society, cannot take full responsibility for everyone's actions; however, from my years of watching devotees leave and speaking to them about why they leave, I have determined that each of us has to take some responsibility for this. In many cases, had there been strong relationships with other devotees, or kind treatment during someone's difficulties, the devotee would not have left.

In a class last November in Vrndavan, Narayana Maharaja expressed his sentiments: "I always pray that those who have left ISKCON, they should come again to ISKCON. You should also see that you give them preference to take them back. If I see them all together I will see in no time that it will spread more and more in this world, your Prabhupada's mission."

My prayer is that one day, each individual in ISKCON can break through the barriers that keep our family from coming together to spread Krishna consciousness for Srila Prabhupada. I invite you to join me in this prayer and meditation.

The title of this essay is somewhat misleading. After all, Prabhupada has built ISKCON already and because ISKCON is Lord Chaitanya's movement and is therefore non-different from Him, it is all-attractive. The statement "building an all-attractive ISKCON" implies that the Movement's all-attractiveness becomes covered at times by our material conditioning and therefore it doesn't look all-attractive from inside or outside. There are things we can do to make it all-attractive.

ISKCON consists of people trying to advance in Krishna consciousness but who are not yet freed from faults, and because the world relates to Prabhupada's mission through the behavior of his servants ISKCON is sometimes seen as having faults. In fact, as devotees, we ourselves have that perception too, so we should take seriously the responsibility of ensuring that the movement's glory shines and attracts many conditioned souls. In the simplest sense, "building an all-attractive ISKCON" means that each devotee must allow the inherent all-attractiveness to come through by good behavior and developing spiritual friendships. In the *Nectar of Instruction,* Srila Prabhupada explains the all-attractive, simple principles by which ISKCON has spread all over the world:

> *dadati pratigrhnati*
> *guhyam akhyati prcchati*
> *bhunkte bhojayate caiva*
> *sad-vidham priti-laksanam*

Offering gifts in charity, accepting charitable gifts, revealing one's mind in confidence, inquiring confidentially, accepting *prasada* and offering prasadam are the six symptoms of love shared by one devotee and another. (NOI 4).

In the purport, Prabhupada writes: "The International Society for Krishna Consciousness has been established to facilitate these six kinds of loving exchanges between devotees. This Society was started single-handedly, but because people are coming forward and dealing with the give-and-take policy, the Society is now expanding all over the world . . . The life of the Krishna consciousness society is nourished by these six types of loving exchanges among the members; therefore people must be given the chance to associate with the devotees of ISKCON because simply by reciprocating in the six ways mentioned above, an ordinary man can fully revive his dormant Krishna consciousness." In the same purport, Prabhupada explains that this principle of loving exchanges is the basis of all activities of our Society. It is the foundation of book distribution, *prasadam* distribution, *harinama,* Sunday Feasts and interactions among ourselves. By this, he has indicated that the foundation of our movement is spiritual relationships – loving exchanges centered on Krishna.

We can speak of various aspects of the development of the ISKCON community or society. Perhaps the first thing that comes to mind is *varnashrama-dharma:* developing farm communities, establishing cow-protection, and educational institutions for children and so on; but I have chosen not to focus on these topics, which are the structure of community. Although it is important to discuss them, I am going to concentrate on the fundamental principle of community – relationships – which lacks a certain necessary quality in our Society.

Before building a structure, the foundation must be solid. If the foundation of our Society is love and trust, and true friendships between devotees are developing, then we have a healthy environment for devotees to advance in Krishna consciousness. The all-attractiveness will bind us to stay, draw back those who've left or who are reserved in their participation and invite the general population to become devotees. There is a great need in our movement to shed superficial interactions among ourselves and develop deep personal friendships – relationships centred on Krishna, but which keep us bound in Krishna consciousness and attached to our true, spiritual family. Such relationships are not *maya*; they are not to be avoided. Allowing ourselves to express human emotions of caring and love is part of the process of bhakti. Bhakti-yoga is one hundred per cent personalism. Personalism means relationships. Each of us has an eternal relationship with Krishna and His devotees. While relationships in the material world are binding, relationships with Krishna's devotees, even the "insignificant" devotees, are liberating. In talking with Ramananda Raya, Lord Chaitanya asked what was the most auspicious activity. Ramananda Raya replied, "the association of the devotees of Krishna is the only auspicious activity." I think we'll all admit that our progress on the path back to Godhead is supported and enhanced by all the devotees in the Krishna consciousness movement. Without the association of Krishna's devotees, there is no chance of our going back to Godhead, but by learning to associate with Krishna's family here, we are being trained to re-enter a relationship with Krishna. Valuing the devotees' association, we should cultivate personal friendships with them.

The very core of our existence is our desire to exchange in a personal relationship with Krishna. Indeed, the reason we exist is to exchange in that relationship to give Krishna pleasure. We know intuitively how to have personal relationships because we are originally persons, and Krishna is a person. Although we are now covered by fear, greed, lust, and envy, and cannot engage in completely spiritual relationships, we have the guiding light of Prabhupada's own example to show us our way back to true spiritual relationships. We need to follow this guiding light.

In this regard, I have some observations to share about our ISKCON family which I've learned from being a mother. I dare speak at all, not because of being a learned spiritualist or having a position in ISKCON, but simply because I have some practical experience being a mother and many things can be applied to our transcendental family. Many devotees disheartenedly refer to the institutionalization and lack of spontaneity of ISKCON since Prabhupada's departure.

Please allow me to make a generalization here, knowing that a generalization doesn't seek to condemn, but to highlight a point: ISKCON as an entity has lost its heart and feeling in the search for order and organization. To a large degree I feel it is because when we lost Srila Prabhupada's personal presence, we lost not only our powerful leader, our founder-*acharya*, but a mother with a heart. Sometimes devotees affectionately refer to Srila Prabhupada as having the heart of a Bengali mother, and indeed, Srila Prabhupada cared for us like an affectionate mother. Our mother has an amazing capacity to love us, accept us as we are, respect and appreciate us. She may see our faults, but she has faith that we will overcome them and our higher traits will prevail. Sometimes her reassuring faith alone helps us conquer our lower nature. She gives us a sense of self-worth and makes us feel that we have a contribution to make in the world. When there's fighting among the brothers and sisters, she knows how to pacify each one and maintain a co-operative spirit for the welfare of the entire family. If she's a good mother, she'll not only take care of us materially, but give spiritual direction as well. Prabhupada had more than a normal mother's capacity for patience and love and we came to know him as our most intimate well-wisher. He brought a nurturing, caring, spiritual relationship which we so much needed. Thus, he gathered his followers around him in love and made the ISKCON family.

We've all seen that devotees join ISKCON because of a personal relationship they develop with a devotee. Naturally there was some introduction like receiving a book or seeing devotees on *harinama,* but mostly devotees have joined due to a personal relationship. We stay because of relationships we develop, or we leave if they are lacking.

Devotees who joined Srila Prabhupada in the beginning almost always relate that they joined because of the personal relationship they developed with him. A relationship with Krishna seems distant, even impossible or unreal, but the relationship we develop with Srila Prabhupada, even if at a distance, is not only real, it fills our whole existence. There is nothing else really attractive in the world when we're in touch with Prabhupada.

Satsvarupa Maharaja relates a powerful experience that bound his heart to Srila Prabhupada. Maharaja had been visiting 26 Second Avenue but felt reserved about surrendering fully to Srila Prabhupada. He even passed up the first initiation. He relates that he wanted a personal invitation from Srila Prabhupada and that Prabhupada expertly caught him in the bond of loving affection by a simple gesture. Once, as Satsvarupa Maharaja was leaving Srila Prabhupada's room, Prabhupada said, in a matter of fact way, "If you love me, I'll love you." This struck Satsvarupa to the core, and he happily surrendered to Srila Prabhupada.

In this exchange and many others, Prabhupada showed us that our love is meant for Krishna's devotees. Although "love" isn't generally accepted in ISKCON as a viable term except in relation with Krishna, Prabhupada didn't hesitate to use it in relation with Krishna's devotees. He expressed it freely and genuinely.

Prabhupada endeared us to him because he really cared about us. He loved and respected us and demonstrated it by practical activity. His feelings for us were genuine; they weren't feigned or superficial. Even though he was so great and we were fallen, he used to ask us our opinion on matters. He would take the extra moment to notice us with his eyes and show that he knew us and loved us. He sincerely appreciated whatever little attempts we made to help him spread Krishna consciousness and he told us so. He liked being with us . He expressed concern when we were ill and he gave us practical advice how to get better. He sincerely empathised with our struggles in becoming Krishna conscious. To us, these were all signs of his genuine love for us.

We are not on the level of Srila Prabhupada and we cannot cause the potent change of heart which he did, but we can go a long way in increasing the number of Krishna's devotees and keeping them, by being personal and sensitive human beings. Although Srila Prabhupada was an exalted paramahamsa, completely beyond this world, he was at the same time very much of this world, very much a real human being, and that was what was so attractive to us.

I want to share a story which exemplifies one of the most important qualities that could be improved among ourselves: "The Rabbi's Gift," from *The Different Drum* by Dr. Peck.

A monastery had fallen upon hard times. Once a great order, as a result of waves of anti monastic persecution in the seventeenth and eighteenth centuries and the rise of secularism in the nineteenth, all its branch houses were lost and it had become decimated to the extent that there were only five monks left in the decaying mother house: the abbot and four others, all over seventy in age. Clearly it was a dying order.

In the deep woods surrounding the monastery there was a little hut that a rabbi from a nearby town occasionally used for a hermitage. Through their many years of prayer and contemplation the old monks had become a bit psychic, so they could always sense when the rabbi was in his hermitage. "The rabbi is in the woods, the rabbi is in the woods again," they would whisper to each other. As he agonised over the imminent death of his order, it occurred to the abbot at one such time to visit the hermitage and ask the rabbi if by some possible chance he could offer any advice that might save the monastery.

The rabbi welcomed the abbot to his hut. But when the abbot explained the purpose of his visit, the rabbi could only commiserate with him. "I know how it is!" he exclaimed. "The spirit has gone out of the people. It is the same in my town. Almost no one comes to the synagogue anymore." So the old abbot and the old rabbi wept together. Then they read parts of the Torah and quietly spoke of deep things. The time came when the abbot had to leave. They embraced each other. "It has been a wonderful thing that we should meet after all these years," the abbot said, "but I have still failed in my purpose for coming here. Is there nothing you can tell me, no piece of advice you can give me that would help me save my dying order?"

"No, I am sorry," the rabbi responded. "I have no advice to give. The only thing I can tell you is that the Messiah is one of you."

When the abbot returned to the monastery his fellow monks gathered around him to ask, "Well, what did the rabbi say?"

"He couldn't help," the abbott answered. "We just wept and read the Torah together. The only thing he did say, just as I was leaving – it was something cryptic – was that the Messiah is one of us. I don't know what he meant."

In the days and weeks and months that followed, the old monks pondered this and wondered whether there was any possible significance to the rabbi's words. The Messiah is one of us? Could he possibly have meant one of us monks here at the monastery. If that's the case, which one? Do you suppose he meant the abbot? Yes if he meant anyone, he probably meant Father Abbot. He has been our leader for more than a generation. On the other hand, he might have meant Brother Thomas. Certainly Brother Thomas is a holy man. Everyone knows that Thomas is a man of light. Certainly he could not have meant Brother Elred! Elred gets crotchety at times. But come to think of it, even though he is a thorn in people's sides, when you look back on it, Elred is virtually always right. Often very right. Maybe the rabbi did mean Brother Elred. But surely not Brother Philip. Philip is so passive, a real nobody. But then, almost mysteriously, he has a gift for somehow always being there when you need him. He just magically appears by your side. Maybe Philip is the Messiah.

Of course the rabbi didn't mean me. He couldn't possibly have meant me. I'm just an ordinary person. Yet supposing he did? Suppose I am the Messiah? O God, not me. I couldn't be that much for You, could I?

As they contemplated in this manner, the old monks began to treat each other with extraordinary respect on the off-chance that one among them might be the Messiah, and on the off, off-chance that each monk himself might be the Messiah, they began to treat themselves with extraordinary respect.

Because the forest in which the hermitage was situated was beautiful, it so happened that people still occasionally came to visit the monastery to picnic on its tiny lawn, to wander along some of its paths, even now and then to go into the dilapidated chapel to meditate. As they did so, without even being conscious of it, they sensed this aura of extraordinary respect that now began to surround the five old monks and seemed to radiate out from them and permeate the atmosphere of the place. There was something strangely attractive, even compelling, about it. Hardly knowing why, they began to come back to the monastery more frequently to picnic, to play, to pray. They began to bring their friends to show them this special place. And their friends brought their friends.

Then it happened that some of the younger men who came to visit the monastery started to talk more and more with the old monks. After a while one asked if he could join them. Then another. And another. So, within a few years, the monastery had once again become a thriving order and, thanks to the rabbi's gift, a vibrant centre of light and spirituality in the realm.

The purport here is that respect and appreciation for each other is the key in allowing the effulgence of spiritual relationships to shine forth and attract others. And how attractive are those relationships! Just consider our attraction to the *Chaitanya-charitamrta*. Although it is full of rigorous philosophy establishing Lord Chaitanya as non-different from Krishna, what most devotees are really attracted to are the very blissful relationships between all the devotees. Don't we each hanker after these types of relationships?

There is no reason why our movement cannot be as attractive. The question may be raised: is it possible to have these types of friendships in a society that is made up of *kanistha-adhikaris* who, by definition, don't know how to interact properly with devotees? Aren't we simply pointing to the need to become *madhyama-adhikari*, devotees manifesting the twenty-six natural qualities of a devotee? Yes and no. Obviously we can't overemphasise the importance of *sadhana-bhakti:* chanting sixteen rounds, following the four regulative principles. By advancement in Krishna consciousness, we automatically develop all good qualities. But that doesn't mean we shouldn't endeavour to act on the platform of ladies and gentlemen, of Vaishnavas. Indeed, my experience and firm conviction is that a little awareness and adjustment in our attitude and outlook can make a big difference.

In Dr Peck's extended studies of communities, he gives repeated examples of how the average non-devotee has applied principles of gentlemanly behavior and attitudes to build communities. Therefore, we don't have to become pure devotees to develop friendships and relationships centered on Krishna that will attract the whole world to Krishna.

Here are some details about personal development of attitudes and behavior in our relationships. I derived the following list from studies of community development combined with the qualities of a devotee. You can use the list to contemplate regularly in your personal attempt to improve Vaishnava *sanga* in your community.

Attitudes needed for development of relationships in community

1. Being conscious of others
2. Good communication
3. Appreciation and respect
4. Transcending individual differences
5. Honesty and humility
6. Self-examination
7. Empathy
8. Resolving conflicts gracefully

1. Being conscious of the needs and emotions of others

The beginning of a relationship is acknowledging that someone exists and that they, like us, have needs and emotions. Of course, this may seem so obvious as to be insulting to even state it, but it is with amazement that I note how we operate at times completely oblivious of another's existence. Most of us tend to focus on our own needs, often at the expense of the needs or emotions of others. We may not even be conscious of offending or hurting another devotee.

The key here is being conscious. Just as Krishna consciousness begins by being conscious, so does developing the requisite skills of interpersonal dealings. We need to become aware of how our behavior, attitudes and interaction with other people affects them. All our interactions have some kind of effect, positive or negative. If we're lucky enough to learn we offended someone, then we're at an advantage to correct the situation. Take the opportunity to address the mistake. Don't let it slide! Sometimes a simple apology is all that is required to mend the relationship. Leaders of our Society need to take special care to see that this is done. Bridge the gaps, heal the hurts, be real people. As with anything, the first step of improvement is understanding the problem and admitting that it exists.

An important builder of being conscious of others is putting ourselves in someone else's position. Taking a moment to reflect on the feelings of another will bring out natural qualities of a devotee, like compassion, empathy, humility and love.

2. Good communication

It is significant that the word "community" has a similar root as the words "community" and "communion." The root word "*communis*" means having something in common. Krishna is the common factor among us. Communication creates communion – or spiritual fellowship – in a community. These three are inextricably linked, and communication is the element that sticks it all together. Communication is the most important feature of community. It creates and sustains community. In fact, it is the basis of all social interactions in the community. With honest communication, one can achieve miracles; without it, even with the most attractive philosophy, we won't be able to develop a lasting community.

I have specifically entitled this attribute "good communication," to indicate that there is a difference between good and bad communication. Good communication is best fostered when we understand a few important aspects of communication. Firstly, it must be two-way. One-way communication is totally ineffectual. Therefore, the type of communication that just passes a message down from husband to wife, parent to child, leaders to rank and file, does not serve the purpose of being a relationship builder and thus it's likely that those on the receiving end are dissatisfied, perhaps to the degree of being rebellious. When we learn to allow the communication to flow back in the other direction, strength is brought to the exchange. And, most importantly, we learn, because everyone has something to offer.

The most crucial aspect in allowing communication to flow back in the opposite direction is listening. Listening has been claimed to be one of the most undeveloped, but most essential skills in communication. So often this is a major cause of a marriage collapsing or unrest between followers and leaders. If someone feels he's going to be judged, he won't be open. If he senses that we don't value him as a person he won't speak. If we can't sympathize with him, he won't share with us.

Listening openly doesn't mean we give up our ability to discriminate right from wrong. Listening openly means being broadminded enough to be open to other viewpoints, realizing that I may not always be right. I listen without passing judgement and I listen with respect and empathy. It means that we have enough integrity to respect others wherever they happen to be on the spiritual path. We clearly understand the standards of Krishna consciousness and practice rigidly ourselves. We preach to them and try to encourage others, but with the utmost respect, knowing that we don't have to play the judge in their lives. Without this attitude true communication becomes impossible.

We all know what it's like trying to communicate with someone who's already judged us or who is unsympathetic with our views. It's an unfruitful endeavor for both people. Real communication is worth working for. It is possible, it is satisfying, and most importantly, it is absolutely necessary for harmony and progress.

3. Appreciation and respect

We could spend a long time on the importance of appreciating others. Srila Prabhupada demonstrated its importance by personal example and he emphasized it in his preaching. Even though he was such an exalted devotee, Prabhupada always saw the good even the smallest of us did, and he wanted his disciples to have this vision also. He wrote to Tamal Krishna Maharaja in 1968, "Your appreciation for the service of your Godbrothers is very much laudable. This is actually a devotee's business that everyone should appreciate the value of other devotees. Nobody should criticize anyone. Because everyone is engaged in the service of the Lord, according to one's capacity, and the thing is, Krishna wants to see how much one is sincere in rendering Him service."

It isn't that we should respect the devotee with a big position and not the devotee with a little position. If we take the time to consider each devotee's contribution and what we need to do to spread Krishna consciousness, it becomes quite easy to appreciate the value of each devotee. Prabhupada wrote in letters that each and every devotee was very important to him. In fact, in one letter he wrote that we were all limbs of his own body. How important we all were to him! Let's reflect on that more often, and see that Krishna, too, appreciates the service of each devotee. If we remember this, we'll appreciate and respect all our godbrothers and godsisters irrespective of position or status. And if we are humble about our own position in Krishna consciousness we can see that others have just as much to offer as we do.

This quality is important for all devotees, but it can be especially difficult for managers to acquire. Several years ago, I was managing the schedules of about twenty lady devotees. As usual, the amount of service outweighed the ability of the available devotee power, so I always felt a strain in covering all the duties. I noticed that I tended to judge a devotee's worth by how much service she did. I didn't think highly of one young mother in particular who spent most of her time taking care of her daughter. I had calculated that she should be doing a lot more to help out. In fact, I started categorizing everyone I was dealing with: good devotee, not so good devotee, and so on.

One day, one of the most reliable stalwarts fell ill and it looked like she would be ill for a while. I didn't know how to help her with her illness and I was certainly hard pressed for time to do so. The devotee I had bad feelings for took it upon herself to nurse the sick devotee back to health with special medicines and *prasadam*. She'd been studying herbal medicine and natural cures, and had a knack for treating devotees. It seemed like a little thing, but I gained a powerful realizsation. By Krishna's grace I saw very clearly how wrong it was to pass judgement on devotees. Each devotee, each living entity, no matter how insignificant, has something valuable to offer the Krishna consciousness movement, even if from our little perspective we don't know what it is. Each devotee has a special place in Krishna's family and I realised I wasn't someone to deny them that, even in my mind. While I still fail at times, I remember the lesson the young mother taught me and I become a little humble and correct my mentality.

The inability to be equal to all is perhaps the most serious violence we can commit and has already created havoc in our movement in various ways. At times we see antagonistic distinctions between Prabhupada's disciples and disciples of other gurus, between men and women, renunciants and householders, leaders and rank and file devotees, core and congregation. Who's better and who's lesser. We think that whoever has a position must be more advanced. But this type of elitist mentality will destroy our movement.

Prabhupada told us that there is no force in the world that can stop our movement's progress – except one. Our movement can be destroyed from within. A controversy surfaced in 1976, between the *grhasthas* and *sannyasis*, which concerned Prabhupada very much. Prabhupada patiently waited to see how we would deal with the controversy, but as the conflict continued, he felt that it wasn't being handled properly, so Prabhupada stepped in with words of advice. He highlighted his deep appreciation for all devotees, even the small ones. One time, while reflecting on the repercussions of that controversy, he pointed out that he could not reject the love and devotion offered in making a small decorative item on his desk. He said that it was his responsibility to help everyone serve Krishna and he commented, "Party politics will spoil everything."

Historically, Prabhupada pointed out how this type of mentality caused a serious decline of Vedic culture. Prabhupada explained that the Mohammedan population in India was not imported from other countries; they were converted from among the lower classes of Hindus. There had been a mass conversion because the *brahmanas*, being arrogant, would treat the *shudras* badly. The *shudras* were not given facility for spiritual culture because the *brahmanas* monopolized it. The *brahmanas* kept the *shudras* downtrodden and because they were neglected, they didn't see a reason to remain Hindu.

Making distinctions of better or worse is extremely dangerous when dealing with devotees (or potential devotees as seen in the story of Dhruva Maharaja). We can't afford to lose any devotees to this narrow view and a simple dose of honest appreciation will control this tendency. One practical way to increase our appreciation is to openly glorify devotees. In one temple on the East Coast devotees got together for a session in which they each glorified one another's good qualities. Devotees said they would always remember the uplifting experience. Even if we don't do it in groups, we can each make a commitment to glorify and appreciate the good qualities of some devotees every day. Just as the Goswamis offered obeisances to devotees a fixed number of times daily we, too, can take vows to openly appreciate the devotees we know and work with every day. It will go a long way to improving our own attitude towards our godbrothers and godsisters, and it will benefit those who hear it.

One devotee in San Diego compiled a book of many devotees, *How I Came to Krishna Consciousness,* and when reading that book it's hard not to appreciate just how exalted each person is. Every one of us has to overcome many obstacles and be very determined to join this transcendental family. Let us not forget how special each devotee is.

4. *Transcending individual differences*

If there was one prominent focus a community should have, based on the findings of Dr. Peck in his book *The Different Drum,* this is it. Dr. Peck studied communities of many different sizes, simple groups of people, large institutions, and so on. In all cases, he concluded that the most important attitude for development of community is the ability of the members to appreciate the differences brought to the community by the individuality of each person. The differences shouldn't be seen as a threat or something to overcome, but should be seen as valuable.

I recently had a discussion with Burke Rochford, a sociology professor at a university in Vermont. He has done a couple of surveys on ISKCON, written a book about the Movement, and has a personal interest in how we are raising our first generation. In fact, he recently taught for a week at the *gurukula* in Alachua. We were speaking about the tensions that exist between the core of our movement and congregation (sometimes manifest as tensions between the householders and renunciants). He commented that in his opinion the most crucial issue for our movement right now is how, or if, our members can learn to face the differences (between statuses or *ashramas*) without being critical. Can we turn petty differences into progressive discussion? Can we build bridges instead of creating greater gaps. I found it interesting that he immediately pointed to our ability to transcend the differences among us as the central issue of our progress.

Transcending individual differences doesn't mean ignoring the natural differences in *varna* and *ashrama* or not observing the roles each of us needs to play. It means to go beyond the differences we find in our varying views and different abilities. To a large degree it means simply appreciating the differences between us as gifts. Some will be book distributors, some will be renunciants, some will be mothers. Not everyone will see eye to eye on every topic in Krishna consciousness, but these are the differences which make us the International Society for Krishna Consciousness.

Prabhupada taught us that differences are natural and desirable for serving Krishna. He would often point out that even among the most elevated devotees, the *gopis*, there are two opposing camps with differing views on how to best serve Krishna. He said that *acharyas* even sometimes disagree on certain points. It is all right and to be expected.

Let us learn to embrace the differences as valuable to Prabhupada's movement. Let us give up our critical, condemning attitudes. The best way to achieve the transformation of attitudes is by being committed to coexistence. Committed to Prabhupada and to each other. No matter what the difficulty or the differences, I will remain participating in Prabhupada's movement through thick and thin.

5. Honesty

Prabhupada taught us that a devotee is straightforward in his behavior. Honesty really shouldn't need much explanation. Sometimes we think that diplomatic dealings are laudable when used for the benefit of the Society. Most of the time this strategy tends to back-fire – perhaps sticking to straightforwardness is best.

6. Self-examination

Just as each devotee must be attentive to self-improvement by self-examination, so too, the community needs to be attentive to improving itself. In order to maintain individual and collective spiritual health, we have to be self-critical, open and thoughtful to the feedback of others. Self-examination for a community naturally occurs when individuals within the community speak out. We should not see this as antagonism or negativity, nor should we ignore the feedback. It is an important chance for improvement and we must always be vigilant to take the opportunity to move forward.

7. Empathy

Only devotees can feel true empathy because we understand the original position of the spirit-soul and how far the soul has strayed from that position. Because a devotee is naturally soft-hearted, his compassion for others is easily aroused. A devotee sympathizes with the suffering of all living entities. Although it should be natural for us to empathize with our fellow godbrothers and godsisters, it's surprising how much we refrain from expressing natural empathy for their struggles or pain. Again, the point needs to be made that we should express sentiments in our relationships.

8. Resolving conflicts gracefully

As everyone knows, conflicts naturally arise; they cannot be avoided. We are realists and a realist will face conflicts or discrepancies head-on. Still we must deal with each other with utmost respect.

So, these are some essential building-blocks for real community among the devotees. When we take practical steps to apply these attitudes in our life, we will see an immediate difference around us. In my experiences in dealing with my son or friends, whenever I become aware of problems it usually takes time to get the resolve to do something to change my behavior. But as soon as I make even little attempts, I see noticeable results in my relationships. I also know best where my shortcomings are. Sometimes I'll take a minute to evaluate where I'm weak and then think about how to improve my next interaction with another devotee. One time a devotee explained to me how she dealt with her husband who was an especially difficult person to get along with. She knew that whenever she had to exchange with him there would be problems. She decided to make sure that all encounters were as smooth as possible and to achieve this she decided to premeditate on being courteous, accommodating and surrendered before she saw her husband. She knew when she would see her husband next and would take a moment to mentally prepare herself for any exchange that may occur. So there's nothing wrong with being thoughtful about our dealings and we can make little practices like this.

There is nothing revolutionary or novel about these things, but at some point we have to decide that it is important and then do something about making changes. As I mentioned earlier, much of what we're talking about here are changes in our daily lives. As one devotee suggested, the importance of building relationships and friendships needs to be preached strongly in our Society alongside our constant reminders to chant sixteen rounds and follow the four regulative principles.

1994

Background for A Proposal for a Women's Ministry
by Sudharma dasi

In 1994 the North American GBC and Temple Presidents met in Dallas, Texas. ISKCON Communications, ISKCON Foundation, and several members of the North American GBC and Temple Presidents body, including Bhaktitirtha Swami, Bir Krishna Goswami, Anuttama dasa, and others had a strong interest in addressing the social incongruencies in our Society. And with good reason: we were in a state of transition after Srila Prabhupada's departure, and the problems were severe. They had rained upon our Society as an intense storm and we often felt like we were standing under that dark rain cloud. The difficulties and fragmentations were real and had cut through the hope, happiness, and trust of too many in our Movement.

It was time now for rebuilding, for mature consideration and healing. We were being called upon to make a difference.

The first step in that healing process was to illuminate the areas where there had been the most hurt. We wanted to begin to address those problems; to make a difference, and help heal our society.

While there were many divisive issues within our communities, including issues of leadership, finance, and initiation, our hearts immediately went to our women and children, where there had been more severe abuse and disenfranchisement.

And in that vein there were a number of symposiums – hearing events – where voices could be heard and programs implemented.

These talks then, in 1996, Children of Krishna and the Child Protection Office was formed. Both initially funded almost solely by the generosity and deep commitments of Rukmini and Anuttama Prabhus.

Given the support and climate of the meetings, it was clear that the time was right for hearing the voices of the women and the youth. Manorama dasa was in attendance as a voice for the *gurukulis*. And with the support of many devotees, I had the proposal for establishing a Woman's Council in hand to address the issues of concern for the Vaishnavis.

We intended to request permission to form a council of thoughtful, mature, senior devotees to hear, identify, and then propose solutions for the pressing issues regarding the women. But Bhaktitirtha Swami pulled me aside and said, "You don't want a council, you want a Ministry. It will empower you, give the discussion longevity, and provide a framework and mechanism for introducing change and education." And it was Burke

Rochford, also in attendance that day, who instructed me how to organize and cultivate relationships in that position.

I had some concerns though. I thought that if we formed a Ministry it meant we would be on our own to address the problems we faced. But Bhaktitirtha Swami assured me that men could be brought in and would support the effort.

That day, we formed two Ministries, one for the Youth and one for the Vaishnavis, which continue to this day.

Sometimes I think it may have been beneficial to start with a council, or better yet, to simultaneously have started with both. A council could have provided more direct opportunity for working together, men and women conjointly, with a broader vision for social understanding in our movement. We also would have benefitted from more hearing and the development of a mutual understanding. But a great deal of work has been accomplished through these Ministries due to the outpouring of support from many in our Society, especially the devotees I mentioned above.

A Proposal for a Women's Ministry
to the North American GBC

To ensure that the legitimate concerns of women receive due attention in ISKCON decision making and that qualified women are included in the decision-making process, we propose that:

1. The North American GBC and Temple Presidents hereby establish the North American Women's Ministry.

2. The Women's Ministry shall be authorized to meet as desired to discuss issues of concern to women in ISKCON.

3. The Women's Ministry representative (Minister) shall be invited to attend the yearly North American GBC / TP meetings, as a voting member, and will receive all relevant correspondence of the body, minutes, etc.

4. The NAGBC/TP shall seek input from the Women's Ministry on matters pertaining to the women of this movement. And the Ministry is invited to bring forward concerns when necessary and/or appropriate to do so.

5. The North American GBC shall further recommend to the International GBC body the formation of an International GBC Women's Ministry.

The creation of a Women's Ministry shall be regarded as an introductory step in the inclusion of senior women in the decision making process of ISKCON.

1995

Presentation for The Association for the Sociology of Religion
by Pranada dasi

The world, of course, takes notice of our organization and in that vein the Association for the Sociology of Religion asked me to speak at their 1995 annual meeting in Washington, D.C.

Dina and Yamuna have just given you a glimpse into the bright side of Krishna consciousness. I'm here to tell you of my experiences. From Yamuna's talk we can understand Prabhupada's equal treatment of his male and female disciples. As in all of his dealings, he acted in accordance with the teachings of ancient, sacred scriptures, and set the example for his international movement. It is an unfortunate fact, though, that some men in the Krishna consciousness movement did not take up Srila Prabhupada's example with regards to dealings with women in ISKCON.

I joined ISKCON in 1975 after a serious search for truth. Srila Prabhupada was not to be with us much longer, and access to him by this time was limited. But I was happy to participate in the movement. I couldn't think of a better way to express my appreciation to Srila Prabhupada for bringing transcendental, blissful knowledge of Krishna, God, than to try to share it with others. And others were happy to receive it. The spiritual exchange I experienced in giving Krishna consciousness to others was so wonderful I decided to focus on this work and nothing else. At this time I had little reason to interact with males in ISKCON, and I didn't notice the situation of other women in the Krishna consciousness movement. Quite frankly, I was young, naive, and oblivious.

But circumstances in my life changed. Soon I had a son and shortly afterward became a single parent. I found myself executing managerial duties, moving in ISKCON's male-dominated managerial hierarchy. My position and abilities were unwelcomed publicly, and males especially threatened by me tried to remove me from my responsibilities through politics. Initially I thought I was just dealing with a local problem, but the situation became so acute it became evident that the obstacles before me were due to my being a woman in ISKCON.

All of a sudden one day I had a shocking vision of just how askew the whole situation was for women in ISKCON. This was in the early '80s, and I began contemplating my years in ISKCON and what I had seen and experienced. Examining my experiences led me to believe that chauvinism in ISKCON was not only prominent, it was a serious problem. The living arrangements at the various temples I stayed at were almost all inferior than the men's. Women were not allowed to give the lectures. Whenever women were discussed in classes it was inevitably with reference to them being less intelligent and objects of enjoyment whom men were to despise. In fact, in the late '70s and through the '80s there was rarely a positive, wholesome reference to women in public forums within ISKCON. The mind-set formed by the constant negative references to women developed a social atmosphere that could only lead to problems. Women had inferiority complexes that led them to silence and acceptance of unhealthy relationships. Women were barred from certain temple worship functions. Certainly I didn't see any women in a position of managerial responsibility extending beyond the kitchen, the nursery, or the altar. In every sphere women were barred by unspoken laws instituted by male leaders. And those laws were not placed by Srila Prabhupada, nor supported by scripture. Rather, in my tracings of the history of female oppression in ISKCON, it was instated and enforced by men in the movement and it was only counterproductive.

I began speaking with senior women around the movement and traced back to when woman were made to stand in the back of our temples, when they were stopped from speaking the scriptural lectures. How they were barred from ever entering the managerial levels of the movement. I saw and heard about abuses to women in marriages which men justified based on the prevalent understanding of women as unintelligent, untrustworthy, and possessions of their husbands.

The more I traced history and current events, the more I saw a very grave situation in ISKCON. The social ills for the women, children and family were undeniable. The commonly accepted view of a woman in ISKCON left the ladies insecure, without any self esteem, and in the words of one man who astutely judged the situation, "systematically de-empowered." I saw many unhealthy marriages; many not lasting. Some female children didn't like being girls because they were prohibited from certain activities they liked; and male children were sometimes punished by being made to stand in the back with the women – a fate very embarrassing for them. One day my 10-year-old son told me he didn't have to listen to his teacher because she was a woman. I couldn't say with absolute knowledge how rampant the problems were; I just suspected it was very widespread from visiting ISKCON centers around the world and being fairly well-connected around the movement. Something had to change.

From my studies and knowledge of Prabhupada's teachings I determined that none of the chauvinism I experienced in ISKCON had a basis in what Srila Prabhupada taught us by his words and actions, nor were they supported by scripture. The prevailing attitudes seemed to be a misunderstanding of how to apply principles of renunciation and separation of male and female for spiritual benefit of both of them. It seemed to me that certain males had their own agenda for position in ISKCON. Some men, though earnest about their spiritual vows of renouncing the world, ignored the needs and rights of others. Some men were probably chauvinists before they arrived at ISKCON's door, it appeared so engrained in them, and some people just didn't seem to have any common sense about how to apply strict spiritual teachings within a social structure of males, females, and children.

But whether the reasons for the problems were innocent or profoundly calculated, I found it impossible to remain silent. I had to speak out on behalf of the many, many women who could not tolerate the injustices any longer. I could not live in denial of the situation; I felt absolutely compelled to be honest, at whatever cost. And there would be a cost to address the situation, for the status quo was deeply engrained and regularly and systematically promoted. To challenge it would literally be heretical, and I would be ostracized. Though an international society, ISKCON was in one way very close knit; therefore, I was risking significant social repercussions. The social pressure was such that no other woman – or man – was prepared to speak out with me, though behind the scenes I had supporters.

After much thought about how to speak up, I wrote a letter addressed to a friend in 1988 discussing points of major concern and backed my statements with scriptural quotes and examples from Prabhupada's life. The letter was widely circulated in ISKCON, and put in the hands of every leader worldwide. It was translated into other languages. As to be expected, it drew antagonism and some actual hatred, and yes, labeled me as the rebel in our movement. But I had given a voice to hundreds of women and they gradually came forward with heart rendering stories and expressed their deep appreciation and relief that discussion had finally started. For some people it took years after my letter was circulated to feel safe enough to come forward.

For a long time the letter I wrote in 1988 was largely ignored. It was quite easy to label me and set the matter aside. But gradually the support from men and women increased, and without a doubt at least dialogue had begun. Some dialogue was negative, some positive, but it paved the way for changes.

I could be patient. I understood that deep-rooted social situations take time to change, and the atmosphere for women was still such it would be impossible for me to make changes any other way than by forcing dialogue in a nonconfrontational way. But things were moving a little too slow; men in positions of leadership were all too willing to keep the status quo. In fact, when I asked the highest governing body for ISKCON law to include resolutions allowing women access to different activities in the Society I received a response saying that no law was necessary since no law existed prohibiting women from the activities. So the unwritten laws continued to reign.

Dialogue seemed to be dying a bit, so in 1990 I began an international newsletter to examine social issues in ISKCON. My editorial mission was to create frank, uncensored, but mature, dialogue that would reach upper level management arid allow the rank and file person to express themselves – this was nonexistent at that time. The circulation quickly increased and people from all age groups and backgrounds around the world began participating.

Dialogue raises awareness and promotes education. When there is dialogue there is an opportunity to increase understanding. From the dialogue about women in ISKCON that began in 1988 many changes have come about. ISKCON still has a distance to walk on the road toward proper treatment of women, but the situation is much improved. There is great hope for further change, and change needs to be instituted evenly throughout all the centers. Right now, not all temples embrace changes or proper views of women and family.

But today if you were to walk into an ISKCON temple you may meet a woman temple president, or hear a woman deliver the class. In some temples you may hear a lady leading the sacred chanting. At least one woman sits on North America's highest managerial board, though they are not yet allowed to sit on the highest international body. This was unheard of 10 years ago.

My experience didn't shake me from the conviction that the path I had chosen was right and the path I wanted to follow for life. I currently still practice Krishna consciousness, though I no longer live in a temple. I've worked in mainstream society for the past 10 years and own an international print brokering business. I have a warm and satisfying relationship with my second husband of ten years. I've enjoyed seeing my son grow, who is now almost 18. And, as you might imagine, I'm deeply satisfied to see the positive changes for women in ISKCON. I hope to see more; they are needed.

And if I can be a part of helping nudge those changes along I will feel honored.

Guidelines for ISKCON Women in Devotee Relationships
by Caroline Constantine, MA
Women's Ministry Special Advisor

In response to the NA GBC resolution condemning abuse, the Women's Ministry published the following pamphlet to educate women about domestic violence. While some of the information is specific to North America other material is applicable around the world. This is one of three brochures that the Ministry published. The other two are no longer available.

Dear Godsisters,

Domestic violence is a growing concern in our world today. Understanding both the signs and the ramifications of domestic violence is important for all women. Whether facing emotional and/or physical abuse in your home, helping a friend or relative in need, or working on an abuse team in your community; most women will encounter domestic violence.

Since minimalization or neglect of a battery situation only increases the probability of further violence, it is essential that proper action is taken both to avoid domestic violence and to rectify or eliminate abusive situations once they occur.

This pamphlet provides you with practical guidelines for dealing with a domestic violence situation. Please be aware that ISKCON does not condone domestic violence, as stated in the following North American GBC and Temple President's resolution of 1995:

The International Society for Krishna Consciousness strongly condemns all spousal abuse and abuse outside the parameters of marriage, including abuse that is physical, verbal, and emotional. Any attempt to justify abuse on the basis of Srila Prabhupada's teachings is misconstrued and firmly rejected.

Do you know anyone who has experienced domestic violence? Or are you yourself in an abusive situation? If so, please don't hesitate or be afraid to get help. All forms of abuse, both gross and subtle, are destructive elements which seriously endanger the spiritual and social fabrics of our movement.

Facts about Domestic Violence

Domestic violence is against the law, and punishment includes immediate detention and enforced therapy. The courts often are sensitive to the victim's needs and will grant restraining orders where necessary as well as child custody and protection of assets in case of separation.

Many women are facing this terrifying and difficult situation. To any women who finds herself being abused, please realize you are not alone.

Traditionally women have endured abuse in silence. Silence, however, perpetuates the abuse. As you find strength and courage to speak out, ending the silence, your action will help make ISKCON a safe community for all women. Your action will also help your abuser realise the seriousness of his offenses.

To determine whether you may be being abused, answer the following questions:

- Has your partner used physical strength to make his point and/or force submission?

- Have you been shoved, hit, or physically restrained?

- Have you been physically forced to break the regulative principles against your will?

- Are you being verbally threatened, intimidated, or put down in front of others?

- Are you forced into isolation or financial dependence?

- Are your belongings being destroyed?

- Are you sometimes afraid or feel that you and your family are in danger living with your spouse?

If you are being abused, here are some guidelines to follow?

1. Know that you are not to blame for the abuse. Nothing you can do or say justifies abuse. The responsibility lies with the perpetrator. Communication problems or dysfunctional behavior may exist within the family, but these are not the causes of the abuse.

2. Often women are old that they are in abuse relationships because of their own psychological problems. This is misleading. Any woman can be abused. Low self-esteem, depression, chronic fatigue, and other problems are frequently the *result* of the abuse, not the cause.

3. Physical abuse is illegal. If you are experiencing physical abuse, we encourage you to take immediate action. If the ISKCON community doesn't provide adequate facility, support, or protection, you can call a local women's shelter or child protection agency. Get the number from information or from the phone book. You can call the police by dialling 911. Domestic violence is a crime. In many states, police will arrest the perpetrator, and the district attorney may file charges. It may be frightening to call the police; however, if you are prepared to take this action, it is the clearest statement you can make that the abuse can no longer be tolerated. Arrest is the single strongest, immediate deterrent to repeated battery as it provides the necessary wake-up call that only the lowest of men would beat their wives. If your husband continues abusive behavior, authority referral agencies will help assure your safety, protect your family, and protect your assets. They may also assist in re-situating your family when necessary.

4. Set up a safety plan of action. Locate a place to go in an emergency. Talk to a friend in advance to arrange to go to her home. If you need to, hide a spare key and some money.

5. Seek assistance and support from a reliable friend. At this time, you need someone to confide in. This person should be a mature person who has the ability to listen, to support, to be an ally, and to be non-judgemental. It is important that this person be fully capable of keeping your confidence.

6. Join a support group where you can break the silence that supports abuse. Bring the situation out into the open.

7. Seek assistance. Find a counsellor or therapist who can help you through this process. Devotee peer counseling is an option, as long as the counselor is trained in the field of domestic violence.

8. The abuser also needs immediate professional help; however, this is not the time for couple's counseling. Joint therapy can be the catalyst for further abuse. Work separately until stability is restored to the relationship and your safety is ensured.

9. A well-qualified, experienced therapist, even if a nondevotee will be able to work with you. Find someone you feel comfortable with. Talk to this person about your religious principles at the beginning of the relationship and work only with someone who you feel has no prejudice against your chosen lifestyle and religious principles. Be aware that many states require the therapist to file a legal report in situations where illegal abuse is taking place.

10. Counselling is often available on a sliding scale or even free when necessary. Contact your local HRS (Human Resource Services) office for information.

11. Document all instances of battery. Writing down your experiences is necessary for many reasons. If you eventually take legal action this documentation will serve as legal evidence. Even if you are not yet ready to take legal action, writing your experience, thoughts, and feelings, validates your experience, helps you notice and track cycles or patterns to the abuse and gives you an outlet for emotions that need release.

Statistics show that 95% of domestic violence victims, also known and physical battery victims, are women: although men may also be victims. These guidelines have been written to 1) Increase understanding of this very serious crime, and 2) identify subtle abuses that may lead to physical battery.

Abuse has no place in devotional service. It is an offence against another Vaishnava. Although sometimes we may chastise a loved one for irresponsible behavior, abuse is an off shoot of bodily identification, lust, pride, and anger. Abuse is about power and control, it is the antithesis of protection.

To help determine whether your behavior may be abusive, the following is a list of common abusive tactics. Use this list to assess your actions in relation to your partner.

- If you forcefully control what your partner does; make it difficult for them to follow their devotional practices; keep them from associating with godsisters /

godbrothers (*as appropriate to their sex and service*) and loved ones; restrict them from leaving the house for practical and devotional activity; treat them disrespectfully or act out of jealousy; this is control by **misusing male or dominant privilege.**

- If you demean your partner; call them names; humiliate; lie to them; shame or make them feel unnecessarily guilty, especially in front of others; threaten to take the children away or put the children in the middle of disagreements; this is **emotional abuse.**

- If you frighten your partner by your looks or actions; by destroying property or displaying weapons; or if you threaten to hurt your partner or commit suicide; this is **coercion and intimidation.**

- If you prevent your partner from having access to adequate funds for the family's needs; make them beg money from you; force them to maintain the family while you remain irresponsible; spend your spouse's family inheritance or financial gifts against their will or without their knowledge; or keep necessary financial information a secret; this could be **economic abuse.**

- If you abandon the family or constantly threaten to leave; neglect their practical needs or speak irresponsibly of their needs to others; this is **irresponsible and neglectful.**

- If you shove, hit or kick; choke, pull hair, or physically restrain; this is **physical abuse.** It is illegal.

- If you minimise the abuse by saying you didn't mean to hurt her/him or by saying the abuse did not happen, or if you tell her/him they caused it; this is **denial or blame.**

Devotees are by nature gentle in their behavior. Although it may be difficult at times to be responsible and keep the family peaceful, you will not benefit by acting irresponsibly, negatively, or violently. Abuse is a choice. It is a learned behavior. If you are abusive towards your partner, you must change your behavior.

The patterns of emotional and subtle abuse are often learned from your past, before you were practicing Krishna consciousness. However, these patterns can sometimes be strengthened by attitudes of disrespect and hatred towards the opposite sex by aspiring renunciates. Abusive tendencies are further accentuated by feelings of dominance and unfulfilled sex desire. Thus, subtle abuse often leads to physical abuse.

To avoid this pattern, we must first recognize our own weaknesses and tendency toward abuse as distinct from other frailties, faults, roles, and actions.

Seventy percent of all abusers come from violent homes. If you are an abuser, you are not alone. You will have wounds of your own to heal. However, you must stop the violent behavior. You must have the courage to reveal the abuse to a trusted devotee friend and/or temple leader who will not minimize the severity of the situation and who will help you overcome your difficulties. Trained counseling, therapy, and a batterer's or other support group can help. Remember that physical abuse is a punishable crime and taken extremely seriously by local authorities.

Although your spouse may have acted improperly, do not hold them responsible for your behavior. Your commitment to change is the most important ingredient in restoring your relationship with your family to wholeness.

Abuse in a relationship is a severe betrayal of trust. As you begin to heal from your wounds, be prepared for a long period of rebuilding before full reconciliation can occur. This difficult work of relinquishing abusive control and dominance over others will secure your advancement in devotional life and improve your relationships with devotee peers.

And, as you work to turn around negative habits and prejudices, your efforts will benefit devotees everywhere. You will be playing an important role in the strengthening and building of our ISKCON society.

- If you are experiencing physical abuse, please get help right away!

- Domestic violence is <u>always</u> condemned both in our spiritual, cultural society and by law in our secular society.

- If you care about the safety of your community, be pro-active.

- Sit together with the women of your community and openly discuss domestic violence.

- Lend support where needed.

- Set up a domestic violence team so you are prepared when tragedy strikes. And discuss what to do in case of physical domestic violence. Who will cook, lend support, speak with the temple president, etc.

Primary reference sources include:
Boulder County Safehouse, Inc. and *Violence in the Family: A Workshop Curriculum for Clergy and Other Helpers* by Marie M. Fortune; The Pilgrim Press: Cleveland, Ohio 1983.

1996

Women's Ministry Celebration
for Srila Prabhupada's Centennial Year
Alachua, Florida January 19-21, 1996

From January 19-21, 1996, as an event for Srila Prabhupada's centennial year, the Women's Ministry sponsored a symposium to celebrate the opening of the new temple in Alachua, Florida. Guest speakers Yamuna Devi, Kausalya Prabhu, and Bhaktitirtha Swami flew in.

From the late 1980's to 1995, the Alachua community had grown from fewer than fifty devotees, to a robust community of many hundreds. Also growing was our sense of community identity and a desire to have strong, supportive relationships with each other.

Gaura-Nitai were the original Deities of our community and they had been housed in a single-wide trailer that needed repairs and couldn't accommodate the number of devotees in the community. The new temple was opened on Janmastami 1995, a few months before the Centennial year. It was equipped with a new kitchen, an expanded altar, and sizable a pujari room, which would allow for the installation of Radha-Shyamasundara and Krishna-Balarama in the near future. Importantly, the temple room could accommodate several hundred devotees as compared to the fifty allowed by fire regulations in Gaura-Nitai's trailer.

Alachua was a very inclusive community. We already had a Vaishnavi temple president, and women featured strongly in the mix of the community. Women maintained the pujari department and kitchen and were regularly giving Srimad-Bhagavatam classes. We assumed that with the increased space in the temple room, we would adjust temple practices to allow for the women to stand on one side of the temple room so we could view the Deities better, to chant in the temple room, and so on. So it took us aback when our GBC asked us to maintain the standard of men in the front and women in the back of the temple during services. He was also opposed to women giving classes, leading kirtans, offering flowers to Srila Prabhupada during his guru-puja, or performing the guru-puja arati.

Was this an accurate representation of the community's desires and thinking?

To answer this question, upon opening the temple, we held a town hall and called for a vote of the community members. The overwhelming majority of devotees wanted the Vaishnavis included in all these seva opportunities and changes were made in the temple functions accordingly.

To support our community decision, we decided to bring together a symposium for discussion and to follow that with a survey so that devotees could share their thinking about women's participation in our community.

We looked to senior devotees, as well as the North American GBC and Temple President leadership. Subsequently, Yamuna, Kausalya, and Bhaktitirtha Swami flew in to elucidate the case for women's involvement in these services and to support the women. After the symposium, community members voted through a confidential ballot. Over 90% of the community supported that the Vaishnavis should have equal access to the front of the temple room, chant japa in the temple room, give class, lead kirtan, offer flowers to Srila Prabhupada during his guru-puja, and offer him his guru-puja arati. All these practices peacefully continue to this day.

The presentations were incredible. Devotees sat enthralled as our esteemed guest devotees shared insights and pastimes with Srila Prabhupada to a full house in our new temple room.

The materials available from this event are four audio recordings. A panel discussion, two sessions of Prabhupada memories with Yamuna Devi and Kausalya Prabhus, and a presentation by Bhaktitirtha Swami.

You can listen to the audio recordings of each presentation by clicking on the title, which is a link.

January 19, 1996

Panel: Learning from Past Mistakes and Successes

Sudharma dasi introduces the panel and she and Bhagavata dasa are the moderators. The panel consisted of Bhaktitirtha Swami, Brahmananda dasa, Kausalya dasi, and Yamuna dasi.

January 20, 1996

Remembering Srila Prabhupada
by Yamuna Devi & Kausalya Prabhu

January 20, 1996

Servant of the Servant
by Bhaktitirtha Swami

January 21, 1996

Remembering Srila Prabhupada
by Yamuna Devi & Kausalya Prabhu

1997

The First Annual Women's Ministry Conference:
"Vaishnavis in ISKCON"

Marina del Rey, Los Angeles, California
December 5 to 7, 1997

Second generation devotees Shakuntala dasi and Krishna Devata dasi of the ISKCON Los Angeles community desired to hold a conference to raise awareness in Southern California about the issues regarding women in ISKCON. The conference organizers had requested permission to hold the conference at their home, the ISKCON temple in Los Angeles. However, permission was denied, so reluctantly they rented a houseboat in Marina del Rey, some distance from the temple.

For this conference, we wanted to create an environment where women felt empowered and safe to openly discuss what was on their minds. Until this time, we hadn't had any opportunity to share as a group. We wanted to underscore the importance of service and relationships, specifically our relationship with Srila Prabhupada. To this end one segment of the conference was titled "How Srila Prabhupada Empowered His Daughters," with presentations by Marge Legaye, Visakha devi dasi, Malati devi dasi, Jyotirmayi devi dasi, and Kausalya devi dasi. These sessions were videotaped. You can view the videos by clicking on the individual's name.

Several papers were also presented at the conference, which we publish here for you. Here's a quick list of the papers presented:

- Women in ISKCON in Prabhupada's Times *by Jyotirmayi dasi*
- The Anomaly of the Single Mother in ISKCON *by Bimala devi dasi*
- Yesterday, Today, and Tomorrow *by Pranada devi dasi*
- Participation, Protection, and Patriarchy *by Radha devi dasi*
- The Importance of Women in ISKCON *by Hridayananda das Goswami*

Hands that Rock the Cradle Rock ISKCON:
A Conference Summary
by Pranada dasi

This conference report was published in the Hare Krishna World Review.

Los Angeles, CA., USA – Anticipation was high as attendees and speakers from around the world gathered for the first annual ISKCON Women's Ministry conference held December 5-7 in Los Angeles.

The conference attracted 116 participants, ranging from as far away as France and London. A group of women in Los Angeles, including second generation devotees Shakuntala dasi and Krishna Devata dasi, organized the event, which was held on a houseboat in Marina Del Rey.

Anuttama dasa, North American director of ISKCON Communications, summed up the enthusiasm: "This conference is the most significant event in ISKCON this year, if not this decade. The level of Krishna consciousness demonstrated here is remarkable. This conference was not what I thought it might be. The visions expressed were intelligent and unifying, not male-bashing, and left me feeling like the changes suggested were going to lend strength in further building the movement."

Topics included Srila Prabhupada's pastimes with his disciples, which demonstrated how he made no distinction between the sexes in services and activities; maturing social relationships and the importance of women's involvement to stabilize ISKCON as a society; standards for women in ISKCON when Prabhupada was still present; investigation of *Bhagavatam* verses about women; a review of protection and of the notable qualities in Vedic and contemporary context; and women in Vaishnava history.

A candid look was taken at encouraging women's involvement in all levels of ISKCON structure, and lively panel discussions evoked audience response. There was healthy balance of presented papers and spontaneous speaking; and presenters, such as Bir Krishna Goswami, Hridayananda dasa Goswami, Mukunda Goswami, Visakha dasi, Jyotirmayi dasi, Radha dasi, Garuda dasa, Titiksa dasi, Bimala dasi, Aniruddha dasa, and Malati dasi examined sensitive topics from many angles.

Throughout provocative and intellectually challenging presentations, the audience responded with applause and cheers. The reception of the discourses was so enthusiastic that many attendees said the conference had changed their lives. Bimala dasi said, "I realized that I was seeing our language change before my eyes. Both men and women at the conference realized the time has come – we're each being called – to accept that we are the leaders. When we say "leader" we're talking about ourselves. And you could hear from the presentations that we have solutions to our Society's problem. We need to restore what Srila Prabhupada has given us. The conference created a sense of belonging that I've never before experienced as a devotee."

A Harvard law graduate, Radha dasi, received a standing ovation for her examination of the international human rights law models and their application to ISKCON. Her parallels with international law and ISKCON's approach to women's positions in the movement elicited both laughter and appreciation.

Bimala dasi spoke briefly about single mothers, their need for respect and compassion, and the necessity for ISKCON to encourage men to take responsibility for their children.

Hirdayananda Maharaja had the audience laughing as he examined the phenomena of men becoming ungentlemanly after becoming devotees, as if unkindness meant freedom from sex desire: "We have to realize now that ISKCON is bigger, it's wiser, it's more mature, and we have to cast off a lot of cultural patterns we adopted when we were young, immature, and ignorant – and that those things are simply suffocating the Society."

Jyotirmayi dasi, who joined the movement in 1969, systematically laid out the historical sequences of ISKCON law as it changed in the mid 70s to exclude women from temple functions, such as giving *Bhagavatam* classes, doing *puja*, and other devotional facilities available to men in the movement. She spoke eloquently of Srila Prabhupada's vision of the man and woman's preaching as "redoubled" strength. Her comprehensive paper detailed these changes, why they were made, and how to right them.

Visakha dasi gave a scholarly explanation about protection, chastity, and humility, with little-known examples from the *Mahabharata* and *Srimad-Bhagavatam*. Her paper challenged many current belief systems in ISKCON.

Workshops generated suggested policies for GBC consideration. The audience emphatically demanded a minimal change of at least two or three voting seats on the GBC be given to women. Bir Krishna Swami, a supporter of the Women's Ministry, assured the audience of his full support in addressing all these issues to the GBC: "Urgent changes need to be made in the consciousness of all the devotees. Impersonalism is a problem. We generally perceive other people as object that are meant to please us."

At the Saturday night banquet attendees raised $10,000 to fund the Women's Ministry activities this year, which will include quarterly newsletter and preparing educational materials for women's issues, such as domestic violence; solidifying a network in the United States and Europe; preparing GBC policy; writing a women's position paper for ISKCON; and preparing for two other conferences in the United States and Europe.

Video Presentations for the Conference Segment:
"How Srila Prabhupada Empowered His Daughters"

Marge Legaye
(attorney and mother of Kshudi dasa)

Visakha devi dasi

<u>Malati devi dasi</u>

<u>Jyotirmayi devi dasi</u>

<u>Kausalya devi dasi</u>

<u>Questions and Answers</u>

Papers Presented at the Conference:

Women in ISKCON in Prabhupada's Time
by Jyotirmayi devi dasi

Jyotirmayi's paper is so comprehensive and authoritative that it was presented to the International GBC body at the 1997 meetings.

Historical Report

From about 1965 up to 1974, time when Srila Prabhupada had to get less and less involved in temple management because of translating work and the tremendous increase of disciples and temples, the women devotee's situation changed very little from what Srila Prabhupada had originally established. From 1974 their situation started to significantly deteriorate and got worse very fast until it reached its paroxysm before Srila Prabhupada's departure.

When Prabhupada decided to accept women in the movement, he did so according to the reasoning he himself quotes in the *Chaitanya-charitamrta, Madhya-lila,* Ch. 23 purport of verse 105: "To broadcast the cult of Krishna Consciousness, one has to learn the possibility of renunciation in terms of country, time and candidate. . . He must avoid the principle of *niyamagraha,* that is, he should not try to perform the impossible. What is possible in one country may not be possible in another. The acharya's duty is to accept the essence of devotional service. There may be a little change here and a little change there as far as yukta-vairagya (proper renunciation) is concerned . . . The essence of devotional service must be taken into consideration, and not the outward paraphernalia . . . A Vaishnava is immediately purified, provided he follows the rules and regulations of his bonafide spiritual master. It is not necessary that the rules and regulations followed in

India be exactly the same as those in Europe, America and other Western countries. Simply imitating without effect is called *niyamagraha*. Not following the regulative principles but instead living extravagantly is also called *niyamagraha* . . . We should not follow regulative principles without an effect, nor should we fail to accept the regulative principles. What is required is a special technique according to country, time and candidate . . . ."

Srila Prabhupada followed this reasoning concerning not only the acceptation of women in the *ashrama*s, but also lots of other subject matters, such as the practice of renunciation, which is being dealt with in the quote, preaching methods, only a partial introduction of Vedic culture, Deity worship, etc. . . . Everything that he introduced or did not introduce was deeply thought about, very carefully and logically analyzed. When he was asked, several years later, if he would have preferred to establish the movement differently, he answered that if it was to be done again he would do it exactly the same way.

Despite the fact that he had been criticized several times in India, because of all the changes he was introducing, Srila Prabhupada kept them and justified his position regarding the women devotees once more in the *Chaitanya-charitamrita Adi-lila* ch. 7, purport of verses 32 and 38: "An acharya who comes for the service of the Lord cannot be expected to conform to a stereotype, for he must find the ways and means by which Krishna Consciousness may be spread. Sometimes jealous persons criticize the Krishna Consciousness movement because it engages equally both boys and girls in distribution of love of Godhead. Not knowing that boys and girls in countries like Europe and America mix very freely, these fools and rascals criticize the boys and girls in Krishna Consciousness for intermingling. But these rascals should consider that one cannot suddenly change a community's social customs. However, since both boys and girls are being trained to become preachers those girls are not ordinary girls but are as good as their brothers who are preaching Krishna Consciousness. Therefore to engage both boys and girls in fully transcendental activities is a policy intended to spread the Krishna Consciousness movement . . . The results of this are wonderful. Both men and women are preaching the gospel of Lord Chaitanya Mahaprabhu and Lord Krishna with redoubled strength . . . Therefore it is a principle that a preacher must strictly follow the rules and regulations laid down in the *shastras* yet at the same time devise a means by which the preaching work to reclaim the fallen may go with full force."

By accepting women in the temples and giving them the *brahmacharini* status, Prabhupada was not pretending; he gave them all the same rights and duties of the *brahmacharis* in the guru's *ashrama*. The same thing applied when he gave them *brahmana* initiation. The women devotees had exactly the same spiritual activities, the same tasks, the same possibilities to progress spiritually and they were entitled to the same respect. At that time everything was done according to the abilities and the spiritual advancement of a person and not according to sex. Prabhupada did not make any distinction.

- Women, as well as men, accompanied Prabhupada when he was traveling and served him as secretaries, as did Arundhati, or served him personally as did Janaki.

- Women led *kirtans:* Yamuna, Kausalya, Lilavati were amongst the best.

- They gave classes and public lectures. The most renowned was Jadurani who was endowed with great erudition.

- Women were in charge of the Deities and performed public *aratis*. Yamuna, Shilavati, Rukmini and Mandakini were the most famous.

- Men and women circumambulated *tulasi* together without mixing, forming a circle separated in two halves, one half for the men, the other half for the women.

- Women paid *dandavats* to Prabhupada.

- Women offered garlands to Prabhupada personally or to his picture.

- Women performed *aratis* to Prabhupada's picture on his *vyasasana* during *guru-puja*.

- Women devotees were on one side of the temple room, men devotees on the other side, during *kirtans* as well as classes and *japa*.

- During *guru-puja*, men and women offered flowers simultaneously to Prabhupada, forming two lines, and women as well as men paid their obeisance's in front of the *vyasasana*.

- When Srila Prabhupada was personally present, women as well as men could stand next to him.

- During *harinamas* (called at that time *sankirtanas*), Prabhupada had asked that the women stand between two groups of men, one in front and one behind so that they could be protected.

- Women wrote articles in magazines. Prabhupada personally asked Bibhavati who had been journalist previously, to do so.

• As far as the service of temple president was concerned, Srila Prabhupada included husband and wife, he recommended them to be father and mother of the devotees they were in charge of.

• Women were doing things that, later on, they were forbidden to do in front of Srila Prabhupada himself; Yamuna was leading *kirtan*s in front of him, Himavati gave public conferences, Jyotirmayi and Rukmini performed *arati* in front of him.

• Women had access to important responsibilities: Jadurani was in charge of the BBT (Bhaktivedanta Book Trust) painting department, Yamuna and Govinda dasi were proposed as the GBC (Governing Body Commissioners) by Prabhupada, Kausalya organized pandals, Varanasi was temple commander, Jyotirmayi the BBT chief translator, etc.

• The *grihastha* status was very respected. Prabhupada was very proud of his couples who were opening temples together.

• Men and women chanted *japa* together in the temple room during the morning program.

The positive results of the way Prabhupada was relating to his women disciples will be presented later on, opposed to the negative results of the decisions taken later on by the leaders, which are going to be discussed now.

After the first six years of the movement, at the beginning of the 1970s, a first change took place, which of course was not contested by anyone. Instead of being mixed in the temple room without any distinction of sex, men and women devotees were separated and were placed on each side of the temple room. In 1973 a second change happened, not very important either, but it was foreboding lots of other changes which were going to follow faster and faster and cause lots of harm to the movement – women devotees were forbidden to do *dandavat*.

Everything began in America and was imported in France only gradually from around 1974. There, a note on the temple room door said that women devotees were forbidden to lead *kirtans* or to give class. Then they were forbidden to circumambulate *tulasi* with men devotees, could not chant *japa* in the temple room, they had to stay behind the men in the temple during *kirtans,* classes, *harinama,* each of their important responsibilities were removed, as well as their right to offer *aratis* to Prabhupada. They were no longer authorized to offer public *arati* (*mangala* and *sundara arati*) to the murtis, to go on the altar and get close to the murtis. They could not pay obeisances in front of the *vyasasana* anymore, they had to offer flowers after the men, and later only after *guru-*

puja was over, etc. Simultaneously with the status of the women, the status of the married men was seriously depreciated, female children became a matter of shame.

As those new decisions were adopted and instead of the simple separation between men and women that Prabhupada wanted, a real segregation was taking place, the women devotees went to see Prabhupada to tell him about it and each time he asked that the standard that he had established remained the same. Two times Jyotirmayi asked Prabhupada about her giving classes, once verbally, another time in a letter; each time Prabhupada told her that it was perfectly all right. Then Prabhupada left his body and there was no one to appeal to any longer concerning this subject and others, even more serious.

Then the effects of those restraints started to really upset the lives of some of the women devotees. Shilavati for example, the most qualified pujari of the movement at that time, had her service removed and was forbidden to go on with the service in which she had put all her heart and soul for so many years. Jyotirmayi also had her responsibility for the BBT removed and today, more than 20 years later, she has to correct all the mistakes that have been made when she could not supervise the work anymore. There are so many other examples. On the whole these unfortunate effects swept away the wonderful spirit established by Prabhupada. Questioned by Gurudas about the difference of atmosphere between the first years and the subsequent ones, Srila Prabhupada answered with regret: "Yes, before it was a family."

• Instead of brotherhood between men and women devotees, aggressiveness, suspicion and fear appeared.

• Instead of caring for one another, there was nothing but indifference.

• Instead of mutual respect, there was contempt of the men for the women and of women amongst themselves.

• Instead of admiration for someone because of his/her material and spiritual abilities, it was only according to the title and the position.

• Submission to the male authorities became blind and fanatical, tinged with "sexuality" (creation of "groupies" and feminine "fan clubs.")

• Instead of being considered full fledged devotees, women were considered only as "women" in the most pejorative sense.

• Women were not considered *brahmanas* anymore (except for the *puja* when this service was given back to them.)

• Women devotees did not consider men as sons anymore and men did not behave with women as mothers but as enemies.

• Instead of kindness, gentleness and courtesy amongst men and women devotees, wickedness, meanness and impoliteness appeared.

• Instead of sane and constructive criticisms aiming at progressing, we could see a fault-finding mentality with an unhealthy purpose.

• Women were not recognized for their services, but often men received the credit for them.

• Instead of being accepted and utilized, women's talents were discredited and rejected if they did not match the new standard.

• The idea came up not to give academic education to the girls, but fortunately Prabhupada did not allow that to happen.

• Women were considered stupid and incapable and became subject to gross mockery.

• Only those who could collect were appreciated.

• Instead of being seen as spirit souls and godsisters, they were only considered as sex objects to be rejected and avoided.

• Adultery and illicit connections, which were excuses to mistreat women devotees, increased instead of decrease.

• Instead of being admired by other women, and example to follow, a goal to reach, intelligent and dynamic women became subject to scorn and malicious talks from other women.

• Spiritual practices of women weakened, enthusiasm went down and services suffered.

• New devotee women, lacking outstanding examples to follow, did not get anymore the motivation that leads to great achievements, to the great detriment of Srila Prabhupada's mission.

• Lots of women lost the spirit of Prabhupada's mission.

• According to their own personality, women either indulged in an easy going situation or lived in frustration and discouragement. It was more difficult for those who had known ISKCON at the beginning when it was lead by the kind but firm hand of Prabhupada, or those who had purely followed his example, and for those who were in charge of important services.

• For most of the women who had not known the movement at the beginning and not met Srila Prabhupada personally, these detrimental psychological effect appeared without their being conscious of it because they did not know anything else and had no other frame of reference.

• Belittled in such a way, lots of women lost confidence in themselves and in their material and spiritual abilities, accepted to be deprived of their human dignity and played the part that was expected from them, being brainless, ignorant and unproductive.

• Exceptionally active and intelligent women, which were numerous in the beginning, no longer joined the movement and women's conditions in our temples became subject to very bad press for our movement.

• Prabhupada's movement, so much in need of arms and heads to accomplish his mission, thus lost a good amount of its strength because on one side the potency of the women in the temple decreased and on the other side fewer women joined the movement.

• The marriages also suffered as a consequence of this new mentality because women were considered as nothing else but an object for sensual desires and not anymore as spiritual personalities: relations between spouses got worse and worse, deprived of the affection and mutual respect required for the good harmony of a couple.

• Women having been put down, so was the married man, internal quarrels between *grihasthas, brahmacharis* and *sannyasis* started.

• Children were of course last on the list of priorities and were very neglected.
It may seem that I depict here a very dark picture, but everything can be confirmed with lots of examples. However, we have to consider that those events were more or less acute according to the temple, the country and the leaders' personality. Most of those abuses took place in America; France was less touched. Moreover, women devotees performing *sankirtana* (book distribution) in France suffered a lot less because their situation was always privileged and protected because of their service. This was not the case in America where unbelievable abuses took place. Moreover, even if ISKCON was deviating from the original teachings regarding this aspect and others, it kept its other

qualities; it was still Lord Chaitanya's movement and the path leading to Krishna and those imperfections did not stop sincere women to know great spiritual joys and progress despite all obstacles. Fortunately the position of women has improved over the years.

PHILOSOPHICAL ARGUMENTS AND PRABHUPADA'S PRACTICAL APPLICATION

Reasons for this Debate

Many of the changes brought in the movement, whether concerning the women or other vital elements of ISKCON, have done great damage to the beauty and the greatness of Srila Prabhupada's contribution to the world. Having known to a certain extent the movement from almost its beginning (from 1969), a number of the first devotees and Srila Prabhupada personally, I feel responsible to share this experience with other newer devotees in order to help correct the faults and give back to ISKCON its original wonderful nature.

Authoritativeness of this Endeavor

Convinced at heart and by practical experiences that Prabhupada was not at the origin of the negative changes of women's position in ISKCON, I personally asked Satsvarupa Maharaja and had someone ask Brahmananda Prabhu, who both associated very intimately and for long periods of time with Srila Prabhupada, if they had ever heard him personally give instruction for these changes to occur. Both said no, that they were instituted by the leading men of the movement.

After a lecture I gave on the subject during a Communication Seminar by Mukunda Maharaja, he told me to take as a special mission the re-establishment of the women's proper situation in ISKCON.

Param Gati Maharaja, the GBC for France, fully backs up my endeavor for informing the devotees about the way things were when Srila Prabhupada directly managed the temples and trained the devotees and about the most wonderful spirit he created.

Authenticity of the Proposed Arguments

Our subject here deals with the social application of Krishna conscious principles, not with the philosophical knowledge. Therefore many of the arguments given here do not come from Prabhupada's books but from conversations between Srila Prabhupada and his disciples in daily encounters, most of which of course did not get recorded. Many devotees do not trust these "Prabhupada's said," but Prabhupada himself gave his opinion about these "Prabhupada said." In a reunion in Mayapur in 1975, the GBC told Prabhupada: "There are so many 'Prabhupada said,' better only accept what is in the books and tapes." Srila Prabhupada answered: 'No, what I say in talks also, many things I say are not in my books.'" (From Himavati.) My information is coming from a notebook in which all along the years, I noted the anecdotes related to me by devotees who lived closely with Prabhupada, or by devotees who received these stories from these first disciples. My other stores, which are irrefutable, are from Srila Prabhupada's letters.

Contradictory Statements

Many devotees are puzzled by the many seemingly contradictory statements appearing in Srila Prabhupada's books and talks, while others choose to quote and act only upon those fitting their own desires and conditioning while completely avoiding to see their counterpart. But devotees must learn, by analyzing scrutinizingly Srila Prabhupada's teachings as a whole, to understand how Prabhupada in his great intelligence and love knew how to change or adapt an instruction according to the spiritual need in a particular time and place. In the following list of anecdotes or quotes showing Srila Prabhupada's attitude towards women in ISKCON, this kind of apparent contradiction will sometimes occur.

Equality and Equal Treatment

Often pushed by his male disciples to minimize ISKCON women spiritual position, Srila Prabhupada reacted for example in the following way:

• Srila Prabhupada: "You dance, she dances. You sing, she sings, you cook, she cooks, there is no difference. You are the same in Krishna's eyes."

• While during a darshan Srila Prabhupada had a *brahmachari* distribute a little *prasadam* to everyone present, the boy gave *prasadam* to all the men and sat down. Srila Prabhupada noticed that he did not serve the only two girls present and said: "Give them also *prasadam*, why don't you serve them?"

Womanly Duties

Srila Prabhupada often stressed that women took up traditional roles:
• "Girls who are living in New Vrindavan should be engaged in the following activities: 1) "Taking care of the children, 2) cleaning the temple, kitchen, etc., 3) cooking and 4) churning butter" (letter to Labangalatika, 1969)

• "A women's real business is to look after household affairs, keep everything neat and clean. . . the women should be sewing." (letter to Chaya Dasi, 1972)
There is not doubt that householder women inside ISKCON or outside, recognize that cooking, cleaning, sewing, taking care of children are their basic activities. As a mother, I spend myself a good part of my time in these matters. But the point is that a

woman is not limited to these activities only, if she has abilities for other activities, as will show the following quotes and anecdotes:

• Bhibavati asked Srila Prabhupada "Should I live like in the Vedic times, and simply serve my husband and child?" Srila Prabhupada answered, "No, you have a talent as a writer, you should write articles for newspapers and propagate Krishna consciousness." (Bhibavati)

• "You have good writing capacity, and good artistic ability. Now devote your life to chanting Hare Krishna and if possible write articles on Krishna Consciousness, as many as possible with your own paintings and send it for publication to Back to Godhead." (letter to Govinda Dasi, 1974)

• "The nursery school program is very good. That is good that the mothers are being freed to increase their devotional service." (letter to Jayatirtha, 1975)

• "All the wives of our students should be trained up for Deity worship and cooking, and when possible they should go on *sankirtana* party with their husband and others." (letter to Hamsadutta, 1970)

• "I am very glad to know that you are engaged as *pujari* there. Try to learn this art of *arcana* very nicely. . . I wish that all our girl devotees be expert in the matter of *arcana* . . . " (letter to Kanchanbala, 1970)

• When the service of Deity worship was being taken away from women, Srila Prabhupada wrote, "Regarding women worshipping the Deity, in the *Bhagavad-gita* it is stated: *striyo vaishyas tatha shudras, te 'pi yanti param gatim*. The idea is that everyone who is properly initiated and following the rules and regulations can worship the Deity." (letter to Uttama Sloka, 1974)

• So far your question regarding women, I have always accepted the service of women without any discrimination, so I have no objection if Yamuna devi contributes her ideas on this construction project. Nothing should be done without group consultation. (letter to Guru Das, 1972)

Women in Posts of Responsibilities

Many men were opposed to women being given posts of responsibilities and refused to work under them.

• Atreya Rsi asked Srila Prabhupada if women could be given great responsibilities. Srila Prabhupada answered, "Yes, if they are Krishna conscious." Then he gave the example of Jahnava, the wife of Nityananda Prabhu, who took charge of the whole Vaishnava community after His departure. (Atreya Rsi)

• "Chanakya Pandita said not to trust those who do not control their senses, politicians and women. But this applies to non-devotee women, not our women, because they do control their senses." (class in Los Angeles 1972)

• When a male devotee refused to be instructed by Jadurani, the head of the art department, because of her being a woman, Prabhupada called him in and ordered him to accept her instructions.

Womanly Qualities Favorable to Devotional Service
• "A devotee should have the courage of an English officer and the heart of a Bengali mother," used to say Srila Prabhupada.

• "Women are better than men because they can accept any position." (Bhavatrini)

Women Leading *Kirtans* and *Bhajanas*
An important apparent contradiction comes from a statement in the scriptures that a *sannyasi* and a *brahmachari* should not hear a woman's voice. But Srila Prabhupada had men and women chant *japa* together, women lead *kirtan*s in the temple and in public engagements and the women gave classes.

• Srila Prabhupada had Yamuna (one of our best singers) lead *kirtan*s in front of crowds of guests and devotees, which included of course *sannyasis* and *brahmacharis*.

• Yamuna, Lilavati, Kausalya and later Parijata, Jyotirmayi and many others used to routinely lead *kirtan*s.

• "I want to organize a women *kirtan* party singing the Gita-Gan. Can you help me?" (letter to Gargamuni Maharaja, 1974)

• In France, when he noticed that Jyotirmayi could pronounce the Sanskrit better than others (she had been taught by Nitai, his personal Sanskrit secretary), Srila Prabhupada said that from then on, she should lead the recitation of the Sanskrit verses before class. (Jyotirmayi, 1972)

• During his massage Prabhupada heard a letter from Jayasacinandana in Los Angeles written on behalf of a group of *brahmacharis*. In every ISKCON temple of the world the assembled devotees offer their obeisances to the Deities in the morning as the Govindam prayers loudly play, George Harrison recorded it and Yamuna sings the mantras. Disturbed by this custom, Jaysacinandana quoted Srila Bhaktivinoda Thakur (as well as Srila Prabhupada) that if a *brahmachari* hears and is attracted to a woman singing, it is a subtle fall down. "In light of this, he wrote, many of the *brahmacharis* approached the temple president to see if it would be possible that when the Deities are greeted in the morning, instead of listening to Gurudasa Maharaja's former wife singing the *Brahma-samhita* prayers, we could listen to Your Divine Grace rather than hear a woman sing." He did not want to change the tape because it has been a standard thing in ISKCON since 1970. "So requested by many devotees, I am inquiring from Your Divine Grace if we could play a tape recording of your singing instead of a woman when the Deities of Rukmini-Dvarkadhisha are greeted in the morning. I am sure that all the devotees would be enlivened to hear you instead of electric guitars, the London symphonic orchestra, etc., etc."

Prabhupada was not pleased. He said that constantly changing things is "our western disease." His reply was short and direct. "No! You have made some discovery. All along you have been hearing the recording of Yamuna dasi and now you want to change. It is not ordinary singing, it is not concert. Many people are singing, so it is not bad. Just like *sankirtana*. I approve of it. Here in the Krishna-Balaram temple we are hearing the same recording every morning. So if it is good here, why not there?" (Hari Sauri, Dec 1975, Vrindavan, *A Transcendental Diary*.)

Women's Advancement

• For a long period of time, women in ISKCON have been considered unfit for real spiritual advancement. Their only hope was to become men in their next life and start spiritual life from that point.

• "Regarding your question, yes woman can certainly reach the perfectional stage of devotion to Krishna." (letter to Krishna Devi, 1969)

• Srila Prabhupada said about Yamuna in the early 70's that she had reached the stage of *bhava*.

• "In the *Bhagavad-gita* we find that women are also equally competent like the men in the matter of Krishna consciousness movement." (letter to Himavati, 1969)

• "We are Vaishnavas. We are not concerned with male or female position in life. That is simply bodily concept of life. It is not spiritual. Whether one is male or female, it does not matter, simply chant Hare Krishna and follow the four regulative principles and your life will be perfect." (letter to Jennifer, 1975)

• It is not that women should only produce children, but they are meant for advancing in devotion." (letter to Jayatirtha, 1975)

Women as Dangerous for Men

Many men in the movement have used various scriptural statements on women's faults to rebuke and humiliate them, hinder their service and advancement, or even try to drive them out of the movement.

• When Srila Prabhupada first said in a class that for a man association with a woman is dangerous because she makes him loose control over his senses, the male devotees started acting very nastily with the women of that particular temple. The ladies expressed their pain to Prabhupada who then called in all the men and said: "I was talking of materialistic women, not of the women of the movement. These are angels."

• Srila Prabhupada also said in another instance: "When we talk of women, we do not talk about those of our movement because by associating with these women, if they are Krishna conscious, you will be liberated." (Madhavananda)

• A disciple of Swami Narayana said to Srila Prabhupada: "My spiritual master said to avoid all women and to never go where there are women." Srila Prabhupada laughed and said: "That is impossible, there are women everywhere." Then, coming back to the temple and watching two women devotees bow down to him, he said: "By associating with these women, you will be purified." (Madhavananda)

• In various occasions, *brahmacharis* complained to Srila Prabhupada that they were agitated by the presence of women in the temple, and Srila Prabhupada replied that if they could not restrain their senses, they should go live alone in the forest.

• "Regarding the disturbance made by the women devotees, they are also living beings. They also come to Krishna. So consciously I cannot deny them. If our male members, the *brahmacharis* and *sannyasis,* if they become steady in Krishna consciousness, there is not problem. It is the duty of the male members to be very steady and cautious." (letter to Gargamuni Swami, 1975)

Women's Well Being

For years men were always given the best facilities (as far as living quarters, chanting *japa*, sitting places in a van or at festivals, *prasadam*, etc.) while the women got what was left. But Srila Prabhupada was always concerned that the women be well protected and taken care of.

• During the Gaura Purnima festival in Vrindavan, Yamuna got sick. Srila Prabhupada had her stay with him until she got better. (Yamuna)

• In 1974, Palika lived in India with Prabhupada, her husband having taken *sannyasa*. While she was taking care of Prabhupada in his office, Srila Prabhupada noticed that her *sari* had a hole and said, "I am going to buy a sari, yours is all torn." As she protested, he continued: "Your husband Bhavananda has now taken *sannyasa*, therefore I shall give you some money." (Dinatarini)

• Srila Prabhupada was informed that there was no running water in the women's living quarters in Bombay for a long time, as the plumbing needed repairs. Srila Prabhupada called in the leaders and said: "You are always talking of big, big things and you do not see that these simple things are being taken care of."

• Srila Prabhupada wanted that for *sankirtana* (chanting in the street), women stay in the middle to be protected.

Women's Level of Intelligence

Srila Prabhupada's statement and the scripture's statements about the women being less intelligent has brought a lot of misunderstanding and men's ruthless behavior towards women. But what does "less intelligent" exactly mean?

• *kalau shudra sambhavat*: in the age of Kali, everyone is *shudra*. In the Vedic times, women were considered on the same level as *vaishya*s and *shudras*. The *brahmana*s and *kshatriyas* of those days were so elevated that women were no doubt on an inferior level. But in Kali-yuga, men have degraded to the level of the women, everyone being *shudra*, and cannot anymore pose themselves as highly superior.

• In *Bhagavad-gita* (3, 42-43), Krishna says: "The working senses are superior to dull matter, mind is higher than the senses, intelligence is still higher than the mind, and he (soul) is even higher than the intelligence . . . .one should steady the mind by deliberate intelligence."

According to this definition, an intelligent person is one able to control the mind with his intelligence. The mind's activities are thinking, feeling, willing. Therefore it can be concluded that a woman is less intelligent because she has harder time than a man to control her emotions than for a man. But it does not mean that a woman is totally deprived of most intelligence, as it has unfortunately often been established in the movement. It is not that one goes from the most intelligent man down to the most stupid, and then only comes the most intelligent women down to the most stupid. If we rate men and women's intelligence on a scale, it is not that man's intelligence occupies the highest section and women's the lowest, but the two overlap. Of course, it is certainly true that if one takes the most intelligent men in the world and the most intelligent women, the men might be on a higher level than the women.

• There are various facets to intelligence – intelligence as controller of the mind, material intelligence, spiritual intelligence – and various definitions. Srila Prabhupada once defined it as "sharp memory and good discrimination." The following examples illustrate its different meanings:

• Srila Prabhupada said to a lady disciple: "Well, if you think you are a woman that means you are less intelligent, because you are suppose to understand that you are a spirit soul and that your real identity is transcendental to these bodily designations." (Sadaputa)

• When Srila Prabhupada was asked if Jyotirmayi should finish her studies in ethnology (study of religions and cultures) in order to teach Vaishnavism in the universities, he answered, "Yes, she is very intelligent girl, she can do it." (Yogesvara)

• "Another examination will be held sometime in 1971 on the four books, *Bhagavad-gita*, *Srimad-Bhagavatam*, *Teachings Of Lord* Chaitanya and the *Nectar of Devotion*. One who will pass this examination will be awarded the title Bhaktivedanta. I want that all my spiritual sons and daughters will inherit this title of Bhaktivedanta, so that the family transcendental diploma will continue through the generations. Those possessing the title of Bhaktivedanta will be allowed to initiate disciples. Maybe by 1975 all my disciples will be allowed to initiate and increase the number of generations. That is my program." (letter to Hamsadutta, 1968)

• "Regarding your questions about the examination to be given, the girls will also be able to take these. In Krishna consciousness there is no distinction between girls and boys. The girls also may become preachers if they are able." (letter to Himavati, 1969)

• "Now I see that in our Society the girls are more intelligent than the boys." (letter to Krishna Devi, 1970)

Women as Preachers

For many years, women have been forbidden to give classes to all devotees in the temple room, to give Sunday lectures to guests, whereas those were common practices from the beginning of the movement to about 1973-74.

• "Regarding lecturing by women devotees: I have informed you that in the service of the Lord there is no distinction of caste, or creed, color or sex . . . . "We require a person who is in knowledge of Krishna, that is the only qualification of a person speaking. It does not matter what he is. Materially a woman may be less intelligent than a man, but spiritually everyone is pure soul. In the absolute plane there is no gradation of higher and lower. If a woman can lecture nicely and to the point, we should hear her carefully. That is our philosophy. But if a man can speak better than a woman, the man should be given the first preference . . . " (letter to Jaya Govinda, 1968)

• "Jadurani has now become a nice preacher, I have report from Satsvarupa that she gives lectures very nicely. If we open a pavilion, I shall take Jadurani also at that time so she will deliver nice lectures." (letter to Mahapurusa, 1968.)

• "So far as girls or boys lecturing in the morning, that does not make any difference. Either girl or boy devotee may deliver lecture if they choose to do. We have no such distinction of bodily designations, male or female. Krishna consciousness is on the spiritual platform. As such, anyone who is a devotee of the Lord, following in this line of disciplic succession, can deliver lecture on the teachings of *Bhagavad-gita*, *Srimad-Bhagavatam*, etc." (letter to Syama Dasi, 1968)

• Srila Prabhupada had Himavati give public lectures in front of crowds of people in India.

• From 1973-74, when stopping women from giving classes began to spread from temple to temple, country to country, different women went to Prabhupada for help.

• "You can also keep giving *Bhagavatam* class if you like. Women in our movement can also preach very nicely. Actually male and female bodies, these are just outward designations; Lord Chaitanya said that whether one is *brahmana* or whatever he may be, if he knows the science of Krishna, then he is to be accepted as guru." (letter to Malati, 1974)

• Excerpt of a conversation about *varnashrama-dharma* between Srila Prabhupada, Yogesvara and Jyotirmayi, 1974, France.
SP: Woman is to help her husband. JM: So the duty of the *brahmana* is to preach. It is to learn the philosophy. SP: Yes, to learn and to preach. JM: And to teach the philosophy. So in our movement, the women have always preached philosophy, given

classes, given lectures. SP: Oh yes, oh yes. With the husband. She is always helping hand to hand the husband . . . . Assistant. JM: Does that mean that the girls should not give lectures and not give classes? SP: Why not? If she is a *brahmana*'s wife, she can give lecture. JM: Jadurani, for example, now she is no longer with her husband anymore., but she is giving classes, she is giving lectures. So is that good? SP: Yes, yes. Why not? This *varnashrama dharma*, woman is according to the husband. That's all. Jadurani is suppose to be a *brahmana*'s wife, her husband has taken *sannyasa*, so she can preach. JM: So women can preach. They can give classes. They can give lectures. SP: Oh yes.

• After receiving the confirmation from Srila Prabhupada, Jyotirmayi went on giving classes in France. But the pressure from the American men became stronger and stronger (such as telling the *brahmacharis* not to attend the classes), and Jyotirmayi wrote to Prabhupada for his renewed support. At that time, Srila Prabhupada did not write his letters himself anymore but dictated his answers to his secretary. As it happened that both Jyotirmayi and Bhagavan had written to Prabhupada at that time, each for a particular question, Srila Prabhupada had his secretary Brahmananda answer them both a common letter. The letter that Srila Prabhupada sent was confirming her right to give classes in the temple. (Jyotirmayi)

Householder Life and *Sannyasa*

As women were being demeaned, householder men and householder life were also heavily put down, to the point that householders were in great numbers trying to convince Prabhupada to give them *sannyasa*.

• "Regarding your separation from Nandarani, nothing should be done artificially. Nandarani is no different from you. She also seeks Krishna consciousness. Your household life is not repugnant. It is favorable. Do not separate artificially. When everyone is engaged in Krishna's service, there is no question of *maya*. I have got good estimation about Nandarani." (letter to Dayananda)

• "If you have taken a wife for *grihastha* life, why are you neglecting? That is not Vaishnava. Vaishnava means he is very much responsible, and if he is householder, then he must be responsible. I cannot give *sannyasa* to any devotee who has not proven himself to be responsible in all respects. Better you prove yourself first by being ideal householder and forget all this nonsense." (letter to Mahatma, 1972)

• "This taking *sannyasa* should not be a whimsical proposition, and should not be an excuse for becoming irresponsible, have no responsibility as *grihastha*, *brahmachari*, etc." (letter to Danavir, 1973)

• "We are suppose to take husband or wife as eternal companion or assistant in Krishna conscious service, and there is promise never to separate. Of course if there is any instance of very advanced disciples, married couple, and they have agreed that the husband shall now take *sannyasa* or renounced order of life, being mutually very happy by that arrangement, then there is ground for such separation. But even in those cases there is no question of separation, the husband, even he is *sannyasa*, he must be certain his wife will be taken care of nicely and protected in his absence. Now so many cases are there of unhappiness by the wife who has been abandoned by her husband against her wishes. So how can I sanction such thing? . . . But if it becomes so easy for me to get married and then leave my wife, under excuse of married life being an impediment to my own spiritual progress, that will not be very good at all. That is misunderstanding of what is advancement in spiritual life." (letter to Madhukara, 1975)

Conclusion

If I usually write "many men" and not just "men," it is that a certain number of them, especially amongst householders, objected against the way women were being treated. But their effort to protect the women was always quickly stopped as they ended up being ridiculed by their godbrothers calling them "henpecked husbands."

The arguments presented here, as well as the anecdotes and letters referred to, are certainly already known to and approved by most of the devotees who have sincerely and objectively tried to understand the matter of women in ISKCON. I have only tried to compile as many of them as possible in a structured way to inform those who never thought over the matter, and those who are reluctant to do the necessary changes, being adverse or insufficiently convinced.

Many of the wrongs done to women for so many years have now been corrected and ISKCON women have recovered some of their rights. Unfortunately, they have been rehabilitated only to higher of lesser degrees according to the different leaders, in different places. Much is still to be done for men to recognize fully women's dignity, and for women to assume again that dignity everywhere. Hare Krishna.

PROPOSAL FOR RE-ESTABLISHING ISKCON WOMEN IN THEIR SPIRITUAL RIGHTS

PROPOSAL ONE

Many of the rights taken away from women have been given back to them since a number of years now, to a different degree in various temples. Again, they are allowed to write articles, perform Deity worship, give classes in the temple, take on various posts of responsibilities previously forbidden to women. (Gurukula headmistress, head *pujari*, photographer, member of temple administration or national council, etc.). Respect and proper behavior towards women has also come back within ISKCON to a certain extent.

Harikesa Swami for example had a memo written to protect women from improper behavior on the part of the men and leaders. Here are some excerpts:

• Whenever *prasadam* is served, it must be served simultaneously to both the men and women . . . This is especially true at festivals. Sufficient sized rooms should be allotted to the men and women for taking *prasadam*. The women should not be made to wait till after the men eat.

• It is a mental concoction to strictly call men "Prabhu" and women

"Mataji" . . . However, calling the ladies "Mataji" is a sign of respect since everyone should respect their mother. It is a very respectful term and should be used in that way. If one uses the term "Mata" in a derogatory sense, then he is using it wrongly. Neither does calling someone "Prabhu" imply automatically that they are superior to a lady. Someone shall be known as higher or lower according to their spiritual status, not according to their gender or social opinion.

• The women should be given equal facilities in the temple. It is not that the men are given a lot of room to live in but the women must be cramped up in their quarters. Both should have proper place to live and both should get equal medical facilities and health care when sick. This principle of equality should be extrapolated into all areas of temple life. All practical considerations should be examined in this light and where there is discrimination, it should be abolished.

• If a women is a temple president, temple commander, *sankirtana* leader or department head, she should be respected by the other devotees, either male or female. Anyone who is a leader in ISKCON has the authority of ISKCON behind them and should be respected. We should not tolerate that some male member of ISKCON will disrespect some female temple president simply because she is female. There must be respect of this position.

• "No guru, *sannyasi* or preacher may speak in a derogatory way about women in classes or in discussions amongst men. They must maintain this spirit of respect between men and women. This does not mean, however, that we should not repeat the message of the *shastras* or what we have heard from Srila Prabhupada regarding the dangers of association between men and women. Rather, this means that there should be no statements wherein the devotee women are seen as lower than the devotee men, and therefore treated improperly . . ." (Memo to the National Council of Germany, from Harikesha Swami, GBC, January 1994)

PROPOSAL TWO

There are very positive improvements but still more has to be done. And these improvements should not be limited to only some temples or some zones, but to the whole movement. To attain this goal, the re-establishment should be one of the prime objectives of the GBC board as it concerns (children included) half of the population of ISKCON.

In addition to what has been instituted by Harikeṣha Swami, in his zone, here is a list of further situations to be corrected in our movement to bring back Srila Prabhupada's original ISKCON.

• Men and women should again both face the Deities, each on one side of the temple room during *kirtan*s.

• Men and women should both again face the speaker of the *Bhagavatam* or *Bhagavad-gita* class, each on one side of the temple room.

• During festivals, both men and women should face the stage, each on one side.

• During special celebrations, both men and women should be invited to sing and talk on stage, both on one side.

• During *guru-puja* and Vyasa-puja, women should be again allowed to offer obeisances in front of the *vyasasana* and not anymore obliged to offer them in the back of the temple.

• While offering flowers to Srila Prabhupada during *guru-puja,* there should be as in the past two lines, one of men, one of women, presenting simultaneously the petals. Out of the two lines, one man goes, then a woman, and so on.

• The same should be done for offering ghee lamps during the month of Damodara.

• *Japa* should again be chanted by both men and women in the temple room, sitting down in front of the Deities, men and women each on their side.

• During public preaching programs, men should be on side, women on the other side.

- While chanting in the streets, both men and women in turn should give a short speech.

- During *tulasi* worship in the temple room, there should be as in the past only one *tulasi* for everyone, both men and women devotees.

- New devotee men should be taught to avoid intimate associate with women (except of course their own wife), but they should not be taught to hate and humiliate women devotee.

- As much as men should be taught to respect women as mothers, women should be taught to respect women as mothers, women should be taught to see the men as sons.

- Women should be taught to respect each other and not feel contempt for each other.

- During festivals, while bathing the Deities, pushing Their swing or reading an offering to Srila Prabhupada, first all the senior men and women should go, then younger men and women; not all the men, then all the women.

- As much as both men and women are taught how to distribute books on *sankirtana*, both men and women should equally be taught how to give classes and public lectures.

- Women able to *kirtan*s and *bhajans* with real devotion and art should be allowed to do so.

- Women should be allowed as before to perform *mangala-arati* as well as 7 o'clock *arati*.

I surely have not covered everything in this list but at least a good part of the problems women have had to face since about 1973, when Srila Prabhupada could not anymore oversee personally ISKCON's management.

PROPOSAL THREE

Because of bad habits acquired for so many years, what was so natural and simple for devotees at the beginning with Srila Prabhupada will be very difficult to institute again now. Most devotees having not known anything else since the time they joined, will not want to change their ways, thinking that doing so will be *maya*. And this attitude will come from women as much as from men. Changing back to the way it was will also be accepted more easily by leaders, by old and advanced devotees than by the mass of devotees. Some will oppose strongly, some will be enthusiastic and some won't dare. It will therefore be necessary for the leaders to free the minds of the devotees all over again, in a very practical way.

• Temple presidents should have regular *istaghosthis* where all there points will be thoroughly discussed until all objections will be defeated, everything clarified and understood, and finally the mentalities changed.

Example 1: It will be objected that some temple rooms are too narrow for men and women to be side by side. Some of our temples in the past were also small and narrow, still there was no problem, just a small space was left between the two lines of men and women, but no one ever sat or stood in the reserved space.

Example 2: Some women will object that they cannot be shy if they come up front. Women in the past were never considered immodest by Prabhupada because of standing in front of the Deities and meditating on Them. So, if Prabhupada did feel that way, so they think they know better than Prabhupada how a woman should behave in Krishna Consciousness?

• Temple presidents, GBC's and heads of departments should see day to day to the application of the reformation of the women's condition.

Example: Stop the men from pushing the women back to the end of the temple room by progressively dancing more and more to their side and on the space left between them and the altar.

Example: Not give in to the blackmailing of some men such as: "If a woman gives class, I won't attend."

• Experienced lecturers should teach the women how to give class and prepare it: proper state of mind, adequate reason for giving class, how to develop erudition, how to capture the attention of the audience, etc. As they never got the chance to practice progressively as the men did, they can start with easier classes such as *Chaitanya-charitamrita* classes or readings of *Prabhupada-lilamrta* (where there is a lot of reading with just a few comments). Once they feel more at ease, they will begin *Bhagavad-gita* classes, then *Bhagavatam* classes when they feel ready. Often, there are no weekly lists of who gives classes, who offers *guru-puja arati*. Just anyone who feels like it goes up. Women won't dare to just go up like that. There should therefore be weekly lists so they may know when it is their turn, especially for classes. Women will not give a spontaneous class as they have no practice. It is better anyway for most devotees to prepare their classes to really teach philosophy to their audience.

• Women are so used to sitting passively back in class, that they have often lost proper behavior. They often go in and out, lean against the wall, sew or do other things rather than really listen and participate actively, let their children move about noisily. They must be taught again adequate behavior in class, respect of the speaker and the listeners. Those who just listen, have no children or services should sit in the front. Those with children or service should sit in the back of the other women. Being side by side with men, the young children will more easily disturb the men, they should therefore be better controlled by their mothers. Srila Prabhupada always wanted the children to behave properly in the temple room. (6)

PROPOSAL FOUR

Recovering Srila Prabhupada's sprit, as far as devotee women are concerned is of the utmost importance for our movement even though many may not be conscious of it.

• To advance spiritually women need examples, just as men have sannyasis, GBC men, gurus, temple leaders, if older women are allowed to express their realizations and knowledge through classes, their devotion through *kirtan*s and taking great responsibilities for their spiritual master, younger women will see them as examples to follow and will advance more and more.

• When on the opposite, they are trained to see all women as unadvanced, unintelligent, incapable, etc., having no female example to admire and follow, being unable to imitate men as their services and association are forbidden to them, they often despise other women and become sexually attracted to advanced men devotees, either grossly or subtly. That is how the phenomenon of "groupies" takes place, and how men leaders fall down.

• Immature men think that despising women and putting them down, "keeping them in their place," proves their own worth. In reality, in societies where men are truly confident of their own worth, women are not merely tolerated, they are valued. Their opinions are listened to with respect, they are given their rightful place in shaping the society in which they live.

• Not only the prejudicial, hurtful behavior towards women has stopped many men and women from joining our movement, but it has made us fail to attract, or loose, the interest and support of educated thoughtful seekers of spiritual truth.

• Whatever progress the movement has made since Prabhupada's arrival is been due at least as much to the efforts of women as of men assisting him. But the women having since 1973 being kept away from almost all decision making and superior responsibilities, the problems and chaotic situations which have befallen ISKCON since cannot be attributed to them, but to the men only. Maybe listening to what the older advanced women had to say would have helped to avoid many blunders.

• Some of the valid positions we have on controversial issues, such as abortion, divorce, sex, birth control, women, children, loose a lot of their impact and are much less convincing in large measure because of their being presented by men instead of women to whom these issues main belong.

• Srila Prabhupada built the movement on the foundation of Chaitanya Mahaprabhu's unique contribution. No one is to be excluded from the *sankirtana* movement, regardless of gender, race, religion, age, social status or any material distinction. He made the necessary adjustment of womanhood to modern western situations as he saw that following the traditional Vedic definition would be completely anachronistic and impede our movement. By not following in his footsteps and trying to overstep his decisions we bring a universal spirituality to the level of a sect, with no contribution to make to the vital issues of our time.

• As we celebrate Srila Prabhupada's Centennial, the world prepares to celebrate the new millennium. Those who wish to see Prabhupada truly honored this year will acknowledge the universality of his message and its relevance to a world in transition, a world in which the role and contribution of women will continue to increase in size and scope. Hare Krishna.

The Anomaly of the Single Mother in ISKCON
by Bimala devi dasi

I originally presented this paper to the leaders at the North American GBC meetings in 1996 in Alachua. I am feeling very optimistic today, because in reviewing it for today's presentation, I had to cross out many of my skeptical comments because I can see that we are making progress. I am also seeing that this weekend we are changing our language.

Originally, the word "leaders" referred to a small elite group of men who, although not leading in the true sense of the word, had assumed the title. I am seeing now that by the word "leader" I am referring to each of us here in this room – and throughout the movement – as leaders. We are each – male and female – being called to assume the role and responsibilities the word entails.

I joined the movement in 1971 with my husband of four years. We had gone to college together, where I received a BA in English and psychology. We chose each other. We were religious and we felt that God had put us together. Once we joined the movement, we were taught that your wife cannot be your friend.

I am here speaking before you today not as myself, but as a voice – a voice representing a growing number of women throughout our movement. This is the first annual ISKCON Women's Conference. When I say women, I mean our daughters, our unmarried women, our wives, and our mothers – our godsisters. But due to the tremendous difficulties the responsibilities of *grihastha* life impose and due to our 25-year emphasis on renunciation, we also have a growing category that is an anomaly in the Vedic literatures – it's the single mother – the woman whose husband is absent.

To the women present here, I am presenting this paper as a means of unification.

There is a vast difference in the lives of married women and single mothers. There's an old North American Indian saying that You can't fully understand a person until you've walked a mile in their moccasins.

I feel that many of you may never have an opportunity to experience these women's lives, so I want to share with you a letter I have written. It addresses many women, your and my godsisters, throughout our movement, many with whom I come into contact daily. I feel this letter is a bridge, for it will enable us better to understand and care for each other.

I should warn you, there is emotion in this letter. I know that can be scary for some of you. But, remember, this is not hysteria. This is neither exaggeration nor distortion. This is the truth. I live it, and many, many of my friends live it. This is my letter.

My dear godsister,

So you tell me your husband has left and you are alone. He has renounced you, and his children.

He is now free to make spiritual advancement. He is giving classes and being adulated by his peers. He is a great devotee. He sits on the asana at the feet of Srila Prabhupada, and silent young *brahmacharis* bring him water and garland him. He folds his hands and speaks our philosophy.

He is doing big service. Other devotees ask his advice. He is absorbing himself in Srila Prabhupada's books. He can quote all the Sanskrit verses. He travels around the world, on pilgrimage, on preaching missions. He is a big devotee. Women look at him and they look at you and they say, "Oh, you're so lucky. He's so advanced. He's so Krishna conscious. You're so fortunate."

And who are you?

You are nobody. You have his one, two, or three children. You are the tiger, your children are little jackals. You're unsubmissive, less intelligent, nine times lustier, and all you want to do is to control men.

[Of course, they'll never know the names he called you, because the words are obscene and ugly in your mouth and shock the sensibilities when heard aloud. They won't know where the bruises were, and they won't know how many times you left and came back, or how many tears you cried. Or perhaps, they won't hear about the other women.]

And what is your reality today? Your little jackals are hungry. They need food. They need clothes, and they want toys. They have to be educated. You can't afford *gurukula*. You don't want to put them in public school. You're lucky, you're on welfare. You need a job, but if you find a job, who'll take care of the kids? You'll lose your medical benefits. You'll lose your food stamps.

You get your job. You go out – you're the father. In the evening you come home – you're the mother. You cook supper, help with homework, throw in a load of clothes at the laundromat, try to wash a floor, run to the store because there's no milk, hope they don't turn off the electricity, bathe the kids, get them to bed, wonder if you heard them, wonder what kind of parent you are becoming, wonder why all you do is worry about money, wonder where your spiritual life went, wonder if you'll ever be able to get up in the morning because you're so tired you want to die, and yes, they did turn off the phone again, but maybe your parents will let you use their credit card just one more time.

And in your heart you remember how life used to be. You were young, new, and eager. You sewed for the Deities – silks and rhinestones, feathers and lace – polished Their silver and brass, cooked the devotees' meals, made the offerings. You distributed Srila Prabhupada's books in airports and malls and parking lots across America. You danced and danced in ecstatic *kirtan*s before the radiant forms of Sri Sri Radha-Krishna, Lord Jagannatha, and Gaura-Nitai. You prayed to Them fervently for devotion, for service.

Now you wake in the middle of the night alone and worry that the food stamps don't last the month, that the kids outgrow their clothes so fast, that you can't pay your bills, that you don't want to end up in a shelter – not again. And you pray to Srila Prabhupada, and you feel so very fallen.

I'm writing this to you because I'm your godsister and it breaks my heart to see your plight. Please don't leave the movement. Don't feel driven away. Don't be discouraged.

There are too few of Srila Prabhupada's children. We need you. We need your strength, your resilience, your incredible determination against overwhelming odds. We need your example of unconditional love that you give your children. We need your compassion. We need your softness and your humor, your gentleness and your nurturing. ISKCON needs you.

I fall at your feet and beg for dust. It is the dust of your feet that I am hungry for, your feet as you trudge to work, stalk the grocery aisles, as you sit with your toddler on your lap, showing him or her pictures of Krishna.

The uninitiated may read this and feel indignant, feel that I'm being melodramatic, that I've exaggerated, that I am speaking harshly. But you know. You know who you are, and believe me, you have no idea how many of you there were and there are now. And you know that what I am saying is exactly true.

I pray to Srila Prabhupada, to Srimati Radharani, and to you, the leaders in our movement.

I am requesting our ISKCON leaders to please consider this letter. In Vedic times, a man choosing renunciation left his wife and children in a village environment. She lived with his family, or she could live with her own parents, or relatives if need be. He didn't leave his family to scavenge for welfare scraps as its daily maintenance, to be branded as social parasites of the government.

With the new welfare reform, in a matter of two years or less, all these women will no longer be eligible for welfare. Know for certain that in the near future we will see women and children living in the streets – and many of them will be ours. Solutions to this impending crisis (if not for most of you, certainly for them) are difficult. I wish I could stand up here and give solutions. But what I would like to believe, however, is that the male leaders would at least deal with the husbands and fathers involved. I would like to know that, as they took their places on the *asana,* you had asked, "Where is your wife? Where are your children? Who is taking care of them? Are they hungry?"

And for the women, well, kindly see them as Vaishnavas. Offer a little respect, a little dignity, a little kindness. *Hear* them.

So that is my plea. Some of you will be moved. Some of you will, to quote one GBC man, see this as "sentimental garbage."

Those who study the behavior of animals have noted that in the face of danger cows will form a circle, the weaker ones and babies inside – and stand with their horns facing outward. Thus their calves and elder cows are protected. The Women's Ministry has been established to form such a circle. It has been established to care for the women, to offer them a voice in our movement – a voice of concern and balance and compassion for the growth and welfare of all devotees, and for the growth of our movement.

Somehow or other we've come into contact with the highest, most sublime philosophy – the Absolute Truth. And we have been fortunate enough to be initiated into the Gaudiya *sampradaya.* How close we are to the goal! We have so much to do for Srila Prabhupada – and there are so few of us. And there are so many discouraged women.

The reality is that this life is but a flash – a brief moment, a few seconds – compared to the eternity that we've been here. And if we view our existence as a straight line back and forward, we will see that our human births have been male, female, male, female, male, female, back, back, back – and forward too. Why, when we are so fortunate, when we are so very near the end of it all, should we not just encourage each other?

I'd like to ask everyone here, how many of you think that at the end of this lifetime you will return back to Krishna, back to the Spiritual Sky? Let's see a show of hands.

Okay. That's nice.

Now, for the majority of you who think that you well may be returning to the material world, don't you agree that you'll probably take birth in this movement? Also, perhaps, isn't there a good possibility that many of you men will be taking birth as women? That's a pretty realistic scenario. So, I'm proposing that if this is the case, then you men had better start seeing that the women are taken care of – because it's really your own futures that you're preparing.

In closing, let's remember that we are a spiritual movement. If we don't have the spiritual vision to see that we are all spiritual beings, that we are all part and part of Krishna, that we are not our bodies but rather we are Vaishnavas – we are Srila Prabhupada's servants – then can't we just pretend?

Also, we may speak about protection of women, and it's a vague and disturbing topic. But the minimal protection is the right to perform devotional practices to the best of our abilities – as we did when Srila Prabhupada was physically present.

So, kindly, let us work together; or let us work together kindly to fulfill Srila Prabhupada's mission. I'm trying to teach my children this fact. Encouragement is free. It costs nothing to give. But it is so powerful and can do so much. So let's cooperate with each other, let's encourage each other, and let's do the work that has to be done – each to his or her own best ability.

Thank you for your attention and your concern.

Yesterday, Today, and Tomorrow
by Pranada devi dasi

I've been asked to speak on my experience of bringing the subject of the treatment of women in ISKCON to the foreground. I wanted to consider the challenges women have faced, what we currently face, and a vision of tomorrow. Therefore, I'd like to look at yesterday, today, and tomorrow.

As a society, we have finally come to understand and accept the abuses our children have suffered in the *gurukula* system. I don't believe we have understood the physical abuses women have suffered. Neither do I want to dwell on this. But it should be stated that from inferior living facilities, to lack of equal *prasadam* facilities, to physical abuse from husbands, women's parties leaders, and others, there is a staggering amount of physical abuses women have suffered in ISKCON. It is not less significant than the abuse our children have faced.

And perhaps more significant is the psychological abuses. This has been casually mentioned at this conference as the de-empowerment of women in our movement. To understand the significance of the damage that has been done is important, but impossible to convey in a few short minutes.

In the not-so-distant past, the climate has been so intolerable, that daily *Bhagavatam* classes proclaimed the position of women as a dangerous element in our Society to be reckoned with. And we reckoned with them by instituting unspoken laws prohibiting them from certain services, keeping their participation in temple programs to an absolute minimum, and allowing an atmosphere in the social status quo to create deep inferiority complexes and fear. Most women were embarrassed to be women, and knew they were thoroughly unwelcome in ISKCON. Even today most women find it difficult to come forward to participate because the climate has been so anti-women for so long.

My own experience with the status quo in ISKCON can hint of the depth of the problem. The atmosphere created by negative thoughts and perceptions about women made it impossible to question the unspoken or invalid laws in public.

I started grappling with issues about women in ISKCON in the early '80s and sought an understanding of just what Prabhupada wanted for women in his movement. It had become evident to me that the status quo was not one administered by Srila Prabhupada. I tried to gather information, but even in private conversations, godsisters were frightened of what might happen to them if they were associated with those discussions. Indeed when it was time to bring facts of physical and psychological abuses, changes made to temple programs not at Prabhupada's request, and how women were becoming increasingly distressed about ISKCON's prohibitions against women, no godsister or godbrothers would stand with me to speak up.

The concerns of my godsisters and godbrothers about speaking out were not unfounded or unwarranted. Although I was gradually becoming known as someone questioning issues, I put my concerns in writing, finally, in 1984. That letter was sent to all the GBC members and was published in the "Vaishnava Journal." That letter also sealed my fate, as I stood alone for my godsisters, as a black sheep of my family. I was told I was a demon destroying Prabhupada's movement, and I received the most controversial label: Pranada is a women's libber. Labels are just labels, but they have the ability to discount human beings and create social rejection. Social rejection is feared by any one of us whose heart has been given over to Srila Prabhupada's movement, and working within his movement is our life and soul. Therefore, labeling was not a light matter. And what was my great sin to receive such rejection? I suggested women should give *Bhagavatam* classes and were authorized to do so by Srila Prabhupada.

Even though social rejection was difficult I promised myself to work toward change. Even if I was the only one who would say something during a *Bhagavatam* class, whose speaker left out a balanced presentation I would say something. If I was in a group and someone made ill reference to women I would state my piece. I would use whatever method of communication available to keep alive a consciousness-raising dialog.

After all, dialog and communication can bring any change. My personal conviction was that there would be change if it was Krishna's desire. Although I didn't know Krishna's desire I had an abiding belief that Krishna's desire was not to see His dear devotee women – who have done so much to build ISKCON and have so much to offer – hurt in the way they have been in ISKCON.

Today

It has been after a long and arduous journey that Vaishnavis find themselves today at this conference. I don't think we should neglect to understand the significance of our coming together to further this goal of healthy relations in ISKCON. This conference is an important event in ISKCON history where women are coming together to make a stand. Abuses, physical or psychological, will no longer be tolerated. Yesterday was only a short time away. It was a time when bringing up even two or three of the hundreds of thoughts we've shared at this conference was so heretical that one feared complete disruption of one's spiritual life. No, it's really no small feat that the swelling of acknowledgment and concern has grown into the formation of a national and international women's ministry, with small changes worldwide in women's services.

Being here today gives me great joy and hope for tomorrow.

But today I still have concerns. I'm concerned that no Los Angeles leaders are here. Women under their care have spent months of their lives to put this conference on. It would be good for the leaders to understand the hopes and desires of those under their care. It is being held only 15 minutes from the temple. I wish they could be here.

I'm concerned that we can't find it within the realm of possibility to allow an exalted soul like Visakha Prabhu to give *Bhagavatam* class.

I'm concerned that there are men in Alachua that won't do something Nanda Prabhu asks of them because they're not convinced it's devotional service.

I'm concerned that the countries opening up in Europe are making the same mistakes we made. Men are leaving their families for renunciation or book distribution, there is spousal abuse, and social issues are suffering in other ways.

I'm concerned that recently in Vrindavan a *gurukula* girl was given permission to lead the bhajanas in the temple, but then a *brahmachari* stopped her and she left crying.

I just spent the past two months with Sesa and Madhumati. They have two little girls, Vraja and Pranaya. Both of them are so endearing. Vraja is very shy, but Pranaya, since she was two or three years old calls people into the temple room and sits down to give *Bhagavatam* class and lead *kirtans*.

Tomorrow

I have a great hope about tomorrow. I want to see that all the Pranayas in the world, wherever they are – Africa, South America, India, Europe, United States, Canada – that all my godsisters, and enthusiastic young women like Shakuntala and Krishna Devata, have facility to use their full mind, body, and words in Krishna's service without fear or insecurity, demeaning attitudes, or abuses. I want to see them fully empowered in Krishna's service.

I want to see a day before I die, where services have opened up for women to the extent that their balancing energy as nurturers and caregivers can make sense of the disastrous social ills that our management to date has created.

I hope to see the day when, around the world, intelligent women see ISKCON family as an attractive alternative to pseudo-religions and material life.

As I was fully confident yesterday that I would see change even though everything seemed dismal and impossible, I am fully confident today that we will continue to see improvements tomorrow. But I know it can only be done with you.

If you share this hope, and can see this vision, then let's join together through the medium of ISKCON's Women's Ministry to make sure we have this tomorrow.

Each one of us individually must make the same commitment I made to myself yesterday. Whatever the cost of our personal social status, let's not remain silent in even one negative *Bhagavatam* class, in even one negative conversation. Let's use every method of communication to raise consciousness. Let us no longer tolerate psychological abuses or the de-empowerment within our Movement.

Let's join together to support the Women's Ministry through finances and time to enable ISKCON policymaking for women, to communicate amongst ourselves through newsletters, and have more conferences nationally and internationally.

Much of yesterday's problem for us was because we weren't a united front. Let's ensure tomorrow by coming together today. Let's overcome any hesitation in doing that for Pranaya, for Shakuntala, for Krishna Devata, for all Krishna's Vaishnavis.

Participation, Protection and Patriarchy:
An International Model for the Role of Women in ISKCON
by Radha devi dasi

Introduction

This paper examines the question of what constitute appropriate roles for women in the International Society for Krishna Consciousness (ISKCON). My purpose is to develop an analytical framework that will be of use to ISKCON in further thinking about the role of women in ISKCON. I use concepts developed in International Law in this examination and I begin by explaining the benefits of a model that incorporates International Law. The second section of this paper addresses the relationship of Human Rights Law to our Vaishnava philosophy and raises problems in our treatment of women up to this point. In the next section I go on to discuss the kind of rights that Human Rights Law embodies. Section four considers the application of those human rights in ISKCON and examines the issue of protection of women from an International Rights perspective. The concluding section highlights actions that ISKCON should take in order to ensure appropriate roles for women.

The benefits of International Law

The first, and most important benefit of an International Law approach in defining roles for women in ISKCON, is that it gives us a coherent framework for resolving many different tensions. The question of the role of women includes a number of different considerations and would have an impact on our Society as a whole. It is, in some sense, artificial to divide our analysis into "men's issues" and "women's issues," because the treatment of women affects every member of ISKCON, regardless of gender – women are wives, mothers, sisters and service colleagues to men. Moreover, the question of the role of women in ISKCON raises other questions, such as the relationship our leaders have with ISKCON's members and the obligations of the individual to ISKCON as an institution. International Law provides an existing model that allows us to integrate these various concerns into a coherent analysis.

The second benefit of International Law is that it allows us to create needed cultural variations in our practices. ISKCON is an international organization facing cultural variations in different regions of the world. If we are going to be an effective organization for all people, and for women in particular, then we have to be sensitive to cultural variations. Srila Prabhupada expressed this thought most easily and eloquently by saying we have to be attentive to time, place and circumstance. International Law has already looked at these cultural variations, and created a way of allowing people some flexibility to tailor a policy to their particular region while maintaining a structure that keeps any adjustment from sacrificing underlying goals.

I do not advocate that we take principles of International Law and replace our own philosophy with International Law. However, I contend that we can effectively use International Law to develop a model within which we can test our adherence to our own philosophy. We have numerous written sources of religious principles, in addition to the examples implicit in the actual behavior of Srila Prabhupada. It is our task to integrate this wealth of instruction into a coherent policy on women in ISKCON. One part of our problem, particularly in our treatment of women, is that we have focused on one or two instructions, which have been taken out of context. We have also used certain words arbitrarily without understanding what those words actually mean. Finally, we have made sweeping statements as justification for our policies even though those statements do not reflect our actual activity. Consequently, we need to revisit this issue of women's participation in a thoughtful and rigorous manner.

Law gives us the tools by which we can integrate numerous instructions on individual issues. Law also teaches us to define our terms and to test our rhetoric against our actions. The need to accomplish these goals is particularly apparent when we examine the role of women in ISKCON. Some of Srila Prabhupada's statements about women have been over-emphasized to the exclusion of other contrary statements. As a result, our policies on women's issues are imbalanced. The particular nature of these misconceptions about women that we have developed in ISKCON is further developed later in this paper.

Human Rights Law and Vaishnava Philosophy

International Law is a particularly useful tool for ISKCON because there is a theoretical similarity between Human Rights Law and our own scripture. That similarity is in the idea of equality. In a sense, it is ironic for members of ISKCON to discuss equality between men and women because so often equality does not occur in practice. However, the principle of spiritual equality is undoubtedly described in our scriptures. There is a similar concept in International Law. International Human Rights Law rests on the principle that everyone is entitled to certain fundamental things because all human beings share the same essence, and that essence is somehow sacred.[1] This fundamental principle is also described in our own scripture. Krishna goes even a little further in the *Bhagavad-gita* when he says that the enlightened sage sees a brahmin, a cow, an elephant, a dog and a dog eater with equal vision.[2] In the related purport, Srila Prabhupada explains that this equal vision arises from the fact that all living entities have the same essence and we all have the same relationship to Krishna.[3] There is, thus, an obvious philosophical basis on which to compare our scripture and International Human Rights Law.

Despite this fundamental teaching, we have not yet accepted this principle of equality in our Society. There is a feeling in ISKCON that souls in women's bodies are not equal, but suffer instead from serious mental and emotional deficits. We are seen as being less intelligent, untrustworthy and over emotional. Jyotirmayi devi dasi described thoroughly in her paper- "Women in ISKCON in Srila Prabhupada's Times"[4] all of these misconceptions about women and explained through Srila Prabhupada's own writings exactly why they are misconceptions. A very brief examination of Srila Prabhupada's statements reveals that he did not view his female disciples as being less intelligent or less able than his male disciples. In the *Chaitanya-caritamrita,* Srila Prabhupada described his disciples, saying, " . . . both boys and girls are being trained to become preachers . . . these girls are not ordinary girls, but are as good as their brothers who are preaching Krishna consciousness."[5] Srila Prabhupada made a similar statement about equality between Vaishnavas and Vaishnavis in a lecture in which he described how women, *vaishyas,* and *shudras* are transformed through Krishna consciousness:

"[It is] Not that even though they become interested they keep behind. No . . . with equal force with men, they also promoted. So Kunti, out of her humbleness, meekness, she is presenting herself that 'We are women, *striya*.' But she's not ordinary woman. She's devotee. Similarly, any devotee woman is as good as Kunti."[6]

Srila Prabhupada never intended his female disciples to be disparaged on the basis of their bodily forms. Rather, he clearly instructed us that women engaged in the practice of Krishna consciousness make equal advancement with male devotees. Indeed, to believe otherwise would indicate a profound lack of faith in the process of Krishna consciousness.

However, the belief that women are inferior is often reflected in our policy and in our practice. Women are dehumanized and devalued by our rhetoric and by accusations used to marginalize them. At the "Vaishnavis in ISKCON" conference, one woman described how she was marginalized when she spoke out on the need for women to give *Bhagavatam* class. She said it led to the end of her career in ISKCON management. Having lived in the same community, I can comment on her treatment from personal experience. Many women who looked to her as a leader, including myself, were told that she did not want to give *Bhagavatam* class because she was more interested in making money than in working in ISKCON management. Thus, she was presented as avaricious and the true facts of her conflict with ISKCON management were concealed. Moreover, I have heard the Women's Ministry dismissed as a "group of women who never cover their heads." This statement, in addition to being inaccurate, misses an important point. The real issue is the purpose and effectiveness of the Women's Ministry; the extent to which the Women's Ministry does or does not propose and implement sensible, useful policy for ISKCON. The fact that some of the members of the Women's Ministry may adjust small externalities in their dress according to time, place and circumstance should not determine the value of the Women's Ministry as a whole. The need to separate Krishna consciousness from external rituals has been the subject of much discussion in our *sampradaya*. Similarly, this external consideration is not the proper measure by which to judge the Women's Ministry.

There are even more insidious, subtle, day-to-day minimizations of women that may be harder to observe. The language we use marginalizes women. When we say "devotees and *matajis*" (*mataji* means mother) we are saying that women are in a category separate from devotees. Such distinctions create a psychological space in which women can be ranked just a little bit lower than the rest of the Vaishnavas, who are the men. Clearly, everyone does not use the statement for such a negative purposes, and the distinction may be genuinely made out of a mood to offer respect, or used blindly simply because the terms used have become the norm in our communities. However, the language creates the space in which the minimization of women is possible. Those who are immature in their faith naturally find these spaces and take advantage of them.

Another example of the minimization of women involves the Mayapur *pushpa samadhi* of Srila Prabhupada.[7] In his presentation, His Holiness Bir Krishna Swami very accurately described the historical photographs that have been reproduced as paintings decorating the *samadhi*. Surprisingly, the female disciples of Srila Prabhupada are not in the paintings although they were in the original photographs. It is without doubt disrespectful and a devaluation of women when they have been deleted from our institutional history. More importantly, this deletion involves the Mayapur samadhi, a place of enormous significance in our movement. Thus, the message that we as women get is multifaceted and extremely negative. First, we are told, "Don't speak." If you do speak, you run the risk of being one of those women who never covers her head. In other words, you become someone who should not be listened to, someone who is not reliable. We are also told, "Don't act," "don't dance in the temple," "don't stand in front of the Deities," "don't give class," "don't lead *kirtan*"[8], and do not participate in many other activities. And the murals in the Mayapur samadhi go even further and say, "Don't exist." Women leave ISKCON and we are surprised. To paraphrase Srila Prabhupada, rather we should be surprised that women have stayed.

Applying the principles of International Law to our Society

Having identified some of the main problems in the treatment of women, we must first ask how the law can help us in solving these problems. The law is relevant here because law involves relationships. Law is a way of governing relationships by creating structure and space in which those relationships can take place. When law works well, it is because it has minimized conflict. We need such a structure in ISKCON. We have many spaces where it is possible for the interests of women and the need of women to be devalued or ignored.

One of the things which we have not yet examined and which is critical for all of our social development policies is the question of what constitutes the proper relationship between ISKCON and its members. At one point, though it may not have been articulated, the relationship was viewed as an autocratic tie with ISKCON functionaries giving pronouncements that could not be questioned by individual members. This relationship led to situations that were destructive to both ISKCON as an institution and to individual members of ISKCON. Srila Prabhupada himself specifically rejected this type of relationship between institutional leaders and those in their care.[9] A new relationship between ISKCON and its members has yet to be articulated. However, there is currently much discussion of the need for ISKCON to support and nurture its members.[10]

In the law we call this type of relationship a social contract. It is a mutual relationship. There is plenty of evidence in the Vaishnava scriptures to support the position that the relationship between institutional leaders and members is based on a social contract. Krishna Himself and Srila Prabhupada have both indicated that the relationship between individual and spiritual leader is a mutual reciprocation. In the verses that Srila Prabhupada liked to quote so frequently from the last chapter of the *Bhagavad-gita*, Krishna says, "Engage always in thinking of Me, become My devotee, offer obeisances to Me, worship Me. In this way you will come to Me. I promise you this because you are so dear to Me."[11]

This verse describes a promise – Krishna tells his devotees, worship Me and I will reciprocate. In the next verse, Krishna says abandon all varieties of religion and I will deliver you.[12] Again, Krishna is describing a reciprocal relationship. The devotee has an important duty to be obedient to the Lord and to surrender to him, but they also have an equally important promise of support and deliverance on the part of the Lord.

This principle of mutuality is highlighted in the pastimes of Lord Ramachandra. An example is when Ravana's brother, Vibhishana, attempts to surrender to Rama. Rama's followers advise Rama to reject Vibhishana saying that he may be an enemy. Lord Rama replies "I cannot reject anyone who surrenders to me. I have no choice." So the Lord is bound, as Srila Prabhupada says, by His devotee's love.[13] That principle can apply to ISKCON as well. If we, the members, surrender and serve Srila Prabhupada's movement, then we fulfil our duty to participate and to obey the laws of the Society. At that point, ISKCON has an obligation to reciprocate and to see that the devotees are cared for.[14] In Human Rights terminology one would say that there is a mutual relationship of rights and duties. In order to articulate what ISKCON's duties would be, we could talk about rights that we would have.

In Human Rights Law, at the international level, there are two types of rights. There is an International Covenant on Civil and Political Rights which covers rights such as citizenship, voting and ability to hold office.[15] There is a second International Covenant on economic, social, and cultural rights which includes rights such as housing, food and education.[16] For the purposes of our discussion in this paper, I will refer to these two categories as participation rights and substantive rights. My theory is that devotees in general, and women in particular, are entitled to both kinds of rights in ISKCON. I further contend that there is an important link between these two categories of rights.

Women are clearly entitled to participation rights in ISKCON at some level. We are allowed to become members of ISKCON. We are allowed to take initiation. We are allowed to chant the holy names. The *maha-mantra* is not a secret mantra given only to men. So we participate at some level. There has been some controversy about what that level of participation should be. This topic is thoroughly covered in the paper presented by Jyotirmayi devi dasi that is available through the Women's Ministry. In her paper, Jyotirmayi devi dasi makes a compelling case for equal levels of participation for men and women based on Srila Prabhupada's own writing and practices.

In *Chaitanya-charitamrita, Adi Lila,* chapter seven, Srila Prabhupada describes how Lord Chaitanya adapted many of the rules of Vaishnava etiquette to increase the effect of His preaching and the spread of Krishna consciousness. In the purport to verse thirty-two, Srila Prabhupada writes:

"Not knowing that boys and girls in countries like Europe and America mix very freely, these fools and rascals criticize the boys and girls in Krishna consciousness for intermingling. But these rascals should consider that one cannot suddenly change a community's social customs. However, since both boys and girls are being trained to become preachers, these girls are not ordinary girls, but are as good as their brothers who are preaching Krishna consciousness. Therefore, to engage both boys and girls in fully transcendental activities is a policy intended to spread the Krishna consciousness movement."

There are two points raised by this purport which we ought to carry into further discussions on this issue.

First, Srila Prabhupada indicates that the test of whether a woman's participation role is appropriate is not whether it is Vedic.[17] Srila Prabhupada says here that the test of whether a woman's role is appropriate is whether it helps to spread Krishna consciousness. If we truly thought in terms of what is effective for spreading Krishna consciousness, many of the controversies between men and women would disappear.

The second point is one I previously discussed in section two of this paper, that Srila Prabhupada has created an analytical exception to the statements that women are less intelligent or untrustworthy.[18] Women engaged in transcendental activities, that is women who are devotees, are, according to Srila Prabhupada, just as intelligent as men engaged in devotional activities.

We can now examine the presumptions that are prevalent in ISKCON against the standard Srila Prabhupada has articulated. My perception, and others may disagree, is that we have a presumption against women's participation in ISKCON. That presumption does not mean that women do not participate in our movement. However, we begin by presuming that women should not participate, and then place the burden on women or their supporters to show why women should be included. This presumption needs to be reversed if we are to give women equal encouragement to develop in their spiritual lives and serve Srila Prabhupada's mission to the best of their abilities. We should have a presumption of equal participation for both genders. The burden then should be on those who argue that the role of women should be circumscribed, for reasons of etiquette or social custom, to articulate why and how such restriction relates to our goal of spreading Krishna consciousness.

When we examine our treatment of women in a logically rigorous manner, many of our practices appear unreasonable. For instance, we often speak of "protecting" women whenever we are accused of gender discrimination. Disparate practices are held to be necessary and even beneficial to women on the grounds that women need special forms of protection.[19] However, this justification for discriminatory practices is incomplete. Those who would use it must define what it is that women are being protected from. Current ISKCON practice supports best the argument that women are being protected from participating. Moreover, we must also decide what the form of that protection should be. For instance, American law requires that restrictions that limit rights must relate to an important governmental purpose and be as narrowly defined as possible. ISKCON could use similar principles in its treatment of women, requiring that restrictions on their participation be related to the goal of spreading Krishna consciousness and that these limits be as narrow as possible.

We must first ask what Srila Prabhupada intended ISKCON to protect women from. For this, we can consult his writings on the subject. The most obvious context in which Srila Prabhupada discussed protection occurs in the first chapter of the *Bhagavad-gita*. Arjuna tells Krishna that when irreligion is prominent, women are prone to degradation. Arjuna informs Krishna that such women may bear unwanted children to the detriment of society. In his purport to this verse, Srila Prabhupada says that women are prone to being misled by irresponsible men and that the cause of their fall down is mixing too freely with men.[20] If that is the kind of protection we are discussing, then I do not understand how the dearth of women on the Governing Body Commission (GBC)[21] or discouraging women from accepting management positions in our movement protects us from sexual exploitation. Such an argument requires a belief that the men we would be working with under such circumstances are irresponsible men. The rules ISKCON uses in this context do not appear rationally related to the purposes Srila Prabhupada has described for us.

The next question is what form should this protection take? In ISKCON, we have an unspoken assumption that protection means restriction. We protect women by telling them "you can't," and taken to its extreme form, this instruction becomes "you can't leave the house."[22] Even in slightly less restrictive contexts which permit women to attend worship at ISKCON temples, making flower garlands for the Deities is sometimes seen as the most suitable service for a woman. There is some similarity between the protection model currently applied to women in ISKCON and the techniques I use in raising my children. I give my children crayons and coloring books and protect them by instructing them to sit quietly and color. Women in ISKCON get colorful bundles of carnation blossoms along with tapestry needles and string. We are instructed to sit quietly and make flower garlands. In ISKCON, the current perception seems to be that women are comparable not only to children, but to very young children.

I do not believe that this "woman as small child" model is the one Srila Prabhupada intended. In fact, examination of the histories told by many of his early female disciples reveals that Srila Prabhupada himself did not treat women in this way. Their stories reveal that Srila Prabhupada protected them in three ways. First, he educated his female disciples about their true identities as spirit souls. Second, Srila Prabhupada engaged women in devotional service, a process by which they could attain liberation from death and rebirth, the ultimate protection from worldly suffering and evil. Finally, as Kausalya devi dasi detailed in her presentation, when limited facilities were available for the devotees' use, Srila Prabhupada protected his female disciples by giving them the lion's share of those physical resources.[23]

In examining Srila Prabhupada's actual behavior toward his female disciples, it seems fair to conclude that far from comparing women to children who need protection, Srila Prabhupada desired a model in which women would be nurtured and supported and above all encouraged to contribute as much as they could to the Krishna consciousness movement, rather than being reviled and restricted. Perhaps we should redirect our efforts toward a model designed to ensure that women are educated, engaged and provided with sufficient physical resources in order to perform their various services effectively within our organization.

This question of protection through the provision of resources raises the second category of Human Rights, that is, substantive rights. If protection really were our goal, then as an external academic observer of the institution I would expect to see policies directed towards that goal. The Women's Ministry and other members of ISKCON have engaged in significant discussion concerning policies that would be necessary to protect women members of ISKCON. That list is legion, but if we examine protection from sexual exploitation specifically, I would expect to see, among many other things, education about the proper roles of men and women, ashrama[24] facilities for women, and a policy prohibiting sexual harassment. In fact, we have some of these things. We have training manuals for our new members, but they do not often include material on how to respect and protect women. We have ashrama facilities. However, we spend more resources on men's training and men's ashramas than we do on comparable programs for women. The Women's Ministry is drafting a policy on sexual harassment, but without effective support from ISKCON's management, that policy is unlikely to result in meaningful social change. Thus, in spite of our rhetoric about protecting women, an outside observer will find that we give more substantive rights to men than to women.

In ISKCON we find ourselves in the position of telling our women members that they do not need participation rights because we will protect them. But we then fail to provide the resources by which that protection might come about. Human rights analysts will tell you that when you decrease somebody's participation rights without a corresponding increase in their substantive rights, that person will be worse off than they were at the beginning.[25] This type of situation is the very definition of oppression and dictatorship, which is surely not what Srila Prabhupada intended.

There is another aspect of the protection issue that raises a slightly different philosophical basis for a duty on ISKCON's part. That issue is domestic violence. In his presentation, His Holiness Bir Krishna Swami mentioned a letter he had seen in which a male member of ISKCON expressed his understanding that our Vaishnava etiquette permitted him to beat his wife as long as he used only a leather belt on her back or a sapling on her legs. Some male members in Southern California have expressed the belief that Srila Prabhupada stated that both a wife and a mridanga required beating. I have personally not seen any proof that Srila Prabhupada endorsed wife beating. Moreover, ISKCON's Governing Body Commission has specifically rejected the claim that our philosophy justifies spousal abuse in any way.

Given this institutional force which misguided members are using to promote domestic violence, ISKCON has a duty to create policies which will counter domestic violence. While the ISKCON Women's Ministry has undertaken to create some policies and substantive programs to meet this need, we often hear excuses for institutional inaction on this issue. The excuses we hear, lack of resources and an inability to interfere between husband and wife, are clearly insufficient. Given our somewhat checkered history which includes (at the very least) the public perception that we have a poor record on domestic violence, we have a duty to find the resources to counter this destructive influence. Moreover, having given numerous, repeated public instructions on the duty of the wife to tolerate any of her husband's abuses and having given men some (false, but well promoted) basis on which to justify their abuses, it seems a little late to make the claim that we cannot become involved in the marital relationship. If we make the claim that we protect women, then we must become responsible and actually protect them.

I want to return now to the issue of participation rights because there is a clear link between participation rights and substantive rights. The best way to ensure that people have substantive rights is to give them participation rights.[26] So, the claim that we can safely relinquish our participation rights in exchange for protection is simply untrue. Even with the best of intentions, our leaders will be unable to safeguard our substantive rights if we have too few participation rights. I am deeply suspicious of anyone who tells us that we do not need participation rights. Experience shows that we do need such rights.[27]

There are two reasons why ISKCON needs to pay particular attention to this link between participation rights and substantive rights. The first is that we have a limited ability to enforce any substantive rights we create. We have no functioning justice system in our movement. Although we have a Justice Minister and have developed some grievance policies, our Justice Ministry has no staff and no financial resources. Hence, our grievance policies are routinely ignored. It would be unreasonable to assume that substantive policies protecting women can be enforced effectively in this environment.

Furthermore, there are important transaction costs which function as barriers preventing our leaders from developing and enforcing policies which would truly meet the needs of ISKCON's women in an environment which excludes women from upper management. Basic economic theory informs us that the development of any policy to protect women will bring with it transaction costs including the costs of gathering the information necessary to develop that policy. Those transaction costs will include both monetary costs and opportunity costs. If our leaders wish to develop substantive policies to protect ISKCON's women, rather than allowing the women to participate in management and work out for themselves what they need, then our leaders must be willing to invest both time and money in this project.

These costs will operate as a significant barrier to the development of substantive rights for women in ISKCON. ISKCON leaders already plead lack of financial resources to explain lack of substantive social development policies in our movement. Furthermore, our leaders are consistently over engaged, that is, they have less time available than they need to accomplish the tasks already assigned to them. So there is little realistic likelihood of them as a group, or even more than one or two individuals, making it their business to find out what the women of ISKCON really need and to develop the structures to meet those needs. Again, we return to the idea that women need participation rights if they are going to have a meaningful role in ISKCON and if ISKCON can truly claim to protect them.

There is another kind of transaction cost that is raised by the exclusion of women from positions of authority in ISKCON. That cost is the difficulty for women in identifying other women who are spiritual role models. There are many visible male role models, advanced spiritual leaders, whom we can easily identify because they have visible symbols of advancement. They have *dandas*[28]; they have titles such as GBC representative or temple president. At the very least, they sit on the *vyasasana*[29] during the morning program and give *Bhagavatam* class. The women in our movement, many of whom have been practicing Krishna consciousness longer than some of the male role models, are very hard to find. They lack the visible symbols of advancement. Thus, it has taken me more than ten years just to begin to identify the women who can act as my spiritual mentors. Giving women participation rights that permit them to give *Bhagavatam* class, to run projects and temples, to sit on the GBC, allows the women of ISKCON to find the role models we need to advance in Krishna consciousness.

Conclusion

There are three points that are essential to any policy that would permit ISKCON to ensure appropriate roles for women.[30] First, as I mentioned before, there should be a presumption against limiting women's access to spiritual resources. Where women's access is limited, policymakers must provide a written justification for their decision, articulating how their policy is necessary to increase the spread of Krishna consciousness.

Second, we need women in leadership roles from the highest levels down to the local temple communities. We need women in leadership roles in significant numbers to prevent these leaders from being isolated or marginalized by male administrators. One aspect of this issue of female leadership that we have not yet addressed is the extent to which men get a significant amount of informal support in rising up through the ranks in ISKCON. This phenomenon is not necessarily a sign of malice on the part of our leaders. Rather, men develop intimate relationships with men in our Society, as they should. However, anyone in an intimate relationship with a leader has access to a great deal of support and resources. Women do not have that opportunity and will not have that opportunity until we have significant numbers of women at high levels. Thus, ISKCON has a duty to foster the development of women leaders. It is not sufficient for ISKCON's management to say, find some qualified women and bring them to us. ISKCON has the duty to find women who can lead and also to find women who have the potential to be leaders and to give these women the same opportunity to develop that is given to similarly qualified men.

When we have done these two things, we can progress to the final prong, developing substantive policies, more effectively. We must identify the needs of the women so that we can do two further things. We must empower the women to meet some of their own needs and we must develop structures that will provide women with the resources and facilities they need. The focus of the Women's Ministry has been, in large part, on providing women with a forum for working together to meet their own needs. This "Vaishnavis in ISKCON" conference embodies that philosophy, involving women from across North America who worked together under the direction of Sudharma devi dasi to organize what His Holiness Hridayananda Swami has described as an historic event which could vastly improve our movement.

Finally, we must all work together as a movement to develop the structures and policies which will provide women with the substantive rights they need for their protection and in order to meet our goals of advancing Krishna consciousness. However, we will work most effectively together if we increase participation roles for women in ISKCON.

Footnotes

[1] Ritter, Matthew A., *Human Rights: Would you know one if you saw one?* A philosophical hearing of International Rights Talk, *California Western International Law Journal*, 27 (1997), p. 265.

[2] Bhaktivedanta Swami, A. C., The *Bhagavad-gita As It Is*, Los Angeles, California: Bhaktivedanta Book Trust, 1994, 5.18.

[3] Reference missing.

[4] Jyotirmayi's paper was presented at the "Vaishnavis in ISKCON" Conference held in Marina Del Rey, California, on 5-7 December, 1997 and is available through the North American ISKCON Women's Ministry I discuss this same topic in further detail in section four, infra.

[5] Bhaktivedanta Swami, A. C., *Chaitanya-charitamrita*, Los Angeles, California: Bhaktivedanta Book Trust, 1994, *Adi-lila* 7.2.

[6] Lecture by A. C. Bhaktivedanta Swami, Mayapur, 30, September 1974.

[7] A *samadhi* is a burial ground for great Vaishnavas. In this case it is the shrine dedicated to the founder of ISKCON, and is a place of worship and pilgrimage in India.

[8] The congregational chanting of the names of God.

[9] In his purports to the *Srimad-Bhagavatam*, 4.9.65-66, Srila Prabhupada writes, "Formerly this earth was ruled by one saintly king only. Kings were trained to become saintly; therefore they had no other concern than the welfare of the citizens. . . . Although it is misconceived that formerly the monarchical government was autocratic, from the description of this verse it appears that not only was King Uttanapada a *rajarshi*, but before installing his beloved son Dhruva on the throne of the empire of the world, he consulted his ministerial officers, considered the opinion of the public, *and also personally examined Dhruva's character*." (Emphasis added.)

[10] I note here that the interaction of His Holiness Bhakti Tirtha Swami, and his disciples in the Bhaktivedanta Institute are a wonderful example of how the relationship between an institution and its members can work in a positive form.

[11] Bhaktivedanta Swami, *Bhagavad-gita*, 18.65.

[12] 18.66.

[13] Bhaktivedanta Swami, A. C., *Krsna*, Los Angeles, California: Bhaktivedanta Book Trust, 1994, Vol. 1, p. 89.

[14] There is a duality in this statement, because we, the members are ISKCON in a sense, and this duty of care and reciprocation devolves upon us as well as on our leaders.

[15] For the text of these and other United Nations documents on the topic of human rights see *United Nations, Human Rights: A Compilation of International Instruments*, U.N. Document ST/HR/1/Rev. 1 New York:1978.

[16] Reference missing.

[17] As a society, ISKCON has failed to define the meaning of the term "Vedic." To the extent the term means in line with the purposes or teachings of the *Vedas,* ISKCON must more clearly articulate how the *Vedas* describe women's roles. So far, ISKCON spokespersons have failed to address the plurality of women's roles described in our own texts, focusing only on one or two examples from one or two women's stories. Currently, the term has a more common usage as a substitute for the phrase "vaguely historical." Women are often told that they cannot lead *kirtan* or give *Bhagavatam* class, for instance, because it would not be considered proper in "Vedic" terms for them to do so, in spite of examples of women in our own *sampradaya* who have done so.

[18] Srila Prabhupada also mentions many times that men in the current age of Kali yuga are less intelligent than men in former ages. Thus, the question of whether the statements about the relative intelligence of men and women apply at all in this age remains undecided.

[19] We should not entirely dismiss this concept of protection, because women do have special circumstances that require additional resources. In particular, women engaged in child rearing have specialized needs which our entire society ought to participate in satisfying.

[20] Bhaktivedanta Swami, *Bhagavad-gita*, 1.40.

[21] This is the main management and law forming body of ISKCON.

[22] On a trip to the ISKCON temple in Bombay in the spring of 1992, I was informed by one male *pujari* (priest) that the reason why there were so few women at the morning program was that the truly sincere *matajis* preferred staying chastely at home to worshipping the Deities in the temple. I was also instructed not to speak while taking *prasadam* and informed that women were not permitted to speak in the *prasadam* hall. Thereafter, I took my meals in the temple restaurant.

[23] Oral Presentation by Kausalya devi dasi at the "Vaishnavis in ISKCON" conference, California, 5-7 December 1997.

[24] *Ashrama* is the accommodation offered to devotees living and serving at the temple. The accommodation is separated into male and female quarters and is usually a facility for unmarried devotees only.

[25] Yamin, Alicia Ely, "Reflections on Defining , Understanding, and Measuring Poverty in Terms of Violations of Economic Social Rights Under International Law," *Georgetown Journal On Fighting Poverty*, 4 (1997), pp. 273, 284-5.

[26] Ibid, p. 287.

[27] One example for the difficulty of protecting substantive rights in the absence of participation rights was documented by Amartya Sen in "Freedom and Needs," *The New Republic*, 10-17 January, 1994, p.31. Sen describes how governments such as India, which are electoral democracies with a relatively high level of participation rights have managed to prevent or contain food shortages to a greater extent than more repressive societies such as communist China.

[28] A long stick carried by a *sannyasi*, a senior devotee of the renounced order, commanding high respect from the community.

[29] A raised comfortable seat offered to the teacher while they give a class from the scriptures. This is usually offered to senior devotees, namely *sannyasis*.

[30] The precise form and language of such a policy must, of course, be arrived at by consensus among the various components of our movement.

The Importance of Women in ISKCON
by Hridayananda dasa Goswami

In the time allotted to me, I want to speak on three related topics, firstly, how I think this topic affects myself personally and also the men in ISKCON, as we sometimes say "the male bodied devotees"; secondly, how from listening I think it is important for the women themselves; and thirdly, how the topic is important for the world and Srila Prabhupada's mission.

I became convinced some time ago that what was about to happen here was of great historical importance, and I am now even more so convinced that this meeting is not only Krishna conscious but it is an important event that will be recorded historically. It is not the beginning, of course, but it is certainly one of the first powerful, organized manifestations of a process which I think will bring tremendous good to ISKCON and to the world. I feel I must express my most profound appreciation for the women and men who have spoken here, and I say this with great sincerity, it's been very moving and very enlightening to say the least, and I think the eloquence, intelligence and Krishna consciousness of the women who have spoken practically proves the point they were making. I would like to thank all of them.

So, the first point, what the process of trying to facilitate and empower the women in ISKCON means to me. When I went home last night from the conference, the realization that came to me was that by the women striking forth to re-establish their proper position in ISKCON and in Vaishnava culture, they were also restoring to me part of myself, and I'll explain what that means. Prabhupada used to say that we are not impersonalists, we do not see Krishna alone. One time, Prabhupada saw a poster of Krishna, one of those things you sometimes see in India. Krishna was in front of the syllable "Om" with some light behind him, no cowherd boys or girls, no cows, no Vrindavan, and Prabhupada said this is not bona fide because we are not impersonalists, we don't see Krishna alone. As we have heard from Krishna-devata who has been speaking very eloquently about this point of the family, we have to understand that ultimately there is, as I say, that "big family up in the sky" in Krishna-*loka*. We are eternally a family and to understand that is to understand Krishna consciousness. When, due to injudicious polices or our own immaturity and ignorance, basically half the family in ISKCON is cut off from what could be much more meaningful participation, then all of us are cut off. That was my realization last night, that if we are denied the normal spiritual relationships with mothers, aunts, sisters, daughters, and nieces, we are being denied our own self-realization. Because to be Krishna conscious, to be able to go back to the spiritual world and participate with Krishna and with the pure devotees there, to be up to speed, so to speak, with the spiritual world, means that one has to fully realize one's own self as an eternal spiritual person, and the realization of that eternal spiritual personality comes through relationships, because to be a person means to have relationships with other persons.

By artificially denying those fortunate great souls who have taken birth as women, to deny our own relationships with them on the spiritual platform, to try to subjugate them or relegate them to a type of sub-human or sub-devotional status within ISKCON, is to deny our own spiritual identity and to deprive ourselves of the types of relationships that we personally need in order to develop our own understanding of ourselves, to develop ourselves as spiritual persons. So that is the understanding I had last night, that among many other things, this is also a self-realization experience for me. All the men, I think, are really depriving themselves of the full richness of Krishna consciousness; they cannot fully understand themselves as spiritual persons if they deny these relationships. Also, as some speakers mentioned, the symptom of a pure devotee or Krishna conscious person is to see Krishna in everyone, to see everyone in Krishna. We all know that famous verse in the *Bhagavad-gita*:

> *tad viddhi pranipatena*
> *pariprasnena sevaya*
> *upadeksyanti te jnanam*
> *jnaninas tattva-darsinah*

"Just try to learn the truth by approaching a spiritual master. Inquire from him submissively and render service unto him. The self-realized souls can impart knowledge unto you because they have seen the truth." (*Bhagavad-gita* 4.35)

The next verse is also very significant because Krishna says, "One who has understood this knowledge given by the spiritual master hears the truth." Krishna says that when you have understood this knowledge, which comes from the spiritual master, then one understands that "all living beings are part of Me and are in Me and are Mine." Without this ability to see all living beings as part of Krishna, especially those who are directly engaged in the Lord's service, one cannot become Krishna conscious. I think it should be philosophically obvious that without offering the proper respect to the devotees who are appearing as women, without caring about them, without appreciating them, one cannot understand spiritual knowledge. One will be unable to really understand Krishna consciousness. I think any sane person who is practicing Krishna consciousness can recognize this point of offering proper respect.

One thing that keeps coming to my mind is that I'm now very convinced that the very best women in the world are in the Hare Krishna movement. According to all the descriptions we have in the Vedic literature they are great souls, they are worshipable. If we don't see things this way we are devaluing Krishna, because if great souls in whatever bodies dedicate their lives to serving Krishna and we don't give importance to them, we're not giving importance to Krishna. Again, in many ways I think that this process of offering to the women in ISKCON what is owed to them is essential for the men's spiritual advancement, for their own spiritual understanding, for them to go back to Godhead. I don't think that men can go back to Godhead if they don't respect women. So that was my first point.

The second point is that as far as the women themselves are concerned, the greatest violence is to cause someone to forget Krishna. Prabhupada, of course, said the absolute good is to give Krishna consciousness to others, and the absolute evil is to take Krishna consciousness away from someone. Certainly in our present conditioned state we do need some encouragement to be Krishna conscious – this has already been said by so many other speakers, so I'll just refer to it – but to deny to the women what Krishna wants for them, what Prabhupada wants for them, is the greatest violence. It means not to represent Krishna but to represent Kali. This movement is meant for spreading knowledge, so to create ignorance or to create illusion within the Hare Krishna movement is the greatest disservice. To deny that the women are able to perform outstanding devotional service – to make a significant historical difference to the salvation of the world – is to create illusion within the community of Vaishnavism. I think that point has been made very well by so many other people; by listening to the speakers here I feel that I am in the presence of great souls, and I think not to recognize that is ignorance.

The third point I want to make is that just as the men cannot become pure devotees of Krishna if they don't recognize that there are also great devotees who are women, this movement cannot mature and flourish unless we recognize the women. I think that in many ways the women are saving the Hare Krishna movement. For example, this emphasis on *ishtagosthi*. Just by demanding – as I hope they will demand – that the men, as I sometimes say, "wake up and smell the *kafta*," by insisting that the men be Krishna conscious, the women are making a tremendous contribution to our personal advancement and to the preaching.

Although the women have done so much service, this is perhaps historically one of the greatest contributions the women are making. This process of the women becoming organized is making a contribution which will be historically recorded, and it has made a tremendous and outstanding contribution to the salvation of the world, to the empowering of the Krishna consciousness movement. It is clear from our scriptures that men often fall into illusion and have to be brought out of illusion by their wives, mothers, sisters or daughters.

There are many examples one can give: the wives of the *brahmanas* – Oh, the *brahmanas*! Krishna sent his cowherd boyfriends to the *brahmanas* to ask for food, but they couldn't appreciate this request, they couldn't appreciate Krishna, and they flatly refused. Then Krishna said, "Ask their wives, they're much more intelligent." The wives, of course, were pure devotees of Krishna. So, as I sometimes ask, why did Vyasadeva put this story there if the real point was to hammer into everyone's head that men are always more intelligent? Why wasn't the opposite story described? So that is one example where the wives enlightened their husbands. In the *Mahabharata*, Pandu wants Kunti to have sons with another man, a pure *brahmana* or demigod, but Kunti is reluctant. At one point, Pandu says, "A woman has to follow her husband; whether he's right or wrong, she has to follow him," and I'm sure some people will quote that. But what happens a few paragraphs later is that when Pandu is wrong, Kunti corrects him and he surrenders to her, just after he said that "a woman has to follow her husband, right or wrong." So there are many cases like that. Kunti had to correct Pandu, the wives of the *brahmanas* had to correct their husbands.

Draupadi had to chastise and correct her five husbands, the Pandavas, who were pure devotees of Krishna. Still, Draupadi knew better. Kunti gave the instruction that the alms should be shared equally between the brothers, and then it turned out that the "alms" were of course Draupadi. At that point Yudhishthira said, "Well, it was just a joke, she didn't understand, therefore we really don't have to follow this," and Kunti chastised Yudhishthira and said, "No, why are you trying to degrade me by making me go back on my word?," and Yudhishthira, of course, accepted what his mother said.

If we look in the scriptures there are many, many examples where the men were in illusion and the women had to save the men from illusion by giving them Krishna consciousness knowledge. I am personally convinced that for some time the men of ISKCON have been in a type of illusion – there are still some men who are in illusion about this – and that the women are giving us knowledge and bringing us back to Krishna consciousness. So I think that this is an outstanding contribution which is not only bringing us back to Krishna consciousness on one particular point but, on an institutional level, bringing the entire society back to a higher state of Krishna consciousness.

As far as what this means for the preaching, the women are, of course, at least half of the International Society for Krishna Consciousness and therefore we want to double this. As Prabhupada said, we should double it. Obviously, the easiest way to double it is to simply recognize that half of us are women and that they are, as Prabhupada said, equal to their brothers. This simple act of waking up, of coming out of the ignorance which is based on the bodily concept of life, and acknowledging the women, will not only double this community and give us twice as many empowered devotees, but it will also mean we won't have devotees working at cross purposes.

Those are basically the points I wanted to make but there are a few other details I could mention. Having traveled around many countries this year, and everywhere I went trying to explain some of these points as best I could, my own observation is that it's not just simply a question of Vedic culture. I found in Poland, in Italy, in Brazil, in Argentina and around America that there is a type of unconsciousness on the part of the men. As a typical example, in the temple room the men somehow or other have developed the illusionary understanding that the temple room is theirs and that the women can take their remnants in the form of whatever spaces they don't choose to occupy, and if they choose to occupy all of them, the women can take a walk. So I tried to explain to the men that the women are an equally important part of ISKCON and that it is also their temple room, it's Krishna's temple room. I have noticed, for example, that the men sit down for a class and we try to make an equal space for the women, and then some men – I think they've simply become crude and uncultured – simply sit down in front of a woman without thinking, "I'm sitting down in front of another person."

As has already been mentioned, a *guru-puja* may be going on where the women are offering the flowers but then whatever man walks in feels that because he is a member of the master race, the master sub-race of the human race, he can simply butt in line and that all the women, immediately becoming ashamed of their existence by seeing a male body, should immediately flee and run back and apologize and then wait until the last man has finished and then come back again. This type of behavior is uncivilized. It's crude, uncultured behavior, and my experience from going around the temples was that when we were having very heavy *ishtagosthis* on this point – in the temples where I was allowed to have *ishtagosthis* – the men were relieved and they thanked me, and the relief was that finally somebody had told them that it was bona fide to be a gentleman.

My personal perception – some of my best friends have male bodies – is that when we joined the Krishna consciousness movement we had to sort of reject everything, so we just pressed that button on our computer that says "erase" and we erased all the programs and then we just started getting all this new information. As you know, we rejected a lot of simple, normal culture, like being a gentleman, being kind, being compassionate, and instead a type of male mafia arose in ISKCON. It is a type of consciousness where the men, even men who would be much more satisfied being kind and gentlemanly, feel that it is somehow not bona fide to be nice to women. That somehow, it's like you're not a man unless you play this role, and they were very relieved and grateful that someone had authorized them to be gentlemen.

I would like to make a further point about the actual way to conquer lust. I think Jyotirmayi spoke so nicely and so much better than I can, also Malati and many other ladies. I remember 1970 in Boston in the *sankirtana* van, I was *sankirtana* leader, we just all piled in, there was no women's or men's section of the van, what to speak of a men's and women's van. You can still see these pictures in the Back to Godhead magazine. We're all just in the van, smiling and waving at the cameras. There was no lust, and there was no lust because there was great respect. I was a *brahmachari* for one and a half years and it was one of the best times of my life, it was super ecstatic, always thinking of Krishna, and I can honestly say – you know, after a few weeks I got the hang of it – that there was no question of lust. I was actually thinking of Krishna, and I had tremendous respect for the ladies. I don't think it was just because I loved my mother, which I did – I have a nice mother – it was not only that I was brought up with great affection for my mother, but also that was just the consciousness. As a *brahmachari* I felt great respect for the ladies, I felt they were transcendentalists, *bhakti yoginis*, and there was no question of lust. The idea that the way to conquer lust is to despise the woman enough so you don't fall down, cultivating hatred and hostility towards women, has obviously totally failed.

Everyone already knows that the men who are the most averse to women are the ones who are going to fall the hardest.

So my recommendation to the men, which is what I've been preaching to my own disciples and *brahmacharis* in general around the movement, is that the real way to conquer lust is by learning to offer all respect to women. If you feel reverence for women as your mother, if you have this reverence, this deep respect, if you very sincerely feel this, then this is the way to conquer lust because you can't simultaneously respect someone and want to exploit them. After all, lust is the desire to exploit and the opposite of that is the desire to serve. I know if my mother came to the temple, I wouldn't ask her to stand at the back while I went to the front.

I would like to express my great, deep gratitude to the women who are organizing this event. To sum up, I am personally very convinced, and I think on very good grounds, that this is historically, in an incalculable way, proving ISKCON, in many ways saving ISKCON. I think that this process is bringing ISKCON to the point of finally becoming an adult movement, where we have young people, but it is a mature movement. If we want to talk about families, I mean my own family I came from – my material family – it's my mother that really keeps things together. There's no question that if my mother wasn't there the family would not have the same sense of family.

So perhaps as a final point I would like to point out real ways, not abstract general points such as if you respect women then you can come to the *brahma-bhuta* platform and so on and so forth. But women make a real contribution. Half of what it means to be a society is the women in it, so if we don't engage the women and encourage them properly, we will never really have a society. We will have a somewhat dysfunctional and incomplete society like we have now. I think perhaps one of the reasons our society still is, in some ways, dysfunctional as a society is because of the lack of women's roles. I didn't come from a matriarchal background, yet still my mother played a very strong role in my personal upbringing and plays a very strong role in keeping the family together, in the mundane sense of the term, and if she wasn't there it wouldn't really be a family the way it is now. And I think ISKCON cannot become a family, we cannot realize that we are a family, we cannot be functional as a movement unless the women are there, unless the women have their important role to play.

In my own *ashrama* – many of you come to visit there over by Wilshire and Roberts where I live – one experience I repeatedly have, not only there but everywhere I've lived, is that if I just depend on the *brahmacharis* I'm going to live in a dump. There would be no flowers, there would be no cleanliness and half the time there wouldn't be great *prasadam*. Not that I want to limit the women's roles to these things. I have always believed women can do everything if that is what their natural inclination is. What I mean to say is that my personal conception has always been that we're all soldiers in Lord Chaitanya's army, everyone should just do what they have to do. In my opinion women can do anything that Krishna inspires them to do and I don't think there are any limits to it. I mean a woman can save the world if a woman turns out to be the greatest devotee of the Lord, the greatest preacher, which is possible. If in Prabhupada's service some woman saves the world, that's fine with me. I have no problem with it. It's not that I hope a man saves the world.

I want to make that clear, that the women can do anything that Krishna inspires them to do. In 1975, when Prabhupada was discussing the academic program that we're now trying to carry out, some devotee man asked, "Is this only for men or do women also participate?" and Prabhupada was surprised by the question. He said, "Why not, what's the problem? Of course, it's for the women, just not cats and dogs."

So, even though women can do anything, it's still crystal clear to me that in my own *ashrama*, if the women aren't there doing service it's basically going to be a filthy mess. In many ways the women civilize the *ashrama* and create the proper atmosphere for spiritual life, an atmosphere for spiritual advancement. The lack of women in prominent positions in ISKCON, the lack of women being empowered by us in ISKCON, I think has very much impoverished ISKCON's movement in many serious ways, has made it dysfunctional, has in many ways obstructed the spiritual advancement of the men, what to speak of what it's done to the women. I see this project the women are carrying out now – and it really is the women, we're here now just to participate but really the credit goes to the women – as a major renaissance within ISKCON, and that's why I'm pushing it so hard because it's the right thing to do. I think that the movement is at the present time, in many ways, stuck in the mud and cannot move forward unless this process of empowering the women becomes successful.

Let's Mend Our Social Fabric
by Pranada dasi

News article published by Chakra, an online news site.

How can we revitalize and strengthen ISKCON? Devotees attending ISKCON's first annual women's conference, held in Los Angeles last December, came up with a solution that includes a mix of arithmetic, common sense, and realization of verses about the equality of all souls, and a few attributes like honesty and compassion. The conference gave attendees new hope for fulfilling Srila Prabhupada's prophecies of ISKCON becoming a powerful worldwide movement for spreading Krishna consciousness. The conclusions of the seminar can provide a foundation for ending the negative propaganda and internal strife that tear at the fabric of the ISKCON family and weaken our potential for spreading Krishna consciousness.

The essence of the solution is simple: Put the heart (mom) back into the family (ISKCON), and the family will grow and galvanize. As the motherly abilities of women

1998

The Power of Words
by Gaurangi Dasi

This paper was delivered at the Women's Ministry Conference in Radhadesh, Belgium, June 1998.

Introduction

The importance of words and sound vibrations.

Everything proceeds from sound: in the beginning was the word of God and the entire cosmic manifestation is generated from the sound of Krishna's flute.

We transmit ordinary and spiritual knowledge through words.

The exchange of words and communication is an essential element in relationships.

A few sweet words is the humblest gift the poorest person on this planet can offer to anyone.

We all have experienced the power of words in our own life:

Sweet and kind words stay with us for life, we cherish them.

Sharp and cruel words hurt, cut, and discourage us; they are hard to forget and can even kill our spirit.

Double function of the language and the words we use.

The words and language we use have a double function.

1) They express and reflect our interior world, our thoughts, and ideas.

The kind of words we use to describe things or talk about others express and reveal who we really are: our frame of mind, feelings, intentions, motivation, level of realization, degree of culture, etc.

We've all made some lapses in the past, spoken some words apparently by mistake and unwillingly, but these words were exactly expressing what was on our mind at that particular time, even while we were trying to conceal our true thoughts and feelings in the first place.

2) They also influence the way we think and perceive the world and reality.

The eskimos have at least fifteen different words to describe "snow." There are many words in Sanskrit that have no english equivalent: in Sanskrit there are several words to describe varieties of love (*kama, priti, prema, bhava,* etc), whereas in English there is only one word (love): you love God, ice cream, swimming, your wife, your country, or your dog. The English language is less refined: it uses the same word to express totally different realities and experiences.

A few remarks about my presentation.

I was strongly encouraged to refer to specific quotes from *shastras* and from what Srila Prabhupada said. But then I realized a few things:

• This is a monumental work. For example, if I had wanted to analyze all the contexts in which Srila Prabhupada refers to women as "less intelligent," and what he meant by that, I would still be doing the research work and not speaking today. Of course this would be a very helpful research, which could be done later on.

• I assume that you all know well the *shastras* and what Srila Prabhupada said and that you are also aware of his overall mood.

This presentation is mainly addressed to devotees who have been in ISKCON for some time, know the philosophy, and have practical experience of life in ISKCON temples.

• By using quotes and counter quotes, we could definitively get a better understanding of Srila Prabhupada's teachings and mood, but this could also be a lengthy debate, and right now we have no time for that. My intention is to appeal to the essence of the philosophy, common sense, basic psychology and human decency. In other words, to bring things to the level of our every day life in examining how certain words we use affect us and our environment. I will also examine a few examples of non-verbal language, since it is a very good part of communication: expression, gestures, intonation, etc.

In preparation for this presentation, I read through the articles and posts of the International Women's Conference on the internet. Among the topics discussed were the "inauspicious character" of widows, whether the *grihasthas* producing baby girls were "fallen" or not and the males sexually "weak," what the word "Vedic" really refers to, whether women equal to *shudras,* etc. There were many different quotes from the *shastras* and Srila Prabhupada on these topics, but what interested me the most were the words of wisdom spoken by various devotees. These words helped me reconfirm my intuition that we have to deal with things at a practical level, examine how we understand, or misunderstand, the philosophy, and apply, or misapply it, and the effect it has on our members, ISKCON as an institution, and the public in general.

I studied linguistics, the analysis of language, which made me aware of the importance and the power of words. That is why I choose a more scientific analytical approach rather than a philosophical one, even though the two are obviously linked.

A. The language of the anticult movement and other oppressive or repressive groups.

Since I am now working in the Communications Department I have read plenty of newspaper articles presenting "cults," new religious movements, and the Hare Krishna movement in particular, in very unkind and unfair terms. In France we even received the official label of being a "dangerous cult." I realized how difficult it is to get rid of the influence of negative designations and I read many reports showing how these designations have ruined people's lives and careers. Once someone has been labeled a member of a cult, the stigma seems to be very hard to remove, whether the accusations made were true or not.

So I thought that a brief analysis of the language of the anticult would be interesting to show the impact of the words we choose to describe someone or represent them.

I also listed expressions used by other oppressive or repressive groups to give further striking examples of the tactic of labeling people and groups.

1) Comparison of words used by the anticult movement to describe an established religion or a cult.

The word "religion" indicates something serious and respectable.	The word "cult" (or "sect") evokes something strange, unusual, weird, unauthorized, bizarre, irrational , or even dangerous.
A religion is spreading its influence.	A cult is proliferating (like a cloud of dangerous insects). People get contaminated by a cult. The influence of a cult is compared to a tidal wave (synonym of catastrophy, danger).
Proselytism	Propaganda
Believer (he is sincere)	Adept (it implies he chose the wrong path)
Priest, pastor, monk, rabbi, etc (respectful words)	Guru (genrally used in a demeaning way), charismatic leader, cheap messiah (self-proclamed, not legitimate).
Spiritual influence of the priest or pastor. Religious conversion. ransmission of religious values. Religious vocation	Mental manipulation. Brainwashing. Mind control. Mental destabilisation. Coercitive (by force) persuasion
Apostles, disciples	Accomplice (for criminal activities)
Catechetism (legitimate and honorable transmission to the children of religious ideas and values in which the parents believe)	Indoctrination Recruitment
Faith (it seems solid and sincere)	Belief (relative and subject to controversy, qualified as being outrageous and irrational), myths, legends
Lithurgy: Vesper, morning prayer, etc	Strange incantations, mascarades Weird nocturn rituals
Religious clothes and paraphernalia	Disguises, silly costumes, trinkets

2) Words used by different oppressive groups.

Group	Words used	Reality behind the words
Nazis	The final solution	Extermination and torture of millions of Jews in concentration camps.
Abortion	Tissue removal Voluntary ending a pregnancy	Cold blooded murder of the baby in the womb of the mother
American army during the Vietnam war	Hamlet pacification	Setting population on fire with napalm, torturing and killling men, women and children.
Anticult groups and deprogrammers	Deprogram	Kidnapping and violent actions (physical, sexual, mental and psychological) against people professing different faiths or ideas
Communists in Cambodia	Reeducation	Sending all the intellectuals to work in the rice fields and/or killing them by the thousands.

3. Consequences of using this language.

Mukunda Goswami made a few interesting remarks in his article "New Religious Movement is a four-letter word," the language of oppression (ICJ, Vol 3 N°2):

• Calling or labeling another person or group differently of the way he, she or they wish can wage **psychological warfare.**

• **People or groups that accept false labeling can lose important battles for their God-given rights,** even before a single shot is fired.

• In recent decades we invented hate words for citizens of other countries especially when "our country" was at war with them, we used slurs for racial and religious groups. Systematic and calculated misnaming and disinformation campaigns have become part of the century's shame.

Effects of the words and labeling tactics used by the anticult groups, the enemical governments and the medias in general.

• To deny, denigrate, insult, ridicule and blaspheme minority religions

• To create fear, hatred, intolerance, prejudice, and promote ignorance amongst the ignorant or innocent population

• To ruin the lives of individuals: it is very hard to recover from calumny as the wrong labels and harsh words used stick in the minds of the individual victim and of the public in general.

• To hide or justify atrocities committed against some groups: illegal actions, harassments, tortures, crimes, etc.

B) The use of language in ISKCON, especially in relation to women.

Before I present the lists I have compiled, I would like to stress that this kind of language is not used systematically in all ISKCON centers or by the majority of its members, but extremes behaviors did exist and still do, and all these examples are true. I chose the worse and most striking ones to make my point. Some derogatory words such as "fringie" have almost disappeared from the ISKCON scene, at least in some areas. I heard a few stories that made me think that what is going on in some temples in Eastern Europe now is what happened in the US and Western Europe around 20 years ago. In order to avoid an unhappy history to repeat itself, devotees must become aware of the way they speak to each other and about each other and present the philosophy.

1)   Derogatory or demeaning language used towards certain ISKCON groups.

Life situation	Language used
A devotee not agreeeing with the leaders' policies or decisions	an envious snake
Devotee living outside a temple	a fringie
A husband who is considerate to his wife, loving and caring	a henpecked husband
Children (spirit souls, devotees of God)	products of sex life
Any man who behaves normally towards women, is appreciative and supportive of them.	a man controlled by women
Acting as obnoxious jerks, pushing women, standing in front of them, being rude and disrespectful.	putting women in their place, being a real man, a real *brahmachari* (and not a lusty one)
Demeaning of women, not giving them participatory rights, giving them the worse facilities, treating them like little children, etc	protection of women

2)   Demeaning, derogatory language towards women: labeling and name calling.

Life situation	Language used
A woman (me) making a wrong maneuver while driving a car	stupid cow
A *sannyasi's* comment while looking at a group of female devotees	the herd of cows
Woman being fed up and angry	hysterical woman
11 year old girl not covering her head or women with problems living in the *ashram*	prostitute prostitute
Married women devotees whom the husband is preparing to leave to take *sannyasa*	hot piece of stool
Young *brahmacharinis* who want to get married	Maya devis
Sick *sankirtana* devotees needing rest (as addressed by a temple president)	witch, in *maya*
Young *brahmacharinis* who have been approached by male devotees for association for marriage, either through proper channels or directly	unchaste women of bad reputation
Women devotees who are doing full time temple service	half a person half a devotee
Older female devotees interested in retiring in the holy *dhama* (a swami's comment)	lusty, loose, licentious and lazy Western ladies
Dedicated and intelligent female devotees concerned about the welfare of women in ISKCON and the future of the preaching mission.	• women's libbers, women activists, • revolutionaries • frustrated women (in need of a man) • women who don't cover their heads • immature new women with problems • women needing 3 or 4 kids to cool down

Further analysis of the principle of scapegoatism and name calling:

A. *The principle: call the dog a bad name and hang him.*
    • Call a religious or alternative group a "cult" and oppress and persecute them.
    • Call the women "stupid, less intelligent, agents of *maya,* etc," and ignore, disrespect and abuse them.

B. *What does this accomplish?*

　　• By labeling people, we are discounting human beings and creating social rejection.

　　• We avoid facing our own imperfections and problems by accusing the other.

　　• We justify unethical or cruel behavior by hiding behind words.

　　• We avoid hearing what the other person has to say, or how he/she feels by hiding a disturbing reality behind technical words.

　　• We avoid taking personal responsibility for a situation.

　　• We create destructive results: emotional dammage, loss of self-esteem, fear, anxiety, depression, devotees leaving the movement or taking great distance from it, suicidal thoughts, etc.

3. Selective language.

　　By selective language I refer to the fact that some devotees and *Bhagavatam* speakers choose to quote only certain verses or emphasize specific words, at the detriment of all the others presented in the *shastras* or by Srila Prabhupada.

　　I will only give here a few brief examples to illustrate the principle without getting into any lengthy analysis.

a. *Most quoted words and expressions.*

　　• Women being the agent of maya, or maya personified, less intelligent, possessing the heart of a sly fox, lusty, untrustworthy, spiritually inferior and more materialistic.

　　• You cannot trust a woman or a politician (Canakya Pandita)

　　• Woman compared to a witch during the day and a tigress at night, by sucking the blood of the husband (*Bhag.* 5.14.3).

b. *Less quoted verses and expressions.*

　　• All the verses describing the good qualities of women: how she is the goddess of fortune, a great friend, more simple and devotional, the other half of a man, etc. An exhaustive list needs to be done.

　　• "When one is elevated to the plaform of Krishna consciousness, man or woman, everyone is equal."

c. *Incompletely quoted words and expressions, not always presented in the original context in which they were introduced.*

　　One example: <u>Women being less intelligent.</u>

　　• Srila Prabhupada said "generally."

　　• He said this applies to materialistic women, not devotees.

　　• He gave the following explanations:

"They are more prone to material enjoyment" (SB 3.23.54). However, by this definition, many men are also less intelligent.

• When they let themselves be exploited by men.

• Srila Prabhupada mentions many times that in Kali-yuga men are less intelligent than in former ages. Thus the question of whether statements about the relative intelligence of men and women apply at all in this age remains undecided.

• Srila Prabhupada uses that word in an archaic sense, as a synonym for "rational," whereas the modern meaning is "smart." Nobody is going to argue that men are more rational than women, but plenty would argue against the idea that men are smarter than women, since neither direct observation, nor *shastra,* nor Srila Prabhupada's activities give credence to such an idea.

• Psychologists say there are so many kinds of intelligence and so many kinds of intelligence tests.

4. Distortive language.

By distortive language I refer to the fact of giving correct and innocent words a subtle meaning and negative connotations. A good example of it is the word "mataji."

a. Original meaning and connotations of the word.

The word "mother" evokes many positive things: the first guru, love, care, affection, protection, understanding, comfort, etc.

b. Proper use ot the term.

By seeing all women, except one's wife, as mothers, men will develop respect and affection for them, because one is not supposed to feel lusty towards his mother or want to exploit her.

c. Negative connotations of the term.

Because of poor treatment of women and mothers in ISKCON, many women even came to the point of cringing when they were addressed with that term.

Men in ISKCON do not always treat women as mothers, because some of them might have treated their own mother rather poorly or their mothers treated them poorly.

With the institutionalization of the inferiority of women, the words "mataji," "mother" or "woman," became associated with some inferior status and a lot of negative qualities.

The word "matajis" is sometimes used to put women "back in their place," the back of the temple or some corner. Several times in ISKCON, I have seen thes kinds of signs: "Devotees" on this side, and "Women" or "Matajis" on the other.

What are the implications of this sort of language? As Radha dasi was observing, we thus marginalize women. This statement creates a psychological space in which women can be ranked a little bit lower than the rest of the Vaishnavas, who oddly enough, turn out to be all men. The language creates a space in which this minimization of women is possible. Clearly, not everybody uses these statements in a negative way, but those of us who are immature and have not completely overcome their conditioning naturally find those spaces and take advantage of them.

Intonation alone, coupled with unfriendly facial expressions, can also convey a very derogatory meaning to a very innocent word.

5. Words in need of a definition.

Many words we use in ISKCON need a very clear definition, such as the word "Vedic." Even amongst scholars of religion, there are endless debates going on about its meaning. As Radha dasi pointed out in her presentation in Los Angeles, so far ISKCON has failed to define this term. To some extent, it means "in line with the purposes and teachings of the *Vedas*," but ISKCON must more clearly articulate how the *Vedas* describe women's roles. So far, ISKCON spokespersons have failed to address the plurality of women's roles described in our own texts, focusing only on one or two examples from one or two women's stories. Currently, the term has a more common usage as a substitute for the phrase "vaguely historical." Women are often told that they cannot lead kirtan, for instance, because it would not be Vedic for them to do so, in spite of the example of women in our own *sampradaya* who have done so.

In one of the famous purports glorifying the preaching efforts of his lady disciples (Cc. *Adi-lila,* Chapter 7, verse 32) "These girls are not ordinary girls, they are as good as their brothers preaching Krishna consciousness," Srila Prabhupada indicates that the test of a woman's participation role being appropriate or not is not whether it is Vedic or not, but whether or not it helps spread Krishna consciousness.

Even though ISKCON is not really clear about the meaning of the word "Vedic," it has been used in specific contexts, usually to get women to become humble, submissive, and cooperative, or to prevent them from rendering certain services and taking positions of responsibility. It seems that the term has been used in political ways, sometimes very inconsistently, when the men wanted to achieve a specific result from women. For example, women were prevented from leading kirtans in the temple, because it was not Vedic, but nobody objected when these same ladies were sent on "*sankirtana*" to collect donations by flirting with men and pinning a flower on their suit while speaking sweet words, running the risk of being raped on door to door, running around dark parking lots or going to sinister bars at night to get donations. I used to do some of these things and go out with another tall black lady, who was carrying a knife and a club, in case of some attack. In case you have in mind an image of the perfect "Vedic woman," I am sure she would not match that dream picture.

Here are a couple of true stories to show you how words and philosophy can get perverted by immature and unscrupulous people.

shine and gain respect, ISKCON leaders will better understand the needs of devotees and how to care for them. They'll find that instead of valuing projects of people (and consequently losing members and support), they'll have successful projects filled with happy, committed devotees. The genuine caring of women will extinguish the fire of anger, sadness, frustration, and hopelessness shared by many who have left our association. Even one small step – putting women on the GBC – will bring balance and heart to high-level discussions.

The vision put forward by speakers at the women's conference of an ISKCON where men and women work side-by-side with redoubled strength to spread Krishna consciousness, an ISKCON where women and men perform responsible preaching services according to their abilities, propensities, and level of Krishna consciousness. The vision reveals an ISKCON that has broken through incorrect stereotypes and distorted philosophy to respect the integrity of women; an ISKCON where women give *Bhagavatam* class, lead *kirtans*, serve on the GBC, initiate disciples; an ISKCON where women are no longer stifled and use their natural talents and abilities to give ISKCON unity, strength, and enthusiasm.

Give full participation to women, and we at once significantly increase our preaching force. Empower the women, and those who have left or resigned themselves to the status quo become enlivened to take part. We can practically double our strength overnight with this one strategy. What intelligent manager – spiritualist or materialist – wouldn't be willing to pay what's needed to get such a quick result?

Women have shown all over the world that they can be as intelligent and competent as men. Unless ISKCON acknowledges and values this reality, it will not gain the respect and participation of intelligent women or men.

Women bring to humanity a required element – heart. They also bring unity to the social structure. Krishna says in the first chapter of *Bhagavad-gita* that women are essential to the spiritual progress of society. As one half of the married couple, they support the preaching of the renunciants, an arrangement that would greatly benefit ISKCON today. How much further could ISKCON have progressed if we hadn't ignored this important principle?

If we choose to ignore this common sense, and instead make women feel unwanted, devalued, and unempowered, then everyone loses. Women lose their inspiration, their hopes, their dreams of serving Krishna to their full potential. And the whole society loses. When we stifle the women, children's needs are unmet and they become unprotected, even abused. We lost women's natural contribution of nurturing, balancing, and bonding the social structure. We reduce our effectiveness to resist negative forces from outside and even within ISKCON. We commit offenses, and our spiritual lives suffer. We lose the support of people who know you can judge a society by how it treats its women and children. And we don't gain new members when people can't quite reconcile the philosophy of Krishna consciousness with what they see practiced socially.

We've read and heard the point many times: all souls are equal. Even a newcomer will at once recognize this basic tenet of our philosophy. Yet, this has conflicted with ISKCON policy and unspoken laws.

We have too often heard scriptural verses about women quoted only to disparage them. How do we apply shastric statements about women? With full realization of all the imports of *shastra*, just as Srila Prabhupada showed us. Srila Prabhupada engaged women in all temple functions – offerings *aratis*, leading *kirtans*, giving *Srimad-Bhagavatam* class. He authorized the women's participation at all levels of managerial service, from temple president to GBC. And he wanted women to function as spiritual leaders and to initiate disciples ("all my sons and daughters").

If we are honest and compassionate, we will be happy to see to it that women devotees are offered the same facilities as men. We will want to see the spark of Krishna consciousness in our young girls fanned and encouraged. We will be happy to see girls growing up in the movement, thankful to be able to fully take part in Krishna consciousness. We will be impressed and encouraged to see highly intelligent women from all walks of life helping the movement, and relived to know that our godsisters feel protected and safe. We will see a decline in outside propaganda trying to make ISKCON look like a cult, and we will feel the benefits of having a true spiritual family.

We will see the truth in Srila Prabhupada's statement that girls are as good as boys in spreading Krishna consciousness movement. And we will grasp how brilliant he was to engage women in preaching, and how important that is for our movement's observers to see.

Pulling all the elements of the formula together, we gain the inspiration to reinstate women devotees to the position Srila Prabhupada gave them: valuable spiritual participants in a worldwide effort to bring people back to their constitutional position as servants of the Supreme Personality of Godhead, Sri Krishna.

The women's conference was more than a gathering of like-minded people. I hope it will be seen as a momentous event that forever changed the position of women in ISKCON. I hope we can look back and see how well that change served ISKCON's preaching and all devotees – men, women, and children.

As one *sannyasi* put it, "By putting forward the fact of this matter, the women are bringing the men back to Krishna consciousness, where we have strayed in this regard. We should thank the women for this."

One male devotee who wanted to go see a prostitute was asking his wife to be "Vedic" by allowing him to do so; she would have thus followed in the footsteps of that great devotee often quoted as a most chaste lady, because she accepted to do menial service for a prostitute so that her husband could use her services without any cost on his part.

Bir Krishna Maharaja recounts how he was accused of being non-Vedic, weird, disobedient to Prabhupada's instructions and deviating from Krishna consciousness, just because his eating habits happened to be different from other people and he could not take his meals in the middle of the day.

So much for the word "Vedic"!

6. Unspoken language.

a. *The Mayapur samadhi:*
• The *pushpa samadhi* of our founder-*acharya*, His Divine A. C. Bhaktivedanta Swami Prabhupada, is certainly one of the most important memorials in ISKCON. Unfortunately it seems to convey a rather negative unspoken message since the bas-relief going around the *samadhi* representing the *sankirtana* movement of Lord Chaitanya features hundreds of men (1,071, I counted them), 8 women and 3 children, even though the original photos from which the paintings were done had women in them. We do not want to minimize the hard labor and sincerity of the artists who executed this work, but we wonder how such a mistake happened in such a prominent pilgrimage place which will become the spiritual capital of the world. Many devotees have commented on it and expressed their shock and surprise.

What is the unspoken message to all the women in ISKCON, most of them very actively engaged in the *sankirtana* movement of Lord Chaitanya?

• You do not count because you have the wrong kind of body
• Tough luck, girls, you are not fortunate enough to have a male body in this life. Hopefully you'll get one in your next life.
• You are not valued.
• All your hard work and sacrifices on *sankirtana* (usually refering to collecting lots of *laksmi*) do not mean anything to us.
• You are not part of the movement of Lord Chaitanya.
• You do not exist.
• You should not exist.

b. *ISKCON publications.*

At one time, ISKCON reviews and magazines were only or mainly portraying male devotees, and usually the *brahmachari* or *sannyasi* section. Happily in general, things have changed over the years.

c. *Bodily language.*

It is said that action speaks louder than words. Unfortunately we have seen many rude gestures and behaviors towards women in our movement.

• Men snapping fingers at their wives or other ladies, to order them to do something.

• Rude gestures to indicate that someone should move to a different location.

• Men not opening doors for ladies with bags, boxes, or babies.

• Men abruptly closing the door in front of women, as they are going in or out.

• Men sitting in the space usually reserved for the women.

• Men obstructing the view of the *murtis* for the women (when they could stand someplace else and still see Them also).

C. Why these language problems in ISKCON are serious ones?

1. The treatment of women in ISKCON is one of the main points the anticult movement strongly objects to.

The anticult people have valid reasons to be alarmed.

a. *What they see and hear going on in some ISKCON temples (what have just been described).*

• By systematically using negative and derogatory expressions, one commits verbal abuse, which has serious psychological repercussions already listed above; a person may even start to believe all these negative things and identify with them.

• Verbal abuse is often followed by physical abuse. Unfortunately there are many cases of wife beating in devotees families.

b. *What they have heard about India and the situation of women there*

To some extent it is true that India has a cultural bias towards women. When people hear these strong statements made in ISKCON without proper explanations and understanding, they might think that our books also represent this cultural bias and it simply reinforces all the negative things they have heard taking place in India.

• Women being treated as servants or sometimes slaves to men and their husbands.

• Men usually being given preference in the family (general facilities, education, access to food and clothing, medical facilities, etc).

• Women having no freedom or power to decide for themselves.

• Women being killed and tortured in many ways because of the dowry system.

- Baby girls being killed in or outside the womb.
- The ancient *sati* rite still being forced sometimes upon unwilling women (there was a time when women entered the fire willingly, but due to abuses, this practice has been made illegal by the British.)

2. We have institutionalized the crude and rude behavior of men towards women.

Hridayananda Maharaja spoke very eloquently on that topic. The following is just a summary of the points he made at the last Women Ministry's conference in Los Angeles.

- When devotees joined the Krishna consciousness movement, they also rejected a lot of simple normal culture, like being a gentleman, being kind, and compassionate. At the beginning of the movement, there was respect and affection betwen men and women, then things began to change.
- Somehow some men thought and are still thinking that it is not bona fide to be nice to women; they are not a man if they do it; they are supposed to play this role, to be obnoxious, rude, crude, and inconsiderate, and that is the proof that they are not lusty.
- It is a false idea to think that you can conquer lust by despising women. You think that you will not fall down if you despise a woman enough and so you pump yourself up, cultivating hatred and hostility towards women. This false idea of conquering lust like that has totally failed and everyone knows that the men who are the most adverse to women are the ones who are going to fall the hardest.
- The real way to conquer lust is by learning to offer all respects to women. If you feel reverence for women as your mother and feel deep respect, you will conquer lust. Because you cannot simultaneously respect someone and want to exploit them. The opposite of exploitation is a desire to serve."

Happily there is hope in that area as we see that things have improved over the years.

Hridayananda Maharaja's experience of going around the temples and having *ishthaghostis* with the men was that they felt quite relieved that someone finally told them it was bona fide to be a gentleman and many of them even thanked him. The men want to be devotees and do the right thing but they adopted an illusion and they have been taught the wrong thing.

3. We are creating obstacles to the preaching of ISKCON.

This derogatory language and negative attitudes towards women is very detrimental to the preaching.

- It is not based on the philosophy: we are not these bodies, the greatest devotees are Krishna are the *gopis* and Radharani is in charge of Goloka.

- Intelligent men and women are turned off.
- It is Vaishnavi *aparadha*.
- Devotees are embarassed to bring intelligent people to the movement or the temples.
- We might mainly attract men who already have bad feelings towards women.

4. We are insulting Srila Prabhupada's character.

Women have been and are being insulted or ill- treated because of our lack of understanding the fundamental principles of our philosophy taught to us by Srila Prabhupada. To even imply that Srila Prabhupada would in any way accept or condone the mistreatment of women in our society is to insult and defame his character and morality. A true Vaishnava cannot tolerate the infliction of harm on any other living being, what to speak of another Vaishnava. Jyotirmayi dasi in her report and many other lady disciples of Srila Prabhupada can tell you how Srila Prabhupada treated them, with love, affection, respect, and encouragements.

Some male members in ISKCON expressed the belief that Srila Prabhupada said that "you can beat a wife and a *mridanga*." One male member even believed that our Vaishnava etiquette permits wife beating as long as he used a lether belt on her back or a sapling on her legs. We can see how some misguided and misinformed members of our movement quote Srila Prabhupada to justify their abuse. Srila Prabhupada may have quoted that common saying, but to imply that he was endorsing such action is misleading and dangerous.

5. We are doing the same thing anticult groups are doing against the Hare Krishna movement: using derogatory language.

How can we expect to be treated fairly as a movement when we ourselves use the same unfair tactics towards a group of people inside our movement?

Recently one honest reporter confessed to one of our leaders that he could not use friendly words when describing us, otherwise he might lose his job and be labeled a cult lover or supporter. Similarly some men in ISKCON wrongly think that they cannot speak nicely to and of women (their wives, co-workers, etc), without loosing their face and reputation and be called a dancing dog in the hands of women, someone controlled by the fair sex, lusty, in other words not a real man.

The same element of bad faith can be found in the anticult and some men in ISKCON: they select only what fits their purpose or hidden agenda, whether consciously or not, and ignore all the rest.

D. Practical Suggestions for Improvements.

Here are a few humble suggestions I am making. Your suggestions are also welcomed of course.

We can then discuss these together, as well as the means to implement them.

1) Understand correctly the *shastra's* and Srila Prabhupada's strong statements.

The fact is that there are strong statements in the *Bhagavatam* and other *shastras* about women, made by the speakers in the *shastras* or Srila Prabhupada in his purports. Unfortunately we have some devotees in ISKCON who now think that the bad treatment towards women is justified in the philosophy, and they will quote these strong statements to justify them. Even though the mass of ISKCON devotees do not think like that happily, they may wonder what to do with these strong statements.

Here are a few alternatives.

a. Reject these statements and the whole philosophy with them.

Some people will throw out the whole philosophy of Krishna consciousness because of reading or hearing some of these strong statements. This points out the need to correctly understand these statements, present and explain them properly, in a faithful but palatable way. Obviously most devotees will not reject statements coming from the scriptures or Srila Prabhupada, or try to change what he gave us, but they are sometimes perplexed or confused about what to make of them.

b. Figure out ways to get around what Srila Prabhupada said.

It is a tricky thing to do for sure and could be dangerous for one's spiritual life because it leaves room for interpretation, choosing and picking what one likes to hear and rejecting the rest.

c. Find ways to understand what Srila Prabhupada said in a way that is not offensive to the women or to Srila Prabhupada himself.

This is what I have been trying to do all these years in ISKCON. I was thus very happy when I heard Hridayananda Maharaja formulating it in a clear manner. So I will more or less repeat what he said on this topic in Los Angeles.

• Some generalizations are valid, otherwise you could not have a *varnashrama* system, you could not classify people's external propensities according to certain standards.

• The way he understands a lot of these heavy statements is that they are the worse cases. If you make a list of all the strong statements about men, you'll find very quickly: they're hogs, dogs, camels, asses, and many other things. Just the way the Vedic literature is presented in terms of Sanskrit and Srila Prabhupada's English, whenever heavy statements are made about the stupidity and sinfulness of human beings, it is the masculine that is used. It says that the men have all these bad qualities, so they take the brunt of that also.

• In practice we see that there are many great women. It cannot be the case that Srila Prabhupada or the *Bhagavatam* want us to think that these great women like Kunti, or Draupadi, or other Vaishnavis present in this conference, are lusty, greedy, envious and so on. Obviously that is not the conclusion we are meant to come to.

So Hridayananda Maharaja's personal understanding is that although some generalization must be valid (otherwise there could not be coherence or sanity in the world), these generalisations are exceptions, and they are the worse case scenario: if a man or woman gives in to their lower propensities, that is what it can lead to. Obviously these heavy statements do not apply to Vaishnavis or to Vaishnavas.

2) Follow Srila Prabhupada's example.

Try to absorb his mood (caring, compassionate, encouraging, equal vision), adopt his attitudes and behavior.

3) Compile a booklet of words, expressions and clichīs in need of a definition or explanation.

Briefly analyze the different contexts in which these words were presented and make a synopsis of it in the light of all the other statements made by Srila Prabhupada on the topic, his own personal example, basic psychology, our preaching tactics, sheer common sense and human decency.

Here is a partial list of expressions that require investigation:
• Women are like children
• The Vedic woman
• You can beat a wife and a *mridanga*
• You cannot trust a woman or a politician
• Women are less intelligent
• Women are ten times more lusty than men
• How Madhavi was half a devotee of Lord Chaitanya
• Why widows are considered inauspicious

4) Encourage male lecturers to follow certain guidelines.

• **Speakers should avoid derogatory words and expressions towards women: stop the denigration of the feminine principle and qualities.** The *Bhagavatam* class or any other lecture is not a forum to let out one's personal frustrations and feelings.

• **Speakers should try to make balanced presentations: not focusing exclusively on negative aspects of certain class of people.**

Srila Prabhupada often said that woman is *maya* for men and man is *maya* for women. It is always good to keep the balance and not focus exclusively on one group, especially when many women still do not get the opportunity to give *Bhagavatam* classes and express themselves.

• Speakers should define their words and put them in the right contexts, instead of making sweeping generalizations.

• Male speakers should avoid making fun in a covert way of ladies having problems.

Conclusion

There is a definite need in ISKCON to watch out for our language, analyze it, understand it, and rectify it when necessary. The psychology of a population, a group or an individual is revealed very clearly in his vocabulary. Our vocabulary is revealing who we are: loving and compassionate people, true Vaishnavas and transcendentalists, or bigotted, hard hearted, narrow-minded, and sectarian people.

I will end with a couple of relevant quotes.

"Nothing so violently opposes men against each other as the fact of putting opposed realities behind the same words."

"It happens very often that men kill each other for words they do not understand. They would embrace each other if they could understand each other." Anatole France

So let's keep on trying to understand Srila Prabhupada, the *shastras* and also each other. We might not all end up embracing each other, but we will make ISKCON a better place and what Krishna and Srila Prabhupada intended it to be.

Hare Krishna!

Second Annual Women's Ministry Conference
Alachua, Florida
September 25-30, 1998

The Women's Ministry was established to encourage the service and association of Vaishnavis, and to bring forward the voices of each devotee in a safe and supportive environment.

In a materialistic society the "important" voices are those that hold power. They are the voices that are given a platform, as they are the decision makers. It was our intention, however, to hear from a wide array of Vaishnavis and share our devotional understandings, our service experiences, and our cares and woes. In essence, we wanted to provide a forum for each Vaishnavi to feel connected and valued through discussion, thought, and interaction.

It was so encouraging to put these principles into action. We found that everyone had something relevant and thought provoking to share. Rather than generating dissension and dissatisfaction, as some may assert would be the purpose of a women's conference, we found deep gratitude, appreciation, and integrity. Everyone had something to share, something to give, and that enriched our hearts and minds.

This five-day event was held from September 25-30, 1998 and nearly 300 Vaishnavis attended. On September 25, 26, and 27 twenty-seven seminars were offered. The following day was a retreat at the local springs with swimming, reading, kirtan, and a bonfire as well as activities for children. The final two days of the retreat were reserved for the conference.

Vaishnavis had flown and driven in from across the United States. If you look over the presentations (see the Appendixes for the brochure we printed) you will see just how varied and encompassing the presentations were, as well as how competent the speakers were.

There were entrepreneurial discussions, managerial presentations, hands-on-service activities, and talks on how to run an effective household. There were presentations on the struggles single women faced, discussions on how to have a happy marriage, and what it meant to be a renounced woman in our Society. There were voices of advocacy, voices of chastity, voices of gentleness, voices of strength, voices of wisdom, and voices of care: men's voices and women's voices. There was also great prasadam, kirtan, *appreciations, and a day for everyone at the springs.*

This conference generated a mood of loving exchange and gratitude in service and association. It also highlighted the wide array of God-given talent and propensities in the Vaishnavi community. There is room for everyone in devotional service, as long as we value, rather than compare and compete. If any member of our Society feels disenfranchised, we suffer. It is our weakest link, not our strongest, that will break the heart of our community. We need to always include, hear, value, and understand the voices and experiences of every member.

We had a fantastic time together. And everyone went home strengthened and enlivened in their individual services.

Of the twelve presentations made at the two-day conference, we present here three papers by Radha dasi, Burke Rochford, and Visakha dasi, as well as a news report.

Fundamental Human Rights in ISKCON
by Radha devi dasi

This paper was published by the International Cultic Studies Association (ICSA) *in 2001. But Radha's initial draft was presented at the 1998 ISKCON Women's Conference under the name "Krishna Conscious Rights and Responsibilities: The Relationship Between Individuals and ISKCON." Although this sounds like an official document, it was not one that was presented to or accepted by ISKCON's managerial body.*

As ISKCON looks to solidify its institutional machinery, it will need to look very seriously, at the relationship between the institution and its individual members. ISKCON is a young society and is in the process of development towards maturity. Radha devi dasi examines some of the problems that arise if the relationship between the individual and the institution are not solidified in a formal contract, she argues that every member of the Society should be secure and protected in their execution of service to the Society. She presents a Bill of Rights for discussion that may begin the process to help fulfill this purpose.

Everyone has an equal right to execute devotional service. That is the platform of oneness and the basis for a classless society.[1]

Oppression is not a spiritual phenomenon. Yet, the history of organised religion abounds with examples of oppression in various forms at various times. From early

Christian martyrs to the Spanish Inquisition, from the Salem witch trials to abuses of the caste system and the treatment of "untouchables" in India, there has always been a risk of oppression in the name of God.

Research shows that there are certain universal factors that cause or contribute to oppression within institutions and nations, and there is also firm evidence that legal structures in the form of Human Rights can minimize the tendency toward oppression. For these reasons, a Declaration of Fundamental Human Rights for the protection of both the institution and the members of the Society would benefit the Society.

Oppression is defined as an "unjust or cruel exercise of authority or power".[2] We must guard against oppressive behavior in our Society. We understand as devotees, that oppression is a phenomenon of Kali-yuga, the age of quarrel and hypocrisy in which we now reside, rather than being a symptom of religion. In fact, *Srimad-Bhagavatam* predicts that the age of Kali will be characterized by a lack of justice. As H.H. Hridayananda Swami points out:

"Already in many nations justice is available only to those who can pay and fight for it. In a civilized state, every man, woman and child must have equal and rapid access to a fair system of laws. In modern times we sometimes refer to this as Human Rights. Certainly Human Rights are one of the more obvious casualties of the age of Kali."[3]

Unfortunately, many of us have had an opportunity to observe the "unjust or cruel exercise of authority or power" within our Society. Vulnerable groups, particularly women and children, have been neglected and abused in numerous ways, which allegedly range from dismaying to truly abominable. The purpose of this article is not to catalogue or recount the various injustices that have been perpetrated by individuals acting in the name of ISKCON. Although naming the abuse is a vital step in eliminating the wrongs, that important task has been and continues to be done in other places.

However, we must go further than simply identifying the behaviors we wish to change. To some extent, we have been naive in believing that sincerity alone could rectify the abuses which we seek to eradicate. We must address the underlying causes of the abuse if we are to arrive at meaningful solutions.

From a psychological point of view, oppression and other forms of injustice spring from a separateness of vision that is based on material conditioning. A necessary precondition to abusing others is learning to see those others as fundamentally different from oneself. The *Srimad-Bhagavatam*, one of our main scriptures, describes this phenomenon as *prthak-drstih*, which Srila Prabhupada translates as "the vision of duality".[4] In the related purport, Srila Prabhupada explains that this dual vision is the result of material conditioning, which causes one to identify with the body, rather than with one's identity as a servant of Krishna. Perceptions based on body, Srila Prabhupada writes, cause one to think in terms of "my body, my wife, my child, my home." Such perceptions permit us to see others as objects of our own enjoyment rather than as servants of the Lord.

This ability to artificially separate oneself from others is the root of oppression. Scholars have noted that one of the common roots of racial, gender and animal oppression is the use of linguistic devices that put the oppressed group into a different category from the oppressor.[5] Carol Adams writes that oppression involves a three-part cycle of objectification, fragmentation and consumption; it is the first stage, objectification, which begins the process of rationalizing unjust treatment.[6]

Animals are objectified by language that treats them as objects rather than as living entities. For instance, we eat "beef" rather than "cows." This objectification permits us to avoid the truth about our actions. The second stage, fragmentation, can be symbolic or literal. In the case of animals, they are literally fragmented in the butchering process. We then deal with "chops" and "joints" rather than living creatures. We say "I am having pork chops for dinner" rather than "I'm having a pig for dinner." The final stage of the process, consumption, occurs when we have so divorced ourselves from the real identity of other beings that we can abuse them. This abuse takes the form of literal consumption in the case of animals.

These three processes may be more symbolic, but no less harmful, in the case of humans. For instance, the Nazis successfully objectified European Jews, convincing other European citizens that the Jews did not deserve the protection of Civil Law because they were less than human. The Nazis then used fragmentation to isolate the Jews physically and psychologically from the rest of the population. The Jews were then "consumed" by the Nazis in the concentration camps. Objectification begins a process which permits fragmentation, both within society and on a concrete, individual level. The final step in the cycle, consumption, occurs when the oppressed being is seen as a mere possession for the enjoyment of the oppressor. Such vision could support acts such as rape and murder.[7]

While ISKCON is a society founded on spiritual truth, we are not exempt from material influences that plague other institutions. In particular, we sometimes suffer from the same separateness of vision that leads to oppression in the larger society: we witness a separation of vision from the principles of our philosophy, to our actual practice of faith. For instance, when we speak of the society outside our own institution, we have our own jargon that both isolates us and condemns those who are not members of our organization. Those outside our movement are called "*karmis*," "demons," "*mlecchas*" and "*shudra*." We describe ourselves as "devotees," "Vaishnavas," "*devas*" and "*brahmanas*."[8] These labels shape our vision of others and ourselves in ways that divide us from the very people we are trying to reach.

Language is also used to marginalize those who oppose the current power structure. For instance, anyone unsatisfied with the local status quo can be labeled as "in *maya*".[9] When one is "in *maya*" one's integrity, intelligence and loyalty to ISKCON are automatically suspect and many temple communities feel no compunction regarding harsh or unfair treatment of someone who is "in *maya*". It is ironic that many of the positions and policies that are in favor today were dismissed as being "in *maya*" ten years ago. Moreover, we must not isolate ourselves from constructive reform, otherwise those elements of our Society that are marginalized will resort to more disruptive methods of ensuring that their voices are heard within the Society. For this reason we must build the institutional framework that allows all of our members to have their voices heard and their needs met. A Bill of Rights for every member is one of the first steps to meeting this objective.

Similarly, our language divides male and female members of our movement. When we say "devotees and matajis," (devotees and mothers) as we frequently do, we place women in a category separate from devotees. We may use or at least sanction by listening to others use derogatory names for women such as "witch," "*maya-devis*"[10] with "no souls" and "razor like hearts." One of the most telling examples of this phenomenon is found in *Srila Prabhupada Lilamrta* where the presence of devotees at one event is described by listing the names of the men present and adding "and their wives" at the end to acknowledge the presence of the female attendees. Thus, in one of the official histories of our movement, women have been, at least at times, robbed of their individual identities. This use of language , which in many cases is benignly motivated, facilitates the dangerous process of objectification.

Objectification poses a particular difficulty for religious organizations seeking to eliminate oppressive behavior. That difficulty is the tendency of religious institutions to transform customary behavior into sacred behavior. For instance, in many Christian churches during the 1960s the use of musical instruments such as guitars or drums, in preference to the traditional church organ, were viewed as heretical, in spite of the fact that the Christian religion did not prohibit the use of any particular musical instrument for worship.

Similarly, women in ISKCON face enormous difficulties in eliminating the "women in the back" policy in some of our gender segregated temple rooms in spite of the fact that ISKCON's original policy permitted men and women to stand on different sides of the temple room with equal access to the altar.[11] Part of the resistance to changing that policy is the mistaken belief that the "women in the back" is the traditional policy when, in fact, it is not a traditional practice in Vrindavan, India, nor is it the policy implemented by Srila Prabhupada. In ISKCON, as in other religious institutions, unjust behavior may be codified and protected in the mistaken belief that such behavior is spiritual. Hence, the material process of objectification can pose a special danger for religious institutions.

I do not contend that we must always avoid distinctions between groups, or that we cannot engage in evaluations of our members. Such distinctions and evaluations are a necessary part of operating an international organization. However, I hold that we require some structural limits on our power to distinguish and label. In the absence of such limits, as we have discovered to our cost, power can sometimes become abusive.

Human rights provide one measure of protection from abuse of power. While classification of people into different groups is a necessary part of a social institution, the presence of certain fundamental entitlements that are available equally to everyone will help to prevent classification from becoming objectification and oppression.

Fundamental Human Rights are entirely consistent with Vaishnava philosophy. Srila Prabhupada himself recognized the existence of universal rights. In fact, he went so far as to stress that there are certain rights belonging to both human and non-human living entities. In a lecture he gave in Johannesburg, South Africa, in 1975, Srila Prabhupada told his followers that all living entities have a birthright to use sufficient economic resources to maintain life. He said that a failure to understand this right springs from material conditioning.[12]

Srila Prabhupada also taught that human beings have equal spiritual rights to opportunities for advancing in the service of Krishna. The Gaudiya Math, the institution in which Srila Prabhupada took initiation, has been considered controversial for preaching a doctrine that holds that those born in *varnas* (social positions) outside brahminical society can be given *brahmana* initiation. Srila Prabhupada was criticized by spiritual practitioners in India who held that non-Indians could never become *brahmana*s. In defence of his practice of initiating non-Indians, Srila Prabhupada said that all living entities have a right to serve Krishna and to make advancement in Krishna consciousness. In a lecture he gave in Toronto, Canada in 1976, Srila Prabhupada told his disciples that these rights apply to both female and male disciples.[13]

Thus, it is not the existence of fundamental Human Rights that are at issue in ISKCON, but the nature of those rights. Nor can we ignore, however, the practical effects of the policies we adopt. The type of rights we integrate into our social fabric will have a profound impact on the type of society we form.

Systems of governance that do not grant Human Rights, however well intentioned, are systems with little accountability. Adding Human Rights to a system of governance creates a standard against which a leader's conduct can be measured. Human rights are a codification of a leader's duties to his or her followers and help to hold that leader accountable for his actions. Open societies in which rights are granted are more stable and productive societies with less conflict, and with fewer behaviors that are destructive to other groups and to the environment as a whole than are societies that fail to grant such rights.[14] Adopting a declaration of Human Rights will help ISKCON to become a more productive and stable society.

A system of fundamental Human Rights is consistent with a spiritual philosophy based on surrender. In fact, surrender, submission, and humility are internal qualities that cannot be legislated. Any attempt to use institutional structures to impose the external appearance of these qualities would result in oppression as well as foolish and ineffective policy.

Srila Prabhupada's descriptions of submission and surrender clarify the voluntary nature of these qualities. In these descriptions Srila Prabhupada explains that devotees can offer their submission to Krishna in three ways. He writes that one can surrender by offering prayers, humbly submitting oneself, or by desiring some stage of perfection.[15]

All three of these processes are voluntary. Similarly, Srila Prabhupada often cited Arjuna's voluntary surrender to Krishna in the second chapter of the *Bhagavad-gita* as the perfect example of the quality of submission. His words make clear that submission is an internal quality that transforms the attitude and external behavior of an individual and has to be cultivated by each member. For this reason, submission cannot be legislated by our Society. Hence, the grant of Human Rights is consistent with the spiritual qualities we seek to acquire.

The Declaration of Fundamental Human Rights which follows is a proposal intended to begin discussion on this issue. No one person can define the rights that our Society should adopt. However, it is my hope that the members of ISKCON can work together to create institutional safeguards which will protect us from the mistakes we have made in the past. Rights to participate freely in the activities of our Society are essential to creating the vital and productive society that will be most pleasing to Srila Prabhupada.

DECLARATION OF MEMBERS' RIGHTS FOR THE INTERNATIONAL SOCIETY FOR KRISHNA CONSCIOUSNESS

Whereas, recognition of the inherent dignity and of the equal and inalienable rights of all living beings is a fundamental tenet of Vaishnava philosophy;

Whereas, compassion and mercy are essential qualities of Vaishnavas;

Whereas, disregard and contempt for the rights of living beings have resulted in injurious acts (both inside and outside the Hare Krishna movement) which outrage the conscience of all compassionate beings; and

Whereas, it is essential to the continued existence of ISKCON that we promote loving relations between all Vaishnavas and Vaishnavis;

Now therefore, we adopt the following Bill of Rights for all of the members of ISKCON:

Article 1

All human beings are born free and equal in dignity and rights. They are all members of Krishna's family endowed with reason and conscience and should act toward one another in a spirit of love and compassion.

Article 2

Membership in ISKCON is available to all people who desire such membership and who agree to the conditions of such membership. No one shall be denied membership in ISKCON on the basis of race, national or social origin, language, birth status or gender.

Article 3
Every member of ISKCON is entitled to all the rights and freedoms set forth in this Declaration, without distinction on the basis of race, national or social origin, language, birth status, age, gender, or identity of the member's initiating guru as long as that guru is authorized by ISKCON to give initiation.

Article 4
Every member of ISKCON has the right to freedom from violence, torture, cruel or degrading treatment and abuse. It is the duty of ISKCON leaders to provide environments that are free from violence, torture, cruel or degrading treatment and abuse.

Article 5
ISKCON is a voluntary society and no member of ISKCON shall be held in a condition of involuntary service.

Article 6
All members of ISKCON are equal before the law and are entitled without any discrimination to equal protection of the laws which govern our Society.

Article 7
Every member of ISKCON has the right to an effective remedy by ISKCON's Governing Body Commission (GBC) for acts violating the fundamental rights granted him or her under this Declaration.

Article 8
No member of ISKCON shall be subjected to any arbitrary sanction or punishment by any ISKCON authority.

Article 9
Every member of ISKCON is entitled in full equality to a fair hearing by an independent and impartial tribunal in the determination of his or her rights and obligations in relationship to ISKCON.

Article 10
No member of ISKCON shall have his or her membership rights in ISKCON limited or terminated without a full and fair hearing by an independent and impartial tribunal. It is essential to such a full and fair hearing that the accused ISKCON member be given (a)

reasonable notice of the hearing, (b) the opportunity to present witnesses and evidence on his or her own behalf, and (c) the opportunity to confront the witnesses and evidence against him or her.

Article 11
Every member of ISKCON shall have the right to freedom of movement and residence. Every temple dependent resident member shall have the right to leave his or her temple *ashrama* for the purpose of establishing his own separate residence at any time. However, any ISKCON member who seeks residence in a temple *ashrama* must abide by the rules of that *ashrama*, including the rules of admission to that *ashrama*.

Article 12
Every member of ISKCON who is of full legal age, without any limitation due to race, national or social origin, language, birth status, gender or religion, shall have the right to marry and to found a family.

Both male and female members of ISKCON are entitled to equal rights under ISKCON and secular law as to marriage, during marriage, and at its dissolution. However, this article does not itself create any right to dissolve a marriage.

Marriage shall be entered into only with the free and full consent of the intending spouses.

The family is the natural and fundamental group unit of society and is entitled to protection by ISKCON.

Article 13
Motherhood and childhood are entitled to special care and assistance. It is the duty of ISKCON leaders to provide protection to the women and children in their area. It is also the duty of ISKCON leaders to provide resources and programs for the development and enrichment of the children in ISKCON.

Article 14
Every member of ISKCON shall have the right to freedom of thought and conscience. While ISKCON leaders may place reasonable restrictions on a member's public expression of ideas which conflict with ISKCON's position, no member of ISKCON shall be sanctioned for ideas or beliefs which differ from official ISKCON positions or for ideas or beliefs which contradict those of ISKCON leaders. However, this provision shall not prevent ISKCON from requiring that its members ascribe to ISKCON's official positions in order to hold leadership positions.

Article 15
Every member of ISKCON shall be entitled to such education and service opportunities as

will assist his or her full development in Krishna consciousness without discrimination on the basis of race, national or social origin, language, birth status, gender, or identity of the member's initiating guru as long as that guru is authorized by ISKCON to give initiation.

Article 16

Every temple dependent resident member of ISKCON shall be entitled to a standard of living adequate for the health and well-being of himself or herself and his or her family, including food, clothing, housing and medical care, rest, and necessary social services, and the right to security in the event of, sickness, disability, widowhood, old age or other lack of livelihood in circumstances beyond his control.

While ISKCON leaders are not responsible for the standard of living of non-temple dependent members of ISKCON, they have a duty to foster the development of necessary economic support skills among the members in their care and to avoid setting policies which would interfere with the ability of non-temple dependent members to provide an adequate standard of living for themselves and their families.

Article 17

Each member of ISKCON shall have the right to information about the process by which ISKCON is governed and, in particular, shall be entitled to information about:

the nature and content of proposals made at each annual Mayapur meeting of the GBC;

the identification of those proposals which are adopted at each annual Mayapur meeting of the GBC; and

the nature and outcome of formal disciplinary proceedings undertaken by ISKCON authorities against ISKCON leaders;

Article 18

In the exercise of his or her rights and freedoms, each member of ISKCON shall be subject only to such limitations as are determined by ISKCON leaders to be essential for the purpose of securing recognition and respect for the rights and freedoms of others and of meeting the just requirements of morality, public order and the general welfare of ISKCON.

Footnotes

[1] Bhaktivedanta Swami, A. C., *Chaitanya-charitamrita, Madhya-lila,* Los Angeles, California: Bhaktivedanta Book Trust, 1994, 25.121 purport.

[2] *Webster's Ninth New Collegiate Dictionary*, Springfield, Massachusetts: Webster Inc., 1986, p. 828.

[3] Bhaktivedanta Swami, A. C., *Srimad-Bhagavatam*, Los Angeles, California: Bhaktivedanta Book Trust, 1994, 12.2.2. purport.

[4] Bhaktivedanta Swami, *Srimad-Bhagavatam* 4.2.21.

[5] Adams, Carol J., *The Sexual Politics of Meat: A Feminist-Vegetarian Critical Theory*, New York: The Continuum Publishing Company, 1995. Also see Spiegel, Marjorie, *The Dreaded Comparison: Human and Animal Slavery*, Philadelphia: New Society Publishers, 1988.

[6] Adams, *The Sexual Politics of Meat*, p. 47.

[7] Ibid.

[8] 1) *karmi;* materialist 2) *mlecchas;* a derogatory term for those that consume meat 3) *shudra;* members of the laboring class, usually used to imply that they are less intelligent 4) Vaishnavas; devotees of Lord Vishnu 6) *devas;* demi-god 7) *brahmanas;* the priestly class.

[9] If one is "in *maya*" then one is said to be "in illusion" by not acting on the instructions of the Lord, but acting under the material energy that binds one to the material world.

[10] *maya-devi; maya* is the illusory energy of the Lord and serves him by enticing living entities to enjoy in the material world. As a consequence the individual becomes more bewildered by the fleeting nature of happiness in the material world and in this way the individual's progress toward freeing themselves from the cycle of birth and death is retarded. Women have been compared to Maya-devi as a detriment to the spiritual lives of men.

[11] See Jyotirmayi devi dasi, "Women in ISKCON in Prabhupada's Times" electronic publication online at www.chakra.org (1997).

[12] 22, October 1975.

[13] 18, June 1976.

[14] Shattuck, "Human Rights and Democracy in Asia," 5 U.S. Dept. State Dispatch 480-1 (18, July 1994).

[15] Swami Bhaktivedanta, A. C., *The Nectar of Devotion*, Los Angeles, CA: Bhaktivedanta Book Trust, 1994, pp. 80-81.

Women's Voices and the Mobilization of Women within ISKCON[1]
by E. Burke Rochford, Jr.

I've never so much regretted being born in a woman's body since I joined the ISKCON movement. I've never been so much criticized, abused, slandered, misunderstood or chastised, because I have this woman's body. It makes it very difficult to do my service and/or assist others with their service, if they are always thinking about these bodily designations, instead of the constructive things I could do or say to help them in their service and to help this movement go forward. If you are a single woman (brahmacharini) *every man thinks he is an authority and will yell at you if he feels like it. But, it's worse when you're married, because you have one authority and you have to surrender to his inflexible, lord-it-over nature, whether he is right or wrong, and whether he is nice or cruel about how he relates to you. It's hellish and I hope I get the opportunity to leave this body as soon as possible.* (Woman who joined ISKCON in 1975, disciple of Prabhupada, married, from 1980 North America Devotee Survey)

By accepting women in the temples and giving them the brahmacharini *status, Prabhupada was not pretending, he gave them all the same rights and duties of the* brahmacharis *in the guru's* ashrama. *The same thing applied when he gave them* brahmana *initiation. The women devotees had exactly the same spiritual activities, the same tasks, the same possibilities to progress spiritually and they were entitled to the same respect. At that time, everything was done according to the abilities and the spiritual advancement of a person and not according to sex. Prabhupada did not make any distinction.* (Jyotirmayi Devi Dasi 1997:2)

My presentation today addresses the emergence of devotee women's collective voice and their recent mobilization to promote change within ISKCON. I organize my thoughts by employing a number of theoretical frameworks and perspectives familiar to scholars of social movements. After briefly detailing the history of women and their roles within ISKCON, I then turn to a discussion of a number of factors that have either promoted a context for women's activism, or have more directly promoted protest. My effort, however, is not limited to explaining *why* women have stood up against abuse, neglect, and mistreatment, as I also account for the *timing* of women's protest and *how* it has successfully gained political influence.

The four factors considered to account for the rise of ISKCON women's protest are: (1) Women's grievances; (2) Consciousness raising and the challenge to traditionalist views of women; (3) The declining labor force within ISKCON's temples and the expansion of women's organizational roles; and, (4) The declining authority of ISKCON's leadership and the emergence of political opportunities. I conclude by considering what responses we might expect to the progressive changes achieved by women activists and how and where future changes in gender relations is likely to occur. Because I have much more to research and think about, I encourage audience members to challenge my observations, or to otherwise offer your own views.[2]

Back to the Future: Rights Lost and Reclaimed

A quick survey of the social landscape of ISKCON reveals a number of apparent gains by women. A woman – Malati Devi Dasi – was elected this year in Mayapur to serve as a member of the GBC. Two women devotees that I am aware of presently serve as temple presidents in the United States (here in Alachua and at New Vrindaban), and a number of others also lead temples in Europe. In addition, several women hold high-level administrative positions at the national and international levels within ISKCON. Significantly, the GBC recently approved the creation of both a Women's Ministry as well as a Youth Ministry. In many temples in North America both men and women serve on the altar, worship side-by-side, and chant together each morning. No longer is it unusual (though not commonplace) to see women give class in the temple. Far less common is women taking the lead in temple *kirtans* or public *harinams*.

I must emphasize that the majority of the above "changes" in actuality represent reclaiming the past. In an important paper tracing the history of women within ISKCON, Jyotirmayi Devi Dasi makes clear that during ISKCON's early years women held roles and responsibilities that differed little from their godbrothers. Remarkably, this history has been largely lost to the collective memory of many ISKCON members. In part this is a consequence of changes that occurred in women's lives beginning in the early 1970s when women's identities were successfully reconstructed by newly appointed *sannyasi* leaders. Thereafter, women came to be seen as "unintelligent," "spiritually dangerous" to men, and incapable of little more than cooking, cleaning, and looking after children. (Also performing *sankirtana* which I will return to momentarily.) This newly formed gender ideology was used by *sannyasis, brahmacharis,* and others, to demean women and to deprive them of the rights and responsibilities provided by Srila Prabhupada. What now looks like *newly* gained rights, in fact, is a revival of women's former ISKCON identities.

The struggle to reclaim women's roles and identities has been accompanied by a significant shift in the perceptions and attitudes of both ISKCON leaders and rank-and-file members. Recently, a number of ISKCON leaders have publicly acknowledged the abuse and mistreatment women have endured within the movement. Note the words of the then chairman of the GBC in a letter to ISKCON members worldwide: "We have not offered proper protection and respect to the women in our movement. We have not understood woman's role as mother of society. We have hurt women by insisting that they behave according to Vedic standards, yet we have not been able to offer the proper standard of Vedic protection . . . (Letter from the Executive Committee of the GBC, signed by Harikesa Swami, June 1998).

The open acknowledgement of past injustices faced by ISKCON women has helped reshape gender attitudes. Finding from the Prabhupada Centennial Survey conducted in 1995-96 highlight how gender attitudes have changed (For more information on the Centennial Survey, see Rochford 1998a). Table 1 presents findings revealing how large majorities of *both men and women reject significant elements of ISKCON's traditionalist gender ideology.* Although there are significant differences in *strength of agreement,* both women and men generally embrace gender equality. Both sexes agree that women should be allowed to chant in the temple with men, have equal access to the Deities during worship, and have the same opportunities as men to realize their potential in devotional service. In addition, both agree that performance, not gender, should be the criterion for placement in an ISKCON position. Women and men alike also agree that women are the spiritual equals of men and that Prabhupada never intended for his women disciples to be treated as other than equal to their godbrothers. Finally, and tellingly, there is strong agreement that over time, male attitudes have become increasingly accepting of devotee women.

Table 1. Select Agree-Disagree Items
Regarding Women's Roles within ISKCON
By Gender

Statement	Women		Men	
	Strongly Agree/ Agree		*Strongly Agree/ Agree*	
Women and men should be able to chant japa together in the Temple.	49% (76)	34% (52)	23% (55)	53% (128)
Men and women should worship on different *sides* of the temple so that both have equal access to the Deities.	49% (72)	35% (51)	31% (74)	51% (120)
Women should have the same opportunities as men to realize their full potential in devotional service.	73% (111)	24% (36)	53% (131)	42% (104)
Performance not gender should determine who is placed in a given ISKCON position.	62% (91)	28% (41)	45% (106)	39% (92)
Women are the spiritual equals of men.	66% (100)	29% (44)	49% (120)	45% (110)
Prabhupada never intended for women to be treated as if they were less than equal to men.	61% (90)	28% (41)	39% (91)	45% (107)
Over the past several years I have seen the attitude of devotee men toward women devotees become more accepting.	7% (10)	76% (105)	9% (20)	80% (172)

In what follows, I will have occasion to return to these findings but, for now, my point is to stress how collectively they highlight how men's attitudes towards women and their ISKCON involvement are generally positive, and presumably this has become increasingly so in recent years.

Women's Collective Voices and Mobilization

Women's Grievances

The fact that women have suffered mistreatment, abuse, and neglect within ISKCON comes as no surprise to any devotee who has been around the movement for any length of time. Even observant visitors to an ISKCON temple can quickly find "evidence" of sexism, at least to the contemporary liberal Western mind. Clearly, many contemporary women and men have been turned off by what they see, and reject any idea of becoming involved in ISKCON.

When asked on the Prabhupada Centennial Survey whether they agreed or disagreed with the statement, "As a woman, I sometimes encounter a degree of sexism in our movement that is a barrier to my spiritual advancement" nearly half (48% of 148 women respondents) agreed or agree strongly with the statement. However, the most compelling, if not systematic, evidence comes from personal testimonies, as seen in the words of the woman quoted at beginning of my presentation. Another devotee woman concluded: "In general we have allowed spousal abuse. Men have always been right, allowed to hit wives, accepted in big, big positions in the movement even if they are known abusers, etc."

Unfortunately, the abuse and mistreatment of women by leaders, husbands, and other men, has often been justified on the basis of ISKCON's religious beliefs. As Jyotirmayi Devi Dasi (1997) argues, "Many men in the movement have used various scriptural statements on women's faults to rebuke and humiliate them, to hinder their service and advancement, or even try to drive them out of the movement."

Beyond outright abuse and mistreatment, women's contributions to Prabhupada's movement have often been dismissed and minimized. Not uncommonly, for example, women have been pushed out of responsible positions, not because they were incompetent, but because they were women (Jyotirmayi Devi Dasi 1997). Sexist ideas also influenced the different ways that men and women successful at book distribution and fundraising were viewed. Successful men were often portrayed as "spiritually advanced" and they commanded the respect of other devotees. Yet I remember during the 1970s and early 1980s successful women often received a very different response. In conversations with male *sankirtana* devotees, I was told that while it was true women were often successful at distributing Prabhupada's books, this was *only* because they used their feminine charm and/or sexuality to their advantage. Women weren't successful on the basis of spiritual qualifications, as were men. Men, who I might add, were known to use deceitful, and even illegal, tactics when distributing Prabhupada's books and when fundraising (e.g., picking).

A critically important concern for many devotee women was the neglect and abuse of children who attended ISKCON's gurukulas (see Rochford 1998b). For women who might have otherwise quietly endured their personal mistreatment at the hands of men, the abuse of children was unforgivable and revealed the corruption of ISKCON's leadership. As one long-time devotee mother commented, the abuse of children was itself directly tied to the marginalization of ISKCON's women.

[T]he widespread disgust with child abuse, and women finally just not taking the nonsense [any longer] have all contributed to making the women's voice finally being heard. . . . Admitting to the child abuse – most all of it committed by men, and probably only allowed to go on because of the de-empowerment of women (the mothers) – is admitting to the abuse of women and how the devaluation of them contributed to our problems, socially and with the children. Gradually that point is dawning on people. (September 1998)

Although I have only partially and incompletely dealt with these issues, it should be clear that during the 1970s and early 1980s many devotee women suffered various forms of neglect, mistreatment and outright abuse. Most did so in silence, whether they accepted, or not, the justifications offered by ISKCON's leadership. However, the hostile sexual-politic within ISKCON proved detrimental to the psychological well-being of many devotee women.

Instead of being considered full-fledged devotees, women were considered only as "women" in the most pejorative sense. . . . Women did not consider men as sons anymore and men did not behave with women as mothers but as enemies. Instead of kindness, gentleness and courtesy amongst men and women devotees, wickedness, meanness, and impoliteness prevailed. . . . Women were considered stupid and incapable and became subject to gross mockery (Jyotirmayi Devi Dasi 1997).

And it appears that threats to women's self-esteem continues into the present as nearly three-quarters (72%) of the women responding to the Prabhupada Centennial survey agreed, or strongly agreed, that women devotees "suffer from low self-esteem because of mistreatment by devotee men."

Consciousness Raising and New Frameworks of Understanding

While it is logical to assume that people collectivize on the basis of shared grievances, the research on social movements and revolutionary situations suggests that grievances are often insufficient. Critical to the formation of organized protest is the realization that the adversity people face is ultimately caused by groups and/or structures within society.

At least since the writings of Karl Marx, scholars have understood the critical role intellectuals play in promoting social protest. Beyond helping to articulate grievances, intellectuals provide alternative frameworks that allow aggrieved groups to see grievances in relation to the willful self-interest of elites and other powerful groups. Grievances thus become matters of injustice instead of personal misfortune.

Many, perhaps most, ISKCON women during the 1970s viewed their mistreatment as *misfortune* growing from their psycho-physical characteristics as women. While aligned with ISKCON's religious beliefs, such an interpretation effectively undercuts the potential for social protest. As the woman quoted at the beginning of this paper implied, her mistreatment at the hands of men was difficult for sure but it hardly constituted a basis for protest and change. Rather, and sadly, she thought giving up her female body was the answer to the distress she felt. Over time, however, devotee women have come to understand their mistreatment in terms of *injustice*. They challenged the ideological justifications offered by ISKCON's male leaders seeing them as little more than self-serving propaganda. Although there are references from Prabhupada, and from scripture, portraying women as less intelligent, etc., the derogatory characterizations employed by ISKCON's leaders represented one-sided attempts to demean and control women's lives.

I want to suggest that this and the previous Women's Conference have played a significant role in promoting a *new* understanding of women's lives within ISKCON. In essence, they represent consciousness raising events that promote alternative interpretations of women's lives in ISKCON. Participants at last year's women's conference in Los Angeles, for example, learned what was for many a new and comprehensive history of women within ISKCON. This history shattered the prevailing traditionalist gender paradigm that legitimated the mistreatment of women. Women heard from the mouths, and subsequently the written texts of Jyotirmayi Devi Dasi, Pranada Devi Dasi, Radha Devi Dasi, and others, how women during ISKCON's early years were treated respectfully and, for the most part, equally by a majority of their godbrothers. This respect grew from Prabhupada's high regard for his female disciples. Women – with Prabhupada's approval – held responsible positions, gave classes, led public *kirtan*s, performed public *aratis,* worshipped *tulasi* together with the men, presented flowers to Prabhupada during *guru-puja* and offered their obeisance's to Prabhupada in front of his *vyasasana* along with the men.

Only because of the brave efforts of women willing to risk their standing in ISKCON did Prabhupada's more favorable views and treatment of his female disciples become widely known. Because of their efforts, large numbers of women came to understand that they, and their godsisters, had been wrongly subjected to neglect, mistreatment, and abuse. Thereafter, pro-change women took up the fight to reclaim their identity as worthy, responsible, and productive people and devotees. As a leader in this effort makes clear, overturning the idea that Prabhupada was behind the maltreatment of women was critical to changing women's lives.

I think the mobilization of women and their issues has increased because of the educating we have been doing. It was a widespread belief that the status quo of women in ISKCON was Prabhupada's doing. It has become increasingly evident that this is not the case. Therefore, changing it and questioning it has become acceptable. Indeed, ten years ago no one would hear the discussion because it was heretical against Prabhupada. Now I would venture to say that there are a rising number of people convinced that what happened to women in ISKCON was NOT what Prabhupada intended. That was a big shift. So, education, communication, discussion has done a lot to change the atmosphere. (September 1998)

Declining Labor Supply and Increasing Responsibilities/Roles for Women

The pragmatic requirements of religious organizations as *communities* of believers require, as we all know, a great deal of human time and energy. Women often disproportionally contribute. They fill houses of worship, do much of the work of maintaining congregations, and are largely responsible for socializing children to religious values and practices. In recent years, women have also gained a growing presence as professionals in religious denominations working as ordained clergy (Chaves 1997). Although a number of explanations have been offered for the rising number of female clergy, research points to the shortage of male clergy, and the declining numbers of men seeking clerical vocations. Men have rejected clerical careers because of the declining prestige and modest compensation associated with clerical roles and duties.

I want to suggest what is probably self-evident to many in this room. The growth in opportunities for women to work as temple presidents, managers, administrators, and the like, are at least in part – perhaps in large part – a function of the fact that ISKCON temples in North America and elsewhere lack a sufficient supply of men to fill these critical roles. Stripped of prestige, sufficient income, and authority, men have abandoned the very idea of becoming temple presidents. The glamour and status are gone; only headaches remain. As a result, many temples are left to be poorly run by men not up to the task, or, in a few but growing number of cases, by women. While women's managerial careers are only at a beginning stage, and could be reversed, it seems plausible to argue that ISKCON is undergoing a process not unlike many mainline religious denominations facing a male clergy shortage.

In a letter to me outlining their thoughts on the issues raised in this presentation, two long-time devotee women, and Prabhupada disciples, offered the following analysis concerning the relationship between (literally) manpower shortages and the increasing responsibilities afforded women in ISKCON.

In most temples there is a severe shortage of manpower and of male devotees willing to take up responsibilities. There are less men overall, and among those present, less are willing now to take up responsible positions. . . So, women are invited to take up responsibilities more and more, because there is nobody else to do the job. If there would be available men, we have no doubt or illusion that they would get a chance first. We are not so naive to think that the men leaders appreciate us so much more than in the past; in a way they became forced by circumstances to engage us and give us more responsibilities. (September 1998)

They go on to acknowledge that while there are some sincere male leaders, the fact is, "Maybe Krishna is tricking them a little bit." Circumstances (created by Krishna) are forcing men to put aside traditionalist notions of gender for the sake of maintaining temples. One of them commented further about the dilemma she recently faced with respect to a new service opportunity:

Before leaving (location), I was asked to take up two important posts of responsibilities, to my great astonishment, in the very temple where I had suffered so much, attending *tulasi puja* in the cold outside the temple in the winter time, and never being invited to give a class, which I love to do. When they asked me to take up these posts, I thought they were really desperate, and had quite some guts to ask, knowing my feeling on the matter. (September 1998)

Because most devotee men, out of necessity, are employed outside of ISKCON to provide for their families, they are largely unavailable to fill ISKCON positions. Their unavailability is made all the more so given the limited compensation generally offered for positions within ISKCON. By default, temple communities have been forced to turn to capable women to fill temple positions, including temple management.

I want to offer one more analytic piece to this puzzle by returning to something I said earlier regarding the findings in Table 1. As you will remember, men and women both tended to reject a number of traditionalist ideas related to women in ISKCON. I would argue that men's changing views of women and their place in ISKCON are in part a function of the fact that ISKCON's communities require women to perform critical organizational roles. Because of this, traditionalist ideas concerning women no longer fit the changed realities of ISKCON's communities. Therefore, these ideas required substantial revision to align with the fact that women now hold responsible and demanding positions within ISKCON's management structure. How can women be "less intelligent," "incapable," "a threat to men," and so forth, while at the same time women are taking up complex, demanding, and important managerial and administrative work? In a very real sense, the ideals that define the women's movement within ISKCON (i.e., equal standing with men spiritually and materially, performance being the relevant criteria rather than gender, and so on) are increasingly compatible with ISKCON's need for women to perform significant organizational positions *in the absence of men*. In sum, because of pragmatic organizational needs, the *content* of women's resurgent voices is becoming co-opted into ISKCON's organizational culture and, perhaps, into its' religious culture as well.[3]

The Declining Authority of the Leaders and Political Opportunity

Scholars of social movements and political protest have often been perplexed about the timing of insurgency. Often groups of people suffering from extreme and unjust hardships fail to collectively mobilize. In other cases, people mobilize into organized movements when grievances appear less severe and urgent. The question is why? One response is that protest activity is more likely to occur when political elites are under siege; internally fragmented and incapable of acting in unison to crush or otherwise undermine dissent. In other words, when elites are in disarray greater opportunities emerge for staging protest and for activism to prove successful. As political scientist Sidney Tarrow suggests, political opportunity structures are " . . . dimensions of the political environment that provide incentives for people to undertake collective action by affecting their expectations for success or failure" (1994:85).

Without belaboring this point, the longstanding scandals and controversies surrounding the guru institution and the GBC, and the related loss of authority attributed to each (see Rochford 1998b), has produced political opportunities for a variety of aggrieved groups; the second generation, women, as well as householders. All of these challenging groups have been able to gain influence and political leverage because of political opportunities arising from a seriously weakened leadership. One guru and GBC member characterized ISKCON's *sannyasi* leadership as "dinosaurs," largely out of touch with the realities of today's ISKCON. No longer able to take for granted the commitment of ISKCON's membership, the leaders were left defenseless against the challenge of pro-change women.

Gender Relations and the Future of ISKCON

I realize I have gone on for some time so allow me to quickly conclude by making a few final observations and then invite your questions.

It remains a possible that the success women activists have achieved thus far could be overturned in the face of a traditionalist backlash. This has occurred in a number of Christian denominations that granted women ordination (Chaves 1997). On its face, however, the likelihood of a successful backlash seems unlikely in light of the diminished authority of ISKCON's leadership. Even so, it would not be surprising to see a grassroots attempt by conservative minded devotees to reassert traditionalist ideas in an effort to overturn the gains women have achieved thus far.[4]

There is reason to argue that in the coming years women's (and men's) lives are likely to occur largely outside of institutional ISKCON. This is because the movement as it currently exists in North America is almost entirely congregationally-based (Rochford 1995, 1997). ISKCON's previous communal structure has given way to the nuclear family as the foundational structure in which devotees live and practice Krishna consciousness. Beyond the reach of institutional control, male and female devotees necessarily negotiate issues of gender on the basis of the circumstances that define their family life. Moreover, because devotees have increased involvements in the larger society through work, school, recreation, and the like, it seems likely that mainstream societal gender norms will directly and indirectly shape their views of what constitutes appropriate gender roles. Each of these developments together are likely to raise still further questions about traditionalist conceptions of gender and the roles and behavior deemed appropriate for devotee women and men alike. Even so, I expect there will be continued conflict going forward given that women's equality is a hallmark of the mainstream liberal culture to which many within ISKCON continue to resist.

FOOTNOTES

[1] This is a slightly revised version of my 1998 presentation at the second annual Women's Ministry Conference in Alachua, Florida.

[2] A more complete treatment of these issues can be found in my book *Hare Krishna Transformed* (New York University Press, 2007). I call the reader's attention to two chapters in particular – "Women's Voices" and "Male Backlash."

[3] It is worth pointing out that the need for women to assume positions such as temple president has apparently become less urgent in the 2000s as ethnic Hindu men, aligned with ISKCON, have assumed these roles in a number of North American temples (e.g., Houston, Dallas, Chicago, Atlanta).

[4] Such an effort did in fact occur. In September 1998, while 150 devotee women were attending the second annual Women's Conference, a group composed of men and a single woman launched a secret Internet conference called General Headquarters, or GHQ. The formation of the GHQ appears to have coincided with the appointment of Malati Devi Dasi to the GBC. The group's objectives included, no women in positions of leadership, the termination of the Women's Ministry, women not allowed to give classes or lead *kirtans*, and that no ISKCON temple should allow "feminist" (i.e., women's) meetings. For a detailed account of the GHQ, see Rochford 2007:139-160). A more recent and consequential threat has emerged in India among devotees who are vigorously challenging a proposal being considered by the GBC to allow women to serve as *diksha* gurus.

REFERENCES

Carrol, J. , B. Hargrove, and A. Lummis. 1983. *Women of the Cloth: A New Opportunity for the Churches.* San Francisco: Harper and Row.

Chaves, Mark. 1997. *Ordaining Women.* Cambridge, MA: Harvard University Press.

Devi Dasi, Jyotirmayi. 1997. "Women in ISKCON in Prabhupada's Times." *Chakra* web site.

Rochford, E. Burke, Jr. 1995. "Family Structure, Commitment, and Involvement in the Hare Krishna Movement." *Sociology of Religion* 56 (2): 133-175

Rochford, E. Burke, Jr. 1997. "Family Formation, Culture, and Change in the Hare Krishna Movement." *ISKCON Communications Journal* 5(2):61-82.

Rochford, E. Burke, Jr. 1998a. "Prabhupada Centennial Survey Report," submitted to ISKCON's International GBC, November (unpublished). A summary was published in1999, "Prabhupada Centennial Survey: A Summary of the Final Report," *ISKCON Communications Journal* 7(1):11-26.

Rochford, E. Burke, Jr,. 1998b. "Child Abuse in the Hare Krishna Movement." *ISKCON Communications Journal* 6(1):43-69.

Rochford, E. Burke, Jr. 2007. *Hare Krishna Transformed.* New York: New York University Press.

Tarrow, Sidney. 1994. *Power in Movement.* Cambridge: Cambridge University Press.

Femininity Honored
by Visakha dasi

sristi-sthiti-pralaya-sadhana-saktir eka
chayeva yasya bhuvanani bibharti durga
icchanurupam api yasya ca cestate sa
govindam adi-purusam tam aham bhajami

"The external potency, *maya*, who is of the nature of the shadow of the cit [spiritual] potency, is worshiped by all people as Durga, the creating, preserving and destroying agency of this mundane world. I adore the primeval Lord Govinda, in accordance with whose will Durga conducts herself." *Brahma-samhita* 5.44

Material nature, the external energy of the Supreme Lord, is also known as Durga, or the female energy that protects the great fort of this universe. The word *Durga* means "fort." This universe is just like a great fort in which all the conditioned souls are kept, and they cannot leave it unless they are liberated by the mercy of the Supreme Personality of Godhead. Durga is a confidential maidservant of Krishna, but she has to punish the conditioned souls by keeping them in this material world. How does she do this? Lord Krishna Himself explains her foremost technique: "Just try to understand the mighty strength of My *maya* in the shape of a woman, who by the mere movement of her eyebrows can keep even the greatest conquerors of the world under her grip" (*Bhag.* 3.31.38). *Maya* or Durga's fort has many insurmountable walls, and for men the most insurmountable of them is their attraction to women. Of course, in actuality we are neither men nor women, for these designations refer only to the outer dress, the body. We are all actually Krishna's servants. However, heterosexual men in conditioned life are imprisoned in the fort of this material world by the form and behavior of beautiful women.

For devotees in Krishna consciousness, this is the familiar dark aspect of femininity, but it is not the only aspect. In fact it is the secondary, inferior aspect of this powerful energy. Srila Prabhupada explains that "Lakshmi has two features: *maya* [or Durga] and the goddess of fortune; the same Lakshmi according to position. Just like a government has got two departments: criminal department and civil department. So the government is the same, but there are two departments. This *maya* is criminal department, and Vaikuntha is civil department. Vaikuntha means there is no anxiety, and *maya* means always anxiety" (*Bhag.* 5.6.6 lecture 11/28/76). Today I'd like to explore with you the idea of restoring the force of femininity to its true sublime beauty.

1. Femininity and the *Grihastha Ashrama*

In our traditional spiritual culture, girls were raised to become agents of Lakshmi rather than Durga. These pure, vivacious, innocent, shy, and inwardly powerful young women were always welcome members of society because they, as Lakshmidevi's servants, evoked the presence of Narayana for Lakshmiji never leaves His side. Srila Prabhupada writes, "*Kumaris,* or unmarried girls untouched by the hand of any member of the opposite sex, are auspicious members of society. . . When thus protected, women as a class remain an always auspicious source of energy to man" (*Bhag.* 4.21.4 purport). Kumaris did not manipulate or seduce or project hidden agendas onto anyone or anything. Being pure in eating, sleeping, fearing, and mating, they were pure in action. Being pure in action, they were pure in mind. And to the extent they were pure in mind, they desired to serve God. The core value of the *kumaris* was their desire to serve God.

When these *kumaris* married, their homes became a fortress, but unlike Durga's fortress, which keeps conditioned souls in the material world, theirs protected conditioned souls from Durga's influence. Srila Prabhupada writes, "The bodily senses are considered plunderers of the fort of the body. The wife is supposed to be the commander of the fort, and therefore whenever there is an attack on the body by the senses, it is the wife who protects the body from being smashed" (*Bhag.* 3.14.20). And: "One who is situated in household life and who systematically conquers his mind and five sense organs is like a king in his fortress who conquers his powerful enemies . . . The senses are considered very powerful enemies. As a king in a strong fortress can conquer powerful enemies, so a householder in *grihastha-ashrama,* household life, can conquer the lusty desires of youth and be very secure when he takes *vanaprastha* and *sannyasa*" (*Bhag.* 5.1.18).

Thus in the traditional *grihastha ashrama* the husband protects the wife by keeping her and the family safe, spiritually on track, and provided for. Such a gentle man awakens and clarifies his wife's spiritual strength. And the wife also protects her husband and family from their own moods, excesses, vulnerabilities and other dangers of the inner world. Qualified women are essential for the success of the *grihastha ashrama*. And a strong *grihastha ashrama* is essential for the success of *varnashrama dharma*. And *varnashrama dharma* is necessary so that human society can progress back home, back to Godhead. "There are four social orders for cooperation in the endeavor for liberation from material existence. The orders of *brahmacharya,* or pious student life, household life with a wife, retired life and renounced life all depend for successful advancement on the householder who lives with a wife" (*Bhag.* 3.14.18). If the family unit is healthy, then society is healthy; when the family falls apart, society falls apart.

A Krishna conscious wife can remind her Krishna conscious husband of the best that is in him. She sees and can show him his own self-worth, as he shows her hers. Her surrender inspires his greatness and his greatness inspires her surrender. As his masculine spirit is evoked, her feminine one is; cared for and cared about, she is his solace and inspiration. Both her emotions and his spirit are honored and gradually husband and wife mature in spiritual realization.

2. Femininity and the Four *Ashramas*

Without being trained in the purifying *ashrama* of *bramacharya,* or celibate student life, a young man may become a womanizer – seeing women only as objects of his sensual

- 216 -

desires. Or, by improper *brahmachari* training, he may become a woman hater – aware not of the positive feminine qualities a woman embodies but only of the distraction her body is to him. Lacking honesty and honor, this ill-fated *brahmachari* blames women for his own weakness. When such a person later enters the renounced order of *sannyasa* (generally he avoids the *grihastha ashrama*), he is a repository of unrealized knowledge, he is unable to establish heartfelt relationships, and, although vacuous inwardly, outwardly he stubbornly refuses to see his own shortcomings. The very qualities that he needs to grow – femininity – he ignores or harshly condemns.

However, with proper *brahmachari* training a young man recognizes the dignity of femininity. In other words, he realizes and acknowledges the intrinsic worth of feminine qualities like mildness, compassion, warmth, tenderness, patience, kindness, tolerance, understanding of others, and nurturing.

When this *brahmachari* enters the *grihastha ashrama*, his dominating male ego is tempered by his wife's precious qualities of femininity. And as he matures he gradually internalizes those exalted feminine qualities. His realizations and humility increase during his decades in the *grihastha ashrama*, while his sensuality decreases until it becomes nil and he enters the vanaprastha stage. Finally, when he accepts the renounced order of *sannyasa*, he has fully recognized and developed his own inner feminine life – of forgiveness, softness, nurturing, relatedness – and does not rely on his former wife to offer hers. (Although it is the exception, it should be noted that there are highly conscious men who can become mature sannyasis without the interim *grihastha-vanaprastha* experience.) Such a secure renouncer is not threatened by a woman's power but on the contrary, evokes it in Krishna consciousness by his dynamic Krishna conscious words and deeds. As he travels and is an example of Krishna consciousness, women other than his wife (whom he no longer sees) may respect and encourage him, and he in turn, respects and encourages them. When he sees men as well as women remembering and acting in their glorious position as servants of Srila Prabhupada, he, as a man of goodwill, is filled with happiness.

For an example of this mature stage of *sannyasa* we can remember how our founder-*acharya* was as hard as a thunderbolt (his masculine side) – kicking with boots on the heads of materialistic scientists, *Mayavadis*, pseudo-Christians, and *sahajiyas*; and when time, place and circumstance warranted it, he was also as soft as a rose (the feminine side) – having nurturing, loving exchanges with his followers, including women, children, and men. In fact, in the Supreme Personality of Godhead Himself, Lord Chaitanya Mahaprabhu, we also see an example of masculine and feminine qualities: on one side He defeated the logicians, the impersonalists, the Buddhists, and the ruffians, and on the other side He tasted Radharani's love for Krishna. In Her mood He swooned at the sight of Jagannatha and at the sound of the Lord's holy name. Srila Prabhupada writes, "Srimati Radharani is a tenderhearted feminine counterpart of the supreme whole, resembling the perfectional stage of the worldly feminine nature" (*Bhag.* 2.3.23 purport).

It is the will of Radha and Krishna that each of us, every woman, child, and man, in every *varna* and *ashrama*, be happy, whole, and successful. The unspoken belief that someone's else's success limits or threatens mine fails to allow others to shine and to allow me to shine fully too. Another's Krishna conscious success never robs you and me of this possibility. Quite the opposite. Their success is our success, if we allow ourselves to applaud instead of criticize. As eternal parts and parcels of Krishna originally, we are all beautiful and powerful and strong. We deserve love and acceptance and support. We would all be glorious if we could only express who we are, for we are, each one of us, a portion of the Lord.

3. Feminine and Masculine Values

Both men and women have both masculine and feminine qualities, the masculine qualities usually predominating in men (with the feminine side subordinate), and feminine ones in women (with the masculine side subordinate). It's important to note that both qualities have assets and weaknesses which complement each other, and so, by the arrangement of the Lord, both are necessary for a balanced, healthy life in individuals, families, communities, and society. For example, a masculine asset is the power of analysis; a feminine weakness is a proneness to be misled. A weakness on the masculine side is insensitivity; a strength on the feminine side, soft-heartedness. Srila Prabhupada comments, "Women in general are unable to speculate like philosophers, but they are blessed by the Lord because they believe at once in the superiority and almightiness of the Lord, and thus they offer obeisances without reservation" (*Bhag.* 1.8.20 purport). Srila Prabhupada also points out that philosophy without religion is mental speculation (the masculine side), while religion without philosophy is sentiment (the feminine). Both philosophy and religion are required. And either men or women can be too influenced by one or the other and thus overcome by either dry erudition or fanaticism. Balance is essential. Overemphasis on masculine qualities such as rational analysis, authority, control, competition, and power causes us, both men and women, to demean the softness, simplicity, and weakness of the feminine. By neglecting and denigrating these gentle and humbling aspects in each of us, by making the feminine seem trivial, our lives become progressively more rigid, sterile, inert, and empty. We unconsciously allow authority to eclipse feeling, prestige and adoration to eclipse warmth and authenticity. The feminine qualities of nurturing and compassion perish when pitted against the masculine lust for power. Our most noble spiritual path, when denied feminine values, degenerates to a prideful quest for distinction. And that quest destroys relationships and evokes hypocrisy rather than devotion.

Similarly, achievements created at the cost of our capacity for feeling, warmth, contentment, and serenity have limited value. If we invalidate the spiritual feminine principle it may be so destroyed that even women will lose touch with it. It is time to bravely and without sensuality affirm the feminine, to heal the wounds of our spiritual woman and at the same time contribute to the healing of our children and our Society. Let us move from a place of arrogant weakness to one of humble strength.

The more brusque of men will cast off this appeal as sentiment and remain fixed in their ways. Yet credit is due them, for often their service has seen millions of books distributed, has seen thousands of devotees initiated, and has fathered hundreds of temples. But without their nurturing mother, without feminine tenderness, these offspring are not whole. They are imbalanced. To become healthy we must allow the feminine to reclaim its natural place. A child is comforted when father and mother are present. Let us all be comforted by the masculine and feminine working together.

4. Femininity and Children

In a letter to Arundhati dated July 30th, 1972, Srila Prabhupada wrote: "For you, child-worship is more important than Deity worship. If you cannot spend time with him [your son], then stop the duties of *pujari*. . . . These children are given to us by Krishna, they are Vaishnavas and we must be very careful to protect them. These are not ordinary children, they are Vaikuntha children, and we are very fortunate we can give them chance to advance further in Krishna consciousness. That is very great responsibility, do not neglect it or be confused. Your duty is very clear."

What could be more important for the future of our world than that we raise happy and well-adjusted, empowered children? If the relationship between parents – especially the mother – and children is the relationship Krishna intended it to be, then children will grow up to know that neither money nor fame nor prestige nor power is nearly as important as a life lived for a noble purpose. And there is no greater nobility than to live in Krishna consciousness, that is, with knowledge, with renunciation, with respect for all living things, and with a mood of devotion to the Lord. The best possible heritage for a child is this clean consciousness. "To become a pure devotee of Lord Krishna, two things are very much essential, namely having a chance to be born in the family of a devotee and having the blessings of a bona fide spiritual master" (*Bhag.* 2.4.1 purport).

Parents who attempt to raise their children in Krishna consciousness are doing an incredibly difficult and demanding service which requires – especially of the mother – almost endless selflessness, patience, deep listening, and understanding. Perhaps only they know the physical, emotional, and spiritual energy it takes to do this service well. Perhaps raising a happy Krishna conscious child takes at least as much focus, sensitivity, and intelligence as any other service. Children who receive respect and patience learn to respect and be patient. Such loved children find their own spiritual strength and genius. The personalities of their mothers are the space that prepares them psychologically and spiritually to become Krishna conscious.

We did not create our children; Krishna did. And it's primarily their mothers who supervise their development; the children are their own beings and their mother gives them the environment to realize themselves. Who among us dares to minimize a mother's service to our Society?

5. Femininity and Women Today, Part I

Although we may be oblivious of it, it is a documented fact that expectations have an extraordinary influence on us. Children who are told that they are underperfomers underperform. Men who are told that they are inferior lose their self-esteem. So, logically, what do you suppose happens to women who are told that they are less intelligent, lusty, envious, untrustworthy sense gratifiers with fox-like hearts? Such expectations draw out the Durga in a woman, defeat her, and stifle her confidence and good intentions. She herself will wonder about her integrity and character. Every time a woman is denied an opportunity because she is a woman, every time she's told she's not good enough because she's a woman, that's she's an agent of *maya*, she is massacred; her feminine strength is denied and her spiritual potential squelched. Such denials and negativity have poisoned our past and toxify the present.

By contrast, tell women that among them Krishna is "fame, fortune, fine speech, memory, intelligence, steadfastness and patience" (Bg 10.34) and the power of such positive expectations will draw out those qualities. Tell them that they are the natural repository of warmth, kindness, caring, relatedness, nurturing, compassion, gentleness, forgiveness, love, and devotion, and these will blossom forth from within them. Srila Prabhupada writes, "Women in general, being very simple at heart, can very easily take to Krishna consciousness, and when they develop love of Krishna they can easily get liberation from the clutches of *maya*, which are very difficult for even so-called intelligent and learned men to surpass" (KB Ch 23). Do not ignore the feminine; do not tear her down. Help her a little and she will fly. Her life is meant to be used in the service of the greatest and most holy cause.

When women are reading and chanting, hearing, inquiring, speaking, and following Srila Prabhupada in spirit; when they are offering their mind, body, and words in the service of Krishna they are a great blessing to this spiritual movement and to the world.

With this in mind I propose that the women in our Society be forevermore seen as agents of Lakshmidevi rather than Durga. Even if women, individually or collectively, are presently unworthy of this vision, simply by being seen in this way the vestiges of Durga that dwell within them will soften, melt, and finally be Lakshmi-ized. The Krishna conscious wisdom of the Vaishnavas and Vaishnavis, their patience, their courtesy and respect will evoke Lakshmi-like behavior in women. With Lakshmi-Narayana's illuminating presence, Durga will exit.

6. Femininity and Women Today, Part II

It is often women themselves who make the world even harder for other women, perhaps in their attempt to survive in our imbalanced world. These women may take one of two stances: in one they say, "I am strong like a man. I view the feminine as weak and unworthy, unnecessary and unimportant; it is the masculine that is glamorous and meaningful." To such a woman, feminine Krishna conscious emotion is a weakness; masculine lack of emotion is a strength. Thus she repudiates feeling or love and finds a masculine niche for her feminine powers. But this woman who succeeds at the expense of her Krishna conscious tenderness does not succeed. Her denial of spiritual emotion through suppression or withdrawal is a weak move, not a courageous one.

Krishna Himself values Krishna conscious emotion. He says, "When I was away from Draupadi, she cried with the words "He Govinda!" This call for Me has put Me in her debt, and that indebtedness is gradually increasing in My heart" (NoD Ch 21). So, Krishna conscious feelings are not less important than achievements, and a woman who honors her feelings for Krishna and Srila Prabhupada and their teachings will find others also honoring them. After all is said and done, our final goal is the most sublime of all possible feelings: to love Krishna unconditionally.

The second stance a woman may take says, "I am in a traditional woman's role as a housewife, mother, cook, seamstress, etc., and all other women should also be in a traditional role." Thus she holds back women who desire unconventional services, even though these women feel drawn to those nontraditional roles and are qualified for them. In the same mood, this second type of woman insists that women should not stand near the Deities in the temple room, sing for Them, or give lectures, even though Srila Prabhupada himself gave directions otherwise. When Srila Prabhupada first established the Governing Body Commission (GBC), he personally appointed two women – Govinda dasi and Yamuna – to be on it. And he often asked his women disciples, like Malati, Hemavati, Kaushala, and Yamuna, to speak and to sing. There is also precedent from the *Srimad-Bhagavatam* for women to precede men: "Suta Goswami said: Thereafter the Pandavas, desiring to deliver water to the dead relatives who had desired it, went to the Ganges with Draupadi. The ladies walked in front" (*Bhag.* 1.8.1).

In response to these two stances, let us say this: when Krishna conscious women go into the world to serve Srila Prabhupada with an authentic balance of intelligence with compassion, every woman can show her support, extend her generosity and her enthusiasm. There cannot be too many glorious women, whether in the home or out. Our Society is crying for them. These glorious women can only help us. They treat others with dignity; without compromise they respect themselves and they respect others. They honor each and every devotee. In their association our hearts are harmonized and uplifted. Let us seriously support others reaching for unmotivated, uninterrupted devotional service to the Supreme Lord, whether their reach is from the home or temple or community or society.

And in response to these stances, let us also say this: devotees encourage Krishna consciousness in one another. We're meant to do this and it increases the Krishna consciousness within us. We fail in our deepest responsibility to Krishna and to ourselves each time we discourage the Krishna conscious efforts of another devotee or allow ourselves to become discouraged in our Krishna conscious efforts. Our joy in seeing a Vaishnavi doing the service she desires for the pleasure of the Lord demonstrates our willingness to relinquish the petty and negative preoccupations that stand in the way of our Krishna consciousness. This beautiful, positive attitude lifts a heavy burden from our minds and hearts and allows a more joyful life to emerge.

When a woman touches the magnificent spiritual possibilities within herself, the internal and external forces that would limit those possibilities hold less and less sway over her. When she is very clear that she wants to be glorious for Srila Prabhupada's pleasure, and that she has permission to be femininely powerful in Krishna consciousness, she will be so. And we will all benefit.

7. Femininity and Aging

Age is magnificent if we take our spiritual lives seriously. In age we can reflect with joy on the richness of the life we have lived. What we have experienced, all we have done, whatever great thoughts we may have had, and all we have suffered, all this is not lost, though it is past, and no power on earth can take this wealth from us. Instead of the uncertain future that youth face, we have the reality of a lifetime of growth in devotion behind us.

The longer we live, the more time we have to pursue the things that make life meaningful. The older we get the more buoyant we become – from fewer anxieties, from more realizations, and from shedding meaningless things and negative preoccupations. We become not harder with age but softer, more gentle. We are blessed with quieting senses, a clear mind, and steady intelligence.

While *sannyasis* travel to preach the science of Krishna consciousness, mature Krishna conscious women – perhaps grandmothers now – remain in the community to exemplify and pass on the eternal family tradition of Krishna consciousness. The children of the community naturally imbibe the Krishna conscious mood of these enlightened ladies; the *kumaris* become wise from their wisdom; the brahmacharis respect them without sensual innuendos; the *grihasthas* feel blessed by their sobering, joyful presence. And on their side, these ladies, who form the foundation of the community, know that they have gained the greatest gain, Krishna consciousness.

Conclusion

In his purport to text 27 of chapter nine in the First Canto of *Srimad-Bhagavatam*, Srila Prabhupada writes: "As far as the women class are concerned, they are accepted as a power of inspiration for men. As such, women are more powerful than men."

In other words, that which inspires a person is more powerful than the person. Therefore, as Srila Prabhupada says, women are more powerful than men. The pages of

Srimad-Bhagavatam and *Mahabharata* offer ample examples of this: due to Devahuti's feminine power, Kardama Muni was inspired to create an incredibly magnificent palace in the sky; due to Sukanya's feminine power, Chyavana Muni transformed his aged, deformed body into that of a young man; due to Gandhari's feminine power, her eldest son, Duryodhana, received a body impervious to weapons. Due to Savitri's feminine power, her husband Satyavan was rescued from death. Due to Cintamini's inspiration, Bilvamangala Thakur gave up material life and completely devoted himself to Krishna. Due to the inspiration of Sudama *brahmana*'s wife, Sudama *brahmana* went to Dwaraka and was reunited with his friend, Krishna. This is the example of the Krishna conscious masculine-feminine dynamic: the Krishna conscious husband cares for his Krishna conscious wife and she inspires him in Krishna consciousness. Srila Prabhupada says, "The protection of women maintains the chastity of society, by which we can get a good generation for peace, tranquility and progress of life" (*Bhag.* 1.8.5 purport).

However, we may note with caution that Krishna conscious feminine power can create havoc in the lives of those who lack Krishna consciousness: the unscrupulous Kauravas perished due to their dishonoring Draupadi.

Honor femininity. Failing to do so has created and will continue to create havoc. Failing to do so inspires edicts instead of dialogues, resolutions instead of relationships, indifference instead of intimacy. This failing costs us our laksmi, our members, and our enthusiasm. It renders us unable to represent Srila Prabhupada and to attract Radha Krishna. Our external achievements, however grandiose, ring hollow.

Want each woman to grow, more each passing day, into the person Krishna would have her be. Enthuse her to be inspired by Lakshmi. Remind her of her worth. She is a servant from the spiritual world. In her heart lies Krishna. And she is here to love Him. Help her lay down her false ego that she might be used as a connecting link between this material world and the spiritual one. Help her take responsibility for her own state of mind; remind her that, whatever the circumstances, she is not a victim, but a heroine. Help her become true to her principles and loyalties, and to expect the causeless mercy of Krishna.

We are all souls that have nothing to do with the physical world; we are nonmaterial, nonphysical. We are God's precious parts, meant to do His service. From following the regulative principles and from the daily spiritual practices of *japa* meditation, reading, associating with devotees, honoring prasad, and engaging in all other varieties of devotional service, our spirituality is revived. At that time we – women, children, and men – will regain our normal position in the Lord's pleasure-giving, feminine potency.

USA and European Conference Report
by Radha devi dasi

Radhadesh, Belgium 28-29 June 1998
New Ramana Reti, Alachua, USA, 25-30 September 1998

If the truth is to be told, it is everyone – men, women and children – in our Society who require recognition, honor, and respect with sufficient opportunities for devotional service, free from impositions of culture, race, or gender. It's about opening a solid, recognizable platform of services in all areas of equal proportion and recognizing, identifying, correcting and preventing areas of mistreatment against any devotee in ISKCON by any other ISKCON member.

The Women's Ministry of ISKCON has sponsored two conferences in the last four months where members of ISKCON met to discuss the position of women in ISKCON and the contributions which women can make in improving our Society. Following on the heels of the historic First Annual "Vaishnavis in ISKCON" conference in Los Angeles last December, the conferences in Radhadesh (Belgium) in June and Alachua (USA) in September 1998 sought to deepen and extend the examination of issues which affect women. In addition to analyzing institutional structures that challenge the participation of women in ISKCON, participants at both conferences discussed the extent to which the treatment of ISKCON's women has affected our movement as a whole.

The European Conference

The first European conference of the Women's Ministry took place at Radhadesh.

The conference was organised by Jyotirmayi devi dasi and Hari devi dasi, working in conjunction with Sudharma devi dasi. Over fifty women and men gathered for the conference which opened with presentations by Jyotirmayi devi dasi and Radha devi dasi summarizing the work of the International Women's Ministry, the Los Angeles conference, and the response of the GBC to the Ministry's work. The conference attendees were inspired to learn of Malati devi dasi's appointment to the GBC and the support she received from many of the GBC members. Other presentations included Gaurangi devi dasi on "ISKCON Language and Women," Radha devi dasi's paper titled "Participation, Protection and Patriarchy: Roles for Women in ISKCON," and a panel discussion on "The Impact of the Women's Situation in ISKCON on Preaching."

One of the conference's most moving moments was a testimonial by second generation devotee, Chakrini devi dasi, who used her personal experiences to explain some of the ways in which our Society has failed women. Describing her childhood as a time when her mother was pressured to neglect her, Chakrini noted that she and her friends "felt, as we grew up, that the role of women was very much frowned upon. We were told that it was just our bad *karma* to be women." Her maturity and insight were evident when she concluded that ISKCON needs "mothers who are happy and confident in their capabilities as women and who therefore pass on those feelings to their children, because those children will grow up to be the parents of the future."

The balance of the conference was spent in lively and thoughtful discussions between the participants on the roles which women can and should undertake in ISKCON as well as the importance of their contributions in helping the larger society to overcome the social difficulties which currently trouble our organization. The conclusion of the participants was that ISKCON's women and men must co-operate, not compete with each other, in an atmosphere of equal spiritual rights to devotional service and spiritual advancement.

The North American Conference

The Second Annual North American Women's Ministry conference in Alachua was an ambitious undertaking which included three days of workshops on a wide range of topics, a one day retreat at a local cold spring spa, and a two day formal conference. Over a hundred devotees participated in some portion of the six-day event.

The workshops that opened the conference were impressive in their range and depth. The twenty-eight classes, all presented by Vaishnavis, covered topics ranging from child rearing, marriage, public speaking, leading *kirtan* (sung prayers), traditional Vedic roles and journal writing, to building self esteem, recovering from mistreatment, organizing events and running a temple kitchen. One of the most enthusiastically received workshops was Arcana Siddhi and Mahendrani's presentation entitled "From Victim to Victor" which focused on healing from past experiences of mistreatment. The wealth of knowledge displayed by the women present was an overwhelming testament to the talent and enthusiasm which women bring to the service of Lord Krishna, and a persuasive argument for the continuing expansion of service opportunities for women.

One of the highlights of the women's retreat day was the panel presentation on Srila Prabhupada's pastimes. Laxmimoni devi dasi, Hari Puja devi dasi, Kusa devi dasi, Visakha devi dasi, Jayasri devi dasi, Malati devi dasi and many others shared their first-hand experiences with Srila Prabhupada. In the process, they inadvertently reminded us all, over and over again, how wonderfully and fully Srila Prabhupada engaged women in service, never limiting them by stereotyped gender roles.

The two-day formal conference included presentations by a number of academics, senior leaders of ISKCON, second generation devotees and women who are making a difference in our Society today. H.H. Bhakti Tirtha Swami opened the conference with a presentation entitled "Putting the Heart Back Into ISKCON." This presentation highlighted how the participation of women at higher levels can help our movement to become more in touch with the needs and concerns of our members. H.H. Hridayananda Swami described how his view of women changed as ISKCON developed, highlighting the transformation which others have previously noted from a family oriented society in which women were accepted, to a more repressive form which devalued women at a later point.

Visakha devi dasi spoke on the topic of femininity, presenting scriptural sources and concluding that strength, service and public roles are not inconsistent with shastric injunctions on the place and treatment of women. Sudharma devi dasi, Rukmini devi dasi, Pranada devi dasi, Vraja Lila devi dasi, and Madhumati devi dasi used their personal experiences as devotees to reflect and comment on the ways in which women have overcome institutional barriers in order to serve and advance in ISKCON.

Sociologist Professor Burke Rochford, spoke on the mobilization of women in ISKCON, noting that his research showed widespread support for more equal roles between men and women amongst ISKCON's membership. Professor Vasuda Narayana, an expert on Vaishnava devotional poetry, shared her research and her personal experience as a woman raised in a Vaishnava culture. She described strong female role models within the Vaishnava tradition.

The conference ended with a presentation by Radha devi dasi that proposed the adoption of a Bill of Rights for ISKCON. Noting the existence of psychological and sociological causes for oppression of women in the larger society outside of ISKCON, Radha devi dasi argued that ISKCON's development institutionalized some oppressive behavior. This, she argued, was achieved by labeling similar types of material discrimination, as experienced in everyday society, as "spiritual" practice. Her presentation concluded with a description of various types of human rights that ISKCON might adopt in seeking to improve the treatment of devotees. While the discussion of women's roles in ISKCON continues, the conferences sponsored by the Women's Ministry leave no doubt that women are making a profound and meaningful contribution to our movement. As H. H. Hridayananda Swami pointed out in his presentation at the women's conference in Los Angeles last December, the eloquence, intelligence and spiritual consciousness shown by the women who participate in these conferences is a loud and persuasive cry that ISKCON open its doors wide to give Vaishnavis unlimited access to devotional service at all levels.

Respect for Individuality
by Urmila Dasi

This paper was published in the ISKCON Communications Journal in December 1998.

The individuality of the self is a central teaching in Vaishnava philosophy, but what is our practical understanding of this term? Individuality is present in all living beings on both a material and a spiritual level. This article translates how this concept needs to relate to education practices in ISKCON today. The author explores evidence in some of

Srila Prabhupada's writings and scripture that deal with the issue of individuality together with some more recent research by academics in the field. With this data, the author builds a persuasive argument for devotees to become more aware of the individual, both in themselves and in others so that they may respond with respectful awareness to the individuals needs.

Every living being is a separate and uniquely distinct individual. The Vaishnava scriptures, such as the *Bhagavad-gita,* teach us that this individuality is present on three different levels: from the physical appearance of a person, to the subtle level which is made up of the mind, intelligence and ego, and also more profoundly, on a spiritual level the spiritual identity of a soul is also unique and individual. Members of ISKCON have a strong understanding of uniqueness in spiritual identity of an individual soul, as this is one of the major teachings of our tradition. Unfortunately, the individual uniqueness of a person on a material level (body and subtle elements) is often overshadowed by our understanding and emphasis of the spiritual ideal.

The need to respond to the needs of a separate and unique individual is an everyday issue for the students and teachers that work in the Society's schools. We need to respond to this need more comprehensively through raising awareness in our teachers. There are a number of well-researched systems that have been put forward by various academics which may be useful for teachers. These will be examined in more detail together with references to the Vaishnava scriptures in the demarcation of personality types. There will also be a few suggestions as to how these concepts can be put to practical use by the teachers in our Movement.

A good education system in Krishna consciousness must show respect for individuality, first by recognizing differences as inherent and value-neutral. The failure either to recognize the existence of distinct personality types or to accept them as value-neutral leads to various problems to the development of an individual or a society, one of the most damaging of which is an understanding that spiritual perfection is an adjustment of material personality. Teachers must then learn to establish a rapport with students based on this understanding, and respect and adjust their teaching methods accordingly to give useful direction for vocation and spiritual service that will be in harmony with each individual's nature. We can then go beyond respecting individuality, to glorifying diversity as a means of pleasing the Lord.

The Gaudiya Vaishnava Position on Individuality

The soul, according to Vaishnava theology, is not simply "light" or existence, it is, in fact, an individual living entity which has an individual relationship with God. When Krishna tells Arjuna, "Never was there a time when I did not exist, nor you, nor all these kings; nor in the future shall any of us cease to be,"[1] the Lord is directly referring to the unending nature of individuality and the immortality of the soul. Srila Prabhupada comments, "The Supreme Personality of Godhead is the supreme individual person, and Arjuna, the Lord's eternal associate, and all the kings assembled there are individual eternal persons"[2] The individuality, to which Lord Krishna and Srila Prabhupada refer to in these examples, means that each soul is a separate and distinct being with an individual relationship with God, and these relationships have been described in the scriptures.

One of the first broad categories of distinctions of spiritually liberated souls is that of their *rasa,* or relationship, with the Lord.[3] According to the various divisions and gradations of devotees, permanent devotional situations can be divided into five categories: peacefulness, service to Krishna, friendship with Krishna, parental affection toward Krishna, and conjugal love for Krishna. Each division has its own different taste and relish, and a devotee situated in a particular division is happy in that position.[4] So one aspect of spiritual individuality is seen in that one perfected soul relates to the Lord as a friend, whereas another perfected soul relates to the Lord as their master, and yet another perfected soul relates to the Lord as their worshipable Deity.

However, even within these five categories, there is great scope for individual expression; it is not that all those who view the Lord as their intimate friend are alike in their mood of friendship, or even alike in their personality. The *Bhagavatam,* one of our main scriptures, relates a story where the demigod Brahma steals not only Lord Krishna's calves but steals His cowherd boy associates as well. Krishna then expands Himself into replicas of each of those boys and calves. It is described that each boy and each calf appeared with their own individual characteristics and personalities and appearance, so Lord Krishna had to replicate each boy and calf with all of these differences.[5] This is a good example to demonstrate that the Lord actually enjoys variety, as each of these boys and calves has an individual relationship with the Lord due to their individual personalities.

Krishna delights in experiencing a variety of relationships with individuals. So, does the Lord have a preference? Many devotees and scholars have analyzed the spiritual variety described in the scriptures in terms of "higher" and "lower." While such an analysis has validity, it is also true that in Krishna's eyes, and in the vision of the devotee of Krishna, all types are good, and wanted. Srila Prabhupada would often say, "Variety is the mother of enjoyment."

In the material world the specifics of our original identity with the Lord are hidden, as we have not only been given a material body, but also a subtle mentality as well. Even though we are not aware of our eternal spiritual rasas with the Lord (unless we are on an elevated spiritual platform), we are still aware that each of us has a unique body and mind. Even if we observe identical twins, they are never exact copies of one another; each has a unique personality.

When dealing with the issue of personality types and individuality, it is helpful to use certain categorizations for the purpose of analysis. It is common to hear criticism, even outrage, whenever one attempts to demarcate personality types. One hears accusations such as that one is trying to "label" or "pigeonhole" people. Presumably, the assumption is that labels for personality types, especially broad labels, are an insult to the very individuality they are meant to honor. Yet, broad descriptions have value, not only for a theoretical, academic purpose, but also as a tool for understanding others and ourselves in the context of our practical interpersonal dealings. Properly understood labels broaden rather than narrow our view, bringing us to a deep and genuine respect for one another.

It is acknowledged though, that as each person is a unique blend of characteristics, categorization can only give a broad idea of a personality.

If we look to one of our main scriptures, the *Bhagavad-gita,* Lord Krishna Himself categorizes people. In fact, we will first consider His categories. Krishna names the categories of personality as follows; "*Brahmanas, kshatriyas, vaishyas* and *shudras* are distinguished by the qualities born of their own natures in accordance with the material modes."[6] *Brahmana*s are the priestly class, *kshatriya*s are warriors, *vaishya*s are the business community and the *shudra*s are the manual workers in society. It is important to note that these are understood differently in the modern context of the term "castes," which is delineated in terms of race, ethnicity, or birth in a higher or lower social group. Rather, Krishna speaks of an individual's personal "qualities" and "nature."

It is common for those who study personality types to conclude that much of our type is "inborn." This is in line with Prabhupda's translation that indicates that these four groups have an "inborn" nature (Srila Prabhupada writes, "born of their own nature"). Dr. Rohm, for example, writes that we are different "by design" and that we are "wired" to be a particular style.[7] If we accept this as fact, then each of us is born with a strong tendency toward a particular type of personality. We find all the above personality types represented in all races and cultures in the world, for all must exist in order to have a heterogeneous society.

To return to the four divisions of individual natures as described in our scriptures, Krishna continues in the *Bhagavad-gita* to describe the psychology of the *brahmana*s. He says, "Peacefulness, self-control, austerity, purity, tolerance, honesty, knowledge, wisdom and religiousness are the natural qualities by which the *brahmana*s work."[8] In the *Bhagavatam,* a similar description is given. The symptoms of a *brahmana* are control of the mind, control of the senses, austerity and penance, cleanliness, satisfaction, forgiveness, simplicity, knowledge, mercy, truthfulness, and complete surrender to the Supreme Personality of Godhead.[9]

The *kshatriya*'s nature is defined as heroism, power, determination, resourcefulness, courage in battle, generosity and leadership.[10] To be influential in battle, unconquerable, patient, challenging and charitable, to control the bodily necessities, to be forgiving, to be attached to the brahminical nature and to be always jolly and truthful – are the symptoms of the *kshatriya*.[11]

The *vaishya* is always devoted to the demigods, the spiritual master and the Supreme Lord; endeavors for advancement in religious principles, economic development and sense gratification; believes in the words of the spiritual master and scripture; and always endeavors with expertise in earning money – are the symptoms of the *vaishya*.[12]

The qualities that are the hallmarks of the *shudra* are offering obeisances to the *brahmana*s, *kshatriya*s, and *vaishya*s, being always very clean, being free from duplicity, serving one's master, performing sacrifices without uttering mantras, not stealing, always speaking the truth and giving all protection to the cows and *brahmana*s – these are the symptoms of the *shudra*.[13]

Brahmana, kshatriya, vaishya and *shudra* – also known as the four *varnas* – can be defined in terms of an individual's situation in what the *Bhagavad-gita* terms the "modes" of nature. Those modes are termed goodness, passion and ignorance. Each of the four *varnas* will gravitate towards one or more of these modes. The relationship between the three modes and the *varnas* is a vast topic and for the purpose of this discussion, it is sufficient to note that a person's alignment with these modes is another indication of his or her *varna*. Very briefly, the *brahmana*s are situated in the mode of goodness, the *kshatriya*s are situated in the mode of passion, the *vaishya*s are situated in the mixed modes of passion and ignorance, and the *shudra*s are situated in the mode of ignorance in terms of material nature.[14]

Acceptance of the personality types described in the *Bhagavad-gita* and *Bhagavatam* do not preclude the validity of some of the classifications which modern researchers have developed. Sometimes modern academic classifications will simply be described in different terminology to those of the Vaishnava scriptures. At other times, personality classifications will be a wholly different way of defining individuality. Below are a few examples of various theories in personality types. They are not presented as the definitive models by which teachers in ISKCON should base their work, but they are presented simply to show that several empirically verifiable models exist which have practical application for teachers.

Models for Classifying Personality Types

The first model is one originally proposed by psychologist, Dr. Howard Gardner. The seven types are linguistic, logical-mathematical, spatial, musical, bodily-kinesthetic, interpersonal and intrapersonal. Recently, those who use this system in education have added a category of "spiritual'. Gardner stresses that most people are a blend of strengths and weaknesses in several of these areas.[15]

Those with linguistic "intelligence" have highly developed auditory skills. They like to read, write and tell stories. Their memory is good, as is their spelling, and they take pleasure in solving puzzles involving words. The logical-mathematical type thinks in concepts, patterns and categories. They are capable of abstract logical thinking and are concerned with philosophical questions. Those with spatial "intelligence" can think well in images and pictures. They love to draw, design things and build. The musical type often remembers by putting information into melody and can discern subtle differences in music that they hear. The bodily-kinesthetic "intelligence" is demarcated by physical restlessness, and either fine-motor coordination or abilities in activities such as sports and dance. Those of the intrapersonal type understand other people, and tend to have positions of leadership. They enjoy and are good at anything that involves relationships between people. The interpersonal "intelligence" types are aware of their own feelings and motives. They often like to work alone and have a sense of independence or strong will. They can motivate themselves, have strong opinions, and are generally self-confident.[16]

We now turn to the categories which psychological researcher Howard Witkin used when conducting experiments for the US Navy. He was seeking to understand why some pilots would fly out of a cloudbank upside-down. He concluded that there are two broad ways in which people gain an understanding of the world: global and analytic. Most people are capable of both types of understanding, but will rely more on one of the two. The analytic types like things ordered step-by-step, observe details, value facts over feelings, want to concentrate on one thing at a time, are self-motivated, rarely become personally or emotionally involved, and may miss the main idea while grasping the facts. The global type is sensitive to others' feelings, flexible, needs reassurance and reinforcement, takes criticism personally, avoids competition and may skip steps and details.[17]

Yet, another way of demarcating personality types is the model that Dr. Anthony F. Gregorc developed. His concern was mostly in the area of the different ways that people process information, although his definitions of types overlap areas of interpersonal interaction, vocational preferences, and so forth. His research has shown that people are primarily concerned with either concrete or abstract information, and then organize this information either sequentially or randomly.[18] Taking all combinations of these mental organizational systems, we can classify four personality types: the concrete-sequential, abstract sequential, abstract random, and concrete random. Again, most human beings can, and to a certain extent do, function in each of these four ways.

The concrete sequential's general qualities are that he or she is hardworking, conventional, accurate, stable, dependable, consistent, factual, and organized. They may have difficulty working in groups, in a disorganized environment, with incomplete instructions, and with demands to use their imaginations. The abstract sequential's general qualities are those of being analytic, objective, knowledgeable, thorough, structured, logical, deliberate and systematic. Their difficulties are with not enough time for research, repetitive tasks, many specific rules, "sentimentality," and being diplomatic.

Abstract randoms are categorized by being sensitive, compassionate, perceptive, imaginative, idealistic, sentimental, spontaneous and flexible. Their challenges are in the areas of having to explain their feelings, competition, giving exact details, accepting criticism, or focusing on one thing at a time. The qualities of concrete randoms are to be quick, intuitive, curious, realistic, creative, innovative, instinctive and adventurous. They struggle with restrictions, formal reports, routines, fixing something after it has been done, keeping detailed records, and having no options.[19]

Dr. W. Lee Carter has analyzed six personality types: oppositional, sensitive, anxious, depressed, self-centered, and deceitful.[20] The difficulty with his understanding is that he focuses on the negative aspects of these types, which is reflected even in the labels he assigns to them. There is little guidance as to how the "negative" qualities can be applied as strengths.

There is also the Barbe-Swassing model of modalities – does a person learn and remember primarily through auditory, visual, or kinesthetic channels? The "modality" model for understanding varieties of human behavior is of great importance to the educator, as it addresses how each of us best assimilate and store information. Fortunately, although most of us have a predominant strategy for the order and circumstances where we use each modality, we can learn and remember in various ways. However, some people have such a strongly dominant mode that learning in other ways may be difficult. Individuals with such an intensely dominant modality will have describable patterns of learning, and, often, behavior.

Finally, the model put forward by Dr. Robert Rohm is particularly well developed.[21] He and other researchers such as Charles Boyd, have extensively applied their research to educational applications, and perhaps most importantly, he defines each type in terms of tendencies that can be either useful or harmful to the person depending on the use and direction of those inclinations.

Dr. Rohm first categorizes people as primarily outgoing-fast-paced-or reserved-slow-paced. Those who are fast-paced generally have the following attributes: confidence, ingenuity, like learning new skills, work in bursts of energy, are future-oriented, have more enthusiasm than patience, and are interested in results. Those who are slow-paced generally have the following characteristics: questioning attitude, like using skills already learned, work steadily at an even pace, are present-oriented, have more patience than enthusiasm, are fine with routine, and are more conscious of problems or procedures than solutions.[22]

Within each broad category of fast and slow-paced, are those who are primarily task oriented and those who are primarily people oriented. The general characteristics of the primarily task oriented are: they value logic over emotions, are truthful rather than tactful, question conclusions, can live without harmony, make decisions impersonally, are firm-minded, guard their emotions, are more decisive than curious, and take pleasure in finishing projects. Those who are primarily people oriented have these general tendencies: they value emotions and traditions over logic, are tactful rather than truthful, have strong relational abilities, accept conclusions, desire harmony, live according to the moment, are more curious than decisive, and take pleasure in starting projects.[23]

By combining the above categories, we arrive at four basic personality types. There are the fast-paced task oriented people, the fast-paced people oriented people, the slow-paced task oriented people and the slow-paced people oriented people.

Those who are fast-paced and task oriented tend to be strong-willed, determined, independent, optimistic, practical, productive, decisive, a leader, and confident if they use their tendencies for good purposes. If they use their tendencies improperly, they are likely to be angry, cruel, sarcastic, domineering, inconsiderate, proud, crafty and unemotional.[24]

The people oriented fast-paced person who uses his or her tendencies well will be friendly, compassionate, carefree, talkative, enthusiastic, personable, and fun. When those qualities are used improperly, they will be weak-willed, unstable, undisciplined, restless, loud, undependable, egocentric, exaggerative and fearful.[25]

A people oriented and slow-paced individual's well-used tendencies will include being calm, dependable, easygoing, trustworthy, efficient, practical, conservative, diplomatic, and humorous. Improperly used, the qualities of this type will be stingy, fearful, indecisive, spectator, self-protective, unmotivated, selfish, timid, and shy.[26]

The slow-paced, task oriented person's tendencies when used well will include being gifted, analytical, sensitive, perfectionist, aesthetic, idealistic, loyal, self-sacrificing, and thorough. When used improperly, such people will be self-centered, moody, critical, negative, rigid, theoretical, impractical, unsociable and revengeful.[27]

What of the differences in the physical appearances of an individual? Of course, we have the two broad distinctions of male and female. Some people are stronger and more athletically/physically able than others, some are healthy and some not, and so on. The differences of gender and physical ability are also certainly part of an individual's material inclinations such as their way of learning and vocational aptitude. Finally, the culture in which we grow up also has a great influence on how we exhibit our personality to others.

Practical application for understanding others

Suppose all the above methods of classifying personality are rejected because we do not want to classify people into types, wishing to relate to, and deal with, one individual in exactly the same way we do others. We may think that everyone is basically the same, or ought to be the same. When we do perceive differences, we will then evaluate against a fixed set of criteria. Charles Boyd writes, "I have yet to meet a person who does not 'put labels' on people. When you meet someone, for example, you make a quick evaluation of him . . . You size up his look, his personality, his intelligence, and how he makes you feel. If you're mature, you'll adjust your evaluation as you get to know this person."[28] So, we are always evaluating – but perhaps only in comparison to some "ideal" or ourselves.

A practical example of this is my observation of two women that were living in the same temple accommodation. One was outgoing and people-oriented while the other was reserved and task-oriented. Each thought that there was something very wrong with the other. They saw each other as inconsiderate, either uncaring or too pushy about the physical environment. Another example is that of a young man who was content to do rather simple and repetitive tasks in the service of the Lord. When he would be called upon to explain why he wished to live as a devotee of Krishna, he would simply explain how much happiness there is in Krishna consciousness. I would sometimes hear others remark that this young man was foolish, and, others felt that this man's spiritual life would not last if he did not quickly became more philosophically learned.

In both of these examples, people were making judgments of "good" and "bad," both in relation to materially and spiritually desirable qualities, using the positive aspects of their own individual type as an absolute criteria. In other words, if I am courageous and heroic, ready to take all personal risk to right the wrongs of society, I may see someone with a more peaceful, forgiving, and tolerant nature as weak and useless. The other person may in turn see me as conceited and reckless. The Sanskrit term for such narrow-minded thinking is *atmavan manyate jagat*, or "everyone thinks of others according to his own position"[29], or in other words, "I see others against the criteria of my own qualities, which I consider as good qualities."

So, if one does not acknowledge the existence of various types of personalities as being fixed and value-neutral, they may think that everyone should be more like himself or herself. Or, conversely, he or she may think a type very unlike him or herself to be the ideal. A person then strives to change one's basic innate nature, rather than to utilize one's nature in the service of the Lord. Such an attempt is generally useless, as the individual will never achieve the "ideal" goal which is in their imagination, because their innate nature and talents are incompatible for achieving this ideal personality. This is acknowledged by Lord Krishna as he points out that, "Even a man of knowledge acts according to his own nature, for everyone follows the nature he has acquired from the three modes. What can repression accomplish?[30] Compelled by the work born of your own nature, you will act all the same."[31]

If one who thinks that spiritual advancement, or even becoming a materially "better" person, means changing their personality, then this person will surely be frustrated. He or she will also be wasting valuable time and energy that could be used to enhance and utilize his or her own personality type for a good cause. It is even more dangerous to present only one "ideal" personality type for a devotee of the Lord. In an extreme case a person may even reject spiritual life as irrelevant if they do not perceive success for themselves in becoming the "ideal" personality type for a devotee. It is more healthy and philosophically correct rather, for an individual to render service to the Lord according to their innate natures, and from these activities every individual can become perfect: "By worship of the Lord, who is the source of all beings and who is all pervading, a man can attain perfection through performing his own work."[32]

Categorization into superficial and unhelpful personality types is another problem that arises when there is a failure to recognize that there are many varieties of personalities. Unhelpful categories are those that are taken as the total description of what the person is, or should be. For example, those relating to age, gender or race are particularly unhelpful. We can illustrate this problem further with an example of personality categorization according to gender. If all women are expected, for example, to be a particular personality type such as that they all should have a *shudra* mentality (suggesting low intelligence) or, they should all be concrete-sequential, or slow-paced people oriented, then women who do not fit into the assumed "correct" behavior pattern would be classed as deviant to the expectation of that society, clearly creating many problems. Some of these problems would be that society would attract only a certain type of woman who naturally had these personality traits, and those already part of that society with different natures to the accepted personality would either feel alienated or attempt to artificially change their natures to the expected ideal; they would not be able to simply be themselves. Similar examples can be drawn from a racial perspective. If a society classed all oriental people as a business orientated and only accepted them if they fit this categorization, then clearly there would be a section of the oriental community which would not be accepted in that society.

Empirical research has shown that whichever of the above models one uses, there is not an equal distribution of personality types in the population in general. For example, in Dr. Rohm's model only 10% of the population are predominantly fast-paced and task oriented. On at least one occasion, Srila Prabhupada described the ideal society as containing 5% *brahmanas*.[33] In the Gregorc model, the smallest group in the population is the abstract-sequential, though interestingly there is virtually an even distribution of each personality type within all models, across gender and cultural lines.

The final difficulty we will consider, that arises when we fail to acknowledge individuality, is intolerance for differences in opinion. We are not referring to differences of opinion about the Vaishnava *siddhanta*, the ultimate goal of life or the Absolute Truth. Rather, we are considering differences of opinion when considering how to accomplish a goal, the order of priorities that we take and the "right" and "wrong" with the actions taken in a particular situation. Srila Prabhupada explained that:

"So far as your question about controversy amongst the disciples . . . that is a fact. But this controversy is not material. Just like in a national program, different political parties are sometimes in conflict and make propaganda against each other, but their central point is always service to the country. Similarly, amongst the disciples . . . there may be some controversy, but the central point is how to preach the mission of His Divine Grace. If the central point is fixed up then there is no harm in such controversy. Every individual being must have his opinion; that is the significance of individuality, but all such differences of opinions must coincide in Krishna. In the battlefield of Kuruksetra were Arjuna and Bhisma who were fighting with one another, and because Krishna was on the side of Arjuna, sometimes Bhisma pierced the body of Krishna also with arrows. But still they remained the greatest devotees of the Lord."[34]

Individuality and the teacher

In order to respect individuality in education, we need to understand that individual uniqueness is an integral feature of reality, both in the material and spiritual worlds. We cannot make everyone the same, and as illustrated earlier, this is opposite to the desires of Lord Krishna, as He enjoys variety. We also need to accept that the innate material characteristics of an individual cannot change in this lifetime. Further, all varieties of personality are neutral, with the possibility of application for good or ill, spiritual advancement or material degradation.

After accepting the above values, we can demonstrate our respect for the individual practically when we work with their nature rather than against it. We can do this if we first recognize our own nature, and, seeing both our strengths and weaknesses, make an action plan for turning our inclinations to good purposes. In a similar way we can teach and relate to others in a more constructive way if we adjust to their individual motivating forces and self-perceptions. Cynthia Tobias lists five stages that one goes through when understanding individual differences. The first is awareness that there are fundamentally different types of people. The second may be to think our style is best. The third stage is appreciation of others, realizing that diversity is necessary for balance in society. Fourth, one may make excuses based on the limitations of one's own nature. And, finally, one can learn to adjust one's style to meet the needs of others that think and act quite differently.[35]

We can also develop understanding and rapport with others by knowing enough about their personality to understand how they experience the world, without which we cannot teach them, or be taught ourselves. We adjust our methods of teaching and explanation to the needs of the student, his or her modalities of learning, ways of intellectual processing or interpersonal dealings, or all three. The specifics of how to adjust according to these considerations is a vast topic beyond the scope of this essay. It is sufficient to say that a good teacher can and will adjust to the student. At the same time, giving a good education requires that we teach our students how to adjust as well, as the world will rarely come to meet them on their terms. Instruction on how to adjust their style is carried out not with the idea that their style is wrong or deficient and that we must "fix" them. Instead, we must know how to be helpful, and this necessarily means that the emphasis is on the teacher to adjust if we wish to give the student a beneficial education.

In the field of vocational training, teachers need to guide students to a career that will resonate with the student's tendencies and thus bring them individual satisfaction and contentment in their lives. Varieties of vocations are meant not only to accommodate various talents and propensities, but also tend to a balanced society. If we look at it in Vaishnava spiritual terms, different vocations are not meant for the gratification of either the individual or society, but for the pleasure of the Supreme Lord, Krishna. Our duties will only truly satisfy ourselves when they satisfy the Lord.

If we understand personality through the models presented in the *Bhagavad-gita*, the corresponding vocational direction becomes easier, as in that model personal qualities and work are closely entwined. Those with *brahminical* qualities work as priests, teachers, physicians, scholars, astrologers and government advisors. *Kshatriyas* administer governments and serve in the military. *Vaishyas* have work related to farming, business and trade. And *shudras* work in manual labor, entertainment, crafts and as general assistants to the other three types in society.

The concept of matching individual personality types to suitable vocations is not unheard of in academic research, from the other models discussed earlier. Each model of personality classifications described earlier also has vocations that naturally fit them; for example, the concrete random would be well suited for creative and innovative work, and the abstract sequential for intellectual pursuits, among other occupations.

For devotees of Krishna, vocation indicates not only one's means of earning one's livelihood, but also the way one serves the Lord. There are services to the Lord that are purely on the spiritual platform and are equally available to everyone, regardless of personality from any angle of vision. These are services such as hearing about the Lord, chanting His name and His glories, remembering Him, and so on. However, when it comes to whether one should manage a temple or a temple garden, be a renunciate or get married we should look not at what is considered "best" in absolute or theoretical terms, but rather what is best for the individual according to his or her nature.

Probably the most significant advantage of respecting individuality for the educator is the ability to encourage everyone as a devotee of Krishna. For example, when a student prefers to talk and be with friends rather than concentrate on his or her work, do we see him as distracted and lazy, or people oriented? When a student wants extra details for assignments, do we see him or her as picky or as analytical? As we can view the qualities of students in two ways – there are almost always two sides to any personal quality – and it is an important responsibility for the teacher to guide a student to utilize their personal characteristics for a positive purpose. A teacher can see every "fault" as a potential good quality that simply needs the right direction and environment to manifest properly. And, as every type of person has a contribution to make in the Lord's service, we can encourage the development of an ability to make a contribution that is in accord with one's nature.

Understanding the nature of others is fundamental to good teaching practice. Without this understanding it is impossible to guide them in their vocation and service. How is that understanding accomplished? Formerly, determination of *varna* was established by the spiritual master observing the student's qualities and studying their astrological chart. Unfortunately, this facility is not available to most of us now, yet we can still guide others based on our observation of their qualities. Of course, there are many modern tests to determine personality and corresponding vocation according to various models, and such tests may be helpful as long as they are used as with other guides rather than being the sole determining factor. Information on this subject should also be gathered from the Vaishnava scriptures for this.

To say that our educational system needs to be founded on respect for individuality does not go far enough. We need to learn to see ourselves honestly, and then engage our strengths while compensating for our weaknesses; if we can attempt to do this, we need not envy nor disparage other personality types in our schools and temples. We need to honor, glorify and teach students in consideration of both theirs, and our own, individual characteristics.

Footnotes

[1] Bhaktivedanta Swami, A. C., *Bhagavad-gita As It Is,* Los Angeles, USA: Bhaktivedanta Book Trust, 1989, 2.12.

[2] Ibid., 2.12 purport.

[3] The word *rasa* is impossible to translate exactly into English; it has a number of different meanings. For the purpose of this essay, we will loosely translate *rasa* as "relationship." For more details see Bhaktivedanta Swami, A. C., *The Nectar of Devotion,* Los Angeles, USA: Bhaktivedanta Book Trust, 1997.

[4] Bhaktivedanta Swami, A. C., *Teachings of Lord Chaitanya,* Los Angeles, USA: Bhaktivedanta Book Trust, 1994, ch.14.

[5] Bhaktivedanta Swami, A. C., *Srimad-Bhagavatam*, Los Angeles, USA: Bhaktivedanta Book Trust, 1987. 10.13.38 purport.

[6] Bhaktivedanta Swami, *Bhagavad-gita*, 18. 41.

[7] Rohm, Robert A., *Who Do You Think You Are, Anyway?*, Atlanta, GA: Personality Insights, 1997, p. xi, 3.

[8] Bhaktivedanta Swami, *Bhagavad-gita*, 18.42.

[9] Bhaktivedanta Swami, *Srimad-Bhagavatam*, 7.11.21.

[10] Bhaktivedanta Swami, *Bhagavad-gita*, 18.43.

[11] Bhaktivedanta Swami, A. C., *Srimad-Bhagavatam*, 7.11.23.

[12] Ibid., 7.11.24.

[13] Ibid.

[14] Bhaktivedanta Swami, *Bhagavad-gita*, 4.13, purport.

[15] Dr. Thomas Armstrong has made Gregorc's work accessible to the lay person. He lays out a method of assessment for the lay person. Armstrong, Thomas, *In Their Own Way*, New York, USA: G. P. Putnam's Sons Publishers, 1987.

[16] Rohm, *Who Do You Think You Are, Anyway?*, ch. 2.

[17] Tobias, Cynthia Ulrich, *The Way They Learn*, Colorado, USA: Focus on the Family, 1994, ch. 9.

[18] For those who feel that "random" has negative connotations, they could use the terms "linear" and "lateral" for sequential and random, respectively.

[19] Tobias, *The Way They Learn*, ch. 2.

[20] Carter, W, Lee, *Kid Think*, Houston and Dallas, TX: Rapha/Word Publishers, 1991.

[21] While there are several other models of personality type that could be listed, we'll end with those of

[22] Rohm, *Who Do You Think You Are, Anyway?*, pp. 34-39.

[23] Ibid. pp. 40-45.

[24] Rohm, Dr. Robert A., *Get Real,* Atlanta, GA, Personality Insights, 1995, p. 12.

[25] Ibid., p. 15.

[26] Ibid., p. 18.

[27] Ibid., p. 21.

[28] Boyd, Charles F., *Different Children, Different Needs,* Oregon, Multnomah, 1994, p. 47.

The North American GBC/Temple President Executive Officers wish to voice our strong disapproval of, and our protest against, the demeaning and ill intended statements made by some members of the GHQ com conference that were recently brought to public attention.

It is our firm position that Srila Prabhupada, the founder-*acharya* of ISKCON, intended his Hare Krishna movement to be free from all prejudice, sexism, racism and other forms of bigotry.

We affirm that the first and foremost principle of our Society is that all people (indeed all sentient beings) are eternal, sacred parts and parcels of the Supreme Lord Sri Krishna, and as such should be respected and affirmed in their individual relationship with the Lord, as well as their service to guru and Krishna.

Multiple statements made by members of this Internet conference ridicule, berate and vilify women, other minorities, and individual Vaishnava devotees. They document an organized attempt to prevent women from their God-given rights of self-expression and service to Srila Prabhupada. We denounce such views. They are opposed to the core values and principles of Vaishnava culture which upholds the devotional offerings of all souls as sacred and worthy of our respect and protection.

While we endorse open debate and dialogue within our Krishna Consciousness movement, we must speak out against any discussion that crosses the line of decency, morality, and Vaishnava etiquette and supports an agenda to exploit or minimize a section of our Society.

Bir Krishna Goswami, Chairperson
Anuttama Dasa
Sudharma Dasi
Vraja Lila Dasi

1999

Third Annual Women's Ministry Conference, New Vrindaban

October 1999

The Women's Ministry's third conference was held in New Vrindavan. For this gathering, we decided we wanted to bring together the broader community. No one exists in a vacuum, and community is very important to the hearts of many women. So, alongside discussions of Vaishnavi seva and sanga, we also considered the grihastha-ashrama and community development. Men were more directly involved in this conference. At the conclusion of the conference, we offered appreciations for the years of dedicated service of the Vaishnavis of New Vrindavan who worked so hard to build that community. Every contribution matters, and at New Vrindavan there were many unsung heroes.

Krishnanandini and Praharana Prabhus were in attendance, and this conference helped bring together some understanding on the need for a grihastha team. Another highlight was that Silavati dasi, a disciple of Srila Prabhupada who had been living for many years as a cloistered nun, attended. Srila Prabhupada had personally trained her in pujari service and had referred devotees to her for training. She was loved by many of our Movement's early devotees. We had not seen her for many years so her attendance was appreciated by many.

Two papers are available from this conference. One by Visakha Prabhu and one by Pranada Prabhu.

Toward Krishna Together
by Visakha dasi

Our Krishna Conscious Heritage of Affection

From the beginning of the creation of the universe, our heritage in Krishna consciousness is a bond of loving affection between devotees: parents and children, husband and wife, friend and friend, spiritual master and disciple. This bond of love originates from Lord Krishna Himself, who expressed great love for His child, Brahma. Lord Brahma in turn had great love for his child, Svayambhuva. Similarly, Svayambhuva Manu and his wife Satarupa raised their children with the deepest concern and love. For example, after they had found a suitable husband for their daughter, Svayambhuva Manu and Satarupa were about to leave the newly-married couple, when "The Emperor was unable to bear the separation of his daughter. Therefore tears poured form his eyes again and again, drenching his daughter's head . . . " (*Bhag.*, 3.21.25) Not surprisingly, the grandchildren of Svayambhuva Manu and Satarupa continued this noble and tender tradition. From these examples and from Srila Prabhupada's abiding affection for us, it is clear that these feelings are an integral aspect of God consciousness. Such concern for others buds within an individual, blossoms in the family, and then is implanted in the next generation.

Children raised with culture and love will become cultured, loving parents who in turn raise children of the same nature. Srila Prabhupada writes, "By bodily union of the husband and wife their qualities are expanded: children born of good parents are expansions of the parents' personal qualifications." (*Bhag.*, 3.23.10 purport) Conversely, a child raised by unqualified parents, especially the mother, may create havoc. Srila Prabhupada writes, "Good population in human society is the basic principle for peace, prosperity and spiritual progress in life . . . Such population depends on the chastity and faithfulness of its womanhood." (Bg. 1.40 purport) And, "Contemptuous sons are born of the condemned womb of their mother . . . This is especially true for boys; if the mother is not good, there cannot be good sons." (*Bhag.*, 3.14.39 purport) And, "If the maternal family is very corrupt or sinful, the child, even though born of a good father, becomes a victim of the maternal family." (*Bhag.*, 4.13.39 purport) "These are very important things, that soft-hearted women, *vama-svabhava (vama*-beautiful; *svabhava*-nature), they should be given protection. They should be trained up how to become faithful wife, affectionate mother. Then the home will be very happy, and without happiness we cannot make any spiritual progress. We must be peaceful. This is the preliminary condition." (Lecture *Bhag.*, 1.7.43 Vrindavan 10/3/76)

Peaceful Women Make a Peaceful Society

For a woman to be peaceful, she must first of all be at peace with herself. She must have a singleness of vision, a purity of intention, a central core to her life that will enable her to carry out her obligations and activities with her natural tenderness. A woman wants to live in inner harmony, which then translates into outward harmony: she wants her outer and inner worlds to be at one. She wants to achieve a state of spiritual grace from which she can function and give as she was meant to, according to her uniqueness.

Certain environments and modes of life are more conducive to inner and outer harmony than others. For example, simplification of life – both inward and outward – can bring extraordinary freedom and serenity. To become simple, devotees may need to remove themselves from conflict, offensive behavior, apathy, manipulation, endless talk with no results, rubber stamping, and the like. These are not a life of peacefulness and simplicity but the life of duplicity that Srila Prabhupada warned us of. They lead not to unification but to fragmentation. They do not bring grace; they destroy it. And this is not only true of women's lives, but of men's also. This is a concern for our communities and society.

A woman who feels her life invaded by duplicity, who feels unloved, is neither peaceful nor protected. She will be unable to inspire, emotionally support, and properly care for her husband and children; she will be unable to have meaningful relationships with her peers; unable to be enthused in Krishna's service. If one is not cared for and cared about, one is a stranger to oneself and estranged from others. What has not been received cannot be given. If we want to build a community, let's take a long look at the necessity of straightforward and affectionate relationships between its members. The deepest need of the soul is to overcome its separateness from the Lord and His servants, to leave the prison of its aloneness in material consciousness. The failure to meet this need means repeated birth and deaths. Without genuine affection between its members, a society crumbles from separatism, faultfinding, callousness, and endless controversy.

It is the softhearted, beautifully-natured, gentle woman who naturally forms the axis within the revolving wheel of relationships in the *grihastha-ashrama*. And it is her sacred time of hearing about, chanting about and serving the Lord that nourishes this all-important axis. In these basic practices of Krishna consciousness she finds and refines her inner strength, perceives the illusion of outward trappings, and enters into relationships with a fullness rather than an emptiness. If women are feeling empty, children and men will suffer. If women's hearts are filled, they will naturally help to fill the hearts of those around them, and their own will be renewed in the process.

To illustrate the effect of such fullness, let us turn to the example of Devahuti, the daughter of Svayambhuva Manu and Satarupa, who served her husband Kardama Muni "with great love and affection, and knew how to please him. . . . Having served him for a long time, she grew weak and emaciated due to her religious observances. Seeing her condition, Kardama, the foremost of celestial sages, was overcome with compassion and spoke to her in a voice choked with great love." (*Bhag.*, 3.23.1, 4 & 5)

As an adult, what Devahuti brought to her remote and austere *grihastha-ashrama* was determined by her background and childhood, her mind and it's education, her conscience and its values, her heart and its desires. From her exalted example we can see how a beloved daughter becomes a beloved wife and a loving mother and plays a vital role in society.

The woman who is not complacent but is satisfied and peaceful can joyfully fulfill her obligations to her family and engage her propensities gainfully in the Lord's service. We know well that during Srila Prabhupada's time with us, many woman served their husbands, raised their children, and painted, photographed, led *kirtan*, lectured, headed departments, traveled, preached, raised funds, participated in construction projects, gardened, served the Deities in the temples, and were generally fully excited about their lives in Krishna consciousness.

Protection Revisited

One who is protected is protected in body, mind, intelligence and spirit. The mind is protected by following certain rules of conduct, and the intelligence by hearing genuine knowledge, knowledge that awakens us to our actual situation and evokes self-realization; such knowledge is compared by Krishna to a sword that cuts through illusion. And the spirit is protected by love. It is the love between the child and parents, wife and husband, friend and friend, disciple and spiritual master, and ultimately the living entity and the Lord, that guides us to right thoughts, right words, and right action. And if by chance we make mistakes (or apparent mistakes) it is love that will bestow upon us the forbearance to tolerate the apparent misfortune that results.

Protection must not be confused with repression, stifling or performing stereotyped functions. Rather, it is similar to what an experienced gardener offers a valuable tree: freedom from disturbance so it can grow to its full capacity. Protection is not the artificial clipping imposed on an espalier or a topiary garden. If you love someone, your goal is that they be all that they can be, and you will encourage them every inch of the way. Every time they do something that helps them grow or learn something to help them become more, you are pleased and may sometimes even dance and celebrate the occasion. You're not growing apart; you're growing together in Krishna's service and for His pleasure.

A devotee is not challenged or threatened by another's growth in Krishna's service, but rejoices in it. A devotee does not impose gender consciousness on aspiring Vaishnavas. Such superficial cutting and clamping is the behavior of those who lack understanding, who confuse Srila Prabhupada's words with their own conceptions.

Allow all to grow in their areas of interest. Let us all blossom for Krishna's pleasure. Srila Prabhupada writes, "No one should try to check a person, no matter what his present position is, from coming to the platform of a *brahmana* or a Vaishnava." (*Bhag.*, 5.26.23 purport) And, "*Vaishnave jati-buddhih*. If anyone considers a Vaishnava, a devotee of the Lord, in the categorical estimation of birth, then that is hellish consideration." (*Bhag.*, 6.1.41-42 lecture), and, "So far as your question regarding women, I have always accepted the service of women without any discrimination . . . " (letter to Gurudasa, 1972)

The exemplary marriage of Kardama Muni and Devahuti produced nine wonderful daughters and Kapiladeva, an incarnation of the Supreme Lord, who, after His father renounced family life, happily stayed with His mother, gave her the ultimate protection of transcendental knowledge, and pleased her.

Thus Devahuti served and received service from her great husband, Kardama Muni, as well as her transcendental son Kapiladeva. Protected by the love of her exalted parents, her husband and her children; fully enlightened by Kapiladeva, the Supreme Lord Himself; not only did Devahuti attain perfection – eternal, blissful residence on a Vaikuntha planet – but she also was instrumental in disseminating Lord Kapiladeva's instructions to the world. Srila Prabhupada writes, "The mission of the appearance of the Supreme Personality of Godhead in the form of Kapila was to distribute the transcendental knowledge of Sankhya philosophy, which is full of devotional service. Having imparted that knowledge to His mother and, through His mother to the world, Kapiladeva had no more need to stay at home, so He took permission from His mother and left." (*Bhag.*, 3.33.12 purport)

As Devahuti was protected and able to grow to her full majesty, so all women should similarly be encouraged to grow to their full and unique majesty.

The Lilas of Three Women

Draupadi's Example

Let us look at several examples of women from the *Srimad-Bhagavatam*. First, Draupadi, the exalted wife of the Pandavas.

When Ashvatthama, the heartless murderer of her five sleeping sons, was brought before her, Draupadi "could not tolerate Ashvatthama's being bound by ropes, and being a devoted lady, said: 'Release him, for he is a *brahmana*, our spiritual master.'" Commenting on this verse, Srila Prabhupada remarked, "Draupadi, being a women, *vama-svabhava*, very soft-hearted, she did not consider whether he (Ashvatthama) is actually a *brahmana* . . . A woman, *varna-svabhava*, she can accept that 'Because he's the son of a *brahmana*, he's *brahmana*.' Therefore the word is used, *vama-svabhava*. Because women are considered less intelligent. . . . Their heart is very soft. Just like children, their heart is very soft. But their intelligence is not very sharp. That is the difference . . . They have been put in one group: women, *vaishyas*, and *shudras*. Because they are not very intelligent. They can be molded by another intelligent man to the proper channel. Therefore they require guidance. They require guidance." (Lecture *Bhag.*, 1.7.43 Vrindavan 3 October 1976)

The next day Srila Prabhupada lectured on the next verse in which Draupadi says, "It was by Dronacharya's (Ashvatthama's father) mercy that you learned the military art of throwing arrows and the confidential art of controlling weapons," and Srila Prabhupada commented. "So this is Vedic civilization. Draupadi advising Arjuna that 'You have learned. Feel always obliged,' . . . this *guru-mara-vidya* (killing the guru after learning from him) should be avoided. That is the instruction in this verse we can get, and that is the Vedic way. It is not that Draupadi is speaking, but Chaitanya Mahaprabhu is also speaking . . . Chaitanya Mahaprabhu was very strict on this point." (Lecture *Bhag.*, 1.7.44 Vrindavan October 4, 1976)

Speaking on the following verse the following day, Prabhupada said, "So, in continuation of the Pandavas' position in relationship with Dronacharya, the guru, so many things are being explained by Draupadi. So she is not ordinary woman. She knows everything of religious principles, and therefore she is teaching the assembly of respectable, learned persons how the spiritual master should be respected . . . That is being explained by even one woman. That is Vedic culture. Draupadi is explaining the importance, and she said, *sa esa bhagavan drona*. She's quite right when she's accepting Drona as Bhagavan. *Se esa bhagavan dronah praja-rupena vartate*. And he is present by his *praja*. So these things should be taken very seriously instruction." (Lecture *Bhag.*, 1.7.45-46 Vrindavan, 5 October 1976)

The following day Prabhupada continued with the next verses, in which Draupadi says to Arjuna, "My lord, do not make the wife of Dronacharya cry like me. I am aggrieved for the death of my sons. She need not cry constantly like me. . . . " Srila Prabhupada remarked, "So, in these two verses the important point is that Draupadi is sympathetic. That is Vaishnava. She is Vaishnavi. This is the attitude of the Vaishnava . . . They never think that he is very advanced. Never . . . So the feeling of Vaishnava is like that. Similarly, Draupadi is Vaishnavi. She is feeling more than herself, the wife of Dronacharya, mother of Ashvatthama, how she will feel. Therefore Vaishnava's qualification is, *para-dukha-duhkhi*. Personally a Vaishnava is not unhappy, but a Vaishnava becomes unhappy for others' distress." (Lecture *Bhag.*, 1.7.47-48 Vrindavan, 6 October 1976)

The next verse the next day was, "Suta Gosvami said: O *brahmanas*, King Yudhisthira fully supported the statements of the Queen (Draupadi), which were in accordance with the principles of religion and were justified, glorious, full of mercy and equity, and without duplicity. Nakula and Sahadeva (the younger brothers of the King) and also Satyaki and Arjuna, the Personality of Godhead Lord Sri Krishna, son of Devaki, and the ladies and others all unanimously agreed with the King." And Prabhupada confirmed, "Then the statement of Draupadi was accepted by all the gentlemen, or the kings. Everyone accepted." (Lecture *Bhag.*, 1.7.49-50 Vrindavan, 7 October 1976)

Here we see that the statement of Draupadi, an elevated Vaishnavi, is first considered that of a less intelligent woman. Then we find that her statement is confirmed by Vedic culture, by Lord Chaitanya, and by all the elevated personalities present, including Lord Krishna Himself. Is this contradictory? Only apparently. Queen Draupadi spoke from her heart and, as her heart was pure, her words were wise, pleasing to the Lord and appreciated by great souls.

Srila Prabhupada informs us that if we try to become Krishna conscious alone it will not be possible; it will be a failure. We are in this together. So to achieve our goal of becoming Krishna conscious, we are obliged to study the nature of our relationships and exchanges. It is exchanges that are steeped in mutual humility, respect and affection that will bless us in our efforts to purify our hearts and move toward Krishna together. Such exchanges will give the Lord pleasure, as did Draupadi's exchanges with Arjuna.

Sati Offers Us More Instructions

From Canto Four of the *Srimad-Bhagavatam*: "Vedic material relationship existed between Lord Shiva and Sati, but sometimes, due to weakness, a woman becomes very much attracted by the members of her father's house, and this happened to Sati. In this verse it is specifically mentioned that she wanted to leave such a great husband as Shiva because of her womanly weaknesses . . . " (*Bhag.*, 4.3.3, purport)

After this we find that Sati "wanted to see whether or not her husband was being respected. To see her relatives, her sisters and mother, was not so important; even when she was received by her mother and sisters she did not care, for she was most concerned that her husband was being insulted in the sacrifice . . . Since Sati was a chaste woman and the wife of Lord Shiva, it was her duty to establish the elevated position of Lord Shiva, not only by sentiment but also by facts . . . She did not actually come to her father's house to participate in the function, although before coming she pleaded with her husband that she wanted to see her sisters and her mother. That was a plea only, for actually at heart she maintained the idea that she would convince her father, Daksha, that it was useless to continue being envious of Lord Shiva. That was her main purpose." (*Bhag.*, 4.4.9 &16, purports)

From this we discover that Sati's intent, cloaked in womanly weakness, was in fact to preach to her father who insisted on dishonoring the best of the Vaishnavas, Lord Shiva.

Next, Sati reveals her humility: "Sati decided to give up her body because she thought herself to be among the *shudras* and *vaishyas*. As stated in *Bhagavad-gita* (9.32), *striyo vaishyas tatha shudrah*. Women, laborers and the mercantile class are on the same level. Thus since it is recommended that *vaishyas* and *shudras* should immediately give up their bodies upon hearing the blasphemy of an exalted person like Lord Shiva, she decided to give up her life." (*Bhag.*, 4.4.17, purport)

And again, we visit other aspects of the reality of this situation: "Since Sati was the representation of the external potency of the Lord, it was in her power to vanquish many universes, including many Dakshas, but in order to save her husband from the charge that he employed his wife, Sati, to kill Daksha because he could not do so due to his inferior position, she decided to give up her body." (*Bhag.*, 4.4.18. purport)

If we read these pastimes with intent to establish our own point of view (whatever it is), their sublimity will elude us. They are not a denigration of women but an exaltation of Vaishnavas and Vaishnava behavior, here portrayed by Sati's selfless love for her husband, her attempt to reform her proud father, and her impeccable sense of propriety.

Parvati's Example

For our third and final example, we turn to Parvati. From *Srimad-Bhagavatam* Canto Six: "Lord Shiva tried to convince his wife, Parvati, that her cursing of Chitraketu was not very sensible." Srila Prabhupada comments, "Here is a difference between male and female that exists even in the higher statuses of life – in fact, even between Lord Shiva and his wife. Lord Shiva could understand Chitraketu very nicely, but Parvati could not. Thus even in the higher statuses of life there is a difference between the understanding of male and that of a female. It may be clearly said that the understanding of a woman is always inferior to the understanding of a man. In the Western countries there is now agitation to the effect that man and woman should be considered equal, but from this verse it appears that woman is always less intelligent than man . . . These were all friendly jokes; there was nothing serious for which Parvati should have cursed

Chitraketu. Upon hearing the instructions of Lord Shiva, Parvati must have been very ashamed for cursing Chitraketu to become a demon. Mother Parvati could not appreciate Chitraketu's position, and therefore cursed him, but when she understood the instructions of Lord Shiva she was ashamed." (*Bhag.*, 6.17.34-35, purport)

This certainly seems like a clear fault of womankind. Yet, as in the other examples, there are other aspects to this pastime: "The difficulty was that Chitraketu, having become a great devotee of Lord Visnu, Sankarshana, was somewhat proud at having achieved Lord Sankarshana's favor and therefore thought that he could now criticize anyone, even Lord Shiva. This kind of pride in a devotee is never tolerated. A Vaishnava should always remain humble and meek and offer respects to others. . . . Chitraketu thought himself a better controller of the senses than Lord Shiva, although actually he was not. Because of all these considerations, Mother Parvati was somewhat angry with Chitraketu . . . Mother Parvati was justified in punishing Chitraketu, for Chitraketu impudently criticized the Supreme Father, Mahadeva, who is the father of the living entities conditioned within this material world. The goddess Durga is called mother, and Lord Shiva is called father. A pure Vaishnava should be very careful to engage in his specific duty without criticizing others. This is the safest position. Otherwise, if one tends to criticize others, he may commit the greatest offense of criticizing a Vaishnava . . . It is to be understood that mother Durga was justified in punishing Chitraketu. This punishment was a boon to Chitraketu because after taking birth as the demon Vrtrasura, he was promoted directly to Vaikuntha." (*Bhag.*, 6.17.10 and 15, purports)

"Srila Visvanatha Cakravarti Thakura comments that Maharaja Chitraketu being cursed by Parvati should be considered the mercy of the Lord. The Lord wanted Chitraketu to return to Godhead as soon as possible, and therefore He terminated all the reactions of his past deeds. Acting through the heart of Parvati, the Lord, who is situated in everyone's heart, cursed Chitraketu in order to end all of his material reactions. Thus Chitraketu became in his next life and returned home, back to Godhead." (*Bhag.*, 6.17.17, purport)

So, are we witnessing a woman's inferior understanding, or that woman meting out unjustified punishment, or that woman delivering a divine boon, or the Lord's supreme plan? We are witnessing all of them. Again any contradiction is only apparent; and again it is resolved in relationships steeped in uplifting, mutually beneficial feelings:

Lord Shiva doesn't want his friend, Chitraketu, to be cursed for his jokes.

Parvati, in the mood of a mother, corrects Chitraketu for his pride and criticism of the greatest Vaishnava, Lord Shiva.

As a "son," Chitraketu humbly accepts Parvati's curse, although he could have done otherwise, and benefits as a result.

The whole affair is an exchange of respect, love and humility. Such exchanges can only be grasped through the culture of Krishna consciousness and the development of genuine affection for Vaishnavas. Those of us under the grip of passion will either be turned off by the statements of women, or be turned on by them, and either way unable to incorporate contrary statements.

A theme of womanly selflessness gently arises from these lilas: while Ashvatthama so craved conquest that he ignored humanness, Draupadi so desired relationships that she ignored Ashvatthama's inhumanity. A Vaishnava is one of infinite compassion.

In apparent weakness Sati left her husband to strongly object her father's treatment of him. A Vaishnava's life cannot include blasphemy.

Parvati corrects Chitraketu for proudly criticizing a Vaishnava. A Vaishnava's life means shedding false ego and ambition, shedding one's mask and armor. In each case the actions of these beautifully-natured women was born of a desire to do good to others in Krishna consciousness. In each case one could say they were ignorant or weak or mistaken, as well a woman may be, and in each case one could also correctly say their words and actions were Krishna conscious. In a dance, what may appear as a misstep, may not be. The dancer may be following a rhythm that we are not yet aware of; when we do become aware of it, then we can appreciate the dancer's movements. A Vaishnava's life is meant for this broadness and clarity.

Srila Prabhupada's *Lila*

Srila Prabhupada introduced us to relationships steeped in respect, humility, and affection without sensuality, and he himself was the personification of such relationships. Here are excerpts from letters that he himself wrote to one fortunate Vaishnavi: "I am so much obliged to you for your devotion and affection for me. I thought of you all throughout my journey from San Francisco to New York and I was praying to Lord Krishna for your more and more advancement in Krishna Consciousness." (4/10/67) "Every minute I think of you and as you asked me to go to San Francisco while returning from India, I am trying to fulfill my promise." (11/4/67) "With the greatest satisfaction I have just now read over your nicely composed and hand-written letter . . . and I thank you so much for the kind sentiments you have expressed therein. I had also been thinking of you because you were thinking of me, but as your letter has arrived first it is for me to answer it. Actually, I always think of you as my naughty daughter and from the start of the movement, you and your very good husband have always shown to be very sincere and I will always appreciate this." (9/9/68) "I was thinking of you since about a week why are you silent, and all of a sudden I got your letter with a golden ring enclosed. It was so much ecstatic. I thank you very much for your kind presentation which you have given . . . immediately upon receipt of this ring I pushed it on my finger, and it is very nice." (1/18/69) "I lost my mother when I was only 14 years old. So I didn't get much of my mother's affection in my childhood. But in my old age, Krishna has given me so many young mothers to take care of me." (2/20/69) " . . . even I am far away, as you say you are remembering me, so also I am remembering you, and in that sense we are never separated." (12/27/72)

The relationship between the spiritual master and the disciple is not simply functional – the master giving knowledge and instructions and the disciple learning and obeying – but it is also a fully personal exchange into which, in the highest sense, two people enter with the interest of the other and the Supreme Lord at heart. Each does not serve limited and partial ends. The value of their exchange lies in its *bhakti* and for that reason transcends all materially-based relationships. The affection between them is transcendentally fulfilling, infinitely considerate, gentle and enthusing.

The light shed by this relationship illuminates all relationships. The disciple loses herself in her service to a worthy person, Srila Prabhupada, and in doing so finds herself in the highest sense. And thus finding herself she can weather the pettiness of useless controversy, of life's endless details, and always thirst for the magnitude and magnanimity of Srila Prabhupada's gift. In the service of her master, her inner life nourished, she can become whole, centered, and free from distraction: she gives of herself fully for his sake. It is from this spiritual strength that an individual, a family, a community and a society can flourish.

Making Our Heritage Relevant Today

In our Krishna conscious heritage all relationships, between husbands and wives, parents and children, spiritual master and disciple, friend and friend, are marinated in mutual respect, humility and affection. Subtract these vital ingredients and simply demand submission, subordination and service (in the name of Krishna consciousness), and the exchange quickly decomposes. Let us not dwarf the individual next to us, dear to us, by the enormity of our own ego. Hear from that person. Be awakened to his or her dignity.

What we seek is for the members of a family and a community to work with the same vision. Drawn together in Krishna's service, we stretch to understand each other and are invigorated by the stretching. We move through life like dancers coming together and then moving into their separate spaces yet always to the same rhythm. Together creating a pattern and being invisibly nourished by it. The joy of such a pattern is not only the joy of creation or participation, but also the joy of living it, of each person completely in touch with the music, poised on the beat in the present, free of innuendoes from the past and omens of the future, moving so harmoniously that who is leading and who is following is immaterial. Each individual feels accepted, appreciated and valued. And the individual is the special concern of the woman, as Ashvattama was for Draupadi, Daksha for Sati, Chitraketu for Parvati. The woman never forgets the particular uniqueness of each member of the family; she wants the best for that person, and she will sacrifice for that person. Awareness of others and giving to them is the basic substance of community.

This dance of community begins with our personal growth in humility; it begins when our fear of others is exorcised by respect for them. It begins when our relationships are not only functional, but are also the affectionate unification of devotees who are developing in all they can be and who are encouraging others to do the same.

These are the essential elements that form a community. We may neglect these realities. And we may witness our community fragment. We may emphasize these realities and move toward Krishna together.

Continuing the Journey
by Pranada dasi

How many of you have seen the September/October issue of BTG?

For me this issue is very telling. In fact, this single issue spoke volumes to me about women in the Krishna consciousness movement.

My initial introduction to the magazine was common enough. As I was reading I was quite impressed with the quality of the articles. The visuals seemed improved over other issues. The magazine was engaging. Overall I had this good feeling about my time with this issue. I turned to the back cover and thought, "Great, something else new, too." Then I picked up the magazine to return it to the bookshelf having completed my review.

I didn't realize that my review was just beginning.

As I went to put the magazine down it dawned on me, "Hey, most of the articles in here are written by women and they are good articles. This wasn't just filler stuff. There was refreshing depth of realization on a wide range of subjects. This has substance!"

As I examined this magazine, the whole history of women in ISKCON became clear. What is currently happening for women also became clear, and in seeing that, I got a glimpse of the future – a very bright future.

As I stepped toward the bookshelf this flash of clarity was confirmed by my recent experiences in Alachua and I felt reassured of the truth of my insight. This issue indeed pointed to a trend in our movement.

Women's participation in ISKCON is increasing – sometimes in areas where previously they were unseen. And overall their contribution is noteworthy. It's not that doors are opening, some women are coming forward, and we're amused by the cute attempts. Rather, I'm overwhelmed by the impressive contribution they are making.

In Alachua there are about nine women on the *Bhagavatam* class schedule. Ladies are giving class and leading *kirtans* a few times every week. It's starting to feel very natural and we're getting a chance to see how much talent has been carefully tucked away for so long. It's like taking valuable gems from the closet and seeing, as if for the first time, their sparkling beauty.

I'm responsible for asking the ladies to do these services, so I regularly see how they respond. They go from fear and horror or terror or completely discounting my request as a valid one, to happiness – actually ecstasy – once they finally find the courage to do the service.

On Vyasa-puja day our godsister Sunita Prabhu spoke some homages to Srila Prabhupada for the first time ever. It was very difficult for her to relate just one pastime about Srila Prabhupada in front of everyone. But afterward she came up to me with this effulgent smile and with a slight tear in her eyes and said," I just want to thank you so much for getting me to finally do that. It was such a wonderful experience I want to do it again. I never thought I could do that!"

I am regularly moved to see this transformation in my godsisters. Here are ladies that have been deeply programmed for many, many years, that they have no value, or very little worth to our movement. And they have believed it and lived it for as many years. To break free of this is an immense challenge, requiring us to really apply ourselves to change.

As I'm watching women around the movement come forward more and more I see parallels of our collective journey to an individual's journey of recovering from mistreatment.

Initially there is blind acceptance of the mistreatment, or perhaps simply denial that it exists. Then gradually the person awakens to the fact they are being mistreated and they decide not to accept that anymore. Even after that determination occurs, though, there is a long journey of putting the pieces of self-worth back into place. As the person is finding their way back to health and balance, they may venture out of their previous boundaries with great caution and trepidation. They test the water here and there to make sure it's safe and no more peril awaits them. As they do this they receive confirmation of their value as human beings and can further blossom in their true glory. Then they start manifesting qualities and abilities even they themselves were not aware of.

If you look at BTGs from the 70s and 80s they starkly contrast this current issue. One or two women were writing even then, but for the most part women all but disappeared from sight in ISKCON and thus those BTGs document the dark time in history when women in ISKCON were convinced of their lack of worth both as human beings and devotees. Actually BTG simply mirrored the climate prevalent all over ISKCON which had systematically de-empowered, de-valued and marginalized women.

The current issue has simply mirrored another a time in history and this one tells of progress: Women in Krishna consciousness are healing. Gradually we're becoming empowered and we're understanding we have contributions to make to Srila Prabhupada's movement in ways we didn't think possible before. It is in recognizing the signs of recovery then that this BTG showed me there's no stopping the ladies' journey to full health and participation. And that's why this moment in history is so exciting and full of hope.

Today I just want to urge each one of you in this room to help each come out of hiding; in whatever way you are currently withholding from expressing your full contribution for Srila Prabhupada. I'm here to tell you unequivocally you each have immense value and can do much to spread Srila Prabhupada's movement. Take courage that you're not alone in the fear and uncertainty and feelings of lack of qualification. As each of us face our fears – not letting them dictate to us – then we'll each get additional courage and strength to go forward.

I see this happening in our little microcosm in Alachua. As women and young ladies regularly see that it is all right for women to perform these services and they see women doing them, then they start to see the possibility that they too can do the services. They gain courage. It is contagious. It's not only *kirtana* and *Bhagavatam* class, but also any service where previously women were prohibited. We need women showing by example in all services.

Don't think there aren't opportunities for you. There are unlimited opportunities. Every other day I have someone ask me if there is a woman somewhere that would be willing to be a temple president here, or could be the manager of a PR office for the GBC, or could be on the editorial review board of ISKCON World Review, or work with the development of Mayapur to make sure women are represented there or could help children. The list is endless. In fact, perhaps the Women's Ministry could function as a clearinghouse connecting you to service opportunities in the movement. Aside from particular services, though, the journey we're on is more about rebuilding our sense of dignity and our place in the Krishna consciousness movement.

Each one of us will come forward or express ourselves in our own way. But please do come forward, please give full expression to your talents and thus give hope and courage to others; make sure this contagious effect of healing spreads. Whatever hesitation or obstacles you face in fully expressing and offering your best service, or finally doing that service you've secretly cherished doing for Srila Prabhupada, please overcome that, for yourself but also for others, for the Movement all around the world. As we continue to gain strength in North America, the rest of the world will gain conviction and the healing process successfully underway here will spread to women on other continents and give them strength to begin their journey.

It's important to understand that while we're continuing our journey, some have not yet begun theirs. There are women in some countries who are still facing the *Bhagavatam* classes condemning women; women and children are being abandoned for book distribution and many other social ills that we saw in the 70s and 80s are repeating themselves elsewhere in our movement. Indeed it doesn't take a psychic to foretell of child abuse to come in those areas due to de-empowering the women. Therefore, I ask you not to forget these godsisters, these children. Move forward yourself and this will help them; it will make it impossible for the misogyny that drives this mistreatment to flourish.

The more we continue to break through our fears and obstacles to offer what we are best qualified to do, individually and collectively – taking courage, strength and hope from each other – then the more the Krishna consciousness movement will be benefited, we will be benefited, and the world will be benefited.

What's a Woman to Do?
by Visakha dasi

This article was printed in Back to Godhead *magazine. The two-part brochure of the same title found in the Appendix of this anthology is an expanded presentation and should not be missed.*

"These women are not ordinary women. They are preachers. They are preachers. They are Vaishnava. By their association, one becomes a Vaishnava." (Srila Prabhupada, morning walk, March 27, 1974)

Srila Prabhupada, India's greatest emissary to the Western world, established *ashramas* and temples in the west, as well as an entire spiritual society. To do this he inspired women as well as men to become devotees of Lord Krishna and he authorized these women to live in *ashramas* and to serve the Lord in a wide variety of ways, some of them unconventional, although exactly in accordance with the teachings of Lord Krishna. So, what is the position of women in the society that Srila Prabhupada founded, the International Society for Krishna Consciousness (ISKCON)?

To answer, let's first look at the purposes of ISKCON. In its founder's vision, the members of ISKCON are dedicated to distributing spiritual knowledge and techniques to others, and to practicing the same themselves. It is a spiritual movement based on rendering transcendental loving devotional service to the Supreme Lord, Sri Krishna.

Devotional service means to engage all our senses in the service of the Lord, the Supreme Personality of Godhead, the master of all the senses. When we render service unto the Supreme, there are two side effects: we are freed from all material designations, and, simply by being employed in the service of the Lord, our senses are purified.

In other words, Srila Prabhupada wanted all of his followers – men, women, and children – to become free from all material designations and restored to their pure identity, engaging their senses in the service of Lord Krishna, the proprietor of the senses. In this way their spiritual life is revived.

Another way to understand Srila Prabhupada's message and mission is to reflect on the Sanskrit word *dharma*. *Dharma* is the essential function or nature of a thing and that characteristic that constantly exists with it. Thus one can say that the *dharma* of fire is heat, the *dharma* of water, liquidity, and the *dharma* of sugar, sweetness.

And what is our *dharma*, the *dharma* of the living being? To render service. Srila Prabhupada writes, "we can easily see that every living being is constantly engaged in rendering service to another living being. A living being serves other living beings in various capacities. By doing so, the living entity enjoys life. The lower animals serve human beings as servants serve their master. . . one friend serves another friend, the mother serves the son, the wife serves the husband, the husband serves the wife and so on. If we go on searching in this spirit, it will be seen that there is no exception in the society of living beings to the activity of service. . . and therefore we can safely conclude that service is the constant companion of the living being and that the rendering of service is the eternal religion [*dharma*] of the living being." (introduction to *Bhagavad-gita As It Is*)

In the material world every living being dwells within a body made of material elements. Each of us is a living being (soul) who is presently covered with a gross and subtle material body. Due to our original nature, which is spiritual, and due to our covering, which is material, each of us has two types of *dharma*: eternal (*sanatana*) *dharma* – our spiritual service to the Supreme spirit, Lord Sri Krishna; and our own (*sva*) *dharma* – the service that is appropriate for our particular mind, intelligence, and senses.

Concerning our own *dharma*, Lord Krishna says (*Bhagavad-gita* 4.13) that this service is not determined by our birth but by our qualities and activities. According to the qualities and activities of human beings, the Lord has established four general types of occupations for the smooth functioning of human society: *brahmanas* – learned priests, teachers, and advisors; *kshatriyas* – government leaders and military men; *vaishyas* – agriculturalists, businessmen, and cow-protectors; and *shudras* – laborers. (In our present confused age, many persons don't fit neatly into any one occupation, but express their talents in several of them.)

Whatever one's position in this societal scheme, the persons who fill these various roles generally do not do so alone, but together, as a husband-wife team. In other words, men and women marry based on their compatible natures and propensities and the wife assists her husband and takes primary charge of the home and of raising their children. Srila Prabhupada writes, "a wife should not only be equal to her husband in age, character and qualities, but must be helpful to him in his household duties" (*Srimad-Bhagavatam* 3.22.11 purport). And the *Srimad-Bhagavatam* declares, "Marriage and friendship are proper between two people who are equal in terms of their wealth, birth, influence, physical appearance and capacity for good progeny, but never between a superior and an inferior" (10.60.15). Thus a *brahmana*'s wife is like a mother for her husband's students, the queen is considered as a mother by the citizens, the agricultural women are expert in utilizing milk and other products of the cows and land, and so forth. In this way both husband and wife are fully and fulfillingly engaged, and in a society composed of such families, peacefulness, happiness, and a cooperative spirit prevail.

However, our own *dharma* is not complete unless it is also bonded with eternal *dharma*. "The occupational activities a man performs according to his own position are only so much useless labor if they do not provoke attraction for the message of the Personality of Godhead." (*Bhag.* 1.2.8) In his explanation to this verse, Srila Prabhupada writes, "The self [soul] is beyond the gross body and subtle mind. He is the potent active principle of the body and mind. Without knowing the need of the dormant soul, one cannot be happy simply with emolument of the body and mind. The body and the mind are but superfluous outer coverings of the spirit soul. The spirit soul's needs must be fulfilled. Simply by cleansing the cage of the bird, one does not satisfy the bird. One must actually know the needs of the bird himself.

"The need of the spirit soul is that he wants to get out of the limited sphere of material bondage and fulfill his desire for complete freedom. He wants to get out of the covered walls of the greater universe. He wants to see the free light and the spirit. That complete freedom is achieved when he meets the complete spirit, the Personality of Godhead."

It was to this end, to enable persons to get out of the limited sphere of material bondage and to meet the Supreme Lord, that Srila Prabhupada founded ISKCON. Although he was in the renounced order of life (a *sannyasi*), Srila Prabhupada arranged and sometimes performed the ceremonies for the marriages of his disciples – acts unprecedented in the history of *sannyasa* – and Srila Prabhupada engaged these young people in a myriad of services both according to their propensities (*sva dharma*) and as their service to the Lord (*sanatana dharma*). Thus, under Srila Prabhupada's direction, there were devotee men and women artists, writers, typists, speakers, singers, Deity caretakers (*pujaris*), book distributors, managers, and so on. For example, my husband, Yadubara das, and I were both trained in photography and served in ISKCON together, my husband as a cinemaphotographer, and I as the sound person and photographer. In this way we sometimes filmed and photographed Srila Prabhupada, who, on more than one occasion, commented, "Husband and wife working together in Krishna consciousness, this is very nice."

For another example, when three householders couples successfully started a Krishna conscious center in London, Srila Prabhupada praised their efforts and noted that his spiritual master had wanted such a center in London many years before, but his spiritual master's *sannyasi* disciples had been unsuccessful in starting one. Srila Prabhupada's young, western Krishna conscious householders had succeeded where mature Indian renouncers had not.

Thus Srila Prabhupada's vision was for his disciples to marry and serve the Lord together, in harmony. He writes, "a wife is necessary to assist in spiritual and material advancement. It is said that a wife yields the fulfillment of all desires in religion, economic development, and sense gratification. If one has a nice wife, he is to be considered a most fortunate man" (*Srimad-Bhagavatam* 3.21.15 purport). Srila Prabhupada wanted to see happy Krishna conscious couples, of like dispositions and proclivities, offering their services to the Lord, making their home conducive for spiritual life, raising their children to be godly, and making gradual, solid spiritual advancement. "By worship of the Lord who is the source of all beings and who is all-pervading, persons can attain perfection by the performance of their own work." (Bg. 18.46).

While this ideal is quite attractive for most people, it also raises some questions: what, if anything, can a woman do beyond assisting her husband, beyond her housework, and beyond her sacred duties as a mother? And what of women who are unmarried, widowed, married but childless, or married with grown children? For such women, their

must be protected (the other four being *brahmana*s, women, children, and cows), Srila Prabhupada sees himself as protected. Yet at the same time he was an unparalleled leader.

In the Hare Krishna movement, Srila Prabhupada trained men to see all women – except their own wife – respectfully as "mother," and women to see all men respectfully as their "sons." As the son's duty is to protect his mother, so one of the duties of Srila Prabhupada's men is to protect Srila Prabhupada's women. A Vaishnavi leader is protected by her husband and/or by her "sons."

Therefore in the Lord's spiritual society and for His pleasure, a woman may do whatever service is suited to her particular qualities and activities. While this principle may seem straightforward and clear to some, it is a point of great controversy for others. These others believe that due to her birth a woman may not do certain services for the Lord, even though she may be qualified for them. Sometimes this line of thinking is culturally based, for example, traditionally in India women don't perform certain Deity services in the temple – a standard that Srila Prabhupada respected in India in order to preach successfully to the people there. And in other cases, especially in reference to a woman leading, disqualifying a woman simply due to her being a woman may be a product of the male ego (a version of the false ego) that is easily identified as "the temperament of always wanting to be in a superior position" (*Bhag.* 9.3.10 purport).

To function successfully in such a difficult milieu, a woman spiritual leader must be soft-hearted, sensitive, astute, guileless, clear-headed, and fixed in Krishna consciousness, seeing herself as a servant of all. It is her natural, humble service attitude which is her saving grace, as well as her gracious and urgently needed contribution to Srila Prabhupada's society.

Srila Prabhupada's established ISKCON so that devotees could please the Supreme Lord Sri Krishna by serving Him with devotion. The Lord is pleased by all service sincerely rendered to Him; in one sense there are no "superior" and "inferior" services. And, from the perspective of the Lord and His pure devotees, all the servants rendering those services are equal. Srila Prabhupada explains, "Therefore in the bhakti platform, Krishna consciousness, there is no such distinction, Here is American, here is an Indian, here is an African, here is this and that." No. Everyone is Krishna conscious. So actually if we want equality, fraternity, then we must come to Krishna consciousness. This is the purpose of Krishna consciousness movement. And actually, it is becoming fact, factual. These boys and these girls, they are no more thinking that they are American or European or Canadian or Australian and Indian also. They are equal. So if you want equality, fraternity, friendship, love and perfection, solution of problems, all problems, economic, political, social, religious, then come to Krishna consciousness. Come to this platform. Then all your ambitions will be fulfilled and you will be perfect." (*Bhagavad-gita* lecture, 13.4)

And let us be enlightened by the perspective Srila Prabhupada reveals in this conversation:

Srila Prabhupada: In the spiritual platform there is no such distinction, man, woman, or black, white, or big or small. No. Everyone is spirit soul. *Panditah sama-darsinah. Vidya-vinaya-sampanne brahmane gavi hastini suni caiva sva-pake ca panditah,* one who is actually learned, he is *sama-darsinah.* He does not make any distinction. But so far our material body is concerned, there must be some distinction for keeping the society in order.

Woman: The women could become *panditas,* then.

Prabhupada: Oh, yes. *Te 'pi yanti param gatim.* Not only [be]come, she can also attain perfection. There is no such restriction. Krishna said.

Woman: Do you have any panditas in the Western movement?

Prabhupada: There are so many Western woman, girls, in our Society. They are chanting, dancing, taking to Krishna consciousness. Of course, because superficially, bodily, there is some distinction, so we keep women separately from men, that's all. Otherwise, the rights are the same." (June 18, 1976, Toronto)

In order not to be distracted from the goal of our lives – rendering uninterrupted, pure devotional service to Krishna – Srila Prabhupada here emphasizes that men and women should not mix (except if they are married). And he also says that men and women have the same rights. What are those rights? Their right – their privilege – to serve the Lord according to their propensity, according to their hearts' desire. Ultimately the real occupational duty, *dharma,* of women is nondifferent from the *dharma* of all living beings: to eternally serve Krishna. A woman who is sincerely and seriously serving the Lord in whatever capacity she chooses should be honored and encouraged rather than being designated as a "woman" and discouraged in this divine service. Those who discourage her reveal their own lack of spiritual awareness and create a godless disruption. Srila Prabhupada clearly declares: "Everyone should be allowed to render service to the Lord to the best of his ability, and everyone should appreciate the service of others. Such are the activities of Vaikuntha. Since everyone is a servant, everyone is on the same platform and is allowed to serve the Lord according to his ability." (*Bhag.* 7.5.12 purport).

Available in German here.

2000

"Healing the Heart of ISKCON":
A Delegation of Vaishnavis to the
Annual Mayapur GBC Meetings

Introduction to the 2000 GBC Meetings
by Visakha and Sudharma dasis

The status of women in ISKCON has long been a contentious issue. Is ISKCON's attitude to women a reflection of Vaishnava values or is it a perversion of them? Are ISKCON members following Srila Prabhupada's instructions or manipulating them to support their own agendas? This year, for the first time, ISKCON's Governing Body Commission (GBC) heard presentations by representatives of the ISKCON Women's Ministry. We present here a brief history of women in ISKCON, the presentations made at the GBC meetings and the 2000 GBC apology and resolutions that they prompted.

In New York, in the spring of 1966, shortly after Srila Prabhupada had coined the acronym "ISKCON" and had laughed playfully with the new word, he initiated the legal work of incorporating the Society. Stephen Goldsmith, a young Jewish lawyer, fascinated by the idea of setting up a religious corporation for an Indian *swami*, began to help. On 11 July 1966, Mr. Goldsmith came to Prabhupada's lecture and *kirtana* at 26 Second Avenue to get signatures from the trustees for the new Society. To the surprise of the people gathered, after Srila Prabhupada's lecture, Mr. Goldsmith stood up and made a short announcement asking for signers on an incorporation document for the Swami's new religious movement. The first trustees – those sympathizers with enough reverence towards the Swami to want to help him – were Michael Grant, his girlfriend Jan Marie Campanella, and James Greene.

Two months later, on Srila Prabhupada's Vyasa-puja day – 9 September 1966 – Srila Prabhupada held the first initiations in ISKCON. Michael Grant became Mukunda Dasa and Jan became Janaki Dasi, Srila Prabhupada's first woman initiate and one of three ISKCON trustees. Three days later, Prabhupada performed a marriage ceremony for them. In those early years, Prabhupada established a personal, warm rapport with each of his disciples and nurtured them in spiritual life. This was true of both men and women. Excerpts from letters that Srila Prabhupada wrote to Janaki over the years reveal how he spiritually transformed her life: "I am so much obliged to you for your devotion and affection for me. I thought of you all throughout my journey from San Francisco to

New York and I was praying to Lord Krishna for your more and more advancement in Krishna consciousness."[1] "Every minute I think of you and as you asked me to go to San Francisco while returning from India, I am trying to fulfill my promise."[2] "With the greatest satisfaction I have just now read over your nicely composed and hand-written letter . . . and I thank you so much for the kind sentiments you have expressed therein. I had also been thinking of you because you were thinking of me, but as your letter has arrived first it is for me to answer it. Actually, I always think of you as my naughty daughter and from the start of this movement, you and your very good husband have always shown to be very sincere and important members of our Society. So I know that both of your services are most sincere and I will always appreciate this."[3] "I was thinking of you since about a week why you are silent, and all of a sudden I got your letter with a golden ring enclosed. It was so much ecstatic. I thank you very much for your kind presentation which you have given . . . immediately upon receipt of this ring I pushed it on my finger, and it is very nice."[4] "I lost my mother when I was only fourteen years old. So I didn't get much of my mother's affection in my childhood. But in my old age, Krishna has given me so many young mothers to take care of me."[5] ". . . even I am far away, as you say you are remembering me, so also I am remembering you, and in that sense we are never separated."[6]

As Srila Prabhupada expressed fatherly emotions towards his disciples, sometimes addressing them as "my dear sons and daughters," so the early temples that he established had a family spirit. Women served side by side with their male counterparts, opening centers, giving class, singing and chanting, performing varieties of other service, and personally caring for their elderly spiritual father. However, as the movement grew, the camaraderie of the early years dwindled. A growing number of Srila Prabhupada's male disciples accepted the renounced order of *sannyasa;* and subsequently devotee women were no longer viewed as partners in a spiritual renaissance, rather they were categorized as personifications of the illusory energy, Mayadevi, who threatened to cause men to deviate from their noble spiritual quest. Women were tolerated more than welcomed. In some temples they were relegated to the back of the temple room where they would not distract the men (rather than the side, where they could see the Deities without peering over the heads of their male counterparts). Generally, women were no longer asked to give classes, to lead *kirtans* or to manage. They had to sit through many discouraging and disparaging lectures in which the intelligence, motives and capabilities of womankind were criticized or scorned.

Women's *ashramas* began to close. Those who were provided *ashrama* facility were often expected to perform disproportionate service or sell paraphernalia on the streets for the Society's income (thus the evolution of the infamous women's parties). Women's role as mother was also called into question, and patience lacked with women who refused to take up temple service rather than care for their children. These conditions were exacerbated by the complete social and financial dependence each temple resident had on the management.

By 1974, this mood reached a zenith: women were now unwelcome. Tamala Krishna Goswami writes of the Radha-Damodara Traveling Sankirtana Party (RDTSKP), which he led:

"The [male] visitors felt strengthened by the atmosphere of renunciation, not so easily available in the temples, where there were so many women. Vishnujana strictly maintained a principle of not preaching to women. Seeing that I was bent on making new devotees, men or women, he had sagaciously directed, 'Whenever you make a woman a devotee, you lose one man.' [Referring to the fact that women had to be married eventually, and there was the possibility that the men would become absorbed in household life and thus be diverted from preaching activities.] At least for our party of *sannyasis* and *brahmacharis* living on a bus, it was sober and practical advice. (Tamala Krishna Goswami, ch. 13)

Several years of this kind of preaching created a major controversy between *grihasthas* (householders) and *sannyasis*. In Sridham Mayapur on 14 March, 1976, it was reported to Srila Prabhupada that: "*Brahmacharis* were being told that if they remained in the temples they would end up married, entangled in family affairs, and therefore useless. On the other hand, they could accept the alternative of a carefree life, traveling and preaching with the RDTSKP buses." However, "Tamala Krishna Maharaja was adamant, defending his party and their record-breaking book distribution. He proclaimed the accusations as outright lies." Srila Prabhupada settled the issue by "wonderfully preaching to everyone that it does not matter what one is, one can do anything and go anywhere for Krishna. We are not to discriminate against anyone on the basis of external dress. One is to be judged on the basis of one's advancement in Krishna consciousness." (Hari Sauri Dasa, Vol. 1, Ch. 9)

Although Srila Prabhupada's words were unequivocal and from that day the Radha-Damodara Party never again had the same mood or influence, the attitude towards women in the Krishna conscious movement was never restored to the original, family-like warmth that Srila Prabhupada had instituted in the early days. While the standards and expectations regarding women varied from place to place, in general women were not considered for any managerial positions, their counsel was not sought in any decision-making, they were still obliged to stand in the back of the temple, they were not asked to lecture in the temples, and women as a class were still denigrated in lectures. There was no system of grievance resolution or channel for communication when difficulties and exploitation arose.

Then, in 1977, the Society's spiritual leader, father, solution provider and counsellor passed away from this world.

Times were difficult. "As a single woman living in the temples in the late 70's and 80's I witnessed a social demoralization of women and families," recounts one female devotee. "Women acted more and more as men. Men lost touch with their feminine qualities. Children felt isolated. Growing numbers of families left behind their temple services and moved out of the temples, sometimes forced, to seek stability and financial independence elsewhere. Domestic violence was on the rise. Conditions for women living in the temples became abysmal, and the terms 'protection' and 'exploitation' seemed practically interchangeable."

Yet, through the difficulties, rays of hope began to emerge. When an elderly woman of 70 travelled from the United States to Mayapur for the yearly festival there, she was told to stay on the roof of one of the buildings. That night brought a downpour. Many were outraged. A letter was written to the Mayapur authorities decrying this travesty. Women galvanized their efforts and thinking and began to seek support, which they found in the Communications arm of the Society. Discussions ensued, papers were written, and *Priti-laksanam*, a publication of uncensored presentation, was established by Pranada Dasi.

Other developments were afoot. In 1992 a conference was held by ISKCON Communications on the subject of women in ISKCON at the German farm (Nava-jiyada-nrsimha-ksetra), then widely viewed as a bastion of male dominance. Ravindra Svarupa Dasa gave an influential address at this conference. Within a year the German National Council decided to reserve a third of its seats for women and by 1994 three German temples had women serving as temple presidents.

In 1995 Harikesa Swami, at that time GBC for Germany, declared that "where there is discrimination, it should be abolished."[7] He stressed that women be given equal facility in temple life and be respected according to their position. This statement cleared the way for abolition of such practices as women being left to stand at the back of the temple room during *aratis*, being ignored for any management position, or not being invited to give *Bhagavatam* class in major European temples such as Radhadesh (Belgium), Bhaktivedanta Manor (UK) and Heidelberg.

In the US, women were attending the North American GBC and temple presidents' meetings. After a moving presentation on the women's issues by a mixed panel of men and women, Sudharma Dasi was elected an executive officer for ISKCON North America. That position entitled her to be a guest of the international GBC body (Governing Body Commission, the highest managerial arm of ISKCON) in Mayapur. There, with the help of several male GBC members, she formed the International Women's Ministry, which was officially approved as an ISKCON ministry in 1996. Later, Malati Dasi, with the help of the Women's Ministry and the support of her local GBC, was recommended as a regional GBC candidate. Together the two began attending the International GBC meetings in Mayapur.

The Women's Ministry began holding conferences in the United States and Europe. These conferences afforded women the opportunity for training, uplifting positive association within ISKCON, and dialectic experience. Women's Ministry conferences are held annually in the US with an average of more than 150 attendees. Many attended these conferences, including male and female leaders of ISKCON, professional counsellors and professors of religious study.

Sudharma's repeated requests for the GBC to examine the situation of women in ISKCON was postponed year after year until, in September 1999, a crisis brought the topic to the forefront. One morning, just before *mangala-arati*, in ISKCON's International Krishna-Balaram Temple in Vrindavan, the *brahmacharis* formed a human chain, linking arm-and-arm, to prevent the women from taking close *darshana* of the Deities. Some women tried to break through this chain and were physically rebuffed. When news of this went out on the Internet, devotees throughout the world were alarmed. Dozens of versions and hundreds of opinions about what happened were exchanged. Using this incident as a catalyst, the Women's Ministry was able to put the women's topic on the table at the annual international GBC meeting in Mayapur. On 1 March 2000, nine women spoke to the assembled GBC representatives. It was the first time in the movement's 30-year history that such a testimony was heard. As a result of these presentations, the GBC wrote an apology into their 2000 resolutions.

The presentations that follow will lend insight into the struggle of the women of the Krishna consciousness movement – a struggle that has encountered and helped synthesize the apparent contradictions between Eastern and Western lifestyle and culture.

What follows are the texts of their talks. These papers were published in *ISKCON Communications Journal* 8.1 in June 2000 issue.

Bibliography

Tamala Krishna Goswami, *Servant of the Servant*. Hong Kong: The Bhaktivedanta Book Trust, 1984.
Hari Sauri Dasa, *A Transcendental Diary*, Vol. 1. San Diego: HS Books, 1992.

Footnotes
[1] Letter to Janaki, 10 April 1967.
[2] Letter to Janaki, 4 November 1967.
[3] Letter to Janaki, 9 September 1968.
[4] Letter to Janaki, 18 January 1969.
[5] Letter to Janaki, 20 February 1969.
[6] Letter, 27 December 1972.
[7] Memo to the German National Council, 6 January 1994.

Srila Prabhupada's Transcendental Sweetness and Beauty
by Yamuna Devi

What a week of Vaishnava *sadhu-satsanga* this has been! I leave the richer, having exchanged with my family members, old and new, godbrothers, godsisters, nephews and nieces. While I feel most unqualified to speak to you today, I am honored and privileged to join my godsisters in voicing my concerns as a woman in ISKCON.

As the GBC body, all of you are responsible for establishing Srila Prabhupada's legacy, which, in these difficult and turbulent times, is at stake. One realm of that legacy – the rapport Srila Prabhupada established with his Vaishnavi disciples – is the topic of our discussion today, because over the years since his disappearance it has been largely forgotten. Perhaps my personal service and association with him, along with his later guidance and instructions, offer some insights in this area.

As a strong and independent young woman, I met Srila Prabhupada in 1966 and took initiation in 1967. Had Srila Prabhupada demanded conformity to orthodox roles for women as a condition of surrender, I, along with many of my godsisters, would probably not have joined ISKCON. That he did not is testament to his spiritual vision. He lovingly encouraged and engaged us in the service of the *sankirtana* movement, and he consistently revealed himself to be *panditah sama-darshinah* – equal to all.

In both men and women, Srila Prabhupada observed our propensities and expertly dovetailed them in his preaching mission. For many years, in different countries and circumstances, I had the good fortune to render personal service to him. He trained me, urged me to accept more and more responsibility, and regularly asked me to lead *kirtans*, give classes, arrange programs, manage departments, provide comforts for visiting devotees, meet with leaders, and actively promulgate Krishna consciousness. In ISKCON India, where previously no women were allowed, he sent me to various temples to learn cooking and Deity worship, and he repeatedly asked me to train others in the same.

It would take much longer than the limited time I have here to give you a glimpse into the numerous exchanges that illustrate Srila Prabhupada's demeanor and mood. However, one such exchange is what I call the Chanakya Pandita episodes. I was present on four occasions when Srila Prabhupada repeated the Chanakya adage: "Never trust a woman or a politician." On each occasion Srila Prabhupada looked me in the eye to see my response. On the last occasion, in Bombay in 1973, he quoted the saying, heartily laughing in front of a small group of men. Then he said: "What do you think, Yamuna?" Immediately I retorted: "Of course it is true, Srila Prabhupada," whereupon he became grave, looked at me with great feeling, and said, "But you are not a woman, you are a Vaishnava."

Another series of exchanges centered on leading *kirtana*. Srila Prabhupada often had me lead the first *kirtana* before he spoke at a program, whether in front of twenty people or ten thousand people. There were occasions when I felt uncomfortable with this. At the Jaipur *pandal* at Radha Govinda temple, I refused to lead *kirtana*. Srila Prabhupada called me over and said, "Lead *kirtana*." I said, "I can't. My throat hurts." He said, "No. Lead *kirtana*." So, croaking like a frog, I led *kirtana*.

In late 1974, not long after I had left my householder *ashrama*, Srila Prabhupada pronounced it "good that you have left your husband," and encouraged me to become a "*sannyasini*." Although I was not in the traditional role of being protected by my father, husband or son, in both his personal *darshanas* and written instructions, Srila Prabhupada offered me unfettered encouragement and astonished me with unexpected answers to my questions.

After settling in Oregon with my godsister Dinatarini, Srila Prabhupada, while pronouncing us "independent" to a concerned godbrother, at the same time twice rebuked us when we approached him to leave. "You westerners are so restless," he admonished. "Why can't you remain in the same place? Stay where you are." We questioned, "But Srila Prabhupada, they are saying that if we aren't in ISKCON, we lose your blessings and cannot make advancement." Prabhupada replied, "ISKCON is where you are chanting the holy name – that is ISKCON." We rejoined: "They are saying we don't have any association here and are therefore in *maya*." He replied: "Association can be two or two hundred. If you are two and compatible, you can become perfect in Krishna consciousness. If you are 200 and are not, then no one will make advancement."

To conclude, Srila Prabhupada trained me to be concerned about his movement, and at this time I am deeply concerned. Now more than ever, it is time to revive and imbibe Srila Prabhupada's mood with his disciples. If we neglect this, an aspect of his greatness will remain unknown to future generations.

I appeal to the GBC that along with the laudable projects you are managing and those you are contemplating – especially the magnificent temple that will arise here in Sridham Mayapur – consider that the behavior of the ISKCON devotees who participate in these projects must also be magnificent. Any other behavior will make the projects less than worthy of Srila Prabhupada's name. This grave responsibility falls on you. In other words, let us instill in every person who comes into contact with Srila Prabhupada's movement the healthy spiritual relationships that he had with his followers – his mood of encouragement, protection and kindness.

The closer we come to individually appreciating and honoring Srila Prabhupada's personal dealings with his disciples, the closer we will come to his sense of completeness in Krishna consciousness, to his joyfulness, to his transcendentally attractive nature.

With great care, our service is to create a devotional environment where men, women and children can thrive in Krishna consciousness, rendering service according to their desire and inclination. Our service is to empower rather than inhibit the service propensity in others.

Finally, let us search our intelligence and hearts for ways to help the women who are sincerely looking for spiritual life. Without properly nurturing them, we as a society have no future. Women in Krishna consciousness are an intricate, essential part of Srila Prabhupada's legacy. In our effort to move forward, let us not put Srila Prabhupada's example behind us, but in front of us – our divine beacon – to guide us together towards the lotus feet of Sri Sri Gaura-Nitai and Sri Sri Radha-Krishna.

Srila Prabhupada left us with clear directives for women: being the weaker sex, in every stage of her life a woman must be protected, either by her father, her husband or her grown son. A woman is dependent and chaste; she must learn to cook and to be a faithful wife.

Are Prabhupada's female followers questioning or have they forgotten these clear guidelines? The women who today are examining the mood and restrictions that some male members of ISKCON have imposed or would impose on them, are doing so on the strength of Prabhupada's teachings and personal example.

Whatever contradictions we may find in these are only apparent. Closer examination and realization will reveal that Prabhupada's legacy is harmonious in all its aspects, including the important aspect of womankind and her duties. It is only in the mature reconciliation of apparent contradictions that Srila Prabhupada's priceless legacy will be left balanced and complete for future generations of his followers.

Regarding the women's issue, apparent contradictions repeatedly originate from statements concerning the principles of *bhakti-yoga* on one side and statements concerning the principles of *varnashrama-dharma* on the other. Srila Prabhupada describes bhakti in this way: "*Sarvopadhi-vinirmuktam.* You have to understand that 'I am not this body. I am neither Indian, nor American, nor Russian. I am part and parcel of God. Therefore my business is to serve God.' This is called bhakti. That is the definition of bhakti. *Sarvopadhi-vinirmuktam.* You have to get yourself cleansed from all these designations, the 'I am Hindu,' 'I am Muslim,' 'I am Christian,' 'I am American,' 'I am this,' 'I am cat,' 'I am dog.' These are all designations because I am pure spirit soul, *aham brahmasmi.* And these conceptions are designations. So you have to be educated how to become free from designations . . . So our request is, let us wash ourselves from the designations. How it will be possible? . . . The dirty things are within my heart, so if we cleanse our heart, then we become free from this designation." (Lecture on *Bhagavad-gita* 13.4, Miami, February 1975.)

Prabhupada's personal lila exemplifies his own pristine heart. For example: "Jadurani helped Govinda dasi gather flowers and the two girls talked together. Both had heard the men say that women were less intelligent, and they felt discouraged. Later Govinda dasi told Prabhupada about the problem. 'Is it true,' she asked, 'that because we are women we won't make advancement as quickly as the *brahmacharis?*'

"'Yes,' Prabhupada answered. 'If you think of yourselves as women, how will you make any advancement? You must see yourself as spirit soul, eternal servant of Krishna.'" (*Srila Prabhupada-lilamrita,* Volume 3, page 150.) And: "Prabhupada was smiling and looking directly from one devotee to another. 'I want each of you to go and start a center.

What is the difficulty? Take one *mridanga*. Then another person will come and join you – he will take *karatalas . . .* '

"'The girls also?' Rukmini asked.

"'There is no harm,' Prabhupada said. 'Krishna does not make distinction – female dress or male dress. I mean to say, the female body is weaker, but spiritually the body does not matter. In the absence of Lord Nityananda, His wife, Jahnavi devi, was preaching. First you must understand the philosophy. You must be prepared to answer questions. Krishna will give you intelligence. Just like I was not prepared to answer all these questions, but Krishna gives intelligence.'" (*Prabhupada* by Satsvarupa dasa Goswami, pages 146-147)

And, in his purport to *Adi-lila* 7.31-32, Srila Prabhupada emphasizes the same principle: " . . . those girls are not ordinary girls but are as good as their brothers who are preaching Krishna consciousness." On the other side of the issue, in Chicago in July of 1975, when asked, "Where do women fit into this [*varnashrama*] social structure? You keep referring to a man." Srila Prabhupada responded that according to the status of her husband, a woman became first, second, third or fourth class. Discussing the same topic on a walk the next morning, Prabhupada said, "Our policy should be that at Dallas Gurukula we shall create first-class men. And we shall teach the girls two things: how to become chaste and faithful to their husband and how to cook nicely."

While Prabhupada and the group of devotees returned to the car, the topic changed to the political troubles in India. Prabhupada commented, "If Indira Gandhi [Prime Minister of India at the time] takes my advice, then I can keep her on the post, and she can do greater service to India. Immediately the whole public will give her support. My first step would be to capture all the hoarders and distribute the grains free. Immediately the public will be obliged to her . . . But to remain the leader she requires spiritual knowledge, otherwise it will be another disaster. If she wants to remain leader then she must be a spiritual person. She must become a Vaishnavi." (*Srila Prabhupada-lilamrita* Volume 6 pages 67-68, 73-75.)

Here, Prabhupada first explains the traditional, home-centered, subservient role for women in the *varnashrama* system, and then explains how a female leader can best remain in power – through her development in *bhakti-yoga*. So, as conservative as some consider Prabhupada's stance regarding women in the *varnashrama* system, those same people will find Prabhupada's stance equally liberal regarding women in *bhakti-yoga*.

From a letter: "The actual system is that the husband is the spiritual master to his wife, but if the wife can bring her husband into practicing this process [of Krishna consciousness], then it is all right that the husband accepts the wife as the spiritual master. Chaitanya Mahaprabhu has said that anyone who knows the science of Krishna should be accepted as spiritual master, regardless of any material so-called qualifications, such as rich or poor, man or woman, or *brahmana* or *shudra*." (Silavati, June 14, 1969.)
From a conversation: "In the material world, is there any prohibition that a woman

cannot become a professor? If she is qualified, she can become a professor. What is the wrong there? She must be qualified. That is the position. So similarly, if the woman understands Krishna consciousness perfectly, she can become guru." (June 18, 1976.)

The Caste System

Our duty, as the custodians of Srila Prabhupada's legacy, is to synthesize the principles of *bhakti-yoga* on one side, with the principles of *varnashrama dharma* on the other. If we are presently forbidding certain services to qualified Vaishnavis, we may be quickly gliding toward the caste system, the convoluted and stultifying misapplication of *daiva-varnashrama*, Lord Krishna's divine social arrangement. Due to this perversion of Krishna's plan, in India today we may find a child born to simple laboring parents who would make an able leader, but is forbidden. Or a child born of priests who wants to farm but cannot, or a farmer's child who is a natural scholar but is obliged to raise okra. These are travesties.

Is this the direction we want ISKCON to go? By not protecting the right of a woman to serve according to her capacities, by squeezing her into a box that all women are supposed to fit in, by default this is the direction we are going unless we take definite steps to change. The suppressive, rigid society that refuses to acknowledge or accept individual proclivities harms itself and harms those it suppresses. In Krishna's divine arrangement, by contrast, one's duties are determined by one's activities (*karma*) and qualities (*guna*), not by one's birth (*janma*).

In November 1971, when Srila Prabhupada returned to Vrindavana with his Western disciples, he enjoined the caste conscious *brahmanas* and *goswamis:* "Our purpose should be to serve Krishna with our senses purified of false designations. This is the transcendental stage. A Vaishnava should not be considered European or American. No. These boys and girls have forgotten that they have come from Europe and America or that they once belonged to a Catholic group or Jewish group. Similarly, we should forget, 'I am a Hindu, I am *brahmana.*' We have to become designationless. We should forget all these false identities . . . So many nonsense things are going on for want of actual spiritual education . . . This Krishna consciousness movement proposes that nobody should think of himself as belonging to a certain family, sect or nation. All these designations have created havoc in the world."

Similarly, discriminative policies and attitudes toward women have created and will continue to create havoc in ISKCON. As, in 1971 Srila Prabhupada requested the Brijbasis not to see his disciples in terms of their birth, so in 2000 – twenty-nine years later – Prabhupada's ladies request the other members of his Society not to see them in terms of their birth.

How long will ISKCON continue to squelch many of the unique contributions of its women in the name of Krishna consciousness? How long will Prabhupada's ladies confront sexism in the name of Krishna consciousness? Were we to put pen to paper on the subject of sexism in ISKCON, devotee women who've been around even for a short time could write volumes, and the older generation could fill bookshelves.

Lord Sri Krishna's practical and dynamic system of social organization enables persons to do what they are able regardless of their birth and, with his unique genius, Srila Prabhupada pushed forward that social system. Under his watchful and caring tutelage, qualified women, like qualified men, did what they were able, and part of these women's qualification was that they were protected, dependent, faithful and chaste. Thus Prabhupada's instructions about women and his practical example in relation to women were and always have been in harmony.

Barring a qualified person, male or female, from devotional service due to their birth is a kind of violence to the soul that not only reveals a critical lack of common sense, but also reveals a materially conditioned mentality, a mentality born not of transcendental realization, but of the modes of material nature. Lord Chaitanya said, "I am not a *sannyasi, vanaprastha, grihastha,* or *brahmachari*; I am not a *brahmana, kshatriya, vaishya* or *shudra*, I am the servant of the servant of the servant of Krishna."

Similarly, Prabhupada's female followers are not women, they are the servant of the servant of the servant of Krishna. One who denies their right to serve in the capacity they are able is violating these saintly souls. Women who are encouraged rather than suppressed will, by the grace of Krishna, develop a keen sense of propriety and act in such a way that pushes on Krishna's mission.

Srila Prabhupada often quoted the aphorism that "Men are like butter and women are like fire. In the presence of fire, butter melts." As far as is practical, women and men always remain separate and make gradual advancement in Krishna consciousness. In this way, the woman's fire becomes not a fire to melt butter but, due to the purity of her intent, a fire of knowledge, a fire that burns ignorance to ashes. The flames of such a fire can consume the fire of lust that threatens to burn every unmindful conditioned soul.

Conclusion

ISKCON needs all the help it can get in the years ahead. Unless it succeeds in convincing the female devotees that they have an equally important role to play – not only physically, but also intellectually and spiritually if they so desire – an immense resource will be wasted; more important, ISKCON's prospects for the future will be seriously undermined. It seems to me that the role of women must be reconstructed in ISKCON. ("ISKCON at the Crossroads?" by Julius Lipner, British scholar of Hindu studies, *ISKCON Communications Journal* 3, 1994)

One's eligibility to attain the highest goal, the Lord's abode, depends on one's development of pure love of God (*suddha-bhakti*) and corresponding freedom from the influence of the modes of goodness, passion and ignorance. It is entirely a matter of one's personal spiritual evolution and has nothing to do with bodily dress. Srila Prabhupada emphatically states, " . . . in devotional service there is no discrimination between lower and higher classes of people. In the material conception of life there are such divisions, but for a person engaged in the transcendental service of the Lord, there are not." (*Bhagavad-gita* As It Is, 9.32 purport.)

In other words, as women are eligible to attain the supreme destination based on their development of surrender to the Lord, so in *daiva-varnashrama*, the organization of society in which one develops that surrendered mood, women are eligible to do whatever they are able in the Lord's service.

In 1972 Srila Prabhupada wrote to Gurudas, "So far your question regarding women, I have always accepted the service of women without discrimination." The basic point is one of common sense: in *daiva-varnashrama* individuals, whether male or female, accept duties according to their qualities and activities and do those duties as an offering to the Lord. This is a fundamental principle of a peaceful, co-operative, spiritual society of fulfilled and satisfied individuals, and as it manifests in our Society, dignity and respect for all women will manifest with it. ISKCON will have begun to heal its heart.

" . . . a living entity is conditioned by a particular type of body. The body is certainly an impediment, but one who associates with a pure devotee and follows his instructions can avoid this impediment and become a regular *brahmana* by initiation under his strict guidance. Srila Jiva Goswami states how a non-*brahmana* can be turned into a *brahmana* by the association of a pure devotee. *Prabha vishnave namah:* "Lord Vishnu is so powerful that He can do anything He likes. Therefore it is not difficult for Vishnu to change the body of a devotee who is under the guidance of a pure devotee of the Lord." (*Sri Chaitanya-caritamrita Adi-lila,* 7.47 purport.)

ISKCON's Social History from a Woman's Perspective
by Sitala dasi

Many of you may be wondering what this women's presentation is all about. So, before setting the scene, I would like to assure you what this presentation is not about.

- It is not about promoting feminism.
- It is not about disregarding Vedic culture.
- It is not about accusing, complaining or blaming.
- It is not about women versus men.

What this presentation is about is looking at ISKCON's social history, specifically from the female perspective, for if we cannot clearly understand the mistakes of the past, we cannot successfully move forward to a healthy future. I would like to read a portion of an article written by Thomas Hopkins in the *ISKCON Communications Journal*, where he describes the importance of ISKCON studying its own history:

"There is a tendency in ISKCON today, however, to look on Prabhupada and his teachings as a source of proof-texts for ad-hoc policies and decisions rather than try to understand him and the tradition in which he stood more systematically. In what may seem a paradoxical way, it may be necessary to pay less attention to specific statements that Prabhupada made in order to preserve the vitality of what he stood for. Prabhupada himself was constantly changing – not in his essential beliefs and devotional relation to Krishna, but in the decisions he made to meet new circumstances and take advantage of new opportunities. Prabhupada was a living person, and it was his personal application of devotional principles that gave life to ISKCON rather than any one teaching or even the whole body of his teachings.

Nevertheless, it is his teachings and the memory of his living presence that ISKCON now has to rely upon, along with – and he would certainly be the first to say this – the guidance of Krishna, the Divine Godhead. How does one use these properly to keep ISKCON a vital tradition? The answer certainly is not to use them in bits and pieces to support decisions made for more materialistic or egocentric reasons. It is rather to approach Prabhupada, his teachings and the tradition in which he stood – the tradition of Chaitanya Vaishnavism as mediated through earlier scriptures and the teachings of Bhaktivinoda Thakura and Bhaktisiddhanta Sarasvati – in a more systematic manner to provide a dialogue with the past on behalf of the future. [. . .]

The purpose . . . of ISKCON history is rather to maintain a continuous check of the present against the core values and essential doctrines of the larger tradition and the spirit of the Founder. It is, in other words, to keep the bright light of trained and devout attention on the way the Lord's human agents are presenting His teachings and managing His affairs."

So this presentation is about:

- Sharing our realizations and experiences of the last thirty years.
- Generating deeper understanding between leaders and the people they lead.
- Seeking balance, working towards social sanity.
- Expressing our love and concern for Srila Prabhupada and his movement.
- Protecting Srila Prabhupada's legacy for future generations (we will not be around that much longer).
- Addressing the difficulties in our human relationships. This is not exclusively a women's issue. We are all suffering due to the lack of deep loving relationships, and the fragmentation of our Society is proof of this. We have a long way to go in living our philosophy.
- It is also about encouraging a shift in emphasis from buildings and institutional concerns to emphasizing the importance of appreciating, valuing and encouraging all individual devotees.

Finally, I would like to humbly request that during these presentations we all try to step out of our own autobiography – to set aside our own glasses and really try to see the ISKCON world through the eyes of others. Make it an exercise in empathic listening – in trying to understand – for not seeking to understand will lead to judgment, rejection and manipulation, whereas seeking to understand will lead to understanding, acceptance and participation. We really have no other choice. To survive in these difficult times we must focus on what unites us, not what divides us.

Symptoms of Disease
by Sudharma dasi

To understand the seriousness of a disease it is important to recognize its symptoms. Otherwise, by minimizing or ignoring the symptoms, the body may be invaded by a terrible, even fatal, illness.

During the following testimonials, we ask that you keep an open mind, attentive ear, and most importantly, a non-prejudiced heart. These histories are important because they exemplify the severity of disregard for women in our Society during the middle to late 1970s. At this time, as documented in Jyotirmayi's paper,[1] many women were relieved of their services, had to stand in the back of the temple rooms during *aratis* and were sent out of the temple rooms for *japa*. There was even talk of asking all the women to leave the temples and move to Australia.

In total, there were at least five women's parties operating just before Srila Prabhupada's disappearance. Each party had approximately twenty-five or more members. More than sixty women were asked to serve on Jiva's party. Of these, at least twenty were approached by Jiva for illicit sex. Five of these women were "legally" married to Jiva. There have been reports of at least three abortions.

These women had little or no shelter because the women's parties were apparently supported by both temple leaders and Governing Body Commissioners. When women went to temple authorities they were sent back to the party where they were publicly admonished and punished. Three GBCs were sent to investigate Jiva's party more than a year before its final demise but no action was taken, perhaps because the cash collections were very high.

Many of you have probably wondered why we felt it was so important to establish the Women's Ministry. I can shed some light on this by sharing a few personal experiences and thoughts. Perhaps also, through my testimony and what you have heard from my godsisters, you will understand that this is not feminism, but rather a sincere attempt to create an environment conducive to devotional service for Vaishnavis. I hope that you will also recognize that the seeds of injustice towards, and prejudice against, women still bear fruit today.

Hearing this, Lord Chaitanya Mahaprabhu said, "My dear Vallabha Bhatta, you do not know religious principles. Actually, the first duty of a chaste woman is to carry out the order of her husband. The order of Krishna is to chant His name incessantly. Therefore one who is chaste and adherent to the husband Krishna must chant the Lord's name, for she cannot deny the husband's order" (Cc. *Antya* 7.103-7).

Similarly, a chaste, Krishna conscious woman who is encouraged by her Krishna conscious father, husband, or son, may render whatever service she's qualified to do, whether a mother, a cook, a temple president, a GBC, or a spiritual master.

In a letter to Shilavati devi, Srila Prabhupada wrote, "Now if you can induce all the women of Los Angeles to place an altar in their homes and help their husbands have peaceful, happy home life in Krishna consciousness, that will be very great service for you. The actual system is that the husband is Spiritual Master to his wife, but if the wife can bring her husband into practicing this process, then it is all right that the husband accepts wife as Spiritual Master. Chaitanya Mahaprabhu has said that anyone who knows the science of Krishna, that person should be accepted as Spiritual Master, regardless of any material so-called qualifications; such as rich or poor, man or woman, or *brahmana* or *shudra*." (June 14, 1969)

This same point was confirmed again, years later, when Professor O'Connell asked Srila Prabhupada, "Is it possible, Swamiji, for a woman to be a guru in the line of disciplic succession?" Srila Prabhupada replied, "Yes. Jahnava devi was – Nityananda's wife. She became. [Jahnava devi was an initiating spiritual master who had male disciples.] If she is able to go to the highest perfection of life, why it is not possible to become guru? But, not so many. Actually one who has attained the perfection, she can become guru. But man or woman, unless one has attained the perfection . . . . *Yei krishna-tattva-vetta sei guru haya.* The qualification of guru is that he must be fully cognizant of the science of Krishna. Then he or she can become guru. *Yei krsna-tattva-vetta, sei guru haya.* In our material world, is it any prohibition that woman cannot become professor? If she is qualified, she can become professor. What is the wrong there? She must be qualified. That is the position. So similarly, if the woman understands Krishna consciousness perfectly, she can become guru" (June 18, 1976, Toronto).

In spiritual circles gender is not a disqualification

As being dependent and being a leader are not necessarily contradictory, so being protected and being a leader are also not contradictory. A woman can be protected (as all women must be throughout their lives) and yet be a leader also. In Srila Prabhupada words, "The child must be taken care of. That is good. Similarly, woman also. Just like old man like us, I am always taken care of . . . That is civilization" (lecture, *Srimad-Bhagavatam* 1.8.51). Although he is a topmost Vaishnava, Srila Prabhupada here humbly identifies himself as an "old man," and, since old men are one of the five groups that services to their children are nonexistent or minimal, and their services in the home also minimal.

In answer, the first point is that women must always be protected. Srila Prabhupada criticized the so-called "woman's liberation" movement which encouraged women to become unprotected and thus available to be exploited by unscrupulous men. Srila Prabhupada noted how the unwanted progeny from such unfortunate combinations are an embarrassment for the government, which is obliged to provide for many husbandless mothers and fatherless children. In the culture Srila Prabhupada introduced, a young man is trained to be a responsible, first class person, and he then marries a compatible, faithful young woman. In such a culture women are protected and children grow up in a peaceful, stable, two-parent home.

However, it is certainly possible for a woman to be protected and at the same time to serve the Lord according to her unique ability. Srila Prabhupada encouraged and occasionally insisted that his women disciples lead *kirtan*s, speak, and distribute his books. And, while Srila Prabhupada did not approve of women leading a country, he found no fault with women being leaders within his spiritual society. For example, in the late 1960s, when his movement was still quite young, he put one of his first women disciples, Jadurani devi dasi, in charge of all the men and women artists who were creating paintings to illustrate his books.

A little later, in the spring of 1970, when Srila Prabhupada was forming the Governing Body Commission (GBC) as the management arm of ISKCON, he personally wrote down the names of GBC appointees and included women in the list. (As it happened, these women declined the position.)

When asked if a woman could become a temple president (in Chicago, July 5, 1975) Srila Prabhupada replied unequivocally, "Yes, why not?," and then explained that women should remain dependent on either her first-class father, first-class husband, or first-class son. (In the final analysis there is only one person who is not dependent, namely the Supreme Lord Sri Krishna, but women are specifically enjoined to remain dependent on their intimate male relation.)

Here, on one hand, Srila Prabhupada states that a woman may be a temple president, but on the other he says that she also must be dependent. Is this contradictory? To gain some insight, we can turn to a conversation between Vallabha Bhatta, Advaita Acharya, and Lord Chaitanya Mahaprabhu:

One day Vallabha Bhatta said to Advaita Acharya, "Every living entity is female [*prakrti*] and considers Krishna her husband [*pati*]. It is the duty of a chaste wife, devoted to her husband, not to utter her husband's name, but all of you chant the name of Krishna. How can this be called a religious principle?"

Advaita Acharya responded, "In front of you is Lord Chaitanya Mahaprabhu, the personification of religious principles. You should ask Him, for He will give you the proper answer."

Within two weeks of my joining the Hare Krishna movement, Jiva's party was formed. I became one of its initial three members and remained a member from the day it was formed until the day it ended. By Krishna's grace and kindness, I was naive and thus unaware of Jiva's sexual intimations towards me or my godsisters. Looking back, the significance of many experiences have become apparent and are shocking, but worse was bearing witness to the suffering of my devoted godsisters. Even though unaware of the details, the pain was evident, immeasurable and unbearable to watch. Clearly, these experiences reflected a perversion of the edicts of protection for women.

After Jiva's party broke apart, I was given the opportunity to increase my preaching role. Thus I moved overseas and began preaching in Hong Kong, the Philippines, Malaysia and Singapore. By Krishna's mercy, despite many difficulties, I was able to meet dignitaries and hold large preaching engagements as I traveled alone, or with a small team of *brahmacharinis*, from town to town.

At one point, I and four other ladies maintained a center in Bagio, Philippines, which prospered until we were told to leave. Next, through our own efforts, we were able to open a beautiful restaurant in Manila. When the restaurant became successful, I was told it was now time to put someone serious in charge; that a woman's nature did not allow her to bear the managerial responsibility of such a project. Unfortunately, the restaurant closed within weeks of my departure.

After a pilgrimage to Vrindavan I returned to the USA. Because I was recovering from malaria, I was not able to go out and collect, so I was given a van and a younger *bramacharini*, and told to go out and do something. Again, through Krishna's grace, we were able in one month to sell many books, including two full sets of *Srimad-Bhagavatam* and a complete set of *Sri Chaitanya-charitamrita*. We had made six new devotees and were offered the opportunity for radio and television spots, as well as a gift of 100 acres of land. Upon returning to the Portland temple happy and exuberant, I was physically assaulted by the temple president (who had warmly received us only a few weeks earlier) and told to never come back. After returning to my home center, I was told not to mention a word of my preaching program to anyone, or I would be asked to leave the temple.

I do not know if the opposition to my efforts was due to a fear of losing collectors – who may prefer to preach – or to being a successful woman preacher, or both. I can only tell you that these were the most empowered days of my Krishna consciousness, and that every night I went to sleep with a smile on my face, every day having had a mystical experience in preaching.

In New Vrindaban, I was able to open a bookstore in the basement of the Palace of Gold. From there, with very little support from the management, and with my young baby girl in tow, by Srila Prabhupada's mercy I was able to distribute a sizeable quantity of Srila Prabhupada's books. This effort was easy because of the grandeur of the Palace and the sincerity of the devotees. Unfortunately, like so many previous efforts, it was not to last. I had just completed a Labor Day weekend of book sales that totaled $10,000 when I was once again informed that it was now time to bring in a more qualified individual. I will not dwell here on the demoralising manner in which the transition took place, but I will say that after my departure from the New Vrindaban book store, the sales immediately decreased to less than a tenth of what they had been when it was under my care.

More detrimental to me than the ill fate of being on a women's party was my arranged marriage. It was determined that the solution to the numerous fall-downs of New Vrindaban's residing spiritual leader would be to give many of the men *sannyasa* and to marry off all of the women. Upon hearing of this decision, I approached one of the leading household couples in our community to inquire about one godbrother I thought might be interested in marrying me. Unfortunately he was one of the candidates for *sannyasa* and thus I was kicked out of the *ashrama* and forced to live outside, alone in the *sankirtana* van.

After returning to the *ashrama*, it became apparent that I was earmarked to marry a man of very low character. Understanding the intention, I began fasting and praying to the Lord for understanding. After several days, I had no answer, so I also stopped drinking water. After four days of not drinking water and not eating, I received a phone call: "Please break your fast, I will not force you to do anything against your will." You can imagine my surprise and dismay when less then two weeks later, my marriage to this very same man was unexpectedly announced at *guru-puja*.

I was tired and weak from the fast and had no fight left in me. I felt that for some unknown reason, Krishna wanted me to surrender. Thus, after years of ardent service and unflinching dedication to the regulative principles, book distribution and preaching, I found myself married to a low-class, disturbed individual who smoked, drank, stayed out nights roaming the streets of the gay sections of San Francisco, regularly forced himself upon me sexually, beat me and tore up everything I owned. He even gave me a disease that is a known link to cervical cancer, a disease for which I have recently undergone extensive surgery in what then appeared to be a life-threatening circumstance.

Finally, I moved to Philadelphia, where I was blessed with mature and rational Krishna conscious association. Our temple president never infringed on my devotional service, in fact he encouraged me and provided facility in numerous ways.

More importantly, for the first time in my Krishna consciousness, I had the association of my older godsisters: Vaishnavis who knew Srila Prabhupada, who had travelled with him and been given personal instruction. I felt a sense of belonging. These ladies endeared themselves to me, reinstated my trust in Srila Prabhupada's movement, and reinvigorated my heart. I was indebted to them in the deepest sense possible. I came to understand that the unpleasant experiences of my past were not isolated incidents. In fact, a seeming majority of my godsisters had undergone similar experiences, and as I listened, I found each story more unbelievable than the last. It was at this time that I resolved to do everything I could to help my godsisters, whatever the cost.

The stories I've mentioned represent a minute segment of the misfortune I and others experienced. If you believe these are tales of ISKCON's distant past, my present service to the Women's Ministry has taught me otherwise.

One vivid and unforgettable impression I have received while in the service of Women's Minister came from a note scrawled at the end of a confidential survey which read, "in dedication to . . . Dasi, a dear friend who has been killed at the hands of her husband." I have also been told several heartbreaking stories of forced marriages that resulted in molestation and physical and sexual assault of wives and children.

We sit before you now, a ragtag remnant of Srila Prabhupada's female disciple army. Each one of us had considerable reservations about making this journey and each of us came at substantial personal sacrifice. One of the ladies here has even lost her means of livelihood as a result of taking extended time off work. But we came out of a sense of duty and concern; concern that extends, in truth, beyond our compassion for other female devotees.

It is our perception that our movement is becoming more and more fragmented due to a lack of empathy, understanding, honesty, and trust amongst our Society's members, and thus our Society's heart is being torn apart. Perhaps the desire to renounce the object of sense gratification has led to a denouncement of women devotees, which in turn results in a denial of the more feminine Vaishnava qualities that each one of us holds within the core of our hearts – qualities that may now be needed to re-instill the trust and faith of our Society's members.

Despite the sufferings of the past, our concern is not for ourselves, but rather for the health and well-being of our Society. Please give us the opportunity to serve co-operatively and respectfully together, so that we may all fully contribute our talents and abilities in the service of our spiritual master.

Footnote
[1] "Women in ISKCON in Prabhupada's Times." Presented to GBC annual meetings in 1997.

Diverse Voices of an Enriched Culture
by Rukmini dasi

We have been enriched in ISKCON by the *sannyasa* culture many of the GBC represent. Perhaps no other spiritual organization has this strength of austerity. But in our efforts to follow Srila Prabhupada in his austerity and carefulness in dealings between men and women, the women of ISKCON have been denigrated. We are becoming more impoverished by not honoring our diversity.

One example of how a culture is enriched by diverse voices is given in the *Bhagavatam* story of the Pandavas' judgement against Ashvatthama for killing the sleeping sons of Draupadi. Bhima wanted an eye for an eye. Draupadi, the bereaved mother of the slain children, thought compassionately of the mother of Ashvatthama, their family relationship and the honor owed Ashvatthama as a *brahmana*, and urged that Ashvatthama's life be spared. Arjuna, by his keen intelligence, sought the counsel of all and, balancing all, made the decision that pleased Lord Krishna.

In our Society, unscrupulous men, often in managerial positions, have abused and neglected women. Under these conditions, women lose their sense of worth as beloved daughters of Srila Prabhupada and lose their voice within the assembly of devotees. With no standing in the devotional community, women, especially those abandoned by their husbands, become degraded and cannot protect their children. Children become like orphans, "unwanted progeny," as Arjuna says in *Bhagavad-gita*, not recognized as the "Vaikuntha children" they are by birthright. Instead of the "future saviors of the world," as one *gurukula* promotional piece states, second-generation devotees become angry, frustrated, and want to sue ISKCON because of their pain.

Our Society is being judged by how we treat our most vulnerable members. As Jesus Christ said: "As you do unto the least of these, you do unto me." Similarly, what we do to the least of these, we do to Srila Prabhupada. The abuses and neglect of women and children must be corrected immediately, as our sexist and inhumane behavior reflects badly on Srila Prabhupada and taints his movement in the eyes of the world.

Instead of Vaishnava etiquette we have elitism – a culture of those who have and those who have not – and women occupy the lower rungs. Many gurus and *sannyasis*, as they grow elderly or infirm, will have the finest medical care in the homes of wealthy disciples and admirers. Women – especially women without husbands – children, second-generation devotees, and soon-to-be elderly persons, are treated as second and third-class citizens in our Society. What will happen to these devotees as they grow older? Where are the systems for their protection?

We are hearing the call for accountability from all sides. In the 1996 survey requested by the GBC, sociologist Burke Rochford, after interviewing hundreds of devotees, concluded that the community of devotees has little trust in ISKCON's leadership.

About two years ago my husband (Anuttama Dasa), Ravindra Svarupa Prabhu and I met with the leaders of the anti-cult movement in North America. In a private meeting, we requested that they no longer refer to us as a cult. They said that for them to refrain from calling us a cult they would have to see evidence of accountability. They requested a position statement enumerating point-by-point how we are caring for our devotees. Krishna is speaking to us through our so-called enemies.

How can we expect our devotees to offer love and surrender if their human needs are not met and if our leaders do not love them? It is the responsibility of the GBC to maintain the quality of life of the devotees. Each devotee should feel enveloped in a loving network. If devotees felt supported spiritually, emotionally and practically, there would be little danger of being vulnerable to *ritvik* or other aberrant philosophies. Philosophical deviations are a symptom of the vacancy that devotees feel in their hearts when they are seen only as a means to fill a service or collect money. As leaders, you meet women in the course of your preaching. Often you give more deference to these women than to your godsisters, whom Srila Prabhupada considered Vaishnavis and more intelligent than ordinary women.

We all hope to remember Srila Prabhupada's lotus feet at the time of death. But if we fall short of our goal because of offences or sins remaining in our hearts, some of us may take our next birth as women in this Society. The GBC decisions you make now will determine whether or not some of us will walk in fear of abuse in the future ISKCON.

We need each other – *sannyasis, grihasthas*, women – all have diverse and enriching roles to play. Jayadvaita Swami says that what ISKCON needs is grandmothers. In a culture where we feel safe to give and receive love – *dadati pratigrhnati*[17] devotees who have some difficulty will not fear being ostracized and will not leave ISKCON to seek community or compassion elsewhere.

I recently spent two days at the Chowpatty temple in Mumbai. It is a striking example of an ISKCON community that works. The resident *sannyasi* is not micro-managing – he is not managing at all. Instead, he is inspiring the *grihasthas*, who are fathering and mothering the *brahmacharis* and enthusiastically financing the community projects. The *brahmacharis* are not hustling for money, but are engaged in preaching, study, and worship of the Deity. We should study this and other examples of successful communities within our movement and try to replicate that success.

When I see the beautiful *pushpa-samadhi* of Srila Prabhupada with all the male figures in *kirtana*, I feel excluded. Half of Srila Prabhupada's disciples are not represented. My godsisters and I are also part of that *kirtana*. Srila Prabhupada's glory is that he brought so many diverse people to worship Lord Chaitanya here at Sridham Mayapur and fulfilled the prediction of Srila Bhaktivinoda Thakura. Chinese, Africans, Europeans, Americans – and women – all should be represented. Whose movement is this? Is it your movement, or does it belong to all of us? As Srila Prabhupada wrote to Atreya Rishi, "You must learn to get along with your godbrothers because in the spiritual world Brahmananda will be there, Shyamasundara will be there." So in the spiritual sky, Yamuna will be there, Kausalya will be there, Visakha will be there, all joining in the *kirtana*.

If ISKCON is to be considered relevant, the voices of our women need to be heard. Yamuna, Visakha, Sitala, and other women are highly intelligent, glued to Srila Prabhupada's lotus feet, and their *sadhana* is impeccable. How enriched this GBC body would be to regularly receive their wise perspectives.

Before I conclude I'd like to quote Radha devi dasi, a Harvard law graduate:

"I have been asked to express some thoughts on the roles and treatment of women in our ISKCON society. There are a number of viewpoints on this issue, but I would like to raise two points that I believe are at the heart of the apparent dilemma we face. First, we misunderstand our own philosophy and misrepresent our founder-*acharya*, Srila Prabhupada, if we develop institutional structures that operate as barriers to the integration of women into our ISKCON society. Second, if we truly wish to build a Vaishnava community as well as a religious institution, then it is imperative that we permit women's voices to be heard in our public discourse.

Our own Vaishnava traditions and heritage are the best possible evidence that women have a valuable voice in our Society. It is a mistake to contend that Vaishnava philosophy requires that women fill one, and only one, social role. In the first place, Srila Prabhupada made clear that our Vaishnava heritage is one of flexibility and adaptation with the goal of bringing as many people as possible to the practice of Krishna consciousness. It is essential that we remember words spoken by Srila Prabhupada in the purport to Text 1, Chapter 4 in the First Canto of the *Srimad-Bhagavatam*:

"Personal realization does not mean that one should, out of vanity, attempt to show one's own learning by trying to surpass the previous *acharya*. He must have full confidence in the previous *acharya*, and at the same time he must realize the subject matter so nicely that he can present the matter for the particular circumstances in a suitable manner. The original purpose of the text must be maintained. No obscure meaning should be screwed out of it, yet it should be presented in an interesting manner for the understanding of the audience. This is called realization."

Our Vaishnava history is not intended as a set of chains which will bind modern persons to an historic lifestyle which has not existed anywhere on this earth in a pure form for thousands of years. Used in such a way, our Vaishnava history becomes a bar – prohibiting others from approaching Krishna – and we fail to fulfill the injunction laid upon us by Sri Chaitanya Mahaprabhu to become spiritual masters and free the entire world. Our preaching, no matter how emphatic, is flawed if we cannot convince others to take up the practice of serving Krishna.

This discussion of the uses and place of our history and tradition has a profound impact on the actual operations and effectiveness of our institution. By arguing that women must keep to traditional roles for which they may not be suited, by preventing them from participating in services where they could excel, and by forcing them to "stand in the back" both literally and figuratively, we diminish our ability to function as Srila Prabhupada desired.

It is no secret that ISKCON's treatment of women and children has drawn criticism from anti-cult groups, rights organizations and even governmental bodies. It is easy, but foolish, to dismiss such criticism as envy or the uninformed opinion of materialists. In taking such a position we force ourselves to defend the indefensible. Our own history includes women who served as spiritual masters and engaged in public *kirtana* and preaching. Srila Prabhupada himself engaged women in management, public preaching, his personal service, in fact, in virtually every aspect of his newly formed ISKCON organization. Why should we offend half the world's population in order to uphold a "tradition" with which even Srila Prabhupada was willing to dispense?

Most women in ISKCON are engaged in traditional roles. We are mothers, wives, cooks, housekeepers and caretakers. We cook, we clean, we care for the children and the men in our Society, as well as caring for each other. But these tasks are not the whole of our abilities or of the contribution we have to make to Srila Prabhupada's movement.

In fact, it is our very participation in the "private sphere" that gives us a unique contribution to the public discourse. There are important gender differences that cannot be ignored. This fact, often used as an argument for silencing women, is actually a reason why they should be involved in ISKCON's public discourse.

Psychologists and others who have studied gender differences have concluded that women are, either through biology or socialization, more invested in personal relationships than men are. They are more concerned with the welfare of others and more likely to be forgiving, insofar as they are more concerned with the facts of the case than the letter of the law. These findings are no different in their essentials from traditional Vaishnava thinking about the nature of women. As a consequence of these differences, women have a unique contribution to make to our Society.

Our Vaishnava society suffers when women are excluded from its public life, from decision-making, management, and formation of policy. Our institution is then off balance, with too much weight given to legalistic concerns and not enough to human ones, just as a family without a mother may lack a warm and nurturing center.

The viewpoints and contributions of both men and women are needed if ISKCON is to grow and flourish in the future.

In conclusion I have three requests for you to consider:

1. Lend credibility to the Women's Ministry by increasing the representation of women on the GBC on some level and inviting senior women to your zones and temples to associate with your women devotees.

2. Issue an apology to women for lack of protection and exploitation under your management and the management of those who came before you.

3. Return to your respective zones and hold *istagosthis* in each temple. As you travel, establish the priority of providing equal facilities, full encouragement and genuine care and protection to the women members of our Society. Hold meetings with leaders and women to openly address their needs and problems.

You are the leaders of our Society. If you make the correction of these abuses a priority, the position of women could be turned around within one year. As I mentioned earlier, the 1996 GBC-authorized survey of devotees told you that the devotional community has very little faith and trust in you as leaders. These steps would be very significant in re-establishing the community's faith in your leadership.

Srila Prabhupada's Mood Was Not Compromise
by Saudamani dasi

There was a rumor going around that we ladies were in Mayapur to present some feminist agenda. The idea was that, under the influence of the modern women's rights movement or the theology which denies the hierarchical nature of existence, we would plead with the GBC to change the philosophy or adjust Srila Prabhupada's teachings in order to fit in with the times. You can feel reassured that the ladies here before you are among the most philosophically conservative in our movement. Confronted with serious questions about the philosophy Srila Prabhupada has given us, any one of them could give a very satisfactory and strictly bona-fide explanation. The difficulty is not in defending or explaining the philosophy, but rather in trying to defend or explain our behavior and, even more so, trying to defend our policies, unofficial and official.

Some of these ladies were among Srila Prabhupada's very first disciples. They experienced Srila Prabhupada's personal interaction with women first-hand, so you can be sure they were paying attention and asking him pertinent questions. There is speculation that Srila Prabhupada dealt with the ladies very liberally in the early days because he was very kind and could see that they weren't up to a very high standard; that the early examples of what Srila Prabhupada did or said are irrelevant to his actual desire. The speculation is that because of his kindness and mercy and out of necessity, Prabhupada allowed ladies to do things he really didn't want them to do.

As we know, Srila Prabhupada went to America to preach Krishna Consciousness on the order of Srila Bhaktisiddhanta Sarasvati. Srila Prabhupada had the idea that he would present the *Srimad-Bhagavatam* to the intellectual and political leaders of America and then eventually the common people would follow. Srila Prabhupada was surprised to find that the people who came forward and took an interest were mostly from the counter-culture. He was perhaps even more surprised to see that it wasn't just boys that were coming forward but girls too. Rupanuga's wife, Kalindi, told me that Srila Prabhupada was amazed to see that we drove cars. We should appreciate how naturally Srila Prabhupada saw everything and everyone as coming from Krishna and how as a pure devotee, he was able to engage everything and everyone in Krishna's service.

Srila Prabhupada was not ungrateful to Krishna for what he provided; nor was he an atheist who saw who and what came as a matter of chance. Because of Srila Prabhupada's purity and full surrender to executing his spiritual master's order, he received instructions and guidance directly from Krishna. Bhaktivinoda Thakura gave us the vision, Srila Bhaktisiddhanta Sarasvati gave the order and Srila Prabhupada executed that order. The early instructions and examples establishing principles and strategies for spreading Krishna consciousness all over the world are extremely important because they

were coming directly from Lord Chaitanya to his pure devotee. As time went on, more and more was left to his disciples.

It is my contention that we should not portray Srila Prabhupada's early personal mood, his preaching strategy, example and instructions as some sort of compromise to necessity, while arrogantly thinking that after a few years we became so advanced that we were able to understand and improve upon the foundational instructions. When Srila Prabhupada first came to Mayapur and asked Malati to give class in front of his own Gaudiya Matha godbrothers (" . . . and in front of our godbrothers with their big sticks, too," as Malati puts it.) Srila Prabhupada knew exactly what he was doing. Should we think he was just being provocative for no purpose? It is a testament to Srila Prabhupada's intense faith in the chanting of the holy name that he left the awesome responsibility of spreading Krishna consciousness in our incompetent hands. His faith was that the holy name would purify us so that we would eventually follow his instructions and example and that we too would receive instructions from Krishna. It would be such a blessing to be united by the Supersoul, rather than by e-mail.

Prajapati: In the early days of this movement, Srila Prabhupada, in New York, devotees said they did not know how to treat Your Divine Grace. They did not know your exalted position. I think we are still very much offensive.

Prabhupada: No, I am servant. I have no exalted position. Servant. Chaitanya Mahaprabhu sat down in a place where people were washing their feet. Yes . . . a representative of Krishna. I came to preach Krishna consciousness, and Krishna has sent so many representatives to help me. I consider like that. Without your help I could not do. So I wanted Krishna's help, so Krishna has sent you. Therefore you are representative of Krishna. That is my conception.[1]

Footnote
[1] Morning Walk, 15 December 1973, Los Angeles.

Austerity of Speech
by Kusha dasi

These past few days I have relished participating in the application of *vaisnava-siddhanta* to management. Thank you!

Burke Rochford's report, submitted to the GBC last year, states: "I recommend that ISKCON leaders immediately move to restore the rights and responsibilities afforded women by Srila Prabhupada. Men should be educated accordingly. Guru and non-guru leaders should teach respect for women; women should again be viewed as capable devotees in the service of Prabhupada's movement rather than as temptresses or other

such derogatory characterizations. To do so would immediately increase the self-esteem of women and make them more productive members of ISKCON. This will also make the movement more attractive to potential members who view ISKCON's position on women as antiquated and morally objectionable."

Calling women temptresses and using other such derogatory characterizations is, in part, due to our failure to practice austerity of speech. In *Bhagavad-gita* 17.15, Lord Krishna states: "Austerity of speech consists in speaking words that are truthful, pleasing, beneficial and not agitating to others, and also in regularly reciting Vedic literature." Profound speech invigorates receptivity and trust within our Gaudiya Vaishnava family. So, why do we sometimes utilize denigrating speech in relation to women? Perhaps it is because when a man is improperly trained, rather than taking responsibility for his own sex desire, he blames women and thus speaks harshly about them and to them. This harshness towards women, and along with it, harshness towards the householder *ashrama*, intimidates, alienates and lessens the esteem and dignity of women and *grihasthas*. Gender-biased speech wounds our Society; spoken from the *vyasasana*, it strikes a thorn in our hearts.

The *Bhagavatam's* wisdom is not gender-exclusive. A small adjustment in the speaker's elaboration of a *shloka* could make the instruction applicable to the whole audience. For example, if the text reads, "regarding associating with women for illicit sex," the speaker could purport that one should guard against associating with anyone for illicit sex. While reflecting guru, *sadhu,* and *shastra* it behooves us to consider our audience and practice austerity of speech.

Pleasing and beneficial speech comes naturally with proper training. A *brahmachari* who has been properly trained honors rather than denigrates women. When such a *brahmachari* enters the *grihastha-ashrama*, his dominating male ego is tempered by his wife's precious qualities. His realizations and humility increase during his decades as a householder, while his sensuality decreases until it becomes nil and he enters the *vanaprastha* stage.

Finally, having fully developed his own inner, gentle life – of forgiveness, softness, nurturing and relatedness – the satisfied gentleman accepts the renounced order. Such a secure renunciate is not threatened by a woman's power; on the contrary, he evokes it.

Srila Prabhupada set the example of this mature stage of *sannyasa*. He was as hard as a thunderbolt, kicking with boots on the heads of materialistic scientists, Mayavadis, pseudo-religionists and *sahajiyas* when time, place and circumstance warranted it. He was also as soft as a rose, having nurturing, loving exchanges with his followers – women, children and men.

Overemphasis on qualities such as rational analysis, authority, control, competition and power causes us, men and women, to demean softness, simplicity and gentility. By neglecting and denying these kind and humbling aspects in each of us, by making the feminine seem trivial, our lives become progressively more sterile, inert and empty. The

feminine qualities of nurturing and compassion perish when pitted against the masculine lust for power. Our most noble spiritual path, when denied feminine values, degenerates to prideful hypocrisy rather than devotion.

It is time to bravely and without sensuality affirm the feminine, to heal the wounds and at the same time contribute to the healing of our children and our Society. Let us move from a place of arrogant weakness to one of humble strength.

In his purport to text 1.9.27 of *Srimad-Bhagavatam*, Srila Prabhupada writes: "As far as the women class are concerned, they are accepted as a power of inspiration for men. As such, women are more powerful than men."

Due to Devahuti's feminine power, Kardama Muni was inspired to create an incredibly magnificent palace in the sky; due to Gandhari's feminine power, her eldest son, Duryodhana, received a body that was impervious to weapons. Due to Savitri's feminine power, her husband Satyavan was rescued from death. Due to Chintamani's inspiration, Bilvamangala Thakura gave up material life and completely devoted himself to Krishna.

Honor all Vaishnavas. Failing to do so inspires edicts instead of dialogues, resolutions instead of relationships, indifference instead of spiritual intimacy. Vaishnavis are agents of Lakshmi, not Mayadevi. They summon the presence of Narayana, for Lakshmi is always in her Lord's company.

We may also note with caution that Krishna conscious feminine power can create havoc in the lives of those who don't respect Vaishnavis: the unscrupulous Kauravas perished due to dishonoring Draupadi. If those of us who are not on the level of Draupadi are disrespected, we may live down to those expectations and become representatives of Mayadevi. Respecting a woman as an agent of Lakshmi will do much to encourage her most precious devotion to the Lord. Expectation, especially from those we respect, has an extraordinary influence on us.

We have experienced Sri Chaitanya's, Srila Bhaktivinoda's, Srila Bhaktisiddhanta's and Srila Prabhupada's mercy. We now request the mercy of the assembled Vaishnavas. Our ISKCON social body needs a change of heart!

A Response to Women in ISKCON
by Urmila dasi

It was with great satisfaction that I read the introduction and texts of presentations to the GBC from respected Vaishnavis. It is due, in great part, to their dedication that there is now a greater mood of including women as full ISKCON members. For instance, to my amazement, H. H. Gopal Krishna Maharaja invited me to deliver a *Srimad-Bhagavatam* lecture in Delhi in April although he was scheduled to do it.

In Mayapur, I was happy to have a place to see Radha-Madhava for *mangala-arati* without fear of the men bumping into me. I could even chant *japa* in the temple room!

However, when I was invited to deliver a scriptural lecture in Mayapur, during the usual morning class, it was in a facility outside of that normally given for the English *Bhagavatam* class. There is no objection to a woman speaking on the scriptures to devotees and guests on temple property during the official class time, as long as the class is in a separate place. Clearly the Mayapur administration knows that the spirit of its restrictions is incorrect, but it still enforces them to the letter. In Mumbai I encountered the same situation – an invitation to speak on *Bhagavad-gita* during the morning class, but not in the temple room.

Besides the simple fact of inertia – these rules and procedures have existed for a while and we may find it hard to change course – I read in all the presentations the pull between our external and spiritual duties.

The many times that Prabhupada speaks and writes about women's position in society, or the psychological differences between men and women, he is dealing with our external duties. I do not agree with some of the authors that the societal/economic model of *varnashrama* is antiquated or irrelevant. Perhaps it cannot be fully established in the present age, however, its establishment to any degree will help all of us achieve the spiritual platform. A sane and stable society makes spiritual progress easier, whereas a disrupted society makes it more difficult. The lack of engaging everyone, not only women, in their external duties according to their propensities, and the lack of solid, functioning families with a pious economic base, has led to many ISKCON members being without a foundation for their spiritual practices. Prabhupada writes that the purpose of marriage is to make the mind peaceful for spiritual life. A peaceful marriage is much more likely when both the man and woman work with their natural differences.

To promote a revival of ancient mores of female behavior is laudable. However, as the presentations indicate, it has been very difficult to practically apply these within ISKCON. I would suggest that there are three reasons for this. First, we do not understand ancient *varnashrama*. Second, we often practice our already distorted understanding hypocritically. Third, we do not distinguish between external and spiritual duties.

Our modern understanding of *varnashrama*, especially as it relates to a woman's place in it, is often grossly inaccurate. For many years ISKCON leaders described women as a fifth class. However, the scriptures clearly describe women in all four *varnas* as having distinct psychological natures befitting their class. We think women made little economic contribution in ancient times, whereas in reality they had duties in both their *varna* and *ashrama*. In terms of women's interactions with their male protectors, there are many stories of chaste women, glorified as socially ideal, who do not fit our modern conception of "submissive." Sometimes ISKCON members equate the culture of a part of modern India with *varnashrama*, although it is well known that there are many practices there which are a result of British and Muslim influence or just degradation over time. We have to carefully sort out what is and is not Vedic culture.

We have also applied our misunderstood ideas about women's social place in a hypocritical manner. For example, many temples have forbidden women from various services yet send the same women away from their husbands and young children in order to earn money for the temple.

The fundamental problem of using Prabhupada's good, clear and applicable instructions on the cultural place of women in order to deny women spiritual facility, is not misunderstanding or hypocrisy, but the confusion between external and spiritual duties. Most of the women who made presentations stated how Prabhupada distinguished between the two, both in theory and in his own example.

Prabhupada writes in the purport to *Bhagavad-gita* 9.30, "In the conditioned state, sometimes devotional service and the conditional service in relation to the body will parallel one another. But then again, sometimes these activities become opposed to one another."

Our spiritual duties of hearing, chanting, remembering, offering prayers, and so on, are fully on the transcendental platform and, while usually in harmony with our external duties, may sometimes appear to conflict with them. For example, culturally, the women serve the men in the family and eat when they are done, but spiritually the men and women equally view the Deity of the Lord.

I can only echo, therefore, the requests of the women who spoke so eloquently – let us live our philosophy. Let us live the traditional cultural aspects Prabhupada taught us as much as we can in our present time, as ISKCON shares with the rest of the world a desperate need for societal stability. And let us also live, simultaneously, the principles of equality of spiritual service that he taught us.

Are We Feminists or Prabhupadanugas?
by Pranada dasi

Dhanistha Prabhu wrote to the GBC in the 70s about the women's parties. She never received a response. Saudamani Prabhu and I wrote you in 1988, asking that women be allowed again to give *Bhagavatam* classes. We never received a response. In 1990 I sent a proposal that women be allowed to give *Bhagavatam* class. Though women were not being allowed to give class in most temples, I was told that no ruling allowing women to give class was required, as no ruling denied women the right to give classes. For the last three years, the Women's Ministry has asked for time at the GBC meetings, and that request has been denied each year. Over the years, women around the world have stated their troubles to members of the GBC and to other leaders.

Our simple request has been that women be protected and allowed to take part in activities Srila Prabhupada allowed. Despite the grief we've endured, we maintain a sincere desire to be Srila Prabhupada's followers and stay faithful to his Society. In return, we've been scorned and labeled feminists, prostitutes, troublemakers, and women's libbers.

Over the past ten years, as women have started revealing a piece of ISKCON history all but unknown to many, we've heard many stories of Srila Prabhupada's engaging women in *kirtan* in front of their godbrothers, including *sannyasis*. Srila Prabhupada asked women to give classes even in the presence of qualified, senior men, again including *sannyasis*, and even in India. Women offered Srila Prabhupada his *guru-puja arati*. He asked women to offer *dandavats*, and sometimes insisted they offer them. He insisted that his leaders give women equal opportunity for Deity *darshana* and *japa* in the temple. He engaged women in managerial work, even when men protested. He said that men unwilling or unable to work side by side with their godsisters should go to the forest. But that was not proper renunciation, he said. He wanted us to work together to preach.

Your godsisters sitting with you now can give you abundant details of specific events, dates, places, etc., when these activities took place. They had the good fortune, under Srila Prabhupada's care, to engage in all the services most women in ISKCON are currently denied. Additionally, you can refer to Jyotirmayi Prabhu's paper, "Women in ISKCON in Prabhupada's Times," which was given to you three years ago, and which is still available from the Women's Ministry.

One response I've heard, questions whether these examples are still applicable today. Visakha Prabhu addresses this doubt in her paper "Prabhupada's Ladies and Soul Concerns," where she points to the harmonious understanding of bhakti and *varnashrama*.

Another response questions whether these examples are applicable in India. One Indian manager wrote, "The local devotees however feel that some activities are traditionally not acceptable for those in women's bodies to perform in Mayapur due to the prejudice of the local Gaudiya Maths and *brahmanas*. They have researched and cannot find anywhere where women doing public Deity worship in an established temple was allowed by any of the four Vaishnava *sampradayas* bona fide branches. So Mayapur doesn't want to be criticized for breaking with tradition. . . . So in India there is a public-opinion problem if women do public Deity worship. . . . Mayapur is the world spiritual headquarters and we are compelled to not change things for our local situation unless Mayapur gets some clear evidence in *shastra* about it."

From my casual reading I've found evidence to the contrary:

In *Rasika Mangala*, Gopijanavallabha dasa relates the story of how Shyamananda dasa appointed Rasikananda's <u>wife</u>, Iccha Devi, head priest of the temple in Gopiballabhpur. Pishima Gosvamini is known to have worshiped Murari Gupta's Gaura-

Nitai Deities in a temple in Vrindavan. There are amazing stories of how the Deities insisted on her worship. In Orissa, male devotees came from all over to hear Gangamata Gosvamini lecture on the *Bhagavatam*.

Prasanta dasi knows of a Madhvacharya *math* in South India where women have been taking part in the worship of *shalagram shila* at the *math's* temple for hundreds of years.

Kusha Prabhu can tell you about Bhagavadiya Shree Goswami Indira Betiji of the Vallabha Sampradaya, who lectures all over the world. Wherever she goes she takes her Thakurji with her. She daily does Thakurji *seva*. She has her own temple, Giriraj Mandir, in Baroda, where she worships Giriraj. She worships Gopala, Srinathji, in the Pusti Marg headquarters at Nathdwar, Rajastan, with the approval of the Tilikyt (the leader of the Marg).

Malati will tell you that Prabhupada asked her to speak in Mayapur. And, of course, Yamuna can give you more examples.

Srila Prabhupada wanted a women's *Gita-gan* singing party to travel all over India.

Harikesa relates a pastime in *On Social Issues*, page 280: "In 1973 in Mayapur, Srila Prabhupada and one of his godbrothers were sitting on a *vyasasana* together. The godbrother had brought his whole *math*, and Srila Prabhupada asked one of the ladies, Saradiya-devi dasi, to please give a lecture. Everyone was shocked: 'A woman giving a lecture?' In Mayapur, that was unheard of. But she gave a good lecture and Srila Prabhupada was appreciative."

These examples in Vaishnava *sampradayas* and in Prabhupada's preaching show that it is not against tradition for women to worship, speak, and sing in public. Women have performed and continue to perform these activities in India.

As for the argument that ISKCON does not want to disturb the Gaudiya Math or local *pandas*, I question the logic of wanting to please the Gaudiya Math at the expense of following Srila Prabhupada's example. Srila Prabhupada is a powerful *acharya* of the *sampradaya*. He proved by practical example the basic spiritual premise that Krishna consciousness is not a question of the body.

In some ways, Prabhupada's preaching broke free of tradition to enable everyone, regardless of birth, to take part in Krishna consciousness. We all gratefully acknowledge this innovation as one of Prabhupada's most outstanding contributions to the world. If we don't follow his example, we dim the brilliance of his preaching and change his contribution to the world.

On the opening day of the Krishna-Balaram Temple, when Prabhupada was most keen not to disrupt local *panditas*, he still had Laksmimoni dasi dress Gaura-Nitai. Why did he do this? He wanted to pacify the *pandas* up to a point, but that didn't mean he was going to change the authorized way he was engaging his disciples, men and women. Srila Prabhupada had a woman go on the altar – and it wasn't due to a lack of men in Vrindavan – even on that significant day.

Why would Prabhupada ignore conventions of our *sampradaya* if they needed to be upheld? More important, why do we need proof from other *sampradayas* to support Prabhupada's own example? Srila Prabhupada himself did not seek approval from the Gaudiya Math in asking Malati or Saradiya or other women to speak in front of the Gaudiya Math visitors in Mayapur.

Srila Prabhupada was proud of his Western devotees. He was happy to see them open and run temples in India and eventually initiate. He did this in the face of opposition and criticism, especially in India and from the Gaudiya Math. His activities were often against public opinion.

ISKCON leadership hasn't found it necessary to seek proof from *sampradayas* to support Prabhupada's engaging Western men born in the families of *mlecchas* and *yavanas* in Deity worship or speaking on the *Bhagavatam*.

It is to Srila Prabhupada's immense credit that as an *acharya* he included women in all devotional activities, disregarding social conventions. It will be to our credit if, as his disciples, we boldly support and defend his vision and behavior and by example prove the brilliance of his actions. Rather than hinder preaching, we will attract people from all over who want to see – if only out of curiosity – women preach on *Bhagavatam*, lead *kirtana*, and worship the Deity.

I have heard devotees say that women's issues are just coming from America. This statement aims to minimize the seriousness of the issues, but it is simply not true. The Women's Ministry regularly receives inquiries from women all over the world – Europe, London, Australia, South America, India, Africa – asking how to deal with the sexism, abuse, hatred, and intolerance they experience daily. Fearing repercussions, they might hesitate to speak openly, but if things don't improve, they certainly will.

The day Kulaja dasi left ISKCON, she told me that she would instigate the Murphy vs. ISKCON lawsuit to send a message to the men of ISKCON about the treatment of women. I know how much Kulaja painfully struggled with this issue, because I was with her every day during her last year in ISKCON. Since that time, other women have considered lawsuits, but I have dissuaded them. And I have heard of other women convincing godsisters not to take legal action against ISKCON.

Sitting here today are just a few of your exalted godsisters. The injustices they've endured include being kicked in the stomach by a godbrother while offering him obeisances, being spit on, being struck with a *danda*, being raped while on a woman's party, and more. Each of these women has suffered many abuses. Women all over ISKCON have had similar experiences. The list of abuses is long and ugly.

I can't even begin to tell you of the psychological damage my godsisters have suffered. A large number of them are impaired. They are demoralized. They can't confidently preach to women to join ISKCON, fearing what these new devotees might have to go through. They feel anxiety, or depression, or a lack of self-worth.

Few women remain to tell their story, since so many have left ISKCON because of the abuse. Many hearts have been shattered.

I have generalized based on speaking with hundreds of women from around the world over the past 25 years. I've not gone into details, because I don't want to put all the abuses into writing. If necessary, they could be more fully documented, but I think you can get a clear picture by simply hearing from the women attending the GBC meeting.

The problems are still going on. Sudharma and others can give you examples of how women continue to struggle with sexism and hatred every day.

I am compelled to make a personal comment. Something has disturbed me for a long time. It is most amazing to me that a society that has been predominantly managed by men who witnessed the civil rights movement in the United States could do to their spiritual sisters what was done to African-Americans. I had thought that those with this type of conscience would recognize and never again tolerate hate, denigration, discrimination, or abuse toward another human being after being part of that time in history.

This is my simple request: Respecting your godsisters and daughters, give us the same dignity to live in ISKCON that Srila Prabhupada gave us. We want to fully participate in our spiritual family. To accomplish this will require international policies that allow us to take part. It will also require caring leaders who, after leaving this room, will explain to the devotees where we went wrong and how to properly respect and protect women so that our participation is guaranteed.

2000 GBC Resolutions

Women's Participation
618 [LAW]

WHEREAS, the Women's Ministry presentation on March 1st, 2000 to the GBC Body brought a clearer understanding of the mistakes of the past and the need to provide equal and full opportunity for devotional service for all devotees in ISKCON, regardless of gender, and

WHEREAS, it is clearly following in our line that all people are welcome to join Lord Chaitanya's *sankirtana* movement and are capable of developing full love of God, and

WHEREAS, it is our belief that many of the social issues that confront us are exacerbated because the voice of our women, who are the mothers and daughters of our Krishna conscious family, have been hushed and stifled due to misinterpretation of our

Vaishnava philosophy, and thus the human and interpersonal needs of our devotees have been minimized,

THEREFORE IT IS RESOLVED THAT:

501 [STATEMENT] 1. The members of the Governing Body Commission of the International Society for Krishna Consciousness offer their humble apologies to the women of Srila Prabhupada's society who, because of our own shortcomings and those of the Society, have suffered due to a lack of protection, support, facility and appreciation for their service, devotion and vast contributions to the Society, and

2. [ACTION] All GBC Body members and other leaders shall hold *istagosthis* [meetings] in each of their respective temples to establish the priority of providing equal facilities, full encouragement and genuine care and protection for the women members of ISKCON. Also, separate meetings should be held with the leaders and women of each temple to address the women's needs and concerns,

Women's Participation 19 [LAW]

A. All ISKCON temples are to allow all qualified devotees, regardless of gender, to speak on *Srimad-Bhagavatam*, *Bhagavad-gita*, etc. during the regular temple class.
B. All ISKCON temples designate half of the temple room area, divided in the center from the altar, for the ladies.
C. If the management in a particular temple feels it is unable to implement these proposals, the Executive Committee will appoint a small team of senior devotees, including women, to sensitively review the particular local situation.

The Reassertion of Women within ISKCON
by Kim Knott

The small number of articles written about women in ISKCON before the mid-1980s appeared in publications intended for a wide audience, especially *Back to Godhead*. Not wishing to expose internal problems to public view, they asserted not only the spiritual equality at the heart of the movement's philosophy but also the equality of opportunity for women within it. It was not until later in the decade that a greater openness about the reality of women's situation came about. But this was not without cost. In a lecture delivered at the first conference of the ISKCON Women's Ministry in 1997, Pranada Dasi looked back on her endeavors some ten years previously to share her concerns with the GBC (in a letter that was then published in the *Vaishnava Journal*):

"That letter sealed my fate, as I stood alone for my godsisters, as a black sheep of my family. I was told I was a demon destroying Prabhupada's movement, and I received the most controversial label: Pranada is a women's libber. Labels are just labels, but they have the ability to discount human beings and create social rejection. . . . And what was my great sin to receive such rejection? I suggested women should give *Bhagavatam* classes and were authorized to do so by Srila Prabhupada."

Female and male devotees gradually began to acknowledge publicly the degree of damage that had been done through the failure to tackle women's second-class status. The newsletter *Priti-laksanam,* an uncensored channel of communication in which women's issues could be aired, was established. A conference was organized by ISKCON Communications in Europe in 1992 on the issue of women, at which women and men spoke. In 1994 the Governing Body Commissioner for Germany, Harikesha Swami, declared that discrimination against women must stop in his area, and instituted a new regime of equality for women in temple life. Then, in 1996, an American woman devotee (Sudharma Dasi) attained guest status on the GBC where, with the help of sympathetic members, she was able to form the ISKCON Women's Ministry. The new ministry held its first international conference in Los Angeles in December 1997.

Sudharma Dasi was joined on the GBC by Malati Dasi in 1998. Their presence, together with the active work of the women's ministry, led to the issue of women in ISKCON being given a serious hearing at the annual Healing the Heart of ISKCON GBC meeting in Mayapur in 2000. The presentations by senior women devotees called for an apology for the mistakes of the past, recognition of the importance of women for the health of the movement, and the reinstatement of women's participatory rights. These were accepted, and resolutions were passed with the purpose of prioritizing the provision of "equal facilities, full encouragement, and genuine care and protection for the women members of ISKCON."

Presenting these positive steps in this way may give the impression that they were attained systematically without a struggle. In fact, there was much opposition to change. The most organized campaign took the form of an electronic conference (GHQ) started in 1998 with the intention of gathering support to contest the demands of reformers and those involved in the women's ministry. Using military images, contributors saw their purpose as the organization of "a counteroffensive against the feminists who are a plague in our movement."

An early contribution to the e-mail conference was more specific, listing the following objectives: no women in leadership positions, no women allowed to give classes or lead *kirtana*, the termination of the women's ministry (and the removal of its concerns to the Grihastha ministry), the banning of "feminist philosophy," and the censorship of ISKCON media for "feminist" contributions. The conference continued to generate short contributions and longer articles (e.g. "Women's Rights . . . and Wrongs," "ISKCON Law: What About Husbands?," "Critical Analysis of 'Women in ISKCON'") in response to reforms and initiatives by women.

Opponents of progress for women focused their attention on challenging the claims made by senior Vaishnavis. Against the examples of Prabhupada's inclusion of women they set counterexamples, citing his statements about the inferiority of women's intelligence, their untrustworthiness and weakness. Drawing on the call for participation rights and substantive rights for women in the movement, they cited Prabhupada's negative responses to secular, liberal calls for equal rights for women. They rejected statements made by women devotees who distanced themselves from secular feminism. Attempting to offer a positive suggestion in addition to counterclaims, they called for the formal reestablishment of the "Vedic" notion of womanhood, thus repudiating the commonly cited principle at the heart of calls for reform for women, of "time, place, and circumstance."

Vaishnavi Ministry Mission Statement

Originally formed as the Women's Ministry, this year the Vaishnavi Ministry published a revised mission statement.

To develop a healthy devotional community by encouraging Vaishnavis through association, education, representation, support, and service.

<u>Purposes</u>
1. Promote full facility for Vaishnavis to associate together and become strengthened by that association through various sanga networks.

2a. Promote devotional training for Vaishnavis.
b. Promote Srila Prabhupada's legacy in relation to Vaishnavis.
c. Inspire inquisitive women about bhakti.

3. Facilitate the Vaishnavi voice in all aspects of devotional life.

4. Encourage an enduring network of personal support for Vaishnavis through guidelines, referrals, counseling, and friendship.

5. Promote opportunities for Vaishnavis to be fully engaged in devotional service according to their God-given talents and inclinations.

2001

Serving Krishna as Husband and Wife
by Visakha dasi

This article was published in the ISKCON Communications Journal in 2001

What Makes It Rough, What Makes It Smooth

"I am not a *brahmana*, I am not a *kshatriya*, I am not a *vaishya* or a *shudra*. Nor am I a *brahmachari*, a householder, a *vanaprastha* or a *sannyasi*. I identify Myself only as the servant of the servant of the servant of the lotus feet of Lord Sri Krishna, the maintainer of the *gopis*." (Cc. *Madhya-lila* 13.80)

Although each of us must carefully follow the particular principles of the role we are playing in society – whether as a wife or husband, a brahmachari or sannyasi – our true identity is that we are the eternal servants of the servants of the devotees of Lord Sri Krishna. By playing our present day role in the proper consciousness, we can realize our original identity – who we actually are – and rejoin Krishna in His home. Krishna says, "By worship of the Lord, who is the source of all beings and who is all-pervading, one can attain perfection through performing one's own work." (Bg 18.46)

To be a husband or a wife is, in Srila Prabhupada's words, "actually a duty performed in mutual cooperation as directed in the authoritative scriptures for spiritual advancement. Therefore marriage is essential in order to avoid the life of cats and dogs, who are not meant for spiritual enlightenment." (*Bhag.* 3.14.19) We accept the husband or wife role so that we can gradually become the best devotee we are capable of being. The first and overriding principle in the husband-wife relationship is the unrelenting desire of both individuals to make their marriage work through Krishna consciousness. If that desire is in place, then there are scores of books and discussions, counselors, scriptural directions and the Lord in the heart to help. For now, based on Srila Prabhupada's teachings, let us briefly look at six items that can hamper one's service as a husband or a wife. Then, using the same source, we will look at six items that can enhance that service.

What Makes It Rough
1. Weakness of Character

Srila Prabhupada writes, "When a young boy or girl sees a member of the opposite sex there is a natural attraction without the need for any introduction. Without any training there is a natural attraction due to the sex impulse." (NOD Chapter 9) Prior to marriage, this natural attraction for the company of the opposite sex may lead to flirting, dating, and dallying in coyness and sexual innuendos. Such casual premarital relationships deny the young man or woman involved the fortitude that celibacy in mind, word and deed creates, deny the magnificence of carefree sailing over choppy waves of unnecessary indulgences, and deny a sense of completion to one's formative years. By indulgence, material tendencies expand, one's neediness expands, and one hankers and laments. Young persons, who avoid the gifts that come from voluntary self-discipline, may later find themselves handicapped householders, that is, householders who have difficulty controlling their senses, who are dissatisfied and frustrated. Why? Because they have not taken the time to find the quiet confidence of emotional fulfillment and happiness within themselves, so they crave that from their partner. But fulfillment and happiness are not to be found there. Srila Prabhupada explains: "Unfortunately, in this present civilization both men and women are allowed to be attracted to one another from the very beginning of life, and because of this they are completely unable to come to the platform of self-realization. They do not know that without self-realization they suffer the greatest loss in the human form of life . . . The span of youth expires very quickly. One who wastes his life simply by committing sinful activities in youth immediately becomes disappointed and disillusioned when the brief period of youth is over." (*Bhag.* 4.27.4-5)

Our goal is to reestablish our relationship with God and we cannot expect to do that by defying His social standards. Moreover, when one is thinking of a qualified companion for a qualified young devotee, one is attracted to a person with inspired devotion, a kind heart and spiritual wisdom, in short, a good devotee, not one who is needy, intemperate and who defies Srila Prabhupada's directives. If we would be married, we must make ourselves marriageable by becoming disciplined human beings.

We find this description in the *Srimad-Bhagavatam* (4.21.4): "As the King entered the gate of the city . . . he was received by many beautiful unmarried girls whose bodies were bedecked with various ornaments." In his purport, Srila Prabhupada explains, "A welcome offered by unmarried girls who are internally and externally clean and are dressed in nice garments and ornaments is auspicious. Kumaris, or unmarried girls untouched by the hand of any member of the opposite sex, are auspicious members of society." The *kumaris* and the *brahmacharis* (described elsewhere in the *Bhagavatam*), separately learn to serve God, to worship Him, to become absorbed in enriching, spiritual arts and to explore their unique gifts. By developing their inner and outer lives with same-sex peers, these young people discover their personal mettle, thrive in that discovery, and have a strong sense of self worth. Their noble and godlike character is not a thing of favor or chance, but is the natural result of continued effort, self-control and good association, and their presence is always auspicious. Those who would achieve much, must also sacrifice much. When young people with a solid personal foundation in self-discipline later enter household life, they also make it auspicious. "Before entering household life, a student is fully trained to become *jitendriya*, a conqueror of the senses. Such a mature student is allowed to become a householder . . . " (*Bhag.* 5.1.18) By

Krishna's grace, the future husband and the future wife find fullness and beauty first within themselves and then in each other.

After several decades, when the challenging journey of householder life finally ends, the singular strength one found in youth and maintained in mid-life can fortify one at life's closure. Srila Prabhupada writes, " . . . at the end of life, when one has to go back home, back to Godhead, everyone has to take care of himself without help rendered by another . . . Draupadi had five husbands, and no one asked Draupadi to come; Draupadi had to take care of herself without waiting for her great husbands. And because she was already trained, she at once took to concentration upon the lotus feet of Lord Vasudeva, Krishna, the Personality of Godhead." (*Bhag.* 1.15.50) The ultimate goal of life is the spiritual growth of the individual; it is our personal journey to the lotus feet of the Lord. Successful training and a successful marriage nurture this most significant journey. In fact, training and marriage exists for nurturing that journey. "If husband and wife are attached to one another for advancement in Krishna consciousness, their relationship of cooperation is very effective for such advancement." (*Bhag.* 6.18.34)

2. Incompatibility

Worse than being alone is to be with a person who doesn't like you; too many devotees have experienced the anguish and chaos caused by an incompatible marriage. Such travesties are systematically avoided in Vaishnava culture because, besides training and restraint prior to marriage, all care is taken in matchmaking: "Formerly, boys and girls of similar dispositions were married; the similar natures of the boy and girl were united in order to make them happy." (*Bhag.* 3.21.15) "The central idea is that if the boy and girl were on an equal level the marriage would be happy, whereas inequality would lead to unhappiness." (*Bhag.* 9.18.23) "Marriage and friendship are proper between two people who are equal in terms of their wealth, birth, influence, physical appearance and capacity for good progeny, but never between a superior and an inferior." (*Bhag.* 10.60.15) We want our life's companion to be a true peer.

Besides conscientiously matching a suitable young man with a suitable young woman, compatibility also includes the husband having like-minded male friends and the wife like-minded female friends. All our dialogue need not fall on just one pair of ears, but in confidence, we reveal our mind to and have dedicated and loving ties with handpicked friends. If at some point our marriage is rocky, qualified friends can help us learn from the difficulties and acquire skills to improve our relationship. Marriage is a process of changing and accepting change, of settling differences and living with differences that will never be settled, of drawing close and pulling apart and drawing close again. Good friends smooth the bumps on this long journey.

Compatibility also includes living with our spouse's faults. Anyone can live with another's good qualities, but can you live with that person's weaknesses? After the initial period of guarded good behavior, the character flaws we brought with us to the marriage surface and we face the pain of dealing with both our own and our spouse's shortcomings and the conflicts those create. No two people are completely compatible and not all incompatibilities in marriage can be worked out. Sometimes inevitable differences can be laughed at, sometimes coped with, sometimes negotiated, sometimes accepted, and sometimes they are complementary. Sometimes waiting and praying is the answer. It is rewarding when, after thousands of these tribulations have come and gone, you know and honor your spouse despite the differences between you. Focus on closeness and differences are manageable, but focus on differences and closeness disappears.

The more one advances in consciousness, the less affected one is by another's failings, and conversely, the more neophyte we are, the more those will irritate us. Not everyone can be like Mandodari, the chaste wife of Ravana, who was fully aware of her husband's lowly nature and activities and yet remained loyal to him to the end: "Ravana's wife Mandodari knew very well how cruel a person Ravana was. The very word 'Ravana' means 'one who causes crying for others' . . . Thus Ravana was condemned not only by Lord Ramachandra but even by his own wife, Mandodari, who said to the slain body of her husband, 'By your deeds you have made your body fit to be eaten by vultures and your soul fit to go to hell.' " (*Bhag.* 9.10.26-28)

3. An Inability to Hear

Our prayer is not, "Dear God, help him (her) see it my way," but, "Please God, show us the way." Even with spiritual progress as a common goal, even with inner strength and compatibility, a marriage will still be painfully difficult if the couple cannot empathetically hear from each other. If we only listen enough to protect our own territory, we lose common ground. If we only hear what we want to hear we will remain inflexible and unaware of the other's needs. But, when we don't impose our self on the other or allow the other to impose him or her self on us, hearing is an opportunity for lifetime learning, for responding to healthy needs and for reconciling divergent opinions. A rewarding marriage creates an atmosphere that encourages each person to talk honestly. Emotions need not be repressed; they can be expressed, but expressed considerately, so the other can hear.

True hearing, total concentration on the other, is to value the other and extend oneself for mutual growth. An essential part of this process is to temporarily set aside our prejudices, frames of reference and desires as to experience our spouse's world from the inside, stepping into his or her shoes. Sensing this acceptance, the speaker feels inclined to open up more to the listener and the listener appreciates the speaker more and more. Unfortunately, most couples do not truly hear each other.

The art of knowing what to say when and the craft of give and take is part of hearing, as illustrated in this pastime from the Sixth Canto of the *Bhagavatam*, explained in Srila Prabhupada's purports:

"Mother Parvati could not appreciate Chitraketu's position, and therefore she cursed him, but when she understood the instructions of Lord Shiva [her husband] she was ashamed . . . and covered her face with the skirt of her sari, admitting that she was wrong in cursing Chitraketu." (*Bhag.* 6.17.35, 36)

However, earlier in this wonderfully intricate narrative, we learned that, "The difficulty was that Chitraketu, having become a great devotee of Lord Vishnu, Sankarshana, was somewhat proud at having achieved LordSankarshana's favor and therefore thought that he could now criticize anyone, even Lord Shiva. This kind of pride in a devotee is never tolerated . . . Mother Parvati was justified in punishing Chitraketu, for Chitraketu impudently criticized the supreme father, Mahadeva . . . Acting through the heart of Parvati, the Lord, who is situated in everyone's heart, cursed Chitraketu in order to end all his material reactions." (6.17.10, 15, 17)

Given this explanation, was there a need for Parvati to hide her face in shame? Yes, for by doing this, instead of an argument to establish who was "right" and who was "wrong," we find Parvati acknowledging her husband's greatness, his joking exchange with Chitraketu and Chitraketu's amazing devotional qualities. Yet, at the same time, her curse remains in tact for the reasons Srila Prabhupada mentions above. The exchange is a beautiful interplay of maturity, humility, knowledge and detachment – a tapestry of harmony despite differences.

The inability to hear and the inability to speak in such a way that we can be heard, creates, in the *Bhagavatam*'s words, a husband and wife who "constantly make material endeavors to eliminate their unhappiness and unlimitedly increase their pleasure but who inevitably achieve exactly the opposite result." (*Bhag.* 11.3.18)

4. Self-righteousness

At the time we were initiated we solemnly vowed to avoid intoxication, illicit sex, meat eating and gambling and to chant 16 rounds of the *maha-mantra* daily. To preserve these holy vows that we took before the Deity, before the fire and before the Vaishnavas are the most important practices in spiritual life. Caring for one another means protecting these principles in each other's lives by our example and by our words.

Yet, if the husband or the wife is not following these principles, we do not have the right to reject that person because we feel superior. The day may come when the roles are reversed, for pride leads to a loss of austerity. Without being condescending and self-righteous, whoever is strict can humbly help the lax one and the lax one must be willing to accept that help. This is teamwork, an exchange of affection in which one person's misfortune of distraction becomes turned around by the other person's gift of focus.

If we have too high an estimation of ourselves, we will make our *ashrama* into a war zone and this war may not be over fundamentals, like the regulative principles, but more minor infractions – wasting time, wasting money, inappropriate behavior, harsh language, and so forth. Whatever the cause of upset, the exchange about it and the mood toward it can still be good-natured and hopeful instead of angry and accusative. Contempt is a corrosive that over time breaks down the bond between husband and wife. Instead of contempt and pride we find light-heartedness and submission in the above exchange between Parvati and Shiva. Since both of them are honorable it is natural for them to honor each other.

For one who cares about another, confronting that person is not easy; the act has a great potential for arrogance, for to confront is to assume a position of moral superiority over the other – we confront because we want to change the course of that person's life. The reality is that at times, one does know better about a certain matter than the other and one is obliged to confront the other with the problem. To do this effectively, we must stringently examine the value of our "wisdom" and our motives behind offering it. This self-scrutiny and self-doubting requires the unusual combination of meekness and strength. To fail to confront when confrontation is required is as detrimental as self-righteous condemnation. When circumstances require it, a partner must, sparingly and carefully, confront the other, and in turn, submit to being confronted by the other.

5. Quitting (in a non-abusive relationship)

The Latin root of "com" means "jointly," and "mittere" means, "to send." In marriage, commitment is a journey by two people who have oneness in purpose. When we unearth the taproot of commitment, we come to our commitment to the Supreme Lord Krishna, from Whom the quality of commitment originally emanates, in Whom it eternally reposes, and Who Himself is the perfection of commitment. Sri Krishna says: "To those who are constantly devoted to serving Me with love, I give the understanding by which they can come to Me. To show them special mercy, I, dwelling in their hearts, destroy with the shining lamp of knowledge the darkness born of ignorance." (Bg 10.10-11) The Lord is unwaveringly committed to selflessly serve those who serve Him selflessly.

Marriage is difficult and once that fact is accepted, the fact that marriage is difficult no longer matters. Sometimes, due to the nature of false ego, there may be tremendous conflict and disagreement between husband and wife but if, in this darkness, their mutual commitment to their relationship prevails, that commitment can carry their relationship beyond its troubles to greater intimacy. When quitting is not an option and is not justified, the alternative – sooner or later – is overcoming the difficulty. Difficulties are inevitable, but overcoming them – not quitting – is optional and requires our discipline, courage and wisdom. Our reward is to again resonate, to grow in kindness, in trust and in trustworthiness. Problems and conflict are not an opportunity to quit but to move forward, to become unstuck. As Krishna is mystical, so non-negotiable commitment to His service is also mystical because, by His grace, we can deal with a problem when we take responsibility for it. When the Lord sends us a test, He simultaneously gives us the ability to pass that test if we so desire. "The Lord is so kind to His devotee that when severely testing him the Lord gives him the necessary strength to be tolerant and to continue to remain a glorious devotee." (*Bhag.* 8.22.29-30)

Srila Bhaktisiddhanta Sarasvati Thakur spoke on remaining committed despite obstacles in his last speech to the members of the Gaudiya Math, delivered on December 23, 1936. He said, "Living in this world one has to face many kinds of difficulties. It is not our job to try and remove those difficulties. Nor should they depress us . . . We have no attachment or hostility towards anyone in this world. All arrangements of this world are temporary. Everyone has an indispensable need for the Absolute Truth. May all of you with one goal and in harmony with each other, attain the right to serve the original *ashraya-vigraha* [Krishna]."

We become a husband or a wife as a service to Krishna. Difficulties are not a reason to stop that service or to become discouraged. They are an opportunity, however painful, to serve with fewer conditions. In the end, that self-sacrifice becomes self-enhancement because, for a devotee, sacrifice is an offering to please the Lord. Sacrifice is the surrender of something desirable for the sake of something having a higher claim. We surrender quitting so that we can please Srila Prabhupada.

6. Selfishness

If we focus on what we need and negate our partner, the relationship can't last, and if we give up who we are to please our partner, we may suffocate and become frustrated, resentful and depressed. One who is self-controlled doesn't need to over lord another, and neither does that person need to be over lorded by another. Marriage is a balance between satisfying our self and satisfying our partner. It is maintaining an awareness of the other person and that person's desires, even as the other maintains an awareness of us and our wishes. It is putting our self out, when necessary, to satisfy the other person's feelings and needs. Marriage is sincerely and respectfully discerning what is best for everyone.

For example, "the first duty of a chaste woman is to carry out the order of her husband." (Cc. *Antya* 7.106) Yet, in the *Ramayana* we find that when Rama ordered His wife, Sita, to remain in the kingdom until His return from banishment, Sita, renown as one of five supremely chaste women, insisted that she accompany Rama. Rama's reasoning was that He had been banished, not Sita, and that forest life would be difficult and dangerous for her. But Sita felt that her place was to be with Rama instead of alone in Ayodhya. Had Sita automatically subordinated herself to Rama's will, she would not have been true to herself. Similarly, had Rama insisted that Sita remain behind – for many sound reasons – He would have dishonored Sita's desire. Sita gave up a comfortable life so that she could fulfill her need to be with Rama, and Rama gave up His vision of a safe life for Sita so that He could please her by allowing her to come with Him. Reason and logic have been delicately tempered by needs and feelings. Both must be taken into consideration for a couple's well being, so neither feels ignored or suppressed.

Another beautiful interplay of selflessness is when the *brahmana* Sudama's wife suggested that her poverty stricken husband see his friend, Lord Krishna, in Dwaraka. Srila Prabhupada writes, "The wife was not very anxious for her personal comfort, but she felt very concerned for her husband, who was such a pious *brahmana*." Sudama agreed to go to Dwaraka not because he wanted to ask Krishna for help, but because he wanted both to see the Lord and to satisfy his wife, who was so eager to satisfy him.

Selfishness is closely related to the inability to hear, as our preoccupation with our self makes us deaf to another's voice. To overcome this, we can learn to consider all matters thoughtfully with due respect to our spouse's point of view. This honest approach, which avoids manipulation and partiality to one's own insights, facilitates finding a better conclusion than one person alone could have attained. It is unlikely that the best possible decision will be made if one person imposes his or her will on the other. After all, our will, our deep conviction of what is undoubtedly "right" and Krishna conscious, may actually be the zeal experienced by neophyte devotees, who, in the words of Krishnadas Kaviraja Goswami are "very expert in arguing though they have no sense of advanced devotional service." (Cc. *Madhya* 2.93) In other words, without our being aware of it, our dearly held opinion may cloak selfishness.

When differences are humbly honored and balanced, the husband and wife find the room they need for spiritual growth, both individually and as a satisfied couple. A mutual spirit of good will shifts their focus from themselves to the other. Each wants the best for the other and each feels the other is an ally.

What Makes It Smoother
1. Enthusiasm

"Without enthusiasm," Srila Prabhupada writes, "one cannot be successful. Even in the material world, one has to be very enthusiastic in his particular field of activity in order to become successful." (NOI Text 3) When Sukanya, a young princess, was wed to Chyavana Muni, an irritable old *sadhu*, she set her mind not on the apparently unfortunate match, but on making a conscientious effort to do her best. She did not try to change her spouse but fully played her role, surrendered her pride and, by day-to-day perseverance, succeeded in making a marriage that worked. A devotee's enthusiasm crystallizes into industriousness, which solidifies into circumstances of Krishna conscious pleasantness and advancement.

In his introduction to *Bhagavad-gita As It Is,* Srila Prabhupada explains that our inherent nature is to serve and in this world everyone is rendering service to someone just as, for example, the wife serves the husband and the husband serves the wife. Both the wife and the husband can be enthusiastic in this service because, as Srila Prabhupada states elsewhere, "Krishna is pleased when a Vaishnava is rendered service." (Cc. *Madhya* 5.24) If our spouse is a devotee and we are sincerely serving that person we will benefit spiritually. "Anyone who wishes to advance in Krishna consciousness must try to serve the devotees of Krishna." (Cc. *Antya* 13.113)

Marriage is like a fortress created by the husband and wife to protect themselves from the powerful enemies of the uncontrolled senses and peacefully make spiritual advancement. "The bodily senses are considered plunderers of the fort of the body. The wife is supposed to be the commander of the fort, and therefore whenever there is an attack on the body by the senses, it is the wife who protects the body from being smashed." (*Bhag.* 3.14.20) "There is no difference between a good wife and good intelligence. One who possesses good intelligence can deliberate properly and save himself from many dangerous conditions." (*Bhag.* 4.26.16) "One who is situated in household life and who systematically conquers his mind and five sense organs is like a king in his fortress who conquers his powerful enemies." (*Bhag.* 5.1.18) As in any battle, if they would be victorious, the fighters must first be enthusiastic.

2. Gratitude

The health of the marriage depends on the health of the individuals in it, and it is gratitude that keeps those individuals healthy and free from dullness and complacency. As a household dedicated to spiritual cultivation, the *grihastha-ashrama* is founded on the spouses respecting, honoring and appreciating each other as Krishna's devotees. The husband thinks, "My wife is the sacred and holy property of her spiritual master and of Krishna. She is not mine. If I do not honor her, if I do not respect her, if I do not protect her and provide for her, then I am a Vaishnava *aparadhi*. I am offending a Vaishnava and it will seriously impede my spiritual progress." Similarly a wife sees her husband as the sacred and holy property of guru and Krishna and treats him as a Vaishnava and, in his role as her husband, is faithful and assists and serves him in whatever ways possible. Each appreciates the sacrifice of the other, the generosity of the other, the loving intent of the other, and each grows in gratitude, overlooking the other's flaws. A sane person wants nothing less than this in marriage and will make the success of such a relationship a top priority.

An example of marital appreciation from the Krishna Book: when the cowherd boyfriends of Krishna were refused alms by the *brahmanas* who were performing sacrifices, Krishna sent them to the wives of those *brahmanas*, who ecstatically provided varieties of wonderful foods for Krishna, Balarama and Their friends. Later, the *brahmanas* understood their foolishness in refusing the boys and appreciated the spiritual advancement of their wives. They said, "Just see how fortunate these women are who have so devotedly dedicated their lives to the Supreme Personality of Godhead, Krishna . . . They have surpassed all of us in firm faith and devotion unto Krishna." (Chapter 23)

In another place Srila Prabhupada writes, "Everyone should be friendly for the service of the Lord. Everyone should praise another's service to the Lord and not be proud of his own service. This is the way of Vaishnava thinking, Vaikuntha thinking . . . Everyone should be allowed to render service to the Lord to the best of his ability, and everyone should appreciate the service of others. Such are the activities of Vaikuntha. Since everyone is a servant, everyone is on the same platform and is allowed to serve the Lord according to his ability." (*Bhag.* 7.5.12)

Sincere gratitude is an antidote for self-righteousness.

3. Affection

Lord Krishna told Rukmini, "My dear beautiful wife, you know that because we are householders we are always busy in many household affairs and long for a time when we can enjoy some joking words between us. That is our ultimate gain in household life." Srila Prabhupada comments, "Actually, householders work very hard day and night, but all fatigue of the day's labor is minimized as soon as they meet, husband and wife together, and enjoy life in many ways. Lord Krishna wanted to exhibit Himself as being like an ordinary householder who delights himself by exchanging joking words with his wife." Similarly, it is described, "Lord Shiva was sitting in an assembly of great saintly persons and embracing Parvati on his lap with his arm . . . For Parvati to be embraced by Lord Shiva was natural in a relationship between husband and wife; this was nothing extraordinary." (*Bhag.* 6.17.5)

Also, "We always speak of the goddess of fortune as being placed on the chest of Narayana. In other words, the wife must remain embraced by her husband. Thus she becomes beloved and well protected . . . Just as intelligence is always within the heart, so a beloved chaste wife should always have her place on the chest of a good husband. This is the proper relationship between husband and wife. A wife is therefore called *ardhaigani*, or half of the body. One cannot remain with only one leg, one hand or only one side of the body. He must have two sides." (*Bhag.* 4.26.17)

A prerequisite for affection is acceptance, and from acceptance grows a rich understanding and deep trust between the husband and wife. In marriages that have endured for some time, the partners are comfortably and effortlessly together, whether in dialog or in silence. They can always be themselves, with nothing to prove, nothing to get, no need to impress. They feel mutually secure, cared for, wanted, and valued. The strength of their affection allows them to enjoy each other's company – foibles and all. Affection shifts frustration, anger and blame to friendliness, understanding, and kindness.

4. Contentment

Everyone's goal is to enter and remain in the elusive condition called "happiness." To be happy we must be peaceful (in Krishna's words, "How can there be happiness without peace?") and to be peaceful we must be content with the situation we are in, whatever it is. We accept our lot in life and are happy even if we don't completely settle our marital discord. "One should be satisfied with whatever he achieves by his previous destiny, for discontent can never bring happiness." (*Bhag.* 8.19.24) There is no element of chance in the circumstances of our life, they are the result of a law that cannot err, and they are our destiny created by our past activities. It is as futile to rail against our pains and misfortunes, as it is to toil to increase our pleasures. "Without endeavor, one can get the amount of happiness and distress for which he is destined. And one cannot change this. Therefore, it is better to use one's time for advancement in the spiritual life of Krishna consciousness." (*Bhag.* 7.7.42) A content person may still make changes in his or her life, but those emerge from following the path of *dharma* and from a desire to advance spiritually, not from a gnawing dissatisfaction with the status quo. "For spiritual advancement, one should be materially satisfied, for if one is not materially satisfied, his greed for material development will result in the frustration of his spiritual advancement . . . one should not be poverty-stricken, but one must try to be fully satisfied with the bare necessities of life and not be greedy. For a devotee to be satisfied with the bare necessities is therefore the best advice for spiritual advancement." (*Bhag.* 7.15.21)

For an example of a contented *grihastha*, we may look at the life of Maharaja Priyavrata. Before he was married, Maharaja Priyavrata was hearing from Narada Muni when his father, Svayambhuva Maharaja and his grandfather, Lord Brahma, came to convince Priyavrata to become king. A student of Narada Muni, Priyavrata Maharaja was advanced in spiritual understanding and had no desire to rule, but since his superiors requested him, not only did he rule, but he also married Barhismati and became an apparently attached householder. As he had been content as a brahmachari, he was also content as a husband, father and king, for he never forgot his purpose and he conquered the modes of passion and ignorance in all their aspects – including lust, greed and envy as well as anger, bitterness and resentment. Srila Prabhupada explains, "Although Brahma had forced Priyavrata to accept the management of worldly affairs, thus breaking his vow to remain brahmachari and completely engage in devotional service, Narada and Priyavrata did not look upon Brahma with resentment . . . instead of looking upon Brahma with resentment, they very feelingly offered him their respect."

Unlike Narada Muni and Priyavrata, conditioned souls bind themselves to misery by holding resentments. Forgiveness (which does not necessarily mean approval of the act that caused the problem), frees one from this bondage. Contentment, then peacefulness then happiness become a reality when we forgive, and the first person to forgive is oneself. We can't forgive others unless we first forgive ourselves for our mistakes and character flaws.

"One should try to keep himself satisfied in any condition of life – whether distress or happiness – which is offered by the supreme will. A person who endures in this way is able to cross over the darkness of nescience very easily." (*Bhag.* 4.8.33) A contented person remains so through all acts of providence, whether they involve change or a lack of change. Contentment is accepting oneself, one's partner and one's situation with grace.

5. A Long-Term Vision

When King Yayati was cursed to immediately become old, he was also benedicted that he could exchange his old age with another's youth. Yayati approached his son, Yadu, for this exchange but Yadu refused, not out of defiance or a desire for sense gratification but because Yadu had a long-term Krishna conscious vision: he wanted to use his youth to attain the renounced order in the future. Srila Prabhupada explains: "Maharaja Yadu was very eager to engage himself in the Lord's service, but there was an impediment: during youth the material desire to enjoy the material senses is certainly present, and unless one fully satisfies these lusty desires in youth, there is a chance of one's being disturbed in rendering service to the Lord. We have actually seen that many *sannyasis* who accept *sannyasa* prematurely, not having satisfied their material desires, fall down because they are disturbed. Therefore the general process is to go through *grihastha* life and *vanaprastha* life and finally come to *sannyasa* and devote oneself completely to the service of the Lord. Maharaja Yadu was ready to accept his father's order and exchange youth for old age because he was confident that the youth taken by his father would be returned. But because this exchange would delay his complete engagement in devotional service, he did not want to accept his father's old age, for he was eager to achieve freedom from disturbances." (*Bhag.* 9.18.40)

In other words, the husband and wife play their roles expertly so that eventually they will expertly distinguish reality from illusion, become fully self-realized and attain love of God. "If a man is in good consciousness, he consults with his religious wife, and as a result of this consultation, with intelligence, one advances in his ability to estimate the value of life. In other words, if one is fortunate enough to have a good, conscientious wife, he can decide by mutual consultation that human life is meant for advancing in Krishna consciousness." (*Bhag.* 4.27.6)

Our home is Krishna's property and when we orient all the affairs of our home around its proprietor, Krishna – around service to the Deities – then all our household activities are devotional service. If we're Krishna conscious, if we're actually *grihasthas*, then everything we do is spiritual. "According to Bhaktivinoda Thakura, a husband and wife can turn the home into a place as good as Vaikuntha, even while in this material world. Being absorbed in Krishna consciousness, even in this world husband and wife can live in Vaikuntha simply by installing the Deity of the Lord within the home and serving the Deity according to the directions of the *shastras*." (*Bhag.* 4.23.29) When we worship the Deity, when we offer all our food, when we share prasada with our family, when we regularly invite devotees to come and when we serve them prasada, have *kirtan* and discuss Krishna topics, our home is a sacred place.

To the degree that we see our *ashrama* as a means to serve and please Krishna, it will be a facility for advancing in Krishna consciousness. To the degree that we desire material satisfaction, household life will distract us from Krishna consciousness. "Generally a person cannot make much advancement in spiritual consciousness if he is married. He becomes attached to his family and is prone to sense gratification. Thus his spiritual advancement is very slow or almost nil." (Cc. *Antya* 13.112) Whether our marriage helps or hinders is a question of consciousness; in other words, it is up to us.

A Krishna conscious marriage is meant to bring us into greater alignment with our spiritual nature. Sri Chaitanya Mahaprabhu advised the householder Kurma, "Remain at home and chant the holy name of Krishna always. Instruct everyone to follow the orders of Lord Sri Krishna as they are given in the *Bhagavad-gita* and *Srimad-Bhagavatam* . . . If you follow this instruction, your materialistic life at home will not obstruct your spiritual advancement. Indeed, if you follow these regulative principles, we will again meet here, or, rather, you will never lose My company." Srila Prabhupada comments, "Many people come and inquire whether they have to give up family life to join the Society, but that is not our mission. One can remain comfortably in his residence. We simply request everyone to chant the *maha-mantra*: Hare Krishna, Hare Krishna, Krishna Krishna, Hare Hare/ Hare Rama, Hare Rama, Rama Rama, Hare Hare. If one is a little literate and can read *Bhagavad-gita As It Is* and *Srimad-Bhagavatam* that is so much the better. If a devotee follows the instructions of Sri Chaitanya Mahaprabhu, he lives in the company of the Lord. Wherever he lives, he converts that place into Vrindavan and Navadvipa. This means that materialism cannot touch him. This is the secret of success for one advancing in Krishna consciousness." (Cc. *Madhya* 7.128-9) Similarly, when a *grihastha* resident of Kulina-grama asked Lord Chaitanya, "My Lord, kindly tell me what my duty is and how I should execute it." The Lord replied, "You should engage yourself in the service of the servants of Krishna and always chant the holy name of Krishna. If you do these two things, you will very soon attain shelter at Krishna's lotus feet." (Cc. *Madhya* 16.69-70)

Conclusion

"In a restaurant or place for drinking cold water, many travelers are brought together, and after drinking water they continue to their respective destinations. Similarly, living entities join together in a family, and later, as a result of their own actions, they are led apart to their destinations." (*Bhag.* 7.2.21) Srila Prabhupada remarks, "In the material world a so-called family is a combination of several persons in one home to fulfill the terms of their imprisonment. As criminal prisoners scatter as soon as their terms are over and they are released, all of us who have temporarily assembled as family members will continue to our respective destinations."

By Srila Prabhupada's grace, may Lord Sri Krishna's philosophy be our solace, our guide, and a source of enduring strength, patience and determination. As much as we take Srila Prabhupada's words into our hearts and realize them, that much will our present and future circumstances improve, for it is our consciousness that determines the states of being we shall attain.

Each of us is inconceivably fortunate because Krishna, our best friend, is on our side; He wants us with Him. That we are not with Him is due only to our causeless unwillingness. May our service to the Lord as a husband or a wife eradicate that causeless unwillingness.

Hare Krishna Hare Krishna, Krishna Krishna Hare Hare
Hare Rama Hare Rama, Rama Rama Hare Hare

2008

Statement by the GBC Executive Committee
Affirming Vaishnava Respect for Women

May 29, 2008

Today we live in a world that is full of war, strife, hatred and exploitation between people. It is a world based on a bodily conception of life that categorizes and then mistreats living beings on the basis of race, gender, national origin, religion, etc. The Krishna consciousness movement teaches a higher guiding principle based upon the soul. We offer to the world a panacea: We can live together peacefully only when we respect each other as individual spiritual beings, part and parcel of God. All living beings are eternal, all are sacred, and all – in their essence – are equally dear to the Supreme Lord.

To effectively teach this principle, members of the International Society for Krishna Consciousness need to be vigilant that it be properly understood and practiced within our own Society and among our members. We must believe in the principle of loving, respecting, and caring for all beings as parts and parcels of Lord Krishna.

It is our sacred duty to teach, speak, and live the principles of humility and respect for all, as taught by Lord Chaitanya and our founder-*acharya*, Srila Prabhupada. We must also speak out against deviations from those principles.

In 1998, the North American GBC/Temple Presidents Executive Committee found it necessary to speak out against an email conference that claimed to be founded on Vaishnava teachings that was belittling and demeaning to women.

It minimized the contributions of women, and failed to fully appreciate the role women play in our Society, our families, and our temples. (See Appendix 1 below.)

Today, the International GBC Executive Committee is disturbed to learn that a blog site claiming affiliation with ISKCON, and using "Hare Krishna" in its name, has included sexist and misogynist statements. Such writings are not authorized, and they are against the principles of the International Society for Krishna Consciousness and our Vaishnava culture.

We condemn any effort to minimize the contributions and importance of women in our Society. Instead, we offer the women of our Society the highest respect. Women are of great value to our Vaishnava community, and have made immeasurable, indispensable, and saintly contributions as mothers, daughters, wives, pujaris, priests, teachers, and leaders.

We call upon all members of ISKCON to be living examples of the highest respect and appreciation for all living beings and to resist any temptations towards disrespect or prejudice.

Your servants,
The GBC Executive Committee

Appendix 1
1998 Statement by the North American Executive Officers

The North American GBC/Temple President Executive Officers wish to voice our strong disapproval of, and our protest against, the demeaning and ill intended statements made by some members of the GHQ com conference that were recently brought to public attention.

It is our firm position that Srila Prabhupada, the founder-*acharya* of ISKCON, intended his Hare Krishna movement to be free from all prejudice, sexism, racism and other forms of bigotry.

We affirm that the first and foremost principle of our Society is that all people (indeed all sentient beings) are eternal, sacred parts and parcels of the Supreme Lord Sri Krishna, and as such should be respected and affirmed in their individual relationship with the Lord, as well as their service to guru and Krishna.

Multiple statements made by members of this Internet conference ridicule, berate and vilify women, other minorities, and individual Vaishnava devotees. They document an organized attempt to prevent women from their God-given rights of self-expression and service to Srila Prabhupada. We denounce such views. They are opposed to the core values and principles of Vaishnava culture which upholds the devotional offerings of all souls as sacred and worthy of our respect and protection.

While we endorse open debate and dialogue within our Krishna Consciousness movement, we must speak out against any discussion that crosses the line of decency, morality, and Vaishnava etiquette and supports an agenda to exploit or minimize a section of our Society.

Bir Krishna Goswami, Chairperson
Anuttama Dasa
Sudharma Dasi
Vraja Lila Dasi

Appendix 2
Women in ISKCON
International GBC Resolution March 2000

WHEREAS, the Women's Ministry presentation on March 1st, 2000 to the GBC Body brought a clearer understanding of the mistakes of the past and the need to provide equal and full opportunity for devotional service for all devotees in ISKCON, regardless of gender, and

WHEREAS, it is clearly following in our line that all people are welcome to join Lord Chaitanya's *sankirtana* movement and are capable of developing full love of God, and

WHEREAS, it is our belief that many of the social issues that confront us are exacerbated because the voice of our women, who are the mothers and daughters of our Krishna conscious family, have been hushed and stifled due to misinterpretation of our Vaishnava philosophy, and thus the human and interpersonal needs of our devotees have been minimized,

THEREFORE IT IS RESOLVED THAT:

501 [STATEMENT] 1. The members of the Governing Body Commission of the International Society for Krishna Consciousness offer their humble apologies to the women of Srila Prabhupada's society who, because of our own shortcomings and those of the Society, have suffered due to a lack of protection, support, facility and appreciation for their service, devotion and vast contributions to the Society, and

2. [ACTION] All GBC Body members and other leaders shall hold *istagosthis* [meetings] in each of their respective temples to establish the priority of providing equal facilities, full encouragement and genuine care and protection for the women members of ISKCON. Also, separate meetings should be held with the leaders and women of each temple to address the women's needs and concerns,

Women's Participation 19 [LAW]
 A. All ISKCON temples are to allow all qualified devotees, regardless
of gender, to speak on *Srimad-Bhagavatam*, *Bhagavad-gita*, etc. during the regular temple class.

 B. All ISKCON temples designate half of the temple room area, divided in the center from the altar, for the ladies.

 C. If the management in a particular temple feels it is unable to implement these proposals, the Executive Committee will appoint a small team of senior devotees, including women, to sensitively review the particular local situation.

2011

Question & Answer about Srila Prabhupada's Comments about Women
by Hridayanada dasa Goswami

Question: Comments about women being less intelligent and untrustworthy just make me recoil. How are we to understand such comments by Srila Prabhupada?

Hridayananda Goswami: Prabhupada grew up in a different time and culture and this may be reflected in some of his statements on worldly matters. In other words, Prabhupada's teaching on the nature of the soul, God, etc., are based on scripture. He consistently taught us that his statements are infallible when he is citing the scriptures. This means that Prabhupada's statements not based on scripture are not infallible.

Regarding intelligence, science now speaks of a variety of intelligences, such as artistic intelligence, emotional intelligence, mathematical intelligence, administrative intelligence, etc. In this age, we cannot speak meaningfully about a single "intelligence" and say that men are more intelligent. It depends on the context.

As far as trustworthiness, we can now study and measure such things scientifically, and so many of these issues, in my view, should be dealt with through social and neurological science.

There is a growing awareness in ISKCON that we must distinguish between different categories of Srila Prabhupada's statements. In fact, based on my own statements on this topic, the GBC formed a hermeneutic committee which is attempting to rationally categorize Srila Prabhupada's different statements according to sound philosophical, spiritual, and scientific principles.

Prabhupada saved us, he loved us, and therefore he eminently deserves our devotion, despite a few remarks which we may struggle with.

Interestingly, despite some controversial statements about women, in his own life, Prabhupada treated women with great dignity and respect, as virtually all of his female disciples testify. In fact, he braved terrible criticism from Hindus by giving women unprecedented opportunities in his movement.

I suggest that you, again, focus on the unlimited good that Prabhupada is doing, and put aside the few points that deeply trouble you. Even in the material world, children feel great love and gratitude toward their loving, devoted parents, and overlook a few areas in which the generations may have different values.

2013

On the Use of "Prabhu" in ISKCON
by Sudharma dasi and Pranada dasi

In 2013, Sivarama Swami gave a lecture wherein he asserted that calling Vaishnavis Prabhu was a recent concoction that didn't exist in Prabhupada's times. Later he pronounced that no one in his zone should address women as Prabhu. (Lecture is available here

https://iskcondesiretree.com/profiles/blogs/calling-women-prabhu-transcribed-lecture-of-h-h-sivarama)

His lecture and decision were unsettling and came as a surprise to many female devotees in ISKCON who had been using this term to address their godsisters – and godbrothers – since they had joined the movement, 30 to 40 years earlier, or longer. *Even Srila Prabhupada had addressed some of his female disciples as Prabhu.*

Once Sivarama Swami announced his position, several other *sannyasi-gurus* followed suit and instituted the same policy amongst their disciples and in their communities, pronouncing the edict that no one was to use the term *"prabhu"* when addressing women, as it was a concoction, a misuse of the term, and was only a recent development that had never been done in Srila Prabhupada's time.

This put the senior Vaishnavi community in the awkward position of seemingly being outside of the tradition and acting contrary to the disciplic line when using the term *"prabhu"* to address each other. And thus a controversy had arisen, where previously there was none.

Then in 2014, those in opposition to the use of the term brought a proposal to the GBC body that no female devotees of ISKCON be addressed as Prabhu. This proposal was submitted despite statements by the female GBC members and senior Vaishnavis that they had always used the term *"prabhu"* when addressing their godsisters; that Prabhu was in fact used uniformly when addressing all devotees whether male or female. You can find the proposal and resolution in the Appendix of this book by referring to the 2014 GBC resolutions.

Many senior Vaishnavis recall being trained from their first days of Krishna consciousness to always address *all* devotees as Prabhu. We were to consider ourselves as servants of the servant of the servant: *dasa-dasa-dasanudasa* (also in masculine gender), and see all other devotees as Prabhu. And this mantra was ingrained in us right alongside, *aham brahmasmi, nitya svarupa krishna dasa.* (Again, also in a male gender.)

In fact, the term was used so freely, that it became colloquial and was even sometimes used negatively, "You're in *maya*, Prabhu." "Do this Prabhu." "Do that Prabhu."

So what did Srila Prabhupada think about the use of the term *"prabhu"* amongst his disciples? Govinda dasi relates the following story:

"In May of 1968, I was sitting in Prabhupada's room taking dictation when my husband came in and asked, 'Swamiji, can I call Govinda dasi "Govindaji" ?' Prabhupada replied, 'No, "ji" is a very third class form of address.' So I asked, 'Then why are we calling you "Swami-ji" ?' He was very humble, saying it was not so important. But I insisted that it was indeed important to us, and that we wanted to address him in the most respectful manner. He then said, 'Srila Prabhupada is nice.'

"He explained, 'Srila Prabhupada means the great master at whose lotus feet all masters take shelter. Prabhu means 'master.' You are all masters who have taken shelter of me, the Prabhupada. So you should all call one another as Prabhu, all of you who have taken shelter of me, the Prabhupada.'

"He told all of us, boys and girls alike, to always address one another in this way. Prabhupada, who knew Sanskrit, didn't relate it to gender. Rather, it was related to our personal relationship to him as 'the Prabhupada.' He called me 'Govinda dasi Prabhu,' and my husband 'Goursundar Prabhu,' and others, such as 'Malati Prabhu,' even in letters. This had the effect of instilling in us respect for one another, regardless of gender."

We don't expect others to respect us. But we can expect that we can address our godsisters in a manner that is befitting our relationship with them, what they have given us, and how they have given it to us.

We are endeared to our godsisters. They have been there for us when the men have only been distant. We have revealed our minds together, learned important services from each other, served side by side for years, performed austerities together, and taken shelter of each other. Our godsisters have truly been our Prabhus: the devotees we look to, get strength from, are inspired by. They are our teachers, our guides, and our leaders. They are, in fact, our Prabhus.

Therefore many feel disconcerted if we are asked *not to address* our godsisters in a manner we have always thought of them with love and respect, and in the manner that is integral to our devotional lives – integral in its direct connection to Srila Prabhupada.

Furthermore, the terms *"mataji"* and "mother" have many meanings and connotations. Some meanings and uses are beautiful. Some are limiting and at times completely inappropriate: Our godsister-peers are not our mothers. Young girls are also not our mothers; often they may be more like our children. Sometimes Mother is used in a manner that speaks of us as being our bodies, and not on a devotional platform, relegating us to only duties performed in the home. Therefore, this address can dissociate us from the many years of service offered outside our homes for Srila Prabhupada.

There is an underlying principle in this discussion. Srila Prabhupada wanted the men not to be overly familiar with the women, because it was leading to problems. Thus he asked that the men see women as mothers because a mother is to be respected and revered. She is not seen as an object of sensual enjoyment. But Prabhupada did not instruct the women to call other women as mother.

In the following paper, Visakha Prabhu lays down the foundational principles and documented history, including Srila Prabhupada's use of *"prabhu* for his daughters, along with a comprehensive reference of lectures and letters regarding the mood and use of the word *"prabhu"*for all devotional practitioners.

Srila Prabhupada on the use of the Address "Prabhu"
by Visakha dasi

1. Even the Spiritual Master sees his disciples as Prabhu

We are teaching our disciples to address amongst themselves Prabhu. This is not new thing. This is very old. Now Narada is addressing Vyasadeva, Prabhu, his disciple. His disciple, he's addressing Prabhu. So we should give respect. Just like we address, "Kirtanananda Maharaja." Although he's my disciple, but the respect should be given. Here, see, Narada is addressing Vyasadeva: "Prabhu. My dear Prabhu. . ." (lecture, *Bhag.* 1.5.1-4, May 22, 1969)

A spiritual master takes his disciples as his spiritual master. That is the position. He thinks that "Krishna has sent me so many spiritual masters." He does not think himself as spiritual master. He thinks himself their servant. Because they have to be trained. Krishna has appointed him to train them. Therefore he thinks himself as servant of the disciples. This is the position. So when one is advanced, he can see the importance of devotees.

Advanced devotee never disobey or disrespect another devotee. Disrespect to another devotee is a great offense. Vaishnava*aparadha*. Vaishnava *aparadha* is very serious offense. Therefore we teach to address amongst the devotees, "Prabhu," "Prabhu," "Such and such Prabhu." This should not be simply spoken by the lips. It should be realized. Everyone should think other devotee as his Prabhu, master. Not he should try to become master.

> *trnad api sunicena*
> *taror api sahisnuna*
> *amanina manadena . . .*

Manadena. We should be always ready to offer respect to all, not only devotees, but everyone. Everyone. Because every living entity is originally a devotee of Krishna. But circumstantially, being covered by the coat of *maya*, he's playing like demon. But his original nature is a devotee of Krishna. *Jivera svarxpa haya nitya krsnera dasa.* Everyone is eternally servant of Krishna. But being influenced by *maya*, when he gets this body, given by *maya* . . . *Prakrteh kriyamanani gunaih karmani sarvasah,* when he's conducted by the three *gunas* of *maya*, he thinks himself otherwise. He thinks himself independent of Krishna. But actually, nobody is independent of Krishna. (Lecture NOD October 23, 1972)

2. Devotees address each other as Prabhu

We advise everyone to address one another as Prabhu. Prabhu means master, so how the master should be disobeyed? Others, they are also pure devotees. All of my disciples are pure devotees. Anyone sincerely serving the spiritual master is a pure devotee . . . Do not try to make a faction . . . Amongst ourselves one should respect others as Prabhu, master, one another. As soon as we distinguish here is a pure devotee, here is a non-pure devotee, that means I am a nonsense. (letter to Tusta Krishna December 14, 1972)

Any Vaishnava is addressed as Prabhu, but Sri Chaitanya Mahaprabhu is Mahaprabhu, the topmost Prabhu, the master Prabhu. All others are servant Prabhu. . . all Vaishnava should be addressed as Prabhu; that is the etiquette. (Cc*Adi* 7.2 lecture March 2, 1974)

In Krishna consciousness we address our contemporaries as Prabhu. Prabhu means master. And the real idea is that "You are my master, I am your servant." Just the opposite number. Here, in the material world, everyone wants to place himself as the master. "I am your master, you are my servant." That is the mentality of material existence. And the spiritual existence means "I am the servant, you are the master." Just see. Just the opposite number. (lecture Bg 4.9, June 19, 1968)

A real devotee, he does not show any disrespect even to the ant, and what to speak of the demigods, because he is in knowledge that "Every living entity is part and parcel of the Supreme Lord. They're playing different parts only. So in relationship with the Supreme Lord they're all my respectables." Therefore a devotee is taught to address all his contemporaries as "Prabhu, my dear sir, my dear lord." That is the position of Krishna consciousness. (lecture Bg 7.18 October 12, 1966)

3. Women devotees as well as men devotees are addressed as Prabhu

The Lord Chaitanya is called Mahaprabhu. Mahaprabhu. Prabhu, master. There are different kinds of master, but He's the Mahaprabhu, the Supreme Master, Supreme Master, and Purusha at the same time. Prabhu, you can say . . . A woman also can become the master. . . (Cc. *Adi* 7.108 lecture February 18, 1967)

Now another thing, that girls should not be taken as inferior. You see? Sometimes . . . Of course, sometimes scripture we say that "Woman is the cause of bondage." So that should not be, I mean to say, aggravated. (laughs) That should not be aggravated, that 'Woman is inferior,' or something like that. So the girls who come, you should treat them nicely . . . After all, anyone who is coming to Krishna consciousness, man or woman, boys or girls, they are welcome. They are very fortunate. You see. And the idea of addressing Prabhu means "you are my Master." That is the . . . Prabhu means master. And Prabhupada means many masters who bows down at his lotus feet. That is Prabhupada. So each, everyone shall treat others as "My Master." This is the Vaishnava (September 24, 1968 conversation)

From a letter to Himavati devi dasi, June 14, 1968:

Yes, to call one another Prabhu is all right, but not to become Prabhu. To accept others as Prabhu, and remain as servant is the idea. But because somebody is calling you Prabhu, one should not become a Prabhu, and treat others as servants. In other words, everyone should feel himself as servant, and not to think himself Prabhu because he is being called Prabhu. This will make the relationship congenial.

4. Srila Prabhupada addressed his male and female disciples as Prabhu

My Dear Ranadhira,

Please accept my blessings. . . Yes, I have all blessings for the happy marriage of Haladhara Prabhu and Joan Prabhu, so you may immediately do the needful in this regards. (16 February, 1971)

My Dear Rsabhadeva,

Please accept my blessings. . . So long as there is Guru-Gauranga worship, Yamuna Prabhu may act as *pujari*. . . (March 25, 1971)

Anna Prabhu may be initiated also and she has my blessings for being married to Puranda at the earliest convenience. (letter to Mukunda April 13, 1971)

So the stock of *japa* beads I brought with me has been depleted. Malati Prabhu was supposed to have brought some beads with her from India, and so I would like that those beads be sent immediately to N.Y. center by air. (letter to Tribhuvanatha July 4, 1971)

My Dear Kirtanananda Maharaja, Vrindaban Candra, and Silavati,

Please accept my blessings. I beg to acknowledge receipt of your letters just now received by me here in Calcutta and describing your plans for traveling *sankirtana* party, and it is very much encouraging news for me. Silavati Prabhu said that this was her long cherished dream. It has been mine also. . . (November 6, 1971)

In Los Angeles I personally advised them in all the different aspects of Deity worship, so you may consult, especially with Silavati Prabhu (now in Dallas) and do the needful. . . (letter to Sri Govinda, January 31, 1973)

My dear Gangamayi,

Please accept my blessings. . . I am glad to hear that you are determined to stay and live in the temple now and that you are becoming very much attached to the Deity worship and very serious about serving the Deity along with Malati Prabhu. . . (May 9, 1974)

My Dear Sacimata Prabhu,

Please accept my blessings. I am in receipt of your letter dated 3rd October 1976 and I have noted the contents carefully. . .

Conclusion

. . there is a place which is full of eternal happiness. So this life should be engaged for that purpose, not to fight like cats and dogs. That is not very credit. Credit means ruining one's life. If one fights like cats and dogs, he becomes cats and dogs. Nature's law is very strict. Therefore we should be very careful not to become like cats and dogs but to become very humble – humbler than the grass and tolerant than the tree. *Amanina.*

Everyone wants that "I am very honorable man, prestigious man. And you should respect me." That is our material disease. "I do not want to respect you, but you should offer me respect." This is the position. Therefore our system is to call another Vaishnava as Prabhu. "Sir, you are Prabhu, you are Master." But we call Prabhu, but I think, "No, you are not Prabhu; I am Prabhu. You are servant." This cheating process will not help us. Actually, we should believe that he is Prabhu. "He is servant of Krishna; therefore he is my Prabhu." This is Vaishnava mentality. *Gopi-bhartur pada-kamalayor dasa-dasa-dasa-dasanudasa.* One who wants to become servant of the servant of the servant of the servant, he is actually Prabhu. If falsely one thinks that "I am Prabhu," then his life is spoiled. So this word we use amongst ourself, Prabhu, means that "I am your servant, you are my master." But that should be practically exhibited. That is called *tapasya,* to learn all these things. (lecture *Bhag.* 5.5.1, October 23, 1976)

2015

Do women have equal rights in ISKCON?
Interview with Ananga Manjari dasi in Vrindavan

Do women have equal rights as men in ISKCON? You've asked me about a hot topic!

I was in Srila Prabhupada's room in Los Angeles 1972 and one journalist asked Srila Prabhupada, "What about the women in your Movement. You say they are less intelligent. What do you have to say about this? What is their position in your Movement?"

Prabhupada said, "Anyone who comes to this Movement becomes most intelligent, otherwise how can they come? How can they accept this philosophy? So anyone who comes becomes most intelligent."

Prabhupada said that the previous *acharyas* wrote from the man's point of view because that was the culture at the time. Only men were educated and could hear philosophy. So they were speaking from the men's point of view. Prabhupada didn't speak from the man's point of view.

In this same interview Prabhupada said, "My women disciples are doing everything the men are doing. They preach, they do *pujari* work, they lead."

And at that time I *was* leading. I had a *sankirtana* party of ladies that I was leading. We went traveling, we had a little temple, and I was the president. I gave classes, I led *kirtans*, I played *mridanga*. This was going on. That's what Prabhupada wanted. Whatever you do best, do it for Krishna, do it to propagate this movement. This is what he wanted: Propagate this philosophy by doing whatever you do best. This is what he wanted for all his disciples.

But there is an element in ISKCON, and there was an element, and we were told, "You can't play *mridanga*. You can't lead *kirtana*. You can't lecture and preach." This was very hard. It was devastating. Not just for the women disciples, but at some point even Prabhupada's male disciples who were told, "Don't preach in the other guru's zones."

So ISKCON has gone through growing pains. It's a young Movement and it's gone through growing pains. We still have much room for improvement.

Some devotees want to focus on mundane roles, *varna* roles. Prabhupada was not big on *varna* rules. Lord Chaitanya was not big on *varna* roles. He asked, "What is the highest?" The highest is spreading the holy name around. That is Prabhupada's mission.

We need to come together and cooperate. You may think different from me. You may preach different from me. Maybe you don't want to do *harinama* or maybe you need to do *harinama*. Or maybe you want to do certain ways of preaching. Maybe you preach heavy. Maybe someone else preaches light. Maybe someone preaches with a lot of psychology. Maybe someone preaches with lots of stories. We should not fight about these things because some people will be attracted to all these different ways of preaching.

Unfortunately, our movement is stagnant in the West because we stomped on so many devotee's heads: "You can't do that. You can't do it like this. Don't do it like this. Do it this way."

Luckily there is grassroots preaching. My Guru Maharaja, Srila Prabhupada, wrote to me, "Become a great preacher for this Movement." That is the only way I can repay him. I don't have an option. I have no option. Sorry. I will not be stopped by some people who say that I should only roll ghee wicks, or stay in the temple and be quiet, and take care of the children. I have done that. I have taken care of my children and look at them! They are on the front lines of preaching. They are on the front lines in universities and yoga studios where things are happening, where people are looking for spiritual knowledge. My children are there and I will be right there with them.

You can't stop us. We're Prabhupada's disciples. You may have a different philosophy from Srila Prabhupada. Sorry, I can't follow that. It's my duty to follow my spiritual master.

Devotees at the grassroots will find service. They will come forward. You can't stop the transcendental energy that Prabhupada gave us. No one can stop that.

But you are trying to stop that. When you step on the grass, you don't water it, don't nurture it, and don't give it opportunity to grow, then it may grow slower, but it will still grow through the cracks of the concrete.

I'm not saying we should fight with one and another about having equal rights. In America there are magazines like one called *The National Inquirer* that just find dirt on the presidents, actors, and famous people. Sometimes they just make up stories, "Angelina Jolie has three heads," "Brad Pitt was born with an extra finger." They just try to find dirt. So don't be like that saying that Prabhupada's daughters are militant and demanding. Talking like that is like the *The National Inquirer*. We don't even want to address these things. It's sad that senior devotees in our Movement are talking like this and name calling. Putting names on the Srila Prabhupada's disciples who have dedicated their whole life, who were forced to give up their children at one point. In the late 1970s and early 80s and even a little later than that, too.

You're saying, "Be a mother." But many mothers were forced to give up their children to the *gurukulas*! I was personally in Prabhupada's room when one mother came and asked, "Prabhupada, do we have to give our children to *gurukula*? I'm afraid my child will be beaten. I'm afraid my child will become a homosexual." She said that because that's what was happening! She humbly asked, "Do I still have to give my child? If you say so, I will."

Prabhupada said, "No. No. I never said this. I never said you have to. I want the *gurukulas* to nurture the children."

Then he wrote a letter, "Stop this nonsense of hurting the children."

My heart goes out to our children. I want nothing more than to nurture the future generation: as a mother, as a Vaishnava, and as a disciple of Prabhupada. We need to nurture the future generation. And if I have to fight for that sometimes, then I will fight for that. I will fight against those who are saying all this nonsense like *The National Inquirer* finding dirt on different people.

I have personal friends who are still crying *to this day* because their children were molested in our *gurukulas,* and the children obviously don't want to be devotees any more. And now you're criticizing these mothers that they weren't good devotees? You didn't let them nurture the children! You took away their services.

We all revere Mother Yamuna. She was very saintly; she was one of our saints. Prabhupada loved her. One time, Prabhupada hit her on the back and said, "Preach boldly for Krishna!"

He had her sit in front of him at the Cross Maiden festival and give classes. He asked her to be GBC and he asked her to be in charge in Vrindavan. The men gave her such a hard time. It's in her biography. She is very polite about it, but it's there. She had to go into seclusion basically. She had to go; she was forced to go into seclusion.

I was there when Yamuna asked Prabhupada, "Prabhupada what do we do? The men are not accepting me, they don't allow me lead and manage as you requested. The men are fighting me. So I just want to go to a farm and be with one devotee. I will do a little *seva* and Deity worship."

Prabhupada said, "Okay because it's so difficult for you do this. You have my blessing."

But she was forced away! That wasn't her choice. Then they criticized and blamed her. You want to talk about women. I can talk about the women's situation. They criticized and blamed her, "Oh, she left. She blooped. She's in *maya.*" They said these things even though Prabhupada gave her his blessings because she had nowhere else to go.

You didn't give us any other place to go! Some of us stuck it out because of Prabhupada – only because of our love for Prabhupada. But you made it very difficult for us.

So we forgive and we want to forget. But don't continue this nonsense. Don't continue this nonsense. We forgive and forget and we'll go on preaching in our own way wherever we can. Krishna will open opportunities for us, and He is opening those doors for us.

After Yamuna passed away we had a memorial for her in Alachua. It was a beautiful ceremony and many godbrothers and godsisters were there. One devotee stood up and said, "I'm representing the GBC and I want to say that Yamuna changed the face of our Movement."

Actually that statement really upset me. Afterwards I went up to him and said, "How dare you say she changed the face of our Movement? You didn't let her change the face of our Movement. You forced her into seclusion: a great personality like her with so much bhakti and love and knowledge. She was so dedicated to Prabhupada and she was able to lead in *so many ways*. You pushed her into seclusion. You didn't allow her to change the face of our Movement! So now *you* please change the face of our Movement. Open up the preaching mission. Lord Chaitanya opened the storehouse for men, women, children, animals."

So don't tell us how we can preach. Thank you. Hare Krishna.

2017

The Rare Human Form
by Visakha Priya dasi

Preface

The sublime philosophy of simultaneous oneness and difference expounded by Sri Chaitanya Mahaprabhu is the only way to go in the age of quarrel and hypocrisy. We are in the right place at the right time. As Srila Prabhupada explained in his teachings, the cosmic manifestation, which lasts for only one breath of Maha-Vishnu, consists of a vast cluster of universes, each one of which is as significant as a mustard seed in a bagful of mustard seeds. The cosmic creation exists as long as Maha-Vishnu breathes out, and then, when He breathes in, the light goes off and the show is over. Again He breathes out, and again everything becomes manifest. Again He breathes in, and again everything disappears.

Within each universe are three planetary systems: lower, middle, and upper. Planet Earth is situated in the middle, and as such it undergoes periodical devastations whenever four-headed Brahma, the secondary creator of our universe, retires for the night. One day of Brahma comprises twelve hours, and his night is of the same duration. But the time scale on his planet is not the same as on planet Earth. One hour of Brahma is worth four million three hundred and twenty thousand solar years. Srila Prabhupada has explained that "Brahma lives one hundred of such 'years' and then dies. These 'hundred years' by earth calculations total to 311 trillion and 40 billion earth years. By these calculations the life of Brahma seems fantastic and interminable, but from the viewpoint of eternity it is as brief as a lightning flash." We are mentioning these facts as a humble reminder that we should not take ourselves and our own opinions too seriously.

Introduction

In the sixth chapter of *The Nectar of Devotion*, Srila Prabhupada writes:

"Srila Rupa Gosvami states that his elder brother (Sanatana Gosvami) has compiled *Hari-bhakti-vilasa* for the guidance of the Vaishnavas and therein has mentioned many rules and regulations to be followed by the Vaishnavas. Some of them are very important and prominent, and Srila Rupa Gosvami will now mention these very important items for our benefit. The purport of this statement is that Srila Rupa Gosvami proposes to mention only basic principles, not details. For example, a basic principle is that one has to accept a spiritual master. Exactly how one follows the instructions of his spiritual master is considered a detail. For example, if one is following the instruction of his spiritual master and that instruction is different from the instructions of another spiritual master, this is called detailed information. But the basic principle of acceptance of a spiritual master is good everywhere, although the details may be different. Srila Rupa Gosvami does not wish to enter into details here, but wants to place before us only the principles."

His Grace Srutakirti Prabhu recalls asking Srila Prabhupada how to discriminate between principles and details. After a short pause, Srila Prabhupada replied, "That requires a little intelligence." In the presentation that follows, we would like to establish, on the basis of Srila Prabhupada's teachings, what the principles are, as opposed to the details, in connection with the role of women in ISKCON. May the Vaishnava devotees of the Lord bless us with the ability to properly discriminate between principles and details for the pleasure of the *parampara* and the benefit of all concerned.

The Rare Human Form

"In human society all over the world, there are millions and billions of men and women, and almost all of them are less intelligent because they have very little knowledge of spirit soul. Almost all of them have a wrong conception of life, for they identify themselves with the gross and subtle material bodies, which they are not, in fact. They may be situated in different high and low positions in the estimation of human society, but one should know definitely that unless one inquires about his own self beyond the body and the mind, all his activities in human life are total failures." (*Bhag.* 2.3.1 p)

The first principle taught by Srila Prabhupada is that we are not the bodies in which we dwell. Rather, we are eternal spirit souls, equal to God in quality – but not in quantity – eternally related to Him in the same way as fiery sparks are related to a bonfire or as molecules of sunshine are related to the sun globe. We cannot, even for one *truti* (8/13,500 second), be separated from the source of our existence, Sri Krishna. And because we are one with Him in quality, we potentially have – in minute quantity – up to seventy-eight percent of His qualities, which include independence. Being minute, however, our independence is limited to two choices: to serve Krishna or to imitate Krishna. And Krishna, being the loving father that He is, fulfills our desire to imitate Him by dreaming up this whole cosmic situation – the dream of Maha-Visnu. The dream feels real as long as we remain asleep. And we can sleep as long as we want. But because God is not – as Judeo-Christian traditions would have it – an angry God who casts the infidels in hell for eternity after giving them only ONE chance to rectify themselves - He dreams up the cosmic manifestation in such a way that at some point we are bound to realize that it is insubstantial and painful, a complete dead end. And when we reach that conclusion, Krishna sends us His representative to guide us out of our slumber, back to our original position.

So, the most important principle is that we are *krsnera nitya dasa*, the eternal servants of Krishna, and the only way out of this identification is to opt for the dream of Maha-Visnu. Those of us who have opted for the dream will have to learn the hard way –

in this "school of hard knocks" called the material world – that the shadow can never replace the substance.

In a lecture on SB 3.2.21, Srila Prabhupada explained that " . . . the superior energy is dressed in two ways, as male and female. Because without male and female, there is no enjoyment. Therefore they [the conditioned souls] have been dressed falsely by the material nature as enjoyer. Here, either a woman or a man, everyone is trying to enjoy. Nobody is trying to become enjoyed. Everyone is trying to enjoy. But he cannot. . . . **Everyone is she, but someone, some of them, are dressed like he.** Because everyone is *prakrti.* . . . That is called *maya.* He cannot enjoy, but he is posing himself as enjoyer. That is the disease.

"Falsely, he [is] representing himself as *purusha,* as enjoyer. Therefore we have got trouble. . . . If a woman is dressed like a man, does it mean that she is man, or she can enjoy like man? No. False dress. Similarly, here, in this material world, we are falsely dressed with this material body and imitating Krishna, enjoyer . . . . Somebody is dressed like a female, somebody is dressed like a male, **but none of them are male.** Both of them are originally female, *prakrti. Prakrti* means feminine gender."

Srila Prabhupada's point – that both men and women are female and that bodily identification is *maya* – is further reinforced in a lecture on *Srimad-Bhagavatam* (6.1.64 – 65) given on September 1, 1975 in Vrindavan: "You do not think that only woman is woman. **The man is also woman.** Don't think that the woman is condemned; man is not. Woman means enjoyed, and man means enjoyer. So this feeling, this *feeling* is condemned. If I see one woman for enjoyment, so I am man. **And if woman also sees another man for enjoyment, she is also man.** Woman means enjoyed and man means enjoyer. So **anyone who has got feeling of enjoyment, he is considered to be man . . .** Therefore he is *purusha,* artificially. Otherwise, originally, we are all *prakrti, jiva,* either woman or man. This is outward dress."

Despite everything else Srila Prabhupada wrote or said about women according to time, place, and circumstances, it is clear from the abovementioned quotes that in *essence,* the whole of humanity is female. No other living creature within both material and spiritual creations qualifies as male besides the Supreme Lord Himself.

In the spiritual world, depending on the nature of our relationship with Krishna, we exhibit different forms and different moods, and all of them are specifically meant to please Krishna. The cowherd boys do not dress up to attract the girls. The girls do not cast sidelong glances at the boys. Everyone is completely fixed in his or her service to Krishna, and all their interactions are solely meant for the purpose of giving pleasure to Krishna. Because everything in the spiritual world is eternally fresh, *nava yauvana,* there is no birth and no death. No birth and no death means no sex life. The male and female designations are only costumes that devotees wear to take part in Krishna's variegated pastimes.

In the material world, we find that women masquerading as men are generally condemned or ridiculed. But Srila Prabhupada's teachings make it clear that living entities endowed with a male body are also women masquerading as *purusha*.

The conclusion is that the kind of costume we wear in our daily practice of pure devotional service is irrelevant. The material concept of male and female and their interactions is a device meant to keep us bound to this world. As Srila Prabhupada mentions in *Srimad-Bhagavatam* (3.31.41),

"A living entity who, as a result of attachment to a woman in his previous life, has been endowed with the form of a woman, **foolishly** looks upon *maya* in the form of a man, her husband, as the bestower of wealth, progeny, house and other material assets."

In the purport to this verse, Srila Prabhupada comments that "from this verse it appears that a woman is also supposed to have been a man in his (her) previous life, and due to his attachment to his wife, he now has the body of a woman. . . . Similarly, if a woman thinks of her husband at the time of death, naturally she gets the body of a man in the next life. In the Hindu scriptures, therefore, woman's chastity and devotion to man is greatly emphasized. A woman's attachment to her husband may elevate her to the body of a man in her next life, but a man's attachment to a woman will degrade him, and in his next life he will get the body of a woman. **We should always remember, as it is stated in Bhagavad-gita, that both the gross and subtle material bodies are dresses; they are the shirt and coat of the living entity. To be either a woman or a man <u>only</u> involves one's bodily dress.**"

It is interesting to note that Srila Prabhupada refers to "the Hindu scriptures," because, as he himself said (SSR 30), one will not find the word *Hindu* in the *Bhagavad-gita*. It seems that by using this term, Srila Prabhupada is de-emphasizing the importance of what these scriptures teach. This may appear to be my own interpretation, but it is supported by various statements Srila Prabhupada made in his books and lectures, including the purport quoted above to the effect that "both the gross and subtle material bodies are dresses; they are the shirt and coat of the living entity." As such, they have no place in *sanatana-dharma*, wherein every living entity, being classified as energy, is *prakrti*, the enjoyed. Although, thanks to ISKCON, Hinduism is on the rise nowadays, Srila Prabhupada did not consider it on a par with *sanatana-dharma*. The idea is *not* to cultivate chastity and devotion to a man in order to get a man's body in one's next life, but to give up material bodies altogether.

Stri-dharma only perpetuates the misconception of who we are. Although we do not dispute the statement that there is less opportunity to get out of the material clutches in the body of a woman than in a man's body, we can practically observe that men do not always take the opportunity given to them and come back in female bodies. Is someone driving a Mercedes Benz more spiritually advanced than someone riding in a Toyota? The person riding in the Mercedes Benz may go faster than the person riding in the Toyota, but the most important thing is where he or she is going, not how fast he or she goes. Just as Bharata Maharaja retained his spiritual consciousness in the body of a deer, a living entity in a woman's body certainly retains whatever Krishna consciousness she achieved in her previous life. The story of Daksha's head transplant also proves that the consciousness of the living entity has nothing to do with the brain or the size of one's brain. And therefore, to gauge the spiritual level of a living entity according to its material body, either gross or subtle, is futile – and possibly offensive.

The next verse (SB 3.31.42) goes further to clarify our misconceptions:

"A woman, therefore, should consider her husband, her house and her children to be the arrangement of the external energy of the Lord **for her death**, just as the sweet singing of the hunter is death for the deer."

In the purport that follows, Srila Prabhupada explains that "not only is woman the gateway to hell for man, but man is also the gateway to hell for woman. . . . As long as either is attached to the other for such material enjoyment, the woman is dangerous for the man, and the man is also dangerous for the woman. But if the attachment is transferred to Krishna, both of them become Krishna conscious, and then marriage is very nice."

In practice, however, Srila Prabhupada's sublime instructions for householder life have been watered down. And therefore, toward the end of his manifest presence, he strongly advocated reestablishing *varnashrama*, even though, in the second canto of *Srimad-Bhagavatam* (2.4.18) he states that "The system of caste, or *varnashrama-dharma*, is no longer regular even amongst the so-called followers of the system. **Nor is it now possible to reestablish the institutional function in the present context of social, political and economic revolution. Without any reference to the particular custom of a country, one can be accepted to the Vaishnava cult spiritually, and there is no hindrance in the transcendental process.**"

Srila Prabhupada's desire that we should reestablish the *varnashrama* system is not incompatible with his purport to SB 2.4.18. But unless we change our present social, political, and economic context to the kind of context in which *varnashrama* can function, we are not going to go very far in our attempts to fulfill Prabhupada's desire. We need to pay full attention to the principle of *desa-kala-patra* with due regard to each and every devotee's antecedents before recruiting them into the *varnashrama* system. We look forward to seeing five years old *brahmacharis* (born of parents mindful of the Vedic rituals for procreation) instead of twenty-five years old beginners burdened with past sinful samskaras bearing that title. We also look forward to seeing little girls learning how to churn butter and make cow dung patties to serve as fuel to cook the family's homegrown *prasadam* meal. But to expect every so-called *brahmachari* or *brahmacharini* (if the latter have not become an extinct species by now) to conform to a model that blossomed in Treta-yuga is quite unreasonable. First, qualified parents need to produce qualified children in a "plain living, high thinking" environment. *Varnashrama* cannot flourish in a mechanized, polluted, and genetically modified environment. To force aspiring devotees to live on a farm, to force women to conform to a system they are not qualified for, to advocate polygamy, is not the way to reestablish *varnashrama* in this age. It will take time and maturity to recreate a sattvic environment in which the ideals of bygone ages can be somewhat emulated. No doubt, Srila Prabhupada preferred to see women married, but he also cautioned them that if they could not find suitable husbands it would be "*better to remain a Brahmacharini all the life, even though it is little difficult.*" (Letter to Satsvarupa, 8 August 1968). And although Srila Prabhupada spoke favorably about polygamy in the context of the Vedic system, he emphatically condemned it in three letters reproduced here below:

To Karandhar, on 10 February 1973

"I have received your letter of 1/24/73 concerning polygamy and feel that this policy must be strictly prohibited within our Society. If it is not it shall only cause chaos, as what was possible under the system of pure Vedic Culture is impossible at the present time."

To Satsvarupa, on 10 February 1973

"First let us understand that polygamy cannot be permitted in our Society. Legally it is impossible and neither are there many of our devotees who are prepared to assume the responsibility for many wives. Therefore as I have suggested previously as they do in Christian religion they have so many convent where the women stay and they receive protection. The point is that the women must be protected and it is the duties of the leaders of our Society to see that this is carried out."

To Rupanuga, on 14 February 1973

"After conferring with my various GBC representatives I have concluded that polygamy must be strictly prohibited in our Society. Although it is a Vedic institution still there are so many legal implications. Neither are many of our men fixed up enough to tend for more than one wife. Polygamy will simply increase the sex life and our philosophy is to gradually decrease the sex life till eventually there is no sex life. The policy should be that all the women are given the utmost protection. Women are looking for husbands because they feel unprotected so it is up to the senior members to give all protection to the women."

It is sheer lunacy to expect women to behave like Kunti or Draupadi unless their husbands are of the same caliber as Arjuna or Yudhisthira. That will take time. In the meantime, the best thing to do is to try to purify our consciousness by serious, offenseless chanting of the great mantra for deliverance – Hare Krishna Hare Krishna Krishna Krishna Hare Hare / Hare Rama Hare Rama Rama Rama Hare Hare. After all, *kalau nasty eva nasty eva nasty eva gatir anyatha*. When we are sufficiently purified by at least nama-abhasa chanting and have developed equal vision, we may be qualified to establish *varnashrama* for the benefit of the sinful souls who are unable or unwilling to take up the process of devotional service. Our point is that in order to properly implement *varnashrama*, we need self-realized teachers, not struggling souls still hoping to fulfill their material desires in a legitimate way.

ISKCON is meant to be a spiritual society. Every society requires intelligence and organization in order to survive. But a spiritual society is not based on the bodily concept of life, and therefore Srila Prabhupada encouraged his female disciples to preach, go on sankirtana, lead kirtans, give classes in the temple, do Deity worship, and ultimately initiate disciples. Hereunder are a few quotes supporting what we just wrote:

"Concerning the woman's duty, if she gets married, that does not necessarily mean that she must give up any of her service in the temple or on *sankirtana*, but she must also see to it that her household duties are not neglected." (Letter to Sri Govinda, 6 February 1975)

"If she gets married" implies that she might not. In a letter to Rukmini dated 19 December 1968, Srila Prabhupada wrote: "In your letter you have written that you are desiring to remain as *brahmacharini* for a few years longer and this idea is alright. **In India the marriage between a boy and girl is arranged by the parents but in this country such arrangement is not possible so we never request our students to marry if they are not desiring to do this.**"

To Silavati, on 14 June 1969, Srila Prabhupada wrote that "I already have practical experience that many of the American girls and boys are very intelligent and qualified to take up this sublime movement."

Srila Prabhupada also stated that *"Our girls can be engaged for teaching as well as temple worship."* (Letter to: Bhavananda, April 14, 1972)

And to Amsu das on 13 August 1974: "Regarding the worship of our Gaura Nitai by women *pujaris*, we worship Lord Chaitanya in His householder life when He was with His wife, and not as a *sannyasi*. So, it is alright for women to do this service. ***But, besides this, service is spiritual and there can be no material designation.*** In *Bhagavad-gita* it is stated by Lord Krishna: *striyo vaishyas tatha shudras te 'pi yanti param gatim.* The principle is that everyone who is properly initiated and following the rules and regulations can worship. This activity cannot [be] on the material platform.

"According to the *smarta viddhi,* women cannot touch Deity during menstrual period but the *goswami viddhi* allows. But it is better not to do it. One thing is that ***the seva can never be stopped for any reason.*** This also for the cooking."

Regarding preaching, in a letter to Malati dated 25 December 1974, Srila Prabhupada wrote:

"Women in our movement can also preach very nicely. Actually, male and female bodies, these are just outward designations. Lord Chaitanya said that whether one is *brahmana* or whatever he may be, if he knows the science of Krishna then he is to be accepted as guru."

In a letter to Jayagovinda on 8 February 1968, Srila Prabhupada tells us that "Regarding lecturing by woman devotees: I have informed you that in the service of the Lord there is no distinction of caste or creed, color, or sex. In the *Bhagavad-gita*, the Lord especially mentions that even a woman who has taken seriously is also destined to reach Him. We require a person who is in the knowledge of Krishna, that is the only qualification of a person speaking. It doesn't matter what he is. Materially a woman may be less intelligent than a man, but spiritually there is no such distinction. Because spiritually everyone is pure soul. In the absolute plane there is no such gradation of higher and lower. If a woman can lecture nicely and to the point, we should hear her carefully. That is our philosophy. But if a man can speak better than a woman, the man should be given first preference. **But even though a woman is less intelligent, a sincere soul should be given proper chance to speak, because we want so many preachers, both men and women.**"

"I want that all of my spiritual sons and daughters will inherit this title of Bhaktivedanta, so that the family transcendental diploma will continue through the generations. Those possessing the title of Bhaktivedanta will be allowed to initiate disciples. Maybe by 1975, all of my disciples will be allowed to initiate and increase the numbers of the generations. That is my program." (Letter to: Hansadutta, Los Angeles, 3 January, 1969)

As late as June 1976, Srila Prabhupada again explained his position on guruship to three Canadian professors in Toronto:

Prof. O'Connell: Is it possible, Swamiji, for a woman to be a guru in the line of disciplic succession?

Prabhupada: Yes. Jahnava Devi was Nityananda's wife. She became. If she is able to go to the highest perfection of life, why it is not possible to become guru? But, not so many. Actually one who has attained the perfection, she can become guru. But man **OR** woman, unless one has attained the perfection.... *Yei krishna-tattva-vetti sei guru haya*

[Cc. *Madhya* 8.128]. The qualification of guru is that he must be fully cognizant of the science of Krishna. Then he **or** she can become guru. *Yei krishna-tattva-vetti, sei guru haya.* [break] In our material world, is it any prohibition that woman cannot become professor? If she is qualified, she can become professor. What is the wrong there? She must be qualified. That is the position. So similarly, if the woman understands Krishna consciousness perfectly, she can become guru. (Interview with Professors O'Connell, Motilal and Shivaram, June 18, 1976, Toronto)

Sometimes we hear the objection that Jahnava-mata was not an ordinary person and that we cannot imitate her. Yet, Srila Prabhupada gave her as an example to emulate. Whether we like it or not, Srila Prabhupada wanted his female disciples to preach, as evidenced by his letter dated 20-12-1969 to Himavati devi dasi: "In India all the *acharyas* and their descendants later on acted only from the man's side. Their wives were at home because that is the system from old times that women are not required to go out. But in *Bhagavad-gita* we find that women are also equally competent like the men in the matter of Krishna Consciousness Movement. Please therefore carry on these missionary activities, and prove it by practical example that there is no bar for anyone in the matter of preaching work for Krishna Consciousness."

One very nice passage glorifying the preaching work of devotees in women's bodies is found in *Sri Chaitanya-charitamrita, Adi-lila*, 7.31-32. The verse tells about a trick Sri Chaitanya Mahaprabhu devised to drown reluctant Mayavadis in the inundation of love of Godhead. In the purport that follows, Srila Prabhupada makes the point that an acharya "cannot be expected to conform to a stereotype, for he must find the ways and means by which Krishna consciousness may be spread." Jealous persons, he says, "criticize the Krishna consciousness movement because it engages equally both boys and girls in distributing love of Godhead. Not knowing that boys and girls in countries like Europe and America mix very freely, these fools and rascals criticize the boys and girls in Krishna consciousness for intermingling. But these rascals should consider that one cannot suddenly change a community's social customs. However, since both the boys and the girls are being trained to become preachers, those girls are **not** ordinary girls but are **as good as** their brothers who are preaching Krishna consciousness. **Therefore, to engage both boys and girls in fully transcendental activities is a policy intended to spread the** Krishna **consciousness movement . . . .** Therefore, what we are doing is perfect by the grace of Lord Chaitanya Mahaprabhu, for it is He who proposed to invent a way to capture those who strayed from Krishna consciousness."

We sometimes hear that Srila Prabhupada saw things differently toward the end of his manifest presence – as if he meant to replace his previous teachings on pure devotional service with the *varnashrama* system. Well, what about the following statement, spoken on January 7, 1977?

"If one becomes Krishna conscious, then she doesn't require husband . . . . She knows that 'Krishna is my protector. **Why shall I artificially seek after father or...[husband]** And what protection, for a few days, either the father or the son or the husband may give? Real protection is Krishna. This is temporary. But because we have got this material body we require some." (Room Conversation, Bombay)

Even though it is a fact that most women do want to get married, if even one percent of the women in ISKCON are inclined to follow the path of renunciation, it will still amount to a fair number of women. Why should they not be engaged according to their propensies, when *guna* and *karma* (acquired in previous lives), **not** *janma*, constitute the essence of *varnashrama*? How many times have we heard that a person is a *brahmana* by qualification, not by birth? And who are we to legislate devotees' spiritual inclinations when Srila Prabhupada himself has given the go ahead.

Just so that women could be protected and make progress in Krishna consciousness, Srila Prabhupada established *brahmacharini ashramas* all over the world. And he also suggested that we should follow the example of the Christians, who "have so many convent[s] where the women stay and they receive protection. The point is that the women must be protected and it is the duties of the leaders of our Society to see that this is carried out." (Letter to Satsvarupa, 10 February, 1973)

One of our members recalls that when she joined ISKCON in 1978, such *ashramas* gave full protection to women and that the devotees considered the temple president as their father and protector. As late as 1989, even after the demise of the zonal *acharya* system, many of us still had faith that the temple would maintain us, and one devotee remembers being shocked when one disciple of Srila Prabhupada from Australia advised her to start putting money aside for her old age.

"Why should I do that?" she asked.

"Well, you don't expect the temple to take care of you after you stop collecting, do you?"

"Of course I do! Why not? I have given my life to the Movement and collected so much money. Why shouldn't they take care?"

"Don't be so sure. You really should start thinking about the future."

So, the devotee decided to ask her GBC about it, and he replied that "*brahmanas* do not stock money. They have full faith in Krishna and depend fully on His mercy." And the fact is that in those days we were striving to become *brahmanas*, not just in name but in deed also.

Later, we built the Kirtan Ashram in Vrindavan with the idea of giving protection to women. It didn't quite serve the role we were hoping it would – a residential community of mature devotees (*vanaprasthis*) sharing their spiritual wealth with the younger women who come to Vrindavan for association – but as Srila Prabhupada said, "A blind uncle is better than no uncle." The point is that it is *not maya* to not want to get married. It is *not maya* to want to live and serve in a temple as *pujari*, cook, teacher, or whatever. And it is *not maya* to live in a convent or an *ashrama* without interference of so-called male devotees.

It is quite clear that Srila Prabhupada's emphatic instruction that women **must** be protected doesn't necessarily mean that they should receive protection in the traditional Vedic way. His Divine Grace Srila Bhaktisiddhanta Sarasvati Thakura himself was concerned that women be given all facilities to practice devotional service – as evidenced by the excerpt hereunder:

"We now have *mathas* at many places, where at numerous *sannyasis, grihasthas,* and *brahmacharis* have facility to reside and receive training in *sadacara*, yet for a long time we have also been trying to provide the mothers similar opportunities for *Hari-bhajana*. Of course those mothers who have the opportunity for *Hari-bhajana* in their own homes do not need a separate residence. But we often hear that they get impeded in their *Hari-bhajana* due to bad association. It will be highly beneficial for them if we can build Sri Visnupriya-palli in Sridham Mayapur, near the abode of Sriman Mahaprabhu, wherein they can live apart from their families and perform *-bhajana*. They belong to the group of Sri Visnupriya-devi, so it is proper that they live in the house of Sriman Mahaprabhu and serve Him under the shelter of Sri Visnupriya-devi. There should not be any bad association or mundane male relationship for them. Only a few devotees who are like Ishana [Mother Sachi's male servant in Chaitanya-*lila*] should stay at a distance and take care of them. If the mothers do not quarrel, and live only for the sake of serving the Lord – by daily reciting *shastra* and discussing devotional subjects, always chanting the holy name, taking care of the paraphernalia for Sriman Mahaprabhu's service, giving up all luxury, living a model saintly life, and serving Mahaprabhu in all ways – then it is necessary to have such an ideal neighborhood." (Excerpt from a lecture given by Srila Bhaktisiddhanta Sarasvati Thakura on 21 September 1925)

At the beginning of our presentation, we quoted Srila Prabhupada's statement that "In human society all over the world, there are millions and billions of men and women, and almost all of them are less intelligent because they have very little knowledge of spirit soul." It is for **them** that our merciful *acharyas* were pushing for the reestablishment of the *varnashrama* system. And Srila Prabhupada also was pushing for it, especially in later years, when he realized that many, if not most of his students, were not on the platform he had hoped they could be. In our early years as still-aspiring devotees, we were told that when Srila Prabhupada was asked whether all of his disciples would go back to Godhead at the end of their life, he replied, "No. Only the most serious," and that most of his disciples only wanted to go to the heavenly planets.

So the choice is ours: the staircase or the elevator. Surely, ISKCON is big enough to accommodate both. To become a pure devotee is not a cheap thing. But Srila Prabhupada always encouraged the devotees – at least some of them – to shoot for the rhinoceros. And who are we to discourage them? To quote Srila Prabhupada quoting Napoleon Bonaparte, "Impossible is a word in a fool's dictionary." Yes, we need *varnashrama*. But we also need pure devotees to encourage those who want to shoot for the rhinoceros. As stated in the Preface of this presentation, our philosophy promotes simultaneous oneness and difference. Things are not black **or** white. They are both black **and** white and we need both *varnashrama* **and** pure devotional service. But we cannot forcibly bring everyone down to the lowest common denominator. Ultimately *varnashrama* is a means to an end. A noble means, but nevertheless just a means, to the ultimate goal: Krishna-*prema*.

Hare Krishna Hare Krishna Krishna Krishna Hare Hare
Hare Rama Hare Rama Rama Rama Hare Hare

2018

In 2018, more than one hundred women from around Australia attended a Vaishnavi retreat there. This next paper is one of the presentations made at that gathering.

History of Women in ISKCON
by Krishnarupa dasi

Gaudiya Vaishnavism has historically had transcendental trailblazers who have had a unique vision regarding ways Krishna consciousness could be spread.

The *acharyas* are always adjusting according to time, place, and circumstance. Bhaktisiddhanta Sarasvati Thakura was one such transcendentalist. For example, he gave *brahmana* initiation to men not born in *brahmana* families. This was unprecedented at the time.

Spiritual Revolutionary

Following in his spiritual master's footsteps, Srila Prabhupada, ISKCON's founder-*acharya*, was also a transcendental trailblazer. He used everything in the service of Krishna and engaged all his disciples – men and women – in carrying on his mission.

Srila Prabhupada very much encouraged his female disciples to lead *kirtans* and preaching programs. He gave his female disciples *brahmana* initiation with the full mantras. This was indeed revolutionary in the history of our *sampradaya* and revealed his unique vision. Prabhupada also permitted women to live in the temples, which was not allowed in the Gaudiya Matha at the time. In India, he made an exception – single Indian ladies were not permitted because of the Indian culture and family restrictions.

He indeed expected the Vaishnavis to perform services according to qualification, not the body, including opening temples.

A Paradigm Shift

Especially pre-1972/1973, Vaishnavis were given equal opportunity in ISKCON temples and Srila Prabhupada gave services to perform in accordance with their propensities.

He even said that the *sannyasis* in India were criticizing him for allowing women to live in the temples, but that when he went to the US, he realized that boys and girls were accustomed to working alongside each other.

Jyotirmayi devi dasi, a senior disciple of Srila Prabhupada's, wrote in a paper that, "Women were doing things in front of Srila Prabhupada himself that later on they were forbidden to do."

Yamuna dasi was leading *kirtans* in India in front of Srila Prabhupada and often at his instruction, Himavati dasi gave public talks in India, and Jyotirmayi and Rukmini dasis performed *arati* in front of him. Many other Vaishnavis were given such opportunities as well, such as Jadurani dasi was put in charge of the BBT painting department, Kausalya dasi organized large preaching programs in India, Varanasi dasi was temple commander, and Jyotirmayi was the BBT chief French translator. Janaki dasi, Mukunda Goswami's former wife, was one of the trustees when ISKCON was incorporated.

Vaishnavis from that era often scratch their heads trying to conclude why suddenly women were treated differently inside ISKCON around 1972 and 1973. Was it because some devotees had gone to India and were living in the traditional Gaudiya Matha or others, who were spending more time in India, brought back to the West a whole wave of more bodily conscious, *smarta* type behavior. I believe it is a combination of factors.

Suddenly, there was a prevailing attitude that women were a burden, a distraction and often in the way – yet women in ISKCON were hugely successful fund-raisers and contributors.

Equal to All

Srila Prabhupada built a house the whole world could live in – and this included men and women.

When *brahmacharis* would complain to Srila Prabhupada that the ladies in the temple were a distraction, he would remind them, "These ladies are like angels, and if you offer your obeisances to them, you will become liberated."

In the *Chaitanya-charitamrita, Adi-lila,* Chapter 7, purport to verses 31 and 32, he writes, "Both boys and girls are being trained to become preachers. Those girls are not ordinary girls but are as good as their brothers who are preaching Krishna Consciousness. Therefore to engage both boys and girls in fully transcendental activities is a policy intended to spread the Krishna Consciousness movement."

On the material platform there are distinctions between men and women, but Srila Prabhupada said those women who have taken shelter of Lord Chaitanya's mission are acting on the spiritual platform and he gave them equal opportunities to serve.

Yamuna devi dasi writes, "I was present on four occasions when Srila Prabhupada repeated the Chanakya Pandit adage: 'Never trust a woman or a politician.' On each occasion Srila Prabhupada looked me in the eye to see my response. On the last occasion, in Bombay in 1973, he quoted the saying, heartily laughing in front of a small group of men. Then he said: 'What do you think, Yamuna?'"

"Immediately I retorted: 'Of course it is true, Srila Prabhupada,' whereupon he became grave, looked at me with *great feeling*, and said, 'But you are not a woman, you are a Vaishnava!'"

During Yamuna's presentation to the GBC in the year 2000, she said, "Srila Prabhupada lovingly encouraged and engaged us in the service of the *sankirtana* movement, and he consistently revealed himself to be *panditah sama-darsinah* – equal to all."

Lynchpins

Despite obstacles, the future of women in ISKCON is one of optimism. Inspired and inspiring Vaishnavis perform *sankirtana* and book distribution, they have leadership roles, such as SABHA membership and GBC membership, they are organizers of large events, engage their artistic sensibilities in Deity worship, have community leadership in roles as educators and Vaishnava Care initiatives – and not the least, they are the lynchpins of the family, training the very future of ISKCON.

As Srila Prabhupada said, "The reason I was so successful, was because I allowed both boys and girls to serve in this movement."

Women generally have a different perspective on issues than men do. They are more empathetic and see things in relationship to the individual. They are excellent problem solvers, and expert at multi-tasking. Generally women also have more emotional intelligence.

Krishna Himself says in *Bhagavad-gita* (10.34), "Among women I am fame, fortune, speech, memory, intelligence, faithfulness and patience."

A neuroscientist Dr Louann Brizandine wrote in her book, *The Female Brain* that women's brains are indeed smaller than men's, but even accounting for bodily size and weight they have the same *number* of brain cells as men. Those brain cells are just packed in tighter, like a corset. So despite a "smaller brain," the number of brain cells are the same, according to Dr Brizandine!

So how do we make further headway in ensuring successful pathways for Vaishnavis in ISKCON? There are many ways this can be done.

We can be the best devotees we can be. We can study Srila Prabhupada's books avidly, and take up the responsibility of giving classes. We can see all men except our husbands as sons, and take our service to Srila Prabhupada and our gurus very seriously. We can be active bystanders if we see Vaishnavis in trouble and we can be pro-active in developing mentorship programs in our temples in order to encourage the younger devotee women and spearhead Vaishnava Care initiatives.

If we have low expectations of ourselves, or if others have low expectations of women and the roles they can play, then we will not avail ourselves of every opportunity we can find to enhance our service attitude.

We want to inspire each other, nurture each other and empower each other to increase our service to Srila Prabhupada's mission. Indeed, women in Krishna consciousness are an intricate, essential part of Srila Prabhupada's legacy.

Dealing with Dysfunction
by Radha dasi

I recently read an online post by a woman who was born and raised in India that covered the topic of "How should a woman behave in the *brahmana* culture?" I'll refer to her as Krishna dasi in this essay, although that is not her name. In the post she describes her experience in a physically abusive marriage and how her *diksha-guru* advised her to stay in her marriage. She offered her experience as a model for other women to follow.

I don't intend to criticize this woman for the choices she has made in her married life. However, having worked with survivors of serious domestic violence, I have learned that an abusive relationship can seriously threaten a woman (and most survivors of domestic violence are women) and her children. A "one size fits all" approach to abusive relationships literally puts lives at risk.

We tend to assume that what works in an ideal situation is going to work even when the situation is less than ideal. Srila Prabhupada instructed Vaishnavis to be humble and submissive to their husbands so that their marriages would be peaceful. Some take this instruction to an extreme, opining that a woman may never disagree with her husband. While there is give and take in any healthy relationship, many Vaishnavis will choose more feminine communication styles in their marriages. These less confrontational communication styles can be part of strong marriages.

On the other hand, a chronic domestic abuser does not, as many think, become abusive due to his wife's behavior or other factors such as stress or financial worries. Stress and financial difficulties, including addiction of any kind, are not the cause of domestic abuse, but rather they can act to exacerbate a domestic violence situation. Domestic violence is used by the abuser to exercise power and control over the vulnerable partner and is a systematic course of behavior employed to achieve these ends. This is the dysfunctional pattern the abuser has developed to manage his own painful emotions. This pattern gives rise to the classic "cycle of violence" in which an abuser first courts his wife, then becomes more and more angry as his stress builds, explodes with violence, returning to the courting stage with remorse and promises of change. His violence is independent of anyone else's behavior, including his wife's.

Krishna dasi's post makes it clear that her husband's behavior was beyond her control. Although she was a model wife, she was frequently beaten and describes her husband as "cruel" (somewhat of an understatement!). Her guru advised her to go to her brother's house when her husband beat her and then return when her husband calmed down, but not to divorce her husband for any reason. Krishna dasi is an ardent defender of "*stri-dharma*" and believes a woman should never "leave your husband." She was uncomplaining and submissive in the face of horrific abuse. No one will argue that she caused her husband's violence.

It's important to acknowledge this violence as aberrant behavior. Beating one's wife is not normal, not a healthy response to life's challenges, and a serious form of Vaishnava *aparadha*. It can also harm children who become anxious and distressed when witnessing such violence or who may be on the receiving end of such violence. Children who witness domestic violence are more prone to mental illness, drug abuse and more likely to be violent with their families as adults. Marital violence can also undermine a family's faith in Krishna.

An often overlooked point is the fact that abusers actually kill their wives. Sometimes they go so far as to kill their children, family members, neighbors, co-workers, or law enforcement along with their spouses. Would we encourage a woman to stay in a marriage knowing that it could end in her death and the death of her children? No. We need to recognize that some women are in life-threatening situations. All devotees should be able to live in peace and safety.

And despite her claims and her advice to others, Krishna dasi did in fact leave her husband. When the violence was at its height, she would typically leave her home and stay with her brother. This kind of safety planning is essential to surviving domestic violence. What Krishna dasi means is that she did not divorce her husband or refuse to live with him after his beatings.

Why is it acceptable to leave the home temporarily to protect oneself, but not permanently? The truth is, Krishna dasi found a safety plan that worked for her and balanced her social and cultural considerations with her safety. Kudos to her. Where she goes off track is in assuming that her compromise should be adopted by any woman in a violent marriage.

Krishna dasi was fortunate in having a brother who offered her a safe haven. Many Vaishnavis lack that resource. Getting out of the house while her husband was violent was, by her own admission, key to Krishna dasi's safety. For those who lack a welcoming relative, that choice is not available.

Krishna dasi was also fortunate that her husband did not beat their children. However, abusers who hit their wives are also more likely to hit their children. Should we expect women to allow their children to be abused in order to comply with a traditional vision of *stri-dharma*? Part of a mother's *dharma* is to protect her children. There are many ways in which another Vaishnavi's situation might differ from Krishna dasi's and we should not expect all women to make the same choices.

Krishna dasi's choice to remain married to her abuser was also driven by her culture and social environment. Although she writes that "everybody" told her to leave her husband, she also writes that her decision to stay in the marriage protected her daughter's social status. If Krishna dasi had left the marriage she writes "who would have married her?" If the decision to stay in an abusive marriage is based on the idea that it is a woman's duty, then do these social considerations even matter? The truth is, Krishna dasi was predisposed by culture to make particular choices. There is no reason to expect other Vaishnavis to make similar choices.

Ultimately, we have to understand that a marriage with recurring domestic violence is a terribly dangerous environment and destructive to everyone involved (husband, wife, children, extended family, and community). Each situation is different and each Vaishnavi should be able to choose her response based on what protects her and her children and what provides an environment where their spiritual lives can flourish.

The Roles of Vaishnavis in ISKCON
by Radha dasi for the Vaishnavi Ministry

Women's roles in ISKCON have been a subject of much confusion, contention, and polarizing debate in which we tend to ascribe the worst motives to those whose conclusions differ from our own. Even more troubling, we tend to characterize Srila Prabhupada's teachings on this issue in absolute terms without considering the nuances of instructions he gave to different devotees at different times and in different circumstances.

At one extreme, devotees say that Srila Prabhupada's instructions on women's roles were based on a social system that is no longer practical in modern society and that, under the principle of time, place, and circumstance, we can dispense with much of his teachings on men's and women's social roles. This position rests, in part, on the idea that traditional male/female social roles are disfavored in modern society and the cause of much exploitation of women. In order to attract intelligent, well-rounded people, the theory is that we must adapt the traditional male/female roles to something more like the roles in modern society.

At the other extreme, devotees argue that Srila Prabhupada did not want women to have any role outside the home. This position rests on Srila Prabhupada's instruction that women must be protected at every stage of life by their father, husband, or son, and by his instruction to institute *varnashrama dharma*. For example, proponents of this position would not allow women anywhere in ISKCON to perform temple Deity worship, speak or lead *kirtan* in public, or have any management or leadership role. They argue that Srila Prabhupada gave women a larger role in ISKCON as a temporary concession to their Western conditioning, that only the instructions in his books and not his letters and conversations should be considered in understanding the role of women, and that *varnashrama dharma* is reflected by a historical Indian society in which women did not leave their homes except to visit the temple or other women.

In the understanding of the Vaishnavi Ministry, both extremes are wrong and both are right to some degree. They are wrong in that they assume that Srila Prabhupada had only one response to every situation. They are right in that they have each focused on some aspect of Srila Prabhupada's teachings. To understand Prabhupada's desire for the role of women in ISKCON, however, these aspects need to be seen from the perspective of the entirety of his teachings on this issue – especially his pivotal statements.

Protection

Srila Prabhupada was unapologetic and unequivocal in his statements that women need to be protected at all stages of their lives. Often, however, we make assumptions about what form that protection should take. There's no evidence that Srila Prabhupada intended "protection of women" to mean they could not perform Deity worship,[1] lead *kirtans*,[2] speak in public,[3] live in temple *ashramas*,[4] or manage departments.[5] To accept that understanding we would have to accept that Srila Prabhupada failed to protect Malati devi dasi, Silavati devi dasi, Yamuna devi dasi, and many others when he engaged them in such activities.

It is unacceptable to assume that Srila Prabhupada did not intend to do something he actually did, such as engage Vaishnavis in these services. Moreover, Srila Prabhupada gave no indication that these engagements for women were temporary. Had he intended such a thing, he would have expressed that instruction in some way. But the opposite is true. When Vaishnavis wrote to Srila Prabhupada inquiring about their roles, he encouraged them to participate in temple/spiritual activities and gave no indication that such participation should be temporary or limited.[6]

When he was informed that certain *brahmacharis* were feeling distracted by the presence of Vaishnavis in the temple room during *japa*, Srila Prabhupada's response was that the *brahmacharis*, not the Vaishnavis, should "go to the forest."[7] Another time, Prabhupada said that he wanted Vaishnavis to live in temple *ashramas* because they needed that protection.[8] He never indicated that *brahmacharini ashramas* or women's presence in the temple were temporary measures.

In a letter to Malati devi dasi, Srila Prabhupada, wrote that whoever was qualified, male or female, could give *Srimad-Bhagavatam* class. Acknowledging differences between men and women, he defined the qualification for speaking in the temple as "how much one understands about Krishna and surrendering to the process."[9] Had he intended this opportunity for women to speak as a temporary concession, why didn't he indicate that? In the clear absence of any such indication, it is dangerous to assume that we understand Prabhupada's intention better than he himself did. We should neither put words into Srila Prabhupada's mouth by assuming a hidden motive he never mentioned, nor take words out of his mouth by ignoring clear instructions on the implementation of women's social roles in our Society.[10]

The Weight of Historical Social Practices

Srila Prabhupada was willing to change tradition in order to shelter women. For example, both Srila Bhaktisiddhanta Saraswati and Srila Prabhupada gave *diksha* initiation to women. Further, Srila Prabhupada gave *brahmana* initiation to women. Both practices constitute a change from tradition. Neither Srila Bhaktisiddhanta Saraswati nor Srila Prabhupada ever indicated that the practice of initiating women was temporary or somehow a lesser initiation than that given to men.

Giving initiation is deeply significant spiritual practice that creates an eternal relationship. In changing tradition in this way, Srila Bhaktisiddhanta Saraswati and Srila Prabhupada also made a statement about the weight we should give historical social practices in determining proper roles for women in ISKCON. In other words, it is clear that our *parampara* is not bound by social custom in regards to the treatment and status of anyone in society, including women. (Lord Chaitanya, a *brahmana*, embraced and was instructed by Ramananda Raya, who was considered a *shudra* – equally maverick, you could say, as Prabhupada giving women second initiation.)

Thus, the argument that something has historically been the custom is not definitive on this issue. In Srila Prabhupada's words, "In India all the *acharyas* and their descendants later on acted only from the man's side. Their wives were at home because that is the system from old times that women are not required to go out. But in *Bhagavad-gita* we find that women are also equally competent like the men in the matter of Krishna consciousness movement. Please therefore carry on these missionary activities, and prove it by practical example that there is no bar for anyone in the matter of preaching work for Krishna Consciousness." (Letter to Himavati, London, 20 December, 1969)

Varnashrama

Some argue that *varnashrama dharma* means women have no roles outside the home. This is an assumption. In fact, women in our tradition have always had larger roles that take them beyond the home. In Krishna-*lila*, there are descriptions of the gopis engaging in commerce by traveling to Mathura to sell their milk products. The fruit seller who traded Krishna fruit for a handful of grains was a woman engaged in the economic life of the village. Draupadi and other *kshatriya* queens managed logistics for large households and even armies! Some women lived as ascetics and others are mentioned in the *Srimad-Bhagavatam* as "expert in transcendental and Vedic knowledge."[11]

Srila Prabhupada told a story praising the chastity of a particular woman he remembered from his college days. This woman was a street sweeper who routinely worked surrounded by men. However, she conducted herself with such grace and care as to be remembered by Srila Prabhupada many years later. He did not indicate that it was wrong for her to be working outside the home or in the company of men, but cited her as one example of how such a thing could be done.

Some argue that under the tenets of *varnashrama dharma*, it is improper for any woman to give instruction to a man. In fact, virtually every man begins his life by taking instruction from a woman. The mother is the first guru. As men in our Society are told to see all women as mother, there is no barrier to taking instruction from a qualified woman.[12]

Historically, women in our tradition have engaged in such activity. Kunti's instructions carried so much weight with her sons that they broke tradition when all five brothers married Draupadi. Even though Kunti's instruction was given based on a misunderstanding ("share whatever you have found"), her sons placed such importance on her instructions that they agreed to share a wife. The prayers of Queen Kunti are included in *Srimad-Bhagavatam*. Clearly, there is no barrier to anyone in taking instruction from a qualified woman.[13]

Jahnava Mata, Lord Nityananda's wife, was the head of His disciples after His departure and also initiated disciples of her own. Not only did she give spiritual instruction, she acted as the spiritual and managerial head of all of Lord Nityananda's disciples. Gangamata Goswamini was initiated in Lord Chaitanya's line and also became an initiating guru.

When Haridasa Thakura converted the prostitute through his pure chanting, he accepted her as a disciple and engaged her in sharing spiritual knowledge with others. Without doubt, the qualification to give spiritual instruction is not based on the body. The idea that women are somehow disqualified from spiritual leadership is not supported by our tradition, our scriptures, or Srila Prabhupada's instructions.[14]

There's no doubt that Srila Prabhupada noted the differences between the sexes and gave his disciples instructions based on those differences. He was strict in how he expected his female disciples to dress, for instance, requiring a degree of modesty that he did not require of his male disciples. When he traveled with his disciples in India, he was sometimes personally attentive to the protection of his female disciples, having them travel with him to programs and stay in the same home or *ashrama*, while he expected his male disciples to make do.

It seems that Srila Prabhupada expected that most of the leaders/managers in ISKCON would be men. In appointing temple presidents, BBT managers, GBC members, and project members, the number of men appointed greatly exceeded the number of women appointed or approached regarding appointment. One might conclude that Srila Prabhupada envisioned a society in which a female leader was not common, but was possible.

In arguing for limited roles for women, devotees quote Srila Prabhupada's request that we institute *varnashrama dharma*. However, there is no statement of Srila Prabhupada's indicating that *varnashrama dharma* excludes women from leadership or management. In fact, the opposite is true. "I am so glad to learn that our London Temple is very, very well managed under your supervision. Kindly continue this standard of

Temple management – that will make me very happy." (Letter to Yamuna, Calcutta, 16 September, 1970)

Beyond *Varnashrama*

Varnashrama dharma is a social system designed to give society's members the best possible opportunity for spiritual advancement. When the *bhakti-yoga* tradition is combined with *varnashrama dharma* the result is called *daiva-varnashrama*, "the transcendental system of four social orders and four spiritual orders." (*Bhag.* 5.1.24 purport) Prabhupada writes, "One of the objectives of the Krishna consciousness movement is to establish this *daiva-varnashrama*, but not to encourage so-called *varnashrama* without scientifically organized endeavor by human society." (*Bhag.* 7.14.10 purport) The distinction between so-called *varnashrama dharma* and *daiva-varnashrama dharma* is profound. Under *varnashrama dharma*, only members of certain *varnas* can engage in scriptural study and temple worship. *Shudras* were not allowed to study the Vedas or be *pujaris,* according to the traditions of *varnashrama dharma.* So-called *varnashrama* is a caste system based on birth. *Daiva-varnashrama* is based not on birth but on one's qualities and activities. In Srila Prabhupada's powerful and clear words, "The *acharyas* who advocate the *daiva-varnashrama* (the social order of *chatur-varnyam* mentioned in *Bhagavad-gita*) do not accept the proposition of *asura-varnashrama*, which maintains that the social order of *varna* is indicated by birth." (Cc. *Madhya* 3.6 purport)

Daiva-varnashrama dharma is based on the understanding that spiritual life and spiritual advancement and engagement are open to everyone regardless of birth. No one in our ISKCON society would ever think of saying that a man born in a *shudra* family could not study Srila Prabhupada's books or engage in Deity worship or manage a *yatra*. Similarly, Srila Prabhupada makes it clear that women can also have responsible positions in his ISKCON society.[15] Thus, if we decide that a particular service is not available to women, it is only for social reasons, not spiritual ones.

Conclusion

In *daiva-varnashrama*, the social system that Srila Prabhupada and Lord Krishna advocate, one's occupation is not determined by one's birth but by one's activities and qualities (Bg 4.13). Prabhupada says: "In *daiva-varnashrama* there cannot be acknowledgement of social status according to birthright because in *Bhagavad-gita* it is said that the determining considerations are *guna* and *karma,* one's qualities and work. It is this *daiva-varnashrama* that should be established all over the world to continue a perfect society for Krishna consciousness." (*Bhag.* 5.1.24 purport)

The question before ISKCON today is: Is *daiva-varnashrama* only for men?

Our considered understanding, based on Srila Prabhupada's teachings, is that *daiva-varnashrama* is for all members of Prabhupada's society. Thus:

1. Prabhupada wants to establish *daiva-varnashrama*,

2. *daiva-varnashrama* is not based on one's birth but on one's qualities and activities, and

3. *daiva-varnashrama* is intended for all members of society, both male and female.

If these three statements are true, then it follows that a woman's position in society should be according to her qualities and activities.

For many, if not most women, this will mean that she is a wife and mother. But this is not all she can be. She may be a wife, a mother, and a temple president. She can give *Bhagavatam* class. Or, if she is so inclined, she may chart a more renounced path, which would allow us to understand why Srila Prabhupada also made statements such as:

> Prabhupada: If one can remain without marriage, that is the first
> class.
>
> Rupanuga: Women also?
>
> Prabhupada: Women also. What is the use of this material husband? Make Krishna husband. Krishna's prepared to become everything – love Him as husband, love Him as son, love Him as friend. (Room Conversation – July 6, 1976, Washington D.C.)

If we accept the principle of *daiva-varnashrama,* if we follow Srila Prabhupada's example in engaging Vaishnavis, we find that women can be wives, mothers, leaders, teachers, worshipers, gurus, and/or whatever else according to their qualities and activities, not their birth.[16] Everyone is an individual. To successfully arouse each person's dormant Krishna consciousness, we must accommodate and encourage each person's individual expression of Krishna consciousness. This will benefit both the individual and our ISKCON society as a whole.

Footnotes

[1] a) "Deity worship means to be very, very clean. You should try to bathe twice daily. The Deities should never be approached without having bathed first and changed to clean cloths after passing stool, etc. Keep teeth brushed after each meal, fingernails clean and trim. Be sure that your hands are clean before touching anything on the altar or the Deities. And cleanse the Deity room, altar and floor daily thoroughly. Shine the various Aratrik paraphernalia after Aratrik. This is described in the booklet for pujaris written by Silavati Dasi. The idea is summit cleanliness – that will satisfy Krsna." Letter to Rukmini, Los Angeles 20 March, 1970.

b) "I am very glad also to know that you are engaged as Pujari there. Try to learn this art of Arcana very nicely. You can consult in this connection Himavati, Yamuna and also Silavati. I wish that all our girl devotees be expert in the matter of Arcana and cooking." Letter to Kancanbala, Los Angeles 20 April, 1970.

c) "I am glad to learn that the Deities are being cared for there in Chicago so nicely by your good self. I personally gave instruction to Silavati how to care for the Deities properly when I was in Los Angeles and you were trained up by her. So I am confident that everything is going on nicely. Proper Deity worship, with all attention to cleanliness, is of the utmost importance. If you can please the Deity by your sincere service, then your temple will flourish. To be able to personally serve the Deity is a great privilege and such a person is very fortunate indeed. So you continue in this way and Kṛṣna will surely bless you." Letter to Hladini, Surat 29 December, 1970.

d) "Please especially see that the Deity worship is going nicely. You are an experienced lady, and you can teach especially the girls there to cook nicely for the Deity, to prepare flower garlands nicely for the Deity, to clean and dress the Deity nicely. You organize this to the first class standard, as I have seen they are doing in Los Angeles and in London. Then people will be automatically attracted. You know how to do these things, and they must take instruction from you. And, you can let me know how things are going on there." Letter to Shaktimati, Bombay 18 August, 1975.

[2] "All along you have been hearing the recording of Yamuna devi and now you want to change. It is not ordinary singing, it is concert, many people are singing, so it is not bad. Just like sankirtana, many voices are there, men and women, so it is the same thing, sankirtana. I approve of it. Here in Krsna Balarama Temple we are hearing the same recording every morning, so if it is good here why not there?" Letter to Jayasacinandana, Vrindaban 12 December, 1975.

[3] "So far as girls or boys lecturing in the morning, that doesn't make any difference. Either girl or boy devotees may deliver lecture if they choose to do. We have no such distinction of bodily designations, male or female. Kṛṣṇa Consciousness is on the spiritual platform. As such, anyone who is a devotee of the Lord, following in this line of disciplic succession, can deliver lecture, on the teachings of Bhagavad-gita, Srimad-Bhagavatam, etc." Letter to Syama, Seattle 21 October, 1968.

[4] "I have received report from Brahmananda Swami that you are still living outside the temple. This is not good, and I would request you to immediately return to the temple. And they must receive you nicely. They are your spiritual sons and daughters, so Mother and children must live together in the temple." Letter to Shaktimati, Bombay 18 August, 1975.

5 a) "Shaktimati is an elderly woman and can do important work with the cultured Indian society, and she also speaks Swahili. She must be given an important position as a manager. She can work under Brahmananda Swami." Letter to Chyavana, Dallas 29 July, 1975

b) The artists whose work so beautifully graces our pages are, to begin with, Jadurani devi dasi, directress of the Art Department. BTG #13 The Artists, June 1967

c) Mrs. Wax: Could a woman be a temple president?

Prabhupada: Yes, why not?

Room Conversation with Mr. & Mrs. Wax, July 5, 1975, Chicago (In this conversation, Srila Prabhupada makes clear that the need of a woman to be protected by husband, father, or son does not preclude a leadership role.)

[6] "Regarding the problem of how to be aggressive on sankirtana and submissive in the temple, my request to you is that you should go on being aggressive on sankirtana." Letter to Jagaddhatri, Pasupati, Sailogata, Pamela, Dallas 30 July, 1975.

[7] "I do not know why these things inventions are going on. That is our only business, to invent something new programme? We have already got our Vaishnava standard. That is sufficient for Madhvacarya, Ramanujacarya, it was sufficient for Lord Chaitanya, six Gosvamis, for Bhaktivinode Thakura, for my Guru Maharaja Bhaktisiddhanta Sarasvati, for me, for all big big saints and acaryas in our line – why it shall be inadequate for my disciples so they must manufacture something? That is not possible. Who has introduced these things, that women cannot have chanting japa in the temple, they cannot perform the arati and so many things? If they become agitated, then let the brahmacaris go to the forest, I

have never introduced these things. The brahmacaris cannot remain in the presence of women in the temple, then they may go to the forest, not remaining in New York City, because in New York there are so many women, so how they can avoid seeing? Best thing is to go to the forest for not seeing any women, if they become so easily agitated, but then no one will either see them and how our preaching work will go on?" Letter to Ekayani, Bombay 3 December, 1972.

[8] "So the problem is there, the women must have a husband to give protection. Of course, if the women can remain unmarried, and if there is suitable arrangement for the temple to protect them, just like in the Christian Church there is nunnery for systematic program of engaging the ladies and protecting them, that is also nice." Letter to Madhukara, Bombay 4 January, 1973.

[9] "So you please continue your devotional service, cooking etc, and you can also keep giving Bhagavatam class if you like. Women in our movement can also preach very nicely. Actually male and female bodies, these are just outward designations. Lord Chaitanya said that whether one is brahmana or whatever he may be if he knows the science of Krsna then he is to be accepted as guru. So one who gives class, he must read and study regularly and study the purport and realize it. Don't add anything or concoct anything, then he can preach very nicely. The qualification for leading class is how much one understands about Krsna and surrendering to the process. Not whether one is male or female. Of course women, generally speaking are less intelligent, better she has heard nicely then she will speak nicely." Letter to Malati, Bombay 25 December, 1974.

[10] "So far your question regarding women, I have always accepted the service of women without any discrimination." Letter to Gurudasa, Los Angeles 26 May, 1972

[11] Svadha, who was offered to the Pitas, begot two daughters named Vayuna and Dharini, both of whom were impersonalists and were expert in transcendental and Vedic knowledge. Bhag. 4.1.64

[12] "The actual system is that the husband is Spiritual Master to his wife, but if the wife can bring her husband into practicing this process, then it is all right that the husband accepts wife as Spiritual Master. Chaitanya Mahaprabhu has said that anyone who knows the science of Krsna, that person should be accepted as Spiritual Master, regardless of any material so-called qualifications; such as rich or poor, man or woman, or brahmana or shudra. So if you can show the women of the community how to help their husbands and children to perfect their home life, and all aspects of life, in Krsna Consciousness by chanting, aratrik ceremonies, and eating Krsna prasadam, then you will improve the conditions of the neighboring communities to an incalculable extent. So try for this as far as possible." Letter to Silavati, New Vrindaban 14 June, 1969

[This principle is also established in Krsna-*lila*: the pastimes of the wives of the brahmanas and the wives of Kaliya.]

[13] a) "If you a have got sufficient devotees to take care of the Deities as you have seen how in the Los Angeles Temple, take instruction from Yamuna and Silavati how they are worshiping and the installation procedure is given on a separate sheet." Letter to Jagadisa, Calcutta 17 September, 1970

b) "Regarding Deity worship, Silavati and Yamuna Devi may be considered expert, so if some new hands come and take their help, that is a good proposition." Letter to Karandhara, Calcutta 19 September, 1970

c) "I am glad to hear that you are taking up the program of deity worship very seriously. This is required. So everything should be first class as you have got full facility, just to the standard of Los Angeles. In Los Angeles I personally advised them in all the different aspects of deity worship, so you may consult, especially with Silavati Prabhu (now in Dallas) and do the needful." Letter to Sri Govinda, Calcutta 31 January, 1973

[14] Prabhupada encouraged his women disciples to preach:

a) "Regarding your preaching work in the schools, colleges, and universities, try to attract the students, they are our great future hope and they will take up this matter very quickly because the students are not very much contaminated." Letter to Kancanbala, Los Angeles 20 April, 1970

b) "It is very good that you and the other girls are preaching in school to your class mates. This will bring the greatest benefit not only to them but also it will help you to progress more and more in your devotional service." Letter to Lilasukha, Los Angeles 17 December, 1968

Prabhupada also encouraged his women disciples to teach:

c) "Satyabhama Dasi is in charge of educating the children in New Vrindaban, and she is very qualified to do this because she is educated and works very nicely with the children." Letter to Silavati, New Vrindaban 14 June, 1969

d) Prabhupada: But by training, by knowledge, one can be elevated. That is gurukula. So these are the general principles. Now arrange.

Jyotirmayi: I was thinking about that, that because the girls are trained like brahmacharinis also in the gurukula, they should be also kept very, very simple, just like the little boys, brahmacharis.

Prabhupada: No, our life is simple. We don't want luxury. We don't want luxury, but as we are accustomed in so many ways, as far as possible. But life should be very simple. To increase unnecessary things unnecessarily, that is material life.

Jyotirmayi: I was thinking in that way – simple clothes, no jewels, just like the boys, simple . . .

Prabhupada: Don't say "no." But give a taste for the good, then it will be automatically "no." Room Conversation, July 31, 1976, New Mayapur

[15] Prof. O'Connell: Is it possible, Swamiji, for a woman to be a guru in the line of disciplic succession?

Prabhupada: Yes. Jahnava devi was – Nityananda's wife. She became. If she is able to go to the highest perfection of life, why it is not possible to become guru? But, not so many. Actually one who has attained the perfection, she can become guru. But man or woman, unless one has attained the perfection . . . yei krsna-tattva-vetta sei guru haya [Cc. Madhya 8.128]. The qualification of guru is that he must be fully cognizant of the science of Krsna. Then he or she can become guru. Yei krsna-tattva-vetta, sei guru haya. [break] In our material world, is it any prohibition that woman cannot become professor? If she is qualified, she can become professor. What is the wrong there? She must be qualified. That is the position. So similarly, if the woman understands Krsna consciousness perfectly, she can become guru. Interview with Professors O'Connell, Motilal, and Shivarama, June 18, 1976, Toronto

[16] "We are Vaishnavas. We are not concerned with male or female position in life. That is simply bodily concept of life. It is not spiritual. Whether one is male or female, it doesn't matter, simply chant Hare Krsna and follow the four regulative principles and your life will be perfect." Letter to Jennifer, Mexico City 15 February, 1975

2019

Some Reasons Why SABHA
Supports Vaishnavi Diksa Gurus (VDG) in ISKCON
by Kalakantha dasa

SABHA stands for "Spiritual Advisors Bhagavata Assembly," and was formed in 2017 as a council to the International GBC.

1. **Srila Prabhupada's Statements.** In a letter intended for wide distribution in ISKCON, Srila Prabhupada stated that his male and female disciples could accept disciples when they were sufficiently qualified. Later, in a recorded interview in Toronto, he specifically stated that qualified female devotees could accept disciples and gave examples from our Gaudiya Vaishnava line, though he acknowledged that generally there were "some, but not so many," VDGs. As these specific statements come from its founder-*acharya,* we accept them as conclusive in ISKCON. The statement from Srila Prabhupada's purport in *Srimad-Bhagavatam*'s fourth canto that Suniti could not initiate her son "because she was his mother and a woman," is not applicable to everyone in all times and circumstances. If it were, Srila Prabhupada would have been contradicting himself with his forementioned direct statements.

2. **The GBC debate** regarding VDGs has been more than sufficient and the GBC committee formed of proponents and opponents has reached a consensus. Though their resolution is unlikely to please everyone, the GBC has addressed a difficult question in a sober way and the significance of their collaborative work should be respected.

3. **With VDGs, all yatras have preaching flexibility. Otherwise, not.** Preaching circumstances in different parts of the world call for different strategies. For example, the Indian Bureau opposes VDGs, but the North American GBC/TP assembly favors them. Under current ISKCON law, devotees become *diksha* gurus only after local committees nominate them. If the local situation does not favor VDGs, local committees will not recommend them. Moreover, if VDGs are nominated and approved elsewhere, local leaders have full authority to ban them from visiting or initiating in their yatras. While any local *yatra* has the authority to deny VDG presence, to deny VDGs throughout ISKCON hurts *yatras* that require "some, but not many" VDGs to preach effectively to local populations.

4. **The views of other *sampradaya*s are not definitive for ISKCON.** Leaders in the Ramanuja *sampradaya* and others who oppose women giving *diksha* generally also oppose low-born men giving *diksha*. Anti-VDG advocates quote them only in their opposition to women.

5. **Guru/disciple gender differences.** It is no less appropriate for a VDG to have male disciples than for *sannyasis* to have female disciples. Many ladies aspiring for *diksha* prefer a female guru.

6. **No Female Ritviks.** In 1977 when his health was failing, Srila Prabhupada appointed 11 senior disciples to accept disciples on his behalf. Opponents of VDGs note that none were female. We note that at that time Srila Prabhupada's female disciples were of child-bearing age. The GBC proposal requires VDG applicants to be 55 or over. We accept this as a reasonable stipulation.

7. *Siddha* **qualifications.** VDG opponents assert that Vaishnavis can only initiate if they are *siddhas,* just as *ritvik* advocates say that Srila Prabhupada's disciples can only initiate if they are *siddhas*. *Shastra* says that anyone who knows the science of Krishna can become a spiritual master. Srila Prabhupada is the PhD in ISKCON; his teaching assistants must be qualified PhD candidates, though not necessarily PhDs themselves. Srila Prabhupada said that when iron comes in contact with fire, it becomes like fire.

8. **Vaishnavi etiquette.** Srila Prabhupada loved his 1,500 female disciples and engaged them without making them feel inferior or intimidated. He encouraged them to perform their service for Krishna, whether it was Deity worship, preaching, or child care, while at the same time developing their feminine qualities of shyness and chastity. Nearly all of Srila Prabhupada's female disciples still active in ISKCON feel offended and discouraged that, even after decades of valuable, devoted service, none of their godsisters inspired to give *diksha* in ISKCON have thus far been allowed to do so.

Protecting someone means not repressing but facilitating their natural serving tendencies. The GBC proposal is an important acknowledgement and furtherance of Srila Prabhupada's mood towards his female disciples and followers, as expressed in his purport to CC *Adi* 7.31-32: "Since both the boys and the girls [in ISKCON] are being trained to become preachers, those girls are not ordinary girls but are as good as their brothers who are preaching Krishna consciousness. Therefore, to engage both boys and girls in fully transcendental activities is a policy intended to spread the Krishna consciousness movement."

9. **Vedic cultural roles.** Although distributing books and raising money are not traditional Vedic female social roles, Srila Prabhupada was pleased by how his female

devotees in North America and elsewhere profusely distributed books and raised money, a large part of which he sent India to start ISKCON there. Today, these same veteran female devotees are being told, notably by some devotees in India, that for some of them to give *diksha* would go against their Vedic social roles. We find this dichotomy unacceptable.

10. **Most ISKCON devotees favor VDGs.** Surveys, petitions, and focus groups conducted by VDG advocates show the vast majority of ISKCON devotees favor VDGs and feel their presence in ISKCON, even on a limited basis, will help ISKCON's worldwide preaching. To dismiss ISKCON devotees' opinion as "vox populi" is to insult them. SABHA is partially meant to represent the body of ISKCON members.

11. *Shiksha/Diksha* **normalization.** We generally favor steps to reduce the present gulf between *diksha* and *shiksha* gurus in ISKCON, which in this context manifests in saying Vaishnavis can give *shiksha* but not *diksha* (unless they are *siddhas*). *Diksha* guru should not be an elite status, and *shiksha* guru should not be seen as for those who aren't good enough to give *diksha*. Srila Prabhupada says this mindset will hinder ISKCON's preaching: "The word *guru* is equally applicable to the *vartma-pradarshaka-guru*, *shiksha-guru* and *diksha-guru*. Unless we accept the principle enunciated by Sri Chaitanya Mahaprabhu, this Krishna consciousness movement cannot spread all over the world." (Cc. *Madhya-lila* 8.128). He goes so far as to say it is an offense: "There is no difference between the shelter-giving Supreme Lord and the initiating and instructing spiritual masters. If one foolishly discriminates between them, he commits an offense in the discharge of devotional service." (Cc. *Adi* 1.47).

12. **Our definition of *brahmana* must be consistent.** The *Bharadwaja Samhita* states that, short of finding a *siddha*, one should seek a qualified *brahmana* as a guru. If the direct interpretation (*brahmana* defined by birth) is applied, then both women and low-born men should give *diksha* only when they are so highly qualified that they are seeing God face to face. If the indirect interpretation (*brahmana* defined by quality) is applied, then both women and low-born men can become qualified as *brahmana*s and thus give *diksha*. There is no indication in *Bharadwaja Samhita* or elsewhere that the direct interpretation applies to women and the indirect interpretation applies to low-born men.

2020

The Suppression of Women in ISKCON
by Hridayananda Goswami

After speaking so much about Indian externals as an impediment to Western preaching, I would like to propose another cause of ISKCON's troubles in the West, a cause that is at least as important, if not more so: the treatment of women. I will argue that the suppression of women in ISKCON has been a major cause of the collapse, and continued flat-lining, of the Western mission.

Prabhupada once wrote to me, "The secret of keeping devotees enthused is to always give them a fresh challenge." Briefly, for most of its existence, ISKCON has systematically denied many women this essential opportunity. As an ISKCON member, but also an ISKCON watcher, for over fifty years, I have seen hundreds of intelligent, dynamic, devoted women join the movement and then leave ISKCON, or move to its outer orbits outside the core mission, because ISKCON did not offer them what Krishna Himself offers them in the *Gita* – the essential opportunity to fully engage their nature and abilities for Him.

Krishna explicitly states twice in the *Gita* that one must perform one's own duty.

3.35 It is better to imperfectly perform one's own *dharma,* rather than expertly perform another's duty. Indeed, perishing in one's duty is better because performing another's duty is (even more) dangerous. Imagine, that performing a duty not born of one's nature is more dangerous than death itself!

18.47 Here Krishna first repeats the same advice as 3.35, "It is better to imperfectly perform one's own *dharma,* rather than expertly perform another's duty." But then he adds a key clarification: "Performing work required [*niyata*] by one's nature, one does not incur sin."

Thus one's duty is determined by one's individual nature, not necessarily by one's gender. It is dangerous to demand that a Vaishnavi deny her propensity for constructive service, since Krishna states at 3.33 that, "Even a wise person acts according to their nature. Living beings follow their nature. What will repression do?" Note that the word for "wise person" here is *jnanavan,* the same word used at 7.19 to describe a soul surrendered to Krishna.

The causal link between nature and duty is strong emphasized again in Chapter 18, where Krishna defines the four *varnas*:

18.41 The duties of the four *varnas* are determined by each one's qualities **born of their own nature.** (*sva-bhava-ja*)

18.42 The duties of *brahmanas* are **born of their own nature.**

18.43 The duties of *kshatriyas* are **born of their own nature.**

18.44 The duties of *vaishyas* and *shudras* are **born of their own nature.**

18.45 A person achieves perfection by dedication to one's **own duty (born of their nature).**

Thus to deny a Vaishnavi full opportunity to serve according to her own nature and ability is to commit violence against her. How cruelly ironic that in the name of "protecting" women, many women were systematically injured.

Now that ISKCON has, more or less, authorized women to serve as gurus, with a few somewhat humiliating conditions, the simple fact is that there are very few women stepping forward to do that service. God only knows how many brilliant, devoted souls distanced themselves from ISKCON, or simply lost their enthusiasm, because of systematic repression.

To complete the logical circle here, I repeat that Prabhupada wrote me that the secret to keeping devotees enthused is to always give them a fresh challenge. It follows that without the chance for that challenge, according to one's nature, it is very hard to maintain one's enthusiasm. And without enthusiasm in spiritual life, one loses one's taste.

Prabhupada insisted that he made adjustments in the West because if the women don't come, the men won't come. The obvious corollary: when the women leave, the men leave, even if the women and their men are simply leaving the arena of active preaching.

Final point: I am inspired and enthused by seeing all the extraordinary Vaishnavis that are coming forward joyfully to serve Krishna West (KW) and of course other ISKCON projects. I believe this is because KW and other projects offer women all opportunity to lead, when to lead is their real nature. Unless we fully encourage sincere, talented Vaishnavis to serve according to their abilities, not according to our bodily prejudice, ISKCON has very little chance of growing in the West.

Excerpts from "Endangered Species"
by Kalakantha dasa and Jitamrta dasi

Since 2006, Kalakatha and Jitamrta Prabhus have been running the Krishna House preaching center in Gainesville, Florida, USA, near the University of Florida campus.

Endangered Species: Ashramites in ISKCON North America, the book they have co-authored, details the principles and practices they put in place to make this one of the most successful centers in North America, where people still join an ashrama environment for full immersion and training in spiritual life and character development. The testimonies from numerous devotees who have joined Krishna House are a beautiful validation of Kalakantha and Jitamrta's loving service and profound insights in how to teach bhakti. With this handbook everyone will have good guidance for serving their community with a modern-day bhakti experience that is attractive and relevant.

I have excerpted whole sections from the book with the permissions of Kalakatha and Jitamrta Prabhus. At each new excerpt I note where it can be found in the book.

(The next section "2. Gender Equity" is from Chapter Six "Five Principles of Sama-darsinah*" of Endangered Species)*

2. Gender Equity

When Srila Prabhupada visited Gainesville in 1971, a reporter asked, "How can one recognize your true follower?"

Srila Prabhupada could have answered in many ways: "My true follower chants Hare Krishna, wears devotional dress, reads and distributes my books," etc. Instead he replied, "My true follower is a very perfect gentleman."

A gentleman is recognized by the way he treats others. Yet in Krishna consciousness, aspiring gentlemen have a problem. In his books and lectures, Srila Prabhupada makes many strong statements critical of women. He describes women as less intelligent, child-like, and a cause of degradation for men. He cites scriptural references saying that women always require protection.

How should a man who wants to be a true follower of Srila Prabhupada view such troublesome creatures?

Let us first look at how Srila Prabhupada treated women. He had some 1500 female disciples whom he loved and who loved him. Once in Mayapur before an assembly of *sannyasi* godbrothers he said of his disciple Malati dasi, "She would cut her throat for me and I would do the same for her."

In the mid-1970's Srila Prabhupada blasted the women's liberation movement of the day as artificial and materialistic. He called it a plot by lusty, lazy men to exploit women sexually and get them to do men's work. At the same time he encouraged his female disciples to do all kinds of "men's work," such as learning and teaching Krishna conscious philosophy, distributing books, worshipping Deities, leading kirtans and more.

Srila Prabhupada inspired and cared for women in spiritual life by making a clear distinction between devotee women and ordinary women. On a morning walk he said to Visakha dasi, "Anyone who thinks they are a woman is less intelligent." On the same point, in *Sri* Chaitanya-*charitamrita* (*Adi* 7.31-32), Srila Prabhupada writes that women spreading Krishna consciousness are, "As good as their brothers."

Although Srila Prabhupada saw and treated his female disciples as spirit souls, equal with their brothers, some of his male followers focus on his critical statements about women in general without his equanimity and love to all, regardless of gender. By maintaining this attitude, some men in ISKCON insult and discourage women in ISKCON – something Srila Prabhupada, nor any gentleman, would never do.

There is no Krishna conscious philosophical basis for such women-averse attitudes. The first teaching of Lord Krishna in the *Bhagavad-gita* is that we are all souls, not our bodies. To see and judge people on the bodily platform is as ignorant as considering oneself one's body. If, as Srila Prabhupada said, anyone who thinks they are a woman is less intelligent, it follows that one who thinks of himself a man and someone else as a woman is also less intelligent.

The first teaching of Krishna conscious philosophy is this: every living being, including male and female human beings, are souls, Krishna's parts and parcels. Yet in another remarkable philosophical gaffe, some male-bodied devotees proudly proclaim their superiority over female-bodied devotees simply because of their gender. Some even profess that the power of Krishna consciousness can transform low-born men to be high-class *brahmanas* and gurus, yet except in the rarest of cases, Krishna consciousness cannot transform women to the same extent because of their unchangeable gender.

Such philosophical speculations reveal the dark and ugly non-Vaishnava trait of misogyny – a congenital dislike or even hatred of women. Mental health literature describes misogyny as an insidious condition, one that the sufferer can almost never recognize on his own. It is generally rooted in a past traumatic experience with a female in one's life, often one's mother.

To see misogyny in ISKCON is discouraging but not surprising, as every conditioned soul come to Krishna consciousness with some baggage. However, if ISKCON men burdened with misogynistic tendencies become leaders, they often take Srila Prabhupada's statements out of context and teach new men that misogyny is part of Krishna consciousness. Thus the misogyny problem in ISKCON proliferates, even in a society dedicated to serving Krishna above the bodily platform.

It is thus vitally important to understand clearly that Srila Prabhupada's critical statements about women as a class does not mean he suffered from misogyny. Nor do they justify misogyny in others. These statements must be taken in context with equally critical statements about low-born men, such as, *kalau shudra sambhavah:* in Kali-yuga, everyone is born a *shudra* or less. We also find Lord Krishna's emphatic urging for everyone, regardless of birth, to become His devotee:

> *mam hi partha vyapasritya*
> *ye 'pi syuh papa-yonayah*
> *striyo vaisyas tatha sudras*
> *te 'pi yanti param gatim*

"Those who take shelter in Me, though they be of lower birth – women, *vaishyas* [merchants] and *shudras* [workers] – can attain the supreme destination." (BG 9.32).

In his purport to this verse Srila Prabhupada writes, "It is clearly declared here by the Supreme Lord that in devotional service there is no distinction between the lower and higher classes of people. In the material conception of life there are such divisions, but for a person engaged in transcendental devotional service to the Lord there are not."

Though this aspect of Krishna conscious philosophy is crystal clear, in ISKCON female devotees often receive inferior care and facility. For example, devotee women have been compared to non-devotee women in countless *Bhagavatam* classes. Devotee women have sometimes been abused mentally, emotionally and sexually by male leaders. In North America, the women's *ashrama*s that Srila Prabhupada said should be standard in all temples are now nearly all closed. In many parts of the world, however qualified they may be, female devotees are rarely or never invited to give class or allowed to worship the Deities. During morning services, women devotees have often had to struggle for the right to have access to the Deities and to Srila Prabhupada's *vyasasana*. During *aratis*, female devotees, however senior, routinely receive Deity *prasadam* only after it has been offered to all the male devotees, however junior. Women devotees are often assigned to limited varieties of service, regardless of their natural talents and inclinations. And as of this writing, Vaishnavis, who otherwise meet all qualifications given in ISKCON law, have not yet been allowed to give *diksha*, spiritual initiation, solely because of their gender.

Do any of these situations appear gentlemanly?

How to address female devotees has also been a controversial question. The masculine "Prabhu," meaning master, does not linguistically apply to females. Yet Srila Prabhupada addressed his early female disciples as "Yamuna Prabhu," "Silavati Prabhu," and "Malati Prabhu." Later he introduced the Chanakhya Pandit aphorism that a learned man sees all women as mothers and thus addresses them as "Mataji."

At Krishna House we returned to Srila Prabhupada's early practice and found it effective. In North America, if a Krishna conscious preacher addresses a 19-year old woman "Mataji," he will usually not get the desired result. Some devotee men fail to understand that the purpose of this admonition is to help them control their own lust, not to pigeonhole women. A preacher who is actually able to see others as spirit souls addresses women only in one way: as they wish to be addressed. As one senior devotee noted, "Where I come from, if you address someone as 'Mother' it is usually followed by another word."

Seeking to teach his young disciples the natural serving mood of the soul, Srila Prabhupada taught them to address each other as "Prabhu" without gender discrimination. This approach is still effective. Srila Prabhupada writes,

"As servants of the Supreme Lord, all living entities are one, but a Vaishnava, because of his natural humility, addresses every other living entity as prabhu. A

Vaishnava sees other servants to be so advanced that he has much to learn from them. Thus he accepts all other devotees of the Lord as prabhus, masters. Although everyone is a servant of the Lord, one Vaishnava servant, because of humility, sees another servant as his master." (SB 7.5.11).

Nowhere in this statement does Srila Prabhupada discriminate between genders.

Despite this basic Krishna conscious teachings, having learned or reinforced latent anti-women attitudes, some devotee men have subjected their wives to domestic abuse, forcing the issue to be addressed by ISKCON's GBC. One impersonalist writer coined a horribly misogynistic phrase that has been bandied about in some ISKCON circles: "Cows, drums and wives improve when they are beaten."

These ungentle, discriminatory practices were all but unknown in ISKCON during its infancy. Doing away with them in ISKCON Gainesville – an easy task, except for the *diksha* problem – has, over the past few years, opened the doors to a steady influx of hundreds of young new female and male devotees moving into the previously empty Krishna House *ashrama*s – a phenomenon found in no other North American ISKCON temple during this time.

Men who value Srila Prabhupada's mission and aspire to become his true followers insure their attitude toward women is firmly rooted in the spiritual vision as expressed in his teachings and actions. Their treatment of women as spirit souls marks them as the gentlemen Srila Prabhupada desired his followers to be.

(The following is from Chapter Seven: "Balanced Temples and Ashrams" of Endangered Species)

2) The benefits of inter-gender temples

Some North American ISKCON temples have tried functioning as men-only centers. These centers generally struggle to attract new devotees. They inadvertently create a sense that women are not welcomed in ISKCON, simply tolerated, as if their presence is a problem and their very existence a disturbance.

By contrast, Srila Prabhupada, himself a *sannyasi*, welcomed and facilitated female devotees in his temples. When we applied his approach in the ISKCON Gainesville center, giving young men and women devotees measurably equal facility, respect and treatment, we were pleasantly surprised to find young devotees joining ISKCON again, their sex desire actually diminished in the spiritually charged co-ed environment.

Though it may seem counter-intuitive, by associating respectfully and informally with young women in public situations – just as they have done in school all their lives – young men in the West find their sex impulse more manageable than in a cloistered, "forbidden fruit" environment. The resulting family atmosphere, disciplined yet loving, has itself proven to regularly attract new people to Krishna consciousness.

Brahmachari life is meant for spreading Krishna consciousness, an activity that inevitably means interacting with women. Some *brahmacharis* respond to women with a cultural shield and interact with them in a strained, artificial way. Not only has history proven this practice unsustainable for *brahmacharis*; this disdainful treatment of women is sheer poison for spreading Krishna consciousness in the West.

3) Driving women away from ISKCON

Imagine you are a young woman entering an ISKCON temple for the first time. When young men come near you, if they acknowledge your existence at all, they avoid eye contact and always seem in a hurry. You might wonder if you might have unknowingly contracted leprosy or some other infectious disease.

Imagine how you, the prospective new bhaktin, would feel if you saw female devotees relegated to the rear of temple rooms, always following the men when greeting the Deities, and not allowed to serve *prasadam* to men or deemed unworthy of being served *prasadam* by men? Would you be attracted to be part of such a community?

Suppose before visiting you had read, "You're not this body," in Srila Prabhupada's books. When you then saw such discriminatory behavior by men towards women based on their bodies, would you not find the devotees hypocritical, speaking one thing but practicing something else? Would you be interested to get involved with ISKCON?

Where discriminatory practices exist, ISKCON communities typically fail to reach young Westerners. On the other hand, where women are treated kindly and given all the respect and facility of their brothers, ISKCON communities thrive and attract new Western devotees, both male and female.

Srila Prabhupada established his North American temples with this inter-gender mood, dismissing criticism from some godbrothers: "Not knowing that boys and girls in countries like Europe and America mix very freely, these fools and rascals criticize the boys and girls in Krishna consciousness for intermingling. But these rascals should consider that one cannot suddenly change a community's social customs." (Cc. *Adi* 7.31-32, purport).

Even today, Srila Prabhupada's approach has proven to consistently attract educated young American men and women to become serious devotees of Lord Krishna. While living in the *ashrama*, these young men and women develop a natural, relaxed, and blissful mood of mutual respect and devotional friendship while remaining fixed in their vows of celibacy. Such a joyous and memorable experience in their youth helps them remain fixed in Krishna consciousness for life.

4) Why women are so important to Western preaching

If young women are thought of and treated as sex objects to be avoided, they will naturally be discouraged from exploring Krishna consciousness, much to the detriment of Srila Prabhupada's mission. On the other hand, if young women are facilitated and encouraged in devotional service, they empower the Krishna consciousness movement through their spiritual enthusiasm and sincere, effective preaching. When preaching Krishna consciousness, women are, as Srila Prabhupada said, "as good as their brothers."

Female devotees bring other important benefits as well. In the short term, their presence in a temple community makes Krishna consciousness more attractive to young men, who are accustomed to intergender environments. In the long term, fixed up devotee wives enable devotee husbands to peacefully spend their lives in Krishna consciousness.

5) Manageable boundaries

Srila Prabhupada often quoted Lord Krishna's statement, "*striyo vaishyas tatha shudra;*" anyone can approach the supreme destination. (Bg. 9.32). By applying this philosophy, within two years of arriving in America he successfully created many ISKCON communities characterized by rapid growth and friendly Krishna conscious dealings between male and female devotees.

Anyone who knows Srila Prabhupada's books can easily understand this point philosophically. Yet when single men and women become devotees, how does it translate to the practical realm?

At Krishna House, with some easily learned boundaries, young male and female devotees share *sadhana,* preaching, kirtan and other Krishna conscious adventures in a warm, accepting, loving family environment. They learn that living in a temple is a great time to develop a relationship – with Krishna, and with Krishna's devotees. They understand that if they want ordinary conjugal relationships, the rest of the world awaits.

Newcomers interested in Krishna but unable to give up their boyfriends or girlfriends are encouraged to live outside the *ashrama* and gradually develop Krishna consciousness as congregational members. Anyone trying to find a boyfriend or girlfriend while living at Krishna House is warned and, if they persist, promptly escorted out of the *ashrama*.

Serious students, however, easily learn to draw lines so inter-gender interactions can be Krishna conscious yet not so familiar as to disrupt a celibate environment. At Krishna House these strict prohibitions include:

- Never be alone in a closed room or in a car with someone of the opposite sex.
- Avoid deliberate physical contact with the opposite sex.
- Avoid flirtatious and extended mundane conversations.
- Avoid revealing your mind, either in person or electronically, to someone of the opposite sex.
- Instead, reveal your mind to confidential devotees such as authorized senior devotees or respected and trusted same-gender peers.

6) Are women really the problem?

In Los Angeles many years ago, a *brahmachari* complained to Srila Prabhupada about the daily playing of the famous *Brahma Samhita* recording featuring Yamuna Devi's voice. He referred to Lord Chaitanya who said that a *sannyasi* should not even hear a woman's voice and suggested using a recording of Srila Prabhupada chanting the prayers instead.

Srila Prabhupada was not pleased. He replied that the recording was choral. He then suggested that anyone disturbed by the sound of women's voices go to the forest.

Srila Prabhupada's point is clear: if a man is agitated in the presence of women, rather than removing women from his environment he should remove the unwanted desires from his heart.

As Srila Prabhupada demonstrated, a self-realized person will not be agitated in any circumstances (*tams titikshashva bharata . . . Bg. 2.11*). Men who are fighting lust in their hearts will be disturbed when a woman simply enters a room. Men who are transcendentally at peace will not have such feelings. Such men, regardless of their *ashrama*, are *dhiras* (undisturbed persons) treating women as spirit souls in an accepting, compassionate, gentlemanly way.

7) Uniformed Criticism

Some critics of Krishna House call it a loose atmosphere and claim the graduates do not become serious devotees. This opinion is remarkably uniformed. In fact, in the past ten years dozens of Krishna House graduates have taken initiation from fifteen different ISKCON gurus. Many are active in the ISKCON mission, running temples and preaching centers, organizing outreach and serving as some of the top book distributors in North America. Dozens of others have completed their advanced education, established professional careers and begun contributing financially to ISKCON.

One way or another, the great majority of Krishna House's hundreds of graduates have remained active devotees, regularly chanting and following the regulative principles.

Like most of Srila Prabhupada's disciples, Krishna House graduates fondly remember their early days in ISKCON as sweet, peaceful, enlightening days relished in an exciting atmosphere of loving acceptance and encouragement. It is an experience that stays with them, one they want to share with others.

(The following is from Chapter 8: "The Simple '60s to the Zealous '70s." of Endangered Species*)*

1) A Shift in Attitude

In ISKCON's simpler early days, young men and women regularly joined the ISKCON *ashramas* springing up in cities throughout North America, Western Europe, and Australasia. An attractive family atmosphere pervaded the temples, with Srila Prabhupada as the father of a blissful group of spiritual brothers and sisters.

After some time, when these young men and women wanted to marry, they would receive blessings if they were sufficiently "fixed up," mature, and committed to Krishna consciousness. Becoming a *grihastha* was seen as a milestone of spiritual advancement.

Over the next few years, that attitude gradually shifted. Some male devotees began introducing markedly different attitudes and treatment of female devotees. Less mature leaders, rarely with the individual's best interest in mind, began discouraging young men from marrying. From the congenial days of the Simple '60s, the Zealous '70s ensued, bringing a number of new social norms. Young men in ISKCON were encouraged to associate only with those in saffron. Married men in ISKCON were ridiculed. Women in ISKCON were stifled and marginalized.

The word "zealous" comes from the Greek "zelo," the same root as the word "jealous." Though over the years the words have diverged in meaning – zealous being sometimes positive and jealous always negative – both words indicate a sense of intolerance. A jealous person cannot tolerate another's success. A zealous person cannot tolerate another's point of view.

In ISKCON of the mid-1970s, the zealous new attitudes, generally originating from young men pursuing lifetime celibacy, manifested most visibly in the Radha Damodara Traveling Sankirtana Party (RDTSKP). Led by two vibrant young *sannyasis,* this party grew to include hundreds of men in several large converted Greyhound busses and dozens of satellite vans, blanketing North America with unprecedented amounts of distribution of Srila Prabhupada's books.

Srila Prabhupada loved and encouraged their service. But in 1976, when *grihastha* temple presidents complained to Srila Prabhupada that RDTSKP members were urging young men to leave their temples and join them, Srila Prabhupada sided with the temple presidents. He also overrode GBC proposals that would have cemented marginalized positions for women and *grihasthas* in ISKCON. From all appearances, while appreciating his young disciples' zeal, Srila Prabhupada clearly saw its limitations.

One of Srila Prabhupada's confidantes during this time was Abhiram das, the former temple president of ISKCON's Miami and Calcutta branches, whom Srila Prabhupada invited to join his party. Abhiram Prabhu explains, "Srila Prabhupada was concerned with everyone, including women, children and the much broader spectrum of society that he expected would soon be drawn to worship Krishna from within their practical ability. Yet ISKCON's status quo had shifted in the mid '70s to a *sannyasa* aspiration for everyone, including women, which led to broken marriages and unhappy ladies.

"Many men, who were mostly unfit for celibacy, nonetheless chased after the new status quo of being officially declared a saint by dint of wearing saffron cloth. While greatly energizing book distribution and preaching, this trend perverted many aspects of the ISKCON society. Inevitably, fall downs began to increase and the dyke composed of youthful zeal began to crack. Using youthful energies to hold back natural inclinations for the sake of a higher mission proved unsustainable, including for many official *sannyasis.*

"As news of fall downs continued to pour into Srila Prabhupada's mail, He began to worry and vocalize his concern about this trend. This increasing concern, along with Srila Prabhupada's intention to build its God given solution – *varnashrama* farm communities – substantially motivated his last trip west in the summer of 1977.

"As he said to me, 'I will go to Gita-nagari. I will sit down and teach you how to live of the land.' He also said to Tamal Krishna Goswami, Brahmanaanda Swami, Bhakti Charu Swami, Upendra, and myself, 'Fifty percent of my work is incomplete because I have not established *varnashrama*. I have one lamentation, that I have not established *varnashrama*.'"

2) *Varnashrama* and Krishna House

Srila Prabhupada was unable to complete that trip to Gita-nagari and left this world in 1977. Since then, his followers have struggled to understand and implement his desire. Many devotees have established farm communities around the world with mixed results. In economically simpler countries, many of these farming projects have achieved some degree of self-sufficiency. This is not the case in North America. Though some individuals have established simple family farms, the larger ISKCON farm communities have been forced to survive by various means other than simply living off the land.

Thus in North America, most *grihastha* devotees, lacking other good options, have applied *varnashrama* principles in Krishna consciousness by practicing *sadhana bhakti* while living as simply as possible working and preaching in urban environments. At Krishna House we accept this way of life as a reasonable fulfillment of Srila Prabhupada's aspiration for *varnashrama*. Hearing this, and seeing examples among successful devotees, newcomers feel hope and confidence in remaining in Krishna consciousness throughout their lives. We believe that was Srila Prabhupada's essential intention for introducing *varnashrama*.

To implement *varnashrama dharma* in Kali-yuga would require enormous preaching accomplishments, such as influencing political and social leaders to be Krishna conscious. Such accomplishments are very difficult, especially in the West, so some zealous *varnashrama* advocates in ISKCON have turned to an easier target: getting women in ISKCON to "toe the line." Citing Srila Prabhupada's criticism of the Women's Liberation movement of the '70s, they insist that any Vaishnavi who does not fit into a certain social mold is unchaste and unfit for Krishna consciousness. While claiming to champion Srila Prabhupada's teachings, such advocates cannot do the difficult work Srila Prabhupada did, namely bringing Westerners to Krishna consciousness.

Intelligent young men and women in the West will accept Krishna consciousness if doing so requires fitting in a certain social mold. Given freedom to choose, at Krishna House these bright young men and women generally gravitate toward preaching and book distribution. We encourage them and facilitate their desire with whatever they need.

Their efforts have resulted in nearly one million books distributed, hundreds of successful outreach programs held, and dozens of new devotees attracted to Krishna consciousness.

Whether our graduates choose to be preachers or professionals, or to live in rural or urban settings, at Krishna House we encourage everyone to be themselves and find their unique way to serve Krishna. Once they have a clear direction in mind, we then encourage them to seek appropriate mentorship to how to fulfill their dreams and practically apply Srila Prabhupada's teachings in their lives.

3) Lingering Zealousness

A tolerant mood at Krishna House has led to success in recruiting and training devotees that is unprecedented in recent ISKCON North America's history. Nonetheless, challenges from the Zealous '70s remain throughout ISKCON, often centered around the wearing of saffron.

Saffron cloth indicates detachment and spirituality. In traditional Vedic India, saffron worn by *sannyasis,* lifelong celibate monks who are respected as spiritual teachers. So revered is saffron in India that even today it is incorporated in the nation's flag.

However, for the young Westerners in the 70's who lacked deep understanding of Vedic traditions, wearing saffron became a status symbol. For them, being a devotee meant wearing saffron for life. The simpler, more convivial days of ISKCON in the '60s that were so attractive to intelligent newcomers were swallowed up by these hard-line attitudes.

Decades on, we now know that nearly all devotees eventually marry. We also understand that healthy marriages are essential for the growth of ISKCON. Yet some senior devotees, lamenting for the "good old days" of the Zealous '70s, still encourage "saffron-only" and discourage marriage. Here's an example from a book still circulated some ISKCON circles purporting to teach young men how to be *brahmacharis*:

"It is not necessary or compulsory that everyone get married. The actual standard of *brahmachari* life is to go on and take *sannyasa; grihastha* life is a consolation prize. At the marriage, everyone is smiling, but the ex-*brahmachari* new husband should not feel that he has anything to celebrate. But if one is so unfortunate that he cannot maintain the firm determination to stay *brahmachari* and is agitated so severely by material desires that he cannot concentrate properly on service, then it may be better for him to get married and be done with it rather than to flip-flop and totter on the mental platform indefinitely."

In this passage, the author, a sincere and accomplished devotee, expresses his own opinion without reference to *shastra* or to Srila Prabhupada. Marriage, he says, is a "consolation prize," and anyone whose personal shortcomings force them to marry is "unfortunate."

Let's consider these statements in regard to spreading Krishna consciousness. Do they help or hinder?

Were they to read such a statement, educated, cultured people – the sort we aspire to attract to ISKCON – would likely sense fanaticism and lose interest in ISKCON. They would laugh and marvel at the strange cultists who believe a groom should be unhappy at his own wedding.

Ironically, this kind of presentation of Krishna conscious *grihastha* life – demeaning it as a consolation prize – leads men to repress their true natures and "flop and totter on the mental platform indefinitely." The resulting repression, indecision and dishonesty often leads to all kinds of chaos in the lives of sincere devotees who, if encouraged to be themselves, would have been peaceful, progressive and productive preachers or congregational members.

If *brahmacharis* are simply encouraged to be honest with themselves, in consultation with trusted seniors they can peacefully make the very personal decision about if and when to marry. Understanding that marriage and lifelong renunciation are both respectable and acceptable options frees young men from artificial pressure. Such fortunate young men have a much better chance of achieving a sustainable lifelong adventure in Krishna consciousness.

From the Vaishnavi's point of view, we must ask: what thoughtful woman would marry a groom who is unhappy at the wedding? Would any sane woman want a husband who sees her as a "consolation prize," an agent of illusion who has caused him to lose his higher principles?'

In the hard-line circles, a woman's feelings are rarely considered. She is seen more as a sex object that an individual person. As one highly educated young woman put it, after living in a hard-line temple she began to identify with being a woman she ever had before (*see "A Brahmacarini's Story," in the appendices*). This inability to understand or consider another's feelings indicates a lack of empathy that goes ill with spiritual advancement (*para dukha-dukhi*).

Philosophically, disregard for others indicates a degree of impersonalism. Strict impersonalists, unlike Vaishnavas, heavily emphasize Vedic knowledge and renunciation without any reference to the individual's needs, nature or personal relationship with Lord Krishna. This is due, Srila Prabhupada explains, to a fear of individual spiritual identity. (Bg. 4.10, purport).

In contrast, *Srimad-Bhagavatam* 1.2.7 explains that renunciation and knowledge are neither the means to nor the goal of spiritual life; rather, renunciation and knowledge are causeless by-products of devotional service to Lord Krishna.

True renunciation, then, comes from devotion to Krishna, and the true devotee treats all of Krishna's parts and parcels with loving detachment. In this way Srila

Prabhupada, a perfect renunciate, invoked and continues to invoke love and trust in the hearts of thousands of female disciples and devotees.

(The following comes from Chapter 12 "Overboiling the Milk" of Endangered Species*)*

1) *Varnashrama* and ISKCON

Some devotees interpret Srila Prabhupada's statements about *varnashrama* at that time to be a major goal for ISKCON going forward. And yet we also find this statement from Srila Prabhupada:

The *varnashrama* system is for convenience sake in the material world. It has nothing to do with spiritual life. Acceptance of *varnashrama* means a little easy progress to spiritual life, otherwise it has no importance to us.

For example, all my European and American disciples have no *varnashrama* position, but spiritually because they have followed the rules and regulations and also my instructions, their advancement spiritually is being appreciated by everyone. Always remember that *varnashrama* life is a good program for material life, and it helps one in spiritual life; but spiritual life is not dependent upon it. (Srila Prabhupada Letter, Oct. 19, 1974)

So, should we reach out to newcomers or boil the milk by implementing *varnashrama* in ISKCON? How do we resolve these apparently conflicting instructions?

We turn to the example of the pharmacy; all the medicines are there, but a patient needs a prescription from an expert physician to pick the right one.

Right now many ISKCON North American temples are desperate for manpower. For decades many of these temples have relied on religious workers, especially from India, to conduct Deity worship and other services. The system of importing *pujaris* and cooks has been fraught with many difficulties which as of this writing are getting worse. As one senior ISKCON leader put it, at a time like this we ISKCON leaders must "recruit or perish."

In other words, at various times in ISKCON's history it may have been appropriate to set aside recruiting to focus on elevating devotees to a higher standard. However, at this time there are precious few new devotees, particularly Westerners, to so elevate. Recruiting and giving basic training appear to now be a far greater priority.

(The following comes from Chapter 13 "Crippling Offenses to ISKCON Vaishnavis" of Endangered Species*)*

Chapter 13: Crippling Offenses to ISKCON Vaishnavis

stri-bala-vrddha, ara 'candala' 'yavana'
yei tomara eka-bara paya darasana

krsna-nama laya, nace hasa unmatta
acharya ha-ila sei, tarila jagata

"If they see You just once, even women, children, old men, meat-eaters and members of the lowest caste immediately chant the holy name of Krishna, dance like madmen and become spiritual masters capable of delivering the whole world." (Cc. *Madhya-lila* 18.121-122)

When asked what was the greatest innovation made by Srila Prabhupada in spreading Krishna consciousness around the world, devotees generally point out his liberal treatment of women. He accepted female disciples in his temples and facilitated and treated them equally with the male disciples. When some godbrothers criticized him for this, he responded strongly, pointing out how their lack of understanding Western culture left them incompetent to spread Krishna consciousness around the world.

Recreating Srila Prabhupada's approach to Vaishnavis that he originally established in ISKCON North America has worked miracles at Krishna House. As we have discussed, when women are treated properly, young men and women become enthusiastic devotees. Unfortunately, the Society to which we introduce these bright young Westerners does not always share the same *sama-darsinah* values that have initially inspired their spiritual lives. Many graduates find their faith challenged by the lingering varieties of discrimination in ISKCON.

In the past, ISKCON's GBC has recognized gender discrimination in ISKCON as a serious problem caused by deviation from Srila Prabhupada's teachings and intent. In 2000 the GBC passed resolutions [which are published here under the GBC resolutions section]:

Although this GBC apology for chronic mistreatment in ISKCON improved the situation for ISKCON Vaishnavis, gender discrimination lingers. Here are two examples as of this writing:

1) The GBC has recently been forced to take steps to prevent domestic abuse among ISKCON couples.
2) Although approved in principle after twenty years of debate, no Vaishnavis are allowed to initiate disciples, despite hundreds of devotees, mostly women, awaiting that opportunity.

Whatever cultural arguments may be put forward, one unmistakable truth remains: marginalizing female devotees in the name of Vedic culture is much to the detriment of preachers who seek to attract intelligent Westerners to ISKCON.

For more explicit evidence of the mistreatment of women still lingering in ISKCON, read "A Brahmacharini's Story," in the appendices of this book. This firsthand account was written by a bright young woman who joined a major Western ISKCON temple community several years *after* the forementioned GBC resolutions were passed.

For further evidence of lingering gender inequity, read "A Brahmachari's Story," also in the appendices.

(The following two stories are from the Appendixes of Endangered Species)*

A Brahmacharini's Story

This account comes from an educated young women recounting events <u>several years after</u> the GBC's apology to women in ISKCON.

As a young woman of European descent, I started chanting Hare Krishna while I was in college. After many years of intensive study and exams, I received my advanced college degree. It was good to get college behind me, and I decided that I wanted to spend some time living in a temple. I was fired up and enlivened by watching footage from the early days, when Srila Prabhupada's "sons and daughters" were blissfully undergoing extreme austerities serving him and his mission. I wished I could have been there.

I looked forward to austere *ashrama* life, where I would spend twenty-four hours a day engaged in loving service to Krishna. I anticipated cold showers in the early morning hours, cramped *ashrama* quarters, daily kirtans, *harinamas,* maybe even book distribution or quantity cooking, all of which I hadn't done before. I was looking forward to a huge dose of camaraderie and spiritual bliss. I was nervous and excited. This was what I had been looking forward to for so long. Though I had high academic credentials, I didn't want to live my life in a materialistic career. I just wanted to be a full-time devotee and go back to Godhead.

Two weeks after graduating, I moved into the *ashrama*. At first it was quite what I expected. But before long came some experiences that almost destroyed my spiritual life.

Rules and regulations came in cascades and were the main focus of my experience. I thought to be Krishna conscious I would have to be meek and quiet, accept daily chastisements, and do what I was told.

The first thing I was told was to correct my appearance; if I didn't part my hair in the middle, and if my *sari* pleats weren't in the center, then it signaled to one and all that I was a prostitute. I was mortified, for I used to part my hair a little to the side. Had I been sending out the message that I was a degraded loose woman? I felt ashamed. I didn't want to be thought of as a prostitute. I was also told that if I sat with my knees hugged into my chest in the temple, that was another sign of being a prostitute. I complied with every instruction.

We girls were referred to as "spaced-out *brahmacharinis.*" It was a running joke/theme in the temple. We felt that, being Western, we were very much uncultured, and we felt inferior. Our main chance for value and worth was to get married, and the girls who had married senior men were looked up to as the most surrendered girls. By marrying a senior man you would learn to be Vedic, and, especially if they were Indian, by integrating into his family you would be highly honored and respected by the community.

I heard stories of some of the Western girls having difficulties in their marriages to senior men. The husbands would approach the girl's spiritual master to request him to instruct the girl to submit. This seemed to be a standard practice.

Our major flaw was being in a woman's body. We were told to stand in the back of the temple when greeting the Deities. We were not allowed to chant in the temple room with the men during *japa* time. We all had to file out of the temple room after kirtan and chant *japa* elsewhere. I always made sure that I was not the last one to exit, in case it looked like I was lingering.

Women weren't allowed to lead the kirtan during the *aratis*, and I don't remember seeing a woman offering *arati* to the Deities, except on Radhastami. A visiting *sannyasi* told the women that we should not dance at the front of the temple near the Deities during the *aratis*. The complaint was that we were too enthusiastic in our dancing, which was seen as a disturbance and lacking culture, although we were all fully covered by our *saris* and our dancing was no more enthusiastic than the men's side. We congregated meekly at the back of the temple after that, and I was very sad because I used to love dancing for the Deities in the mornings.

Some girls had a service requiring them to go into the temple room to change the flower arrangements for Srila Prabhupapa's *vyasasana* during *japa* time. Although it was their service, many of the girls felt scared or embarrassed to go into the temple room while all the men were chanting *japa* there. I did that service once, and I felt extremely bodily conscious and ashamed when I had to go into the temple room with the flowers. I thought, "I'm not supposed to be here. I better make sure I am covered up and run out as soon as I can. I don't want anyone to think I am lingering with the men, like a loose woman. I just want to be chaste."

The interactions we had with our leaders were most often chastisements, regularly being told everything we were doing wrong. I remember during *ashrama* meetings everyone sheepishly staring at the floor while being told in no uncertain terms what rascals we were. I was afraid of my *ashrama* leader. I wanted to be perfect, and I didn't want to do anything wrong, risk offending anyone, or for anyone to doubt my sincerity. My leader said to me once that we girls were just sponging off the temple financially. We were all working hard in our services, and it was devastating to hear our leader questioning our sincerity.

There was no positive upliftment, no reading groups, very few organized outings, and no focus on building the relationships between us. There was a sense that you didn't know who you could trust. No one asked how I was doing, and although I was externally dutiful, internally I was deeply struggling because of the cold, lonely, and sometimes harsh environment.

The daily *Bhagavatam* classes focused on what a scary place the "outside world" was. I became afraid to live outside the temple, but with no caring and positive connections in the *ashrama*, I began to feel despondent.

The management discouraged mentors and banned some senior women from visiting. Only one senior female devotee was allowed to give class on a regular basis, and the theme of her classes was usually a pastime demonstrating that a woman's primary duty in life is to serve her husband. While there is nothing wrong with this statement according to Srila Prabhupada's teachings, this aspect was emphasized to us so strongly in our training that it almost seemed to eclipse the essential spiritual teachings of our philosophy that I had come for.

The messages we were hearing over and over again, in many different classes and in instructions from our leaders, seemed to be heavily weighted towards telling the women that we were second-class and that we should be restricted to cooking and cleaning. Looking back, I wish there had been more classes about Krishna's qualities and pastimes. As a new devotee, being reminded so often about my position as a woman strengthened my bodily consciousness and inferiority complex.

The male devotees were the most important devotees in the temple. It was understood that men had a rational brain, which was superior to the female emotional brain. Men and women weren't to talk or look at each other. It seemed as if the men were as uncomfortable as we were. Since they were at the top of the pecking order, if a *brahmachari* was coming towards you, as a woman you were to look down and move out of the way. If a *brahmachari* had to talk to you, he would look at the floor or to the side, never talking to you like a person. When this would happen I wished I could sink into the floor and disappear rather than spend another moment in this woman's body. I had come to Krishna consciousness for a transcendental experience, yet I never felt so bodily conscious and ashamed in my life.

Overall I had gotten what I had come for – there were blissful kirtans, service, *prasadam* and scriptural education, but the price was much more than I had bargained for. Then things really got crazy.

After some time a devotee manager took an interest in marrying me. He was very insistent. I became concerned with what was happening because I felt it was wrong. Because my service forced me to be around him, I wanted to change it. When I meekly approached my authorities about it, they said no.

I felt very dejected and increasingly demoralized, as I had taken the inferiority complex of being in a woman's body to heart. After trying to end the forced association and being harassed by the pushy man I could not escape, I gradually submitted to the idea of just going along with what he wanted, and I thought at least if I got married I could get out of the *brahmacharini ashrama* which was so cold, lonely, and harsh. But I was afraid for my future, and I felt like there was no one I could talk to who could help me.

I was trying to just surrender and "accept my fate," but I had never before experienced fear like I felt in that situation. With no mentors or friends with influence, I felt as hopeless and desperate as a trapped animal. I felt like other people were making decisions for me, people I didn't trust to have my best interests at heart. But as a woman I thought I wasn't supposed to be independent, so I didn't say anything and went along with it all.

As preparations started for our wedding, I was feeling increasingly desperate. I worked up the nerve to ask the temple authority for permission to leave the temple for a short break. The response I received was very curt and dismissive. "No, you're not going anywhere. You're just an emotional woman who needs to get married." Somehow Krishna helped me stand my ground and I persisted with my request. Finally I got permission to leave for a few days.

I left the temple with no intention of returning. I just didn't feel safe there. After some time I returned to my parents' home in another state. I was absolutely devastated and confused. On one hand I felt responsible for staying so long in that situation and for my part in letting things get out of hand. But on the other hand I felt that the way I was trained, and the lack of care, groomed me to accept being taken advantage of. I thought that if I wanted to be a devotee there was no other way. If I wanted to practice spiritual life in a temple, I would have to accept everything that came with it. And when it became too much for me, I felt like a failure.

While I kept the regulative principles, due to the fear and shame associated with life in a temple community I drifted away from active devotional life. Though I became distant from ISKCON and devotional service, I never gave up on Krishna. It took quite a few years and regular counseling before I could again visit an ISKCON temple without those painful memories coming back to me.

A Brahmachari's Story

I began practicing Krishna consciousness in my late twenties, having been cultivated from 2010-2014 by devotees in my home town. I began chanting from one round of *japa* per day, gradually increasing to 16 rounds by increasing by one round per day each month. At the same time, I attended kirtan, cooking classes, and *Bhagavad-gita* talks at our local center. Eventually I became part of the team there and I began distributing books and cultivating guests. The guidance I received was quite disciplined in terms of the fundamentals – waking early, prioritizing *japa*, reading, offering food and *sankirtana*. At the same time, I had no standing in any *ashrama* and I found myself attracted more and more to the *brahmachari* lifestyle.

A couple of years later I spent Kartik with my Gurudeva and other advanced preacher-devotees at ISKCON's Govardhana *ashrama*. There I was blissfully absorbed in a regulated schedule, including taking rest and rising early, morning and evening temple programs, 4-5 hours of group reading daily and a simple life, unplugged from the modern world but rich in devotee *sanga*. This was my first immersion in this kind of lifestyle. I experienced a profoundly uplifting effect on my mind and spiritual practices that I could not reproduce on my own. I was convinced that I wanted a lengthier experience of full absorption in chanting, reading, service and *brahmachari sanga*. So with this in mind, I moved to another city in which the local ISKCON temple had an active *brahmachari ashrama*.

When I joined the *ashrama*, I was fortunate to serve under the care of a temple president who took time to get to know me, regularly checked in with me, engaged me in service according to my propensities and made me feel valued and cared for. Living arrangements were simple but sufficient – I shared a room with other *brahmacharis*, I was given traditional attire and storage space for personal effects. *Prasadam* was very good and we learned to make our health a priority. I was given an appropriate amount of responsibility fairly quickly, so I quickly took on a sense of ownership in the local services. I was also encouraged to take the opportunity to travel to the *dhama* with senior devotees for intensive hearing and chanting on a regular basis. All in all, I was very fortunate to have an experience of care, based on a vision of my long-term potential in Krishna consciousness. The local management did a good job of avoiding the traps of neglecting or exploiting their *brahmacharis* and because of that, I still feel very dedicated to the devotees and Deities here.

I was 33 years old when I entered the *ashrama*, older than the average new *brahmachari* and far older than the traditional Vedic ideal of five years old! When I joined, I did not have a clear idea of my future plans. "Could I survive in the *ashrama*? How long would I remain a *brahmachari*?" Although I did not have immediate answers to these questions, I proceeded on the basis of my faith in Krishna bhakti and Srila Prabhupada's instructions on the value of *brahmachari* training for men in Krishna consciousness. I was immensely pleased to discover that not only would I survive and thrive as a *brahmachari*, but that I would learn tremendously important lessons for my spiritual practice and my life in general. Over the past 5+ years, I've committed to training as a *brahmachari* and also guiding and teaching others how to take the most advantage of the opportunities for growth afforded in this *ashrama*.

One aspect of *ashrama* living that I noticed immediately was the concentrated effect of following the same program in the same space with other serious devotees. I observed that I was almost immediately capable of a greater degree of sense and mind control, organization and efficiency than I was otherwise qualified for on my own. This phenomenon wasn't just limited to my early days in the *ashrama* either – almost six years later I still notice the boost that comes from being in close "synergy" with other devotees. This observation, repeated across time and circumstances, makes it progressively easier for me to appreciate Krishna's devotees and feel myself dependent on them.

Brahmacharis receive other tangible proofs of the value of devotee association. For example, *ashrama* life provides many opportunities for both receiving and giving guidance and inspiration. In other words, if I have a sincere desire to serve, I may be called by Krishna at any time to act as either a teacher or a student in relationship with any other *brahmacharis*. I also see that *brahmachari* life deliberately places me alongside devotees of different ages, backgrounds, and personalities, necessitating qualities like tolerance, and skills such as communication, interpersonal sensitivity and conflict resolution. All of these things will offer tremendous practical benefit throughout my life. Much can be said about the deep problems that human society suffers from in the absence of such training. Actually, men generally lack such qualities and abilities without training - I certainly did. I've been fortunate to serve in a very progressive *ashrama*, which deliberately helps the devotees to develop the inward-looking perspective and the external skill sets necessary for both material and spiritual success.

Aside from benefiting through association, I experience that *ashrama* life in general is an ongoing opportunity to introspect and refine myself through personal endeavor. For example, my training has included a strong focus on both abstract understanding and practical application of theory, so I can see that philosophical knowledge has increased side-by-side with practical competence in things such as cleanliness. I can therefore vouch for the truth of Srila Prabhupada's statement (SB 1.9.26, purport) that "[the] *brahmachari-ashrama* is especially meant for training both the attached and detached." I know that my future success will be built on the advancement I'm making now. Because *brahmachari* training is meant to create a foundation for life, it includes setting aside time for mastering life skills and for removing unwanted obstacles to pure devotion. It's clear to me that skill development and *anartha-nivrtti* both progress proportionately to how much I put into them, so it's a great relief and privilege to have full permission to "work on myself"!

Brahmachari training includes the development of a strong work ethic. I have experienced the great satisfaction that comes from surrendering to Krishna's service and to Krishna's devotees. My journey as a *brahmachari* has been characterized by a gradual, steady increase in the quality and quantity of service responsibilities that I have. This dynamic, when guided by experienced leadership, has kept me out of the two trouble areas known as the "comfort zone" and the "burn-out zone." In the comfort zone I simply follow the dictates of my mind and work only as hard (or concentrate as well, or plan as effectively, etc.) as I absolutely have to in order to get the minimum done. Surrender remains theoretical in the comfort zone and knowledge isn't effectively transformed into realization. In the burn-out zone, the opposite problems exist. Due to constantly taxing the body and mind, putting out fires and thinking only in the short-term, I overextend myself and lose spiritual strength. In between these two is the "stretch zone," where I learn how to be comfortable outside my comfort zone, to take on fresh challenges and steadily improve the quality and quantity of my services to Krishna and His devotees.

All of my lessons and the benefits of *brahmachari* life have manifested under enlightened, benevolent leadership. Respect for authority is a fundamental part of our philosophy. Indeed, personal success and capacity for leadership both take their root in one's ability to follow. Surrendering to the association of devotees, to the purificatory processes of *brahmachari* life and to the "stretch zone" is consistently in my best interests. By seeing that, my appreciation and affection for authority has steadily increased. Advancement in *brahmachari* life has also meant being asked to take up leadership responsibilities as I become qualified to do so. The perspective that I've gained from taking leadership positions has deepened my appreciation for the difficulties inherent in leading and guiding others. This in turn has made me more humble, tolerant, and appreciative of spiritual and managerial authority in my own life.

Being a *brahmachari* and having travelled fairly widely through ISKCON, I'm fortunate to have some perspective on my particular *ashrama* in relation to others I've seen. There is some variety in the moods of *ashramas*, due to cultural differences, varieties of leadership styles and local priorities in preaching and service profile. In general, my home *ashrama* is notable for having a very liberal mood, which reflects the character of our *ashrama* leader and of our temple president. I have seen that this focus on supporting new devotees and patiently allowing them to grow into their potential is very much a hallmark of the local flavor and it goes a long way to maintaining rapport and a sense of belonging. Devotees who spend time here are generally very appreciative of this and become inspired to dedicate more and more of themselves to the community's mission. Another defining characteristics of our *ashrama* is a strong focus on hearing and chanting. All *brahmacharis* are expected to read for at least an hour a day, we have a rich schedule of classes, seminars, public reading groups, and a strong culture of relishing and discussing *shashtra* and its application in our lives. I would also say that we have a steady commitment to *sankirtana*/outreach activities, with multiple *harinamas,* college programs, and book distribution events weekly. Our Sunday Feast program attracts a majority of local Western guests and is noted by visitors for its sweetness and accessibility to the modern Western, young person.

Brahmacharis in our *ashrama* also learn how to serve appropriately within the social body of the community. We are trained to be respectful of Vaishnavis and women in general, but to not be familiar in our dealings. The entire social system of our devotional culture is based on mutual respect and we believe that this culture of respect begins with *brahmachari* training. As such, our *brahmacharis* are expected to be exemplary in terms of humility and attentiveness to time, place, and circumstance. All of our *brahmacharis'* actions are rooted in respect for ourselves and others. In terms of interacting with women, this respect manifests as politeness, verbal and emotional cultivation of the conception of all women as mothers and respect for the tremendous power of women by deferring to women in offering physical and emotional space. Senior *brahmacharis* lead by their example, showing how to move in a way that is free of the problematic mentalities of exploitation and aversion.

As our *ashrama* has developed, we have had the privilege of witnessing members move on ("graduate") to the *grihastha ashrama* as well as to roles as senior *brahmacharis*. We take these transitions as a sign of success of the program and our culture reflects that. Because transition is a natural part of human life and because it can also be quite challenging, we began holding change of *ashrama* ceremonies within the *ashrama* and also in the temple with the broader community. These are opportunities to praise the qualities of the transitioning devotee, to offer guidance and blessings, and to send a message about the importance of having healthy transitions under Krishna-conscious guidance. Transitioning devotees find these ceremonies to be very supporting and encouraging. By doing this, we make it clear that transitions are normal and healthy, but should be done under careful guidance. Our *ashrama* devotees are trained to have a realistic view of *ashrama* transitions and to remain friendly with graduated members of the *ashrama*, understanding that devotees who have begun developing their *grihastha ashrama* will have new time-commitments and challenges to face that have to be respected. In our community, *brahmacharis* specifically fill the role of providing support for graduating members of the *ashrama*, acting as reliable sources of friendly care and Krishna-conscious service opportunities to devotees who are navigating the ups and downs of *ashrama* transition.

* * *

Note: Many thanks to these two sincere devotees who have shared their stories for *Endangered Species*. As you may note, the *brahmachari* story reflects many of the values laid out in this book – equal vision, devotee care, and more. However, it is notable that as of this writing there is no equivalent *brahmacharini ashrama* in the progressively managed temple in which the *brahmachari* writer has thrived.

The *brahmacharini's* story, on the other hand, reflects the tragic mistreatment many sincere and capable Vaishnavis have received at the hands of ISKCON leaders, especially since Srila Prabhupada's departure. Sadly, it is a story that is too often repeated, driving women from ISKCON with heavy and often overlooked consequences.

Correcting this imbalance is more than the decent, moral and gentlemanly thing to do; it is imperative if ISKCON is remain a credible international organization, relevant in the modern world, able to attract high-caliber devotees from all over the world as Srila Prabhupada did.

2020: Parting Words

Confusion Due to Misinterpretation of Shastra
by Govinda dasi

Most of us know that *Aha!* moment when we recognize: "Yes! This is the absolute truth! This is what I've been looking for!" The philosophy of Krishna consciousness makes sense and is woven together in a beautiful shimmering brocade of enlightenment, compassion, wisdom, and love – the refinement of Krishna bhakti.

And then, we smack into the brick walls of shastric statements that we find unacceptable – or intolerable – or not understandable in our world of experience. We find statements that don't tally with our view of the world, or they are conveyed by some people in a way that lacks maturity, compassion, and even validity. Yet there they are staring us in the face: statements like "women are less intelligent," or "women are nine times lustier than men."

So how do we make sense of these statements given by *shastra* and by our *acharya* Srila Prabhupada?

In a lecture Srila Prabhupada gave in 1967 he said that Prahlada's mother forgot the teachings given by Narada "because she was a woman." I became alarmed! I was relishing the direct association of Srila Prabhupada and hearing him speak every day. I had finally found the most beautiful philosophy and practice of Krishna bhakti, and I was experiencing the greatest joy I had ever known. Yet because of being female there was a chance I would forget all this? I was more than alarmed! This disturbed me very much.

Shortly after this lecture, I went to his room and asked him about it. He immediately understood my anxiety. Srila Prabhupada, then called Swamiji, not only understood my dilemma, but he also explained everything in a way that I could understand – in a way that we should all understand so that we don't become misled by others' lack of understanding and realization. I paraphrase here what he told me. I remember it well because it was so important for me and has been the beacon my entire life.

"Generally," he said, "women are more attached to family life, to children, husband, and home. These are bodily attachments, they have nothing to do with the soul. When death comes, they will all be gone. But women, usually they are very much attached to these temporary will-o'-the-wisp relationships. That is their nature.

"Hiranyakashipu, he was a very big demon king. His wife, she was queen. She wanted to again be with her husband, the king, and be safe in his palace. So her chastity and simplicity were there. However, her attachment to husband, family – all these things

– stood in the way of her hearing and remembering Narada's instructions. So she could not hear Narada with proper attention.

"Govindasi, don't think that simply because you are in female body you cannot become Krishna conscious. It is not like that. Here we have to make the best use of a bad bargain. Whatever body we have, male or female, it is to be considered a bad bargain. Because we have taken birth in this material world, we are subject to birth, death, disease, and old age – this is a very bad bargain. But we must make the best use of it. We must try to become Krishna conscious in this very lifetime, never mind man or woman, doesn't matter.

"And how long you will be in this body, this American body? Eighty, ninety, maybe one hundred years at most. Never mind it is man or woman, American or Indian, death comes either way. What is important is your development of Krishna consciousness. That is all that will matter when death comes.

"What is important is that you become Krishna conscious. You see, generally the conditioned soul becomes attached to the opposite sex – to husband or wife. So if he is attached to wife at time of death, he takes next birth as woman. And if that soul is attached to husband, next birth she takes as man. Back and forth, in this way and that way. It is coming and going. Male, then female, then male, and again female. Better not to identify with either. Don't become attached to any false identity of either male or female. Better to become Krishna's devotee. That is our real identity.

"There are many examples of great lady devotees: Queen Kunti, Devahuti, Draupadi, Jahnava, Gandhari – they are all shining examples of devotion to Krishna. So you please don't become discouraged in this way.

"By nature, women are mothers. So their hearts are soft. They want to love, so they love their children and their husbands. But they also want to love God. In that way, they are pious. In churches you will see, mostly there are women coming. Have you seen? Whole church is full of ladies, not so many men. So woman's nature is soft and good. But the problem is that women are easily misled, easily swayed by material desires, and they often become victim to some bad association.

"But if they have good teachings, good guru, good husband, and good leaders, they can become advanced in Krishna consciousness very quickly because their hearts are soft. No crookedness, simple hearts. Men have harder hearts, and crookedness is also there. Ambition, duplicity, so many complex conditions are there. Yet men have many other advantages. Main thing is this: you don't become attached to this false notion, 'I am man,' 'I am woman.' Become fixed in 'I am eternal servant of Krishna.' That is your real identity."

In light of Srila Prabhupada's explanations, we can better understand all such similar statements in *shastra* about women.

We all know the goal of Krishna bhakti is to return to our natural position in the spiritual world. And to do this, we must be free of all attachments to the material world. To remain attached to family, children, and home are indeed attachments that will bind us to this world. Even more so are the attachments to false ego, position, and identities as lords of our little universes. So this is what is meant by "less intelligent."

Women often are exploited as pleasure objects by unscrupulous men, not only in our world today, but even historically. The beauty and grace of women is sought after by lusty men focused upon owning them and exploiting them. This is undeniable, we see it everywhere.

Therefore, the need for protection arises. And ideally, such protection is given by a caring husband and loving father. That is the ideal. But we also now know that most often women are not protected by their fathers and husbands. Instead we see situations in our Kali world of abusive, neglectful, or even cruel husbands, and worse, predatory and exploitive fathers and father figures.

Certainly we don't read headlines that women have gang raped any man! It's always the men who have gang raped some helpless woman, even killed her, to satiate their gross physical lust! So what does this "nine times lustier" statement mean? It just doesn't make sense to anyone with normal intelligence!

Lust refers to much more. Their "extended" lust is for nice home, children, nice clothing, and ornaments. Remember, Kardama Muni created "nine palaces" that were all beautifully decorated for Devahuti. These are the entanglements that tie one to this world of *samsara*. Yet, women cannot be safe without the protection of four walls around them. Women cannot wander the world as safely as men can. So the natural need for these entanglements is there. And by remaining attached to these things prevents our liberation from *samsara*, and this is known as "less intelligent."

Srila Prabhupada often said, "A sixteen year old girl and a sixteen year old boy, they are different in that he can roam about the world freely – but a sixteen year old girl cannot. Someone will snatch her!"

So the underlying understanding here is that women, the "fair sex," with their beauty and grace, are desired by the opposite sex. Therefore they need protection from exploitation and abuse. Their "less intelligence" is due to the tendency to become completely engrossed in the world of security, home, family, and the *identification* with these. The *identification* with these temporary arrangements is what is meant by "less intelligent." Not whether or not they have a PhD in science, or are recognized as great writers, scientists, or intellectuals – which they are. It is the attachment to the false identification with a temporary identity that is the less intelligence – which we do see in men also.

As devotee women, we are not primarily interested in the temporary trappings of the material world, such as bangles and baubles, as are most materialistic women. We are drawn to this path perhaps not so much for renunciation, but for dovetailing our natural service to our children and family in Krishna consciousness. Our nature is to have children, and grandchildren, and make our homes into temples for worshiping Lord Krishna. Our focus is on serving Krishna and Srila Prabhupada with the talents and inclinations we have. It's called "dovetailing," a unique use and meaning of the word given to us by Srila Prabhupada.

As devotee women, we "dovetail" our natural love of fabrics and jewelry, for example, by creating lovely apparel and jewelry for our Deities. We dovetail our intelligence by reading and speaking about Krishna and His devotees. We dovetail our lovely feminine voices by singing bhajans or leading kirtans laced with the love in our hearts. Love for Krishna comes easily to women who have the boon of soft hearts. Krishna bhakti is about love of God, and for love of God, one needs to have a heart as soft as butter.

So be inspired to know that as women we have certain strengths and certain weaknesses. It is important that we understand these things so that we don't get confused or lost in despair because others do not understand. There are pros and cons of being female, just as there are pros and cons of being male.

The real issue is to find the best way we can serve Krishna, and to clear away doubts about our worthiness to do so. In this way, we will feel encouraged and empowered to use all the talents and gifts that we have, as explained by Srila Prabhupada.

Once, Srila Prabhupada said to me, "You are not a woman, you are something else." He was referring to the rigors I was undergoing of living a nomadic life, traveling from city to city, preaching, with only one suitcase. Srila Prabhupada also wrote in one letter, "These are not ordinary women, they are Vaishnavis!" Even if others don't understand this, we need to understand this and never forget it.

We are Srila Prabhupada's daughters and granddaughters, and we were sent here to serve Lord Chaitanya's *sankirtana* mission in Kali-yuga. Whatever we can do to become inspired in our service to Them should be our most important focus.

A Letter To Our Future Selves
by Rukmini dasi

Dear Vaishnavis of the Future,

My deepest respects to you all. All glories to Srila Prabhupada.

Several years ago I attended a conference in Geneva, Switzerland sponsored by the Global Peace Initiative of Women. A woman who was a high court judge in India spoke and explained a powerful metaphor.

She said that traditionally in India most people lived in a joint family home. There was usually a courtyard space in the center facing inward, and a veranda around the perimeter facing out. The men would usually be on the veranda, talking about finance, politics, science, and the problems and affairs of the outside world.

The women would be in the courtyard cooking, talking, dealing with domestic problems, and healing the family's illnesses with herbal remedies.

Some are trying to lead by facing out, looking for solutions from outside. Others are looking to lead and heal community by facing in.

Of course, today there are many women in leadership – in government, in finance, in science, and many other fields. In ISKCON in the United States today there are six women temple presidents. In other countries, there are also women leading in different capacities and offering various services. It seems that often women and also men who are spiritually advanced have an ability to lead in a supportive, empathic way, rather than a controlling or domineering way.

To me that this sort of introspective leadership intends to lead as a sort of path smoother, or servant-leader, trying to truly hear others and deeply appreciate each and everyone's unique and diverse contribution to the whole. This inward-facing community-centered leadership seems to be a formula for developing what Dr. Martin Luther King Jr called, "the beloved community."

He defined that beloved community, first of all, as one that offers *radical* hospitality to everyone; an inclusive family rather than an exclusive club, that recognizes and honors the image of God in every human being. Of course, we would extend that to include every living being.

I'm fond of a certain story about Srila Prabhupada. In the early days, a new devotee who was also very young at the time had a chance to serve Srila Prabhupada. Srila Prabhupada was staying for a few days in a house near New Vrindavan, and this young man was given the task of guarding outside the house that night. It began to rain and the young man went into the attached garage to guard from there.

In a few moments, he felt a presence behind him in the garage. He turned around and there was Srila Prabhupada standing behind him. He fell down and offered his obeisance. Then he rose and asked, "Is there any service I can do for you, Srila Prabhupada?"

Srila Prabhupada said, "Yes. You can go where *I* will not go!" The young man was bewildered. Srila Prabhupada had just come from Chicago, Dallas, Caracas, Venezuela, San Francisco, and before that Tokyo. Soon he would be going to New York, London, Paris, and Germany.

He asked, "But where is it that *you* will not go, Srila Prabhupada? You are going everywhere!"

Srila Prabhupada replied, "To the future! And by the way you treat the people there, they will know how much Krishna loves them."

In other words, Krishna cares for us, for all living beings. He patiently travels with us as the Supersoul in our lost wanderings as we try to fulfill our separatist desires in so many species of life. When we feel distress, Krishna feels compassion for our suffering. *"Tat te 'nukampam."* *"Anukampam"* means "to tremble with" (*Bhag.* 10.14.8). And He gives us the understanding by which we can come to Him.

As His aspiring devotees, how can we be more loving and caring as He is? What will enhance our Krishna consciousness and help us go deeper in experience and realization? What parts of ourselves do we want to carry into the future? What kinds of interactions in our communities and beyond can grow into deep loving exchanges that sustain and build faith and trust?

On the path of Bhakti, we learn that at the center of all existence, there is a love affair. The divine masculine, Sri Krishna, and loving the divine feminine, Sri Radha, who is expanded from Him, dance. Radha is His own pleasure potency. In effect, this is God loving God. And we are being invited to join that dance, to live and dance in harmony along with Them in eternity. To live in Bhakti, means to live in harmony with this "rta," or divine cosmic order.

Once, Srila Prabhupada gave an example: If you're sitting on the bank of a still lake and you throw a pebble into the center of the lake, then harmonious concentric circles will radiate outward from that center where you threw your pebble. If you throw another pebble, and another one, and yet another one into that same center, they will all create harmonious circles generating out from that center. But if I throw a pebble to this side or that side, and you throw your pebble here or there, then so many interference patterns will form and begin to clash with each other.

In other words, if we act in this world, loving Krishna and serving Him in the core of our hearts, and at the center of our lives, then as many interests, goals, or pursuits as we may have, they can all be harmonized in peace and sustainability in Krishna. We can have community, family, art, music, intellectual pursuits, environmentalism, all offered into the center point of loving Krishna. And if we act out of self-centered ego, then we will clash – within ourselves, between ourselves and others, and in the world.

How does Srila Prabhupada describe the formula for peace? To understand that everything is owned and controlled by Krishna, that everything is meant for His pleasure, and that He is our dearest friend. (*Gita* 5.29)

In his purport to *Bhagavad-gita* 4.24, Srila Prabhupada explains that,

"Everything that exists is situated in the *brahmajyoti,* but when that *jyoti* is covered by illusion (*maya*) or sense gratification, it is called material. The material veil can be removed at once by Krishna consciousness. . . . the Absolute Truth covered by *maya* is called matter. Matter dovetailed for the cause of the Absolute Truth regains its spiritual quality. Krishna consciousness is the process of converting the illusory consciousness into Brahman, or the Supreme. When the mind is fully absorbed in Krishna consciousness, it is said to be in *samadhi,* or trance."

How can we bring this mood of harmony into our hearts, into our communities, and into the world? We are eager to preach but are we eager to appreciate and to truly hear others?

We are members of an institution meant for giving compassion to others but are we each individually acting with compassion in our personal dealings? Or are we remaining on the neophyte platform judging and criticizing others? Are we offending others and becoming offended by petty things, making assumptions, taking things personally, and acting out of false ego? Are we trying to grow the seeds of Bhakti but instead getting tangled up in the weeds?

I was recently listening to a lecture given by Srila Prabhupada where he was comparing the practice of beginning or *sadhana, vaidhi-bhakti,* to jumpstarting the engine of a car. We try to give our internal battery a jump by our daily practice. But real Bhakti begins when we develop a spontaneous taste for the practice, or when the car engine kicks in and begins to run on its own power.

If we want to carry these sacred teachings into the future, we must ourselves develop the taste for authentic Krishna consciousness. So many religious communities of different traditions exist on a *kanishtha,* or beginner's platform and they judge or criticize others over petty differences of understanding, or class or race or practice.

If we remain on this beginner's platform, how are we any different? Perhaps we have an extraordinary theology, but if we don't practice it with realization, how are we any better? How will we communicate to others how much Krishna loves them if we are not living and showing that love between ourselves?

Recently, we attended a funeral ceremony for a beloved devotee who had taken his own life. It was a tragedy in the community. In the first days after the suicide, there were naturally many unanswered questions, "Why? How could this happen?" As well as much blame and finger pointing to others in leadership which, sadly, also extended out onto social media.

I feared that this mood of negativity would continue at his memorial ceremony. And yet after those first painful days, there seemed to be a shift. At his ceremony, each person spoke of him with such appreciation, telling stories of how kind, selfless, and lovingly serving he had always been. How he treated everyone of every community, both Indian and Western, young and old, new and seasoned members with such affection.

After the ceremony, there was such a sense of peace, of the community having come together. Afterwards, one godbrother of mine said to me, "Why did we have to wait until after his death to appreciate him so much? Why didn't we let him know while he was alive, how much we all loved him? Maybe this tragedy could have been averted, if we had let him know."

We so often speak about higher levels of *rasa,* of *bhava,* and *prema.* But this kind of love is impossible to realize without first learning to act with appreciation and gratitude in this world. Our *acharya,* Srila Prabhupada, was always so grateful. Even Lord Krishna is so grateful for any tiny service rendered.

In conclusion, dear Vaishnavis, I suggest that gratitude and appreciation are the two doors to the palace of Bhakti. There is no back door. Can we *be the change* that creates the future and show the people there how much Krishna loves them?

Hare Krishna. Your sister in service,

Rukmini devi dasi

The Failed Experiment versus Loving Krishna
by Kusha dasi

I share this sad tale of woe in the hope of helping even one innocent Devi who may fall prey to an errant man selfishly dwelling in the illusion of convoluted principles. We need to embrace the truth that we are Krishna's and Krishna is ours.

In my innocence, I believed love could conquer, and love of God could conquer all. I *was* a true romantic.

When my path crossed that of the Hare Krishnas of ISKCON Hawaii, I was instantly attracted to the name of Krishna and I was enthralled by the philosophy. While listening to *Bhagavad-gita* and *Srimad-Bhagavatam* classes, I celebrated each "*aha*" moment, internally with a resounding yes, yes, yes. Everything I heard made me blissful.

But there was trouble in paradise. After some time, some of the young men began discussing taking more than one wife. These fellows were slightly older than most of the women; they were around thirty years old. They were in positions of influence and power but they lacked maturity and wisdom. They influenced the thinking of many a lusty young fellow in the temples. As it says in *Bhagavad-gita,* "What great men do, common men follow."

This created havoc in many temples, including Hawaii. As the chaos increased, which brought on by the temple president who wanted a second wife, the Hawaii temple was abandoned, and what was left was ruins of lost love.

In response, Srila Prabhupada sent eight men to save the Hawaii temple and take care of the Panca-tattva Deities. Our true hero, he swiftly dealt with the problem.

While speaking with Govinda dasi about the situation, Srila Prabhupada slammed his hand on his desk, asserting that she should not associate with her former husband. We understood – with extra emphasis – his objection. He dispelled the conception that a wife should remain submissive to her husband in any condition.

Subsequently, a year and a half into my first marriage, my husband and I performed *garbhardana-samskara* to invite a lovely soul into our lives. We were blessed with a noble son who caught the eye of Srila Prabhupada. On many occasions, Srila Prabhupada blessed my son with praise to encourage him on the path of devotion.

When our son was one year old, my husband, Hb dasa, who had remained influenced by the musings of the "*purusha bhava club*" (the club of desire for lordship and control) began thinking about taking a second wife. His eye wandered over the beauty of the lasses. Hawaii is infamous for its sparkly *maya* and women of striking beauty.

While Srila Prabhupada visited Hawaii in 1975, Hb brought his new beautiful seventeen year old *hapa haole* (part Asian, part Caucasian) additional wife to the temple. The other men were green with envy, seeing his exotic love acquisition, and welcomed him into their fold. I was like a deer before headlights – devastated, bewildered, shocked.

In my family, my parents were everlastingly committed. How could this have happened to me who was now living in a society rich with high spiritual ideals? What happened to our simple living, our regard for austerity, our devotional absorption?

When a Vaishnavi is at her all time low, so many well intended well-wishers come forward to offer their unsolicited advice. That can be confusing and overwhelming. I wished to hibernate and remove myself from public view. I felt vulnerable. Emotionally I was shredded with blame and shame confounded by bad advice.

In my bewildered state, Jayatirtha Prabhu compassionately suggested I write a letter to Srila Prabhupada. This made perfect sense! So I wrote asking what to do and how to act. Prabhupada replied by letter on February 3, 1975:

> I have studied your situation carefully and I encourage you to live in the temple in the association of fixed up devotees who are following my teachings strictly. If your husband cannot follow our principles properly, you are not to think you should let that hamper your spiritual life. You should stay with us and cultivate spiritual life peacefully under Krishna's protection and care. If he is not interested in spiritual life, let him do as he pleases. I have given all of my disciples instructions to follow for making spiritual advancement, but if they do not have the desire to follow, then what I can do? Anyone who is unwilling to follow our regulated principles, you should not live or associate close with such a person.

Jayatirtha flew down the wide, spiral staircase, bubbling over having just spoken with Srila Prabhupada about my situation. "Srila Prabhupada said that this co-wifery is not our philosophy and you should simply increase your hearing, chanting, and reading." Srila Prabhupada also commented, "This will cause chaos in our Society!"

Prabhupada's message to me was unlike what other devotees were telling me. My confusion lifted and I became determined to follow Srila Prabhupada's instructions, feeling great relief and freedom from my suffering.

I share this story because I pray that when heartbreak befalls us, and it will, we will be able to pick ourselves up and resume our joyful practice of Krishna consciousness. There is always a glimmer of hope, a ray of light at the end of every dark night of the soul.

May Vaishnavis everywhere be established in sustainable lifestyles. I pray they can share their truthful healthy confidence and enthusiasm, celebrating joyful Krishna consciousness, adding color and beauty to every occasion.

Reliance upon Krishna is secure; He won't abandon us. He is always there for us all. The more we are self-realized, the more we are able to love with all our hearts.

As the eldest child in a family of three girls, I have a sense of confidence in gentle nurturing leadership. Vaishnavis bring beauty and culture to our Society. Be happy, celebrate the feminine, add light and love to every occasion. Do not hide your light under a basket, sparkle and shine for Srila Prabhupada! We can add to the glory of God because we are Krishna's and He is ours!

You're a reflection of Krishna's beauty, wonderful, shining from the inside out. Let His light and love fill your lives with love of Krishna! Starting with ourselves, love of Krishna conquers us all!

A Call to be Torchbearers
by Govinda Priya dasi

Throughout history, empowering women in society has ensured the stability, progress, and long-term development of nations. This also holds true for our ISKCON society where the contributions made by women are invaluable and undeniable.

This book magnanimously takes us into an enlightening and enlivening journey underscoring the role of women in ISKCON – from the Movement's inception and beyond. We're given a rare glimpse and insight into the life and contributions of many stalwart women disciples of Srila Prabhupada. The papers, articles, and letters unravels a tale of fearless, selfless efforts, and unhesitating sacrifices rendered by Srila Prabhupada's female champion generals. The ripened fruits of their hard work have become the delicacies for us to relish as a legacy for our entire lives!

I was very moved to hear of the concerns and challenges my older godsisters in the post-preceptor era of ISKCON express here. It is truly revealing and insightful and has opened up aspects about Krishna consciousness for me that I hadn't contemplated completely. I'm grateful for the efforts of these senior devotees to change the situation for women in ISKCON and I'm inspired to carry on their work.

On one hand this book provides an ornamental embellishment to the beauty of feminine potency within our Society. On the other hand, devotees and newcomers will happily discover answers to many things that may have confused or confounded them about the role of women in ISKCON. In this anthology we see women as educators, preachers, mothers, managers, and even gurus in our disciplic line.

Reading these pieces was quite encouraging and empowering as it allowed me to envision my truest potential and expanded my scope of where and how I can contribute as a woman in the Movement. I am left brimming with a sense of gratitude for these devotee's lifetime of devotion and undeterred determination.

I want to graciously accept what has been done for me and other women. In many ways I feel like a bridge that I should responsibly carry forward their work into the future. I'm asking myself, How can I be part of the solution? I hope you will ask yourself the same question so that Vaishnavis around the world can come together and support each other.

I want to leave a better situation for Vaishnavis in the future. I want to see expanded opportunities for services based on our god-given talents, not restrictions based on bodily discrimination as to the color of someone's skin or their sex. Let our full offerings be made. It is only a loss to ISKCON if all the talents aren't used. Women will move forward in their lives and their skills will be used elsewhere. I hope our Movement will take advantage of all the services women have to offer and you will join me as a torchbearer of this noble effort.

A Vision for ISKCON's Future
by Shyamala Kishori dasi

I am grateful to all the Vaishnavis who came before my generation and paved the way for us to serve Krishna according to our nature. It is because of their struggles and sacrifices that I grew up having the opportunity to lead kirtan, play *mridanga*, and give lectures. As a young girl, I heard firsthand accounts of how Srila Prabhupada's female disciples steadily served their spiritual master amidst circumstances that were often discouraging. It saddened me to hear how these Vaishnavis, to whom I turned for guidance and wisdom, had been dismissed due to bodily conceptions. Their steady service under such circumstances is a powerful testimony to their spiritual strength and depth of devotion.

Dear Vaishnavis, if we become disheartened, this anthology of resources is here to remind us that we are not alone. Through its pages, we receive the association of a wonderful assembly of kind, caring devotees. Let us come together and support each other on our spiritual journeys. We can encourage each other by not instinctively shying away when someone invites us to give a lecture, write an article, lead a kirtan, or take on another service outside of our comfort zone. Together we can find the courage to use our voices in glorification of Krishna and His devotees. The more we speak about Krishna, the deeper our realizations will grow, and the more we will inspire others to step forward. Let us teach our young boys to hold women in high esteem and value their wisdom. And let us show our young girls by example that they too can play an active role in sharing Krishna consciousness, in their own unique ways.

I envision a future for ISKCON where every Vaishnavi is valued and respected. Communities will seek out the women's wisdom and perspective on important issues.

Vaishnavis will be recognized as spiritual leaders, mentors, educators, and speakers. Every woman will feel inspired and supported in serving Krishna according to her propensity, per Krishna's instructions in *Bhagavad-gita* (3.35), whether that entails running a center, giving class, raising children, or any number of other services. The men in our Movement will be concerned about the spiritual, physical, and emotional well-being of the women. During *Srimad-Bhagavatam* lectures, the feminine pronoun will also be used so that young girls growing up in the Society will know that they too can be devotees of Krishna. Men will appreciate and support the kirtans led by Vaishnavis and encourage their daughters to learn to play the *mridanga* and other musical instruments. Temples will have instruments on both sides of the room so that anyone musically inclined may participate. Men and women will take turns being first to recite *Srimad-Bhagavatam* verses and to receive *maha* during *arati*. Devotees will speak up when they see women being treated disrespectfully. The men will acknowledge and empathize with the struggles that women have gone through in ISKCON and work toward reformation. In this vision for the future, Vaishnavis are not treated as second-class citizens, rather as spirit souls, part-and-parcel of Krishna and invaluable members of our Society.

The vision I describe above is not merely abstract; certain ISKCON communities, centers, and leaders already imbibe it. I grew up in New Goloka, North Carolina, where Bir Krishna Goswami encouraged all the *gurukulis* to lead kirtan. When I was in my twenties, I had the opportunity to live for several years at the Krishna House in Gainesville, Florida, where I observed how, under the guidance of Kalakantha Prabhu, all *ashrama* residents and newcomers are treated with equal respect and care. Regardless of gender, devotees are given equal opportunity and encouragement to lead kirtan, give lectures, and take on various services according to their natures.

Dear Vaishnavis, I hope this anthology will give you inspiration to seek encouraging association on your spiritual sojourns. Ultimately, each one of us needs to nurture our own *bhakti* for Krishna. If our current environment is not uplifting, we can create a *sanga* of like-minded devotees with family, friends, and spiritual seekers. From within that favorable association we can then share the treasure of *bhakti* with others.

Courageous Women Ushering in a New Partnership Paradigm for Relationships
by Vrajalila dasi

When I was requested by Sudharma and Pranada Prabhus to write a short article touching on some personal and relevant questions, my first thoughts were, "*What could I possibly share in this book that has not already been shared by so many exalted Vaishnavi contributors?"* Almost simultaneously, as if by instinct I heard my most favorite sutra resounding in my head and heart, "Humble and Brave."

Whenever my mind starts going down the track of limitations, my trusted friend, this *sutra* surfaces and calls me to take risks, to rise above my mind into the realms of possibilities.

A beautiful lesson I have learned over the last forty-one years on the bhakti path is that as women we carry the best of every generation within us. We are the nurturers, the caregivers, as well as the warriors, and the instruments for change.

One of the questions I was asked was, "If you were to die tomorrow what would I want to say?"

Before I reply to this question, I want to extend my gratitude to the Vaishnavas worldwide for your selfless service to assist Srila Prabhupada carry on the mission of Sri Chaitanya Mahaprabhu. I have deep appreciation for my mentor-guru and those senior Vaishnavis who nurtured me on the path. I am certainly blessed by having had their saintly association. Most especially, since I *am* to die tomorrow, I will take this opportunity to acknowledge a few of those sincere Vaishnavis who were my early mentors.

In the summer of 1979 my life was forever changed. I met my first Vaishnavi at West 55th Street Govinda's Restaurant and temple in New York. She sort of cornered me one day. My friend had paused in the hallway to take in the commotion, which I later learned was a kirtan for the arrival of HH Satsvarupa Maharaja.

I was desperately trying to leave, but the hallway was packed with monks singing and playing loud musical instruments. This devotee spoke sweetly and convincingly, encouraging me – urging me – to enter the temple room. Although I was reluctant, I did not refuse. This was my first encounter with Sri Sri Gaura-Nitai, Sri Sri Radha-Govinda, Jagannatha, Baladeva, and Lady Subhadra. As I stood before Sri Sri Radha-Govinda, I cried and cried and cried for what seem like hours even though it was more like ten or fifteen minutes. This experience made me aware that I had to do some serious soul searching.

I had recently returned to New York to get more involved in the Siddha Yoga Ashram in upstate New York, continue with another degree program and modern dance classes. I was a vegetarian. I loved to meditate and engage in *seva*. I chanted *om nama shivaya* every day to my beautiful picture of Lord Shiva on my altar in my apartment. However, the experience with the Deities had impacted me more than anything else I had ever experienced. I knew I was being called.

After my first Ratha-yatra in Philadelphia a few weeks later, I knew I had to answer the call. Together with my partner, we left New York for the *ashrama* in Los Angeles. I lived in the women's *ashrama* and Jadurani Prabhu was my *ashrama* leader. That was excellent training.

Then HH Bhakti-Tirtha Swami recruited my partner to join him in Washington D. C. After arriving in Washington D. C., I personally meeting HH Bhakti-Tirtha Swami. It felt as if I had known him before; felt safe and understood. As preparation to send me to Africa to preach, he asked me to return to the West 55th street temple to be trained in book distribution, where I lived in the women's *ashrama*. I saw this as most auspicious because Sri Sri Radha-Govinda had brought me back to Their temple.

It was here that I gleaned the benefits of the most sacred, loving, and life-sustaining association in my Krishna consciousness. Vaishnavis that impacted my life were Ragatmika, Pavani, Sadhvi, and Mulaka Prabhus. Their determination, discipline, and love for distributing Srila Prabhupada books was contagious. Nanda Prabhu's joyful, caring mood made *ashrama* life fun. Tulasi Devi served the Vaishnavis and studied the *shastras*. Her daily service was to wash the *sankirtana* devotees clothes and she taught me my first *Bhagavad-gita shloka*. Laxmimimoni Prabhu was an administrative warrior, she had a voice, and appeared fearless. Jai Sri Prabhu became my confidant; and I was hers. As we were both New Yorkers, we could talk about anything.

The New York temple moved to different locations, and as I followed, my association continued to sustain me. When Sunita Prabhu gave birth to a son, her simplicity and excitement was most refreshing and reminded me that Krishna consciousness included having children. Madri and Pallika Prabhus exemplified introspection and silence. They were friendly, but it was clear that they had boundaries that only a very few people were allowed to cross.

Each of these Vaishnavis played an important role in preparing me for my next Krishna conscious adventure in a foreign country.

Serving as a pioneer in West Africa was not easy. I quickly learned that strength comes from being uncomfortable. As I traveled opening temples throughout West Africa, I yearned for the summer months when I would return to America to raise *laksmi*. Then I could be in the association of my Vaishnavi elders and friends who were my inspiration as well as my caretakers.

I share my story with these Vaishnavis to remind us that we are interdependent practitioners in Krishna consciousness. Though my singular authority was my guru, HH Bhakti-Tirtha Swami, who always encouraged, trained, and engaged me in leadership roles, these Vaishnavis were influential in rooting me with priceless training that cements the foundation of who I am today in Krishna consciousness.

After almost ten years in West Africa, I returned to America to assist with pioneering another project. Yasodamayi and I were encouraged by HH BTSwami to go to Belize to open a preaching center. The center was successful, but we returned to America to assist Bhakti-Tirtha Swami with "The Institute for Applied Spiritual Technology."

It was during this time that I met Sudharma Prabhu. She was on fire: fully dedicated to empowering women to find their voices and to speak out about the inequalities many Vaishnavis faced in the bigger organization of ISKCON. Her desires to speak out on behalf of Vaishnavis was fully aligned with the desires of my mentor and guru, HH Bhakti-Tirtha Swami, who always championed women's rights and always gave me autonomy to create many different kinds of programs and to teach women as well as men in our different projects.

HH Bhakti-Tirtha Swami encouraged me to support Sudharma Prabhu as much as possible, given that I was fully engaged with many new people coming to the Institute and therefore I was traveling less.

Sudharma Prabhu is one of my mentors. Although I had been engaged in many different leadership roles, I was a bit shy and not a public speaker. On the other hand Sudharma was an eloquent speaker. She was fearless, determined, and loyal to the women of ISKCON. Most especially to those whose voices that had been silenced for years and whose potential had been minimized.

If I were to die tomorrow, I would write a global letter of gratitude to all of Srila Prabhupada daughters for their loyalty and dedication even though they experienced many adversities and endured the many challenges during the early years of establishing the organization after Srila Prabhupada's departure.

I very much appreciate that some of these stories are now documented and will be available for all generations to come.

What is important in the life of a Vaishnavi?

In my experience modeling genuine sisterhood is extremely important. For me, this means appreciating, acknowledging, listening, becoming a friend, and learning from each other. As sisters, we must keep our voices amplified to construct the future for the next generation.

It takes a lot of grieving to be open for receiving.

As Vaishnavis we have certainly grieved, and may still be grieving, often wishing for acceptance and inclusion within our organization in ways that are meaningful for us. Many of us are now ready for receiving.

The voices of Vaishnavis are now being heard and we are changing obstacles to opportunities. In receiving, it is important to encourage the next generation to care for all the parts of their lives: spiritual, emotional, and physical.

As Vaishnavis, we study the scriptures, we pass this practice on to the next generation, as Visakha Prabhu exemplifies.

As Vaishnavis, we serve our communities by extending ourselves to support other Vaishnavis to walk their talk, to be courageous, to be honest, and to be vulnerable, as Yamuna Prabhu exemplified.

As Vaishnavis, we encourage self acceptance, being patient with our flaws, and at the same time being brave to take risks to speak out. We ought to be ready to be uncomfortable and to be an agent of change like Sudharma Prabhu exemplifies.

As Vaishnavis, we take the communication courses, then we teach them to other Vaishnavis.

As Vaishnavis, we make time for introspection. There is a sweet poem by Ruth Bebermeyer that always remind me of the value of making time for quiet connection.

> I can't be in touch with you
> when I am not in touch with me
> I can't see you when I am looking for myself
> So if I seem to pass you blind
> Please keep in mind
> It isn't you, it's me I cannot find.

As Vaishnavis, we find ways to support the single mother, or the single sister, who needs a friend.

As Vaishnavis, we share the joy of bhakti through kirtan, prayers, poems, writing, or sharing our weakness and our strengths, even if it is to only to one confident.

As Vaishnavis, we create programs to nourish each other's bhakti.

As Vaishnavis, we build bridges to assist women from other traditions to understand we are relevant; we can share the essence of our teachings in any environment.

As Vaishnavis, we learn to look for understandable (not necessarily condonable reasons) for each other's behavior.

A few years ago in Mayapur, a small team of us organized a departure program for my mentor/guru. As I was facilitating the ceremony and calling up speakers, I sat in the front and to the side of the males. The room was packed with friends, well wishers, many distinguished devotees.

A third of the way into the program, someone toward the back of me said, "Get up. Get up." At first I was stunned; I had never heard anyone speak to another person with such a harsh, demanding tone. I turned around. A *sannyasi* behind me, his face flushed red, repeated, "Get up. Get up. I said." He was speaking to me!

I had three choices. I could be rude back. I could give him my chair. Or I could arrange for his need. He needed a seat to sit. I chose option three and requested my husband, who was nearby, to please find him a seat. Then I called on this *sannyasi* to share his memories and glorification of his friend Bhakti-tirtha Swami. I also arranged for the males on our team to personally serve this *sannyasi*. The devotees offered first-class service and the *sannyasi* seem pleased when he left.

The following year in Mayapur this same *sannyasi* was enthusiastic to speak with me. He shared he had just finished taking a leadership course, and he had learned so many tools to help with relationships. He apologized for his behavior the year before and asked if I could forgive him.

I reflected on what some of our senior Vaishnavis may have experienced before our Institution started teaching leadership courses. I also reflected on the value of being humble and brave. I humbly arranged everything nicely for this *sannyasi,* however, I did not get up out of my chair.

As Vaishnavis, we remind each other of the death of this body and the legacies we want to leave behind for the next generation.

As Vaishnavis, we see each other as caretakers for our sisters as they prepare to die.

As Vaishnavis, we constantly remind each other about why we are doing what we are doing. We never forget our goal, our purpose, and our rightful inheritance to love and serve Krishna.

As Vaishnavis, we can build bridges of love.

Dedicated to all Vaishnavis

If we can build great bridges across mighty waves, between distant ridges,
is it too great a task to build a bridge across the depth of hurt?
If we can reach unknown places in our mind's eye,
surely we can find our way from soul to soul, from heart to heart.
Bridges of steel reach from shore to shore, bridges of love reach so much more.
They link our common hopes, our common prayers, our common goal.
We can build bridges of love each day
with our words, our actions, our will to find the way.
For now, more than ever, we need each other
with bridges of love: Their Lordships are waiting.
It's time. We can reach out to each other with bridges of love.

With love and gratitude. Your servant,
Vrajalila dasi

Epilogue: Reflections and Lessons Learned
from the Founder of the Vaishnavi Ministry
by Sudharma dasi

It's been years since I found myself sitting with Visakha at our home in Philadelphia and then in Reston, VA, or in Yamuna and Dinatarini's home nearby, discussing topics that were important to us. It was a time of transition in ISKCON and we had deep concern for the future of our Movement. We wanted to retain Srila Prabhupada's instructions, mood, and spirit. He had set the tone and taught us everything we knew about devotional life – including how to treat each other. Now now there was a great deal of disenfranchisement amongst the devotees, and we no longer could turn to him directly for insight and resolution.

One of the topics we discussed was the disenfranchising of the female devotees, the Vaishnavis. The senior women in our Movement had found their role of partnership in sharing and spreading Krishna consciousness dismissed; and similarly, as you have read here, they also felt dismissed as individuals. The Vaishnavis had been systematically sent to the back of the temple rooms, sent out of the temple rooms during *japa,* forbidden from offering prostrated obeisances, no longer asked to give class or lead a kirtan, placed behind all of the men in all social considerations, and stripped of services, particularly services of responsibility. Emphasis was placed on women as *sankirtana* collectors. In more rare cases for new devotees, as cooks, *pujaris,* and garland makers.

Of course, while women experienced these changes in mood, intention, and thinking, they would still find niches and means to continue their services using their talents and capabilities, albeit with many new obstacles.

Simultaneously, the men thought less of householder life and focused more on renunciation. Renunciation became almost synonymous with seriousness in devotional life and dedication to Srila Prabhupada. Men who had been householders gave up their *grihastha ashramas* in favor of renounced life, leaving wives and sometimes children to fend on their own, because maintaining vows of celibacy meant that women needed to be out of sight and out of mind. This thinking became so extreme that at one point, the male devotees of our Movement asked Srila Prabhupada if all the women could be sent to Australia. Who knows what would have happened if Srila Prabhupada had not still been with us then.

I guess it's already clear that all of these changes to the involvement of women in our Movement were presented as coming from Srila Prabhupada and that they were in line with our disciplic succession. Such declarations still go on today. It is very easy to be dismissive of other people when you don't feel the brunt of the disassociation and attitudes yourself.

Female disciples who were fortunate enough to have Srila Prabhupada's direct association will always hold dear the individual relationships, mood, and instructions from Srila Prabhupada to his female disciples, which were vitally and distinctly different from many experiences of the Vaishnavis in his temples. The individual was always foremost, and everyone was encouraged to be fully engaged, challenged, cared for, and happily situated in devotional life. And while I was a younger devotee and did not have the personal association of my spiritual master, the love, care, encouragement, and training that Srila Prabhupada offered to theses Vaishnavis, was then turned around and offered to me. I learned from these courageous, encouraging, and wise women the importance of being very attentive in everything I did, utilizing every moment lovingly in Krishna's service, and bringing forward the best of what I had to offer, and then to fully engage all that I had, all that I did, all that I could offer and give away, in the service of the Lord.

I also learned the value of true association. "Two or two hundred. But you must be compatible. If you are two, and you are compatible, you can go back to Godhead. But If you are 200 and not compatible, then no one will make any advancement." As Srila Prabhupada had shared this insight at a most important time in their lives, they had in turn offered it to me, at a similar moment of transition in my life.

Srila Prabhupada fully engaged his female disciples according to their desires, talents, skills, and abilities. He was always loving, caring, and concerned for the women. He was never harsh or cruel, or even dismissive, and he always encouraged all devotees to cultivate their individual talents and devotional relationships with guru and Krishna. He would say things like, "You are devotees; you are only women if you think you are women."

In this way, I would watch Yamuna as she gave every drop of her being to each detail of her Deity worship, kirtan, and cooking. All of this she had learned from Srila Prabhupada and in turn I was learning important life lessons about how to tend to my devotional services.

As I spoke with Visakha, Yamuna, Dinatarini and others, we turned to the instruction and directives from Srila Prabhupada in his books, letters, personal instructions, and through his living example. But while the memories and mood lived on for those who had had his association, there was always concern about how these understandings would be passed to future generations.

Srila Prabhupada encouraged women to enter household life. That was natural and practical given the flourishing growth of our Movement which included men and women. He spoke of the need to protect women from exploitation. These directives were offered as a means for care and loving protection, not as a support for dismissing, minimizing, abusing, or exploiting the gifts of Vaishnavis and their beautiful qualities and skilled contributions.

In the 1980s, Pranada had made it her mission to draw attention to the neglect and abuse women were facing. Taking her pen in hand, she sent out letters using a male pseudonym expressing the pain "he" felt when "his" friend, an educated 70-year-old woman with a PhD and years of life experience had traveled to Mayapur as a new devotee. As we now understand much more directly, when you travel as a 70 year old, you need to take the time to ensure everything is properly cared for. S. dasi had paid for a room, but the management couldn't find her room reservation. Without hesitation they put S., sick with dysentery, on the roof of the Long Building, fully exposed to the elements without bathroom facilities.

Unfortunately, all too often, Pranada's repeated efforts to confront leadership and draw attention to the then commonplace abuse or displacement of women met with sarcasm, disdain, name-calling, and condescension, which was one reason why she turned to a male pseudonym.

This correspondence then became the seed for the *Priti-laksanam* publication which has been enclosed within this publication.

As I mentioned, some women were still able to carve out small niches where their service could flourish. I found my niche, first through Sesa dasa, who gave me complete support and facility in service to the Philadelphia temple as a board member, where I headed up self-defined projects, then later through Mukunda Maharaja.

While Mukunda Maharaja was a *sannyasi* at that point, he had come to the Movement with his soon-to-be wife Janaki. The two of them introduced their friends, another couple, Shyamasundara and Malati to Krishna consciousness. And they were of course joined by their friend, and Janaki's sister, Yamuna Devi, who married Guru dasa. As we know, these householder couples did incredible pioneer preaching for Srila Prabhupada – the men and the women.

So many years later, Mukunda Maharaja still had great appreciation for the contributions and capabilities of the women of our Movement, especially as communicators. He engaged several women in his Communications Ministry. He was trusting, empowering, and always humbly supportive. Through my work on the Robin George case, I was eventually asked to take responsibility for North American Communications. Then I was given the choice of maintaining that position or joining the ISKCON Foundation. I joined the ISKCON Foundation. Through these services I was thrust forward into ISKCON management, and found myself attending the North American GBC and Temple Presidents meetings.

Anuttama dasa and I became close through our work in the North American GBC (NAGBC) environment. Anuttama dasa, Naveen Krishna dasa, and Mukunda Maharaja were supportive – each in their distinct ways – with the efforts to help the women. I received a great deal of encouragement from each one of them. My access to leadership allowed me to bring forward a proposal to form a council for mature discussion on the concerns of the women devotees of our Krishna consciousness society. When this happened, the ground was already fertile due to the support of these men and the attention Pranada had drawn to the issues.

Thus, in 1994, the Ministry was formed. In 1995, at the next NAGBC meeting we had a symposium of speakers. I facilitated that panel which Malati, Pranada, Anuttama, and Bhaktitirtha Swami sat on as the speakers. The discussions on that panel were very revealing for the GBC members; they were clearly moved by it. The next day, I was propelled forward by Jayapataka Swami. He nominated me to serve as an Executive Officer of the North American GBC and Temple President (NAGBC/TP) body, an honor no woman in our movement had previously held. The body voted in approval of that nomination.

At our next annual meeting, using my privilege as a North American Executive Officer, I personally invited all of the wives of the North America temple presidents and a variety of Vaishnavi project leaders to attend the upcoming NAGBC/ TP meetings. It was then that the face of those meetings were changed and to this day women remain in attendance.

It is also important to say that on becoming a North American Officer, I received the full support of another important ally for the Vaishnavis: Bir Krishna Goswami. When the moment came, he was immediately supportive of the Ministry effort and remained that way throughout my term in my services, and beyond, despite severe scrutiny and disparagement. I offer my unequivocal gratitude to him. He became a target for those opposed to the Ministry, and he encountered injustice as a result, though he never complained about the criticism and negative actions taken against him.

With the invitation I now had to the International GBC meetings, I was given the privilege of sitting and voting in committee, being able to help facilitate the appointment of a small handful of women to serve as GBC Deputies, and to introduce resolutions to the GBC body. We successfully passed the initiative to make the Women's Ministry an International Ministry with a seat on the international body. I was also able to present additional resolutions that supported women giving class, again standing at the front of the temple room during service, and having room to chant in the temple room. We took a stand against domestic violence and Caroline Constantine, a family therapist from Colorado and a friend of the devotees, developed an educational packet of three well received brochures: one for the leadership, one for the men, and one for the women on the topic.

With the formation of the International Ministry, I had the opportunity to become the International Women's Minister. This position would have given me voting privileges and International GBC membership. Instead of accepting the seat I stepped back. It was not only that I did not want to become the token female member of the GBC body, it was vitally important to me to include as many of my godsisters as possible. I wanted to use the opportunity of the seat to bring other women forward. I began by inviting other women to sit in my stead at the annual GBC meetings. It had been my hope that a more senior Vaishnavi, someone who had come before me and was more deserving, would ultimately and eventually, take on the responsibility as the Minister of the Vaishnavis. In time, Malati dasi became that person.

I continued to serve as the *de facto* International Women's Minister and the factual NAGBC Minister for the next decade. In this position, many women shared their experiences with me; thus I was exposed to a great deal of their pain. Though it was a burden to carry the weight of their accumulated suffering, the service was extremely fulfilling. It molded me as a person and a devotee in a way no other service since has. I enjoyed "being there" for my godsisters and advocating for the women.

I am most grateful to Visakha for the influence she has played in my life. Her daily association, steadfastness, and Krishna conscious wisdom gave me the strength to stand up and make a difference. Her own example helped me remain steadfast in this service. Before my connection with Visakha, I had seen a lot. Sometimes I felt that I had seen it all. But it was Visakha's influence that carried me past all that was disheartening; she reinvigorated my devotional life. She was there at just the right time, in the right way for me; a role that she has played again and again through my life. Therefore, it was only natural that I would want to reciprocate by stepping up to the task at hand for the Vaishnavis: we all needed reinvigoration. Visakha also provided me the philosophical foundation for addressing the concerns of the Vaishnavis as their Minister.

The Vaishnava men who supported the Ministry, as mentioned above, made all the difference too. In earnest they were a day-to-day source of strength and empowerment. In particular, I am indebted to Anuttama dasa, who daily helped to work through quandaries. He spoke up when needed and supported both the Vaishnavis at large and me personally and financially at the most critical junctures in my life. Also, loving appreciations to Bhaktitirtha Swami, who encouraged me to form the Ministry, imbibed the mood of inclusion for all devotees, and shared with me just weeks before his passing that he wanted to do more to support the Vaishnavis and the Ministry itself.

Many Vaishnavis were instrumental in bringing forward the Ministry. Particularly, Radha dasi, and Vraja Lila dasi. I offer my deepest regards also to Yamuna Devi, Rukmini dasi, Prasanta dasi, Sitala dasi, Malati dasi, Dina Sarana dasi, Kusha dasi, and Nandimukhi dasi, as well as others. They all deserve to be remembered in this moment.

Finally, most special appreciation to my dear friend Pranada. For without her, there never would have been a Ministry, and we may all still find ourselves unable to participate in temple activities, without a voice, and in the case of temple devotees, without basic necessities. She really was the pioneer and the one we can turn to and remember for shining a light when it was unpopular to do so. She was the seed that made change happen.

Of course, the difficulties and prejudice still continue. It is not easy to completely erase deeply seeded ideas or social constructs once they are built. As I look to the younger generations of this Movement, I am inspired by their warmth and intelligence. I have no doubt that they will become the voices of reason and a heartfelt inspiration for our Movement.

Lessons Learned

It's been twenty years since I have served as the Minister for the Vaishnavis or been active in ISKCON management. In that time I have had ample opportunity to reflect back on these experiences. As I do, certain thoughts keep coming forward. I would like to share them in hopes that they may help pave a way for a better understanding. However, I recognize that these are my conclusions. Others may not share my views and, as well, these views may not be fully realized on my part. But I offer them for whatever is good and of value in them, as they are in my heart, and important to me, and are in consideration for others. I hope they resonate to some degree for you.

1. If we learn nothing more, I find this the most crucial: *Sastra* **should never be used to support abuse or exploitation; to hurt or diminish; to decry another's service or peace of mind in devotional life.**

2. **Every soul is valuable and dear to Krishna.** I have intense affection for the devotees and my heart is heavy seeing the state of this world. For this reason I say with earnestness: We must learn to genuinely appreciate what each <u>individual</u> has to offer and help each other to always bring our best foot forward. We need to value the integrity of every living being. To those who have felt that I have fallen short in these regards, I offer my obeisance, reverence, and apologies. Good association, loving association, is invaluable. It is the most important thing in my life.

While we know that Krishna loves every living being and that He is in their heart helping them, we also know that it is our nature to act against the desire of the Lord. Thus we behave in a manner that is hurtful to ourselves and others. We must work to uproot the envy in our hearts and help others uproot the envy in their hearts. Envy is the underlying culprit that manifests as hurtful behavior and abuse of others. These steps are necessary for us to reawaken our own devotional natures.

3. We must always **value the individual** above a social construct.

4. Every individual is born with certain propensities. **Whatever gifts Krishna has given the individual need to be fully used in Krishna's service.**

So we work together to support each other and support each other's service in a loving, balanced way. One's birth and propensities may not align exactly with our ideas of *varnashrama;* we need to balance this with a consideration of time, place, and circumstance. As devotional participants we are patient, supportive, tolerant, and willing to help others grow so they can give all that they have to offer.

5. **We must always hear each other.** We should not allow disenfranchisement and prejudice. We shouldn't place individuals into groups and give them a name with negative connotations, thus dismissing them. For instance, our householders are in an *ashrama,*

they are not in *maya*. Our children are young and looking to us for care and direction, they are not simply untrained or unruly. Our elderly have experience; many are wise, not outdated or derelict. Our Vaishnavis are not feminists and insubordinate. They are whole living beings who have integrity and a great deal to offer.

Your birth, cultural beliefs or heritage, gender, race, strength, religion, beauty, affluence, or intelligence really don't matter. It doesn't ultimately matter if you are conservative or liberal, from India, the U.S., or Siberia. It doesn't matter if you are homosexual, bisexual, straight, or asexual. None of these are final determinants in the matters of love, devotion, understanding, equal vision, care or any of the truly valuable qualities in life, nor in the cultivation of our devotional service. Own strength, culture, religion, and intelligence increases when we value each other. So we must always hear and value others. We serve in a devotional mood as the servant of the servant.

6. It is essential that **we disempower extremes** in our devotional society, particularly extremes that support abuse and disenfranchisement. When I use the term *extreme,* I am referring to hardened or emotional positions that create polarities, lack balance, and reason or common sense. I am referring to views that cannot accommodate the whole or are overly self-focused, even subtly. When we make decisions that impact others, we have to consider the impact of our decisions. Will it please the Lord and our *acharyas*? We will consider whether it serves the devotees. To accomplish this, we will try to balance our perspectives with reasonableness, thoughtfulness, and care.

I learned that it is not that one position is always right and the other is always wrong. More generally, I have seen that most everything in this world is mixed. Therefore most vantage points contain information worth considering in making decisions. What is important is reason with devotion in a mood of service and understanding. We need to ask questions and in return, we need to hear. And again, in this mood, we can never allow abusive mentalities and actions to be given credibility, especially in the name of *shastra*.

7. There is a strength in devotional femininity. This is not the power of a female's desires over a male's desires, rather it is **the strength of universal motherhood.** Femininity has the power of an internal knowing that accounts for a loving understanding in the heart. This is not a strength one achieves by removing or denigrating women, rather it is a strength we receive in exchange for love and support.

8. **How relationships are structured within a family will be determined by the individuals involved.** They will affectionately decide among themselves. Often within family structures the gentleness of women will complement the strength of men, though this is not a hardened rule or expectation. Also, women have strengths and the gentleness in men complement those. In other words, we all have strengths regardless of our bodily designations. So, as often as not, there will be individual variances in relationships.

Further, it's not that women are subservient to all men; the idea that women are to be submissive to all men is a perversion. Women may often contribute a loving and supportive mood in society benefitting men, but not at the expense of personal denigration. We all stand on the merit of what we give, not on the merit of what others can get from us.

9. We should never again allow words like "care" and "protection" to equate to force and denigration.

The bodily concept and the idea of "mine" and "yours" are rooted in envy. We shouldn't organize our devotional society in a manner based on an idea of how to protect our future or align our social positions or power. Rather we must align each individual with Krishna and support their devotional growth. When even the subtlest of material motives colors our idea of how to structure our Society it can lead to a great deal of pain for those affected.

For those who identify as men, I would ask:

• If you feel that a soul in a woman's dress is nine times more lusty, then be all the more appreciative when they give that up to be fully engaged in devotional life.

• If you would like to see women more supportive in your life, then be the gentle men you are meant to be. Lead by example.

• Remember too that your negative opinions about women with whom you have no personal relationship represent the opposite of protection. If you criticize women who are giving their hearts to the Society, the Lord, and His devotees because they don't fit your personal views, that means you have become the very person women need protection from. Bondage to material life and material concepts manifest in many ways, not only as sexual attraction.

• And please, don't use terms, or allow others to use terms, like "feminist," "woman's libber," or "salacious" to define or describe Vaishnavis. A woman may determine for herself if she believes in feminist philosophies. You may determine which of these beliefs you agree or disagree with. But please don't use these terms to put large groups of devotees into a corner (because they are born in the West, for example), and denigrate them. On a personal note, while I have been called a feminist by those who opposed the Ministry, I have never read, associated with, or subscribed to feminist movement or ideology. I prefer to think in terms of being grateful, universal, and inclusive. And I believe that entitlement equals false pride and is not a desirable devotional quality. In fact it really has no place and generally leads to abuse and exploitation. My main point is that I am against hurt and abuse, especially in the name of *shastra*. We are servants of the servant of the servant.

For those who identify as women, I would offer the following:

- Do not allow yourself to become a round peg in a square hole. It can be very uplifting to do the needful in life, to fill in and make a difference where there is a need, even if it means being the round peg in the square hole. But at the end of the day, we must know how to stand on our own feet and understand our strengths, and give the best we have to offer to Krishna.

- If we feel that we have been hurt by others then we should not use our power to turn around and hurt others. If we feel that men have caused pain, we should not then act like those men and abuse power too. Rather, we should be the person we want to see in others. This is true for everyone, by the way. And again, I offer obeisance and ask forgiveness for every instance in which I have done the same.

- If we want to be seen as being beyond bodily designation, we should really put our "womanly" frailties aside, not in a spirit of false renunciation, but lovingly, with care, and with an eye to a more broad-minded purpose. At the same time, it is not necessary to act or dress or speak as men. We are self satisfied in the lives Krishna has given us.

In my service as the Vaishnavi Minister, I sometimes felt as hurt by the women as the men. We ought to support each other.

We are individuals walking a path back to Krishna. None of us is perfect; none of us is any less than another. Each of us is tiny and insignificant, but we have value and we can be whole in devotion and integrity. We are just souls on our way home.

I hope and pray in the deepest corners of my heart, from this point forward, that I always feel the gratitude, the warmth, and value of devotional life and for every living being with love for the Lord and His devotees. I pray I may see with equal vision, and that Sri Sri Radha and Krishna may always be at the core center of all of my dealings and heart. I pray that I may always be totally dependent upon Lord Sri Krishna, the transcendental cowherder of Vrindavan. He carries what we lack and preserves what we have. I pray the same for everyone else too.

Signing off on this day of July the 7th, 2020
With affection, Sudharma dasi

"As servants of the Lord, we are one, and there can be no questions of enmity or friendship. If one actually understands that every one of us is a servant of the Lord, where is the question of enemy or friend?

"Everyone should be friendly for the service of the Lord. Everyone should praise another's service to the Lord and not be proud of his own service. This is the way of Vaishnava thinking, Vaikuntha thinking.

"Everyone should be allowed to render service to the Lord to the best of his ability, and everyone should appreciate the service of others. Such are the activities of Vaikuntha. Since everyone is a servant, everyone is on the same platform and is allowed to serve the Lord according to his ability. As confirmed in *Bhagavad-gita* (15.15), *sarvasya caham hridi sannivishto mattah smritir jnanam apohanam ca:* the Lord is situated in everyone's heart." From Srila Prabhupada's purport to *Bhag.* 7.5.12

Note: to download any of the PDFs in this section follow these instructions.

After opening the PDF, click on the double arrow in the top right-hand part of the "PDF screen" as shown to the left.

Choose "Download" and it will immediately begin.

1991-2000: *Priti-laksanam* Newsletters

The newsletter was a groundbreaking international newsletter which created a dialogue between devotees and the GBC. *Many of the articles are excellent and still relevant today.*

Priti-laksanam was conceived, edited, published, and financed by Pranada dasi. All the newsletters can be accessed here:

http://vaishnaviministry.org/history-2/priti-laksanam/

1998: Women's Ministry Conference Brochure

The schedule for this retreat and conference was elaborate and may give you ideas for a Vaishnavi retreat in your own area of the world.

http://vaishnaviministry.org/1998-womens-ministry-conference-brochure/

1998: Conspiracy to Terminate the ISKCON Women's Ministry

An editorial published on Vaishnava News Network (VNN) and written by Ardhabuddhi dasa (which many felt was a pseudonym) includes the leaked email conference called GHQ, "General Headquarters," which was formed by a group of men with the aim of terminating the Vaishnavi Ministry.

The article and leaked email correspondence which exposed the plot and concerted effort to end the Ministry. The participants discredit the devotees working with the Ministry and go so far as to conjecture women have no souls and Yamuna Devi and Visakha dasi are "salacious," meaning they are obscene and lecherous! The documents are here: http://vaishnaviministry.org/anti-vaishnavi-ghq/

2004: Healing the Heart of ISKCON
by Kim Knott

Kim Knott is the Head of the Department of Theology and Religious Studies at the University of Leeds and the President of the British Association for the Study of Religions. You can view the chapter "Healing the Heart of ISKCON" here: http://vaishnaviministry.org/healing-the-heart-of-iskcon/

2004: Female Diksa-gurus in ISKCON
by the Sastric Advisory Council

The GBC asked the Sastric Advisory Council to research the topic. This paper was author by Suhotra Svami, Gopiparanadhana Dasa, Drutakarma Dasa, Purnacandra Dasa, and Devamrta Dasa and considers (1) statements by Srila Prabhupada (2) statements by other Gaudiya Vaishnava *acharyas* (3) statements by other Vaishnava *acharyas* (4) statements from Vaishnava *smrtis* and (5) historical examples. The document can be viewed here: http://vaishnaviministry.org/female-diksha-gurus-in-iskcon/

2013: Did Srila Prabhupada Want Women Diksa Gurus?
by Kaunteya dasa

This is well-produced, extensive investigation and consideration of numerous references about women's gurus. The book can be downloaded here: https://sites.google.com/site/eyeofthestormbooks/

2013: Some Evidence Regarding Education and Guruship for Vaishnavis
by Bhaktarupa dasa and Madhavananda dasa

This paper brings forward and discusses "Women in the Vedas" and refers to quotes from the *Rg Veda*, the *Upanishads, Manusmriti, Manu Samhita, Hari-bhakti-vilasa*, and other ancient texts.
http://vaishnaviministry.org/some-evidence-regarding-education-and-guruship-for-vaishnavis/

2014 : Yamuna Devi's Legacy Project:
Biography, classes, and bhajans.
http://krishnamagic.com/

2018: What's Woman to Do?
by Visakha dasi

Visakha presented this paper in two parts at the 2018 Vaishnavi Retreat in North America. The participants were so happily with the presentation they urged her to make this available to the public.

This paper is substantially different from the BTG article of the same name.

Part Two discusses some of the negative references to women in *Srimad-Bhagavatam*. You can view and download a PDF here:

Part One "Reflections on Womens' Services in Srila Prabhupada's Hare Krishna Movement

Part Two "Why We May Misunderstand Srila Prabhupada's Teachings Regarding Women"

An audio recording of Visakha's presentation can be accessed here:
https://www.vaishnaviministryna.com/what-s-a-woman-to-do

2020: Guru: The Principle, Not the Body
by Madana Mohana dasa

This is a well-documented, thorough response to "Vaishnava-diksha according to Narada-Pancaratra: Can a Female Devotee be a diksha-guru?"

The author is a scholar and this book, though long, is worth reading. We're shown the improper logic and the incorrect use of references – references that have been translated incorrectly! – used by those who oppose Vaishnavi *diksha* gurus.
http://vaishnaviministry.org/guru-the-principle-not-the-body/

1995 Resolutions

The International Society for Krishna Consciousness strongly condemns all spousal abuse, and abuse outside the parameters of marriage, including abuse that is physical, verbal, and emotional. Any attempt to justify abuse on the basis of Srila Prabhupada's teaching is misconstrued and firmly rejected.

GBC Resolutions Pertaining to Women from 1996 to 2014

1996 Resolutions

102. The GBC Body shall establish an International Women's Ministry. This Ministry will address the following concerns in a clear, mature, and deliberate manner:

1. Appreciating the contribution of ISKCON's female devotees.
2. Increasing understanding of the serious concerns of women in ISKCON.
3. Providing facility, communication and support for all female members of ISKCON.
4. Addressing issues of abuse and sexual impropriety in ISKCON.
5. Defining the different female devotee situations (e.g. *grihastha* women, older, renounced women, and *brahmacharinis*).
6. Working with temple authorities and GBCs to identify role models and encourage them to inspire and train junior Vaishnavis.

The first duties of this Ministry:
1. Establishment of Regional Ministers (who will serve on a worldwide Women's Ministerial Council.)
2. Selection of an International Women's Minister.
3. Communication with regional GBC, temple presidents and other leaders as to the purposes, understanding and practical application of the Women's Ministry in each individual region.
4. Positive, regional guidelines for protecting ISKCON women, including domestic violence, sexual impropriety, etc.

The first objectives of this Ministry:

STEP ONE: (Complete by July 1996)

Appoint Regional Ministers. The regional minister will by chosen conjointly by local senior Vaishnavis, GBC, and other ISKCON leaders. Her qualifications include: ability to communicate maturely with local leaders, senior and junior female devotees and female congregation; genuine understanding of the needs and concerns of ladies; ability to proceed with Women's Ministry responsibilities in a non-confrontational yet serious manner.

STEP TWO: (Complete by October 1996)

Choose an International Minister. The International Minister will be chosen as follows:

1. Senior Vaishnavis from each region will nominate appropriate candidates.
2. Discussion of these candidates will ensue via COM, mail and phone.

Sudharma dasi, with the help of Bhaktitirtha Swami, Madhusevita Prabhu, and Bir Krishna Goswami will ensure the completion of these tasks.

103. The GBC hereby requests all temple and congregational leaders to practically engage female devotees in areas of temple sadhana and preaching, giving careful and mature consideration to devotee ability, local culture, devotee seniority, dedication, service, need for encouragement, and temple environment.

ISKCON is a family where everyone should feel welcome. Although temple environments may differ, the underlying principle of facilitating ladies' *sadhana* must remain, based on an attitude of encouragement and respect.

104. [LAW] 620. THAT the following is added to GBC resolution 413-96: "Standards of a temple president: A female temple president should;

– see all men as son except her husband.
– never be alone with a man except one's husband.
– avoid intimate dealings with men.
– as far as possible appoint a senior man to deal with men's affairs.
– in certain conditions it may be prudent for a female president to

have her husband deal with the men, or for a male president to have his wife deal with the women. The general principle is that the temple president should avoid intimate dealings with the opposite sex."

THAT the GBC Body hereby declares that the International Society for Krishna Consciousness does not condone abuse of any kind, especially that which is directed towards dependents such as women, children, aged, and cows. Battery, verbal, and emotional abuse are destructive to the devotional creeper and thus considered serious Vaishnava *aparadhas*. Any attempt to justify this type of abusive mentality on the basis of *sastra* is misconstrued and is firmly rejected by all practicing Vaishnavas.

THAT every ISKCON temple is to provide equal facility for both women and men to chant *japa*. This may mean equal or appropriate facility, or common or alternative use of the temple room as acceptable by everyone.

1999 Resolutions

504. [VISION AND GOAL] VARNASRAMA DHARMA AND CARE FOR DEVOTEES

Whereas Srila Prabhupada repeatedly and consistently advocated the implementation of *varnashrama* as the panacea for all of societies social imbalances, and

Whereas Srila Prabhupada instructed that *varnashrama* must be implemented within ISKCON,

It is resolved THAT

as a humble beginning of the process of implementing *daivi-varnashrama* within ISKCON, the GBC Body emphasizes the need to care for devotees in the following fundamental areas:
Children
Women
Elderly
*Brahmana*s
Cows

2000 Resolutions

Women's Participation
618 [LAW]

WHEREAS, the Women's Ministry presentation on March 1st, 2000 to the GBC Body brought a clearer understanding of the mistakes of the past and the need to provide equal and full opportunity for devotional service for all devotees in ISKCON, regardless of gender, and

WHEREAS, it is clearly following in our line that all people are welcome to join Lord Chaitanya's *sankirtana* movement and are capable of developing full love of God, and

WHEREAS, it is our belief that many of the social issues that confront us are exacerbated because the voice of our women, who are the mothers and daughters of our Krishna conscious family, have been hushed and stifled due to misinterpretation of our Vaishnava philosophy, and thus the human and interpersonal needs of our devotees have been minimized,

THEREFORE IT IS RESOLVED THAT:

501 [STATEMENT] 1. The members of the Governing Body Commission of the International Society for Krishna Consciousness offer their humble apologies to the women of Srila Prabhupada's society who, because of our own shortcomings and those of the Society, have suffered due to a lack of protection, support, facility, and appreciation for their service, devotion, and vast contributions to the Society, and

2. [ACTION] All GBC Body members and other leaders shall hold *istagosthis* [meetings] in each of their respective temples to establish the priority of providing equal facilities, full encouragement, and genuine care and protection for the women members of ISKCON. Also, separate meetings should be held with the leaders and women of each temple to address the women's needs and concerns,

Women's Participation 19 [LAW]

A. All ISKCON temples are to allow all qualified devotees, regardless of gender, to speak on *Srimad-Bhagavatam*, *Bhagavad-gita*, etc. during the regular temple class.
B. All ISKCON temples designate half of the temple room area, divided in the center from the altar, for the ladies.
C. If the management in a particular temple feels it is unable to implement these proposals, the Executive Committee will appoint a small team of senior devotees, including women, to sensitively review the particular local situation.

502 Women's Issue Discussion in India
Whereas, there is a need for a dialogue between the GBC Body and ISKCON leaders in India about implementation of the resolution 618/2000 concerning women in ISKCON;

[ACTION ORDER] Resolved, That the GBC Body hereby appoints a subcommittee, whose members will be selected by the Executive Committee, of three or four devotees to engage in discussions over the course of the next 12 months or longer with the members of the Indian Continental Committee (ICC) with a mandate to:

1. Explain resolution 618/2000 and the intention of the GBC Body as to how it should be implemented in India.
2. Carefully hear the various objections being raised by different members of the ICC.
3. Attempt to isolate whatever genuinely contentious issues exist and prepare a joint statement explaining all viewpoints on these issues.
4. Seek out possible resolutions for these contentious issues and report back to the GBC Body and ICC, possibly with recommendations for further action by either body.

417. Endorsement of the *Grihastha Ashrama* and Community Development

[Statement]
The Governing Body Commission expresses its support and encouragement to devotees serving in the *grihastha ashrama*.

We affirm that the *grihastha ashrama* is a valuable institution that brings great benefit. Those who sincerely serve Lord Sri Krishna and Srila Prabhupada in this *ashrama* will make tangible spiritual advancement.

We also affirm the importance in ISKCON of nurturing strong marriages, encouraging harmony in families, improving the welfare of children, ensuring the protection and care of women, discouraging divorce, and enlivening *grihastha* men and women in Krishna's service.

We hereby pledge ourselves, and will encourage our regional and other senior leaders, to:

- Promote an environment conducive to successful Krishna conscious family life in ISKCON temples and communities
- Encourage on-going support for Vaishnava families in ISKCON communities through Krishna conscious *grihastha* activities, community preaching programs, and other initiatives

- Educate congregations, and particularly youth, about the spiritual and social value of Krishna conscious marriage based on Srila Prabhupada's teachings
- Confront and correct any preaching or teaching that undermines the health and strength of the *grihastha ashrama*, or discriminates against spiritually based *grihastha* life
- Engage in thoughtful and meaningful discourse about the responsibilities, privileges, and goals of *grihastha* life with devotees who are considering marriage
- Ensure that marriages facilitated under our care prioritize the needs of the individuals involved, and the health and longevity of the marriage
- Encourage professionally developed pre-marital counseling for all potential *grihastha* couples
- Match newly married devotees, whenever possible, with mature, spiritually strong couples who can act as mentors and supporters
- Be trained personally, as appropriate, in marital counseling, communication and conflict resolution skills

2006 Resolutions

425. Female Diksa Guru
    [Statement]
    The GBC accepts the basic philosophical conclusion presented in the SAC's Female Diksa Guru Paper, i.e., that a mature, qualified, female devotee may accept the role of an initiating spiritual master. The implementation thereof is pending further GBC consideration.

420. Task Force on Abuse of Women
    [Action Order]
    Whereas it is the duty of the leadership of a spiritual society to protect its members so that they can peacefully perform devotional service to Sri Sri Radha Krishna

    Therefore it is resolved that:
    The GBC Body hereby directs the GBC CCO and Tamohara Prabhu to coordinate a Task Force to define and deal with abuse against women in ISKCON.

421. Women's Ministry Regional Representatives
    [Guideline]
    Whereas women reside in ISKCON temples and communities across the globe where customs, culture, and facility vary greatly. While the basic principles of full

engagement in devotional service, protection, and freedom from exploitation are foundational principles for all women, how they are applied locally may vary. Thus, it is imperative that the Women's Ministry is properly represented in each region of the globe.

Whereas the original GBC resolution forming the Women's Ministry directs the Ministry to appoint regional Women's Ministry representatives.

Therefore the GBC Body hereby recommends that the Regional Governing Bodies (RGBs) work with the ISKCON Women's Ministry to designate, at their determination, either a Women's Ministry representative or a Women's Ministry Council for their respective region. This representative or Council will operate under the direction and auspices of both the Women's Ministry and the RGBs.

2008 Resolutions

311. End Notes or Appendices in Srila Prabhupada's Books
Whereas some of Srila Prabhupada's books contain sentences such as the following, which when taken in isolation may be considered derogatory to and offensive against women:

Although rape is not legally allowed, it is a fact that a woman likes a man who is very expert at rape. (*Bhag.* 4.25.41, p.)

When a husbandless woman is attacked by an aggressive man, she takes his action to be mercy. (*Bhag.* 4.25.42, p.)

Generally, when a woman is attacked by a man – whether her husband or some other man – she enjoys the attack, being too lusty. (*Bhag.* 4.26.26, p.)

Whereas some ISKCON devotees may have used these statements out of context as an excuse to offend, neglect, and abuse women;

Whereas some people who read such statements may consider them to be derogatory or offensive, may misunderstand what Srila Prabhupada actually means, and may not want to further read those books, notwithstanding the many other beneficial statements in them;

RESOLVED: That the GBC Body recommends to the BBT Trustees that the above quotes, and other such statements as determined by the BBT, be explained in Footnotes or in appendices.

305. Female Diksa Gurus
[Action Order]
Whereas there is a factual need for more *diksha-gurus* in ISKCON to accommodate the worldwide preaching;

Whereas there are mature female preachers qualified to take on *diksha-guru* responsibilities;

Whereas there are a number of such qualified women who already have *shiksha* disciples;

Whereas the GBC Body previously issued the following statement in 2005, which has now been given further consideration:

425. Female Diksa Guru
The GBC accepts the basic philosophical conclusion presented in the SAC's Female Diksa Guru Paper, i.e., that a mature, qualified, female devotee may accept the role of an initiating spiritual master. The implementation thereof is pending further GBC consideration.

RESOLVED:
1. That resolution 425/2005 – Female Diksa Guru is amended to read as follows:

The GBC accepts the philosophical conclusion presented in the SAC's Female Diksa Guru Paper that a mature, qualified, female devotee may accept the role of an initiating spiritual master.

2. The GBC Body authorizes local area committees to put forward for approval as initiating guru any devotee in their area, male or female, who is qualified according to existing GBC Law.

309. Female Diksa Gurus
The subject of Vaishnavis initiating in ISKCON is tabled until the GBC Annual General Meeting 2014.

310. Female Diksa Guru Research Paper

Whereas there is a need for clarity in ISKCON's current policy regarding Vaishnavi *diksha* gurus;

And whereas there have been calls for additional references and support from Srila Prabhupada and the sastra to explain and justify that policy:

RESOLVED:

A GBC committee consisting of Bir Krishna Das Goswami (convenor), Bhanu Swami, Badrinarayan Das, and Praghosa Das shall research and write a paper on the subject of female *diksha* gurus based on Srila Prabhupada's teachings, *sastra*, and historical precedents. The committee may enlist the service of other devotees including current members of the Sastric Advisory Council.

The committee will specifically document and provide justification of the current ISKCON policy, or reasons to reconsider that policy.

The committee shall send a draft of its work to the GBC Executive Committee by September 30, 2013 so that it may be circulated to the GBC members in advance of the Midterm GBC meeting in Mumbai in October 2013, and may be discussed there.

The committee will then consider the input from the GBC members and complete a final draft to be sent to the Executive Committee by January 15, 2014. The Executive Committee will circulate that final draft so that it may be discussed and voted upon at the AGM in 2014.

2014 Resolutions

312: Should Women be Called "Prabhu," "Mataji," or "Devi" ?

Whereas in ISKCON men had generally been taught to see all women other than their wives as mother;

Whereas in more recent times a practice has gained momentum that women should not be called "Mataji," but "Prabhu;"

Whereas the word "Prabhu" is traditionally used to address men;

Whereas one section of ISKCON considers addressing women as "Prabhu" to have no cultural or linguistic backing, or any evidentiary or experiential support from Srila Prabhupada's teachings;

Whereas another section of ISKCON cites conversational or correspondence-based evidence that Srila Prabhupada addressed female disciples as "Prabhu;"

Whereas there is increasing discord among the proponents of these two opinions;

Whereas all initiated women also have the title "Devi" as part of their spiritual name, an address that could also apply to the non-initiated

RESOLVED:
That the Sastric Advisory Committee is requested to research the evidence for women being called "Mataji," "Prabhu" or "Devi" and give a conclusive directive as to which of these terms should and should not be used by members of ISKCON.

316: Gender *Kirtan*
[Guideline]
Whereas a new practice has emerged in ISKCON *kirtan* consisting of:
Kirtan Leader Chants Ladies Only Respond
Kirtan Leader Chants Men Only Respond
Kirtan Leader Chants Full Congregation Responds

Whereas there is no description of Srila Prabhupada ever leading *kirtan* like this, nor of any devotee leading *kirtan* like this in Srila Prabhupada's presence;

Whereas this new practice emphasizes the bodily conception of life and our false designations as man and woman;

Whereas when such questionable chanting occurs, some devotees are uncomfortable, alienated, disturbed, or may even refuse to participate in such a *kirtan*, and thus the unity of our movement, even in its most core activity – *sankirtana* – is jeopardized

RESOLVED:
Kirtan leaders in all temple and public programs, should refrain from separating the congregation into responding sections based on bodily considerations like male, female, young, old, etc.

321. Female Diksa Gurus

The subject of Vaishnavis initiating in ISKCON is further tabled until additional discussion at the 2014 GBC Midterm Meeting. In the meantime the GBC Executive Committee will work on the following process:

1. Creating a committee of devotees who have no pre-determined view on this topic who will gather documents from all sources on the subject of female *diksha-gurus*.

2. The committee will sort, summarize, and categorize all documentation. Categories could include Srila Prabhupada's quotations, *varnashrama-dharma*, history within our *sampradaya* and other Vaishnava *sampradaya*s, etc.

3. As far as possible all documentation will be verified for accuracy, authenticity, etc.

4. As far as possible this committee will do whatever other research may be required.

5. The committee will then provide all those documents to the GBC members prior to the Midterm meeting. Thus all GBC members will come to the Midterm Meeting well aware of all the arguments, information, and evidences available. This will then enable the GBC to make either informed progress or an informed decision on this matter.

To view other GBC resolutions, or resolutions about women from subsequent years visit here: http://gbc.iskcon.org/gbc-resolutions/.

Anuttama dasa is the Minister of Communications and a Governing Body Commissioner (GBC) of ISKCON. He was initiated by Srila Prabhupada in 1976 in Vrindavan, India. Anuttama was a founding member of Children of Krishna, the MANtra Retreat, Festival of Inspiration (New Vrindavan), the Vaishnava Christian and Vaishnava Muslim Dialogues, and other efforts to strengthen ISKCON's social fabric. Currently he also serves on the Board of Religions for Peace (USA), the Bhaktivedanta College (Belgium), and the Advisory Board of Religious Freedom Institute. He and his wife, Rukmini, live in Rockville, Maryland, USA, near their son, Gauravani, daughter-in-law Vrinda, and their three grandchildren.

Bhakti Tirtha Swami [1950 – 2005] was initiated by Srila Prabhupada in 1973 and took *sannyasa* in 1979.

Prior to becoming a devotee, at Princeton University, he became president of the student council and also served as chairman of the Third World Coalition. Although his main degree was in psychology, he received accolades in many other fields, including politics, African studies, and international law.

His books are used as reference texts in universities and leadership organizations throughout the world. Bhakti Tirtha Swami gained international recognition as a representative of the Bhaktivedanta Book Trust, particularly for his outstanding work with scholars in the former communist countries of Eastern Europe.

He directly oversaw projects in the United States, West Africa, South Africa, Switzerland, France, Croatia, and Bosnia. He also served as the director of the American Federation of Vaishnava Colleges and Schools.

In the United States, Bhakti Tirtha Swami was the founder and director of the Institute for Applied Spiritual Technology, director of the International Committee for Urban Spiritual Development, and one of the international coordinators of the Seventh Pan African Congress. A specialist in international relations and conflict resolution, Bhakti Tirtha Swami constantly traveled around the world and had become a spiritual consultant to many high-ranking members of the United Nations, to various celebrities, and to several chiefs, kings, and high court justices. In 1990 His Holiness was coronated as a high chief in Warri, Nigeria in recognition for his outstanding work in Africa and the world.

Burke Rochford is Professor Emeritus of Religion at Middlebury College in Vermont. He studied the Hare Krishna movement for over thirty years, and as the movement's friend, has written numerous articles addressing its development. In Rochford's "Hare Krishna Transformed," which he referred to as a labour of love, he addresses social issues within ISKCON.

Govinda devi dasi was a senior at the University of Texas at Austin in 1966 when she and her husband went to San Francisco in search of a spiritual teacher. She explains, "My yoga books said that when the *chela* is ready, the guru will appear. So I was trying to make myself ready with many hours of meditation and purificatory disciplines. One day I went to a book shop and happened to read the description of Srila Prabhupada in Hayagriva's *Back to Godhead* article. Upon reading this description, I saw him in my mind's eye, as if a window had been suddenly opened, and began to weep, 'I've found him, I've found him at last!' I went immediately to the newly opened San Francisco storefront temple, and have never left Srila Prabhupada since that day."

In 1969, Srila Prabhupada sent Govinda dasi and her husband to Hawaii to open Krishna temples in the Hawaiian Islands. Srila Prabhupada then came to Hawaii to join them, and lived with them for several weeks in a beachhouse in Kaawa, on the windward coast of Oahu. He later made many visits to the Islands, which he named "New Navadwip."

Govinda dasi has been a disciple of Srila Prabhupada since 1966. She is also the author and illustrator of numerous children's books, including *Gopal, Nimai, Jagannath, Krishna,* and *Damodar.* She resides in Hawaii and Vrindaban.

Govinda Priya devi dasi was born into a Vaishnava family and is a disciple of His Holiness Radhanath Swami. She became active in ISKCON through ISKCON Chowpatty in her teenage years. Govinda Priya has served as a full-time devotee in India and in New Vrindavan teaching. She served as a member of the Child Protection and Congregational development team. She currently resides in Sacramento, California, with her husband and two children serving as the Vaishnavi Minister for North America. She also serves ISKCON's Governing Body Commissions Nominations committee as a secretary and vetting officer. Govinda Priya has recently taken on more responsibilities serving as the project manager for the GBC Charter Model, which is a project of the GBC Strategic Planning Team.

Hridayananda Goswami began visiting the Berkeley ISKCON temple in 1969 where he would later enroll as a full-time *ashrama* student engaged in monastic service and theological training. H.D. Goswami distinguished himself by his devotion to Prabhupada's message and his eloquence in presenting Prabhupada's teachings to others. In 1972, he accepted *sannyasa.* He spent the following 20 years establishing over 40 ISKCON centeres and supervising the translation, publication, and distribution of millions of Prabhupada's books throughout Central and South America, Italy, and Greece. He also wrote the commentaries for the final volumes of *Srimad-Bhagavatam.*

After graduating from the University of California as a student of World Religions, he continued his studies at Harvard University, where he received his Ph.D. in Sanskrit and Indian Studies in 1996.

He is fluent in seven languages (English, Spanish, Portuguese, Italian, French, German, and Sanskrit), and continues to seek out effective ways in which to preserve yet adapt ancient wisdom to contemporary circumstances. Because people in the West need and deserve the chance to practice genuine bhakti yoga within an external culture that is comfortable and natural for them, H.D. Goswami has established Krishna West to help facilitate ISKCON's outreach to Western audiences.

Jyotirmayi devi dasi met the devotees in Paris in the fall of 1969 and went to London to meet Prabhupada in December. Prabhupada accepted her as his disciple in January 1970 at which time she gave up her Ethnology studies (religion, philosophies, and civilizations) at the Sorbonne in Paris and her aspiration to become a Buddhist nun. Her early services included preaching to guests, cooking, sewing, and painting pictures of Radha-Krishna and Lord Chaitanya.

She served in the temples in the south of France, Paris, and New York and regularly lectured at the temple and universities. She was a head *pujari*, a temple commander, translated Prabhupada's books into French, and headed up the translation team in France. She was in charge of public relations and was the interpretor for Prabhupada during his classes and preaching programs in France. From 1975 to 1978, Jyotirmayi was headmistress, academic, and *ashrama* teacher in New Mayapur Gurukula in France. She also served as regional secretary for GBC Paramgati Maharaja and was a member of the Vaishnavi Ministry.

Currently she has been an activist leader for Animal Rights in Georgia and South Carolina in the United States and France.

Kalakanta dasa and Jitamrta dasi, though raised in Christian homes, in 1972, ten years before they met and married, both moved into local ISKCON *ashramas.* They performed kirtan on the streets, distributed books and *prasadam,* and raised funds for their temples. After marrying they raised three children together. In 2006 they were asked to manage the sleepy ISKCON center in Gainesville, Florida, also known as Krishna House. Since then the preaching center has become a vibrant home of bhakti.

They decided to use the method Srila Prabhupada used in ISKCON's earliest days. To their surprise and delight, three young people moved into the former Krishna House *ashrama* and began seriously practicing Krishna consciousness. Within a few years the Krishna House *ashramas* were stuffed with thirty students. Morning programs at Krishna House became dynamic, uplifting, fun, and attractive. Krishna House expanded *harinama sankirtana,* book distribution, *prasadam* distribution, and cultural programs. Dozens of Krishna House graduates took initiation from fifteen different ISKCON *diksha* gurus.

Hundreds have gone on to perform valuable service in ISKCON communities in North America, South America, Europe, India, and China. They have published *Endangered Species: Ashramites in ISKCON North America* detailing their formula of success.

Kim Knott is a professor of religious and secular studies at Lancaster University in the United Kingdom. She published the chapter "Healing the Heart of ISKCON" in *The Hare Krishna Movement: The Postcharismatic Fate of a Religious Transplant.* She has also written numerous articles such as *Contemporary theological trends in the Hare Krishna Movement: A theology of religions; Insider and outsider perceptions of Prabhupada;* and *In Every Town and Village: Adaptive Strategies in the Communication of Krishna Consciousness in the UK, the First Thirty Years.*

Krishnarupa devi dasi is a senior disciple of His Divine Grace A. C. Bhaktivedanta Swami Prabhupada. She is a member of ISKCON Australia's National Council and was appointed as the inaugural Women's Minister of ISKCON Australia. In addition, she is a member of the BBT's Revisions Review Panel (RRP) and also the SABHA (Spiritual Advisory Bhagavata Assembly), an advisory body to the GBC.

Krishnarupa has developed local woman representatives in all the Australian temples in order to better support the Vaishnavis. Her goal is to provide care, encouragement, and counsel to women in Australia and globally. This prompted her to develop a workshop on the "Identification and Prevention of Sexual Harassment in ISKCON," which resulted in a resolution passed to deliver it to all the temples in Australia. Another seminar she has developed is focused on creating awareness and prevention of domestic related violence entitled "Harmony in the Home," which during the Covid-19 pandemic she has been presenting on YouTube and Zoom.

A professional in the publishing industry for many decades, Krishnarupa now happily uses the skills honed from her career in editing devotees' books.

In the 1970s, she served as Radha-Madhava's seamstress during Mayapur's pioneer days and cared for some of the young Bengali girls at that time. Before moving to Mayapur, she was Lord Jagannatha's head *pujari* in Kolkata temple. These days, Krishnarupa resides some months in Mayapur and the remainder of the time in Australia, near the New Govardhana farming community in northern New South Wales.

Kusha devi dasi became a devotee at 17 and moved into the temple at 18 in 1969. Govinda dasi deputed her and Jayasri Prabhu to grow the first *tulasi* plants in the western world. She assisted Govinda dasi to make Gaura-Nitai Deities and sculpted the first clay form of Lord Chaitanya in ISKCON.

She has been on the board of trustees for the Vrinda Kund Project near Nandagaon in India for many years. She was instrumental in producing Srutakirti's book *What is the difficulty!* and produced a website called "Srila Prabhupada Uvacha" for Srila

Prabhupada's Centennial. Kusha worked for three years to improve hospice conditions at ISKCON Hospice in Vrindavan and was on the Vrindavan Management Council for two years.

When kirtankar Chakarini was forcibly stopped from singing *Damodarastaka*, Kusha went to ISKCON management and Gopal Krishna Maharaja to ask for an apology and a policy so it would not happen again. The matter was settled, but frictions between men and women increased and they erupted the following Gaura Purnima: Parvati dasi was manhandled in front of Radha-Shyamasundar's altar in Vrindavan. This event intiated the Vaishnavi Ministry's delegation of women to the 2000 international GBC meetings called "Healing the Heart of ISKCON."

Kusha atttended the international GBC meetings as a Vaishnavi Ministry member for three years. Through her work, she was able to place Vrindavan's "Kirtan Ashram" under the protection of the Vaishnavi Ministry.

In 2003, as ISKCON's representatives, Rukmini dasi and Kusha joined female spiritual leaders at the "Global Initiative for World Peace" at the United Nations in Geneva, Switzerland.

She was the director of Community Services and Devotee Care in Vrindavan from 2013-2019, during which time she took up a petition to stop the distribution of Bhakti Vikas Swami's book *Masters or Mothers?* The Vrindavan Executive Board agreed to stop the sale of the book. Bhakti Vikas Swami attempted to call Kusha into public debate and ultimately changed the cover of the book and some of the contents.

While organizing, the 45th anniversary of the grand opening of Krishna-Balaram Mandir, she fought diligently for the right of the Vaishnavis to sing during a Vraj Rasa kirtan in front of the Deities. Though previously women had led kirtans in Vrindavan, they hadn't been able to do so for thirty years.

She was the Grihastha Minister from 2001-2003; the regional secretary for Hawaii ISKCON from 2000-2003, and the ISKCON Hawaii temple president from 2001-2003. She is currently serving as the temple president of ISKCON Honolulu.

Pranada devi dasi joined the Los Angeles temple at seventeen years old and Srila Prabhupada accepted her as his disciple in 1976. She distributed books and served *Back to Godhead* magazine in various roles for nearly 30 years. She served as a board member of the ISKCON Foundation, Gita-nagari Press, the Alachua temple, and the Alachua Learning Center. As the KCF president, she spearheaded the building of the ISKCON Alachua temple. She was the co-director of the BBT Special Projects division for five years and launched Krishna.com with three other devotees in 2000.

She published the quarterly newsletter *Priti-laksanam* to educate devotees about the role of women in ISKCON and provide an avenue for devotees to communicate with the GBC about other topics of concern. She founded Adopt-a-Child that served to place devotee children from disadvantaged families into devotee homes who could care for them. With Sudharma dasi and others, she helped establish the ISKCON Women's Ministry, now known as the Vaishnavi Ministry.

To have the facility to offer these volunteer services, as an entrepreneur, Pranada established and managed two successful businesses to support her family. She is a mother and grandmother, and the author of award-winning _Wise-Love: Bhakti and the Search for the Soul of Consciousness_ (available as a print, digital, and audio book) which was re-published by BBT South Africa. She has issued a free online course to accompany _Wise-Love_ called _Journey into the Heart of Bhakti._ Her second book, _Bhakti-Shakti: Goddess of Divine Love_ will be released in 2021 by Mandala Publishing. She is a featured speaker in the film _Women of Bhakti_ and her writing has appeared in numerous online and print publications for outside audiences. She lives with her husband, Nagaraja dasa, in their home in Alachua and is working on her third book. www.pranadacomtois.com.

Radha devi dasi is a disciple of His Holiness Mukunda Goswami with a lifelong interest in issues concerning women and children. She currently serves as ISKCON's International Vaishnavi Minister which gives her the opportunity to work with ISKCON's Governing Body Commission on issues affecting Vaishnavis. Her past service includes work with ISKCON Communications and the Child Protection Office, as well as congregational preaching. Radha is a graduate of Harvard Law School and practices law in the U.S, with an emphasis on helping victims of domestic abuse. She is a trained peer counselor for domestic abuse issues and previously taught at Chapman University School of Law and the University of San Diego School of Law.

Rukmini devi dasi first met the devotees in San Francisco in 1968. A few weeks later, she traveled to Montreal, Canada with the six householder couples who were on their way to open the London temple. She took initiation from Srila Prabhupada there.

She served as a _pujari_ in the Boston and New York temples until 1972. At that time she was part of a group of artists who were sent by Srila Prabhupada to Mayapur to learn the art of "_putul,_" a Bengali doll-making technique. Srila Prabhupada wanted dioramas to be used to present Krishna consciousness in innovative ways.

In 1974 she continued this work as part of a group in Los Angeles, under the name, the "First American Theistic Exhibition," or FATE. Multimedia exhibits were created in the Los Angeles and Detroit temples.

She served in the Colorado temples from 1986 until 1993, when she and her husband, Anuttama dasa moved to Washington, D. C. to establish a national office for ISKCON Communications. They are involved in outreach through interfaith dialogue.

For twenty-five years they also owned a business with three locations in the Washington, D. C. metro area called "As Kindred Spirits" that helped to fund various ISKCON and social welfare projects.

Since closing their business in 2017, Rukmini has been teaching and leading workshops and retreats. She is on the board of directors of Bhakti Center in New York City, as well as the ISKCON Sabha (Spiritual Advisors Bhagavata Assembly) International Advisory board. She is the founder of the Urban Devi collective, which hosts a website and a women's *sanga* each month at Bhakti Center in New York City. The kirtan artist, Gaura Vani is her son. She has three grandchildren, Revati, Kairava, and Kirtan Simha. You can follow Rukmini on FaceBook, Patreon, and Urban Devi.

Saudamani devi dasi graduated from the University of Pennsylvania and married before she joined the Philadelphia temple. Srila Prabhupada initiated her in July 1971. Her first service was *harinama-sankirtana*. She served Sri Sri Radha-Saradbihari as a their head *pujari* and helped manage the Philadelphia temple for decades.

Shyamala Kishori devi dasi grew up in the ISKCON New Goloka community in North Carolina with parents who are disciples of Srila Prabhupada. She is a disciple of Indradyumna Swami. Shyamala Kishori has an M.A. in women's studies and a certificate in gerontology from the University of Florida. She is a certified hypnotherapist. She enjoys writing, kirtan, enlivening discussions, and visits to Vrindavan.

Sitala dasi moved into the ISKCON temple in Detroit, Michigan in 1970, and was initiated by Srila Prabhupada in 1971. The first years of her devotional life, were spent in daily *harinamas,* book distribution, preaching programs, cooking, sewing, and transcribing of Srila Prabhupada tapes. She also assisted in opening temples in Cleveland, Ohio and Bloomington, Indiana.

In the mid-70s she moved to France where she was engaged primarily in Deity services in Paris and New Mayapur. In 1975 she began visiting India regularly to arrange for the carving of Deities, making of outfits, and procuring of paraphernalia required for temples throughout Europe. She eventually opened an embroidery shop in Vrindavan wherein hundreds of outfits were made for numerous temples throughout the world. This service required her to spend four to six months per year in Vrindavan, a pattern which carried on for over four decades. During her spare time in Vrindavan, she worked for the Institute of Vaishnava Studies, helping with research and editing.

From 1975 thru 1986, when not in Vrindavan, she was sent to various countries (France, Spain, Italy, Holland, England, Denmark, Israel) for a variety of services; assisting in installing Deities, helping to open restaurants, doing traveling *sankirtana,* secretarial work, taking care of the Bhaktin program, and acting as the zonal Deity minister.

In 1986 she moved to Vrindavan to work full time for the Institute of Vaishnava studies and continued making outfits for temples.

In 1989 she married Hari Sauri dasa, moved to Alachua, Florida, and began assisting her husband in bringing out his *Transcendental Diary* series (books describing his time as Srila Prabhupada's servant), while also starting her own book on the life of Srila Narottama dasa Thakura.

In 1995 she moved with her husband and daughter to Mayapur, where they continue to live today. While caring for her family, as well as her work in Vrindavan, she helped to set up the first committee to care for the needs of the growing Mayapur community, as well as participating on the Masterplan Team, Vision Team, and Strategic Planning group.

Over the years, she has become a regular speaker particularly on the lives of our Vaishnava *acharyas*, especially on Indradyumna Swami's yearly Kartika *parikrama*. She recently published *The Glorious Life of Srila Narottama Dasa Thakura*.

Sudharma devi dasi began practicing Krishna consciousness and took initiation from Srila Prabhupada in 1976. In her 43 years of devotional life she has served as a *sankirtana* devotee, *sankirtana* leader, temple board member in Philadephia and Alachua temples, temple president in the Philippines, itinerant preacher in the Pacific Northwest and in Southeast Asia where she helped to develop congregational communities from devotees homes. She developed and managed of book distribution at Srila Prabhupada's Palace in New Vrindavan, where she personally distributed many hundreds of Srila Prabhupada's books each week.

She served as the ISKCON Communications Director for North America, a member of the ISKCON Foundation, the founder of the North American and International GBC Women's Ministry (now known as the Vaishnavi Ministry), and a North American GBC / TP Executive Officer for six years.

She was the wife of Sundararupa Prabhu who was initiated in 1974, and served as a preacher in our movement, passing on in 2008. Her two daughters, Prema and Braja are 25 and 36 respectively. Prema is working on her PhD at the University of Florida, while her older sister Braja graduated with a Master's Degree from Goddard College in Vermont. Braja is currently employed at the University of Florida.

Sudharma is working to develop a radio platform with the goal of bringing together podcasts and music from across the spectrum of our Krishna consciousness movement that highlight the incredible aspects of our Vaishnava society: its intelligentsia, lifestyle, and devotional practices, geared for devotees and Western audiences. She feels a great deal of gratitude and affection for Srila Prabhupada and the devotees for her services, association, meditations, and the *Srimad-Bhagavatam*.

Urmila devi dasi (Dr. Edith Best) has served ISKCON continuously since her initiation by Srila Prabhupada in 1973. She and her husband are in the *vanaprastha* order since 1996. They have three married children, 14 grandchildren, and two great-grandsons.

She has a PhD in education, was a primary and secondary teacher for 27 years, and has 19 years of experience with school management. Urmila is the chair of the Sastric Advisory Council to the GBC, and formerly a professor of Sociology of Religion at Bhaktivedanta College as well as an associate editor of *Back to Godhead*. She travels worldwide teaching Krishna consciousness. She is the author of <u>Essence Seekers</u>, <u>Dr. Best Learn to Read</u>, an 83-book literacy program, and <u>The Great Mantra for Mystic Meditation.</u>

Visakha devi dasi has been a disciple of Srila Prabhupada since 1971. As one of Srila Prabhupada's official photographers, she traveled with him in the US, Canada, Europe, and India. She has written many *Back to Godhead* articles as well as five books. Visakha also assists her husband, Yadubara dasa, in making films – most recently the ninety-minute, award-winning documentary, *Hare Krishna! the Mantra, the Movement, and the Swami Who Started it All,* which has been translated into twenty-four languages and screened in theaters throughout the world. Visakha is currently the president of Bhaktivedanta Manor.

She has written several books *Photomacrography: Art and Techniques* (as Jean Papert), *Our Most Dear Friend: Bhagavad-gita for Children*; *Bhagavad-gita: A Photographic Essay, a visual guide to the world's greatest spiritual dialog*; *Bhagavad-gita: A Summary Study*; *Harmony and the Bhagavad-gita: Lessons from a Life-Changing Move to the Wilderness.*

Her memoir <u>*Five Years, Eleven Months and a Lifetime of Unexpected Love*</u> can be purchased on by clicking on the link of the title.

Visakha's website is <u>www.OurSpiritualJourney.com.</u>

Visakha Priya devi dasi was born and raised in France. She joined ISKCON in South Africa in 1978. There she helped build the Sri Sri Radha-Radhanath Temple of Understanding, started the Food for Life cum *harinama* programs in the African townships, and organized the first translation and publication of *The Perfection of Yoga* in Zulu. In 1991 she moved to India, where she served first as one of Giriraja Swami's personal assistants in Mumbai and then, from 1996 onwards, at the Vrindavan Institute for Higher Education, first as treasurer, then as a teacher, and then as the director's secretary. She was residing at the crumbling old Kirtan Ashram for senior ISKCON women when the Vaishnavi Ministry became its official caretaker. And although she had no desire to get involved, by Krishna's will and the help of His Holiness Giriraj Swami, she ended up getting an entirely new building constructed on the site, which she continues to manage to this day (2020), although from day one she has been looking for someone to take up that responsibility.

Vrajalila dasi is a disciple of HH Bhakti-Tirtha Swami. She started practicing Bhakti Yoga in 1979, where she first met devotees at the ISKCON 55th Street Temple in

New York City. Her introduction to devotional service started with book distribution in NYC. Within a year, she was requested by HH Bhakti-tirtha Swami to go to West Africa to join the late Brahmananda Prabhu with the pioneering of Krishna consciousness in West Africa, starting in Nigeria. She lived in West Africa for almost ten years traveling and assisting with opening temples. She and Yasodamayi Prabhu opened a preaching center in Belize. She assisted HH Bhakti-tirtha Swami with the development of "The Institute for Applied Spiritual Technology " for nine years.

In 1995, she and her husband, Ekavira Prabhu, were requested to take on leadership roles in Gita-nagari, where they served as temple presidents until HH Bhakti-Tirtha Swami was diagnosed with melanoma cancer.

She and her husband were the primary caretakers of their revered Guru Maharaja for one year during his illness. Presently she and her husband is living at the home of HH BTSwami where he left his body. After his departure she served as a member of the GBC Devotee Care Committee and assisted with co-authoring the manual for the GBC Devotee Care Course in Sri Dhama Mayapur.

Both her and her husband currently serve on the Grihastha Vision Team. She recently developed inter-Ifast (International Institute for Applied Spiritual Technology) a team of five Vaishnavis who are currently offering online webinar classes for newbies to Krishna consciousness, as well as a weekly series of "Memories of HH BTSwami."

She is a graduate of Berkeley University and also a certified trainer in Conflict Resolution, Mediation, and Non-Violent Communication.

Yamuna devi, one of Srila Prabhupada's early disciples, joined the Krishna consciousness movement in 1966, initially serving in San Francisco, England, and India. She traveled extensively with Srila Prabhupada, serving as his personal cook, engaging in deity worship and caring for the Vaishnavas. Yamuna became widely known for her ambrosial culinary skills and her melodious singing voice, and was regularly requested by Srila Prabhupada to lead kirtans. After his departure, she wrote her award-winning cookbook, *Lord Krishna's Cuisine, the Art of Indian Vegetarian Cooking,* which won the highest award given in the International culinary profession. Yamuna devi remained a dedicated and devoted disciple of Srila Prabhupada until her passing in 2011 and was much-loved throughout the world. She was well known for her compassion, grace, and loving nature, always encouraging others while remaining humble and kind. Yamuna devi's comprehensive biography and memoir, *Yamuna Devi, A Life of Unalloyed Devotion* is available in hardback and audio editions on Amazon.com and through other retailers.

www.ingramcontent.com/pod-product-compliance
Lightning Source LLC
Chambersburg PA
CBHW050457110426
42742CB00018B/3278